"A crackling exposé" *New York Times Book Review*

"*Blackwater* is the utterly gripping and explosive story of how the Bush administration has spent tens of millions of dollars building a parallel corporate army that functions in Iraq outside the law ... an army so loyal to far right causes it constitutes nothing less than a Republican Guard. The most important and chilling book about the death throes of U.S. democracy you will read in years and a triumph of investigative reporting" Naomi Klein, *Guardian*

"Long before the mainstream media and Congress were paying attention, Scahill exposed the workings of this lawless private army. Its an amazingly researched and well-told story of the nexus between far-right fundamentalists, the Bush-Cheney war machine, privatisation, and profiteering." Matthew Rothschild for The Progressive

"Scahill provided me information ... which I have not been able to get from the U.S. military ... I have read more from Mr. Scahill than I've got from our government." Representative Marcy Kaptur, Defense Appropriations Committee

"Blackwater raises a lot of deeply disturbing questions about where America's military is being led by this new breed of free-market mercenaries" Chris Barsanti, *In These Times*

"Terrifying and thrillingly written" Arundhati Roy, author of *The God of Small Things*

"This is no uninformed partisan screed ... Meticulously documented and encyclopaedic in scope ... it's a comprehensive and authoritative guide ... this book serves as a provocative primer for advancing the debate." Virginian-Pilot

"Andy McNab couldn't have invented this prescient tale of the private army of mercenaries run by a Christian conservative millionaire who, in turn, bankrolls the president. A chilling exposé of the ultimate military outsource." Christopher Fowler, *New Review*

"Fascinating and magnificently documented ... belongs on the reading list of any conscientious citizen." Scott Horton, Columbia University Law School

"The sternest message of this book has to do with the dangers a mercenary army poses, and always has: that it can always be turned on its host." John Freeman, President of the National Book Critics Circle

"Jeremy Scahill's exposé of the Blackwater mercenary firm forcefully demonstrates the grave dangers of outsourcing the government's monopoly on the use of force" Joseph Wilson, former U.S. Ambassador to Iraq

"Jeremy Scahill actually doesn't know anything about Blackwater." Martin Strong, vice president, Blackwater Worldwide

JEREMY SCAHILL is an international journalist who has covered the war in Iraq; the downfall of Milosevic's government in Serbia; the role of the Chevron oil corporation in the massacre of protesting villagers in the Niger Delta; and the involvement of mercenaries in New Orleans following Hurricane Katrina. He was among the few western reporters to gain access to Abu Ghraib prison when Saddam Hussein was in power. A frequent contributor to *The Nation* magazine and a correspondent for U.S. radio and television, Scahill has won numerous awards for his investigative journalism. *Blackwater* is his first book.

BLACKWATER

THE RISE OF THE WORLD'S MOST POWERFUL MERCENARY ARMY

JEREMY SCAHILL

A complete catalogue record for this book can
be obtained from the British Library on request

The right of Jeremy Scahill to be identified as the author of this work
has been asserted by him in accordance with the
Copyright, Designs and Patents Act 1988

First published in the USA in 2007 by
Nation Books, a member of the Perseus Books Group

This updated paperback edition published in 2008

First published in the UK in 2007 by
Serpent's Tail,
an imprint of Profile Books Ltd
3A Exmouth House
Pine Street
Exmouth Market
London EC1R 0JH
website: *www.serpentstail.com*

ISBN 978 1 84668 652 8

Printed by CPI Bookmarque, Croydon, CR0 4TD

Mixed Sources
Product group from well-managed
forests and other controlled sources
www.fsc.org   Cert no. TT-COC-002227
© 1996 Forest Stewardship Council
FSC

1 3 5 7 9 10 8 6 4 2

For unembedded journalists, particularly Arab media workers, who risk and often lose their lives to be the eyes and ears of the world. Without their courage and sacrifice, history would indeed be written by self-declared victors, the rich, and the powerful.

CONTENTS

AUTHOR'S NOTE

THIS BOOK would not have been possible without the tireless efforts of my colleague Garrett Ordower. Garrett is a remarkable investigative journalist who spent countless hours filing Freedom of Information Act requests, researching complicated people and events, digging up facts and figures, and interviewing sources. He also wrote solid first drafts of some chapters for this book. I am forever grateful to Garrett for his diligent and careful work on this project and his unflinching dedication to old-fashioned muckraking. This book is as much his as it is mine. I look forward to Garrett's future endeavors in law and journalism and would be honored to work with him again.

Additionally, I would like to thank Eric Stoner who provided research assistance in the paperback updates of this book. I also wish to alert the reader to the fact that Blackwater refused to grant me interviews with company executives. A spokesperson did write to "thank" me for my "interest in Blackwater" but said that the company was "unable to accommodate" my request for interviews with the men who run Blackwater. I am indebted to the solid reporting of Jay Price and Joseph Neff of the Raleigh *News & Observer* and Bill Sizemore and Joanne Kimberlin of the *Virginian-Pilot* newspapers. These reporters and their groundbreaking work have done the public a great service in chronicling the Blackwater story and the explosive growth of the private military industry. Special thanks also to T. Christian Miller of the *Los Angeles Times* and Anthony Shadid and Rajiv Chandrasekaran of the *Washington Post,* as well as authors P. W. Singer and Robert Young Pelton. I would encourage readers to read the acknowledgments at the end of this book for a more comprehensive understanding of the number of people who contributed to this process.

THE FACE OF BLACKWATER

October 2, 2007
Washington D.C.

ERIK PRINCE, the boy-faced thirty-eight-year-old owner of Blackwater, marched confidently into the regally decorated chamber of the Congressional hearing room and was immediately swarmed by a mob of paparazzi. Cameras flashed and heads turned inside the packed room. The man at the helm of a small army of mercenaries was escorted not by his elite squad of ex–Navy SEALs and Special Forces operators but by an army of lawyers and advisers. Within minutes, his image would be beamed across the globe, including onto television screens throughout Iraq, where rage against his men was building by the moment. His company was now infamous, and for the first time since the occupation began, it had a face.

It was a moment Prince had long resisted. Before that warm October day in Washington in 2007, he had shunned the spotlight, and his people were known to stifle journalists' attempts at taking his picture. When Prince did appear in public, it was almost exclusively at military conferences, where his role was to extol the virtues of his company and its work for the U.S. government, which consisted, in part, of keeping alive the most hated officials in Iraq. Since September 11, Blackwater had risen to a position of extraordinary prominence in the "war on terror" apparatus, and its contracts with the federal government had grown to more than $1 billion. On this day, the man in control of a force at the vanguard of the Bush administration's offensive war in Iraq would be on the defensive.

Shortly after 10 a.m. on October 2, Prince was sworn in as the star witness in a hearing of Representative Henry Waxman's Committee on Oversight and Government Reform. The muscular, clean-shaven ex–Navy SEAL wore a smartly tailored blue suit—more CEO than cowboy contractor. On the desk in front of Prince's chair was a simple paper sign that read, "Mr. Prince." The Republicans attempted to adjourn the meeting in protest before it started, but the measure was defeated. In classic Waxman fashion, the advertised title of the event was generic and understated: "Hearing on Private Security Contracting in Iraq and Afghanistan." But the reason for Prince's appearance on Capitol Hill that day was very specific and politically charged. Two weeks earlier, his Blackwater forces had been at the center of the deadliest mercenary action in Iraq since the start of the occupation, an incident one senior U.S. military official said could have an impact "worse than Abu Ghraib." It was a massacre some had dubbed "Baghdad's Bloody Sunday."

BAGHDAD'S BLOODY SUNDAY

SEPTEMBER 16, 2007, approximately 12:08 p.m., Nisour Square, Baghdad, Iraq: It was a steamy hot day, with temperatures reaching 100 degrees. The heavily armed Blackwater convoy entered the congested intersection in the Mansour district of the Iraqi capital. The once upscale section of Baghdad was still lined with boutiques, cafes, and art galleries dating back to better days. The ominous caravan consisted of four large armored vehicles with 7.62-millimeter machine guns mounted on top.[1] For Iraqi police, it had become a standard part of their workday in occupied Iraq to stop traffic to make room for U.S. VIPs, protected by heavily armed private soldiers, to blaze through. Ask U.S. officials and they'll say the reason was to prevent an insurgent attack on U.S. convoys.

More often, though, the Iraqi police did this for the safety of Iraqi civilians who risked being gunned down merely for getting too close to the most highly valued lives in their country—those of foreign occupation officials.

As the Blackwater convoy was entering the square that day, a young Iraqi medical student named Ahmed Hathem al-Rubaie was driving his mother, Mahasin, in the family's white Opal sedan. They had just dropped off Ahmed's father, Jawad, a successful pathologist, near the hospital where he worked. They then had gone on their way to run errands, including picking up college applications for Ahmed's sister. The plan was to finish up and return later to pick up Jawad. As fate would have it, they found themselves stuck near Nisour Square. The Rubaies were devout Muslims and were fasting in observance of the holy month of Ramadan. Ahmed was multilingual, a soccer fan, and was in his third year of medical school, where he was training to become a surgeon. Medicine was in his DNA. Like his father, Ahmed's passenger that day, his mother, was also a doctor—an allergist. Jawad says the family could have left Iraq, but they believed they were needed in the country. "I feel pain when I see doctors leaving Iraq," he said.[2]

Ali Khalaf Salman, an Iraqi traffic cop on duty in Nisour Square that day, remembers vividly the moment when the Blackwater convoy entered the intersection, spurring him and his colleagues to scramble to stop traffic. But as the vehicles entered the square, the convoy suddenly made a surprise U-turn and proceeded to drive the wrong way on a one-way street.[3] As Khalaf watched, the convoy came to an abrupt halt. He says a large white man with a mustache, positioned atop the third vehicle in the Blackwater convoy, began to fire his weapon "randomly."[4]

Khalaf looked in the direction of the shots, on Yarmouk Road, and heard a woman screaming, "My son! My son!"[5] The police officer sprinted toward the voice and found a middle-aged woman inside a vehicle holding a twenty-year-old man who had been shot in the forehead and was covered in blood. "I tried to help the young man, but his mother was holding him so tight," Khalaf recalled.[6] Another Iraqi policeman, Sarhan Thiab, also ran to the car. "We tried to help him," Thiab said. "I saw the left side of his head was destroyed and his mother was crying out, 'My son, my son! Help me, help me!'"[7]

Officer Khalaf recalled looking toward the Blackwater shooters: "I raised my left arm high in the air to try to signal to the convoy to stop the shooting."[8] He says he thought the men would cease fire, given that he was a clearly identified police officer.[9] The young man's body was still in the driver's seat of the automatic vehicle and, as Khalaf and Thiab stood there, it began to roll forward, perhaps because the dead man's foot remained on the accelerator.[10] Blackwater guards later said they initially opened fire on the vehicle because it was speeding and would not stop, a claim disputed by scores of witnesses.[11] Aerial photos of the scene later showed that the car had not even entered the traffic circle when it was fired upon by Blackwater,[12] while the *New York Times* reported, "The car in which the first people were killed did not begin to closely approach the Blackwater convoy until the Iraqi driver had been shot in the head and lost control of his vehicle."[13] Thiab explained, "I tried to use hand signals to make the Blackwater people understand that the car was moving on its own and we were trying to stop it. We were trying to get the woman out but had to run for cover."[14]

"Don't shoot, please!" Khalaf recalled yelling.[15] But as he stood with his hand raised, Khalaf says, a gunman from the fourth Blackwater vehicle opened fire on the mother gripping her son and shot her dead before Khalaf's and Thiab's eyes.[16] "I saw parts of the woman's head flying in front of me, blow up," Thiab said. "They immediately opened heavy fire at us."[17] Within moments, Khalaf says, so many shots had been fired at the car from "big machine guns" that it exploded, engulfing the bodies inside in flames, melting their flesh into one.[18] "Each of their four vehicles opened heavy fire in all directions, they shot and killed everyone in cars facing them and people standing on the street," Thiab recalled. "When it was over we were looking around and about fifteen cars had been destroyed, the bodies of the killed were strewn on the pavements and road."[19] When later asked by U.S.

investigators why he never fired at the Blackwater men, Khalaf told them, "I am not authorized to shoot, and my job is to look after the traffic."[20]

The victims were later identified as Ahmed Hathem al-Rubaie and his mother, Mahasin. Ahmed's father, Jawad, has a brother, Raad, who worked in a nearby hospital where victims of the shooting were being taken. "He heard the shots," Jawad recalls. "It was a battle, a fight, a war. And, of course, it didn't occur to him that my wife and my son were the victims—among the victims of the incident."[21] Raad "went to the morgue, and the person who was responsible for the morgue told him that they received sixteen bodies as casualties from the incident that day. They were all identified, identifiable, except for two. Two bodies completely burnt. . . . They were put in black plastic bags."[22] Raad suspected that it could be Ahmed and Mahasin but, he said, "my heart didn't want to believe it."[23] He and his wife drove to Nisour Square and found a badly burnt white sedan. The license plate was not on the vehicle, but Raad's wife found an imprint of the numbers in the sand. Raad called Jawad and began reading the numbers on the vehicle and confirmed his worst fears.[24]

Jawad raced to the morgue, where he viewed the charred bodies. He identified his wife through her dental bridge and his son by the remains of one of his shoes.[25] In all, Jawad says, there were some forty bullet holes in their vehicle.[26] He said he never returned to claim the vehicle because he wanted "it to be a memorial to the painful event caused by people who, supposedly, came to protect us."[27]

That attack on Ahmed and Mahasin's vehicle spiraled into a shooting spree that would leave seventeen Iraqis dead and more than twenty wounded.

After Ahmed and Mahasin's vehicle exploded, sustained gunfire rang out in Nisour Square as people fled for their lives. In addition to the Blackwater shooters in the four armored cars, witnesses say gunfire came from Blackwater's Little Bird helicopters. "The helicopters began shooting on the cars," Khalaf said. "The helicopters shot and killed the driver of a Volkswagen and wounded a passenger" who escaped by "rolling out of the car into the street," he said.[28] Witnesses described a terrifying scene of indiscriminate shooting by the Blackwater guards. "It was a horror movie," said Khalaf.[29] "It was catastrophic," said Zina Fadhil, a twenty-one-year-old pharmacist who survived the attack. "So many innocent people were killed."[30]

Another Iraqi officer on the scene, Hussam Abdul Rahman, said that people who attempted to flee their vehicles were targeted. "Whoever stepped out of his car was shot at immediately," he said.[31]

"I saw women and children jump out of their cars and start to crawl on the road to escape being shot," said Iraqi lawyer Hassan Jabar Salman, who was shot four times in the back during the incident. "But still the firing kept coming and many of them were killed. I saw a boy of about ten leaping in fear from a minibus—he was shot in the head. His mother was crying out for him. She jumped out after him, and she was killed."[32]

Salman says as he entered the square that day he was driving behind the Blackwater convoy when it stopped. Witnesses said some sort of explosion had gone off in the distance, too far away to have been perceived as a threat. He said Blackwater guards ordered him to turn his vehicle around and leave the scene. Shortly after, the shooting began. "Why had they opened fire?" he asked. "I do not know. No one—I repeat, no one—had fired at them. The foreigners had asked us to go back, and I was going back in my car, so there was no reason for them to shoot."[33] In all, he says, his car was hit twelve times, including the four bullets that pierced his back.

Mohammed Abdul Razzaq and his nine-year-old son, Ali, were in a vehicle immediately behind Ahmed and Mahasin, the first victims that day. "We were six persons in the car—me, my son, my sister, and her three sons. The four children were in the back seat," Razzaq said.[34] He recalled that the Blackwater forces had "gestured stop, so we all stopped. . . . It's a secure area, so we thought it will be the usual: we would stop for a bit as convoys pass. Shortly after that they opened heavy fire randomly at the cars with no exception."[35] He said his vehicle "was hit by about thirty bullets. Everything was damaged: the engine, the windshield, the back windshield, and the tires.[36]

"When the shooting started, I told everybody to get their heads down. I could hear the children screaming in fear. When the shooting stopped, I raised my head and heard my nephew shouting at me, 'Ali is dead, Ali is dead!'"[37]

"My son was sitting behind me," he said. "He was shot in the head and his brains were all over the back of the car."[38] Razzaq remembered, "When I held him, his head was badly wounded, but his heart was still beating. I thought there was a chance and I rushed him to the hospital. The doctor told me that he was clinically dead and the chance of his survival was very slim. One hour later, Ali died."[39] Razzaq, who survived the shooting, later returned to the scene and gathered the pieces of his son's skull and brain with his hands, wrapped them in cloth, and took them to be buried in the Shiite holy city of Najaf. "I can still smell the blood, my son's blood, on my fingers," Razzaq said two weeks after his son died.[40]

In all, the melee reportedly lasted about fifteen minutes.[41] In an indication of how out of control the situation quickly became, U.S. officials report that "one or more" Blackwater guards called on their colleagues to stop shooting.[42] The word "cease-fire" "was supposedly called out several times," a senior official told the New York Times. "They had an on-site difference of opinion."[43] At one point a Blackwater guard allegedly drew his gun on another. "It was a Mexican standoff," said one contractor.[44] According to Salman, the Iraqi lawyer who was in the square that day, the Blackwater guard screamed at his colleague, "No! No! No!" The lawyer was shot in the back as he tried to flee.[45]

As the heavy gunfire died down, witnesses say, some sort of smoke bomb was set off in the square, perhaps to give cover for the Blackwater convoy to leave, a common practice of security convoys.[46] Iraqis also said the Blackwater forces fired shots as they withdrew from the square. "Even as they were withdrawing, they were shooting randomly to clear the traffic," said an Iraqi officer who witnessed the shootings.[47]

Within hours, Blackwater would become a household name the world over, as news of the massacre spread. Blackwater claimed its forces had been "violently attacked"[48] and "acted lawfully and appropriately"[49] and "heroically defended American lives in a war zone."[50] "The 'civilians' reportedly fired upon by Blackwater professionals were in fact armed enemies."[51] In less than twenty-four hours, the killings at Nisour Square would cause the worst diplomatic crisis to date between Washington and the regime it had installed in Baghdad. Though Blackwater's forces had been at the center of some of the bloodiest moments of the war, they had largely operated in the shadows. Four years after Blackwater's first boots hit the ground in Iraq, it was yanked out of the darkness. Nisour Square would propel Erik Prince down the path to international infamy.

A Deadly Pattern

Even though tens of thousands of mercenaries have deployed in Iraq, private security forces faced no legal consequences for their deadly actions in the first five years of the Iraq occupation. As of Spring 2008, not a single one had been prosecuted for a crime against an Iraqi. In fact, they seldom faced any public outcry from Iraqi officials. Within the Bush administration they were either praised or unmentioned. In Congress, privatized war was almost a nonissue despite the efforts of a few prescient legislators who realized the threat. The belligerent politicians who did pay attention primarily did so to win even more business for the war contractors. Media coverage of mercenary activities in Iraq was sporadic and incident-oriented. Almost no one was looking at the bigger picture. But following Nisour Square, Blackwater and other mercenary firms suddenly lost their fiercely guarded covert status.

While the shooting in Nisour Square put the issue of private forces in Iraq—and Blackwater's name specifically—on the front pages of newspapers around the world, this was hardly the first deadly incident involving these forces. What was new was that the pro-U.S. Iraqi government responded powerfully. Within twenty-four hours of the shooting, Iraq's Interior Ministry announced that it was expelling Blackwater from the country; Prime Minister Nuri al-Maliki called the firm's conduct "criminal."[52] For the Iraqi government it was the final straw.

The Baghdad government's anger would be understandable even if the only incident involving Blackwater were Nisour Square. But this was a four-year pattern, one that had intensified in its lethality the year preceding the killing of the seventeen Iraqis in Baghdad. And, particularly enraging to the Iraqis, there had been no consequences for the company's actions. Contractors in Iraq reportedly had a motto: "What happens here today, stays here today."[53] As one armed contractor informed the *Washington Post*, "We were always told, from the very beginning, if for some reason something happened and the Iraqis were trying to prosecute us, they would put you in the back of a car and sneak you out of the country in the middle of the night."[54]

That is what apparently happened after another fatal Blackwater incident. On Christmas Eve 2006, inside Baghdad's heavily fortified Green Zone, Andrew Moonen,[55] an off-duty Blackwater operative, had just left a holiday party. Witnesses said he was drunk as he walked through the "Little Venice" section of the zone,[56] where he encountered Raheem Khalif, an Iraqi bodyguard of Vice President Adil Abdul-Mahdi.[57] "Between 10:30 and 11:30 p.m., the Blackwater contractor, carrying a Glock 9 mm pistol, passed through a gate near the Iraqi Prime Minister's compound and was confronted by the Iraqi guard, who was on duty," according to a U.S. Congressional investigation. "The Blackwater contractor fired multiple shots, three of which struck the guard, then fled the scene."[58]

Blackwater officials confirmed that within days they whisked the contractor safely out of Iraq, which they say Washington ordered them to do.[59] Iraqi officials labeled the killing a "murder."[60] Blackwater said it fired the contractor, but as of early 2008, he had yet to be charged with any crime. A year after the incident, Erik Prince would say that Blackwater had gotten Moonen's security clearance revoked, which Prince said meant Moonen would "never work in a clearance capacity for the U.S. government again," or that it would be "very, very unlikely."[61] But weeks after the fatal shooting, Moonen was rehired by a Defense Department contractor and was back working on a U.S. government contract in the Middle East.[62]

Representative Dennis Kucinich, a member of the Committee on Oversight and Government Reform, suggested that by facilitating Moonen's secret departure from Iraq, "There's a question that could actually make [Blackwater's] corporate officers accessories . . . in helping to create a flight from justice for someone who's committed a murder."[63] According to a memo from the U.S. Embassy to Secretary of State Condoleezza Rice, after the shooting, Iraqi Vice President Abdul-Mahdi tried to keep the story under wraps because he believed "Iraqis would not understand how a foreigner could kill an Iraqi and return a free man to his own country."[64]

Six weeks later, on February 7, a Blackwater sniper shot and killed a guard with a bullet through the head at the state-funded Iraqi Media Network and then proceeded to snipe two other guards who responded to the initial shooting.[65] The Iraqi government investigated the incident, as did the media network, which concluded, "On Feb. 7, members of Blackwater opened fire from the roof of the Ministry of Justice building, intentionally and without any provocation, shooting three members of our security team which led to their deaths while they were on duty inside the network complex."[66] But the U.S. government, relying on information from Blackwater, concluded that the sniper's actions "fell within approved rules governing the use of force."[67] Blackwater says its forces were fired upon, a claim contested by witnesses and the Iraqi government. Neither the U.S. Embassy nor Blackwater interviewed any of the Iraqi witnesses.[68]

In May 2007, Blackwater forces engaged in back-to-back deadly actions in a Baghdad neighborhood near the Iraqi Interior Ministry, according to a report by Steve Fainaru and Saad al-Izzi of the *Washington Post*.[69] In one incident, Blackwater forces fired on an Iraqi vehicle they said had veered too close to their convoy, killing a civilian driver. As with the September 16 shooting, witnesses said it was unprovoked. In the ensuing chaos, the Blackwater operatives reportedly refused to give their names or details of the incident to Iraqi officials, sparking a tense standoff between Blackwater and Iraqi forces, both of which were armed with assault rifles. It might have become even bloodier if a U.S. military convoy hadn't arrived on the scene and intervened. A day before that incident, in a nearby neighborhood,

Blackwater operatives found themselves in a nearly hourlong gun battle that drew in U.S. military and Iraqi forces, in which at least four Iraqis are said to have died. U.S. sources said the Blackwater forces "did their job," keeping the officials alive.[70]

Shortly after Nisour Square, Ambassador Ryan Crocker said, "I'm the ambassador here, so I'm responsible. . . . Yes, I certainly do wish I'd had the foresight to see that there were things out there that could be corrected."[71]

According to the *Washington Post*, by early June 2007, three months before Nisour Square, "concerns about Blackwater had reached Iraq's National Intelligence Committee, which included senior Iraqi and U.S. intelligence officials, including Maj. Gen. David B. Lacquement, the Army's deputy chief of staff for intelligence. Maj. Gen. Hussein Kamal, who heads the Interior Ministry's intelligence directorate, called on U.S. authorities to crack down on private security companies. U.S. military officials told Kamal that Blackwater was under State Department authority and outside their control, according to notes of the meeting. The matter was dropped."[72]

Iraqi officials alleged that there had been at least six deadly incidents involving Blackwater in the year leading up to Nisour Square.[73] In all there were ten known deadly shootings involving Blackwater from June 2005 to September 2007.[74] Among these was a February 4, 2007, shooting allegedly resulting in the death of Hana al-Ameedi, an Iraqi journalist, near the Foreign Ministry; and a September 9, 2007, shooting during which five Iraqis were killed near a government building in Baghdad. There was also a September 12, 2007, shooting that wounded five people in eastern Baghdad.[75]

"We tried several times to contact the U.S. government through administrative and diplomatic channels to complain about the repeated involvement by Blackwater guards in several incidents that led to the killing of many Iraqis," said Kamal.[76] However, U.S. Embassy spokesperson Mirembe Nantongo said, "We have no official documentation on file from our Iraqi partners requesting clarification of any incident."[77] But that statement was apparently contradicted by another U.S. official, Matthew Degn, who served as a liaison to the Iraqi Interior Ministry until August 2007. Degn told the *Washington Post* that Iraqi officials had sent a flurry of memos to Blackwater and U.S. officials well before the September 16 shootings and had been rebuffed in their requests for action. "We had numerous discussions over [Iraqi government] frustrations with Blackwater, but every time [Iraqi officials] contacted the [U.S.] government, it went nowhere,"[78] Degn said.

"Blackwater Provides a Valuable Service"

The day after the Nisour Square shootings, the U.S. State Department ordered all non-U.S. military officials to remain inside the Green Zone, and diplomatic convoys were halted. It was a stark reminder of how central Blackwater was to the U.S. occupation. As one Iraqi observer joked, the Green Zone became the "Green Zoo."[79] The Iraqi government, acting as though it was in control of the country, announced that it intended to prosecute the Blackwater men responsible for the killings. "We will not allow Iraqis to be killed in cold blood," Maliki said. "There is a sense of tension and anger among all Iraqis, including the government, over this crime."[80]

But getting rid of Blackwater would not prove to be so easy. Four days after being grounded, Blackwater was back on Iraqi streets. After all, Blackwater is not just any security company in Iraq; it is the leading mercenary company of the U.S. occupation. It first took on this role in the summer of 2003, after receiving a $27 million no-bid contract to provide security for Ambassador Paul Bremer, who headed the Coalition Provisional Authority from May 2003 to June 2004. Since then, it has kept every subsequent U.S. Ambassador, from John Negroponte to Ryan Crocker, alive. It protected Secretary of State Condoleezza Rice when she visited the country, as well as scores of U.S. Congressional delegations. From its original Iraq contract to late 2007, Blackwater had won $1 billion in "diplomatic security" contracts through the State Department alone.[81]

Blackwater's presence on Iraqi streets days after Maliki called for its expulsion served as a potent symbol of the utter lack of Iraqi sovereignty. Maliki quickly found himself under heavy U.S. pressure to back off his initial demands of expulsion and prosecution. While Rice immediately called the Iraqi prime minister to apologize, she made a point of emphasizing publicly that "we need protection for our diplomats."[82] A few days later, Tahseen Sheikhly, a representative of Maliki's government, stated, "If we drive out this company immediately, there will be a security vacuum. That would cause a big imbalance in the security situation."[83] Given the carnage of September 16, it was a difficult statement to wrap one's head around.

In a telling 180-degree turn, Maliki swiftly agreed to withhold judgment on Blackwater's status, pending the conclusion of a "joint" U.S.-Iraqi investigation. But he was also under intense pressure from Iraqis, with leading political and resistance figures demanding that Blackwater leave immediately. Clearly aware of this, while visiting the United States a week after the shootings, Maliki went so far as to call the situation "a serious challenge to the sovereignty of Iraq" that "cannot be accepted."[84]

Despite Maliki's wavering, back in Baghdad there seemed to be great and genuine determination to bring the perpetrators of the Nisour Square slaughter to justice. An investigative team made up of officials from Iraq's Interior, National Security, and Defense ministries said in a preliminary report that "the murder of citizens in cold blood in the Nisour area by Blackwater is considered a terrorist action against civilians just like any other terrorist operation."[85] But, as with other deadly incidents, Iraqi investigators claimed that they had received little or no information from the U.S. government and were being denied access to the Blackwater operatives involved in the shootings. A U.S. official appeared to dismiss the validity of the Iraqi investigation, telling the *New York Times*, "There is only the joint investigation that we have with the Iraqis."[86]

Still, Iraqi officials announced their intent to bring criminal charges against the Blackwater forces involved in the shooting, and the Iraqi ministries' report stated, "The criminals will be referred to the Iraqi court system."[87] Abdul Sattar Ghafour Bairaqdar, a member of Iraq's Supreme Judiciary Council, the country's highest court, declared, "This company is subject to Iraqi law, and the crime committed was on Iraqi territory, and the Iraqi judiciary is responsible for tackling the case."[88]

Unfortunately, things were not quite so simple.

On June 27, 2004, the day before Bremer skulked out of Baghdad, he issued a decree known as Order 17.[89] This directive granted sweeping immunity to private contractors working for the United States in Iraq, effectively barring the Iraqi government from prosecuting contractor crimes in domestic courts. The timing was curious, given that Bremer was leaving after allegedly "handing over sovereignty" to the Iraqi government. The immunity conferred by Order 17 continues to this day and was firmly in effect at the time of Nisour Square. Industry representatives and U.S. officials have long argued that Iraq does not have a fair and stable judiciary system in place to handle prosecutions of foreign private contractors. Regardless of the legitimacy of that claim, if the United States took contractor crimes seriously, it would have pursued avenues of alternative prosecution or sanction of alleged killers—if for no other reason than to show the Iraqis that the United States would not simply shrug off their concern and outrage. But the fact is that not a single armed contractor, for Blackwater or any other firm, has ever been charged in any court anywhere with any crime against an Iraqi. As a result, these forces operate in a climate of total impunity, which some observers allege is deliberate and serves a larger purpose for the occupation. "The fact that they have immunity means that there is not even the possibility of them fearing any consequences for acts of killing and brutalization," said Michael Ratner, president of the Center for Constitutional Rights. "None of this is by chance; their very purpose is to brutalize and strike fear into the people of Iraq."[90]

At the time of the Nisour Square shooting, Blackwater was one of more than 170 mercenary firms offering their services in Iraq. While it was viewed widely as the most elite of these companies, there were two U.S. competitors, DynCorp and Triple Canopy, that would gladly have stepped in to fill its shoes in one of the most lucrative private security contracts in modern history. But what happened behind the scenes in the days and weeks after

September 16 spoke volumes as to how deeply embedded Blackwater was in the occupation apparatus and how important Erik Prince's company had become to the White House. Blackwater "has a client who will support them no matter what they do," H.C. Lawrence Smith, deputy director of the industry-funded Private Security Company Association of Iraq, told the *Washington Post* shortly after Nisour Square.[91]

The dirty open secret in Washington was that Blackwater had done its job in Iraq: to keep the most hated U.S. occupation officials alive by any means necessary. "What they told me was, 'Our mission is to protect the principal at all costs. If that means pissing off the Iraqis, too bad,'" recalled former U.S. occupation adviser Ann Exline Starr, who was protected in Iraq by both Blackwater and DynCorp.[92] This "mission" encouraged conduct that placed U.S. lives at an infinitely higher premium than those of Iraqi civilians, even in cases where the only Iraqi crime was driving too close to a VIP convoy protected by Blackwater guards. "Those guys guard my back," Ambassador Ryan Crocker said shortly after Nisour Square. "And I have to say they do it extremely well. I continue to have high regard for the individuals who work for Blackwater."[93] He was hardly alone in coming to the company's defense. "Zero individuals that Blackwater has protected have been killed" in Iraq, said Republican Congressman Patrick McHenry, who represents Blackwater's home state of North Carolina. "That is, I think, the operable number here."[94]

"That's a perfect record," said Connecticut Republican Chris Shays, asserting Blackwater didn't "get any credit for it for some reason."[95]

As media scrutiny of the Nisour Square shootings intensified and Congressional Democrats woke up to the activities of Blackwater in Iraq, it appeared for a moment as though the company's days in Iraq were numbered. Even on a practical level, U.S. officials had to be concerned at the prospect of Washington's bodyguards becoming greater targets than the personnel they were tasked with keeping alive.

A few days after Nisour Square, another scandal involving Blackwater erupted, this one centered in Washington and highlighting the close relationship between the company and the Bush administration. Allegations surfaced that weapons brought into Iraq by Blackwater may have ended up in the hands of the Kurdish militant group the PKK, which is designated a "foreign terrorist organization" by the State Department.[96] According to a September 18 letter sent by Representative Henry Waxman to State Department Inspector General Howard "Cookie" Krongard, a federal investigation into whether Blackwater "was illegally smuggling weapons into Iraq" was obstructed by Krongard, who, Waxman charged, was a "partisan" operative with close ties to the Bush administration.[97]

Waxman cited a July 2007 e-mail from Krongard in which he ordered his staff to "stop IMMEDIATELY" cooperating with the federal prosecutor investigating Blackwater until Krongard himself could speak to him. Waxman said Krongard's actions had caused "weeks of delay" and that by subsequently assigning a media relations staffer instead of an investigator to aid the prosecutor, Krongard had "impeded the investigation."[98] Krongard described the allegations as "replete with inaccuracies including those made by persons with their own agendas." It was later revealed that Krongard's brother, Alvin "Buzzy" Krongard, had accepted a position as a paid adviser to Blackwater, a position from which he resigned after Waxman's committee exposed it. [99] (As discussed in Chapter 3, Alvin Krongard, who served as the number-three man at the CIA, was a player in helping Blackwater win its first private security contract in Afghanistan in 2002.) Howard Krongard subsequently resigned from his State Department post in late 2007.[100] Blackwater, for its part, denied that it was "in any way associated or complicit in unlawful arms activities" and said it was cooperating in the federal investigation.[101]

While Blackwater got hammered for these scandals in the media, behind the scenes, a series of events was unfolding that reeked of a major-league cover-up of the Nisour Square massacre, an effort that appeared to emanate from some of the highest levels of power in Washington. As Waxman prepared for Erik Prince's October trip to Capitol Hill, he discovered that after the shooting, the State Department had ordered Blackwater "to make no disclosure of the documents or information" regarding its Iraq security contract without written authorization.[102] Waxman protested to Rice, saying Congress had a "constitutional prerogative" to investigate Blackwater and telling her, "You are wrong to interfere with the committee's inquiry."[103] Under fire, the State Department shifted its position the day Waxman wrote to Rice, saying that the restriction applied only to classified information.[104]

Unlike many private companies working for the occupation in Iraq, Blackwater reported directly to the White House, not to the military. They "are really an arm of the administration and its policies," charged Kucinich.[105] Both Gen. David Petraeus and Ambassador Crocker made clear that without Blackwater and its ilk, the occupation would not be tenable. "I have a great deal of respect for their work," said Deputy Secretary of State John Negroponte, who was guarded by Blackwater during his time in Iraq. Blackwater, he said, "kept me safe—to get my job done." Without them, he said, "the civilians of the Department of State would not be able to carry out our critical responsibilities in places like Iraq and Afghanistan."[106] Nicholas Burns, the Under Secretary of State for Political Affairs, said, "We have lots of people in Baghdad, it's our largest embassy in the world, and they have to be well protected."[107]

While George W. Bush had, at times, displayed a willingness to throw his allies overboard when his own survival—or that of his pet policies—was on the line, Blackwater would not join Donald Rumsfeld and George Tenet in the open waters of collateral damage. "Blackwater provides a valuable service," Bush said after the Nisour Square massacre. "They protect people's lives. And I appreciate the sacrifice and the service that the Blackwater employees have made."[108] What was probably dawning on members of the Bush administration at this point was that, like it or not, they needed Blackwater. Even if it was politically expedient to let them go, the occupation of Iraq would have been practically impossible to carry on without them. The company and its ilk had become that integral to the military operations of the United States.

Prince of the Hill

The first time Erik Prince was summoned to appear before Congress to answer questions about Blackwater's activities, in February 2007, he sent his lawyer. That was before most people had ever heard of his company. After Nisour Square, he had no choice but to show up in person. On October 2, 2007, the world would meet Mr. Prince.[109] Security was heavy inside the Committee room, and a line of would-be spectators and journalists stretched through the corridors of the Rayburn building. Many would be corralled into an overflow room, but most remained in the halls. Only a few dozen people were permitted to witness the event in person, among them the family members of Blackwater operatives killed in Fallujah, who were suing Blackwater for wrongful death. The entire seating section behind the leather chair where Prince would sit was blocked off with signs that read, "Reserved for Blackwater USA." Several of those chairs would remain empty for the duration of the hearing.

Prince arrived surrounded by lawyers and advisers, including Barbara Comstock, a veteran Republican operative and crisis communications expert, and a number of senior Blackwater executives, among them Prince's right-hand men, vice president Bill Matthews and president Gary Jackson. Prince's consigliere would repeatedly interrupt the proceedings to huddle the advisers around the Blackwater chief like a sports team plotting its next play. In preparation for his appearance that day, Prince's lawyers had enlisted the services of BKSH, the political consulting arm of Burson-Marsteller, a PR giant controlled by one of the barons of spin, Mark Penn.[110] It was an interesting choice, given that Penn was Hillary Clinton's chief strategist, a man some observers have called "Hillary's Rove." Perhaps more telling was the fact that BKSH was led by Charles Black Jr., an adviser to both presidents Bush.[111]

What put Prince in the hot seat was undoubtedly Nisour Square. But amazingly, Prince would face no questions about that incident. On the eve of the hearing, Alberto Gonzales's Justice Department announced it had launched a criminal investigation into the incident. Waxman said the Justice Department had asked him not to take testimony on the shootings to avoid tainting the investigation. Although Waxman asserted Congress "has an independent right to this information," he nonetheless agreed to keep it off the table. The timing of the Bush administration's announcement to investigate—a full two weeks after the alleged crime was committed and on the eve of the appearance of the man in charge of the alleged perpetrators— was suspect, to say the least.

Waxman banged his gavel and brought the meeting to order. "Over the past twenty-five years, a sophisticated campaign has been waged to privatize government services," he declared. "The theory is that corporations can deliver government services better and at a lower cost than the government can. Over the last six years, this theory has been put into practice. The result is that privatization has exploded."

"There may be no federal contractor in America that has grown more rapidly than Blackwater over the last seven years," Waxman said at the hearing's onset. "In 2000, Blackwater had just $204,000 in government contracts. Since then, it has received over $1 billion in federal contracts. More than half of these contracts were awarded without full and open com- petition. Privatizing is working exceptionally well for Blackwater. The ques- tion for this hearing is whether outsourcing to Blackwater is a good deal for American taxpayers, the military, and our national interest in Iraq."

After opening statements, Erik Prince stood before the committee, raised his right hand, and vowed to tell the truth. Prince painted a picture of his company as a patriotic extension of the U.S. military whose men "play defense" in a dangerous war zone where they "bleed red, white, and blue" as they heroically protect "reconstruction officials" trying to "weave the fabric of Iraq back together, to get them away from that X, the place where the bad guys, the terrorists, have decided to kill them that day." He used the phrase "bad guys" at least nine times during his testimony, at one point declaring, "The bad guys have figured out killing Americans is big media, I think. They are trying to drive us out. They try to drive to the heart of Amer- ican resolve and will to stay there."

During nearly four hours of testimony and questioning, Prince boldly declared that in Iraq his men have acted "appropriately at all times" and denied the company had ever killed innocent civilians. His hand never trembled, and he showed no sign of breaking a sweat. To say he was cool under fire would be an understatement. Prince was defiant.

"You do admit that Blackwater personnel have shot and killed innocent civilians, don't you?" Illinois Democrat Danny Davis asked Prince.

"No, sir. I disagree with that," Prince shot back. "I think there's been times when guys are using defensive force to protect themselves, to protect the packages, trying to get away from danger. There could be ricochets, there are traffic accidents, yes. This is war."

Prince added smugly, "We do not have the luxury of staying behind to do that terrorist crime-scene investigation to figure out what happened."

The assertion by Prince that no innocents had been killed by Blackwater was simply unbelievable. And not just according to the eyewitnesses and survivors of the Nisour Square shootings and other deadly Blackwater actions. According to a report prepared by Waxman's staff, from 2005 to the time of the hearing, Blackwater operatives in Iraq opened fire on at least 195 occasions.[112] In more than 80 percent of these instances, Blackwater fired first. These statistics were based on Blackwater's own reporting. But some alleged the company was underreporting its statistics. A former Blackwater operative who spent nearly three years in Iraq told the *Washington Post* his twenty-man team averaged "four or five" shootings a week—several times the rate of 1.4 incidents per week that Blackwater claimed.[113] Waxman's report also described an incident in which "Blackwater forces shot a civilian bystander in the head. In another, State Department officials report that Blackwater sought to cover up a shooting that killed an apparently innocent bystander."[114]

Not surprisingly, Prince said he supported the continuation of Order 17 in Iraq, the Bremer-era decree immunizing forces like Blackwater from prosecution in Iraqi courts. At one point, Prince was asked whether Blackwater operated under the same "rules of engagement" as the military. "Yes, they're essentially the same," Prince said—before fumbling for words and admitting, "Well, well, sorry, Department of Defense rules for contractors. We do not have the same as a U.S. soldier at all."

The truth is that while scores of U.S. soldiers had been court-martialed on murder-related charges in Iraq, not a single Blackwater contractor had ever been charged with a crime under any legal system—U.S. civilian law, military law, or Iraqi law. Prince said that Blackwater operatives who "don't hold to the standard, they have one decision to make: window or aisle" on their return flight home. Indeed, that and being fired seem to have been the only consequences faced by Prince's men for their actions in Iraq. In all, Blackwater had terminated more than 120 of its operatives in Iraq—more than one-seventh of its deployment at the time of the hearing.[115]

On this point, the committee focused on one incident at length: the Christmas Eve killing of the bodyguard to the Iraqi vice president. Prince confirmed that Blackwater had whisked him out of Iraq and fired him, and said the company had fined him and then billed the man for his return plane ticket. Prince said he did not know if the man had been charged with any crime (he hadn't). "If he lived in America, he would have been arrested, and he would be facing criminal charges," Democrat Carolyn Maloney told Prince. "If he was a member of our military, he would be under a court-martial. But it appears to me that Blackwater has special rules." Prince said, "As a private organization, we can't do any more. We can't flog him, we can't incarcerate him." Maloney told Prince, "Well, in America, if you committed a crime, you don't pack them up and ship them out of the country in two days."

When asked directly whether this was a murder, which Iraqi officials had alleged, Prince said, "It was a guy that put himself in a bad situation." Pressed further, Prince consulted with his advisers and said, "Beyond watching detective shows on TV, sir, I am not a lawyer, so I can't determine whether it would be a manslaughter, a negligent homicide, I don't know. I don't know how to nuance that. But I do know he broke our rules, he put himself in a bad situation and something very tragic happened."

The committee also released an internal e-mail from a Blackwater employee to a colleague just after the shooting, noting that an Iraqi TV report had erroneously attributed the killing of the bodyguard to a U.S. soldier. "At least the ID of the shooter will take the heat off us," the Blackwater employee wrote. Representative Elijah Cummings concluded, "In other words, he was saying: 'Wow, everyone thinks it was the military and not Blackwater. What great news for us. What a silver lining.'" Prince responded, "I don't believe that false story lasted in the media for more than a few hours, sir."

This exchange would set off a discussion about one of the main questions of the hearing: was Blackwater hurting the U.S. military's stated counterinsurgency program in Iraq?

"It does appear from some of the evidence here that Blackwater and other companies sometimes, at least, conduct their missions in ways that lead exactly in the opposite direction that General Petraeus wants to go," Democrat John Tierney told Prince. "That doesn't mean you're not fulfilling your contractual obligations." Tierney then read numerous comments from U.S. military officials and counterinsurgency experts raising questions about Blackwater's actions having a blowback effect on official U.S. troops.

Tierney quoted Army Col. Peter Mansoor: "If they push traffic off the roads or if they shoot up a car that looks suspicious, they may be operating within their contract, but it is to the detriment of the mission, which is to bring the people over to our side." He quoted retired Army officer Ralph Peters: "Armed contractors do harm COIN—counterinsurgency efforts. Just ask the troops in Iraq." Brig. Gen. Karl Horst: "These guys run loose in this country and do stupid stuff. There is no authority over them, so you can't come down on them when they escalate force. They shoot people and someone else has to deal with the aftermath. It happens all over the place." And Col. Thomas X. Hammes: "The problem is in protecting the principal, they had to be very aggressive. And each time they went out they had to offend locals, forcing them to the side of the road, being overpowering and intimidating, at times running vehicles off the road, making enemies each time they went out. So they were actually getting that contract exactly as we asked them to—it was at the same time hurting our counterinsurgency effort."

Tierney told Prince, "So when we look at Blackwater's own records that show that you regularly move traffic off the roads and you shoot up cars— in over 160 incidents of firing on suspicious cars—we can see, I think, why the tactics you use in carrying out your contract might mitigate [sic] against what we're trying to do in the insurgency."

"I understand the challenges that the military faces there," Prince responded, adding, "We strive for perfection, but we don't get to choose when the bad guys attack us. You know, the bad guys have figured out—the terrorists have figured out how to make a precision weapon with a car, load it with explosives with a suicidal driver."

Representatives also raised the issue of cost, pointing out that each Black-water operative cost taxpayers $1,222 per day. "We know that sergeants in the military generally cost the government between $50,000 to $70,000 per year," Waxman said. "We also know that a comparable position at Black-water costs the federal government over $400,000, six times as much." Prince was confronted with Defense Secretary Robert Gates's statement a week earlier on the issue of the disparity in pay between soldiers and private forces. "I worry that sometimes the salaries they are able to pay in fact lures some of our soldiers out of the service to go to work for them," Gates had said, adding that he was seeking legal advice on whether a "noncompete" clause could be put into security contracts. Prince said it would be "fine" with him but asserted that "it would be upsetting to a lot of soldiers if they didn't have the ability to use the skills they learned in the military in the private sector."

Toward the end of the hearing, it was noted that General Petraeus makes about $180,000 a year. When asked his own salary, Prince said he didn't know exactly and then, when pressed, offered that it was "more than $1 million." He estimated that about 90 percent of the business of the Prince Group empire (Blackwater's parent company) comes from federal contracts.

He wouldn't say how much the company had made for its work in Iraq, but "as an example" he said under some contracts Blackwater earns a profit margin of about 10 percent, which one Congressman remarked could mean more than $100 million. Prince adamantly refused to answer the profit question directly. "We're a private company," he said. "The key word there is 'private.'"

Connecticut Democrat Christopher Murphy, incredulous, asked, "How can you say that information isn't relevant?" adding, "my constituents pay 90 percent of your salary." Finally, Prince quipped, "I'm not a financially driven guy."

While Blackwater's actions in Iraq over the past four years have consistently resulted in an escalation of violence and bloodshed there, many of the most infamous incidents involving the company were not discussed or only brought up in passing at the hearing. Some of the Democrats on the committee appeared to be reading their briefing papers while Prince was testifying, giving the impression that they were ill-prepared to address Blackwater's central role in the U.S. war machine. Prince did face some tough and important questions, but often his answers were left to stand with no credible follow-up or challenge. All the while, the very reason Prince found himself before Congress that day and the reason the world watched his testimony—the Nisour Square massacre—went undiscussed, the Iraqi victims unmentioned.

The Republicans did their best to portray the hearing as a witch-hunt and heaped praise on Prince for his patriotism and service. "This is not about Blackwater," said conservative California Republican Darrell Issa. "What we are hearing today is, in fact, a repeat of the MoveOn.org attack on General Petraeus's patriotism." Several Republicans thanked Prince for keeping them alive when they toured Iraq, the irony of how this could impact their impartiality apparently lost on them.

It wasn't lost on Massachusetts Democrat Stephen Lynch. He said in his trips to Iraq, he too had been protected by Blackwater, which he acknowledged "did a very, very good job." He added, "I find myself right now with this committee having a difficult time criticizing those employees, because I am in their debt . . . which brings me to my problem. If I have a problem criticizing Blackwater and criticizing the employees and some of the times that you have fouled up, what about the State Department?" Lynch questioned how any effective investigations into Blackwater's conduct could be expected when Blackwater itself is responsible for the safety of those tasked with investigating the company. "The State Department employees, you protect them every single day. You protect their physical well-being, you transport them, you escort them. And I am sure there is a heavy debt of gratitude on the part of the State Department for your service," Lynch told Prince. "And yet they are the very same people who are in our system responsible for holding you accountable in every respect with your contract and the conduct of your employees. . . . That is an impossible conflict for them to resolve." Prince never addressed the matter because Lynch's time expired. But Lynch's point was an important one. According to the Oversight Committee's investigation, "There is no evidence" that "the State Department sought to restrain Blackwater's actions, raised concerns about the number of shooting incidents involving Blackwater or the company's high rate of shooting first, or detained Blackwater contractors for investigation."[116] Indeed, the State Department had not only failed to effectively investigate or rein in Blackwater; there was evidence that it had done the reverse, covering for the company when it landed in the hot seat.

As the duration of the hearing neared four hours, Prince was asked if he wanted to take a break or deal with the remaining questions. "I'll take them, and then let's be done," he shot back. Moments later, Prince's lawyer shot up from his chair behind the Blackwater chief and frantically directed a "T" for "time" with his hands toward the committee. With that, the hearing came to an end. Prince stood up, grabbed the paper with his name on it from the table, and marched with his entourage from the room.

There is no question the Justice Department's intervention at the eleventh hour took some of the heat off Prince over Nisour Square. "He gave a very self-serving testimony to us," said Waxman. "I can understand that that's what he wanted to do. That was in his interest to do it."[117] Blackwater clearly felt its man had won the day. Emboldened by Prince's defiant appearance before Congress, Blackwater would launch a new PR campaign to defend its image, and its star would be Prince himself. Far from facing the heat of a critical media, Prince would find friendly faces and softball questions as he met the press. Shortly after his Congressional testimony, Prince's longtime friend archconservative California Congressman Dana Rohrabacher compared the Blackwater chief to another controversial figure who had once been forced to raise his right hand before Congress. "Prince," Rohrabacher said, "is on his way to being an American hero just like Ollie North was."[118]

In the meantime, in Baghdad, the survivors and victims' families of Nisour Square were learning what U.S. justice really meant.

Nothing You Say Can and Will Be Used Against You in a Court of Law

Any criminologist will tell you that it is essential to seal off the scene of a crime as soon as possible. Evidence must be secured, witnesses interviewed, suspects identified and taken into custody. It is a race against the clock. The Bush administration's handling of Nisour Square was a textbook case in how not to investigate a crime. Perhaps that was the point all along.

Ten days after the shooting, and with the administration facing a mounting scandal, the State Department's "first blush" report on Nisour Square was leaked to the media. Dated September 16, 2007, the day of the shooting, and stamped "Sensitive but Unclassified," it was titled "SAF [small-arms fire] attack on COM team."[119] The report alleged that the Blackwater team entered the square and was "engaged with small arms fire" from "8–10 persons" who "fired from multiple nearby locations, with some aggressors dressed in civilian apparel and others in Iraqi police uniforms. The team returned defensive fire." It made no mention of any civilian deaths or injuries. While it appeared as though the State Department had investigated and was contradicting the widespread allegations of an unpro-

voked shooting, what was not revealed at the time was that the report was
written by a Blackwater contractor, Darren Hanner, and printed on official
State Department letterhead.[120]

It would be two weeks before the Bush administration would get around
to deploying a ten-person team from the FBI—the official investigative
body of the U.S. government—to Baghdad to investigate the shooting.[121] As
the FBI prepared to depart for Baghdad, reports emerged that the agents
were to be guarded by none other than Blackwater itself.[122] Senator Patrick
Leahy quickly raised questions about the arrangement, forcing the Bureau
to announce it would be guarded by official personnel and not personnel
from the same company it was investigating.[123]

In the meantime, the official investigation of the Bush administration
would be conducted by the State Department, whose personnel continued
to depend on the chief suspects to keep them alive. "To rely on non-law
enforcement to conduct sensitive law enforcement activities makes no sense
if you want impartial justice," said Melanie Sloan, a former federal prosecutor who currently serves as executive director of Citizens for Responsibility and Ethics in Washington.[124]

Normally when a group of people alleged to have gunned down seventeen civilians in a lawless shooting spree are questioned, investigators will
tell them something along the lines of: "You have the right to remain silent.
Anything you say can and will be used against you in a court of law." But
that is not what the Blackwater operatives involved in the Nisour Square
shooting were told. They were questioned by State Department Diplomatic
Security investigators with the understanding that their statements and
information gleaned from them could neither be used to bring criminal
charges against them nor even be introduced as evidence.[125]

ABC News obtained copies of sworn statements given by Blackwater
guards in the immediate aftermath of the shootings, all of which began, "I
understand this statement is being given in furtherance of an official administrative inquiry," and "I further understand that neither my statements nor
any information or evidence gained by reason of my statements can be used

against me in a criminal proceeding."[126] CCR's Ratner said the offering of so-called "use immunity" agreements by the State Department was "very irregular," adding he could not recall a precedent for it.[127] In normal circumstances, Ratner said, such immunity was granted only after a grand jury or Congressional committee had been convened and the party had invoked its Fifth Amendment right for protection against self-incrimination. Immunity would then be authorized by either a judge or the committee.

"What the State Department has done in this case is inconsistent with proper law enforcement standards. It is likely to undermine an ultimate prosecution, if not make it impossible," said military law expert Scott Horton of Human Rights First. "In this sense, the objective of the State Department in doing this is exposed to question. It seems less to be to collect the facts than to immunize Blackwater and its employees. By purporting to grant immunity, the State Department draws itself more deeply into the wrongdoing and adopts a posture vis-à-vis Blackwater that appears downright conspiratorial. This will make the fruits of its investigation a tough sell."[128] One U.S. diplomat described the relationship between the U.S. Embassy's security office in Baghdad and Blackwater to the *Los Angeles Times*. "They draw the wagon circle," the diplomat said. "They protect each other. They look out for each other. I don't know if that's a good thing, that wall of silence. When it protects the guilty, that is definitely not a good thing."[129]

But it wasn't just that the State Department was apparently corrupting or stifling the investigation or hindering a successful prosecution of Blackwater. As Congress investigated Nisour Square, what emerged was evidence of a clear pattern of the State Department urging Blackwater to pay what amounted to hush money to Iraqi victims' families. "In cases involving the death of Iraqis, it appears that the State Department's primary response was to ask Blackwater to make monetary payments to 'put the matter behind us,' rather than to insist upon accountability or to investigate Blackwater personnel for potential criminal liability," according to a report of the House Oversight Committee. "The most serious consequence faced by

Blackwater personnel for misconduct appears to be termination of their employment."[130] Congressman Waxman charged that the State Department was "acting as Blackwater's enabler."[131]

On Christmas Day 2006, the day after Blackwater operative Andrew Moonen allegedly shot and killed the Iraqi vice president's bodyguard, the State Department recommended that Blackwater pay off the guard's family. The U.S. Embassy's chargé d'affaires wrote to the regional security officer, Blackwater's handler, "Will you be following in up [sic] Blackwater to do all possible to assure that a sizeable compensation is forthcoming? If we are to avoid this whole thing becoming even worse, I think a prompt pledge and apology—even if they want to claim it was accidental—would be the best way to assure the Iraqis don't take steps, such as telling Blackwater that they are no longer able to work in Iraq."[132]

It was a prophetic warning, coming a full nine months before the Iraqis would demand just that in the aftermath of Nisour Square. The chargé d'affaires initially suggested a $250,000 payment, but the State Department's Diplomatic Security Service said this was too much and could cause Iraqis to "try to get killed so as to set up their family financially."[133] In the end, the State Department and Blackwater reportedly agreed on a $15,000 payment. During his Congressional testimony, Prince corrected that figure, saying Blackwater had actually paid $20,000.[134] In another case, in Al Hillah in June 2005, a Blackwater operator killed an "apparently innocent bystander" and the State Department requested that Blackwater pay the family $5,000.[135] "Can you tell me how it was determined that this man's life was worth $5,000?" Representative Davis asked Prince. "We don't determine that value, sir," Prince responded. "That's kind of an Iraqi-wide policy. We don't make that one."[136] In cases where the government and Blackwater claimed the guards fired in self-defense, though, no money was offered to victims' families. The three victims of the Blackwater sniper at the Iraqi TV station in February 2007, for example, received nothing.[137]

Shortly after the Nisour Square shootings, the State Department began contacting the Iraqi victims' families. Dr. Jawad, whose son and wife were the first victims that day, said U.S. officials asked him how much money he wanted in compensation. "I said their lives are priceless," Jawad recalled.[138] But the U.S. officials continued pressing him for a dollar amount. He said he told a State Department representative "if he could give me my loved ones, I would gladly give him $200 million." To many Iraqis, the U.S. offers were an insult. "If you perceive marriage as half of your life, Mahasin was my best half," Jawad said, talking about his wife. "We were always together. I don't know how to manage my life or care for my other two children without her."[139]

Mohammed Razzaq, whose nine-year-old son Ali was killed, asked, "Why should I ask for compensation? What would it do? Bring back my son? It will not." Ali "was in school, but last year had to leave school because we were displaced. Now the Americans have killed him—why? What did he do? What did I do? After what I witnessed, I now jump out of bed at night, I have nightmares, it's experiencing death, bullets are flying from here and there and here explosions, cars hit. Why? Why did they do this?" he asked. "I only ask why? [I] just want them to admit to the truth."[140]

The Iraqi government eventually demanded $8 million in compensation for each victim.[141] In the end, the State Department, on behalf of Blackwater, offered family members between $10,000 and $12,500,[142] which many of them refused. A U.S. official said the monetary offer was "not an admission of culpability."[143] This would not be the last Blackwater would hear from the victims' families of Nisour Square.

When the FBI finally arrived in Baghdad, some of the Blackwater guards involved in the shooting refused to be interviewed, citing promises of immunity from the State Department.[144] The FBI also discovered that the crime scene had been severely compromised.[145] Blackwater would later claim that proof it had been attacked by Iraqis could be found in damage to the company's armored vehicles. Prince said three vehicles sustained gunfire damage and that the radiator on one had been "shot out and disabled."[146] The initial State Department report (written by the Blackwater contractor) alleged one had been "disabled during the attack" and had

to be towed from the scene.[147] But when the FBI went to investigate the vehicles, it found that Blackwater had already "repaired and repainted them."
The Associated Press reported, "The repairs essentially destroyed evidence
that Justice Department investigators hoped to examine in a criminal case
that has drawn worldwide attention."[148] Blackwater spokesperson Anne
Tyrrell said any repairs "would have been done at the government's direction."[149] The State Department would not comment on it.

In contrast to the Bush administration's approach to Nisour Square, the
Iraqi authorities began their investigation within moments of the massacre,
interviewing scores of witnesses and piecing together a timeline of events.
When the Iraqis released their findings, defenders of Blackwater quickly
stepped up to cast aspersions on Baghdad's integrity. "Iraqis claim that the
Blackwaterites fired indiscriminately and without provocation. There is no
reason to assume—as so many critics do—that the more damning version
is true," wrote Blackwater apologist Max Boot in the *Los Angeles Times*,
"especially because the harshest condemnations have come from the Iraqi
Interior Ministry, a notorious hotbed of sectarianism."[150]

While Blackwater refused to answer specific questions on the incident,
citing an ongoing investigation, the company did, in fact, have its own version of events. The morning of Prince's appearance before the Oversight
Committee, his prepared remarks were released to the media. He would
never publicly deliver them, but they would constitute the most comprehensive account of the incident Blackwater would provide. Prince alleged that
his men came under fire in Nisour Square. "Among the threats identified
were men with AK–47s firing on the convoy, as well as approaching vehicles
that appeared to be suicide bombers. The Blackwater personnel attempted to
exit the area but one of their vehicles was disabled by enemy fire," Prince
claimed in the statement. "Some of those firing on this Blackwater team
appeared to be wearing Iraqi National Police uniforms, or portions of uniforms. As the withdrawal occurred, the Blackwater vehicles remained under
fire from such personnel."[151]

Two months after the shooting, ABC News obtained the sworn statement of Blackwater operative Paul Slough, a twenty-nine-year-old Army veteran. Slough was Blackwater's turret gunner that day and is believed to be the main shooter in the square.[152] His statement was given, with the promise of immunity, to the State Department three days after the incident. In it, he described his version of how the shooting began, describing the car driven by Ahmed, the medical student, and his mother, Mahasin. "As our motorcade pulled into the intersection I noticed a white four door sedan driving directly at our motorcade," Slough alleged. "I and others were yelling, and using hand signals for the car to stop and the driver looked directly at me and kept moving toward our motorcade. Fearing for my life and the lives of my teammates, I engaged the driver and stopped the threat. . . . A uniformed individual then started pushing the vehicle toward the motorcade and again I shouted and engaged the vehicle until it came to a stop."[153] This stood in sharp contrast to the Iraqi version of events, including those of several eyewitnesses, who insisted the shooting was entirely unprovoked. It was also contradicted by major media investigations and aerial photos of the aftermath.[154] Slough went on to describe several more instances in which he "engaged" Iraqis to "stop the threat."[155]

In his Congressional statement, Prince insisted that "based on everything we currently know, the Blackwater team acted appropriately while operating in a very complex war zone." He alleged that "Blackwater and its people have been the subject of negative and baseless allegations reported as truth" and that "many public reports have wrongly pronounced Blackwater's guilt for the death of varying numbers of civilians." Prince concluded there had been a "rush to judgment based on inaccurate information."[156]

There was one force that did rush to the scene to obtain information. And, unlike the Iraqi government, the media, or witnesses, this investigator could not be easily dismissed or discredited: the U.S. military, which arrived on the scene the day of the incident at 12:39 p.m., moments after the shooting ended.[157]

Amid the carnage of Nisour Square, soldiers from the Third Battalion, 82nd Field Artillery Regiment of the Second Brigade, First Cavalry Division,

interviewed witnesses, conducted an on-site investigation, and held talks
with Iraqi police. The forces under the command of Lieut. Col. Mike Tarsa
contradicted almost every one of Prince's and Slough's assertions. They
bluntly concluded there was "no enemy activity involved," determined
that all of the killings were unjustified and labeled the shootings a "criminal event." Tarsa's investigation found that many Iraqis were shot as they
attempted to flee, saying "it had every indication of an excessive shooting."
Combing the scene, Tarsa's soldiers found no bullets from AK–47 assault
rifles or BKC machine guns used by Iraqi military and police that Prince
had alleged were fired. But they did find an abundance of evidence of
ammunition from U.S.-manufactured weapons, including M4 rifle 5.56-
millimeter brass casings, M240B machine gun 7.62-millimeter casings,
and M203 40-millimeter grenade-launcher casings. Tarsa's soldiers also
said they were "surprised at the caliber of weapon being used."[158] Blackwater said at the time, in early October, it would not comment until the FBI
had concluded its investigation, but Prince did attempt to cast aspersions
on Tarsa's conclusions. "It's from one colonel," Prince said. "And I don't
know what his experience is in doing crime scene investigations."[159]

In November, the first glimpse into the conclusions of the FBI probe
emerged in the *New York Times*, which reported that the federal agents had
"found that at least 14 of the shootings were unjustified and violated
deadly-force rules in effect for security contractors in Iraq."[160] The report
added, "Investigators found no evidence to support assertions by Blackwater employees that they were fired upon by Iraqi civilians," quoting one
official as saying, "I wouldn't call it a massacre, but to say it was unwar-
ranted is an understatement." A military investigator "said the F.B.I. was
being generous to Blackwater in characterizing any of the killings as justifi-
able." The military was clearly outraged at the shootings, and some officials
believed it would have a blowback effect on U.S. soldiers. "It was absolutely
tragic," Maj. Gen. Joseph Fil, the Army's top commander for Baghdad, told
the *Washington Post*. "In the aftermath of these, everybody looks and says, 'It's
the Americans.' And that's us. It's horrible timing. It's yet another challenge,

another setback."[161] During this period, a chorus of voices rose against Blackwater from within the ranks of the military. The pay disparity between private contractors and official soldiers was hurting morale, and senior commanders complained that the misconduct of Blackwater and other private forces was damaging the U.S. "counterinsurgency" campaign. This critique was sounded from the highest levels of the military. In an unusually blunt comment a month after Nisour Square, Defense Secretary Robert Gates said the mission of many private security contractors was "at cross-purposes to our larger mission in Iraq," adding that "in the objective of completing the mission of delivering a principal safely to a destination, just based on everything I've read and what our own team has reported, there have been instances where, to put it mildly, the Iraqis have been offended and not treated properly."[162]

What was particularly troubling (aside from the loss of Iraqi civilian life) was that even if Blackwater were not so politically connected to the White House and even if there were a truly independent U.S. Justice Department and even if immunity had not been offered and even if there had been an aggressive investigation, it would not have been enough. When Secretary of State Condoleezza Rice dispatched a team to Baghdad, led by veteran diplomat Patrick Kennedy, to review the department's private security force in the aftermath of Nisour Square, the team returned with the conclusion that it "is unaware of any basis for holding non-Department of Defense contractors [like Blackwater] accountable under US law."[163]

While a fierce debate over the use of private forces raged in the United States, legal scholars debated what—if any—court could hold Blackwater and other mercenary forces accountable for their crimes in Iraq. Not only had the State Department's immunity offerings early on in the Nisour Square investigation potentially compromised the chance of prosecution, as the Justice Department acknowledged in early 2008, but the bottom line was that Blackwater operated in a legal gray zone, seemingly outside the scope of both U.S. civilian and military law and immune from Iraqi law.[164] While a federal grand jury was convened in late 2007 to investigate, serious questions about the potential for a successful prosecution abounded. Many legal analysts concluded that U.S. civilian law on contractors abroad covered only contractors working for the military—Blackwater worked for the State Department.

While the House voted shortly after Nisour Square to expand the law to apply to all contractors, it could not be applied retroactively and still had to clear the Senate. The Bush administration "strongly oppose[d]" the legislation, saying in a statement released the day after Prince appeared before Waxman's committee that the law would have "intolerable consequences for crucial and necessary national security activities and operations."[165] A court-martial seemed unlikely and could possibly meet resistance from civil liberties advocates who would view it as a step toward applying military law to civilians (though some would argue that such a label should not apply to armed mercenaries). Washington was clear it would not hand over U.S. personnel to Iraqi courts, and the Bremer-era ban on Iraq prosecuting contractors remained in place. Some analysts believed the Justice Department would attempt to prosecute at least one Blackwater operative for Nisour Square—indeed, Slough was identified as being "at the center of the investigation"—as a token symbol of accountability. But because of the way the law governing contractors was phrased at the time of the killings, the possibility of failure was significant. Some legal experts argued that the shooters could be prosecuted for war crimes under U.S. law, but that would require not only political will from the Bush administration but also a de facto indictment of the whole system of privatized war, which seemed highly unlikely to happen. The possibility that private soldiers could face prosecution, particularly for war crimes, would also have presented a major disincentive for mercenary companies to work for the Bush administration. "There clearly is jurisdiction and a basis to act against them under the War Crimes Act," said military law expert Scott Horton. "But the Bush administration doesn't want to go there, doesn't want to touch that. I think they've made that point clear."[166] The State Department's acting Assistant Secretary of State for the Bureau of Diplomatic Security, Gregory Starr, admitted, "It might be the case that Blackwater can't be held accountable" for the killings.[167]

Some of the Iraqi victims' families and Nisour Square survivors did not want to wait for Congress and the Bush administration to resolve these questions and didn't have faith justice would be done. So they took the only action they could—they sued Blackwater, not in Iraq but in Washington, D.C.

"War Crimes" and "Extra-judicial Killing"

Days after the shootings, some of the Iraqi survivors and victims' families contacted local Iraqi human rights lawyers who worked with U.S. law firms that had filed cases against other Iraq War contractors for alleged abuses. Attorneys from the Center for Constitutional Rights and two other firms, led by attorney Susan Burke of Burke O'Neil, began interviewing survivors, witnesses, and victims' families. CCR was no stranger to cases involving contractors' crimes in Iraq, having filed a major lawsuit against some of the private forces who were among the alleged perpetrators of the torture and abuse at Abu Ghraib Prison. Burke spearheaded that case as well. "[The Nisour Square families] came to us because they know of our work representing the torture victims at Abu Ghraib, and they asked us whether it would be possible to try to get some form of justice, some form of accountability, against this rogue corporation," Burke recalled.[168]

On October 11, 2007, Blackwater was sued by Iraqi civilians. Burke and CCR filed the groundbreaking lawsuit in federal court in Washington, D.C., on behalf of five of the Iraqis killed at Nisour Square and two of the survivors wounded in the attack. The suit alleged that Blackwater's actions amounted to "extra-judicial killing" and "war crimes."[169] It was filed in part under the Alien Tort Statute, which allows for litigation in U.S. courts for violations of fundamental human rights committed overseas.

"Blackwater created and fostered a culture of lawlessness amongst its employees, encouraging them to act in the company's financial interests at the expense of innocent human life," the suit charged. "This action seeks punitive damages in an amount sufficient to punish Erik Prince and his Blackwater companies for their repeated callous killing of innocents." The suit was believed to be the first U.S. case brought by Iraqi civilians against a private "security" company.

It alleged that "Blackwater heavily markets the fact that it has never had any American official under its protection killed in Iraq" and "views its willingness to kill innocent people as a strategic advantage setting Blackwater apart and above other security companies." Blackwater, the suit alleged, "was and is willing to kill innocent bystanders in order to preserve that 'no death' statistic for marketing purposes. Blackwater benefits financially from its willingness to kill innocent bystanders."

Among the plaintiffs were the estates of the first victims, Ahmed Hathem al-Rubaie and his mother, Mahasin. "She was shot to death by Blackwater shooters as she cradled her dead son's body, calling for help," the suit alleged. The three other Iraqis named in the lawsuit who were killed on September 16—Oday Ismail Ibraheem, Himoud Saed Atban, and Usama Fadhil Abbass—had fourteen children among them, one an infant, according to Burke.

"The rule of law in every civilized nation in the world is that there is no legitimate reason to indiscriminately kill innocent bystanders," Ratner said. "We believe that the acts of Blackwater at Nisour Square were deliberate, willful, intentional, wanton, malicious, and oppressive, and constitute war crimes. Blackwater is harming the United States by its repeated and consistent failure to act in accord with the law of war, the laws of the United States, and international law."[170]

Among the allegations in the suit:

- Despite Blackwater's claim that it is a defensive force, its "mobile armed forces" are "consistently referred to by Blackwater management and employees as 'shooters.'"

- Blackwater should not have been at Nisour Square and defied orders not to go there. At the time of the shootings, "Blackwater shooters were not protecting any State Department official. The

Blackwater shooters had already dropped off the official under its protection prior to arriving at Nisour Square." The "Tactical Operations Center" (manned by both Blackwater and State Department personnel) "expressly directed the Blackwater shooters to stay with the official and refrain from leaving the secure area. Blackwater personnel were "obliged" to follow the directive and did not.

- "Blackwater routinely sends heavily-armed 'shooters' into the streets of Baghdad with the knowledge that some of those 'shooters' are chemically influenced by steroids and other judgment-altering substances. Reasonable discovery will establish that Blackwater knew that 25 percent or more of its 'shooters' were ingesting steroids or other judgment-altering substances, yet failed to take effective steps to stop the drug use. Reasonable discovery will establish that Blackwater did not conduct any drug-testing of its 'shooters' before sending them equipped with heavy weapons into the streets of Baghdad." (Blackwater rejected the steroid allegations, saying its forces face drug tests during their application process and on a quarterly basis while working for the company. A spokesperson said, "Blackwater has very strict policies concerning drug use, and if anyone were known to be using illegal drugs, they would be fired immediately.")

- Blackwater does not have "a valid contract" with the United States: "The Anti-Pinkerton Act . . . prohibits the United States from doing business with '[a]n individual employed by the Pinkerton Detective Agency, or similar organization.' The legislative history of the Act makes it clear that a 'similar organization' means any mercenary or quasi-mercenary organization. Blackwater constitutes such a 'similar organization' and therefore lacks any valid contractual relationships with the United States." (Ironically, a few months after the suit was filed, Blackwater vice president Martin Strong actually compared Blackwater's work directly to Pinkerton's. "Well, I can remember a time when Abraham Lincoln tried to get to his inaugural and he couldn't find anybody to protect him except for the Pinkertons, who were a private-sector solution to protecting the new president of the United States," he said. "This has been going on for a long, long time."[171])

Blackwater publicly declined to respond to the allegations in the suit, citing ongoing government investigations, but its spokesperson, Anne Tyrrell, said Blackwater "will defend itself vigorously."[172] Erik Prince, however, went on the attack—against the Iraqi victims' lawyers. "The lawyers, the trial lawyers that filed this lawsuit are the same guys that defended the World Trade Center bombings in 1993, the blind sheikh, and defended a bunch of killers of FBI agents and other cops," Prince said on CNN two days after the suit was filed. "So this is very much a politically motivated lawsuit, for media attention."[173] In fact, Prince was dead wrong. CCR did not represent "the blind sheikh," nor did it "defend" the 1993 WTC bombing. But Prince's spin was promptly adopted by his right-wing defenders and disseminated in the media.

A few days later, J. Michael Waller, vice president of the Center for Security Policy—a hard-line conservative think tank with deep connections to the Bush administration—wrote an op-ed in the *New York Post* called "Lawyers for Terror."[174] In it, he accused CCR and Michael Ratner of having "a four-decade record of aiding and abetting terrorists, spies and cop-killers" and said they "specialize in defending the enemies of American society." Waller wrote, "As we await the facts to establish responsibility for the Sept. 16 tragedy in Nisour Square, we must demand answers to another question: Of the million-plus lawyers in the United States they could have chosen to sue Blackwater, how did ordinary Iraqis manage to pick the few who aid cop-killers and terrorists?"

Ratner said these claims were "transparent attempts to try and divert attention from Blackwater's actions in Iraq and particularly its role in the Nisour killings. I don't think character attacks fool anyone. Such attempts at character assassination are a smokescreen to cover up the killings. At trial the facts will speak for themselves and the truth will be revealed."[175]

On December 19, 2007, CCR and Burke filed yet another lawsuit against Blackwater. This one stemmed from Blackwater's alleged killing of five Iraqis on September 9 in Baghdad's Watahba Square, one week before the Nisour Square killings. "Blackwater shooters shot, without justification, and killed five innocent civilians," the suit alleged. "Numerous other innocent civilians were . . . injured in the incident."[176] Burke filed the case on behalf of the family of Ali Hussamaldeen Albazzaz. "This gentleman was a rug merchant, and he was gunned down for absolutely no reason, leaving behind a twenty-day-old baby daughter and family. It is again another instance in which Blackwater shooters shot first, asked questions later," Burke alleged.[177]

"If the Government Doesn't Want Us to Do This, We Will Go Do Something Else"

Despite the massive controversy surrounding Blackwater, its forces—and lucrative contracts—remained firmly in place on the ground in Iraq. One Blackwater employee described to the *New York Times* a conversation company representatives had with the State Department's Gregory Starr in November 2007. "He said Blackwater has not lost the contract here in Iraq, and that it entirely depends on our actions from here on out."[178] On December 3, Blackwater posted job listings for "security specialists" and snipers as a result of its State Department diplomatic security "contract expansion."[179]

Rather than hiding out and hoping for the scandals to fade, Blackwater launched a major rebranding campaign, changing its name to Blackwater Worldwide and softening its logo: once a bear paw in the site of a sniper scope, it would become a bear claw wrapped in two half ovals—sort of like the outline of a globe, with a United Nations feel. Its overhauled website boasted of a corporate vision "guided by integrity, innovation, and a desire for a safer world."[180] Blackwater operatives were referred to as "global stabilization professionals." Prince did a series of interviews, many of them conducted by mainstream journalists who were fawning and uncritical, in which he spun Blackwater as a patriotic extension of the military, often repeating almost verbatim his carefully crafted lines. He was named number eleven in *Details* magazine's "Power 50," the men "who control your viewing patterns, your buying habits, your anxieties, your lust . . . the people who have taken over the space in your head."[181]

In one of the company's most bizarre actions in this period, on December 1, Blackwater paratroopers staged a dramatic aerial landing, complete with Blackwater flags and parachutes—not in Baghdad or Kabul but in San Diego at Qualcomm Stadium during the halftime show at the San Diego State/BYU football game. The company also sponsored a NASCAR racer and teamed up with gun manufacturer Sig Sauer to create a Blackwater Special Edition full-sized 9-millimeter pistol with the company logo on the grip. It came with a limited lifetime warranty. For $18, parents could purchase infant onesies from the Blackwater ProShop emblazoned with the firm's logo.[182]

During his media blitz, Prince indicated that Blackwater might quit Iraq. "We see the security market diminishing," he told the *Wall Street Journal* in October.[183] One way of looking at it was that Blackwater had gotten what it needed out of its Iraq work. As Prince told Congress, "If the government doesn't want us to do this, we will go do something else."[184] While its name had become mud in the human rights world, Blackwater had not only already made big money in Iraq; it had secured a reputation as a company that kept U.S. officials in an extremely hostile war zone alive by any means necessary. It's an image that could serve Blackwater well as it expands globally.

Prince vowed that in the future Blackwater "is going to be more of a full spectrum" operation.[185] Amid the cornucopia of scandals, Blackwater was bidding for a share of a five-year $15 billion contract with the Pentagon to "fight terrorists with drug-trade ties."[186] This "war on drugs" contract would put Blackwater in the same league as the godfathers of the war business, including Lockheed Martin, Northrop Grumman, and Raytheon.

In addition to its ongoing robust business in law enforcement, military, and homeland security training, Blackwater is branching out. Among its current projects and initiatives:[187]

- Blackwater affiliate Greystone Ltd., registered offshore in Barbados, is an old-fashioned mercenary operation offering "personnel from the best militaries throughout the world" for hire by governments and private organizations. It also boasts of a "multinational peacekeeping program," with forces "specializing in crowd control and less than lethal techniques and military personnel for the less stable areas of operation."

- Prince's Total Intelligence Solutions, headed by three CIA veterans (among them Blackwater's number-two, Cofer Black), puts CIA-type services on the open market for hire by corporations or governments. (*See Epilogue.*)

- Blackwater is launching an armored vehicle called the Grizzly, which the company characterizes as the most versatile in history. Blackwater intends to modify it to be legal for use on U.S. highways.

- Blackwater's aviation division has some forty aircraft, including turboprop planes that can be used for unorthodox landings. It has ordered a Super Tucano paramilitary plane from Brazil, which can be used in counterinsurgency operations. In August 2007, the aviation division won a $92 million contract with the Pentagon to operate flights in Central Asia.

- In late 2007, it flight-tested the unmanned Polar 400 airship, which may be marketed to the Department of Homeland Security for use in monitoring the US-Mexico border and to "military, law enforcement, and non-government customers."

- A fast-growing maritime division has a new 184-foot vessel that has been fitted for potential paramilitary use.

What Blackwater has done since it first opened for business in the late 1990s is to build up a privatized parallel structure to the U.S. national security apparatus. As of this writing, it continues to receive major contracts for

its various divisions, and the U.S. government remains the greatest con-
sumer of its services. In December 2007, it registered a new high-powered
lobbying firm, Womble, Carlyle, Sandridge & Rice.[188] The disclosure form,
filed with the U.S. Senate in January 2008, indicated the firm would be
lobbying for Blackwater on a wide range of contracts in: defense, homeland security, aerospace, disaster planning, foreign relations, and law
enforcement.

War Is Business. Business Is Good.

In many ways, Blackwater is the embodiment of the Bush administration's
"revolution in military affairs," which has entailed aggressive outsourcing
of core military functions. The company's centrality to the U.S. occupation
of Iraq was emblematic of the new face of the U.S. war machine. But it is
also a symbol of the times in which we live, where every aspect of life is
being radically privatized—schools, healthcare, prisons, homeland security
operations, intelligence, municipal services. While Blackwater certainly
owes its stunning success to the belligerent, offensive foreign policies of the
Bush administration, it is important to remember that Blackwater opened
for business during President Bill Clinton's time in office. It was Clinton's
administration that authorized Blackwater as a vendor to the federal government and awarded the firm its first government contracts.

The fact is that privatization is not just a Republican or a Bush administration agenda—it was rapidly escalated by Bush, but it has been embraced
and nurtured by the power structures of both political parties for decades.
"Even under the Clinton administration, this was a standard operating procedure," said Illinois Democrat Jan Schakowsky, one of the sharpest Congressional critics of war contracting. "But we've seen this enormous
escalation of this industry so that now it's billions and billions of dollars.
This is definitely an expansion."[189] The U.S. government pays contractors as
much as the combined taxes paid by everyone in the United States with
incomes under $100,000, meaning "more than 90 percent of all taxpayers
might as well remit everything they owe directly to [contractors] rather than

to the [government]," according to a 2007 investigative report in *Vanity Fair*.[190] As journalist Naomi Klein put it, "According to this radical vision, contractors treat the state as an ATM, withdrawing massive contracts to perform core functions like securing borders and interrogating prisoners, and making deposits in the form of campaign contributions."[191]

"I think it's extraordinarily dangerous when a nation begins to outsource its monopoly on the use of force and the use of violence in support of its foreign policy or national security objectives," said veteran U.S. diplomat Joe Wilson, who served as the last Ambassador to Iraq before the 1991 Gulf War. The billions of dollars being doled out to war companies, Wilson argues, "makes of them a very powerful interest group within the American body politic and an interest group that is in fact armed. And the question will arise at some time: to whom do they owe their loyalty?"[192]

While the bipartisan privatization virus spreads further, companies like Blackwater become ever more deeply embedded in the most sensitive sectors of government. Blackwater is moving ahead at full steam. Individual scandals clearly aren't enough to slow it down. Even if Blackwater were to go out of business tomorrow, there are scores of companies that would gladly step in to take over its work.

While radical privatization is having a devastating impact throughout society, the privatization of the war machine has been lethal. Blackwater is a company whose business depends on war and conflict to thrive. It operates in a demand-based industry where corporate profits are intimately linked to an escalation of violence. That demand has been tremendous during the presidency of George W. Bush. In particular, the unprecedented militarization of the State Department's Bureau of Diplomatic Security, which has occurred in tandem with the process of rapid privatization, has enriched Blackwater. The department's Worldwide Personal Protective Services was originally envisioned as a small-scale bodyguard operation to protect small groups of U.S. diplomats and other U.S. and foreign officials. In Iraq, the administration turned it into a paramilitary force several thousand strong. Spending on the program jumped from $50 million in 2003 to $613 million in 2006.[193]

According to the Congressional Oversight Committee's investigation, "In fiscal year 2001, Blackwater had $736,906 in federal contracts. By 2006, Blackwater had over $593 million in government contracts, an increase of more than 80,000%."[194] In 2007, Blackwater had two-thirds as many operatives deployed in Iraq as the U.S. Bureau of Diplomatic Security had in all other countries in the world combined. As Ambassador Ryan Crocker said in late 2007, "There is simply no way at all that the State Department's Bureau of Diplomatic Security could ever have enough full-time personnel to staff the security function in Iraq. There is no alternative except through contracts."[195]

As of summer, 2007, there were more "private contractors" deployed on the U.S. government payroll in Iraq (180,000) than there were actual soldiers (160,000).[196] These contractors worked for some 630 companies and drew personnel from more than 100 countries around the globe.[197] Tens of thousands were armed operatives like those who work for Blackwater— exactly how many was unknown, because neither the administration nor the military could or would provide those numbers. This meant the U.S. military had actually become the junior partner in the coalition that occupies Iraq. The existence of a powerful shadow army enabled the waging of an unpopular war with forces whose deaths and injuries went uncounted and unreported. It helped keep a draft, which could make the continuation of the war politically untenable, off the table. It also subverted international diplomacy because the administration didn't need to build a "coalition of the willing": it rented an occupation force. Private soldiers were hired from countries that had no direct stake in the war or whose home governments opposed it, and were used as cheap cannon fodder.

War is business, and business has been very good. It is not just the actions of Blackwater and its ilk that need to be investigated, exposed, and prosecuted. It is the whole system. If the insatiable demand for these mercenary "services," which derives from offensive, unpopular wars of conquest, is not forcefully challenged, Blackwater and other mercenary firms have little to fear. In street parlance, they are the dealers, but the government is the addict. These companies are not simply bad apples. They are the fruit of a very poisonous tree. This system depends on a wedding of immunity and impunity. If the government started slapping mercenary firms with indictments for war crimes or murder or human rights violations—and not just in a token manner—the risk for the companies would be tremendous. This, in turn, would make wars like the one in Iraq far more difficult and arguably impossible. But even after the outrage of Nisour Square, there was no sign of this happening. In early 2008, President Bush once again sought to force the Iraqi government to extend immunity to private contractors, as he negotiated a new "Status of Forces" agreement with Baghdad.[198] He also said he would "waive" a provision of a 2008 law—which he signed—that would have established a bipartisan Wartime Contracting Commission to investigate war contractors, as well as one that provided protections for whistleblowers working for government contractors. In a statement, Bush said these provisions would "inhibit the President's ability" to "protect national security, to supervise the executive branch, and to execute his authority as Commander in Chief."[199]

While Bush undoubtedly has been the war industry's greatest supporter, the prospect for the aggressive action required to confront the mercenary menace, whether a Democrat or Republican replaces him in the White House, is slim. The war industry is an equal-opportunity campaign contributor and has solid support from influential politicians on both sides of the aisle. Representative Schakowsky introduced legislation in late 2007 called the Stop Outsourcing Security (SOS) Act, which sought to end the use of Blackwater and other mercenary firms in U.S. war zones by 2009. "Private contracting companies have forfeited their right to represent the United States," Schakowsky said, asserting that they "put our troops in harm's way, and resulted in the unnecessary deaths of many innocent Iraqi civilians. They have become a liability instead of an asset."[200] Only a small fraction of the 435 legislators in the House signed on to support her bill and, as of spring 2008, only two senators—Vermont Independent Bernie Sanders and New York's Hillary Clinton.

Because of the Bush administration's refusal to hold mercenary forces

accountable for their crimes in Iraq and the Democrats' unwillingness to
effectively challenge the radically privatized war machine, the only hope the
victims of Nisour Square have for justice lies in the lawsuit they filed against
Blackwater in Washington, D.C. In some ways, that is the most logical place
for such a trial to take place, because the violence unleashed by Blackwater
in Iraq is ultimately rooted in the for-profit war machine based in the U.S.
capital. Shortly after Nisour Square, Erik Prince was asked by an interviewer,
"How many Iraqi civilians have been killed by Blackwater employees?"
"That's an unknowable number," Prince replied, in a rare moment of
candor on the subject.[201] The significance of that acknowledgment was not
lost on the lawyers suing Blackwater for Nisour Square. "What these Iraqi
families are doing is a civil service to all Iraqis because they don't want
anyone else to be killed by Blackwater," attorney Susan Burke said. "We are
going to expose the corporate culture that is leading to all this death and
destruction in Iraq."[202]

As the United States debates an Iraq withdrawal, Blackwater doesn't
appear threatened. In April 2008, over the objections of the Iraqi government, the company's Iraq contract was extended for another year. The State
Department's Gregory Starr said the decision was made "after careful consideration of the operational requirements necessary to support the U.S.
Government's foreign policy objectives in Iraq."[203] Some leading Democrats have advocated a gradual military withdrawal that would leave in place
a counterterrorism "strike force," the Green Zone, and security for U.S.
Embassy personnel, who would staff the largest embassy in the world—
potentially tens of thousands of armed forces. This, in turn, means a continued, major role for private forces in Iraq. In fact, one of Blackwater's
senior executives, Joseph Schmitz, seemed to find a gold lining for Blackwater and other war contractors in a U.S. withdrawal from Iraq: "There is a
scenario where we could as a government, the United States, could pull
back the military footprint and there would then be more of a need for private contractors to go in."[204]

CHAPTER ONE

MAKING A KILLING

THE WORLD was a very different place on September 10, 2001, when Donald Rumsfeld stepped to the podium at the Pentagon to deliver one of his first major addresses as Defense Secretary under President George W. Bush. For most Americans, there was no such thing as Al Qaeda, and Saddam Hussein was still the president of Iraq. Rumsfeld had served in the post once before—under President Gerald Ford from 1975 to 1977—and he returned to the job in 2001 with ambitious visions. That September day in the first year of the Bush administration, Rumsfeld addressed the Pentagon officials in charge of overseeing the high-stakes business of defense contracting—managing the Halliburtons, DynCorps, and Bechtels. The Secretary stood before a gaggle of former corporate executives from Enron,

Northrop Grumman, General Dynamics, and Aerospace Corporation whom he had tapped as his top deputies at the Department of Defense, and he issued a declaration of war.

"The topic today is an adversary that poses a threat, a serious threat, to the security of the United States of America," Rumsfeld thundered.[1] "This adversary is one of the world's last bastions of central planning. It governs by dictating five-year plans. From a single capital, it attempts to impose its demands across time zones, continents, oceans, and beyond. With brutal consistency, it stifles free thought and crushes new ideas. It disrupts the defense of the United States and places the lives of men and women in uniform at risk." Pausing briefly for dramatic effect, Rumsfeld—himself a veteran Cold Warrior—told his new staff, "Perhaps this adversary sounds like the former Soviet Union, but that enemy is gone: our foes are more subtle and implacable today. You may think I'm describing one of the last decrepit dictators of the world. But their day, too, is almost past, and they cannot match the strength and size of this adversary. The adversary's closer to home. It's the Pentagon bureaucracy." Rumsfeld called for a wholesale shift in the running of the Pentagon, supplanting the old DoD bureaucracy with a new model, one based on the private sector. The problem, Rumsfeld said, was that unlike businesses, "governments can't die, so we need to find other incentives for bureaucracy to adapt and improve." The stakes, he declared, were dire—"a matter of life and death, ultimately, every American's." That day, Rumsfeld announced a major initiative to streamline the use of the private sector in the waging of America's wars and predicted his initiative would meet fierce resistance. "Some might ask, How in the world could the Secretary of Defense attack the Pentagon in front of its people?" Rumsfeld told his audience. "To them I reply, I have no desire to attack the Pentagon; I want to liberate it. We need to save it from itself."

The next morning, the Pentagon would literally be attacked as American Airlines Flight 77—a Boeing 757—smashed into its western wall. Rumsfeld would famously assist rescue workers in pulling bodies from the rubble. But it didn't take long for Rumsfeld, the chess master of militarism, to seize the

almost unthinkable opportunity presented by 9/11 to put his personal war—
laid out just a day before—on the fast track. The world had irreversibly
changed, and in an instant the future of the world's mightiest military force
had become a blank canvas on which Rumsfeld and his allies could paint
their masterpiece. The new Pentagon policy would draw heavily on the private sector, emphasize covert actions, sophisticated weapons systems, and
greater use of Special Forces and contractors. It became known as the Rumsfeld Doctrine. "We must promote a more entrepreneurial approach: one that
encourages people to be proactive, not reactive, and to behave less like
bureaucrats and more like venture capitalists," Rumsfeld wrote in the
summer of 2002 in an article for *Foreign Affairs* titled "Transforming the Military."[2] Rumsfeld's "small footprint" approach opened the door for one of
the most significant developments in modern warfare—the widespread use
of private contractors in every aspect of war, including in combat.

Among those to receive early calls from the administration to join a
"global war on terror" that would be fought according to the Rumsfeld Doctrine was a little-known firm operating out of a private military training
camp near the Great Dismal Swamp of North Carolina. Its name was Blackwater USA. Almost overnight following the great tragedy of September 11, a
company that had barely existed a few years earlier would become a central
player in a global war waged by the mightiest empire in history. "I've been
operating in the training business now for four years and was starting to get
a little cynical on how seriously people took security," Blackwater's owner
Erik Prince told Fox News host Bill O'Reilly shortly after 9/11. "The phone
is ringing off the hook now."[3]

But the story of Blackwater doesn't begin on 9/11 or even with its executives or its founding. In many ways, it encapsulates the history of modern
warfare. Most of all, it represents the realization of the life's work of the officials who formed the core of the Bush administration's war team.

During the 1991 Gulf War, Dick Cheney—Rumsfeld's close ally—was
Secretary of Defense. One in ten people deployed in the war zone at that
time was a private contractor, a ratio Cheney was doggedly determined to

ratchet up. Before he departed in 1993, Cheney commissioned a study from a division of the company he would eventually head, Halliburton, on how to quickly privatize the military bureaucracy. Almost overnight, Halliburton would create an industry for itself servicing U.S. military operations abroad with seemingly infinite profit potential. The more aggressively the U.S. expanded its military reach, the better for Halliburton's business. It was the prototype for the future. In the ensuing eight years of governance by Bill Clinton, Cheney worked at the influential neoconservative think tank the American Enterprise Institute, which led the charge for an accelerated privatization of the government and military. By 1995, Cheney was at the helm of Halliburton building what would become the U.S. government's single largest defense contractor. President Clinton largely embraced the privatization agenda, and Cheney's company—along with other contractors—was given lucrative contracts during the Balkans conflict in the 1990s and the 1999 Kosovo war. One military consulting firm, the Virginia-based Military Professional Resources Incorporated, staffed by retired senior military officials, was authorized by the Clinton administration in the mid-1990s to train the Croatian military in its secessionist war against Serb-dominated Yugoslavia, a contract that ultimately tipped the balance of that conflict. That contract was a foreshadowing of the kind of private-sector involvement in war that would become standard in the war on terror. But privatization was only part of the broader agenda. Cheney and Rumsfeld were key members of the Project for a New American Century, initiated in 1997 by neoconservative activist William Kristol.[4] The group pressed Clinton to enact regime change in Iraq, and its principles, which advocated "a policy of military strength and moral clarity,"[5] would form the basis for much of the Bush administration's international agenda.

In September 2000, just months before its members would form the core of the Bush White House, the Project for a New American Century released a report called *Rebuilding America's Defenses: Strategy, Forces and Resources for a New Century*. In laying out PNAC's vision for overhauling the U.S. war machine, the report recognized that "the process of transformation, even if it brings revolutionary change, is likely to be a long one, absent some catastrophic and catalyzing event—like a new Pearl Harbor."[6] A year to the month later, the 9/11 attacks would provide that catalyst: an unprecedented justification to forge ahead with this radical agenda molded by a small cadre of neoconservative operatives who had just taken official power.

The often-overlooked subplot of the wars of the post-9/11 period is the outsourcing and privatization they have entailed. From the moment the Bush team took power, the Pentagon was stacked with ideologues like Paul Wolfowitz, Douglas Feith, Zalmay Khalilzad, and Stephen Cambone and with former corporate executives—many from large weapons manufacturers—like Under Secretary of Defense Pete Aldridge (Aerospace Corporation), Army Secretary Thomas White (Enron), Navy Secretary Gordon England (General Dynamics), and Air Force Secretary James Roche (Northrop Grumman). The new civilian leadership at the Pentagon came into power with two major goals: regime change in strategic nations and the enactment of the most sweeping privatization and outsourcing operation in U.S. military history—a revolution in military affairs. After 9/11 this campaign became unstoppable.

The swift defeat of the Taliban in Afghanistan emboldened Rumsfeld and the administration as they began planning for the centerpiece of the neoconservative crusade: Iraq. From the moment the U.S. troop buildup began in advance of the invasion, the Pentagon made private contractors an integral part of the operations. Even as the U.S. gave the public appearance of attempting diplomacy, behind closed doors Halliburton was being prepped for its largest operation in history. When U.S. tanks rolled into Baghdad in March 2003, they brought with them the largest army of private contractors ever deployed in a war. By the end of Rumsfeld's tenure, there were an estimated 100,000 private contractors on the ground in Iraq—an almost one-to-one ratio to active-duty U.S. soldiers.[7] To the great satisfaction of the war industry, before Rumsfeld stepped down, he took the extraordinary step of classifying private contractors as an official part of the U.S. war machine. In the Pentagon's 2006 Quadrennial Review, Rumsfeld outlined what he called a "roadmap for change" at the DoD, which he said had started in 2001.[8] It defined the "Department's Total Force" as "its active and reserve military components, its civil servants, and its *contractors*—constitut[ing] its warfighting capability and capacity. Members of the Total Force serve in thousands of locations around the world, performing a vast array of duties to accomplish critical missions."

Coming as it did in the midst of an open-ended, loosely defined global war, this formal designation represented a radical rebuke of the ominous warnings laid out by President Eisenhower in his farewell address to the nation decades earlier during which he envisioned the "grave implications" of the rise of "the military-industrial complex." In 1961, Eisenhower declared, "The potential for the disastrous rise of misplaced power exists and will persist. We must never let the weight of this combination endanger our liberties or democratic processes. We should take nothing for granted. Only an alert and knowledgeable citizenry can compel the proper meshing of the huge industrial and military machinery of defense with our peaceful methods and goals, so that security and liberty may prosper together." What has unfolded in the ensuing years and particularly under the Bush administration is nothing less than the very scenario Eisenhower darkly prophesied.

While the war on terror and the Iraq occupation have given birth to scores of companies, few if any have experienced the meteoric rise to power, profit, and prominence that Blackwater has. In less than a decade, it has risen out of a swamp in North Carolina to become a sort of Praetorian Guard for the Bush administration's "global war on terror." Today, Blackwater has more than 2,300 private soldiers deployed in nine countries, including inside the United States. It maintains a database of 21,000 former Special Forces troops, soldiers, and retired law enforcement agents on whom it could call at a moment's notice. Blackwater has a private fleet of more than twenty aircraft, including helicopter gunships and a surveillance blimp division. Its 7,000-acre headquarters in Moyock, North Carolina, is the world's largest private military facility. It trains tens of thousands of federal and local law enforcement agents a year and troops from "friendly" foreign nations. The company operates its own intelligence division and counts among its executives senior ex-military and intelligence officials. It recently began constructing new facilities in California ("Blackwater West") and Illinois ("Blackwater North"), as well as a jungle training facility in the Philippines. Blackwater has more than $500 million in government contracts—and that does not include its secret "black" budget operations for U.S. intelligence agencies or private corporations/individuals and foreign governments. As one U.S. Congressmember observed, in strictly military terms, Blackwater could overthrow many of the world's governments.

Blackwater is a private army, and it is controlled by one person: Erik Prince, a radical right-wing Christian mega-millionaire who has served as a major bankroller not only of President Bush's campaigns but of the broader Christian-right agenda. In fact, as of this writing Prince has never given a penny to a Democratic candidate—certainly his right, but an unusual pattern for the head of such a powerful war-servicing corporation, and one that speaks volumes about the sincerity of his ideological commitment. Blackwater has been one of the most effective battalions in Rumsfeld's war on the Pentagon, and Prince speaks boldly about the role his company is playing in the radical transformation of the U.S. military. "When you ship overnight, do you use the postal service or do you use FedEx?" Prince recently asked during a panel discussion with military officials. "Our corporate goal is to do for the national security apparatus what FedEx did to the postal service."[9]

Perhaps the most telling sign that such a transformation had taken place came when the White House outsourced the job of protecting America's most senior officials in Iraq to Blackwater beginning in 2003. As L. Paul Bremer, Bush's envoy in the first year of the occupation, hunkered down in Baghdad to implement the Bush agenda, he was protected by Blackwater, as every successive U.S. Ambassador there has been. In contrast to active-duty soldiers who are poorly paid, Blackwater's guards were given six-figure salaries. "Standard wages for PSD (personal security detail) pros [in Iraq] were previously running about $300 [per man] a day," Fortune magazine reported at the time. "Once Blackwater started recruiting for its first big job, guarding Paul Bremer, the rate shot up to $600 a day."[10] With almost no public debate, the Bush administration has outsourced to the private sector many of the functions historically handled by the military. In turn, these private companies are largely unaccountable to the U.S. taxpayers from whom they draw their profits. Some began comparing the mercenary market in Iraq to the Alaskan Gold Rush and the O.K. Corral. As *The Times* of London put it at the time, "In Iraq, the postwar business boom is not oil. It is security."[11]

As this unprecedented private force expanded in Iraq, Bremer's last act before skulking out of Baghdad on June 28, 2004, was to issue a decree known as Order 17, immunizing contractors in Iraq from prosecution.[12] It was a significant move in a sea of policies (and absence of policies) governing the occupation of Iraq, and one that emboldened private forces. While U.S. soldiers have been prosecuted for killings and torture in Iraq, the Pentagon has not held its vast private forces to the same standards. That point was driven home during one of the rare Congressional hearings on contractors in Iraq, which took place in June 2006. Blackwater represented the industry at the hearing, which also included several government officials. Representative Dennis Kucinich questioned Shay Assad, the Pentagon's director of defense procurement and acquisition, the department in the DoD responsible for contractors. Kucinich pointed out that U.S. troops are subjected to enforceable rules of engagement and have been prosecuted for violations in Iraq, while contractors were not. He said that as of the date of the hearing, "no security contractor has been prosecuted" for crimes in Iraq.[13] He then directly asked Assad, "Would the Department of Defense be prepared to see a prosecution proffered against any private contractor who is demonstrated to have unlawfully killed a civilian?"

"Sir, I can't answer that question," Assad replied.

"Wow," Kucinich shot back. "Think about what that means. These private contractors can get away with murder." Contractors, Kucinich said, "do not appear to be subject to any laws at all and so therefore they have more of a license to be able to take the law into their own hands."

Blackwater has openly declared its forces above the law. While resisting attempts to subject its private soldiers to the Pentagon's Uniform Code of Military Justice (UCMJ)—insisting they are civilians—Blackwater has simultaneously claimed immunity from civilian litigation in the United States, saying its forces are a part of the U.S. Total Force. Blackwater has argued in legal briefs that if U.S. courts allow the company to be sued for wrongful death of its workers, that could threaten the nation's war-fighting capacity: "In order for responsible federal contractors to accompany the U.S. Armed Forces on the battlefield, it is essential that their immunity from liability for casualties be federally protected and uniformly upheld by federal courts. Nothing could be more destructive of the all-volunteer, Total Force concept underlying U.S. military manpower doctrine than to expose the private components to the tort liability systems of fifty states, transported overseas to foreign battlefields. . . . How the President oversees and commands these military operations, including his decisions through the chain of command concerning the training, deployment, armament, missions, composition, planning, analysis, management and supervision of private military contractors and their missions, falls outside the role of [the courts]."[14] Instead, Blackwater claims that its forces operate under the legally impotent and unenforceable code of conduct written by its own trade association, ironically named the International Peace Operations Association. Erik Prince says his forces are "accountable to our country,"[15] as though declarations of loyalty to the flag are evidence of just motives or activities or somehow a substitute for an independent legal framework.

This logic is encouraged not only by the virtual immunity already extended to contractors but also by the Pentagon's failure to oversee this massive private force that is now officially recognized as part of the U.S. war machine. Private contractors largely operate in a legal gray zone that leaves the door for abuses wide open. In late 2006, a one-line amendment was quietly slipped into Congress's massive 2007 defense-spending bill, signed by President Bush, that could subject contractors in war zones to the Pentagon's UCMJ, also known as the court martial system.[16] But the military has enough trouble policing its own massive force and could scarcely be expected to effectively monitor an additional 100,000 private personnel. While the five-word insert hardly establishes a system of independent oversight, experts still predict it will be fiercely resisted by the private war industry. Despite the unprecedented reliance on contractors deployed in Iraq, Afghanistan, and elsewhere, the government has failed to even count them, let alone police them. A Government Accountability Office report released in December 2006 found that the military had no effective system of oversight and that "officials were unable to determine how many contractors were deployed to bases in Iraq."[17] The Army and Air Force were unable to provide the GAO investigators "the number of contractors they were using at deployed locations or the services those contractors were providing to U.S. forces." The GAO concluded "problems with management and oversight of contractors have negatively impacted military operations and unit morale and hindered DOD's ability to obtain reasonable assurance that contractors are effectively meeting their contract requirements in the most cost-efficient manner."

A week after Donald Rumsfeld's rule at the Pentagon ended, U.S. forces had been stretched so thin by the war on terror that former Secretary of State Gen. Colin Powell declared "the active Army is about broken."[18] Rather than rethinking such aggressive policies and wars of conquest, the Bush administration and the Pentagon talked of the need to expand the size of the military. Prince had already offered up a proposal of his own: the creation of what he called a "contractor brigade" to supplement the conventional U.S. military. "There's consternation in the DoD about increasing the permanent size of the Army," he said. "We want to add 30,000 people, and they talked about costs of anywhere from $3.6 billion to $4 billion to do that. Well, by my math, that comes out to about $135,000 per soldier. . . . We could do it certainly cheaper."[19] It was an extraordinary declaration that could only come from a man in control of his own army. Prince likes to position Blackwater as a patriotic extension of the U.S. military, and in September 2005 he issued a company-wide memorandum requiring all company employees and contractors to swear the same oath of loyalty to the U.S. Constitution as Blackwater's "National Security-related clients (i.e. Pentagon, State Department and intelligence agencies)" to "support and defend the Constitution of the United States against all enemies, foreign and domestic. . . . So help me God."[20]

But despite the portrayal of Blackwater as an all-American operation seeking to defend the defenseless, some of its most ambitious and secretive projects reveal a very different and frightening reality. In May 2004, Blackwater quietly registered a new division, Greystone Limited, in the U.S. government's Central Contracting office. But instead of incorporating the company in North Carolina or Virginia or Delaware, like Blackwater's other divisions, Greystone was registered offshore in the Caribbean island-nation of Barbados. It was duly classified by the U.S. government as a "tax-exempt" "corporate entity."[21] Greystone's promotional literature offered prospective clients "Proactive Engagement Teams" that could be hired "to meet emergent or existing security requirements for client needs overseas. Our teams are ready to conduct stabilization efforts, asset protection and recovery, and emergency personnel withdrawal." It also offered a wide range of training services, including in "defensive and offensive small group operations." Greystone boasted that it "maintains and trains a workforce drawn from a diverse base of former special operations, defense, intelligence, and law enforcement professionals ready on a moment's notice for global deployment." The countries from which Greystone claimed to draw recruits were: the Philippines, Chile, Nepal, Colombia, Ecuador, El Salvador, Honduras, Panama, and Peru, many of whose forces have human rights records that are questionable at best. It asked applicants to check off their qualifications in weapons: AK-47 rifle, Glock 19, M-16 series rifle, M-4 carbine rifle, machine gun, mortar, and shoulder-fired weapons (RPG, LAAW). Among the qualifications the application sought: sniper, marksman, door gunner, explosive ordnance, counter-assault team. In Iraq, Blackwater has deployed scores of Chilean mercenaries, some of whom trained and served under the brutal regime of Augusto Pinochet. "We scour the ends of the earth to find professionals," said Blackwater president Gary Jackson. "The Chilean commandos are very, very professional and they fit within the Blackwater system."[22]

With domestic armed forces stretched to the limit—and a draft off the table for political reasons— the U.S. government is left to struggle to find nation-state allies willing to staff the occupations of its "global war on terror." If the national armies of other states will not join a "coalition of the willing," Blackwater and its allies offer a different sort of solution: an alternative internationalization of the force achieved by recruiting private soldiers from across the globe. If foreign governments are not on board, foreign soldiers—many of whose home countries oppose the U.S. wars— can still be enlisted, at a price. This process, critics allege, is nothing short of a subversion of the very existence of the nation-state and of principles of sovereignty and self-determination. "The increasing use of contractors, private forces or as some would say 'mercenaries' makes wars easier to begin and to fight—it just takes money and not the citizenry," says Michael Ratner, president of the Center for Constitutional Rights, whose organization has sued private contractors for alleged human rights violations in Iraq.[23] "To the extent a population is called upon to go to war, there is resistance, a necessary resistance to prevent wars of self-aggrandizement, foolish wars and in the case of the United States, hegemonic imperialist wars. Private forces are almost a necessity for a United States bent on retaining its declining empire. Think about Rome and its increasing need for mercenaries. Likewise, here at home in the United States. Controlling an angry, abused population with a police force bound to obey the Constitution can be difficult—private forces can solve this 'problem.'"

As with Halliburton, the Pentagon's largest contractor, Blackwater is set apart from simple war profiteers by the defining characteristic of its executives' very long view. They have not just seized a profitable moment along with many of their competitors but have set out to carve a permanent niche for themselves for decades to come. Blackwater's aspirations are not limited to international wars, however. Its forces beat most federal agencies to New

Orleans after Hurricane Katrina hit in 2005, as hundreds of heavily armed Blackwater mercenaries—some fresh from deployment in Iraq—fanned out into the disaster zone. Within a week, they were officially hired by the Department of Homeland Security to operate in the U.S. Gulf, billing the federal government $950 a day per Blackwater soldier.[24] In less than a year, the company had raked in more than $70 million in federal hurricane-related contracts—about $243,000 a day.[25] The company saw Katrina as another moment of great opportunity and soon began applying for permits to contract its forces out to local governments in all fifty states. Blackwater executives have met with California Governor Arnold Schwarzenegger about deploying there in the aftermath of an earthquake or another disaster. "Look, none of us loves the idea that devastation became a business opportunity," said the Blackwater official heading up its new domestic operations division formed after Katrina.[26] "It's a distasteful fact, but it is what it is. Doctors, lawyers, funeral directors, even newspapers—they all make a living off of bad things happening. So do we, because somebody's got to handle it." But critics see the deployment of Blackwater's forces domestically as a dangerous precedent that could undermine U.S. democracy. "Their actions may not be subject to constitutional limitations that apply to both federal and state officials and employees—including First Amendment and Fourth Amendment rights to be free from illegal searches and seizures. Unlike police officers, they are not trained in protecting constitutional rights," says CCR's Michael Ratner. "These kind of paramilitary groups bring to mind Nazi Party brownshirts, functioning as an extrajudicial enforcement mechanism that can and does operate outside the law. The use of these paramilitary groups is an extremely dangerous threat to our rights."

What is particularly scary about Blackwater's role in a war that President Bush labeled a "crusade" is that the company's leading executives are dedicated to a Christian-supremacist agenda. Erik Prince and his family have provided generous funding to the religious right's war against secularism and for expanding the presence of Christianity in the public sphere.[27]

Prince is a close friend and benefactor to some of the country's most hard right Christian evangelists, such as former Watergate conspirator Chuck Colson, who went on to become an adviser to President Bush and a pioneer of "faith-based prisons," and Christian conservative leader Gary Bauer, an original signer of the Project for a New American Century's "Statement of Principles," whom Prince has worked alongside since his youth and who was a close friend of Prince's father. Some Blackwater executives even boast of their membership in the Sovereign Military Order of Malta,[28] a Christian militia formed in the eleventh century, before the first Crusades, with the mission of defending "territories that the Crusaders had conquered from the Moslems."[29] The Order today boasts of being "a sovereign subject of international law, with its own constitution, passports, stamps, and public institutions" and "diplomatic relations with 94 countries."[30] The outsourcing of U.S. military operations in Muslim countries and in secular societies to such neo-crusaders reinforces the greatest fears of many in the Arab world and other opponents of the administration's wars.

Most of the world first heard of "private military companies" after the infamous March 31, 2004, ambush of four Blackwater soldiers in Fallujah, Iraq—a gruesome mob murder that marked the moment the war turned and the Iraqi resistance exploded. Many of the media reports at the time (and today) refer to these shadowy forces as "civilian contractors" or "foreign reconstruction workers" as though they were engineers, construction workers, humanitarians, or water specialists. The term "mercenary" was almost never used to describe them. That is no accident. Indeed, it is part of a very sophisticated rebranding campaign organized by the mercenary industry itself and increasingly embraced by policy-makers, bureaucrats, and other powerful decision makers in Washington and other Western capitals. Those men who died at Fallujah were members of Washington's largest partner in the coalition of the willing in Iraq—bigger than Britain's total deployment—and yet most of the world had not a clue they were there. The ambush resulted in Blackwater being positioned in a key role to affect the regulations that would oversee (or not) the rapidly expanding industry, of which Blackwater was the new leader. Three months later, the company was handed one of the U.S. government's most valuable international security contracts: to protect diplomats and U.S. facilities. The highly publicized deaths of four of its private soldiers would prove to be the spark that set Blackwater on a path to success for years to come.

The story of Blackwater's rise is an epic one in the history of the military-industrial complex. The company is the living embodiment of the changes wrought by the revolution in military affairs and the privatization agenda radically expanded by the Bush administration under the guise of the war on terror. But more fundamentally, it is a story about the future of war, democracy, and governance. This story goes from the company's beginnings in 1996, with visionary Blackwater executives opening a private military training camp in order "to fulfill the anticipated demand for government outsourcing of firearms and related security training," to its contract boom following 9/11, to the blood-soaked streets of Fallujah, where the corpses of its mercenaries were left to dangle from a bridge. It includes a rooftop fire-fight in Muqtada al-Sadr's stronghold of Najaf; an expedition to the oil-rich Caspian Sea, where the administration sent Blackwater to set up a military base just miles from the Iranian border; a foray into New Orleans's hurricane-ravaged streets; and many hours in the chambers of power in Washington, D.C., where Blackwater executives are welcomed as new heroes in the war on terror. But the rise of the world's most powerful mercenary army began far away from the current battlefields, in the sleepy town of Holland, Michigan, where Erik Prince was born into a right-wing Christian dynasty. It was the Prince family that laid the groundwork, spending millions of dollars over many decades to bring to power the very forces that would enable Blackwater's meteoric ascent.

CHAPTER TWO

THE LITTLE PRINCE

THE STATELY mansion at 1057 South Shore Drive in Holland, Michigan, is about as far from Fallujah as one could imagine. The home where young Erik Prince, founder of Blackwater USA, grew up sits along the sleepy banks of Lake Macatawa, an inlet of Lake Michigan in the American Midwest. Trees shimmer along the edges of the driveway on a summer day; the sun glints peacefully off the lake. Occasionally, a car clips by or a boat motor starts, but otherwise the neighborhood is calm and quiet, the embodiment of affluent, postcard American society. Two middle-aged women power-walk past a man lazily riding his lawnmower. Other than that, the street is deserted. As they trot by, one of the women glances over to her companion, their sun visors almost colliding, and asks whether the Prince family still owns the mansion.

The estate is well-known, the family more so. In Holland, Michigan, the Princes were indeed royalty, and Erik's father, Edgar Prince, was the king.

Much like Blackwater's compound in Moyock, North Carolina—a seven-thousand-acre peat bog with a constant rattle of machine-gun fire—is Erik Prince's personal fiefdom, the idyllic Dutch hamlet of Holland was his father's. A self-made industrialist, Edgar Prince employed nearly a quarter of the city. He shaped its institutions, planned and funded its downtown, and was among the biggest benefactors to its two colleges. A decade after Edgar's sudden death in 1995, his presence and legacy still permeate the town. On the corner of two of the busiest streets in Holland's soccer-mom-chic downtown, there is a monument to Ed Prince: seven bronze footsteps embedded in the ground lead to a raised platform upon which stand life-sized bronze statues of a trio of musicians—a tuxedoed cello player, a mustached violinist, and a young woman wearing a skirt who is blowing into her flute. Another statue depicts a little girl standing with her arms wrapped around a small boy, holding a book of music notes, their mouths frozen in song. On the pedestal below the group is a small plaque memorializing Edgar D. Prince: "We will always hear your footsteps," it reads. "The People of Downtown Holland honor your extraordinary vision and generosity."

If there was one lesson Edgar Prince was poised to impart to his children, it was how to build and maintain an empire based on strict Christian values, right-wing politics, and free-market economics. But while the landscape of Holland today is dotted with memorials to the Prince family legacy, Edgar was not the town's original emperor. Dating back to the community's founding, Holland had long been run by Christian patriarchs. In 1846, with a sea-weary clan of fifty-seven fellow Dutch refugees, Albertus Van Raalte came ashore in western Michigan. Prince's predecessor had fled his home country because he had "undergone all manner of humiliation and persecution through his defiance of the religious restrictions imposed by the State church," according to the city.[1]

Van Raalte was a member of a sect of the Dutch Reform Church opposed by the Dutch monarchy at the time. After arriving in the United States aboard his vessel, the *Southerner,* Van Raalte led the clan to the shores of Lake Michigan, where he envisioned a community free to live and worship within the tenets of his brand of Dutch Reform, and without any outside influence. After some scouting he came upon a perfect spot, next to a lake that ran into Lake Michigan. On February 9, 1847, Van Raalte's community was founded, on the site where Erik Prince would later spend his youth, perhaps some of it on the creaking dock that sneaks out into the Lake Michigan inlet. But Van Raalte's perfect vision would not be realized quite as he expected, according to a biography produced by Hope College, which he founded and which has seen millions of dollars in donations from the Prince family: "[Van Raalte's] goal of developing a Christian community governed by Christian principles was visionary but was shattered in 1850. Holland Township became the basic unit of government. Van Raalte's ideal of Christian control was lost."[2] But Van Raalte sought alternative means of establishing his Shangri-La in Holland. "His influence was felt because he became active in politics and he continued to own large tracts of land," according to the biography. "Although many of the means to achieve a Christian community broke down, Van Raalte was still the pastor of the only church, member of the district school board, guiding light of the Academy, principal landowner, and a businessman with major property holdings."[3] Virtually the same description could be applied to Edgar Prince and, eventually, to Erik, born nearly a century after Van Raalte's death.

The conservative Dutch Reform Church that provided the religious guidance for Van Raalte, and eventually the Prince family, based its beliefs on the teachings of a seventeenth-century minister, John Calvin. One of the main tenets of Calvinism is that of predestination—the belief that God has predestined some people for salvation and others for damnation. Calvinists believe that people have no business meddling or vainly trying to divine God's decisions. The religion also teaches strict obedience and hard work, acting on the belief that God will steer followers but that they are responsible for the work. Calvinists have long taken pride in their work ethic. The town of Holland boasts that its villagers dug the canal to Lake Michigan—that would prove valuable for trade—with their own hands, and then set down their shovels and immediately constructed the bridge over their new channel.[4]

It was this famed work ethic that found Erik Prince's grandfather Peter Prince, owner of the Tulip City Produce Company, on a truck heading to Grand Rapids, thirty miles away, for a business meeting in the early morning hours of May 21, 1943. Shortly into the trip, Prince complained of heartburn to his fellow wholesale produce dealer, and they pulled over for a few minutes. Soon, they continued on, and near Hudsonville, halfway through the trip, Prince slumped over against his colleague, who was driving. A doctor in the town pronounced him dead on arrival at the age of thirty-six.[5] Peter's son, Edgar, was eleven years old.

A decade later, Edgar Prince graduated from the University of Michigan with an engineering degree and met Elsa Zwiep, whose parents owned Zwiep's Seed Store in Holland and who had just completed her studies in education and sociology at nearby Calvin College.[6] The two married, and Edgar followed family tradition and joined the military, serving in the U.S. Air Force. The couple moved east and then west as Edgar was stationed at bases in South Carolina and Colorado. Though it's unclear whether Peter Prince was a veteran—he came of age for the draft during the window between World War I and World War II—four of Peter's five brothers were in the Army at the time of his death.[7] Though Edgar Prince had traveled far and wide during college and the Air Force, his hometown of Holland beckoned him and Elsa back to Lake Michigan and to the strict religious and cultural traditions embraced by the Prince family. "We find Holland a very comfortable place to live," Edgar Prince said in a book written about Holland's downtown, which included three chapters on the family. "We have family here. We enjoy the recreational opportunities. We like the community's heritage, which is based on the Dutch reputation for being neat, clean, orderly, and hard working. Their standard has always been excellence."[8]

Upon returning to the town, Edgar rolled up his sleeves and started working in die-casting, rising to the position of chief engineer at Holland's Buss Machine Works.[9] But Edgar had much bigger ambitions and soon quit. In 1965, Prince and two fellow employees founded their own company that made die-cast machines for the auto industry.[10] In 1969, he shipped a sixteen-hundred-ton machine capable of creating aluminum transmission cases every two minutes.[11] By 1973, Prince Corporation was a great success, with hundreds of people working for the company's various Holland divisions.[12] That year, the company began production of what would become its signature product, an invention that would end up in virtually every car in the world and put Edgar Prince on his way to becoming a billionaire: the ubiquitous lighted sun visor.[13]

But while wealth and success were in abundance in the Prince family, the sixteen-to-eighteen-hour days had been taking their toll on Edgar, and in the early 1970s, he nearly fell to the same fate as his father when he suffered a serious heart attack.[14] "It was then, while he lay in a hospital bed reflecting on what all his labor had won for him, that he committed himself anew to his faith in Jesus Christ," recalled Prince's friend Gary Bauer, one of the early leaders of the religious right and founder of the conservative Christian lobby group the Family Research Council. "Ed turned his future and the future of his business over to God. From that point forward, the Prince Corporation was blessed with unprecedented growth and financial success."[15] Edgar Prince recovered from the heart attack and steered his company toward amazing prosperity. Prince Corporation soon expanded into map lamps, visors that could open garage doors, consoles with ashtrays, and cup and change holders, among many other products.[16] By 1980, the Prince empire boasted numerous plants and more than 550 employees.[17] As Erik Prince later recalled, "My dad was a very successful entrepreneur. From scratch he started a company that first produced high-pressure die-cast machines and grew into a world-class automotive parts supplier in west Michigan. They developed and patented the first lighted car sun visor, developed the car digital compass/thermometer and the programmable garage door opener."[18] But, Prince said, "Not all their ideas were winners. Things like a sock-drawer light, an automated ham de-boning machine and a propeller-driven snowmobile didn't work out so well for the company. My dad used them as examples of the need for perseverance and determination."[19]

In that respect, it wasn't the only way in which the product itself seemed of secondary importance to Prince. "People make the difference," read the copy from an old Prince Corporation brochure. "It isn't magic that brings excellence to a company; excellence is the result of commitment and hard work by dedicated people. Whether we're talking about products or processes, no wizardry or easy formulas will solve the challenges of tomorrow. People will."[20] Edgar Prince was fond of initiatives like one where executives stuck to a strict exercise regimen. Three days a week from 4:15 to 5:15 p.m. the executives met at the Holland Tennis Club, which Prince also owned.[21] In 1987, Prince opened a sprawling 550,000-square-foot facility spread over thirty-five acres, its fourth manufacturing center and home to many of its now fifteen hundred employees.[22] The Prince "campus" centerpiece featured nearly five thousand feet of skylights and amenities like a basketball and volleyball court.[23] He never made employees work on Sundays and flew executives home from business trips promptly so they could be with their families on the Lord's Day.[24]

Detroit's auto industry may have been suffering in the 1980s, "but you'd never know it from the Prince Corporation," read the lead of a story in the *Holland Sentinel*.[25] "My family's business was automotive supply—the most viciously competitive business in the world," Erik Prince told author Robert Young Pelton. "My father was focused on quality, volume, and customer satisfaction. That's what we talked around the dinner table."[26] But Edgar Prince had more than the success of his business and his employees on his mind, and with the money flowing into Prince Corporation, he finally had the means to achieve the higher goals to which he aspired. That meant pouring serious money into conservative Christian causes. "Ed Prince was not an empire builder. He was a Kingdom builder," recalled Gary Bauer. "For him, personal success took a back seat to spreading the Gospel and fighting for the moral restoration of our society."[27]

In the 1980s, the Prince family merged with one of the most venerable conservative families in the United States when Erik Prince's sister Betsy married Dick DeVos, whose father, Richard, founded the multilevel marketing firm

Amway and went on to own the Orlando Magic basketball team.[28] Amway was a powerhouse distributor of home products and was regularly plagued by accusations that it was run like a cult and was nothing more than a sophisticated pyramid scheme.[29] An investigation into whether Amway was an illegal pyramid scheme was dropped in 1979, but it later ran into legal problems in Canada. The company would rise to become one of the greatest corporate contributors in the U.S. electoral process in the 1990s, mostly to Republican candidates and causes, and used its business infrastructure as a massive political organizing network.[30] "Amway relies heavily on the nearly fanatical—some say cultlike—devotion of its more than 500,000 U.S. 'independent distributors.' As they sell the company's soaps, vitamins, detergents, and other household products, the distributors push the Amway philosophy," reported *Mother Jones* magazine in a 1996 exposé on the company.[31] "They tell you to always vote conservative no matter what. They say liberals support the homosexuals and let women get out of their place," Karen Jones, a former Amway distributor, told the magazine. "They say we need to get things back to the way it's supposed to be."[32] Amway leaders also reportedly used "voice-mail messages, along with company rallies and motivational tapes, to mobilize distributors into a potent domestic political force."[33]

Betsy and Dick's union was the kind of alliance common among the families of monarchs in Europe. The DeVos family was one of the few in Michigan whose power and influence exceeded that of the Princes. They were one of the greatest bankrollers of far-right causes in U.S. history, and with their money they propelled extremist Christian politicians and activists to positions of prominence. For a time, Betsy and Dick lived down the street from the Prince family, including Erik, who is nine years younger than his sister.[34]

In 1988, Gary Bauer and Focus on the Family founder James Dobson began building what would become the Family Research Council (FRC), the crusading, influential, and staunchly conservative evangelical organization that has since taken the lead on issues ranging from banning gay marriage to promoting school vouchers for Christian schools to outlawing abortion and stem-cell research. To get it off the ground, though, they needed funding, and they turned to Edgar Prince. "[W]hen Jim Dobson and I decided that the financial resources weren't available to launch FRC, Ed and his family stepped into the breach," wrote Bauer. "I can say without hesitation that without Ed and Elsa and their wonderful children, there simply would not be a Family Research Council."[35] Young Erik would go on to become one of Bauer's earliest interns at the FRC.[36] It was one of many right-wing causes that the Princes would join the DeVoses in bankrolling, leading to what would be known as the Republican Revolution in 1994, which brought Newt Gingrich and a radical right-wing agenda known as the Contract with America to power in Congress, wrestling control from the Democrats for the first time in forty years. To support the "revolution," DeVos's Amway gave some $2.5 million to the Republican Party in what was the single largest soft-money donation on record to any political party in history.[37] In 1996, Amway also donated $1.3 million to the San Diego Convention and Visitors Bureau to pay for Republican "infomercials" broadcast on Pat Robertson's Family Channel during the RNC convention.[38]

Erik's sister Betsy DeVos would go on to chair Michigan's Republican Party from 1996 to 2000 and from 2003 to 2005; at times she flirted with running for the U.S. Senate.[39] She was also a George W. Bush "Pioneer" fundraiser, bringing in more than $100,000 for his campaign.[40] Her husband, Dick, was the GOP candidate for governor in 2006, a race that he ultimately lost.[41] Seasoned observers of Michigan politics say it would be hard to overestimate the influence the DeVos family has on politics in the state. "Anyone who runs for a significant Republican office in Michigan has to check with the DeVos family," said Calvin College political science professor Doug Koopman. "They are perceived within that community as being not only a source of funds but a judge of [a candidate's] fitness."[42]

The Prince and DeVos clans were also a major driving force behind the Michigan Family Forum (MFF), the state's chapter of Jim Dobson's Focus on the Family.[43] Besides the tens of thousands of dollars that the Prince family poured into the MFF, another of Erik Prince's sisters, Emilie Wierda, has served as its treasurer.[44] The MFF has mobilized voters in conservative churches to support legislators who have backed the Christian right's agenda. Beginning in 1990, the MFF ran what was essentially a backdoor lobbying system, through the establishment of more than one thousand church-based Community Impact Committees (CICs), which operated under the radar, away from public scrutiny.[45] "The CICs offer advantages to political organizing that other Christian Right organizing doesn't have," Russ Bellant wrote in his 1996 book *The Religious Right in Michigan Politics*. "Because they are based in churches, their meetings are not visible in the world of politics. Since laypersons rather than pastors may run these groups, they may not have a high profile even in the church community outside the Family Forum network."[46] The MFF also established the Michigan Prayer Network, which consisted of "prayer warriors" assigned to nearly every legislator in the state.[47] While the groups were prohibited from expressly lobbying, the effect of asking legislators to "pray" for issues like school choice and against gay rights made it, as one Michigan legislator put it, "just another lobbying gimmick."[48]

While opening his wallet to the Christian right, Edgar Prince also became a patron to the entire community of Holland, investing millions of dollars into Hope College, founded by Albert Van Raalte, and its equally devout rival Calvin College, Edgar's wife's alma mater.[49] He and Elsa almost single-handedly reengineered and brought a boom to Holland's downtown, saving it from the fate hundreds of other small towns had suffered throughout the Midwest as they gradually slipped into economic oblivion due to poor urban planning coupled with outsourcing, downsizing, layoffs, and the overall decline of U.S. manufacturing. The Princes helped establish the Evergreen Commons, a popular senior center downtown, and lobbied hard for the preservation and restoration of historic landmarks in town.[50] They fought for a well-planned city that would exist and thrive for generations while maintaining what they saw as a necessary connection to its Dutch roots. They personally took on causes like saving an 1892 stone clock tower that had once been a cornerstone of downtown before falling into disrepair.[51] Some of Edgar Prince's ideas for maintaining a vibrant downtown seemed utterly insane. He envisioned and campaigned hard in the late 1980s for an underground system of heated pipes that would melt snow and ice throughout the downtown business district, ensuring that strollers could be pushed along the sidewalks even during western Michigan's harsh winters.[52] When the city balked at the $1.1 million plan, Prince ponied up a quarter of the funding himself.[53]

All the while, Edgar Prince continued to balance his business and religious obligations, both to his local Dutch Reform Church and the Prince Corporation. "Ed was at his best and was most valuable to [the Family Research Council] during the dark and difficult times—during the confirmation battle over Clarence Thomas, following the bitter disappointment of the Supreme Court's unexpected pro-abortion ruling in Planned Parenthood v. Casey, through the anti-family shift in the Congress in 1992, and in recent months with the wave of efforts by some to redefine the traditional family and undermine marriage," Gary Bauer wrote of Prince in 1995.[54] Prince Corporation continued to flourish, a "boom built on Biblical principles," Bauer wrote.[55] In 1992, the company roster had grown to 2,250 employees.[56] By early 1995, it had ballooned to more than 4,000 employees and $400 million in annual sales.[57] Prince had also married his business acumen with his desire to see Holland thrive and had founded Lumir Corporation, which became Holland's foremost downtown developer, responsible for projects like the $2.5 million Evergreen Commons Senior Center.[58] But tragedy would soon strike the Prince empire.

At about 1:00 p.m. on March 2, 1995, Edgar Prince had one of his usual chats with Prince Corporation president John Spoelhof,[59] a longtime friend with whom he had just gone skiing in Colorado a week earlier.[60] They said good-bye, and the sixty-three-year-old Prince stepped into the elevator at his company's headquarters. Inside, he suffered a massive heart attack and was found on the floor fifteen minutes later.[61] Despite CPR attempts by two Prince employees, Edgar was pronounced dead within the hour.[62] "I saw him probably two minutes before he passed away," Spoelhof said. "I looked at the expression of his face and the color of his face and Ed was Ed. I knew him so well all these years; if he would have been a little ashen, I would have noticed."[63]

As happens with the deaths of kings, patriarchs, and heads of state, the town of Holland entered a period of intense mourning. The flag flew at half-staff.[64] Every newspaper in the region ran front-page stories eulogizing Prince, accompanied with sidebars and pictures and timelines. More than one thousand people gathered at the Christ Memorial Reformed Church to hear evangelical leaders James Dobson and Gary Bauer, who referred to Edgar as his "mentor," eulogize Prince.[65] Bauer remembered how Prince was adamant that the Family Research Council's new headquarters in Washington, D.C., should have a cross atop it, to remind the President, members of the Supreme Court, and Congress "that this is one nation under God's judgment."[66] In the *Grand Rapids Press* Lakeshore supplement, the banner headline read "A Christian Man," and the Rev. Ren Broekhuizen said, "Ed Prince was a gifted and developed individual who never took his eyes off the goal of honoring Jesus Christ in his life."[67] That pastor, a friend of Prince's for two decades, would marry Edgar's widow Elsa five years later.[68]

At the time of his father's death, Erik Prince was a Navy SEAL serving a string of deployments in Bosnia, Haiti, and the Middle East.[69] Even still, he had happened to visit his father just a week before his death, when Edgar made the sign of the cross on Erik's daughter's forehead during her baptism.[70] Erik remembered that his father had taught him never to say, "I can't."[71] At the time of his death, Edgar had been married to Elsa for forty-one years, and they had raised three daughters in addition to Erik. "Dad was definitely the shepherd of his family, and he would bring the whole family together every chance he could. He'd make all the arrangements and take care of all the details," Erik told the *Holland Sentinel* after Edgar's death.[72] Erik seemed elated that his father had been able to meet and baptize his first-born daughter, Sophia, but that elation was tinged with regret: "He loved her. That was the last time I saw him. My regret is my kids will never know him. I wanted them to be able to talk to him, to learn from him."[73]

Erik Prince adored his father and strived to follow in his footsteps from the time he was a child. Erik was an active youth, playing soccer, track, and basketball at the Holland Christian schools he attended as a primary and high schooler, and for which his family also provided financial support. Prince's deeply religious high school featured pages upon pages of Bible quotations and incantations throughout its yearbooks. One year, the third page of his yearbook intoned: "In God's Kingdom all of life is living out the meaning of the New Humanity in Christ. This takes all the inventiveness, creativity and discovering that we can do." Gary Bauer recognized the special bond between Edgar and Erik: "Erik Prince, Ed and Elsa's only son, and one of FRC's first college interns, certainly did know him well."[74] In addition to his work with the Family Research Council, Erik spent his college years increasingly taking up his father's mantle. He entered the Naval Academy after high school intending to be a Navy pilot but resigned after three semesters to attend Hillsdale College, a Michigan Christian liberal arts school that preaches libertarian economics. The campus was rated the most conservative in the country in a 2006 Princeton Review poll.

"He was a smart guy, and pleasant to be around, and he's well spoken," said Erik's professor Gary Wolfram. "What's good about him, he understands the interrelationship between markets and the political system."[75] Prince also had a thirst for adrenaline-pumping action and initially satiated it by becoming the first college student to join the Hillsdale Volunteer Fire Department. "When you've been on a fire an hour and a half and the crowd's gone, some of the guys want to sit on bumpers and have a soft drink," recalled firefighter Kevin Pauken. "Other guys will be rolling hoses and picking up equipment so you can get out of there. That was Erik."[76]

As he grew older, Erik became increasingly active in right-wing politics, landing a six-month internship at George H. W. Bush's White House. It was during this internship that the nineteen-year-old Prince made his first political contribution, giving $15,000 to the National Republican Congressional Committee. Since then, Prince and his late wife, Joan, and current wife, Joanna, have given $244,800 in contributions to federal campaigns, not a dime of it to Democrats.[77] He has supported Jesse Helms, Ollie North, Richard Pombo, Spencer Abraham, Dick Chrysler, Rick Santorum, Tom Coburn, Tom DeLay, Jim DeMint, Mike Pence, Duncan Hunter, and others.[78] Prince also worked for a stint in the office of Republican Congressman Dana Rohrabacher.[79] In 1992, he became enthralled with the renegade presidential campaign of Pat Buchanan, who challenged President Bush for the GOP nomination, running on an extreme anti-immigrant, antiabortion, antigay platform. Erik Prince's backing of Buchanan led the then twenty-two-year-old into a feud of his own with his sister Betsy, who was working for Bush's reelection as chairwoman of a local Republican district.[80] Erik and Edgar, however, didn't seem to care for Bush. "I interned with the Bush administration for six months," Erik told the *Grand Rapids Press* in 1992. "I saw a lot of things I didn't agree with—homosexual groups being invited in, the budget agreement, the Clean Air Act, those kind of bills. I think the administration has been indifferent to a lot of conservative concerns."[81]

Erik began coordinating Buchanan's campaign at Hillsdale, and Edgar contributed to it. But Erik's foray into public politics would be short-lived. The next year, he went back into the military, joining SEAL Team 8 through Officer Candidate School in1992[82] and starting down the path that would bring him to Moyock, North Carolina. It was during his four years with SEAL Team 8 in Norfolk, Virginia, that he met many of the people who would found Blackwater.[83] Erik seemed happy as a SEAL, and his family seemed proud to have him be one. "[Edgar] always wanted his children to do what they wanted to do, not just what he experienced," Elsa Prince said months after her husband's death. "He wanted them to go where their preferences and talents took them."[84]

But during the months after Edgar Prince's death, the future of the Prince Corporation was anything but clear. More than four thousand employees depended on what had largely been the vision of Edgar Prince. The company and many in the family felt that only the Prince family itself could ensure that the reputation of Prince Corporation outlived its founder. Elsa became chairman of the company's board, and Erik came home to help get the company's affairs in order, and to help his family. His wife, Joan Nicole, had just been diagnosed with terminal cancer. Being a full-time SEAL was no longer an option.

But the young Prince would not become the king of Prince Corporation. On July 22, 1996, little more than a year after Edgar's death, the family, after much deliberation and many suitors, agreed to sell the corporation to Johnson Controls for $1.35 billion in cash. They sold under the condition that the Prince name would remain, as would the employees and the community atmosphere they had long fostered. The bevy of stories in the local press took on that same enthusiasm, liberally quoting Elsa Prince gushing over the deal: "The Lord opened the right doors at the right time in an answer to our prayer. His timing is always perfect."[85] Beyond that, Elsa said the buyout would enable her husband's company to have "an influence well beyond the United States."[86] A few years later, that influence could really be felt in Holland, as hundreds of jobs started migrating to Mexico.[87] Johnson Controls eventually stripped the name off the company and shuttered some of the local factories.[88]

Though the influence of industrialist Edgar Prince has steadily receded in Holland, the religious beliefs and politics he promoted, as well as the downtown he created, continue to grow. When Edgar was alive, the Prince family largely shied away from overt political involvement, preferring to let its money do the talking. In the years after her husband's death, Elsa Prince became notably outspoken on behalf of a number of right-wing political causes, including those favored by her late husband. In 2004 she was the single largest donor to the successful campaign to ban same-sex marriage in Michigan, kicking in $75,000 of her own money.[89] She served on the boards of the Family Research Council and Focus on the Family and was active in the Council for National Policy and a host of other right-wing religious organizations.[90] "My main thrust is to do things that Jesus would want you to do to further your knowledge of him and his ways," she told the *Holland Sentinel* in 2003.[91] Edgar, Elsa, and her new husband, Ren, cumulatively donated nearly $556,000 to Republican candidates and political action committees,[92] along with untold millions to right-wing causes. Along with the DeVos family, the Princes remain major players in the conservative Christian movement in Michigan and nationally. One of their recent hard-fought but unsuccessful battles was to implement school vouchers in Michigan. The DeVos family itself spent upwards of $3 million in 2000 pushing the perennial conservative education ideal.[93]

Erik Prince adopted his father's behind-the-scenes demeanor, as well as his passion for right-wing religious causes, but with a twist. "Erik is a Roman Catholic," said author Robert Young Pelton, who has had rare access to Prince. "A lot of people brand him in his father's religion, but he converted to Roman Catholicism."[94] Indeed, many of the executives who would later form the core of Prince's Blackwater empire are also Catholics, and when Prince's first wife, Joan, died, Catholic Mass was celebrated for her both near her hometown outside Schenectady, New York, and near where the family lived in McLean, Virginia.[95] In 1997, Lt. Erik Prince, U.S. Navy SEAL, blurbed a book called *Christian Fatherhood: The Eight Commitments of St. Joseph's Covenant Keepers*, saying that it "provides men with the basic training they need to complete (their) mission."[96] At the time, Prince himself had two young children. The book's author, Stephen Wood, is the founder of Family Life Center International, a Catholic apologist organization specializing in providing "moral media . . . geared toward deepening a family's love and knowledge of their faith and thus hopes to impact today's society. We place a special focus on fatherhood and providing resources which aid fathers in fulfilling their vocation." The "moral media" include books with titles like *A Parent's Guide to Preventing Homosexuality* and *Breast Cancer and the Pill*, among many others.

Taking a cue from his father's funding of right-wing evangelical Protestant causes, Prince became a major funder of extremist, fringe Catholic organizations. In 1999 he contributed $25,000 to Catholic Answers, a San Diego–based Catholic evangelical organization founded by the Catholic fundamentalist Karl Keating. Keating dedicated his life to apologetics and defending Catholicism at all costs. During the 2004 and 2006 elections, the group promoted a "Voters Guide for Serious Catholics," which listed five "non-negotiable" issues that it said are never morally acceptable under Catholic teaching: abortion, homosexual marriage, embryonic stem-cell research, euthanasia, and human cloning.[97] Issues that were identified as "Not Non-Negotiable" included "the questions of when to go to war and when to apply the death penalty."[98] When Prince's wife was dying of cancer, he e-mailed Keating, who in turn asked his followers to pray for the Princes.[99] The following year, Prince provided funding to the right-wing Catholic monthly magazine *Crisis*.[100] He also gave generously to several Michigan churches, including $50,000 to Holy Family Oratory, a Kalamazoo Catholic Church, and $100,000 to St. Isidore Catholic Church and school in Grand Rapids, as well as Catholic churches in Virginia.[101]

But Erik Prince's philanthropy has certainly not been limited to Catholic causes. The Prince family was deeply involved in the secretive Council for National Policy, described by the *New York Times* as "a little-known club of a few hundred of the most powerful conservatives in the country [which has] met behind closed doors at undisclosed locations for a confidential conference" three times a year "to strategize about how to turn the country to the right."[102] The Council was started in 1981 by the Rev. Tim LaHaye, one of the founders of the modern right-wing Christian movement in the United States and author of the apocalyptic *Left Behind* novels.[103] The idea was to build a Christian conservative alternative to the Council on Foreign Relations, which LaHaye considered too liberal. CNP membership is kept secret, and members are instructed that "The media should not know when or where we meet or who takes part in our programs, before or after a meeting."[104] While membership lists are not public, CNP meetings have been attended by a host of conservative luminaries like Jerry Falwell, Phyllis Schlafly, Pat Robertson, Tony Perkins, James Dobson, Gary Bauer, and Ralph Reed. Holland H. Coors of the beer dynasty and Wayne LaPierre of the National Rifle Association, Richard and Dick DeVos, and the likes of Oliver North, Grover Norquist, and Frank Gaffney are also affiliated with

CNP.[105] Guests are allowed to attend "only with the unanimous approval of the executive committee."[106] George W. Bush addressed the group in 1999, seeking support for his bid for the presidency.[107]

The group also has played host to powerful players in the Bush administration. Shortly after the Iraq invasion, Vice President Dick Cheney and Defense Secretary Donald Rumsfeld attended CNP meetings; in 2004 John Bolton briefed the group on U.S. plans for Iran; John Ashcroft has attended meetings; as did Dan Senor, the top aide to Paul Bremer, the original head of the Iraq occupation.[108] Former House majority leader Tom DeLay and several other prominent Republican politicians have also attended meetings.[109] Then-Senate majority leader Bill Frist was given the CNP's Thomas Jefferson Award. In his acceptance speech, he told the gathering, "The destiny of our nation is on the shoulders of the conservative movement."[110] Edgar Prince served a stint as vice president of the CNP from 1988 to 1989 and was CNP vice president at the time of his death.[111] Elsa Prince was also a member of the organization. The DeVos family has donated at least $100,000 to the CNP, and the Princes gave at least $20,000 over a two-year period in the 1990s.[112] While the lack of public records on the group makes it impossible to confirm that Erik Prince is a member, as his father was, the younger Prince has donated money to the CNP[113] and has close relationships with many of its key players.

Erik Prince's philanthropy and politics have also put him in bed with some of the most controversial political figures in recent U.S. history. Prince's Freiheit Foundation, which is German for "liberty," gave $500,000 to the Prison Fellowship in 2000.[114] The Fellowship is a so-called prison reform organization that, among other things, advocates for "faith-based prisons."[115] It is the brainchild of Richard Nixon's "hatchet man," Watergate conspirator Charles Colson.[116] In 1969, Colson was appointed Nixon's Special Counsel; he was seen by many as the "evil genius" in the administration.[117] In 1971, Colson wrote what later became known as Nixon's Enemies List, a catalogue of the President's political opponents, who would be targeted by the White House.[118] Colson was the first person sentenced in the Watergate scandal, after pleading guilty to obstruction of justice in the investigation of the break-in to the psychiatrist's office of Daniel Ellsberg, the whistleblower who leaked the Pentagon Papers during the Vietnam War.[119] Colson also allegedly tried to hire Teamsters thugs to beat up antiwar demonstrators and plotted to raid or firebomb the Brookings Institution.[120] Colson became a born-again Christian before going to prison and after leaving wrote the bestseller *Born Again* about his conversion, the proceeds from which he used to found the Prison Fellowship.

As of late 2006, some 22,308 Fellowship volunteers operated in more than eighteen hundred U.S. prison facilities, while upwards of 120,000 prisoners participated in its monthly Bible study and seminar programs.[121] It boasted of "ministries" in more than one hundred countries.[122] Colson's Fellowship has become so widespread that it actually runs the daily lives of some prisoners, including two hundred in a Texas prison, courtesy of one George W. Bush. "I'll never forget this," Bush said at the First White House National Conference on Faith-Based and Community Initiatives. "When I was the Governor of Texas, one of the early initiatives in my governorship, one of the faith-based initiatives, was to turn over a part of the prison unit to a faith program, Chuck Colson's program. He convinced me that this would be a great opportunity to change lives. And it would be—it would be better than stamping license plates."[123] Bush, whose administration held Colson's work up numerous times as evidence of successful "faith-based initiatives," went on to tell the story of a prisoner "whose life was changed and saved because of faith."[124] From the first week that Bush took office in 2001, Colson has been a regular adviser to the President. The Texas prison Colson ran was in Sugar Land[125]—the district represented by then–majority leader Tom DeLay.

In 2002, Colson gave a speech at Calvin College about his Texas prison: "My friend Erik Prince, who is here tonight, traveled with me recently to a prison in Texas that has been under Prison Fellowship administration for the past eighteen months. This is an extraordinary program because it is not just that men are coming to Christ and being redeemed, as wonderful as that is. They are creating an entire culture!"[126] A similar program at an Iowa prison was found unconstitutional in June 2006 because it used state funding, a judge said, for the indoctrination of "inmates into the Evangelical Christian belief system." Colson has vowed to appeal the ruling all the way to the Supreme Court. He has suggested that his faith-based prison program is "the one really successful antidote" to what he termed "the largely unimpeded spread of radical Islam through our prisons."[127] Colson predicted, "If, God forbid, an attack by home-grown Islamist radicals occurs on American soil, many, if not most, of the perpetrators will have converted to Islam while in prison."[128] He suggested that opponents of his Prison Fellowship program are abetting terrorism and said the efforts to declare his program unconstitutional "leaves jihadists and other radical groups as the only game in town."[129] In October 2006, Colson was given the Faith & Freedom Award by the Acton Institute for the Study of Religion and Liberty,[130] an organization to which Prince has donated at least $200,000.[131] The Grand Rapids–based organization has Prince's stepfather, Ren Broekhuizen, on its board of directors, and its president and founder is the Rev. Robert Sirico, who presided over the funeral of Erik Prince's first wife.[132] "Islam has a monolithic worldview, which sees just one thing: the destruction of infidels and the recovery of territories they've lost," Colson declared at the Acton dinner. "We're in a hundred-year war and it's time to sober up, and Christians understand it because we understand our history, and we understand what makes the religious mind tick, and secular America doesn't get it." Colson said when Mohammed wrote the Koran, "I think he'd had too many tamales the night before."[133]

A few years earlier, in the 2002 speech in which Colson praised Erik Prince, the former Watergate conspirator talked extensively about the historical foundation and current necessity of a political and religious alliance of Catholics and evangelicals. Colson talked about his work, beginning in the mid-1980s, with famed conservative evangelical Protestant minister turned Catholic priest Richard Neuhaus and others to build a unified movement. That work ultimately led in 1994 to the controversial document

"Evangelicals and Catholics Together: The Christian Mission in the Third Millennium."[134] The ECT document articulated the vision that would animate Blackwater's corporate strategy and the politics practiced by Erik Prince—a marriage of the historical authority of the Catholic Church with the grassroots appeal of the modern conservative U.S. evangelical movement, bolstered by the cooperation of largely secular and Jewish neoconservatives. Author Damon Linker, who once edited Neuhaus's journal, *First Things*, termed this phenomenon the rise of the "Theocons."[135]

The ECT document became the manifesto of the movement that Erik Prince would soon serve and bankroll. It declared that "The century now drawing to a close has been the greatest century of missionary expansion in Christian history. We pray and we believe that this expansion has prepared the way for yet greater missionary endeavor in the first century of the Third Millennium. The two communities in world Christianity that are most evangelistically assertive and most rapidly growing are Evangelicals and Catholics."[136] The signatories called for a unification of these religions in a common missionary cause, that "all people will come to faith in Jesus Christ as Lord and Savior."[137] The document recognized the separation of church and state but "just as strongly protest[ed] the distortion of that principle to mean the separation of religion from public life. . . . The argument, increasingly voiced in sectors of our political culture, that religion should be excluded from the public square must be recognized as an assault upon the most elementary principles of democratic governance."[138] But the ECT was not merely a philosophical document. Rather, it envisioned an agenda that would almost identically mirror that of the Bush administration a few years later, when Neuhaus would serve as a close adviser to Bush, beginning with the 2000 campaign.[139]

The signers of the ECT document asserted that religion is "privileged and foundational in our legal order" and spelled out the need to defend "the moral truths of our constitutional order."[140] The document was most passionate in its opposition to abortion, calling abortion on demand "a massive attack on the dignity, rights, and needs of women. Abortion is the leading edge of an encroaching culture of death." It also called for "moral education" in schools, advocating for educational institutions "that transmit to coming generations our cultural heritage, which is inseparable from the formative influence of religion, especially Judaism and Christianity."[141] The document forcefully defended neoliberal economic policies. "We contend for a free society, including a vibrant market economy," the signers asserted. "We affirm the importance of a free economy not only because it is more efficient but because it accords with a Christian understanding of human freedom. Economic freedom, while subject to grave abuse, makes possible the patterns of creativity, cooperation, and accountability that contribute to the common good."[142] It called for a "renewed appreciation of Western culture," saying, "We are keenly aware of, and grateful for, the role of Christianity in shaping and sustaining the Western culture of which we are part." "Multiculturalism," the signers declared, has most commonly come to mean "affirming all cultures but our own." Therefore, the ECT signers claimed Western culture as their "legacy" and set for themselves the task of transmitting it "as a gift to future generations."[143]

"Nearly two thousand years after it began, and nearly five hundred years after the divisions of the Reformation era, the Christian mission to the world is vibrantly alive and assertive. We do not know, we cannot know, what the Lord of history has in store for the Third Millennium. It may be the springtime of world missions and great Christian expansion," the lengthy document concluded. "We do know that this is a time of opportunity—and, if of opportunity, then of responsibility—for Evangelicals and Catholics to be Christians together in a way that helps prepare the world for the coming of him to whom belongs the kingdom, the power, and the glory forever. Amen."[144] In addition to Neuhaus and Colson, the document was endorsed by one of the most powerful mainstream Catholic leaders in the United States, John Cardinal O'Connor of New York, as well as the Rev. Pat Robertson and Michael Novak of the conservative American Enterprise Institute.[145] The manifesto was years in the making and would greatly assist the unifying of the conservative movement that made George W. Bush's rise to power possible. The ECT signers, according to Damon Linker—who worked for Neuhaus for years—"had not only forged a historic theological and political alliance. They had also provided a vision of America's religious and political future. It would be a religious future in which upholding theological orthodoxy and moral traditionalism overrode doctrinal disagreements. And it would be a political future in which the most orthodox and traditionalist Christians set the public tone and policy agenda for the nation."[146]

Six years later, with Bush—the theocons' President—in the White House, Chuck Colson was in Michigan with his buddy Erik Prince at Calvin College talking about his faith-based prisons. During the lecture, Colson played to the largely Protestant crowd's heritage as he advocated his theoconservative movement based on Catholic/Evangelical unity. Colson quoted a nineteenth-century Calvinist scholar who said, "Rome is not an antagonist but stands on our side, inasmuch as she also recognizes and then maintains the Trinity, the Deity of Christ, the Cross as an atoning sacrifice, the Scriptures of the Word of God, and the Ten Commandments as a divinely imposed rule of life. Therefore, let me ask, if Roman Catholic theologians take up the sword to do valiant and skillful battle against the same tendency that we ourselves mean to fight to the death, is it not part of wisdom to accept their valuable help?"[147] Erik Prince has been in the thick of this right-wing effort to unite conservative Catholics, evangelicals, and neoconservatives in a common theoconservative holy war—with Blackwater serving as a sort of armed wing of the movement. As Prince himself once envisioned the role of his mercenaries, "Everybody carries guns, just like Jeremiah rebuilding the temple in Israel—a sword in one hand and a trowel in the other."[148]

In addition to his support for extremist Catholic organizations, Prince has continued to contribute heavily to the evangelical Christian causes that his parents supported, including large donations to a slew of Protestant schools and colleges. Prince has also donated at least $200,000 to the Haggai Institute in Atlanta, Georgia (to go along with the hundreds of thousands more from the broader Prince family).[149] Haggai, one of the leading Christian missionary organizations in the world, boasts that it has "trained" more than sixty thousand evangelical "leaders" around the globe, with a concentration on poor or developing countries.[150] Prince has also served on the board of directors of and donated to Christian Freedom International, formerly Christian Solidarity International, a crusading missionary group active operating everywhere from Somalia to Sudan to Afghanistan and Iraq. Its mission statement reads: "More Christians have been martyred in the past 100 years than in all prior 1900 years combined. And the persecution of Christians is growing. Today more Christians are oppressed for their faith than ever. In many nations—right now—Christians are harassed, tortured, imprisoned, and even martyred for their faith in Jesus Christ."[151] Jim Jacobson, a former aide to Gary Bauer in Ronald Reagan's White House, runs the group, which has taken public positions against the work of the United Nations, calling some of its agencies "merchants of misery,"[152] and has protested that Iraqi self-determination could harm Christians.[153] In calling for the United States to attack Afghanistan after 9/11, Jacobson declared, "Only unequivocal military strikes will express our commitment to world peace and the rule of law."[154] The board of directors includes Blackwater lobbyist Paul Behrends, former Republican Senator Don Nickles, and former Voice of America director Robert Reilly, who began his career as a Reagan White House propagandist for the Nicaraguan Contras and worked briefly for war contractor SAIC on its ill-fated attempt to create a new Iraqi information ministry.[155]

In 2000 Erik Prince was on hand for a Michigan benefit to raise money for one of his family's (and the theoconservative movement's) pet causes—school vouchers. At the event, Prince spoke to the *Wall Street Journal*, saying both his family and the DeVos clan believe in conservative, Christian, free-market ideals, and that his beloved father's business—the one responsible for building up Focus on the Family and the Family Research Council—"was an engine that generated cash that he could use to do good things."[156] He said his sister Betsy was using those "same energies."[157] By that time, the thirty-year-old Prince had his own small cash-generating engine, on the brink of becoming much, much bigger. While Erik continued the Prince family tradition of supporting the right-wing Christian movement, his Blackwater empire was steadily growing in the Great Dismal Swamp of North Carolina. How fast it would grow wouldn't become clear until two planes smashed into the World Trade Center a year later, in a horrible tragedy that would fuel Erik Prince's meteoric rise to become head of one of the most powerful private armies in the world. Prince would soon draw on his father's ideals and money to build up an army of soldiers who would serve on the front lines of a global battle, waged largely on Muslim lands, that an evangelical President Prince helped put in the White House would boldly define as a "crusade."[158]

BLACKWATER BEGINS

ARMY. NAVY. Air Force. Marines. Blackwater.

Erik Prince might now see his empire as the fifth branch of the U.S. military, but his designs for Blackwater started off much more modestly, and they weren't really his own designs. While he served as the hands-on ATM for the creation of Blackwater, the location, plans, and virtually every detail of the new company came not from Prince but rather from one of his mentors in the Navy SEALs: Al Clark, who spent eleven years as one of the elite unit's top firearms trainers. In an interview, Clark said that in 1993, when Prince was just beginning his military career, Clark had already "started drawing the sketches for Blackwater."[1] The concept grew out of Clark's experiences as a Navy firearms trainer, when he recognized firsthand what he saw as an inadequate training infrastructure for what was one of the most vaunted forces in the U.S. military machine. "There were no facilities. We didn't have anything. The Navy never owned ranges, they always had to borrow from the Marine Corps or the Army," he said. "[Private] facilities were out there that had different pieces of the programs we needed, but no one had one-stop shopping."[2]

But one essential element was missing from Clark's plan: money. Little did Clark know that within a few years, one of the wealthiest men ever to serve in the U.S. military would be one of his pupils. In 1996, Clark was transferred to SEAL Team 8 to run its tactical training program. Lt. Erik Prince was in the first platoon that Clark trained there, but "I didn't know he had a gazillion dollars," Clark recalled.[3] Prince went through Clark's training, though the two never discussed any sort of business partnership. Eventually, Prince set off on a deployment with SEAL Team 8.[4] Seven months later, Al Clark had learned not only that his former pupil was loaded with cash but that the two shared a common interest in the burgeoning world of privatized training. When Prince returned to the States after his SEAL deployment, "I hooked it up with him through the request of somebody else," Clark recalled. "Basically, we just kind of started the dialogue from there."[5]

For Prince, that period was a bittersweet time. His father had died in 1995, and every indication suggests that Prince wanted to remain in the SEALs, instead of jumping head first into the family business. But the combination of his father's death and the worsening condition of his first wife, Joan—then sick with cancer—and the needs of their four children left Prince little choice. "Just prior to a deployment, my dad unexpectedly died," Prince recalled a decade later. "My family's business had grown to great success and I left the Navy earlier than I had intended to assist with family matters."[6] In short order, however, the family sold Edgar Prince's empire. The 1996 sale for $1.35 billion in cash allowed Erik Prince to begin building his own kingdom, one that would combine his various religious, political, and military passions.[7] "I wanted to stay connected to the military, so I built a facility to provide a world-class venue for U.S. and friendly foreign military, law enforcement, commercial, and government organizations to prepare to go into harm's way," Prince claimed in 2006. "Many Special Operations guys I know had the same thoughts about the need for private advanced training facilities. A few of them joined me when I formed Blackwater. I was in the unusual position after the sale of the family business to self-fund this endeavor."[8]

But Prince's attempt to claim virtually sole credit for Blackwater's founding spurs sharp reactions from some of his early Blackwater cohorts. According to several sources involved with Blackwater's founding and early history, the story of the company's genesis had never been in dispute until Blackwater rose to prominence after the 2003 Iraq occupation. That was when Erik Prince began peddling what appeared to be a bit of revisionist history. The company Web site boasted, "Our founder is a former U.S. Navy SEAL. He created Blackwater on the belief that both the military and law enforcement establishments would require additional capacity to train fully our brave men and women in and out of uniform to the standards required to keep our country secure."[9] Prince has claimed the Blackwater concept came to him during his time with SEAL Team 8, when he was deployed in Haiti, the Middle East, Bosnia, and the Mediterranean. "As I trained all over the world, I realized how difficult it was for units to get the cutting-edge training they needed to ensure success," he said. "In a letter home while I was deployed, I outlined the vision that is today Blackwater."[10]

Al Clark and other former Blackwater executives hotly dispute that version of Blackwater's history. "[Clark] was the guy that came up with the idea for Blackwater as a training center in the beginning and mentioned it to Erik Prince," says a former Blackwater executive. "Al was the idea [man] and Erik came up with the money. Erik gets the credit for it because he's the owner, but it was actually Al's idea."[11] Moreover, Prince's claim that he laid out "the vision that is today Blackwater" in 1996 is dubious given how closely linked to the "war on terror" the company's success has been. But because of his upbringing and the training he received at the hands of his father and the family's conservative friends and allies, Erik Prince was a committed disciple of free-market economic theory and privatization; he clearly understood what led Al Clark to envision a "one-stop shopping" training facility for the federal government. In many ways, the Blackwater project couldn't have come at a better time—converging as it did with the government's embrace of some of the very policies the Prince family had long advocated.

Blackwater was born just as the military was in the midst of a massive, unprecedented privatization drive that had begun in force during Dick Cheney's time as Defense Secretary, from 1989 to 1993, under George H. W. Bush. "In his first year in office, Cheney reduced military spending by $10 billion. He cancelled a number of complicated and expensive weapons systems, and reduced the number of troops from 2.2 million to 1.6 million. Year after year, from 1989 to 1993, the military budget shrank under Cheney," wrote Dan Briody in his book *The Halliburton Agenda*. "The army depended very little on civilian contractors in the early 1990s and Cheney was inclined to change that. The idea was to free up the troops to do the fighting while private contractors handled the back-end logistics. It was also a tidy way of handling the public relations nightmare that ensued every time the United States committed troops overseas. More contractors meant fewer troops, and a much more politically palatable troop count."[12] At the end of his tenure, Cheney commissioned Halliburton subsidiary Brown and Root (later renamed KBR following a merger with engineering contractor M. W. Kellogg) to do a classified study on how the military could privatize the majority of support services—troop housing, food, laundry, etc.—for U.S. international military operations.[13] Brown and Root was paid $3.9 million to write a report that would effectively create a hugely profitable market for itself by greatly expanding the Pentagon's Logistics Civil Augmentation Program (LOGCAP).[14] Indeed, by late August 1992, the U.S. Army Corps of Engineers had selected Halliburton, soon to be run by Cheney himself, to do virtually all of the support work for the military over the next five years.[15]

That first Halliburton contract burst open the door for the rapid privatization that would culminate in the contracting bonanza in Iraq, Afghanistan,
and elsewhere ushered in by the war on terror.

By the time Al Clark, Erik Prince, and a handful of others began serious
planning for what would become Blackwater in the mid-1990s, the military
had been downsizing for years, and training facilities were some of the casualties of that trend. Those facilities were also some of the most valuable
components of the military machine. But the Base Realignment and Closure Act process that had begun during the Reagan/Bush era, ostensibly as
a money-saving venture, had accelerated under Bill Clinton and had left the
military with what many in the special forces community saw as an inadequate number of training venues. This downsizing would provide fertile
ground for Blackwater to sprout and grow fast. "There was a need for
training for military and for Special Operations units, because most of the
ranges and facilities were World War II and they were antiquated," said Bill
Masciangelo, the first president of Blackwater, who now runs military and
government sales for hotel giant Cendant. "Since they were running out of
places to train, and nobody provided a modern military facility, that was
the whole concept behind Blackwater when it was first conceived."[16] Al
Clark said that at the time of Blackwater's founding it was "not an original
idea. Everybody knew for twenty years there needed to be a place like this
built."[17] Not long after Clark pitched his idea to Prince in 1996, Clark says
his former pupil told him, "Let's do it."[18]

At the time, the United States was in the midst of one of the darkest
moments in recent history for the Republican Party and the religious right. Bill
Clinton's defeat of George H. W. Bush in the 1992 presidential election meant
the end of a twelve-year golden era of conservative governance, molded in large
part by the policies of Ronald Reagan's White House. While the right-wing
political apparatus in which Edgar Prince was a key player did succeed in pro-
pelling the 1994 Republican Revolution and Newt Gingrich's rise to Speaker
of the House, the Clinton administration was viewed by the theocons as a far-
left "regime" that was forcing a proabortion, progay, antifamily, antireligious

agenda on the country. In November 1996—the month Clinton crushed Bob Dole and won reelection—the main organ of the theoconservative movement, Richard Neuhaus's journal *First Things*, published a "symposium" titled "The End of Democracy?" which bluntly questioned "whether we have reached or are reaching the point where conscientious citizens can no longer give moral assent to the existing regime."[19] A series of essays raised the prospect of a major confrontation between the church and the "regime," at times seeming to predict a civil-war scenario or Christian insurrection against the government, exploring possibilities "ranging from noncompliance to resistance to civil disobedience to morally justified revolution."[20] Erik Prince's close friend, political collaborator, and beneficiary Chuck Colson authored one of the five major essays of the issue, as did extremist Judge Robert Bork, whom Reagan had tried unsuccessfully to appoint to the Supreme Court in 1987. "Americans are not accustomed to speaking of a regime. Regimes are what other nations have," asserted the symposium's unsigned introduction. "This symposium asks whether we may be deceiving ourselves and, if we are, what are the implications of that self-deception. By the word 'regime' we mean the actual, existing system of government. The question that is the title of this symposium is in no way hyperbolic. The subject before us is the end of democracy." It declared, "The government of the United States of America no longer governs by the consent of the governed. . . . What is happening now is the displacement of a constitutional order by a regime that does not have, will not obtain, and cannot command the consent of the people."[21] The editorial quoted Supreme Court Justice Antonin Scalia saying, "A Christian should not support a government that suppresses the faith or one that sanctions the taking of an innocent human life."[22]

Colson's essay was titled "Kingdoms in Conflict." "[E]vents in America may have reached the point where the only political action believers can take is some kind of direct, extra-political confrontation of the judicially controlled regime," Colson wrote, adding that a "showdown between church and state may be inevitable. This is *not* something for which Christians should hope. But it is something for which they need to prepare." He asserted, "[A] 'social contract' that included biblical believers and Enlightenment rationalists was the basis of the founding of the United States. . . . If the terms of our contract have in fact been broken, Christian citizens may be compelled to force the government to return to its original understanding. . . . The writings of Thomas Jefferson, who spoke openly of the necessity of revolution, could also be called upon for support." Colson stopped short of calling for an open rebellion, but he clearly viewed that as a distinct possibility/necessity in the near future, saying, "with fear and trembling, I have begun to believe that, however Christians in America gather to reach their consensus, we are fast approaching this point."[23]

The *First Things* symposium sparked great controversy—even within the theoconservative movement. Among those who came to the defense of Colson, Bork, Neuhaus et al. was Edgar Prince's old friend, ally, and beneficiary James Dobson of Focus on the Family. "My deepest gratitude to the editors of First Things for facilitating what history may reveal to be their most important symposium. The moral legitimacy of our current government and the responsibility of the Christian towards it are questions of tremendous moment," Dobson wrote. "I wonder—do we have the courage to act upon the conclusions we may reach in these deliberations?" Dobson said the essays had "laid an indisputable case for the illegitimacy of the regime now passing itself off as a democracy," adding, "I stand in a long tradition of Christians who believe that rulers may forfeit their divine mandate when they systematically contravene the divine moral law. . . . We may rapidly be approaching the sort of Rubicon that our spiritual forebears faced: Choose Caesar or God. I take no pleasure in this prospect; I pray against it. But it is worth noting that such times have historically been rejuvenating for the faith."[24]

It was against this backdrop—a throwing down of the political and religious gauntlet by many of the powerful conservative leaders Prince and his family had supported and built up—that Blackwater was born. A month after the *First Things* symposium explored the possibility of a "showdown between church and state" and a "morally justified revolution,"[25] Erik

Prince would begin building up one of the largest privately held stockpiles of weaponry inside the United States, a few hours outside Washington, D.C. Prince simultaneously strengthened his bonds with powerful Republican legislators and the leaders of the theoconservative movement, becoming a major bankroller on par with his father.[26] On December 26, 1996, three months after being discharged from active duty with the SEALs,[27] he incorporated Blackwater Lodge and Training Center.[28] The next year, he purchased more than four thousand acres in Currituck County, North Carolina, for $756,000 and nearly one thousand acres in neighboring Camden County for $616,000. Prince's new kingdom would be built near the Great Dismal Swamp.[29] The stated idea behind Blackwater was "to fulfill the anticipated demand for government outsourcing of firearms and related security training."[30]

Blackwater USA might now have influence over and access to some of the most powerful operatives roaming the chambers of power in Washington, D.C., but at its inception, the company struggled to convince the planning commission of Currituck County—population twenty-thousand[31]—that Blackwater should be allowed to open for business. In the pre-9/11 days of Bill Clinton's America, the planning commissioners weren't worried about international terrorism and couldn't have even comprehended the company that Blackwater would become. Instead, what concerned them was property values, noise ordinances, and the possibility that the types of militia groups that Oklahoma City bomber Timothy McVeigh had been linked to would come to their community for training. When Erik Prince appealed to the plan commissioners, his project was described as a "$2 million outdoor shooting range."[32] At the time, Prince estimated the facility could create up to thirty new jobs in the county and help to train its sheriff's department. But before Prince could land approval for the facility, he needed to convince the planning commission to create a new ordinance that would allow it to be built, and to spell out the protections that would be put in place to keep the area quiet and stray bullets away from residences.[33]

Local opposition to the Blackwater project was strong. A year earlier, residents had been outraged when stray bullets from a hunter struck a truck and building at a local junior high during school hours.[34] Consequently, county officials raised serious questions that a proposed 900-foot buffer between nearby properties and firing areas would be sufficient. "The 900-foot buffer is no buffer at all, really," County Attorney William Romm said.[35] One resident constructing a home near Blackwater's proposed site said, "Nobody's going to want to live anywhere near a shooting range," while another resident asserted, "I've not spoken to anyone who is in favor of this."[36] One woman at one of the early meetings said she "would never consider buying anything next to a firing range of this magnitude."[37] The commission apparently didn't seem sold on the idea, either, and a month later denied Prince's request for a new ordinance. "We're very disappointed," Prince said at the time. "For a county that claims to be a sportsman's paradise, it doesn't bode well for safe-shooting sports."[38] After being rebuffed by Currituck, Prince went down the road to Camden County, which quickly approved the project.[39]

In June 1997, ground was broken on the Blackwater compound, and in May 1998, the company officially opened for business.[40] Though the company's name sounds ominous, it actually was inspired by the black waters of the Great Dismal Swamp—a 111,000-acre peat bog stretching from southeastern Virginia to northeastern North Carolina—close to where Blackwater was contructed. While many later accounts from company executives and others would portray the early days of Blackwater as slow going, its volume of "black" and confidential contracts makes that difficult to confirm. As Clark remembers it, the company hit the ground running. "The SEAL community came down, because we came from the SEAL community and they were aware of it. They came down at least for the shootouts and the ranges to run their training. It filtered into a lot of law enforcement; the FBI came down, as word got out. The facility was the initial draw to a lot of them because it was something new and big and close by," Clark said.[41] While Blackwater was constructed on a swamp, it was strategically located a half-hour from the largest naval base in the world, the forty-three-hundred-acre Norfolk Naval Station,[42] and not far from the epicenter of the U.S. intelligence and federal law enforcement communities. The facility would also provide various government agencies—federal, state, and local—with a remote and secure location to discreetly train forces. "A lot of the reason some of those agencies came down there was to get away from everybody else, get out of the public eye, for the press and the public," Clark recalled. "Just because they're wearing black outfits everybody want[ed] to come see what they're doing."[43]

Clark said Blackwater's new training facility offered U.S. Special Operations forces another advantage over existing private shooting facilities, many of which were run by competitive "trophy shooters." At Blackwater, Clark recalled, "the training that we exposed them to—mainly that I exposed them to while I was there—kind of gave them a breath of fresh air. You know, finally someone that's not a competitive trophy shooter or some kind of action shooter." Competitive shooting, Clark said, was "all about me, me, me. Second place for them is just a small trophy, but [for] tactical shooters, people who have to kick in doors or go to the desert, second place is not a very good place to be."[44]

By 1998, Blackwater was doing a brisk business in training private and government customers in the use of a wide variety of weapons from pistols to precision rifles to machine guns. It was leasing out the facility to SEALs for their training. Police officers from Virginia, North Carolina, and Canada had enrolled in Blackwater training programs, and the company was starting to get inquiries from foreign governments. The Spanish government was interested in training security details that would protect presidential candidates, while Brazil expressed interest in counterterrorism training.[45] "They are the best of the best . . . to come to a school where you are taught by the best in the world is great," an early customer told the *Virginian-Pilot* in September 1998. "It is an honor to be here."[46]

As word spread about Blackwater's training, Prince and other executives wanted to make sure that Blackwater would earn a reputation as the premiere facility of its kind. "I was a retired Marine officer who had been in the hotel business for fifteen years, so they were looking for somebody that had that balance," Masciangelo, the company's first president, said in an interview. "Blackwater delivered more than training. The whole customer service issue and the ambiance and the setting and the facilities, that was the whole reason for them hiring me."[47] By late 1998, Blackwater boasted a nine-thousand-square-foot lodge with conference rooms, classrooms, lounge, pro shop, and dining hall. A wide variety of ranges including an urban street façade and a pond for water-to-land training were just some of the early offerings.[48]

Steve Waterman, a writer on assignment for *Soldier of Fortune*, visited Blackwater in 1999 and described the facility at Moyock in glowing terms. With "a great chow hall (I would describe it more as a cafeteria), satellite TV systems in the dorms and plenty of hot water in the showers, I would put Blackwater ahead of any of the civilian or military training sites I have visited," Waterman wrote. "When you turn the last corner and are able to see the buildings, it quickly becomes obvious that the operators of this center are quite serious in their endeavors and nothing has been spared to make this a top notch facility. The buildings are brand new . . . and the place is well laid out and neat. Off to the right are the dorm facilities and the tactical house. Straight ahead is the main building which houses the classrooms, store, administrative offices, cafeteria, armory, and conference rooms, lounge, where tall tales may be spun and examples of taxidermy are displayed. A large black bear looms out at you over the fireplace and several other animals watch you through plastic eyes. The gun cleaning area is off to the side of the main building where there is room for more than a dozen people to clean weapons. The benches are chest high and there are compressed air nozzles for blowing dust and dirt out of weapons. The well-lighted rooms have four bunk beds in each with a spacious closet for each occupant. There are two heads (bathrooms to you landlubbers), each with several shower stalls. On both sides of the dorm building is a large room with a couch and several chairs. A TV in each lounge is fed by a satellite system. There is also a refrigerator and water cooler in each of these rooms. Magazines are there for the perusal of the guests."[49] In 1998 Blackwater hosted a police and military handgun competition, the first of many such events, later called the Shoot-Out at Blackwater, that would draw people from all over the world to Moyock. But Blackwater would soon demonstrate its powerful ability to capitalize on tragedy and fear. In fact, 1999 would kick off a string of almost annual high-profile violent incidents that would play out on international television and result in more business and growing profits for Blackwater.

On April 20, 1999, Dylan Klebold and Eric Harris walked into their high school, Columbine High, in Littleton, Colorado, wearing black trench coats and armed to the teeth with semiautomatic weapons and shotguns. The two proceeded to go on a killing rampage that took the lives of twelve of their fellow students and one teacher. The incident would quickly be dubbed the "Columbine massacre." Despite the fact that the number of school shootings had dropped from thirty-two during the 1992–1993 school year to nineteen during 1998–1999, the hype around Columbine encouraged a panic about such incidents that spread throughout the country.[50] It also caused law enforcement agencies at all levels to review their ability to respond to such incidents. "Nobody thought that Columbine could have happened," Ron Watson, a spokesman for the National Tactical Officer's Association (NTOA), said at the time. "So Columbine has changed thinking. It has thrown a new wrinkle into training."[51]

In September 1999, some four hundred SWAT team officers found their way to Moyock for exercises at Blackwater's newly constructed "R U Ready High School."[52] The NTOA kicked in $50,000 to construct the fifteen-room, 14,746-square-foot mock school, but the project likely cost Blackwater much more.[53] As with future projects, Prince had the means and the motivation to spend if he thought there would eventually be a payoff. "Erik had enough money to pay for whatever they needed up front, so he could get his money back, he had plenty of capital," said Al Clark. "He probably inherited $500 million, so he had plenty of money to play with."[54] The mock school featured the sound effects of screaming students, blood spatters, gunshot wounds, and simunition (practice ammo). "You're dealing with chaos—a tremendous amount of confusion," said retired NYPD Emergency Service Unit commander Al Baker. "They are all young and all are unknowns in this large place. There is a tremendous amount of noise. You don't know who the shooter is. We're trying to teach them the techniques of clearing a hostile environment. There is a lot of bleeding. This is not something that can wait."[55]

Blackwater's quick construction and running of "R U Ready High" convinced the NTOA, an organization that trains four thousand police officers annually, to split its sixteenth annual conference between Virginia Beach and Blackwater's Moyock compound. The event drew tactical teams and police officers from every state, Canada, Haiti, Belgium, and England. By April 2000, the NTOA had put more than one thousand officers through training at "R U Ready" as police departments across the country started more and more to hear the name Blackwater. At an NTOA soiree at the time, Prince commented that events like Columbine are "a reminder that vigilance is the price of liberty, and we need well-trained law enforcement and military. There is no shortage of evil in the world."[56]

On February 1, 2000, with its name spreading across the law enforcement community, Blackwater took a huge leap forward as it landed its first General Services Administration contract, creating a government-approved list of services and goods Blackwater could sell to federal agencies and the prices it could officially charge. Winning a "GSA schedule" essentially opened Blackwater up for "long-term governmentwide contracts."[57] The schedule outlined a list of prices for use of Blackwater facilities or to use Blackwater instructors for specialty training. Use of the tactical training area cost $1,250 per day for less than twenty shooters. Use of the urban training area, of which "R U Ready High" was a component, ran $1,250 a day for less than thirty people, $1,500 a day for more. Each range could be rented out to a government agency for $50 per person per day with a $500 minimum. The schedule also provided for $1,200-a-day Blackwater instructors to teach classes in executive protection, force protection, close quarter battle, shipboarding movement, and hostage rescue, and allowed Blackwater to sell its own specially developed targets and other training gear to whatever agency requested it. Offerings ranged from $1,335 bullet traps to $170 "pepper poppers" to $512 turning targets.[58] In and of themselves, those may not seem like big ticket items, but having the GSA schedule in place essentially opened Blackwater's doors to the entire federal government, provided it could politick well enough to score contracts. "It's like having a Wal-Mart to the government," explained Jamie Smith in an interview.[59] Smith is a former CIA operative who spent years working for Blackwater. "Having a GSA contract allows the government to go in and buy things from you without having to go out to bid really." The real work for companies once they win a GSA designation is greasing the wheels at various government agencies and convincing them to use the company's services often and widely. That's where a company's political connections come into play. Halliburton had developed a model that Blackwater and others could mimic. As Smith said, "It's a handshake-type thing and you say, 'Here's our GSA schedule, and let's see what we can do.'" Blackwater's first payment under its GSA contract was for $68,000 in March 2000 for "armament training devices."[60] As it happened, that was the exact amount Erik Prince would donate later that year to the Republican National State Elections Committee in an election year that would see George W. Bush take power.[61]

Blackwater's original five-year GSA contract value (i.e., the government's projection of how much business Blackwater would do with federal agencies) was estimated at a meager $125,000.[62] When it was extended by five years in 2005, the estimate was pushed to $6 million.[63] But all of those projections were far shy of the actual business Blackwater would win under the GSA. As of 2006, Blackwater had already been paid $111 million under the schedule. "This is a multiple-award schedule, indefinite quantity, indefinite delivery contract," said GSA spokesman Jon Anderson. "When the contract is first awarded, we do not know whether or not agencies are going to place orders with the contractor as the contractor has to compete with other . . . contractors for task orders, so we set the estimated dollar value of the contract at $125,000. Blackwater was obviously very successful in their endeavors and was able to build their sales to $111 million over a six-year period."[64] By 2008, the number would reach more than a billion dollars.

In 2000, as business was picking up for Blackwater, all was not well at the Moyock compound. Al Clark, the man many credit with dreaming up the company, found himself at odds with Prince and others at the company. "As time went on, some things took place there that I didn't really agree with, so I left to start another business," recalled Clark, who founded Special Tactical Systems with former Blackwater employee and fellow SEAL Dale McClellan in 2000. "One of the things that started happening was Erik wanted it to be a playground for his rich friends. And I was questioned on why would I train your standard Army guy on the same level that I'd train a SEAL. And my rebuttal was, 'Why would you base the value of someone's life on the uniform they're wearing, because once the bullets start flying they don't discriminate,' and I was basically told my standards were too high."[65]

Clark says during training sessions he "gave everybody everything I had when I had them," but he said company executives "thought there was no incentive for [clients] to come back if I gave them everything, and my argument was, they may not get a chance to come back, so while we've got them, we should give them everything we have. A lot of cops were paying out of their own pocket, taking their vacation time away from their families, to go to a school they thought would give them something their departments wouldn't." As an original founder of Blackwater who left before the company's rise to substantial financial success, Clark may have a tainted view of Prince and the company. Through a spokesperson, Prince declined an interview for this book and, therefore, his views on Clark's allegations are unclear except as they are represented in Blackwater's official history. Clark was reluctant to expand much on his split with Prince, but he summed up his feelings about leaving Blackwater: "Let's put it this way: I wanted it to be a place built by professionals for professionals, and I wanted it to be professional, and it didn't feel to me like it was being that way."[66] Blackwater had already started down the path to success when Clark left in 2000, having landed a couple of hundred thousand dollars in payments on its GSA contract and other awards, but it wasn't until more than a year later that the business really began to boom. That would come courtesy of two terror attacks attributed to Osama bin Laden.

Shortly after 11:00 a.m. on the morning of October 12, 2000, in the Yemeni port of Aden, a small boat approached the U.S. Navy guided missile destroyer the USS Cole, which had just finished up a routine fuel stop. As the boat neared the ship's port side, it exploded, ripping a forty-by-forty-foot hole in the massive ship. Osama bin Laden would later take responsibility for the suicide attack that killed seventeen U.S. sailors and injured thirty-nine others. The second annual tragedy, following 1999's Columbine massacre, that would benefit Blackwater resulted in a $35.7 million contract with the Navy, Blackwater's ancestral branch of the military, to conduct "force protection" training.[67] Traditionally, the average Navy midshipmen didn't train for a combat role, but with increased threats to the fleet, that began to change. "The attack on the USS Cole was a terrible tragedy and dramatic example of the type of threat our military forces face worldwide on a day-to-day basis, emphasizing the importance of force protection both today and in the future," Adm. Vern Clark, the chief of Naval operations, told the Senate Armed Services Committee in May 2001. "The Navy has taken action at home and abroad to meet this challenge, undergoing a sea change in the way we plan and execute self-defense. We have enhanced the manning, training, and equipping of naval forces to better realize a war fighter's approach to physical security, with AT/FP serving as a primary focus of every mission, activity, and event. Additionally, we are dedicated to ensuring this mindset is instilled in every one of our sailors."[68] At the time, the Navy had already committed itself to incorporating "a comprehensive plan to reduce infrastructure costs through competition, privatization, and outsourcing."[69] Among its projects was a review of some 80,500 full-time equivalent positions for outsourcing.[70] While the bombing of the USS Cole significantly boosted Blackwater's business, it would pale in comparison to the jackpot that would come courtesy of the greatest act of terror ever carried out on U.S. soil.

On the morning of September 11, 2001, American Airlines Flight 11, carrying ninety-two passengers from Boston to Los Angeles, abruptly turned course and headed straight toward New York City. At 8:46 a.m., the plane smashed directly into the North Tower of the World Trade Center. Some seventeen minutes later, United Airlines Flight 175 crashed into the South Tower. At 9:37 a.m., American Airlines Flight 77 hit the Pentagon. As fire and smoke burned from two of America's most famous buildings, the attacks almost instantly accelerated an agenda of privatization and conquest long sought by many of the people who had just taken over the White House less than a year earlier. President Bush's Secretary of the Army, Thomas White, a former Enron executive, oversaw the rapid implementation of the privatization agenda kick-started by Dick Cheney a decade earlier.[71] The program would soon see the explosion of a $100 billion global for-profit military industry. Among the greatest beneficiaries of the administration's newly declared "war on terror" would be Erik Prince's Blackwater. As Al Clark put it, "Osama bin Laden turned Blackwater into what it is today."[72]

"The bombing of the USS Cole in Aden, Yemen, sent a ripple through the U.S. Navy, and then 9/11 happened and the ripple was worldwide," Blackwater vice president Chris Taylor said in a 2005 speech at George Washington University Law School. "The Navy appropriately responded realizing that in order to combat today's terrorist threat, all sailors would need substantial training in basic and advanced force protection techniques. The Navy moved swiftly to create a sound training program, the majority of which Blackwater now executes and manages all over the country. Sailors the world over are now better prepared to identify, appropriately engage, and defeat would-be attacks on naval vessels in port and underway. To date, Blackwater has trained some 30,000 sailors."[73] Blackwater was officially awarded the $35.7 million Navy contract for "force protection training that includes force protection fundamental training . . . armed sentry course training; and law enforcement training."[74] The bulk of the work was to be performed in Norfolk, with some in San Diego and San Antonio.[75] A

Blackwater trainer who oversaw the contract commented shortly after it started in 2002 that his instructors were shocked to find many sailors "have never held a firearm, except for at boot camp."[76]

The post-9/11 environment provided Erik Prince and his Blackwater colleagues with a blank canvas on which to paint a profitable future for the company, seemingly limited only by imagination and personnel. Defense Secretary Rumsfeld had come into office determined to dramatically expand the role private companies like Blackwater would play in U.S. wars, and 9/11 had put that agenda on the fastest of tracks. On September 27, two weeks after 9/11, Prince made a rare media appearance as a guest on Fox News's flagship program, *The O'Reilly Factor*. "I've been operating in the training business now for four years and was starting to get a little cynical on how seriously people took security," Prince said on the show. "The phone is ringing off the hook now."[77] The reason for Prince's appearance on Fox was to discuss the air marshal program and the training that marshals would receive, some of it at Blackwater. That month, Blackwater inked contracts with the FBI worth at least $610,000.[78] Soon it would be providing training for virtually every wing of the government, from the Department of Energy's National Nuclear Security Administrative Service Center to the Department of the Treasury's Financial Crime Enforcement Network to the Department of Health and Human Services assistant secretary's office.[79]

But while Blackwater raised its profit margin and profile with its training services in the aftermath of 9/11, its true fame and fortune would not be gained until it formed Blackwater Security Consulting in 2002 and burst into the world of soldiers-for-hire. As with Blackwater's founding, Erik Prince would once again provide the medium for another's idea. This time, it was the vision of former CIA operative Jamie Smith. Smith had been recruited by Al Clark to teach weapons classes while he was a law student at Regent University, "America's preeminent Christian university," in Virginia Beach, not far from Blackwater.[80]

In an interview, Smith said he first thought about the prospects for a private security company while working as a CIA operative during the 1991

Persian Gulf War. "I'm not trying to say that I was some sort of soothsayer a decade prior to all of this, but it was an infantile idea, it looked like it was just going to continue the trends of privatization," Smith said. "There were already companies doing similar things. There wasn't a lot of public knowledge surrounding that. DynCorp was working, there were other companies, SAIC, that were doing something along the same lines." Smith said he realized that the military was beginning to use private forces to guard military facilities, a practice known as "force protection," thus freeing up more forces for combat. It was a trend, and Smith said he "did not think it was something that could be arrested because of the nature of our military being a volunteer service. Do you really want to have your volunteer force standing guard out at the front gate when they could be doing things a lot more valuable for you? So I just didn't see that it would change and that it would probably just continue."[81]

Like Al Clark a few years earlier, Jamie Smith didn't have the means at the time to start his own private security company, and while the demand was certainly there, it was not overwhelming. Then, after 9/11, Smith says Prince "called and said, 'Hey, I'd like you to consider a full-time job and come back to work with us,' and I told him that was interesting to me and that I would consider doing that with the caveat that we could create this security company." Prince agreed. But, Smith contends, Prince didn't see the payoff in what would shortly become Blackwater's biggest moneymaker. "I was told, 'You can't devote all your time to this because it's not going to work.' They said, 'You can devote about 20 percent of your total time to this, but no more than that—you need to stick to what you're doing now,'" Smith said.[82] Smith joined Blackwater full-time in December 2001, and Blackwater Security Consulting was incorporated in Delaware on January 22, 2002.[83] Within months, as the U.S. occupied Afghanistan and began planning the Iraq invasion, Blackwater Security was already turning a profit, pulling in hundreds of thousands a month from a valuable CIA contract.[84]

One of the key players in landing that first Blackwater Security contract was A. B. "Buzzy" Krongard, executive director of the CIA, the agency's number-three position.[85] Krongard, who was named to that post in March 2001,[86] had an unusual background for a spook, having spent most of his adult life as an investment banker. He built up Alex.Brown, the country's oldest investment banking firm, into one of the most successful, eventually selling it to Bankers Trust, which he resigned from in 1998.[87] There have been some insinuations that Krongard was working undercover for the CIA years before he officially joined the agency in 1998 as a special adviser to George Tenet.[88] But he won't reveal how he met the CIA director, except to say that it was through "mutual friends."[89] The Princeton alum, Hall of Fame lacrosse player, and former Marine boasts of having once punched a great white shark in the jaw; and he keeps one of its teeth on a chain and pictures of the animal in his office.[90] Despite his bravado, some at the agency thought Krongard more of a wanna-be, according to a 2001 *Newsweek* story published shortly after his ascension to the number-three spot. "A wanna-be? Maybe I am. Maybe I'm not. That's as much as you're going to get," Krongard responded.[91]

9/11 conspiracy theorists have long been interested in Krongard because the bank he headed until 1998, which was bought out by Deutsche Bank after he left, was allegedly responsible for the unusually high number of put options on United Airlines stock placed just before 9/11, options that were never collected.[92] There is no evidence that he or anyone at the bank had prior knowledge of the attacks. While at the CIA, working under George Tenet, Krongard acted internally, reorganizing divisions[93] and pushing for projects like an intelligence venture capital firm,[94] but he did on occasion speak publicly. In October 2001, he declared, "The war will be won in large measure by forces you do not know about, in actions you will not see and in ways you may not want to know about, but we will prevail."[95]

Some three years later, in January 2005, Krongard made news when he became the most senior administration figure to articulate the benefits of having *not* killed or captured Osama bin Laden. "You can make the argument that we're better off with him (at large)," he said. "Because if something happens to bin Laden, you might find a lot of people vying for his position and demonstrating how macho they are by unleashing a stream of terror. . . . He's turning into more of a charismatic leader than a terrorist mastermind."[96] Krongard also characterized bin Laden "not as a chief executive but more like a venture capitalist," saying, "Let's say you and I want to blow up Trafalgar Square. So we go to bin Laden. And he'll say, 'Well, here's some money and some passports and if you need weapons, see this guy.'"[97]

It's not clear exactly what the actual connection was between Prince and Krongard. Some have alleged that Krongard knew Prince's father.[98] In a brief telephone interview, Krongard would only say he was "familiar" with Prince and Blackwater.[99] A former Blackwater executive, however, asserted, "I know that Erik and Krongard were good buddies."[100] Whatever Krongard's involvement, it was the CIA that handed Blackwater its first security contract in April 2002.[101] Krongard visited Kabul and said he realized the agency's new station there was sorely lacking security.[102] Blackwater received a $5.4 million six-month no-bid contract to provide twenty security guards for the Kabul CIA station.[103] Krongard said it was Blackwater's offering and not his connection to Prince that led to the company landing the contract, and that he talked to Prince about the contract but wasn't positive who called who, that he was "not sure which came first, the chicken or the egg."[104] He said that someone else was responsible for actually signing off on the CIA contract. "Blackwater got a contract because they were the first people that could get people on the ground," Krongard said in the interview. "We were under the gun, we did whatever it took when I came back from Kabul. . . . The only concern we had was getting the best security for our people. If we thought Martians could provide it, I guess we would have gone after them."[105]

The relationship between Krongard and Prince apparently got chummier after the contract was signed. "Krongard came down and visited Blackwater, and I had to take his [family] around and let them shoot on the firing range a number of times," said a former Blackwater executive in an interview. "That was after the contract was signed, and he may have come down just to see the company that he had just hired."[106] Prince apparently became consumed with the prospect of being involved with secretive operations in the war on terror—so much so that he personally deployed on the front lines.[107] Prince joined Jamie Smith as part of the original twenty-man contingent Blackwater sent to fulfill its first CIA contract, which began in May 2002, according to Robert Young Pelton's book *Licensed to Kill*.[108] Most of the team guarded the CIA Kabul station and its assets at the airport, but Smith and Prince also went to one of the most dangerous places in Afghanistan, Shkin, where the United States was establishing a base four miles from the Pakistani border. But after just one week, Prince left the Shkin detail and the mud fortress (that some called the "Alamo") out of which U.S. forces operated. Smith told Pelton that Prince's trip was more like "playing CIA paramilitary" and that he left to go "schmooze" those who could give more work to Blackwater Security.[109] Smith stayed in Shkin for two months and then in Kabul for four months. After leaving Shkin, Prince remained in Kabul for a week. Apparently Prince enjoyed the experience so much that he reportedly tried to join the CIA, but was rejected.[110] Though Prince was denied the status of a full CIA operative, he has apparently maintained close ties with the agency. Prince reportedly was given a "green badge" that permitted him access to most CIA stations.[111] "He's over there [at CIA headquarters] regularly, probably once a month or so," a CIA source told *Harper's* journalist Ken Silverstein in 2006. "He meets with senior people, especially in the [directorate of operations]."[112]

Since CIA and other intelligence and security contracts are "black" contracts, it's difficult to pin down exactly how much Blackwater began pulling in after that first Afghanistan job, but Smith described it as a rapid period of growth for Blackwater. The company's work for the CIA and the military and Prince's political and military connections would provide Blackwater with important leverage in wooing what would become its largest confirmed client, the U.S. State Department. "After that first contract went off, there was a lot of romancing with the State Department where they were just up the road, so we traveled up there a lot in Kabul and tried to sweet talk them into letting us on board with them," Smith said. "Once the State Department came on and there was a contract there, that opened up some different doors. Once you get your foot in the door with a government outfit that has offices in countries all over the world, it's like—and this is probably a horrible analogy—but it's something maybe like the metastasis of a cancer, you know, once you get into the bloodstream you're going to be all over the body in just a couple of days, you know what I mean? So if you get in that pipeline, then everywhere that they've got a problem and an office, there's an opportunity."[113]

For Blackwater, the opportunity of a lifetime would come when U.S. forces rolled into Baghdad in March 2003. Strapped with a GSA schedule and deep political and religious connections, Prince snagged a high-profile contract in Iraq that would position his men as the private bodyguards for the Bush administration's top man in Baghdad, Ambassador L. Paul Bremer III. Referred to as the "viceroy" or "proconsul," Bremer was a diehard free-marketeer who, like Prince, had converted to Catholicism and passionately embraced the neoconservative agenda of using American military might to remake the world according to U.S. interests—all in the name of democracy. The Bremer contract meant that Prince would be at the helm of an elite private force deployed on the front lines of a war long sought by many of the forces that made up the theocon movement. Far from the simple shooting range on a North Carolina swamp that Blackwater was just a few years earlier, the company was now recognized by the Bush administration as an essential part of its war on terror armada. Blackwater president Gary Jackson, a career Navy SEAL, would soon boast that some of Blackwater's contracts were so secret that the company couldn't tell one federal agency about the business it was doing with another agency.[114] Iraq was a pivotal coming-of-age moment for mercenaries, and Blackwater would soon emerge as the industry trendsetter. But less than a year after Prince's forces deployed in Iraq, four of Blackwater's men would find themselves on a fatal mission in the Sunni Triangle that would propel Blackwater to international infamy and forever alter the course of the U.S. occupation and Iraqi resistance to it. It happened in a city called Fallujah.

CHAPTER FOUR

FALLUJAH BEFORE BLACKWATER

"A stranger should be well-mannered."
—Fallujah proverb

LONG BEFORE Blackwater deployed in Iraq—more than a decade earlier, in fact—events beyond the control of Erik Prince and his colleagues were setting in motion the epic ambush that would take place on March 31, 2004, when Iraqi resistance fighters killed four Blackwater contractors in broad daylight in the center of Fallujah. The killing of those Americans would alter the course of the Iraq War, spark multiple U.S. sieges of Fallujah, and embolden the antioccupation resistance movement.

But to begin the story of what happened to the Blackwater men that day with the particular details surrounding the ambush of their convoy, or even the events of the immediate days and weeks preceding the killings, is to ignore more than a decade of history leading up to the incident. Some would say the story goes even further back, to Fallujah's fierce resistance to the British occupation of 1920, when an antioccupation rebellion in the city took the lives of some one thousand British soldiers almost a century before the United States invaded Iraq. Regardless, there is little question that the city of Fallujah has suffered like no other in Iraq since the U.S. invasion began in 2003. On several occasions, U.S. forces have attacked the city, killing thousands and displacing tens of thousands, and occupation troops have fired on unarmed demonstrators several times. Since the invasion, U.S. officials have brutally sought to make an example of the rebellious city. In the U.S. press and among the punditry, policy-makers, and military commanders, Fallujah has been portrayed as a hotbed of pro-Saddam resistance and as the seat of foreign fighters angered at the regime's overthrow and furious at the U.S. occupation. But that is a very narrow, incomplete, and misleading presentation of history that serves only Washington's agenda. As Pulitzer Prize–winning *Washington Post* correspondent Anthony Shadid noted, "[Fallujah's] historical links with the former government constituted only part of the story. It was also a region shaped by rural traditions and reflexive nationalism, stitched together by a fierce interpretation of Islam and the certainty it brought. This fundamental identity and its attendant values became even more important as the community sank deeper into the sense of disenfranchisement voiced so often in this swath of Sunni land."[1] What is seldom acknowledged in the media is that before the first U.S. troops rolled into Iraq, before the Blackwater killings and the ensuing sieges of the city, before it became a symbol of Iraqi resistance, the people of Fallujah knew suffering at the hands of the United States and its allies.

During the 1991 Gulf War, Fallujah was the site of one of the single greatest massacres attributed to "errant" bombs during a war that was painted as the dawn of the age of "smart" weaponry. Shortly after 3:00 p.m.

on the afternoon of February 13, 1991, allied warplanes thundered over the city, launching missiles at the massive steel bridge crossing the Euphrates River and connecting Fallujah to the main road to Baghdad.[2] Having failed to bring the bridge down, the planes returned to Fallujah an hour later. "I saw eight planes," recalled an eyewitness. "Six of them were circling, as if they were covering. The other two carried out the attack."[3] British Tornado warplanes fired off several of the much-vaunted laser-guided "precision" missiles at the bridge. But at least three missed their supposed target, and one landed in a residential area some eight hundred yards from the bridge, smashing into a crowded apartment complex and slicing through a packed marketplace.[4] In the end, local hospital officials said more than 130 people were killed that day and some eighty others were wounded.[5] Many of the victims were children. An allied commander, Capt. David Henderson, said the planes' laser system had malfunctioned. "As far as we were concerned, the bridge was a legitimate military target," Henderson told reporters.[6] "Unfortunately, it looks as though, despite our best efforts, bombs did land in the town." He and other officials accused the Iraqi government of publicizing the "errant" bomb as part of a propaganda war, saying, "We should also remember the atrocities committed by Iraq against Iran with chemical warfare and against [its] own countrymen, the Kurds."[7] As rescue workers and survivors dug through the rubble of the apartment complex and neighboring shops, one Fallujan shouted at reporters, "Look what Bush did! For him Kuwait starts here."[8]

Whether or not it was an "errant" bomb, for the decade that followed that attack, it was remembered in Iraq as a massacre and would shape the way Fallujans later viewed the invading U.S. forces under the command of yet another President Bush.[9] Already, the overwhelmingly Sunni population of Fallujah was one of Saddam Hussein's most loyal populations within Iraq and the home of many of his elite Revolutionary Guard soldiers.[10] "Even though Saddam Hussein regarded Fallujah as a city which had supported his regime, the Iraqi government couldn't insulate Fallujah's hospitals and clinics from the devastating effects of US-led economic sanctions," recalled veteran human rights activist Kathy Kelly, founder of Voices in the Wilderness.[11] "We visited hospital wards before the invasion in Fallujah that were like 'death rows' for infants because of shortages caused by the sanctions." Kelly has been to Iraq scores of times since first traveling there during the 1991 Gulf War. In a visit to Fallujah before the 2003 invasion, she said she and some British activists went to the city in an effort to acknowledge U.S./U.K. culpability in the marketplace bombing of 1991 and to interview survivors. Kelly got separated from the group and recalled, "One man began to shout at me, in English: 'You Americans, you Europeans, you come to my home and I'll show you water you wouldn't give your animals to drink. And this is all that we have. Now, you want to kill our children again. You cannot kill my son. My son, he was killed in the first Bush war.'" After shouting at her, Kelly recalled, the man calmed down and offered her tea at his home. To her, that was evidence that "even in Fallujah, there might have been a chance to build fair and friendly relations, in spite of the suffering inflicted on ordinary Iraqis. But those chances were increasingly squandered by maintenance of economic sanctions and eventual bombing of the no-fly zones." When U.S. Forces rolled into Iraq in April 2003, it didn't take long for them to pour gasoline on the already volatile anti-American rage born in Fallujah at least twelve years earlier.

U.S. Special Forces took Fallujah in April, early on in the invasion, but soon left the city.[12] Local Iraqis said they agreed to surrender the conservative Sunni city without a fight on the condition that U.S. troops would not occupy it for more than two days.[13] As in many Iraqi communities, the people of Fallujah began to organize themselves and to take stock of the consequences of the earth-moving developments in their country. They even assembled a new city council.[14] As the occupation spread and various U.S. commanders fanned out to different regions in Iraq, the Eighty-second Airborne Division ultimately moved into Fallujah.[15] Like their countrymen elsewhere, the people of Fallujah did not immediately resist the occupying forces. Instead they watched and waited. It didn't take long for resentment to build, as the Americans would speed up and down the streets in their

Humvees; checkpoints humiliated local people and invaded their privacy, and some complained the soldiers were staring at local women inappropriately.[16] There were also allegations that soldiers were urinating on the streets.[17] A clear consensus was building in Fallujah that the Americans should at least withdraw to the city limits.[18] It took only days before the situation in the city took a decisive and bloody turn for the worse. Hundreds of troops from the Eighty-second quickly spread out across Fallujah, and on Friday, April 25, a few days before the birthday of Saddam Hussein, they occupied Al Qaed (The Leader's) School on Hay Nazzal Street, converting the two-story compound into an occupation headquarters in Fallujah.[19]

The takeover of the school, attended by both primary and high school students, immediately sparked anger in the city for a number of reasons. Among them, parents and teachers were trying to return their children to some semblance of normalcy, and school was viewed as central to that. But also, rumors were rampant that the U.S. soldiers were using their night vision goggles to peer through windows at Iraqi women from the roof of the school and that troops were gawking at women without head coverings in the privacy of their own backyards.[20] Local Iraqi leaders met with U.S. soldiers throughout the weekend, urging them to leave the school. The weekend passed, and on Monday, April 28, Saddam Hussein's 66th birthday, some 150 soldiers continued to occupy the school.[21]

That night, with tensions rising in the city over the presence of the troops, a local imam preached against the United States occupation from the pulpit in his mosque during evening prayers and decried the continued occupation of the school.[22] In the face of the heavy U.S. presence in their city, local clerics had been reminding people of the adage "Better to be strong than weak."[23] After the prayers ended, people began to assemble in what would become the first organized demonstration against the United States since troops moved into Fallujah.[24] A week earlier, U.S. forces had killed ten demonstrators in the northern city of Mosul, but that did not deter the people of Fallujah. At around 6:30 the evening of April 28, people began to gather outside the former Baath Party headquarters, which had also been commandeered by U.S. forces and converted into a command post. Next door was the U.S.-backed mayor's office, where the local U.S. commander was holding a meeting.[25] The crowd chanted slogans like "God is great! Muhammad is his prophet!" as well as "No to Saddam! No to the U.S.!"[26] Military officials claim that some in the crowd were firing weapons in the air, a common practice at Iraqi demonstrations. Local residents say that is untrue, and many Iraqi witnesses contend that no weapons were fired.[27] The U.S. commander in Fallujah, Lt. Col. Eric Nantz, said his forces warned the protesters to disperse, announcing, he claims, in Arabic through a loudspeaker that the demonstration "could be considered a hostile act and would be engaged with deadly force."[28] The crowd moved from the mayor's office and made its way through the streets of Fallujah gathering momentum and size. By the time it reached the school, there were hundreds of people. In the crowd, someone held a large picture of Saddam, which residents say was the clearest symbol of opposition to the occupying forces.[29] "There is no God but Allah, and America is the enemy of Allah," demonstrators chanted on Hay Nazzal Street, as Americans looked down from sniper positions on the roof of the school. "We don't want Saddam and we don't want Bush," said Mohamed Abdallah, a retired accountant. "The Americans have done their job and they must go."[30]

What happened that night is a matter of great dispute between the U.S. occupation forces and local Fallujans. According to scores of Iraqis interviewed by major media outlets at the time, no Iraqis fired on the school or at U.S. forces. Some locals describe random shots fired into the air, while others deny that any Iraqis in the crowd fired guns; and Iraqi witnesses categorically deny that shots were fired at U.S. forces. Every Iraqi witness and demonstrator subsequently interviewed by Human Rights Watch said no one in the demonstration had arms. Several said there was shooting in other Fallujah neighborhoods, but not near the school. Nantz claimed that as the demonstration went on, the crowd was "hostile, throwing rocks, and occasionally firing a number of weapons into the air."[31] A U.S. soldier, Nantz said, was hit by a rock. Then, he says, the school came under attack from gunmen within the crowd. Iraqis there that night say that is not true. U.S. commanders say their troops threw smoke grenades and were then given orders to respond with fire.[32] Within moments, bullets were raining into the crowd. The Americans say they wore night-vision goggles and fired only at muzzle flashes.[33] Iraqis say the shooting was unprovoked and uncontrolled. "We were shouting, 'There's no god but Allah,'" recalled Fallujah resident Ahmed Karim, who was shot in the thigh. "We arrived at the school building and were hoping to talk to the soldiers when they began shooting at us randomly. I think they knew we were unarmed but wanted a show of force to stop us from demonstrating."[34]

"We had one picture of Saddam, only one," said nineteen-year-old Hassan. "We were not armed and nothing was thrown. There had been some shooting in the air in the vicinity, but that was a long way off. I don't know why the Americans started shooting. When they began to fire, we just ran."[35] A fifteen-year-old boy, Ahmed al-Essawi, who was shot in both the arm and leg said, "All of us were trying to run away. They shot at us directly. The soldiers were very scared. There were no warning shots, and I heard no announcements on the loudspeakers."[36]

Within moments, the demonstration on Hay Nazzal Street turned into a bloodbath. Many people described a horrifying scene of wounded people—among them children—lying in the streets and U.S. forces firing on people attempting to rescue them.[37] "They suddenly started shooting at us," remembered Falah Nawwar Dhahir, whose brother was killed that day. "There was continuous shooting until people fled. They shot at people when they came out to get the wounded. Then there was individual shooting, like from snipers."[38] Mu'taz Fahd al-Dulaimi saw his cousin Samir Ali al-Dulaimi shot by U.S. forces: "There were four [U.S. soldiers] on the roof—I saw them with my own eyes. There was a heavy machine gun. It was full automatic shooting for ten minutes. Some of the people fell to the ground. When they stood up, they shot again." Ambulance drivers also report being told to "Go away!" by U.S. forces.[39]

"We were sitting in our house. When the shooting started, my husband tried to close the door to keep the children in, and he was shot," said thirty-seven-year-old Edtesam Shamsudeim, who lives near the school and was herself shot in the leg.[40] More than seventy-five people were injured that night, and at least thirteen were killed. Among the dead were six children.[41] "The engagement was sharp and precise," said Nantz. Soldiers, he said, "returned fire with those firing at them, and if others were wounded, that is regrettable."[42] Almost immediately, the U.S. version of the events came under serious scrutiny when journalists toured the area. In a dispatch from Fallujah, correspondent Phil Reeves of *The Independent* of London, wrote:

> [T]here are no bullet holes visible at the front of the school building or tell-tale marks of a firefight. The place is unmarked. By contrast, the houses opposite . . . are punctured with machine-gun fire, which tore away lumps of concrete the size of a hand and punched holes as deep as the length of a ballpoint pen. Asked to explain the absence of bullet holes, Lt-Col Nantz said that the Iraqi fire had gone over the soldiers' heads. We were taken to see two bullet holes in an upper window and some marks on a wall, but they were on another side of the school building.
>
> There are other troubling questions. Lt-Col Nantz said that the troops had been fired on from a house across the road. Several light machine guns were produced, which the Americans said were found at the scene. If true, this was an Iraqi suicide mission—anyone attacking the post from a fixed position within 40 yards would have had no chance of survival.
>
> The American claim that there were 25 guns in the crowd would also indicate that the demonstrators had had a death wish or were stupid. Iraqis have learnt in the past few weeks that if they fail to stop their cars quickly enough at an American-manned checkpoint, they may well be shot.[43]

In its on-the-ground investigation, Human Rights Watch (HRW) found that "the physical evidence at the school does not support claims of an effective attack on the building as described by U.S. troops."[44] This, HRW's researchers asserted, "contrasts sharply" with the homes across the street from the school, which bore "the marks of more than 100 rounds—smaller caliber shots as well as heavy caliber machine gun rounds—shot by U.S. soldiers. The facades and perimeter walls of seven of the nine homes across from the school had significant bullet damage, including six homes that had been hit with more than a dozen rounds each. . . . No bullet marks were found on the upper levels of the houses, despite U.S. soldiers' claims that they had targeted gunmen on the roofs across the street."[45]

Any hopes the United States had about its "winning hearts and minds" rhetoric resonating in Fallujah were obliterated that blood-soaked night. The morning after the shooting, funerals were held for the dead in accordance with Islamic tradition. A bloodied Iraqi flag hung outside the emergency room at a local hospital, [46] which was struggling to treat the wounded as word was spreading fast across Fallujah and the country about the massacre. "We won't remain quiet over this," said Ahmad Hussein, as he sat in a Fallujah hospital with his eighteen-year-old son, who doctors predicted would die from the gunshot wound to his stomach. "Either they leave Fallujah or we will make them leave."[47] Some in the international press were comparing it to the "Bloody Sunday" massacre of 1972, when British troops opened fire on Irish Catholic protesters, killing thirteen, an event that helped popularize and mobilize the Irish Republican Army.[48]

On the Wednesday morning after the killings, as many as a thousand people poured into the streets of Fallujah to protest the massacre and to demand that the U.S. troops leave the city. They assembled in front of the old Baath Party headquarters, which—like the school—had been taken over by the Americans. UPI reported that "the street scene was chaotic, with U.S. troops aiming weapons into the crowd from buildings the United States has been using as a base camp, while a pair of Apache attack helicopters circled overhead training their guns on the gathered crowd throughout the morning."[49] Once again, the protest ended in bloodshed, as U.S. forces shot and killed four people and injured at least fifteen others.[50] As with the incident at the school, U.S. commanders claimed their forces acted in self-defense. But journalists from mainstream news organizations on the scene contradicted this account. The UPI correspondent in Fallujah, P. Mitchell Prothero, reported that "none of the dead and wounded in Wednesday's incident appeared to have been armed, and none of the gathered protesters displayed weapons of any kind. In over a dozen interviews with witnesses of the shooting, the Iraqis denied any shots were fired at U.S. troops. The only shell casings found within the vicinity were 5.56 mm rounds used by U.S. forces, not 7.62 mm rounds commonly used in AK-47s, the Iraqi weapon of choice."[51]

Witnesses said one man was shot in the face and chest. His friends said the man was the father of four children.[52] People interviewed by the *Washington Post* described U.S. forces in Fallujah patrolling neighborhoods and "firing with little regard for civilian life."[53] "This is exactly like what's happening in Palestine," geography professor Ahmed Jaber Saab, whose two nephews were wounded by U.S. forces, told the paper. "I didn't believe it until I saw it myself."[54] As he prepared a body for burial after the killings, Sunni cleric Sheik Talid Alesawi mocked U.S. rhetoric. "We understood freedom by making demonstrations," he said. "But the shooting that greeted us was not freedom. Are there two types of freedom, one for you and one for us?"[55] That sentiment was widespread in the city. "Is this Bush's freedom and liberation?" asked Fallujah resident Faleh Ibrahim as he marched with hundreds of others to a cemetery with the coffins of two of the dead. "We don't want Bush, and we don't want to be liberated. The Iraqis will bring their own liberation."[56]

A few hours after the second round of killings happened in Fallujah, Defense Secretary Donald Rumsfeld landed at the Basra airport, at the time making him the most senior U.S. official to visit Iraq.[57] "What is significant is that large numbers of human beings, intelligent, energetic, have been liberated," Rumsfeld declared. "They are out from under the heel of a truly brutal vicious regime and that's a good thing."[58] In Fallujah, U.S. soldiers abandoned Al Qaed School, consolidating their headquarters in the former

Baath Party offices in Fallujah. Nearby, someone hung a banner that read: "Sooner or later, U.S. killers, we'll kick you out."[59]

That day as well, a letter from Saddam—at the time still underground—was published, calling on Iraqis to "forget everything and resist the occupation," declaring, "There are no priorities other than driving out the infidel, criminal, cowardly occupier. No honorable hand is held out to shake his, but, rather, the hand of traitors and collaborators."[60] The White House, meanwhile, announced that President Bush would, the following day, declare an end to major combat operations in Iraq aboard the USS Abraham Lincoln—his infamous "Mission Accomplished" moment. In reality, though, the real war was just beginning, and the events of the previous forty-eight hours would play a decisive role. That night, a grenade was thrown into the new U.S. headquarters in Fallujah, wounding seven American soldiers.[61] After meeting with U.S. representatives in an effort to avert further bloodshed, Imam Jamal Shaqir Mahmood, of the Grand Fallujah Mosque, said the Americans argued that the troops were needed to provide security, "but the people of Fallujah told them we already have security."[62] To Fallujans, their city was now officially occupied. "After the massacre, we don't believe the Americans came to free us, but to occupy and take our wealth and kill us," said local leader Mohammed Farhan.[63]

It didn't take long for the story of the U.S. massacres in Fallujah to spread across Iraq and the Arab world. Within a few weeks, folk songs appeared on the radio, praising the people of Fallujah for bravely confronting the occupation forces.[64] DVDs went on the market with footage of the aftermath of the massacres interwoven with images of resistance attacks against U.S. patrols and scenes of epic Arab movies. In one DVD, footage from the movie Black Hawk Down depicting the slaughter of U.S. forces in Somalia is accompanied by the voice of Fallujan singer Sabeh al-Hashem, who sings: "Fallujah, attack their troops and no one will be able to save their injured soldiers. Who brought you to Fallujah, Bush? We will serve you the drink of death."[65] In another song, Hashem declares, "The people of Fallujah are like wolves when they attack the enemy."[66]

All of this would prove eerily prophetic in less than a year's time, when four Blackwater soldiers found themselves driving through the center of Fallujah. In the meantime, back in the suburbs of Washington, D.C., a neoconservative "terror expert," L. Paul Bremer, was preparing to head for Baghdad, where he would direct the occupation for the Bush administration. Erik Prince would soon ready his private soldiers to serve as the elite personal bodyguards for Bush's man in Iraq.

CHAPTER FIVE

GUARDING BUSH'S MAN IN BAGHDAD

L. PAUL Bremer III arrived in Baghdad on May 12, 2003, and moved into Saddam Hussein's former Republican Palace on the banks of the Tigris River.[1] Perhaps Bremer's greatest legacy in Iraq, where he served as the proconsul of the U.S. occupation for a little more than a year, was overseeing the transformation of the country into the epicenter of anti-U.S. resistance in the world and presiding over a system in Iraq that resulted in widespread corruption and graft within the lucrative world of private contracting. At the end of Bremer's tenure, some $9 billion of Iraqi reconstruction funds were unaccounted for, according to a comprehensive audit done by the U.S. special inspector general for Iraq. Bremer responded that the audit held his Coalition Provisional Authority to "an unrealistic standard."[2]

Like Erik Prince, Bremer is a conservative Catholic convert who cut his teeth in government working for Republican administrations and was respected by right-wing evangelicals and neoconservatives alike. In the mid-1970s, he was Secretary of State Henry Kissinger's assistant. During the Reagan administration, he served as Executive Secretary and Special Assistant to Alexander Haig, Reagan's imposing and powerful Secretary of State. At the height of Reagan's bloody wars in Central America, Bremer was promoted to Ambassador at Large on terrorism. In the late 1980s, Bremer left government, joining the private sector as the managing director of Henry Kissinger's consulting firm, Kissinger and Associates. A favorite "terrorism expert" among neoconservatives, Bremer was influential in developing the concepts for what would become the "war on terror" and the Department of Homeland Security.[3] A year before 9/11, he protested CIA guidelines that "discouraged hiring terrorist spies," arguing that they should be lifted to permit the CIA to "actively recruit clandestine informants."[4] When the 9/11 attacks happened, Bremer was already a fixture in the "counterterrorism" community, having been appointed in 1999 by House Speaker Dennis Hastert as chair of the National Council on Terrorism. At the time of the attacks, Bremer was a senior adviser on politics and emerging risks for the massive insurance firm Marsh & McLennan. The company had a headquarters in the World Trade Center staffed by 1,700 employees, 295 of whom died in the attacks.[5]

Forty-eight hours after 9/11, Bremer wrote in the *Wall Street Journal*, "Our retribution must move beyond the limp-wristed attacks of the past decade, actions that seemed designed to 'signal' our seriousness to the terrorists without inflicting real damage. Naturally, their feebleness demonstrated the opposite. This time the terrorists and their supporters must be crushed. This will mean war with one or more countries. And it will be a long war, not one of the 'Made for TV' variety. As in all wars, there will be civilian casualties. We will win some battles and lose some. More Americans will die. In the end America can and will prevail, as we always do." Bremer concluded, "[W]e must avoid a mindless search for an international 'consensus' for our actions. Today, many nations are expressing support and understanding for America's wounds. Tomorrow, we will know who our true friends are."[6] In an appearance on *Fox News* at the time, Bremer said, "I would hope that we would conclude that any state which was involved in any way, giving any kind of support or safe haven to that group, will pay the ultimate price."[7]

A month after 9/11, Bremer headed up a new division at Marsh & McLennan, specializing in "terrorism risk insurance" for transnational corporations. The division was called Crisis Consulting Practice and offered companies "total counterterrorism services." To sell this expensive insurance to U.S. corporations, wrote Naomi Klein in *The Nation*, "Bremer had to make the kinds of frank links between terrorism and the failing global economy that activists are called lunatics for articulating. In a November 2001 policy paper titled 'New Risks in International Business,' he explains that free-trade policies 'require laying off workers. And opening markets to foreign trade puts enormous pressure on traditional retailers and trade monopolies.' This leads to 'growing income gaps and social tensions,' which in turn can lead to a range of attacks on US firms, from terrorism to government attempts to reverse privatizations or roll back trade incentives."[8] Klein likened Bremer to a computer hacker who "cripples corporate websites then sells himself as a network security specialist," predicting that "in a few months Bremer may well be selling terrorism insurance to the very companies he welcomed into Iraq."[9] Shortly after Bremer arrived in Baghdad, his former boss at Marsh & McLennan, Jeffrey Greenberg, announced that 2002 "was a great year for Marsh; operating income was up 31 percent. . . . Marsh's expertise in analyzing risk and helping clients develop risk management programs has been in great demand. . . . Our prospects have never been better."[10]

In mid-April 2003, Dick Cheney's then Chief of Staff, I. Lewis "Scooter" Libby, and Deputy Defense Secretary Paul Wolfowitz had contacted Bremer about taking "the job of running the occupation of Iraq."[11] By mid-May, Bremer was in Baghdad. His appointment as both Director of Reconstruction and Humanitarian Assistance and the head of the Coalition Provisional

Authority in Iraq was met with immediate controversy, even among those who had worked with him. One former senior State Department official who served with Bremer labeled him a "voracious opportunist with voracious ambitions," saying, "What he knows about Iraq could not quite fill a thimble."[12] Klein argues that, in Bremer, the Bush administration was not looking for an Iraq specialist, but rather tapped him because he "is an expert at profiting from the war on terror and at helping US multinationals make money in far-off places where they are unpopular and unwelcome. In other words, he's the perfect man for the job."[13] That certainly seemed to be the view of Henry Kissinger, who said of Bremer at the time, "I don't know anyone who could do it better."[14]

Bremer replaced Gen. Jay Garner, who seemed intent on building an Afghan-style puppet government and maintaining the public veneer of Iraqi self-governance, while ensuring a permanent U.S. presence in Iraq.[15] Garner himself was heavily criticized during his three-week tenure in Iraq, but he certainly was less ambitious than his successor when it came to realizing Iraq as the free-market laboratory envisioned by many within the administration and the neocon intelligentsia. Garner was, by most accounts, a military man, not a committed ideologue. The *Washington Post* described Bremer as "a hard-nosed hawk who is close to the neoconservative wing of the Pentagon."[16] This was further emphasized by the fact that Dick Cheney sent his own special assistant, Brian McCormack, to Baghdad to serve as Bremer's assistant.[17] Bremer also reportedly relied heavily on the disgraced Iraqi exile, Ahmad Chalabi, for advice on internal politics in Iraq. Almost immediately upon Bremer's arrival in Baghdad, some Iraqis viewed him as another Saddam, as he began issuing decrees like an emperor and quashing Iraqi hopes of self-governance. "Occupation is an ugly word," Bremer said upon his arrival in the country. "But it is a fact."[18]

During his year in Iraq, Bremer was a highly confrontational viceroy who traveled the country in a Brooks Brothers suit coat and Timberland boots. He described himself as "the only paramount authority figure—other than dictator Saddam Hussein—that most Iraqis had ever known."[19] Bremer's

first official initiative, reportedly the brainchild of Defense Secretary Rumsfeld and his neoconservative deputy, Douglas Feith, was dissolving the Iraqi
military and initiating a process of "de-Baathification,"[20] which in Iraq
meant a banishment of some of the country's finest minds from the reconstruction and political process because party membership was a requirement for many jobs in Saddam-era Iraq. Bremer's "Order 1" resulted in the
firing of thousands of schoolteachers, doctors, nurses, and other state
workers, while sparking a major increase in rage and disillusionment.[21]
Iraqis saw Bremer picking up Saddam's governing style and political witch
hunt tactics. In practical terms, Bremer's moves sent a firm message to many
Iraqis that they would have little say in their future, a future that increasingly looked bleak and familiar. Bremer's "Order 2"—disbanding the Iraqi
military—meant that four hundred thousand Iraqi soldiers were forced out
of work and left without a pension. "An Iraqi soldier was getting $50 a
month," said one Arab analyst. "Keeping these men and their families in
food for a year would have cost the equivalent of three days of U.S. occupation. If you starve a man, he's ready to shoot the occupier."[22] In his book
on the Iraq War, *Night Draws Near*, Pulitzer Prize–winning *Washington Post*
correspondent Anthony Shadid wrote, "The net effect of Bremer's decision
was to send more than 350,000 officers and conscripts, men with at least
some military training, into the streets, instantly creating a reservoir of
potential recruits for a guerrilla war. (At their disposal was about a million
tons of weapons and munitions of all sorts, freely accessible in more than
a hundred largely unguarded depots around the country.)"[23] One U.S. official put the number of out-of-work Iraqi soldiers higher, telling *The New
York Times Magazine*, "That was the week we made 450,000 enemies on the
ground in Iraq."[24] According to Bremer's orders, some soldiers were given a
month of severance pay, while Iraqi commanders were given nothing.
Shortly after Bremer's order was issued, former Iraqi soldiers began to
organize massive demonstrations at occupation offices—many housed in
former palaces of Saddam's. "If we had fought, the war would still be going
on," said Iraqi Lt. Col. Ahmed Muhammad, who led a protest in Basra. "The

British and the Americans would not be in our palaces. They would not be on our streets. We let them in." Muhammad warned, "We have guns at home. If they don't pay us, if they make our children suffer, they'll hear from us."[25] In an ominous warning of things to come, another former Iraqi military commander, Maj. Assam Hussein Il Naem, pledged: "New attacks against the occupiers will be governed by us. We know we will have the approval of the Iraqi people."[26]

In the meantime, Bremer exacerbated the situation as he stifled Iraqi calls for direct elections, instead creating a thirty-five-member Iraqi "advisory" council, over which he would have total control and veto power. Bremer banned many Sunni groups from the body, as well as supporters of Shiite religious leader Muqtada al-Sadr, despite the fact that both had significant constituencies in Iraq. The future prime minister of Iraq, Ibrahim al-Jaafari, said that excluding these forces "led to the situation of them becoming violent elements."[27] Within a month of Bremer's arrival, talk of a national uprising had begun. "The entire Iraqi people is a time bomb that will blow up in the Americans' face if they don't end their occupation," declared tribal chief Riyadh al-Asadi after meeting with U.S. officials who laid out the Bremer plan for the country.[28] "The Iraqi people did not fight the Americans during the war, only Saddam's people did," Asadi said. "But if the people decide to fight them now, [the Americans] are in big trouble."[29] Bremer staunchly ignored these Iraqi voices, and as the bloody impact of his decision to dissolve the military spread, he amped up his inflammatory rhetoric. "We are going to fight them and impose our will on them and we will capture or, if necessary, kill them until we have imposed law and order upon this country," he declared.[30]

By July 2003, Bremer began referring to Iraq in the first-person plural. "We are eventually going to be a rich country," Bremer said. "We've got oil, we've got water, we've got fertile land, we've got wonderful people."[31] According to *Time* magazine, he toured the Iraq National Museum that month, in the aftermath of the massive looting of Iraq's national treasures— including by U.S. forces and journalists. As museum officials showed

Bremer a collection of ancient gold and jewelry, Bremer quipped, "Which one can I take home for my wife?" As he made the remark, according to *Time*, "a member of his security detail interrupted, informing him of reports of four grenade attacks near Bremer's palace headquarters. Minutes later Bremer climbed into a waiting SUV and headed back to the office, managing a few hurried handshakes as he left. Later that day a U.S. soldier was shot and killed while guarding the museum."[32]

He also made no bones about his religious influences. Taking a page from the Christian zealot Gen. Jerry Boykin, Bremer spoke of his divine guidance. "There is no doubt in my mind that I cannot succeed in this mission without the help of God," Bremer said a month after arriving in Baghdad. "The job is simply too big and complex for any one person, or any group of people to carry out successfully. . . . We need God's help and seek it constantly."[33] This perspective seemed to be a family affair. Bremer's brother Duncan ran for Congress in 2006 in the home district of James Dobson's Colorado-based Focus on the Family. "I want to be God's man in Washington,"[34] he said. He ran on a far-right platform and opposed exceptions to any abortion ban that would allow abortions for victims of rape or incest, saying, "We're killing the wrong person in that case."[35] During his unsuccessful campaign, Duncan Bremer held up his brother's role in Iraq as evidence of his own foreign policy experience, saying he had visited Iraq while Paul Bremer was heading the occupation. Duncan Bremer declared during his campaign, "While I prefer that the Islamic Jihadists convert to my world view and receive the benefits of it, my point is that they must give up their world view and their particular version of Islam in order for us to have a peaceful world. From a geopolitical point of view, it does not matter whether they convert to 'peaceful Islam' if that be a religion, or Buddhism or whatever, as long as they give up their religious ideology."[36] Paul Bremer's wife, Francie, whom Dobson called a "prayer warrior,"[37] told a Christian publication that "her husband viewed his work in Iraq as a chance to bring the light of freedom to the people of Iraq after decades of darkness there."[38]

But Bremer's zealotry was not confined to his religion. Upon his arrival, he moved swiftly to begin building the neoconservative vision in Iraq, ushering in a period that Naomi Klein labeled "Baghdad Year Zero." True to form, after just two weeks in the country, Bremer declared that Iraq was "open for business."[39] The centerpiece of his plan was the rapid privatization of Iraq's oil industry. Klein, who traveled to Iraq during Bremer's tenure in the country and has written extensively on his rule, described the effects of his edict-based governance as such:

> [Bremer] enacted a radical set of laws unprecedented in their generosity to multinational corporations. There was Order 37, which lowered Iraq's corporate tax rate from roughly 40 percent to a flat 15 percent. There was Order 39, which allowed foreign companies to own 100 percent of Iraqi assets outside of the natural-resource sector. Even better, investors could take 100 percent of the profits they made in Iraq out of the country; they would not be required to reinvest and they would not be taxed. Under Order 39, they could sign leases and contracts that would last for forty years. Order 40 welcomed foreign banks to Iraq under the same favorable terms. All that remained of Saddam Hussein's economic policies was a law restricting trade unions and collective bargaining.
>
> If these policies sound familiar, it's because they are the same ones multinationals around the world lobby for from national governments and in international trade agreements. But while these reforms are only ever enacted in part, or in fits and starts, Bremer delivered them all, all at once. Overnight, Iraq went from being the most isolated country in the world to being, on paper, its widest-open market.[40]

Shortly after Bremer took over in Baghdad, economist Jeff Madrick wrote in the *New York Times*: "[B]y almost any mainstream economist's standard, the plan, already approved by L. Paul Bremer III, the American in charge of the Coalition Provisional Authority, is extreme—in fact, stunning. It would immediately make Iraq's economy one of the most open to trade and capital flows in the world, and put it among the lowest taxed in the world, rich or poor. . . . The Iraqi planners, apparently including the Bush administration, seem to assume they can simply wipe the slate clean." Madrick stated boldly that Bremer's plan "would allow a handful of foreign banks to take over the domestic banking system."[41]

It seems appropriate, then, that Bremer, the senior U.S. official in Iraq, the public face of the occupation, would not be protected by U.S. government forces or Iraqi security but rather by a private mercenary company— and one founded by a right-wing Christian who had poured tens of thousands of dollars into Republican campaign coffers.

By mid-August, three months after Bremer arrived in Baghdad, resistance attacks against U.S. forces and Iraqi "collaborators" were a daily occurrence. "We believe we have a significant terrorist threat in the country, which is new," Bremer said on August 12. "We take this very seriously."[42] As with other violent incidents and situations in preceding years, the chaos in Iraq would convert to financial success for Blackwater. On August 28, 2003, Blackwater was awarded the official "sole source," no-bid $27.7 million contract to provide the personal security detail and two helicopters for Bremer[43] as he carried out the all-important work of building the neoconservative program in Iraq. "Nobody had really figured out exactly how they were going to get him from D.C. and stand him up in Iraq," recalled Blackwater president Gary Jackson. "The Secret Service went over and did an assessment and said, 'You know what? It's much, much more dangerous than any of us believed.' So they came back to us."[44] Blackwater's presence, Bremer wrote, "heightened the sense that Iraq had become even more dangerous."[45] The man who would head Bremer's Blackwater security team was Frank Gallagher, who served as head of Henry Kissinger's personal security detail in the 1990s when Bremer worked for Kissinger.[46] "I knew and liked Frank," Bremer recalled. "I trusted him totally."[47]

Employing Blackwater mercenaries as his personal guards was made possible by the very neoliberal policies Bremer had advocated for throughout his career and was now implementing in Iraq. It was a groundbreaking moment in the process that then-Defense Secretary Dick Cheney launched in the early 1990s when he hired Brown and Root "to explore outsourcing logistical activities."[48] It also represented a major shift away from the long-held doctrine that the "U.S. military does not turn over mission-critical functions to private contractors," according to Peter Singer, author of *Corporate Warriors*. "And you don't put contractors in positions where they need to carry weapons. . . . A private armed contractor now has the job of keeping Paul Bremer alive—it can't get much more mission-critical than that."[49] The privatization of the Bremer detail marked an almost immediate watershed moment for mercenary firms.

"Standard wages for PSD (personal security detail) pros [in Iraq] were previously running about $300 a day," *Fortune* magazine reported. "Once Blackwater started recruiting for its first big job, guarding Paul Bremer, the rate shot up to $600 a day."[50] Blackwater described its Bremer project as a "turnkey security package."[51] Company vice president Chris Taylor said the job "was no ordinary executive protection requirement; it really amounted to a hybrid personal security detail (PSD) solution that had yet to be used anywhere. In response, Blackwater developed an innovative combat PSD program to ensure Ambassador Bremer's safety and that of any ambassador who followed."[52] The company provided him with thirty-six "personnel protection" specialists, two K-9 teams, and three MD-530 Boeing helicopters with pilots to taxi him around the country.[53] In October 2003, a Blackwater spokesman said the company had just seventy-eight employees in Iraq, a number that would soon explode.[54] A month after winning the Bremer contract, Blackwater registered its new security division with the North Carolina Secretary of State.[55] Blackwater Security Consulting LLC would specialize in "providing qualified and trained Protective Security Specialist[s] (PSS) to the U.S. Department of State, Bureau for Diplomatic Security for the purpose of conducting protective security operations in Iraq."[56] The Bremer contract had officially elevated Blackwater to a status as a sort of Praetorian Guard in the war on terror—a designation that would open many doors in the world of private military contracting. It wouldn't be long before Blackwater was awarded a massive contract with the State Department to provide security for many U.S. officials in Iraq, not just the Ambassador. Paul Bremer's picture would soon grace the top banner on the new Blackwater Security division's Web site, as would images of Blackwater's mercenaries around Colin Powell and British Prime Minister Tony Blair.[57]

Blackwater's men brought a singularly Yankee flair to the Bremer job and, by most accounts, embodied the ugly American persona to a tee. Its guards were chiseled like bodybuilders and wore tacky, wraparound sunglasses. Many wore goatees and dressed in all-khaki uniforms with ammo vests or Blackwater T-shirts with the trademark bear claw in the cross-hairs, sleeves rolled up. Some of them looked like caricatures, real-life action figures, or professional wrestlers. Their haircuts were short, and they sported security earpieces and lightweight machine guns. They bossed around journalists and ran Iraqi cars off the road or fired rounds at cars if they got in the way of a Blackwater convoy. "You see these pictures in the media of Blackwater guys loaded to the hilt with pistols and M-4s and their hand out grabbing the camera. There's a reason for that," said former Blackwater contractor Kelly Capeheart, who protected John Negroponte, Bremer's successor in Iraq. "I don't want my face on Al-Jazeera. Sorry."[58]

Helicopters with snipers would hover above some Blackwater transport missions, as a menacing warning to everyone below. "They made enemies everywhere," recalled Col. Thomas X. Hammes, the U.S. military official put in charge of building a "new" Iraqi military after Bremer disbanded the old one.[59] "I would ride around with Iraqis in beat up Iraqi trucks, they were running me off the road. We were threatened and intimidated. [But] they were doing their job, exactly what they were paid to do in the way they were paid to do it, and they were making enemies on every single pass out of town."[60] Hammes said Blackwater's high-profile conduct in guarding Bremer broke the "first rule" of fighting an insurgency: "You don't make any more enemies."[61] Hammes said, "They were actually getting our contract exactly as we asked them to and at the same time hurting our counterinsurgency effort."[62]

An intelligence officer in Iraq told *Time* magazine, "Those Blackwater guys . . . they drive around wearing Oakley sunglasses and pointing their guns out of car windows. They have pointed their guns at me, and it pissed me off. Imagine what a guy in Fallujah thinks."[63] Al Clark, one of the founders of Blackwater, helped develop the company's training procedures. In the U.S., Clark said, "we get upset about a fender-bender." But, he said, "you've got to get over that in Baghdad. Your car can be a 3,000-pound weapon when you need it. Hit and run. Trust me. The police aren't coming to your house because you left the scene of an accident."[64]

An apparent deadly case of contractor impunity allegedly involving Blackwater guards took place in May 2004. The incident was thoroughly investigated and reported by *Los Angeles Times* correspondent T. Christian Miller.[65] The U.S. Embassy spokesman in Baghdad, Robert J. Callahan, was finishing up his tour of duty and was making the rounds to say his good-byes to various journalists and media organizations around the Iraqi capital. "As was typical for State Department officials, Callahan relied on Blackwater for transport around Baghdad," according to Miller. Returning from one media compound, Callahan's "five-vehicle convoy turned onto a broad thoroughfare running through Baghdad's Masbah neighborhood, an area of five-story office buildings and ground-level shops." At the same time, according to Miller, a thirty-two-year-old Iraqi truck driver named Mohammed Nouri Hattab, who was moonlighting as a taxi driver, was transporting two passengers he had just picked up in his Opel. "Hattab looked up and saw Callahan's five-car convoy speed out of a side street in front of him. He was slowing to a stop about fifty feet from the convoy when he heard a burst of gunfire ring out, he said. Bullets shot through the hood of his Opel, cut into his shoulder, and pierced the chest of nineteen-year-old Yas Ali Mohammed Yassiri, who was in the backseat, killing him," according to Miller. "There was no warning. It was a sudden attack," said Hattab.

Miller reported that, on background, "one US official said that embassy officials had reviewed the shooting and determined that two Blackwater employees in the convoy that day had not followed proper procedures to warn Hattab to stay back; instead they opened fire prematurely." The official said the two had been fired and sent home. As of this writing, they have not been prosecuted. Miller obtained hundreds of pages of incident reports involving private military contractors in Iraq. He reported, "About 11 percent of the nearly two hundred reports involved contractors firing toward civilian vehicles. In most cases the contractors received no fire from the Iraqi cars."[66]

Blackwater's style fit in perfectly with Bremer's mission in Iraq. In fact, one could argue that Bremer didn't just get protection from Blackwater's highly trained mercenaries but also from the all-powerful realities of the free-market lab he was running in Iraq. Indeed, it seems that those forces were what Bremer banked on to survive the Iraq job—if he died, Blackwater's reputation would be shot. "If Blackwater loses a principal (like Bremer), they're out of business, aren't they?" asked Colonel Hammes. "Can you imagine being Blackwater, trying to sell your next contract, saying, 'Well, we did pretty well in Iraq for about four months, and then he got killed.' And you're the CEO who's going to hire and protect your guys. You'll say, 'I think I'll find somebody else.' . . . The problem for Blackwater [is] if the primary gets killed, what happens to Blackwater is they're out of business. For the military, if the primary gets killed, that's a very bad thing. There will be after-action reviews, etc., but nobody's going out of business."[67]

For Blackwater, keeping Paul Bremer alive would provide the company with an incredible marketing campaign: *If we can protect the most hated man in Iraq, we can protect anyone, anywhere.* Indeed, in less than a year Osama bin Laden would release an audio tape offering a reward for Bremer's killing. "You know that America promised big rewards for those who kill mujahedeen [holy warriors]," bin Laden declared in May 2004. "We in the Al Qaeda organization will guarantee, God willing, 10,000 grams of gold to whoever kills the occupier Bremer, or the American chief commander or his deputy in Iraq."[68] The resistance, too, reportedly offered a $50,000 reward for the killing of any Blackwater guards.[69] "We had prices on our heads over there," recalled ex-Blackwater contractor Capeheart. "We all knew it."[70]

Bremer said that soon after Blackwater took over his security, "at Rumsfeld's request, the U.S. Secret Service had done a survey of my security and had concluded that I was the most threatened American official anywhere in the world. . . . One report Blackwater took seriously suggested that one of the Iraqi barbers in the palace had been hired to kill me when I got a haircut." After that, Blackwater moved Bremer into a villa on the palace grounds that reportedly had housed Qusay Hussein's mother-in-law.[71]

In December 2003, a few months after Blackwater began guarding Bremer, came the first publicly acknowledged resistance attack on the proconsul. It happened the night of December 6, right after Bremer saw Defense Secretary Rumsfeld off at the Baghdad airport. "It was after 11:00 p.m. when [Bremer's aide] Brian McCormack and I got into my armored SUV for the run back to the Green Zone," Bremer recalled. "Our convoy, as usual, consisted of two 'up-armored' Humvees sheathed in tan slabs of hardened steel, a lead-armored Suburban, our Suburban, another armored Suburban following, and two more Humvees. Overhead, we had a pair of buzzing Bell helicopters with two Blackwater snipers in each."[72] Inside the SUV, Bremer and McCormack were discussing whether Bremer should attend the World Economic Forum in Davos, Switzerland. Bremer was thinking that he "could now use some of the ski resort pampering" when a "deafening" explosion happened, followed by automatic gunfire. The lead vehicle in the convoy had its tire blown out by an improvised explosive device (IED), and resistance fighters were attacking with AK-47s. According to Bremer, a bullet had hit a side window in his SUV. "We'd been ambushed, a highly organized, skillfully executed assassination attempt," wrote Bremer. "I swung around and looked back. The Suburban's armored-glass rear window had been blown out by the IED. And now AK rounds were whipping through the open rectangle." As he sped toward the safety of the palace, Bremer recalled that "with the stench of explosives lingering in the car, I considered. Davos, all those good meals. . . . Francie could fly over and we could ski. That was about as far from Baghdad's Airport Road and IEDs as you could get."[73]

Bremer's office intentionally concealed the attack until two weeks later, when news of the ambush leaked in the U.S. press and Bremer was confronted at a press conference in the southern city of Basra.[74] "Yes, this is true," he told reporters.[75] "As you can see, it didn't succeed,"[76] adding, "Thankfully I am still alive, and here I am in front of you."[77] Despite Bremer's later description of the attack as "a highly organized" assassination attempt, at the time his spokespeople dismissed it as a "random" attack that was not likely directed at Bremer personally,[78] perhaps in an effort to downplay the sophistication of the resistance. After the attack was revealed, Bremer's spokesperson, Dan Senor, praised Blackwater: "Ambassador Bremer has very thorough and comprehensive security forces and mechanisms in place whenever there is a movement, and we have a lot of confidence in those security personnel and those mechanisms. And in this particular case, they worked."[79]

As Bremer traveled Iraq, his policies and the conduct of his "bodyguards" and the other contractors he had immunized from accountability increasingly enraged Iraqis. Meanwhile, he continued to reinforce the Iraqi characterization of him as another Saddam, as he carried out expensive renovations to the Baghdad Palace. In December 2003, Bremer spent $27,000 to remove four larger-than-life busts of Saddam's head from the palace compound. "I've been looking at these for six months," said Bremer as the first head was being removed. "The time has come for these heads to roll."[80] With much of Iraq's civilian infrastructure in shambles, it seemed a questionable use of funds, but Bremer's spokespeople characterized it as compliance with the law. "According to the rules of de-Baathification, they have to come down," said Bremer deputy Charles Heatly. "Actually, they are illegal."[81]

For most of the time Blackwater guarded Bremer, the company remained under the radar. There was rarely a mention of Blackwater in media reports; instead, the men were simply referred to as Bremer's security detail or as his bodyguards. Sometimes, they were identified as Secret Service agents. Within the industry, though, Blackwater's men were viewed as the elite, the trendsetters among the rapidly expanding mercenary army in the country.

Around the time Blackwater won its Bremer contract, mercenaries quickly poured into Iraq. Firms like Control Risks Group, DynCorp, Erinys, Aegis, ArmorGroup, Hart, Kroll, and Steele Foundation, many of which already had some presence in the country, began deploying thousands of mercenaries in Iraq and recruiting aggressively internationally. In a throw-back to the Vietnam War era, the positions were initially referred to as "pri-vate security consultants" on the job boards. Some companies, like Blackwater, won lucrative contracts with the State Department, the U.S. occupation authority, or the British government; others guarded oil proj-ects, foreign embassies, or government buildings; while still others worked for major war contractors like Halliburton, KBR, General Electric, and Bechtel, or as part of security details for journalists. Among the highest paid mercenaries were former Special Forces: Navy SEALs, Delta Force, Green Berets, Rangers and Marines, British SAS, Irish Rangers, and Australian SAS, followed by Nepalese Gurkhas, Serbian commandos, and Fijian troops. Meanwhile, the prospect of tremendous profits depleted official national forces, as soldiers sought more lucrative posts with private companies, which also aggressively headhunted Special Forces men for private work in Iraq. "We were bigger than life to a lot of the military guys," said ex-Black-water contractor Kelly Capeheart. "You could see it in their eyes when they looked at us—or whispered about us. A lot of them were very jealous. They felt like they were doing the same job but getting paid a lot less."[82]

In addition to these "professionals," there were many seedier elements that got in on the action, charging less money than their corporate col-leagues and acting with even greater recklessness, among them former South African apartheid forces, some from the notorious Koevoet, who apparently entered Iraq in contravention of South Africa's antimercenary laws. By November 2003, the United States was explicitly telling companies wishing to do business in Iraq to bring their own armed security forces into the country.[83]

When Bremer left Iraq in June 2004, there were more than twenty thou-sand private soldiers inside the country's borders and Iraq had become known as a "Wild West" with no sheriff. Those mercenaries officially hired by the occupation would be contracted for more than $2 billion of security work by the end of the "Bremer year" and would account for upwards of 30 percent of the Iraq "reconstruction" budget. That, of course, does not take into account the private entities that widely hired mercenaries in Iraq. According to *The Economist* magazine, the Iraq occupation shot British military companies' revenues up from $320 million before the war to more than $1.6 billion by early 2004, "making security by far Britain's most lucrative postwar export to Iraq."[84] One source cited by the magazine estimated that there were more ex–Special Air Service soldiers working as mercenaries in Iraq than on active duty there. Within a year, the British firm Erinys had built up a fourteen-thousand-man private army in Iraq,[85] staffed by locals— among them, members of Ahmad Chalabi's "Free Iraq" forces—and commanded by expatriates from the company, some of whom were South African mercenaries. "[T]he massive demand for protection, and the fear of almost daily killing of foreign workers, has overstretched market supply, spawning an upsurge in cowboy contractors and drawing on a pool of international guns for hire that, according to reputable firms, are as much a liability to themselves and Iraqis as to their clients," reported *The Times* of London.[86]

What these forces did in Iraq, how many people they killed, how many of them died or were wounded, all remain unanswerable questions because no one was overseeing their activities in the country. As of this writing, not a single U.S. military contractor has been prosecuted for crimes committed in Iraq. Still, stories trickled out of Iraq, sometimes through the bravado of the contractors themselves. One such case involved a Blackwater contractor bragging about his use of "non-standard" ammunition to kill an Iraqi.

In mid-September 2003, a month after Blackwater won the Bremer contract, a four-man Blackwater security team was heading north from Baghdad on a dirt road in an SUV when they say they were ambushed by gunmen in a small village. That morning, one of the Blackwater contractors, Ben Thomas, had loaded his M4 machine gun with powerful experimental ammunition that had not been approved for use by U.S. forces. They were armor-piercing, limited-penetration rounds known as APLPs.[87] The product of a San Antonio company called RBCD, they are created using what is called a "blended metal" process. According to *The Army Times*, the bullets "will bore through steel and other hard targets but will not pass through a human torso, an eight-inch-thick block of artist's clay or even several layers of dry-wall. Instead of passing through a body, it shatters, creating 'untreatable wounds.'"[88] The distributor of these experimental rounds is an Arkansas company called Le Mas, which admits that it gave Thomas some of the bullets after he contacted the company. During the short gun battle that day, Thomas says he fired one of the APLP rounds at an Iraqi attacker, hitting him in the buttocks. The bullet, he said, killed the man almost instantly. "It entered his butt and completely destroyed everything in the lower left section of his stomach . . . everything was torn apart," Thomas told *The Army Times*. "The way I explain what happened to people who weren't there is . . . this stuff was like hitting somebody with a miniature explosive round. . . . Nobody believed that this guy died from a butt shot."[89] Thomas, an ex–Navy SEAL, said he has shot people with various kinds of ammunition and that there is "absolutely no comparison, whatever, none," between the damage the APLP bullet did to his Iraqi victim that day and what would be expected from standard ammo. When Thomas returned to base after the shooting, he says his fellow mercenaries "were fighting over" the bullets. "At the end of the day, each of us took five rounds. That's all we had left."[90]

These bullets have been a source of some controversy in Congress, and the manufacturer has lobbyists trying to get them approved for use by U.S. forces, calling it "an issue of national security."[91] In fact, Thomas says he was threatened with a court-martial for using unapproved ammunition after he was mistakenly understood by a Pentagon official to be an active-duty soldier.[92] It was the first recorded kill using the bullets, which had been tested for several years at the *Armed Forces Journal* annual "Shoot-out at Black-water" at the company compound in Moyock.[93] After Thomas allegedly killed the Iraqi using the APLP round, he sounded like a paid spokesman on a commercial for the bullets. "I'm taking Le Mas ammo with me when I return to Iraq, and I've already promised lots of this ammo to my buddies who were there that day and to their friends," Thomas told an interviewer during a leave from Iraq. "This is purely for putting into bad guys. For general inventory, absolutely not. For special operations, I wouldn't carry anything else."[94] The *Armed Forces Journal* excitedly chronicled Thomas's experience with the rounds, calling them "reason enough for Pentagon officials to insist that Special Operations Command immediately begin realistic testing of the blended-metal ammunition."[95] Thomas later posted on his MySpace Web page a link to a news article about his use of the armor-piercing bullets in Iraq with a note that said:

OSAMA BIN LADEN IS MY BITCH
And here is why [story link]
Fucker wants me dead now.[96]

As mercenaries roamed the country freely, there was no official explanation given to Iraqis as to who these heavily armed, often nonuniformed forces were. It would be a year before Bremer would officially get around to issuing an order that defined their status—as immune from prosecution. Iraqis killed or wounded by these mercenaries had no recourse for justice. Many Iraqis—and some journalists—erroneously believed that the mercenaries were CIA or Israeli Mossad agents, an impression that enraged citizens who encountered them. The mercenaries' conduct and reputation also angered actual U.S. intelligence officers who felt the mercenaries could jeopardize their own security in the country.[97] As 2003 neared its end, much of Iraq lay in ruins, while the oft-promised "reconstruction" projects, ostensibly to be funded by Iraqi oil revenue, were overwhelmingly nonexistent or flat-out failing. For mercenary companies, though, business was booming. In early 2004, the situation in Iraq would begin to descend even further into chaos, bringing more business for private military companies.

In February 2004, Bremer's office engaged in an incredible act of either vast miscalculation or wanton (and deadly) disregard for reality. According to a report at the time in the *Washington Post*, "U.S. officials courting companies to take part in the rebuilding insist that security is not an issue for contractors and said accounts have been overblown. 'Western contractors are not targets,' Tom Foley, the CPA's director of private-sector development, told hundreds of would-be investors at a Commerce Department conference in Washington on Feb. 11. He said the media have exaggerated the issue."[98] On the contrary, Foley asserted, "The risks are akin to sky diving or riding a motorcycle, which are, to many, very acceptable risks."[99] By mid-March 2004, mercenary firms were basking in what had become a tremendous "sellers' market" in Iraq. "What it cost to hire qualified security personnel in June (2003) is a fraction of what it costs today," said Mike Battles, founder of the U.S. firm Custer Battles,[100] which was contracted to guard the Baghdad airport.

On March 18, word hit the streets that the United States was putting up a contract worth $100 million to hire private security to guard the four-square-mile Green Zone and its three thousand residents.[101] "The current and projected threat and recent history of attacks directed against coalition forces, and thinly stretched military force, requires a commercial security force that is dedicated to provide Force Protection security," read the solicitation.[102] As Blackwater's Bremer detail succeeded in keeping its high-value "noun" alive, the company's management seized opportunity in the chaos of Iraq. They opened several new offices, in Baghdad, Amman, and Kuwait City, as well as headquarters in the epicenter of the U.S. intelligence community in McLean, Virginia, that would house the company's new Government Relations division. Plans were under way to expand Blackwater's lucrative business in the war zone in a profit drive that would end with four American contractors dead in Fallujah, Iraq in flames, and Blackwater's future looking very bright.

CHAPTER SIX

SCOTTY GOES TO WAR

BY EARLY 2004, Blackwater was firmly entrenched in Iraq, while Erik
Prince, Gary Jackson, and other Blackwater executives were aggressively
exploring new markets and contracts for their thriving business. Its men
were guarding the head of the U.S. occupation and several regional CPA
offices around Iraq, giving Blackwater a pole position for prime contracts,
and its forces were the envy of the burgeoning private security business in
Iraq. This was made possible by the ever-worsening security situation in the
country. In January 2004, the *Financial Times* reported, "Contractors say
there have been more than 500 attacks on civilian and military convoys in
the last two months alone." That month, Blackwater executive Patrick
Toohey "advised" businesses looking to operate in Iraq, "You should be

adding a further 25 percent for security."[1] Some began comparing the mercenary market in Iraq to the Alaskan Gold Rush and the O.K. Corral. As *The Times* of London put it, "In Iraq, the postwar business boom is not oil. It is security."[2] Almost overnight, a once-despised industry was emerging from the shadows and thriving, and Blackwater was at the head of the pack. Eager to expand its business and profits, the company quickly put the word out that it was looking for highly qualified ex–Special Forces guys to deploy in Iraq. The company offered wages to "qualified" candidates that dwarfed basic military pay—and almost any other job's salary. A contractor with Blackwater could make $600 to $800 a day, in some cases even more. Plus, the short-term contracts the company offered—two months—meant that a small fortune could be made quickly in a defined number of days. In many cases, contractors could extend for more terms if they wished. There were also major tax breaks offered to would-be mercenaries.

The privatization of the occupation also offered a chance for many combat enthusiasts, retired from the service and stuck in the ennui of everyday existence, to return to their glory days on the battlefield under the banner of the international fight against terrorism. "It's what you do," said former Navy SEAL Steve Nash. "Say you spend twenty years doing things like riding high-speed boats and jumping out of airplanes. Now, all of sudden, you're selling insurance. It's tough."[3] Dan Boelens, a fifty-five-year-old police officer from Michigan and self-described weapons expert, went to Iraq with Blackwater because it was "the last chance in my life to do something exciting," saying, "I like the stress and adrenaline push it gives me."[4]

"When a guy can make more money in one month than he can make all year in the military or in a civilian job, it's hard to turn it down," said ex-SEAL Dale McClellan, one of the original founders of Blackwater USA. "Most of us have been getting shot at most of our lives anyway." Their skills—urban warfare, sniping, close-quarter combat—McClellan said, are "all worthless in the civilian world." Plus, there's an added bonus McClellan calls the "cool-guy factor." "Let's face it," he said. "Chicks dig it."[5]

"You're not trained for a lot of other things," said Curtis Williams, another ex-SEAL. "That adrenaline rush is addicting. It's something that never goes away."[6] Many Special Forces soldiers who served in the "peace-time" of the 1990s also felt robbed of the overt combat of different eras and viewed the war on terror as their chance at glory. "We are trained to serve our country in an elite fashion," said Williams. "We want to go back and kill the bad guy. It's who we are."[7] A Blackwater contractor who served in Afghanistan admitted that money is a major factor. "But that's not all of it," he said. "After 9/11, I wanted some payback."[8] Among those lured to Iraq by Blackwater's offer was a thirty-eight-year-old former Navy SEAL named Scott Helvenston.[9]

A tan, chiseled, G.I. Joe action figure of a man, Helvenston was like a walking ad for the military. Literally. His image—shirt off, running on a beach at the head of a pack of jogging SEALs—once graced the cover of a Navy promotional calendar. He came from a proud family of Republicans, and his great-great-uncle, Elihu Root, was once the U.S. Secretary of War and a winner of the 1912 Nobel Peace Prize. Helvenston's father died when he was seven, and he helped raise his younger brother, Jason. Scott Helvenston was, by all accounts, a model soldier and athlete. He made history by becoming the youngest person ever to complete the rigorous Navy SEAL program, finishing it at seventeen. He spent twelve years in the SEALs, four of them as an instructor. "It's the longest and most arduous training of its kind in the free world," Helvenston said of the SEAL program's Basic Underwater Demo-lition School. "When you make it through, you say, Hey, I think I can handle anything."[10] But, like many ex–Special Forces guys, Helvenston struggled to figure out what to do with his life after he left the service in 1994. His combat skills didn't exactly transfer into the "real world" all that well, and he had no interest in being anybody's rent-a-cop. His real passion was fitness: he had made several workout videos through his company, Amphibian Athletics, and had dreams of opening his own fitness center.

For a while in the 1990s, Helvenston tried his luck with Hollywood. He trained Demi Moore for her film about the SEALs, *G.I. Jane,* was an adviser on John Travolta's film *Face/Off*, and he even had a cameo as a stunt double in a movie here and there. He also did a few stints on reality television, including a starring role in the Special Forces military reality show *Combat Missions*, which was produced by *Survivor* creator Mark Burnett. One reviewer described Helvenston as having "a spitfire temperament" on the show, and he was widely seen as the villain.[11] "He's very emotional, and he reads things a certain way and is of a mind about how he's perceived," said Burnett of Helvenston. "But you know what? Put a gun on him and send him into battle. You'd want him on your side. He's a great Navy SEAL and one of the best athletes in America."[12] In another series, *Man vs. Beast*, Helvenston was the only contestant to defeat the beast, outmaneuvering a chimpanzee in an obstacle course.

Not for lack of effort, the acting work wasn't panning out for Helvenston, and he was struggling to make ends meet. "It was good money but it was never enough," his mother, Katy Helvenston-Wettengel, remembers. He was divorced from his wife, Patricia, but continued to support her and their two teenage children, Kyle and Kelsey. Helvenston was also in debt, and when he heard through the SEAL grapevine that serious money was to be made as a high-risk bodyguard, he began looking around. He was offered a job by DynCorp protecting Afghan President Hamid Karzai, but he ultimately declined because it required a one-year commitment and Helvenston didn't want to leave his children.[13] Then, in late 2003, when he heard that Blackwater was hiring—and that he could deploy for just two months—the idea immediately appealed to him. Scott's mother says he viewed it as an opportunity to turn his life around. "He said, 'I'm gonna go over there, make some money, maybe make a difference, then I'll be coming back starting my new job. I'll only be away from my kids for a couple of months.' That's why he chose Blackwater," she recalls.

When he would talk about it with his family or friends, Scott Helvenston would tell people that he was going to be guarding the U.S. Ambassador in Iraq. After all, that's what Blackwater was known in the private security world to be doing over there. Plus, the company was run by ex-SEALs like

Helvenston—he'd be right at home and around guys who'd have his back in Iraq. "Scott had a warrior mindset," said his friend Mark Divine, a Navy SEAL reservist trained by Helvenston. He said Helvenston planned to make $60,000 in Iraq, but that he also was looking forward to seeing the kind of action he'd trained for but hadn't really seen during his "peacetime" years in the SEALs. "When you're not in the game, you feel a little bit like a caged animal. Like training your whole life to be a pro football player and not getting to suit up for the game," Divine said.[14] Helvenston's brother, Jason, said that although Scott had participated in covert operations as a SEAL, he felt none were risky enough to feel fulfilled. "He sometimes felt he never served his country because he didn't encounter enough danger," Jason Helvenston said. "That's why he went to Iraq."[15] Divine spoke to Helvenston two days before he shipped out. "This was a last hooray for Scott," he said. "It was his last opportunity to get back in the arena." As for the serious risks of deploying in Iraq, Divine said, "His feeling was, 'If your time is up, there's going to be a bullet out there with your name on it.'"[16]

If it had been up to Katy Helvenston-Wettengel, her son wouldn't have gone to Iraq at all. "We had argued about him going over there," she recalls. "I believe that we should have gone into Afghanistan, but I never believed we should have gone into Iraq. And Scott bought the whole story about Saddam Hussein being involved with Al Qaeda and all that. He believed in what he was doing." Except guarding the Ambassador—or any other U.S. official, for that matter—is not what Scott Helvenston would be doing in Iraq.

In early March 2004, Helvenston arrived at the Blackwater training center in the wilderness of Moyock, North Carolina, where he would spend two weeks preparing for deployment in Iraq. He was surrounded by ex-SEALs and other Special Ops guys. Also at the compound were some of the first batch of non-U.S. mercenaries Blackwater would hire: Chilean commandos—some of whom had trained under the brutal regime of Augusto Pinochet—whom Blackwater had flown to North Carolina a few days earlier.[17] Like Helvenston, they, too, were destined for deployment in Iraq as part of the rapidly expanding privatized forces. "We scour the ends of the earth to find professionals," Blackwater president Gary Jackson said at the time. "The Chilean commandos are very, very professional, and they fit within the Blackwater system."[18]

Shortly after Scott Helvenston arrived in North Carolina, trouble started. One of the men heading the training at Blackwater was a man some of the guys called Shrek,[19] presumably after the green ogre movie cartoon character. By all accounts Helvenston was excited to be working for Blackwater and heading into action. But shortly after the training, he alleged in an e-mail to Blackwater management that a conflict had developed between him and Shrek. Among other things, Helvenston alleged that Shrek was an "unprofessional" manager, and he portrayed Shrek as becoming defensive when Helvenston would ask questions of him during training. "In my class participation, I truly attempted to serve my comments in a manner that would not imply [Shrek] was wrong but that this was the experience I gained while going through a Department of State Certification course,"[20] Helvenston alleged, adding that because of how Shrek reacted to his comments and suggestions, he stopped offering them. After the training session in North Carolina, Helvenston and Shrek ended up deploying to Kuwait together, flying over in mid-March with the team of Chilean commandos recently contracted by Blackwater.[21]

Despite what Helvenston saw as a conflict with Shrek, the deployment seemed like a decent situation for him, as two of his friends from his days on the reality TV show *Combat Missions* were helping to run the Blackwater operations: John and Kathy Potter. "I spent a week in Kuwait with Scott right before he went into Iraq," recalled Kathy Potter, who was running Blackwater's Kuwait operations while her husband was in Baghdad. "We were able to have some wonderful conversations about his family, life, and lessons learned. Scott was a totally changed man from the last time I saw him."[22] She described Helvenston as "a joy to be around! There wasn't a day I wasn't cracking up at him and his comments!"

"His favorite saying (which he used every opportunity he had) was 'I'm just damn glad to be here!' This would make me laugh and bring a smile to all of our faces when he said this," Potter wrote. She described Helvenston as supporting her in the face of other Blackwater "guys coming in with a very negative and disrespectful attitude, and a chauvinistic and challenging demeanor."[23] But it took only a few days before things started to go very wrong for Helvenston.

When he set off for the Middle East, Scott Helvenston's family thought he was going to be guarding Paul Bremer. As it turned out, he was slated to carry out a far less glamorous task. As part of Blackwater's power-drive for more business, the company had recently teamed up with a Kuwaiti business called Regency Hotel and Hospital Company, and together the firms had won a security contract with Eurest Support Services (ESS), a Halliburton subcontractor, guarding convoys transporting kitchen equipment to the U.S. military. Blackwater and Regency had essentially wrestled the ESS contract from another security firm, Control Risks Group, and were eager to win more lucrative contracts from ESS, which described itself as "the largest food service company in the world," in its other division servicing construction projects in Iraq. Blackwater was quickly pulling together teams to begin immediately escorting the convoys, and it was one of these details that Helvenston would ultimately be assigned to in Iraq. In the meantime, unbeknownst to him, there were secret business dealings going on behind the scenes.

Blackwater was paying its men $600 a day but billing Regency $815, according to the contracts and reporting in the Raleigh News and Observer.[24] "In addition," the paper reported, "Blackwater billed Regency separately for all its overhead and costs in Iraq: insurance, room and board, travel, weapons, ammunition, vehicles, office space and equipment, administrative support, taxes and duties." Regency would then bill ESS an unknown amount for these services. Kathy Potter told the News and Observer that Regency would "quote ESS a price, say $1,500 per man per day, and then tell Blackwater that it had quoted ESS $1,200."[25] In its contract with Blackwater/Regency, ESS made reference to its contract with Halliburton subsidiary

KBR, apparently indicating that Blackwater was working under a KBR sub-contract with ESS. The *News and Observer* reported that ESS billed KBR for the Blackwater services and that KBR in turn billed the federal government an unknown amount for these same services.[26] KBR/Halliburton, which makes a policy of not disclosing its subcontractors, said they were "unaware of any services" that Blackwater may have provided to ESS.

In February of 2007, representatives of ESS, KBR and Blackwater appeared together before a Congressional Committee investigating waste and abuse among Iraq War contractors.[27] A representative from Regency was scheduled to appear but did not attend. In sworn testimony during the hearing, Black-water's legal counsel, Andrew Howell stated, "the assumption that anything other than the amount paid in labor costs is pure markup and pure profit is wrong," saying the difference reflected other costs incurred by Blackwater. The ESS representative made a similar claim. Howell said Blackwater would have made just over $10 in profit per man per day on that contract, which he claimed Blackwater was never paid for. During the hearing, Rep. Dennis Kucinich disputed Blackwater's portrayal of its billing practices, charging that Howell's statements didn't "square with some facts." This would remain a point of contention as Congress continued its investigation.

The original contract between Blackwater/Regency and ESS, signed March 8, 2004, recognized that "the current threat in the Iraqi theater of opera-tions" would remain "consistent and dangerous," and called for a min-imum of three men in each vehicle on security missions "with a minimum of two *armored* vehicles to support ESS movements."[28] [Emphasis added.] But on March 12, 2004, Blackwater and Regency signed a subcontract that specified security provisions identical to the original except for one word: "armored." It was deleted from the contract, allegedly saving Blackwater $1.5 million.[29]

John Potter reportedly brought that omission to the attention of Black-water management and Regency.[30] Further delays could have resulted in Blackwater/Regency losing profits by hindering the start of the ESS job, and they were gung-ho to start to impress ESS and win further contracts.

"Regency, all they cared about was money," Kathy Potter alleged. "They didn't care about people's lives."[31] But the call to go ahead with the project without armored vehicles would have been Blackwater's to make. As the *News and Observer* reported, "The contract gives Blackwater complete control over how and when the convoys move, based on its judgment and the threat level. Kathy Potter said that Blackwater signed off on the mission."[32] On March 24, Blackwater removed John Potter as program manager, allegedly replacing him with Justin McQuown, who lawyers for Helvenston's family allege was the man known as "Shrek" whom Helvenston had clashed with at training in North Carolina.[33] McQuown, through his lawyer, declined to be interviewed. Word reached Helvenston in Kuwait that both Kathy and John Potter had been removed. "The one thing I do know is that both John and Kathy put their hearts and souls into this job," Helvenston wrote. "It is my opinion that whatever the severity of their wrongdoing they should not have been fired."[34]

In the meantime, Helvenston had been shuffled around a bit in Kuwait before being assigned to the Blackwater team he was slated to deploy to Iraq with in a few days. "We spent the last two days working, going out for meals, getting to know one another and in general bonding," he wrote on March 27, 2004. "We have been told that we are scheduled to leave two days from now to escort a bus up to Baghdad."[35] Helvenston wrote that he and his new team went out for dinner that night in Kuwait to continue their bonding and then to a "hukha bar" when a series of fateful events began to unfold, beginning with a call on Helvenston's mobile. "At roughly 2200 hrs. this evening I receive a call asking me if I can leave tomorrow 0500 with a new team leader," he wrote. "God's honest truth. . . . I am sitting there with a fruit drink and a piece pipe in my mouth (completely legal) feeling . . . well . . . dizzy as shit and a bit nasuated and my response was no. My bags were not packed and i just didn't feel up to it." Helvenston said he returned to his room in Kuwait and his team leader "went to speak with Justin. He frankly did not want to lose me as a team member and I think he felt that there was a hidden agenda. 'Lets see if we can screw with Scott'" [sic].[36]

Then, according to Helvenston's e-mail, things got ugly. He alleged that Shrek and another individual came to his hotel room late that night "to front me. No, not confront me. FRONT ME!" The man with Shrek, Helvenston wrote, called Helvenston a "coward" and "Stands as if he wants to fight Justin does the same. I draw my ASP [handgun] and this coward is ready to rock & roll. I just had a premintion [*sic*] it was going to happen. My roommate Chris breaks it up and Justin says I am fired and on a plane tomorrow. We exchange pleasantries and the result is him assuming my GLOCK [pistol] for which he has giving [*sic*] me permission to keep in my room."[37] Helvenston's family would later allege that McQuown "threatened to fire Helvenston if he did not leave early the next morning with the new team."[38] Regardless of the alleged conflict that night, Helvenston would soon find himself in Iraq. McQuown's lawyer said his client lacked any "involvement in the planning or implementation of [the] mission,"[39] on which Helvenston would be dispatched a few days later. The e-mail Helvenston sent the night before he deployed to Iraq was addressed to the "Owner, President and Upper Management" of Blackwater. Its subject: "extreme unprofessionalism."[40] It was the last e-mail Scott Helvenston would ever send.

CHAPTER SEVEN

THE AMBUSH

AROUND THE time Scott Helvenston arrived in the Middle East, in mid-March 2004, the situation in Fallujah was reaching an incendiary point. Following the massacre outside the school on Hay Nazzal Street in April 2003, the U.S. forces withdrew to the city's perimeter. Like Muqtada al-Sadr's Shiite followers in the Sadr City section of Baghdad, Fallujans had organized themselves and, before U.S. forces entered the city, created a local system of governance—appointing a Civil Management Council with a manager and mayor—in a direct affront to the authority of the occupation. According to Human Rights Watch, "Different tribes took responsibility for the city's assets, such as banks and government offices. In one noted case, the tribe responsible for al-Falluja's hospital quickly organized a gang of armed men to protect the grounds from an imminent attack. Local imams urged the public to respect law and order. The strategy worked, in part due to cohesive family ties among the population. Al-Falluja showed no signs of the looting and destruction visible, for example, in Baghdad."[1] They were also fierce in their rejection of any cooperation with the United States and its Iraqi allies. In January 2004, Maj. Gen. Charles Swannack, commander of the Army's Eighty-second Airborne Division, said the region was "on a glide path toward success," declaring, "We have turned the corner, and now we can accelerate down the straightaway."[2] But Swannack's forces had largely operated on the outskirts of the city, which, to the great consternation of Bremer and other U.S. officials, remained semiautonomous and patrolled by local militias. "Iraqis consider this period only a truce," said Fallujan shopkeeper Saad Halbousi in the weeks following the massacre at The Leader School and the subsequent U.S. withdrawal to the city's perimeter. "They will eventually explode like a volcano. We've exchanged a tyrant for an occupier."[3] In February, in a highly organized, broad-daylight raid, resistance fighters stormed a U.S.-backed Iraqi police center in Fallujah, killing twenty-three officers and freeing dozens of prisoners.[4] The next month, with militia openly patrolling Fallujah and antioccupation sentiment rising across Iraq, the U.S. determined to make an example of the city. "The situation is not going to improve until we clean out Fallujah," declared Bremer. "In the next ninety days [before the official 'handover' of sovereignty], it's vital to show that we mean business."[5]

On March 24, the First Marine Expeditionary Force took over responsibility of the city from the Eighty-second Airborne and immediately attempted to impose U.S. dominance over the antioccupation residents of Fallujah. A few days earlier, Marine commander Maj. Gen. James Mattis had outlined his strategy for dealing with Fallujah and the other areas of the largely Sunni Anbar province at a "handover" ceremony. "We expect to be the best friends to Iraqis who are trying to put their country back together," Mattis said. "For those who want to fight, for the foreign fighters and former regime people, they'll regret it. We're going to handle them very roughly. . . .

If they want to fight, we will fight."[6] Less than a year later, Mattis spoke about his time in Iraq and Afghanistan, telling an audience, "Actually it's quite fun to fight them, you know. It's a hell of a hoot," adding, "It's fun to shoot some people. I'll be right up there with you. I like brawling."[7]

As Mattis's forces took Fallujah, the Associated Press reported from inside the city, "Newly arrived U.S. Marines are leaving no one in doubt about their resolve to defeat insurgents. Residents are awed by the show of force but remain convinced that the Marines will fail to stamp out the resistance."[8] In a message to arriving troops, Mattis compared the Fallujah mission to battles in World War II and Vietnam: "We are going back into the brawl. . . . This is our test—our Guadalcanal, or Chosin Reservoir, our Hue City. . . . You are going to write history."[9] Khamis Hassnawi, Fallujah's senior tribal leader, told the *Washington Post*, "If they want to prevent bloodshed, they should stay outside the city and allow Iraqis to handle security inside the city."[10] Two days after they arrived, the Marines engaged in street battles with Iraqis in the working-class al-Askari neighborhood that raged for hours. In the end, one Marine was killed and seven were wounded. Fifteen Iraqis—among them, an ABC News cameraman[11] and a two-year-old child[12]—died in the fighting. A Marine crackdown quickly followed that "many residents say was unlike any they'd seen in nearly a year of U.S. occupation."[13] The Marines' aggressive move into Fallujah also presented many residents with a harsh sea of choices: surrender to foreign occupation, flee their homes, or resist. While some chose to leave, the more civilians that died, the more emboldened people in Fallujah became.

There was also another significant incident around that time that was fanning the flames of Sunni resistance. It happened not in Iraq but in Palestine. The Israeli military openly assassinated the spiritual leader of Hamas, Sheikh Ahmed Yassin, in Gaza. As he was being wheeled in his chair out of a morning prayer session on March 22, 2004, an Israeli helicopter gunship fired a Hellfire missile at his entourage, killing Yassin and at least a half-dozen others.[14] The "targeted assassination" enraged Muslims globally, particularly Sunnis like those living in Fallujah. Right after the assassination, more than fifteen hundred people gathered for prayers in the city to remember Yassin, with Sunni clerics saying the killing presented "a strong case for jihad [holy war] against all occupation forces."[15] Shops, schools, and government buildings were shut down as part of a general strike in Fallujah. For many in Iraq, the U.S. occupation of their country was part of the broader pro-Israel agenda in the region, and the Israeli occupation of Palestine and the U.S. invasion of Iraq were seen as intimately linked. "The assassination of an old man on a wheelchair, whose only weapon is his fierce drive to liberate his land, is an act of cowardice that proves the Israelis and the Americans do not want peace," said sixty-four-year-old Muslih al-Madfai, a Fallujah resident.[16] The timing of the assassination, which happened as the aggressive Marine takeover of Fallujah was beginning, fueled the belief that the United States and Israel were working in concert. As it was, many ordinary people in Iraq believed private security contractors to be Mossad or CIA.

As the Marines began fanning out across Fallujah, residents began reporting house-to-house raids and arbitrary arrests. "If they find more than one adult male in any house, they arrest one of them," said Fallujah resident Khaled Jamaili. "Those Marines are destroying us. They are leaning very hard on Fallujah."[17] On Saturday, March 27, the Marines issued a statement saying they were "conducting offensive operations . . . to foster a secure and stable environment for the people." It went on to say, "Some have chosen to fight. Having elected their fate, they are being engaged and destroyed."[18] The Marines blockaded the main entrances to the city with tanks and armored vehicles and dug foxholes along the roads. Graffiti began popping up on buildings in the Askari neighborhood with slogans like "Long live the Iraqi resistance," "Long live the honorable men of the resistance," and "Lift up your head. You are in Fallujah." Many in the city began hunkering down as the U.S. forces escalated their campaign to take Fallujah. "We are all suffering from what the Americans are doing to us, but that doesn't take away anything from our pride in the resistance," said Saadi Hamadi, a twenty-four-year-old graduate of Arabic studies from Baghdad's al-Mustansiriyah University. "To us, the Americans are just like the Israelis."[19] Tension was mounting inside Fallujah as the Americans began warning people—using patrols with bullhorns—that their neighborhoods would be turned into a battlefield if the "terrorists" did not leave.[20] By then, some families had already begun to flee their homes.

"The American forces had withdrawn from Fallujah over the winter, saying that they were going to rely on Iraqi security forces to do the work there for them, and so as not to be provocative," the veteran *New York Times* foreign correspondent John Burns said at the time. "The Marines, who took over authority for the Fallujah area from the 82nd Airborne Division, only last week changed the template. They decided to go back into Fallujah in force, and take a real crack at some of these insurgents. That resulted in a whole series of running battles last week, in which a number of marines were killed. Quite a few Iraqi civilians [were killed], 16 in one day last Friday."[21] It was part of a Marine strategy to draw the "insurgents" out. "You want the fuckers to have a safe haven?" asked Clarke Lethin, the First Marine Division's chief operations officer. "Or do you want to stir them up and get them out in the open?"[22] According to *Washington Post* defense correspondent Thomas Ricks, "Marine patrols into Fallujah were familiarizing themselves with the city, and in the process purposely stirring up the situation. Inside the city, insurgents were preparing to respond—warning shops to close, and setting up roadblocks and ambushes with parked cars." Even still, on March 30, 2004, Brig. Gen. Mark Kimmitt told reporters, "The Marines are quite pleased with how things are going in Fallujah, and they're looking forward to continuing the progress in establishing a safe and secure environment and rebuilding that province in Iraq."[23] In reality, the United States was swatting a hornets' nest in Fallujah, one in which Scott Helvenston and three other Blackwater contractors would find themselves less than twenty-four hours later.

Like "Slaughtered Sheep"

Jerry Zovko was a private soldier years before the "war on terror" began.[24] He had joined the U.S. military in 1991 at age nineteen and fought his way into the Special Forces, eventually becoming an Army Ranger.[25] The Croatian-American was deployed, by choice, in Yugoslavia, his parents' homeland, during the civil war there in the mid-1990s, where his family says he participated in covert operations. He was independent-minded, stubborn, and ambitious, and after Yugoslavia he trained to become an elite Green Beret but was never given a team assignment. In 1997, Zovko left the military. "He did something for the government that he couldn't tell us about," recalls his mother, Danica Zovko.[26] "We don't know what it was. You know, I never knew what he was doing. To this day, I do not." She says her son once showed her some small copper "tokens" the size of a silver dollar that he said would prove who he was to people who needed to know. She remembers a conversation where Jerry said, "Mom, it's easy to be an Army Ranger—that's physical work. But going into Special Forces, that's where your intelligence comes in."

In 1998, Zovko headed for the relatively unknown (to the public) world of private security. He was hired by one of the largest of these companies, DynCorp, and was stationed in the Arab Gulf nation of Qatar, working at the U.S. Embassy, where he learned Arabic. That assignment grew into a career as a soldier for hire. He traveled a lot and did a stint in the United Arab Emirates. Whenever Danica Zovko would ask her son about what exactly he was doing in all of these exotic places, he would always tell his mother the same thing. "He would tell me he was just taking care of the Embassy and working in the kitchen. But then, all his life in the military—a good seven years—he was always in the kitchen," she recalls with a doubtful tone. "Now I found out that he wasn't really in the kitchen." When the occupation of Iraq took hold, Zovko took a job, in late-August 2003, with the Virginia-based Military Professional Resources Incorporated, training the new Iraqi army. A few months before he left for Iraq, his mother had asked him, "Would you want to be a hired gun or something like that? Why would you put your life in danger for someone else?" He said, "Mom, I'm not. I'm going to train the Iraqis." The job was short-lived, though, as many Iraqi recruits never returned after a Ramadan break a couple of months later. So Zovko was picked up by Blackwater, which was in the midst of its aggressive recruitment drive for Iraq deployment. It was a good gig for Zovko, especially because his buddy Wes Batalona, a tough former Army Ranger from Hawaii who had been in Panama in 1989 and Somalia in 1993, was by his side.[27] The two had hit it off during their brief stint training the Iraqi army, and Batalona was ultimately drawn back to Iraq in February 2004 by Zovko to work with Blackwater after the training job fell apart.[28] "Around that time, Jerry called me," remembers his mother. "He was serious. He said I needed to write something down. I asked, 'What is it?' He said it was the number of the insurance policy, and I told him, 'If I need to write down an insurance policy number, then you need to get your you-know-what home.' And I hung up on him." Danica Zovko instructed her other son, Tom, to tell Jerry the same if he called. "That was the first time we'd ever argued with Jerry or ever asked him to come home. He did not tell me he was working for Blackwater," Danica says. The next time Jerry called, "he promised my husband and me that he would be there for Easter dinner, that we'd go to church together and that he'd take over the family business."

But a few weeks before Easter, on the morning of March 30, Zovko and Batalona got teamed up with another Blackwater contractor, thirty-eight-year-old Mike Teague from Tennessee, a former member of the 160th Special Operations Aviation Regiment, the "Night Stalkers." Known as "Ice Man" to his friends, Teague was a twelve-year Army veteran who had been in Panama and Grenada before becoming a reservist.[29] Most recently, he'd won a Bronze Star for his time in Afghanistan after 9/11.[30] After Afghanistan, he returned to the States and took a low-paying security job before joining up for more lucrative work with Blackwater in Iraq.[31] "This was the kind of work Mike loved," his friend John Menische told *Time* magazine. "He was a soldier and a warrior."[32] That day in Iraq, Teague had sent an e-mail to a friend, saying he loved Iraq and the excitement of his new six-figure-salary job.[33] The fourth member of this hodgepodge team was a face Zovko and Batalona had never seen in Baghdad, an ex-SEAL named Scott Helvenston. Their assignment was to escort some trucks to pick up kitchen equipment near Fallujah and then drop it off at a military base.[34] It was one of the first missions under Blackwater's new contract to provide security for ESS's catering convoys. Before the mission, Batalona complained to a friend that the group had never worked together.[35] On top of that, they were sent off that morning short two men, who were allegedly held back for clerical duties at the Blackwater compound.[36] Then, there were the vehicles. Instead of armored trucks, the men were provided with two jeeps that had been recently equipped with a single improvised steel plate in the back.[37]

On March 30, 2004, Scott Helvenston's first real workday in Iraq, he found himself behind the wheel of a red Mitsubishi Pajero jeep, speeding through the eerie, empty desert of western Iraq. Next to him was Teague. Helvenston had just met the others a day earlier—not the ideal procedure for men about to deploy to one of the most dangerous areas in the world. Following close behind the red jeep, hulky Jerry Zovko was at the wheel of a black Pajero; next to him was Batalona—at forty-eight, the oldest of the group. The mission they were on that day had nothing to do with Paul Bremer or diplomatic security. They literally were putting their lives on the line for some forks and spoons and pots and pans. The men, though, weren't getting paid $600 a day to set the priorities or to question the bigger picture, just to make sure the job got done right and that their "noun" of the moment was protected. Today it's kitchen equipment; tomorrow it's the Ambassador.

In retrospect, there were all sorts of reasons those four men shouldn't have gone on that mission. For one, they were shorted two guys. The CIA and State Department say they would never send just four men on a mission into the hostile territory these guys were heading into—six is the minimum. The missing man in each vehicle would have been wielding a heavy SAW machine gun with a 180-degree scope to mow down any attacker, especially from behind. "I am a designated driver so I am pretty dependent on my buds to pick up field of fire," Helvenston had e-mailed to his ex-wife, Tricia, a few days before he set off for Fallujah.[38] Without the third man, that meant the passenger had to navigate and defend from attacks pretty much alone. The men should have been in better-secured vehicles than SUVs, which are widely referred to as "bullet magnets" in Iraq because of their wide use by foreign contractors.[39] The men also were supposed to be able to do a pre-operation intelligence assessment and review the threat level along the route they'd be traveling, but the mission was reportedly pulled together too fast. To top it all off, Helvenston was allegedly sent out that day without a proper map of the dangerous area into which he would be driving.[40] It's easy to look back and say the four men could have said, "No way, screw this, we're not going." After all, they were not active military and would not have faced a court-martial for disobeying orders. In the end, all they had to lose in refusing to go was their reputations and possibly their paychecks. "We just shouldn't have gone [on the mission]," Helvenston's friend and former Blackwater employee Kathy Potter told the *News and Observer*. "But these guys are go-getters, and they'll make do with what they get."[41]

So off they went into the quiet of the western Iraqi desert. It's hard to imagine that the men didn't talk about the short stick they seemed to have drawn. Going anywhere near Fallujah in those days was scary business for non-Iraqis, and they didn't need any intel to know it. The U.S. Marines were in the midst of a major offensive in the city, and nobody from the military in their right mind would have headed through Fallujah with only four men and without serious firepower. Blackwater management was very well aware of this. In its own contract with ESS, Blackwater laid it out, recognizing that with "the current threat in the Iraqi theater of operations as evidenced by the recent incidents against civilian entities in Fallujah, Ar Ramadi, Al Taji and Al Hillah, there are areas in Iraq that will require a minimum of three Security Personnel per vehicle. The current and foreseeable future threat will remain consistent and dangerous. Therefore, to provide tactically sound and fully mission capable Protective Security Details, the *minimum team size is six operators*."[42] [Emphasis added.]

In the immediate days preceding this particular mission, the situation in Fallujah was already spiraling out of control. U.S. soldiers had been ambushed in the city, civilians had been killed, and word was getting around that "the city of mosques" was quickly becoming the city of resistance. A day before the four Blackwater men set off for Fallujah, a Marine convoy near the city had hit an improvised explosive device. Within moments resistance fighters had moved in on the vehicle, opening fire with AK-47s, killing a Marine and wounding two others.[43] The next morning, as Helvenston and the others headed to Fallujah, the Marines shut down the main highway from the city to Baghdad.[44] Nine Marines had died in the past eleven days around the city. After months of relative calm, a giant was rising from the rubble of "Shock and Awe," and Scott Helvenston and the other three Blackwater contractors would soon find themselves in the middle of it all.

As luck would have it (or perhaps because they didn't have a map), on the night of March 30, Helvenston and the three others got lost. They drove around for a while in the Sunni Triangle before making contact with the U.S. military in the area. They made their way to a Marine base that had recently been renamed Camp Fallujah and arranged to spend the night before heading off. It is well-known in Iraq that a lot of active-duty soldiers harbor resentment toward mercenaries. Most soldiers knew that guys like Helvenston and the other three were making in a day what an average grunt makes in a week. So it isn't surprising that the Blackwater men wouldn't have exactly been guests of honor at the base. Still, the four men crashed there and ate alongside the troops. One Marine officer from the base angrily called the men "cowboys" and said the Blackwater men refused to inform the commanders—or anyone on the base for that matter—about the nature of their mission.[45]

According to a 2007 Congressional investigation, KBR personnel at Camp Fallujah reported that "the Blackwater personnel seemed disorganized and unaware of the potential risk in traveling through the city of Fallujah. One of the KBR contractors said he felt that 'the mission they were on was hurriedly put together and that they weren't prepared'."[46] The KBR contractors told Congressional investigators that they gave the Blackwater men "multiple warnings to avoid driving directly through Fallujah and informing them that there were ambushes occurring there. After one warning, one of the Blackwater personnel said that they would not go through Fallujah. After a different warning, however, the response of the Blackwater personnel was that 'they would see how it went when they got out there.' According to one KBR contractor, 'It almost felt like they were being pressured to get there and get there as quickly as possible'."[47]

At some point before they set off the next morning, Helvenston called his mother, who said she was already sick with worry about her son being over there. But the fact that he hadn't called in days made her even more concerned. It was the middle of the night back in Leesburg, Florida, and the ringer was off on his mother's phone, so Helvenston left a message: *Everything's fine mom. Please don't worry. I'm gonna be home soon. I'm gonna take care of you.*

A short while later, Scott Helvenston was behind the wheel of the Pajero driving down Highway 10, heading straight for perhaps the most dangerous city in the world in which four lightly armed CIA-looking Americans wearing wraparound sunglasses could find themselves. It was about 9:30 a.m., and the city of mosques was awake and waiting.

The main drag through Fallujah is a congested strip, lined with restaurants, cafes, *souks*, and lots of people milling around. At some point before the men arrived in Fallujah that morning, according to witnesses, a small group of masked men had detonated some sort of explosive device, clearing the streets and causing shopkeepers to shutter their doors.[48] From the moment the convoy entered the city limits, the men stood out. In fact, it was very possible that the whole thing was a setup from the start. In a video purportedly made by an Iraqi resistance group, insurgents claimed they had been tipped off to the movements of the Blackwater convoy, which they believed consisted of U.S. intelligence agents. "A loyal mujahideen arrived who was a spy for the Islamic Jihad Army," said a masked insurgent on the video. "He told our commander that a group of CIA will pass through Fallujah en route to Habbaniyah."[49] The insurgent said, "They would not have bodyguards with them and they would wear civilian clothes—this to avoid being captured by the mujahideen, because every American that passes through Fallujah will be killed."[50] Blackwater representatives later alleged that units purportedly from the U.S.-installed Iraqi police had escorted the men into the city.[51] A senior U.S. intelligence official "with direct access to that information" later told journalist Thomas Ricks that there had been a leak out of the Green Zone about the Blackwater convoy's movements.[52] Claims of Iraqi police involvement were later contradicted by the findings of a CPA investigation provided to Congress.[53]

As it happened, Zovko and Batalona—who had been in country much longer than Helvenston—led the way, followed by three flatbed trucks, that were to be stocked up with kitchen equipment on the other side of Fallujah. Taking up the rear, Helvenston and Teague were in the red Pajero. Shortly after they rolled into the city, the convoy began to slow. To their right were shops and markets; to the left, open space. As the vehicles came to a standstill, witnesses say a group of four or five boys approached the lead vehicle and began talking to the Blackwater men inside. Before Helvenston or Teague could figure out what was happening, the unmistakable rip of machine-gun fire bellowed out on Fallujah's streets. Bullets tore through the side of the Pajero like salt through ice.

It was the worst thing that could happen to a Special Forces guy—the realization that you're trapped. No one knows for sure the last thing Scott Helvenston saw before he breathed his last breath, but there is no doubt it was terrifying. He may have lived long enough to know that he would die a gruesome death. As his fatally wounded body lay in the jeep, blood gushing from him, a mob of men jumped on the hood of the Pajero, unloading cartridges of ammo and pounding their way through the windshield. Next to Helvenston lay Mike Teague, blood spitting from his neck. Chants of "Allahu Akbar" (God is Great) filled the air. The attackers had moved in swiftly, like hawks on fatally wounded prey. Soon, more than a dozen young men who had been hanging around in front of a local kebab house joined in the carnage.[54] According to one eyewitness, one of the Blackwater men survived the initial attack after being hit in the chest with gunfire, only to be pulled from his vehicle by the mob, begging for his life. "The people killed him by throwing bricks on him and jumping on him until they killed him," the witness said. "They cut off his arm and his leg and his head, and they were cheering and dancing."[55]

By the time Helvenston's jeep was shot up, Jerry Zovko and Wes Batalona realized an ambush was under way. Batalona slammed on the gas, rammed over the median, and tried either to rescue the other two or get the hell out. According to a former private military-company operator, Blackwater trains its men "not to aid the other when one vehicle is hit in an ambush. They are taught to get off the X. Your own survival is the ultimate monkey."[56] But with little armor on the jeep and only one gunner, Batalona and Zovko were as good as dead. Within moments, they found themselves in a hail of gunfire as their jeep slammed into another vehicle. Zovko's head was blown apart. Batalona's Hawaiian shirt was full of bullet holes; his head slumped over. Down the road, the mob was tearing apart Helvenston's Pajero. Their weapons and gear had been looted; someone brought in gasoline and doused the vehicles and the bodies. Soon they were in flames. The eerie soundtrack to the massacre, captured on videos made by resistance fighters, was a mix of horns blaring and random screams of "Allahu Akbar!"

In the midst of the carnage, journalists arrived on the scene and captured images that would soon become infamous. The crowd swelled to more than three hundred people, as the original attackers faded into the side streets of Fallujah. The scorched bodies were pulled from the burned-out jeep, and men and boys literally tore them apart, limb from limb. Men beat the bodies with the soles of their shoes, while others hacked off burned body parts with metal pipes and shovels. A young man methodically kicked one of the heads until it was severed from the body. In front of the cameras, someone held a small sign emblazoned with a skull and crossbones that declared, "Fallujah is the graveyard of the Americans!" Chanting broke out: "With our blood and our souls, we will sacrifice for Islam!" Soon the mob tied two of the bodies to the back of a dark red Opel sedan and dragged them to the main bridge crossing the Euphrates.[57] Another body was tied to a car with a poster of the assassinated Hamas leader Sheik Yassin.[58] Along the way, someone tied a brick to one of the men's severed right leg and tossed it over a power line. At the bridge, men climbed the steel beams, hanging the charred, lifeless remains of Helvenston and Teague over the river, forming an eerily iconic image. Their bodies dangled over the Euphrates for almost ten hours—like "slaughtered sheep" in the words of one Fallujan.[59] Later, people cut the bodies down and put them on a pile of tires, setting them ablaze once again.[60] When the fire died out, men tied what was left of some of the bodies to the back of a gray donkey cart and paraded them through Fallujah, eventually dumping them in front of a municipal building.[61] Dozens of Iraqis followed the cart in a macabre procession chanting, "What makes you come here, Bush, and mess with the people of Fallujah?"[62] One man warned, "This is the fate of all Americans who come to Fallujah."[63]

It was the Mogadishu moment of the Iraq War, but with two key differences: the murdered men were not U.S. military, they were mercenaries; and unlike Somalia in 1993, the United States would not withdraw. Instead, the deaths of these four Blackwater soldiers would spark a violent U.S. siege, ushering in a period of unprecedented resistance to the occupation almost a year to the day after the fall of Baghdad.

CHAPTER EIGHT

"WE WILL PACIFY FALLUJAH"

THE CHARRED bodies of the Blackwater contractors were still hanging from the Fallujah bridge when news of the ambush began to spread across the globe. "They can't do that to Americans," said Capt. Douglas Zembiac as he watched the scene on TV in a mess hall at a military base outside Fallujah.[1] But there would be no immediate response from the thousands of nearby U.S. Marines. Perhaps that was because that same morning, five Marines were killed near Fallujah after hitting a roadside bomb. Maybe it was because the Blackwater men were not "official" U.S. forces. In any case, the contractors' bodies hung over the Euphrates for hours as a grim reminder that one year after the fall of Baghdad, eleven months after President Bush declared an end to major combat operations, and ninety days before the official "handover of sovereignty" to the Iraqis, the war was just beginning. U.S. military spokesperson Brig. Gen. Mark Kimmitt initially tried to downplay the significance of the ambush, calling it an "isolated" and "small, localized"[2] case, part of a "slight uptick in localized engagements."[3] Fallujah, Kimmitt said, "remains one of those cities in Iraq that just don't get it."[4] "While this one incident was happening in Fallujah, throughout the rest of the country, we are opening schools. We're opening health clinics. We are increasing the amount of electrical output. We are increasing the amount of oil output,"[5] Kimmitt declared at a press briefing the day of the ambush. "So is this tragic? Absolutely it's tragic. There are four families in this world today that are going to get knocks on the doors. And you don't want to be on either side of that door when it happens, either hearing the news or delivering the news. . . . But that isn't going to stop us from doing our mission. In fact, it would be disgracing the deaths of these people if we were to stop our missions."[6] Paul Bremer's spokesperson, Dan Senor, told reporters that "the people who pulled those bodies out and engaged in this attack against the contractors are not people we are here to help," saying, "Those are people we have to capture or kill so this country can move forward."[7] Senor said the people who carried out the ambush and supported it represented "a tiny, tiny minority" of Iraqis. "The overwhelming majority of Iraqis are grateful for the liberation—95, 98 percent are the numbers that come up," he said.[8]

Meanwhile, thousands of miles away in Washington, D.C., President Bush was on the campaign trail, speaking at the posh Marriott Wardman Park Hotel at a Bush-Cheney dinner. "We still face thugs and terrorists in Iraq who would rather go on killing the innocent than accept the advance of liberty," the President told his supporters. "This collection of killers is trying to shake our will. America will never be intimidated by thugs and assassins. We are aggressively striking the terrorists in Iraq. We will defeat them there so we do not have to face them in our own country."[9] The next morning Americans woke up to news of the gruesome killings in Fallujah. "Iraqi Mob Mutilates 4 American Civilians," screamed the banner headline in the *Chicago Tribune*. "U.S. Civilians Mutilated in Iraq Attack," announced the *Washington Post*. "Americans Desecrated," proclaimed the *Miami Herald*. Somalia was being mentioned frequently.

After Kimmitt's initial downplaying of the ambush, the White House— and Paul Bremer—recognized the prolonged, public mutilation of the Black-water men as a major blow in the propaganda war against the fast-emerging anti-U.S. resistance in Iraq. Some went so far as to believe the ambush was a direct attempt to re-create Somalia in 1993, when rebels shot down a U.S. Black Hawk helicopter, killing eighteen U.S. soldiers and dragging some of their bodies through the streets of Mogadishu, prompting the Clinton administration to pull out of the country. With less than three months before the much-hyped "handover," the Bush administration faced the undeniable reality of an emboldened resistance to an occupation that was increasingly unpopular, both at home and inside Iraq. "The images immediately became icons of the brutal reality of the insurgency," wrote Bremer, saying they "underscored the fact that the coalition military did not control Fallujah."[10] Bremer says he told Lt. Gen. Ricardo Sanchez, the commander of U.S. forces in Iraq, "We've got to react to this outrage or the enemy will conclude we're irresolute."[11] Sanchez, according to Bremer, responded, "We're dusting off the operation we planned last fall . . . the one to clean out Fallujah."[12] Almost immediately, plans for crushing the "city of mosques" were put on the fast track. "We will not be intimidated," declared White House spokesperson Scott McClellan. "Democracy is taking root and there's no turning back."[13] Senator John Kerry—then the Democratic candidate for President—concurred, saying, "These horrific attacks remind us of the viciousness of the enemies of Iraq's future. United in sadness, we are also united in our resolve that these enemies will not prevail."[14] Rep. Nancy Pelosi, the House Democratic leader, said, "We're not going to run out of town because some people were lawless in Fallujah."[15] Meanwhile, political pundits on the cable networks called for blood. Bill O'Reilly of Fox News spoke of a "final solution,"[16] saying, "I don't care about the people of Fallujah. You're not going to win their hearts and minds. They're going to kill you to the very end. They've proven that. So let's knock this place down."[17]

Later, in calling for the United States "to use maximum force in punishing the Fallujah terrorists,"[18] O'Reilly declared, "Fear can be a good thing. Homicidal terrorists and their enablers must be killed or incarcerated. And their punishment must be an example to others. How do you think Saddam controlled Iraq all these decades? He did it by fear."[19] Meanwhile on MSNBC, former Democratic presidential candidate Gen. Wesley Clark said, "The resistance is not declining in Fallujah, so far as I can determine. It's building and mounting. And we can't have that challenge to our authority."[20]

Many questioned why—with four thousand Marines positioned around Fallujah—such a prolonged mutilation of the bodies of the Blackwater contractors was possible and why their charred corpses were left for hours to hang from the bridge. "[E]ven while the two vehicles burned, sending plumes of thick, black smoke over the shuttered shops of the city, there were no ambulances, fire engines or security dispatched to try and rescue the victims," UPI reported. "This time, there were no Blackhawks to fly to the rescue. Instead, Fallujah's streets were abandoned to the jubilant, chaotic, and violent crowds who rejoiced amid battered human remains."[21] Col. Michael Walker, a Marine spokesman, said: "Should we have sent in a tank so we could have gotten, with all due respect, four dead bodies back? What good would that have done? A mob is a mob. We would have just provoked them. The smart play was to let this thing fade out."[22]

Responding to a reporter's question about whether the Marines did not go into Fallujah right after the ambush to confront the mob attacking the Blackwater men because it was "too dangerous," Kimmitt shot back, "I don't think that there is any place in this country that the coalition forces feel is too dangerous to go into."[23] That day on CNN, *Crossfire* host Tucker Carlson said, "I think we ought to kill every person who's responsible for the deaths of those Americans. This is a sign of weakness. This is how we got 9/11. It's because we allowed things like that to go unresponded to. This is a big deal."[24]

Within twenty-four hours, Kimmitt's tone had changed. "We will respond. We are not going to do a pell-mell rush into the city. It's going to be deliberate, it will be precise and it will be overwhelming," he declared at a press briefing in Baghdad.[25] "We will be back in Fallujah. It will be at the time and the place of our choosing. We will hunt down the criminals. We will kill them or we will capture them. And we will pacify Fallujah."[26]

Paul Bremer made his first public remarks on the killings during an address in front of nearly five hundred new graduates from the Iraqi police academy in Baghdad. "Yesterday's events in Fallujah are a dramatic example of the ongoing struggle between human dignity and barbarism," he declared, warning that the killing of the Blackwater men "will not go unpunished." The dead contractors, he said, "came to help Iraq recover from decades of dictatorship, to help the people of Iraq gain the elections, democracy, and freedom desired by the overwhelming majority of the Iraqi people. These murders are a painful outrage for us in the coalition. But they will not derail the march to stability and democracy in Iraq. The cowards and ghouls who acted yesterday represent the worst of society."[27]

In most U.S. news reports on the ambush, Fallujah was described as a Sunni resistance stronghold filled with foreign fighters and Saddam loyalists. The dominant narrative became that the Blackwater men were innocent "civilian contractors" delivering food who were slaughtered by butchers in Fallujah. At one point after the incident, Kimmitt told reporters that the Blackwater men were "there to provide assistance, to provide food to that local area,"[28] as though the men were humanitarians working for the Red Cross. But inside Fallujah and elsewhere in Iraq, the ambush was viewed differently. The news that the men were technically not active U.S. forces did not change the fact that they were fully armed Americans who had traveled into the center of Fallujah at a time when U.S. forces were killing Iraqi civilians and attempting to take the city by force. The *New York Times* reported, "Many people in Falluja said they believed that they had won an important victory on Wednesday. They insisted that the four security guards, who were driving in unmarked sport utility vehicles, were working for the Central Intelligence Agency. 'This is what these spies deserve,' said Salam Aldulayme, a 28-year-old Falluja resident."[29]

On CNN's *Larry King Live*, *ABC News* anchor Peter Jennings, who had just returned from Iraq a few days before the Blackwater killings, said, "There is a sort of second army of Americans out there now in the form of security personnel, who can be seen almost anywhere in the country there is a member of the coalition doing something. And they struck me as being very high-profile targets. They're armed to the teeth. A lot of them look like they come out of a Sylvester Stallone movie. And so, and they move around the country. And I think that the insurgents, whomever they are, have picked up on them and may be tracking them. So when it happened in Fallujah, as bad as it was, I must say I wasn't deeply surprised."[30]

Others described the ambush as a response to the recent U.S. killing of civilians in Fallujah, particularly the gun battle the previous week that left more than a dozen Iraqis dead. "Children and women were killed. They were innocent," said Ibrahim Abdullah al-Dulaimi. "People in Fallujah are very angry with the American soldiers."[31] Leaflets began circulating in Fallujah claiming that the killings were carried out as revenge for the Israeli assassination of Hamas leader Sheikh Ahmad Yassin.[32] A Fallujah shop assistant named Amir said, "The Americans may think it is unusual, but this is what they should expect. They show up in places and shoot civilians, so why can't they be killed?"[33] These sentiments were even echoed among the ranks of the U.S.-created Iraqi police force. "The violence is increasing against the Americans," said Maj. Abdelaziz Faisal Hamid Mehamdy, a Fallujan who joined the police force in 2003 after Baghdad fell. "They took over the country and they didn't give us anything. They came for democracy and to help the people, but we haven't seen any of this, just killing and violence."[34]

A local Fallujan official, Sami Farhood al-Mafraji, who had been supportive of the occupation, said, "Americans are not meeting their promises here to help build up this country. . . . I used to support the military. But they have put me in a very difficult situation with my people. Now, they tell us to hand these people over?"[35] He said the dire humanitarian situation and the violence of the occupation had "made people depressed and angry." "Hungry people will eat you," he said. "And people here are very hungry."[36] This context even seemed clear to some U.S. troops as well. "The people who did this heinous crime were looking for revenge," said Marine Lt. Eric Thorliefson, positioned on the outskirts of Fallujah. He added, "We shall respond with force."[37]

While U.S. officials condemned the public mutilation of the bodies, they refused to answer questions about the U.S. policy of distributing gruesome photos of the mangled corpses of "high value" Iraqis killed by U.S. forces, like Saddam's sons Uday and Qusay in July 2003, as proof of death. Similar to the outrage expressed by Washington over the mauling of the Blackwater contractors, Iraqis were furious over this U.S. propaganda technique. At the White House the day of the Blackwater killings, McClellan was asked if the administration did "not see hypocrisy [when showing] embalmed bodies as proof of death is condemned but the dragging of American bodies through a street goes on without a comment?"

"It is offensive. It is despicable the way that these individuals have been treated," McClellan responded, ignoring the question. "And we hope everybody acts responsibly in their coverage of it."[38] Indeed, most of the images of the ambush and its aftermath that were broadcast on U.S. networks and in newspapers were edited or blurred. Even so, the message was clear. With the Somalia comparisons increasing in the international media, the administration shot back. "We are not going to withdraw. We are not going to be run out," Secretary of State Colin Powell, the first senior Bush administration official to comment directly on the Blackwater killings, told German television. "America has the ability to stay and fight an enemy and defeat an enemy. We will not run away."[39]

Meanwhile, reporters began questioning who these four contractors were and what they were doing in the middle of Fallujah. "I will let individual contractors speak for themselves on the clients they have inside Iraq. My understanding is Blackwater has more than one. But again, I would have you contact them to get that information. I certainly do not have it," said Dan Senor, the occupation spokesperson in Baghdad. "They—we do have a contract with Blackwater, with—relating to Ambassador Bremer's security. They are involved with protecting Ambassador Bremer," Senor said.[40] On CNN, Senor was asked, "So with all due respect to the men who lost their lives, any concern that this security company is up to the task?"

"Absolutely," Senor shot back. "We have the utmost confidence in Blackwater and the other security institutions that protect Mr. Bremer and provide security throughout the country."[41]

In North Carolina, meanwhile, Blackwater's phones were ringing off the hook as the identities of the four "civilian contractors" became public. The company refused to officially confirm the names of the dead, a Blackwater policy. "The enemy may have contacts in the U.S.," said former Blackwater vice president Jamie Smith. "If you start putting names out there—any names—and they start finding out who your friends are and asking questions, it could become a security problem."[42]

The day after the ambush, Blackwater hired the powerful, well-connected Republican lobbying firm the Alexander Strategy Group (founded and staffed by former senior staffers of then–House majority leader Tom DeLay) to help the company handle its newfound fame.[43] Blackwater released a brief statement to the press. "The graphic images of the unprovoked attack and subsequent heinous mistreatment of our friends exhibits the extraordinary conditions under which we voluntarily work to bring freedom and democracy to the Iraqi people," the Blackwater statement said.[44] "Coalition forces and civilian contractors and administrators work side by side every day with the Iraqi people to provide essential goods and services like food, water, electricity and vital security to the Iraqi citizens and coalition members. Our tasks are dangerous and while we feel sadness for our fallen colleagues, we also feel pride and satisfaction that we are making a difference for the people of Iraq."[45] Republican Congressman Walter Jones Jr., who represents Currituck County, North Carolina (where Blackwater has its headquarters), said the contractors had "died in the name of freedom."[46] Republican Senator John Warner, head of the Senate Armed Services Committee, praised the Blackwater men at a hearing, saying, "Those individuals are essential to the work that we're performing in Iraq, primarily the rebuilding of the infrastructure."[47]

In the "Chaplain's Corner" section of Blackwater's newsletter, *Blackwater Tactical Weekly*, right after the ambush, Chaplain D. R. Staton continued the misleading characterization of the men as "humanitarian" workers who came to Iraq "to save a people," writing, "Those four Americans were there because they were hired to provide security to food caravans delivering life giving substances to native Iraqis. . . . This one incident points up the hatred of Islamic militants for anyone not Islamic militant and especially those who are called by them the white devils or the 'great Satan' or simply 'infidels.' Did you study those individuals in the mob as they were displayed to us via television? Did you note their attitudes and their ages? They are brainwashed from birth to hate all who are not with them. . . . And especially us!!! . . . And the Israelis!" The attackers' message, Staton wrote, "is to discourage our forces from entering Fallujah and the special claimed area around that city!!! The message will backfire!!!" Staton ended his sermon with a plea to his readers: "Make the enemy pay dearly for every action brought against us as we stand for liberty and justice!!!"[48]

But not everyone working for Blackwater was on the same page. "I think they're dying for no reason," said Marty Huffstickler, a part-time electrician for the company in Moyock. "I don't agree with what's going on over there. The people over there don't want us there."[49]

To the Marines, which had just taken over command of Fallujah, the Blackwater ambush could not have come at a worse moment because it dramatically changed the course of Maj. Gen. James Mattis's strategy. The local commanders wanted to treat the killings as a law enforcement issue, go into the city, and arrest or kill the perpetrators.[50] But at the White House, the killings were viewed as a serious challenge to the U.S. resolve in Iraq—one that could jeopardize the whole project in the country. President Bush immediately summoned Rumsfeld and the top U.S. commander in the region, Gen. John Abizaid to ask for a plan of action.

According to the *L.A. Times*:

> Rumsfeld and Abizaid were ready with an answer, one official said: "a
> specific and overwhelming attack" to seize Fallouja. That was what
> Bush was hoping to hear, an aide said later. What the president was not
> told was that the Marines on the ground sharply disagreed with a full-
> blown assault on the city. "We felt . . . that we ought to let the situation
> settle before we appeared to be attacking out of revenge," the Marines'
> commander, Lt. Gen. James T. Conway, said later. Conway passed this
> up the chain—all the way to Rumsfeld, an official said. But Rumsfeld
> and his top advisors didn't agree, and didn't present [Lt. Gen.
> Conway's reservations] to the president. "If you're going to threaten
> the use of force, at some point you're going to have to demonstrate
> your willingness to actually use force," Pentagon spokesman Lawrence
> Di Rita said later. Bush approved the attack immediately.[51]

In Fallujah, word of the President's go-ahead for an attack reached the Marine
base positioned on the city's outskirts. "The president knows this is going to
be bloody," Sanchez told the commanders there. "He accepts that."[52] One
officer characterized the orders as, "Go in and clobber people."[53] By April 2,
2004, forty-eight hours after the ambush, "Operation Vigilant Resolve" was
put on the fast track. Marine Sgt. Maj. Randall Carter began to pump his
men up for their mission. "Marines are only really motivated two times," he
declared. "One is when we're going on liberty. One is when we're going to
kill somebody. We're not going on liberty. . . . We're here for one thing: to
tame Fallujah. That's what we're going to do."[54] Inside the city, meanwhile,
Fallujans, too, were preparing for a battle many believed was inevitable.

Before the U.S. troops launched the full assault on the city, Bremer
deputy Jim Steele, the senior adviser on Iraqi security forces, was sent
covertly into Fallujah with a small team of U.S.-trained Iraqi forces and
people Steele referred to as "U.S. advisors."[55] Steele had most recently been
an Enron executive before being tapped for the Iraq job by Paul Wolfowitz.[56]
Perhaps most appealing to the administration, Steele had a very deep

history with U.S. "dirty wars" in Central America. As a colonel in the Marines in the mid-1980s, Steele had been a key "counterinsurgency" official in the bloody U.S.-fueled war in El Salvador, where he coordinated the U.S. Military Group there,[57] supervising Washington's military assistance and training of right-wing Salvadoran Army squads battling the leftist FMLN guerrillas.[58] In the late 1980s, Steele was called to testify during the Iran-Contra investigation about his role in Oliver North's covert weapons pipeline to the Nicaraguan Contra death squads, running through the Salvadoran Air Force base at Ilopango.[59] He also worked with the Panamanian police after the United States overthrew Manuel Noriega in 1990.[60]

Steele played a similar role with U.S.-trained Iraqi forces in the early days of the occupation and was central to a program some refer to as the "Salvadorization of Iraq."[61] Under this strategy, "U.S. soldiers are increasingly moving to a Salvador-style advisory role," wrote Peter Maass in *The New York Times Magazine*. "In the process, they are backing up local forces that, like the military in El Salvador, do not shy away from violence. It is no coincidence that this new strategy is most visible in a paramilitary unit that has Steele as its main adviser; having been a central participant in the Salvador conflict, Steele knows how to organize a counterinsurgency campaign that is led by local forces."[62]

After the Blackwater ambush, Steele claimed his "undercover" mission in Fallujah in April 2004 was to recover the corpses of the Blackwater men and to "assess the enemy situation."[63] Shortly after that mission, he laid out what he thought should happen. "In Fallujah, a heavy hand makes sense," he said. "That's the only thing some of those guys will understand. Down south, too [where the United States faced a mounting Shiite rebellion]. We can't be seen as weak. Otherwise, this kind of thing can happen everywhere."[64] The "city of mosques" would soon find itself under siege as Bremer's dreams of "cleaning out" Fallujah found their justification. While U.S. commanders readied their troops to attack, Blackwater's stock was rising in Washington, and Erik Prince's men would soon find themselves in the middle of the second major resistance front exploding against the occupation—this time in the Shiite holy city of Najaf.

CHAPTER NINE

NAJAF, IRAQ: 4.04.04

AS THE Marines began preparing to invade Fallujah, back in Washington, D.C., Erik Prince's stock was rising dramatically. In a matter of days, Prince and other Blackwater executives would be welcomed on Capitol Hill as special guests of some of the most powerful and influential Republican lawmakers—the men who literally ran Congress—where Blackwater would be hailed as a "silent partner" in the war on terror.[1] As his schedule began to fill, Prince found himself monitoring yet another crisis with his mercenaries at the center. But unlike Fallujah, where the deaths of four Blackwater men had provided the spark for a U.S. onslaught, this time Blackwater forces would be active combatants in the fighting, engaging in a day-long battle against hundreds of followers of the fiery cleric Muqtada al-Sadr in the Shiite holy city of Najaf, where Blackwater had been contracted to guard the U.S. occupation authority's headquarters.

In the weeks preceding the March 31 Fallujah ambush, the Bush administration had been building toward an intense crackdown on Sadr, whom Bremer and the White House viewed as an obstacle to the central U.S. goal at the time—the so-called "handover of sovereignty" scheduled for June 2004. The son of a revered religious leader assassinated by Saddam's forces, Sadr had emerged in occupied Iraq as commander of the Mahdi Army—named for a Shiite messiah—and perhaps the most vocal and popular opponent of the U.S. occupation.[2] The administration and Bremer believed that like the rebellious Sunnis of Fallujah, Sadr and his insurgent Shiite movement had to be stopped. In April 2004, as the U.S. launched simultaneous counterinsurgency wars in Iraq against the country's main Sunni and Shiite resistance movements, Blackwater would play a decisive role in perhaps the most pivotal moments of the Iraq occupation, a period that would irreversibly alter the course of the war and go down as the moment the anti-U.S. insurrection exploded.

While the killing of the Blackwater men in Fallujah grabbed international headlines for days and is remembered as an iconic moment of the war, the significant role of Blackwater's forces in Najaf during the Shiite uprising five days later was barely noticed at all. And yet this episode, which found Blackwater mercenaries commanding active-duty U.S. soldiers in battle, starkly dramatized the unprecedented extent to which the Bush administration had outsourced the war. Like the ambush in Fallujah, the fate of Blackwater in Najaf was guided by history.

During his year in Iraq, Paul Bremer presided over various U.S. policies that greatly accelerated the emergence of multiple antioccupation resistance movements. In April 2004, it all came to a head. "The British took three years to turn both the Sunnis and the Shias into their enemies in 1920," wrote veteran British war correspondent Robert Fisk from Fallujah. "The Americans are achieving this in just under a year."[3] The disbanding of the Iraqi military combined with the firing of thousands of state employees under Washington's "de-Baathification" program had put tens of thousands of Iraqi men of fighting age out of work and into the resistance. Iraqis watched as foreign corporations—most of them based in the United States—fanned out across their country to reap enormous profits while ordinary Iraqis lived in squalor and insecurity. What's more, victims of U.S. crimes had almost no recourse as contractors were basically immunized from domestic prosecution, giving the overwhelming appearance of total impunity.[4]

At the same time, the dire humanitarian situation in the country and killings and disappearances of Iraqi civilians had opened the door for religious leaders to offer security and social services in return for loyalty. This phenomenon was perhaps seen most clearly in the ascent of Muqtada al-Sadr to the status of a national resistance hero. In the chaos and horror that followed "Shock and Awe," Sadr was one of the few figures within the country actually addressing the extreme poverty and suffering, establishing a sizable network of social institutions in his areas of influence, among them the vast Baghdad slum of Sadr City, whose 2 million residents had long been neglected by Saddam's regime. At a time when Bremer's de-Baathification was dismantling social institutions and protections, Sadr's network was building alternatives and winning thousands of new followers. "Immediately after the invasion, Mr. Sadr deployed black-clad disciples to patrol the streets of Baghdad's Shiite slums," reported the *New York Times*. "His men handed out bread, water and oranges. They also provided much-needed security. Mr. Sadr had seen a void and filled it."[5] While other religious and political figures vied for power within the new U.S.-created institutions, Sadr rejected all components and supporters of the U.S. regime. In August 2003, his militia numbered roughly five hundred members. By April 2004, it had swelled to an estimated ten thousand.[6]

Sadr's rising credibility and popularity, combined with his fierce rhetoric against the occupation—and Bremer in particular—would soon earn him the U.S.-imposed label of "outlaw."[7] With the June 2004 "deadline" fast approaching, the United States believed that, like the militant Sunnis of Fallujah, Sadr had to be stopped.

Washington had long viewed Sadr as a primary enemy in the "new" Iraq, and top U.S. officials, including Deputy Defense Secretary Paul Wolfowitz and the senior commander in Iraq, Gen. Ricardo Sanchez, had for months discussed plans to neutralize him. "There was a conclusion early on that this guy was trouble and needed to be contained," a senior U.S. official told the *Washington Post*. "But there was not a clear plan on how to go about it."[8] That changed in March 2004, when Bremer launched his all-out war on Sadr, his institutions, and his followers. As Bremer and the Bush administration engaged in a major propaganda campaign leading up to the "handover," Sadr was railing against the occupation and its collaborators within the country. He was calling for the United States to pull out and had declared his Mahdi Army the "enemy of the occupation."[9] Sadr was not just a Shiite religious figure; he was also an Iraqi nationalist who spoke the language of the streets, often peppering his sermons with slang and cultural references.

According to the *Washington Post*, there had long been concerns that if the United States went after Sadr, it would boost his already rising popularity and possibly make him into a martyr. By March, the *Post* said, "Bremer's calculus had changed."[10] On March 28, U.S. troops raided the Baghdad office of Sadr's small antioccupation weekly newspaper, *Al Hawza* (The Seminary), ejecting the staff and placing a large padlock on the door.[11] In a letter written in "sparse, understated" Arabic, bearing the official stamp of the CPA,[12] Bremer accused the paper of violating his Order 14, charging that *Al Hawza* had the "intent to disrupt general security and incite violence."[13] While U.S. officials could not cite any examples of the paper encouraging attacks against occupation forces, Bremer provided two examples of what he characterized as false reporting. One of them was an article headlined "Bremer Follows in the Footsteps of Saddam."[14] The move against Sadr was carried out with senior Bush administration officials fully behind it. "We believe in freedom of press," said Bremer spokesman Dan Senor. "But if we let this go unchecked, people will die. Certain rhetoric is designed to provoke violence, and we won't tolerate it."[15] The crackdown would prove to be a disastrous miscalculation on Bremer's part. *Al Hawza* was named for a thousand-year-old Shiite seminary that historically encouraged revolt against foreign occupiers, most notably in the 1920s against the British.[16] "In recent months, al-Sadr had been losing popularity," wrote Newsday's veteran Iraq correspondent Mohamad Bazzi. "But after U.S. soldiers closed al-Sadr's weekly newspaper in Baghdad on March 28, accusing it of inciting violence, the young cleric won new support and established himself as the fiercest Shiite critic of the U.S. occupation."[17] The shutdown of Al Hawza immediately sparked massive protests and fueled speculation that Bremer intended to arrest Sadr.[18] Eventually the protests spread to the gates of the Green Zone, where demonstrators chanted, "Just say the word, Muqtada, and we'll resume the 1920 revolution!"[19]

Even before the United States began its attacks against Sadr, there were serious rumblings across Iraq of a national uprising of Shiites and Sunnis. Two days before Bremer shut down Al Hawza, U.S. forces had raided a neighborhood in Fallujah, killing at least fifteen Iraqis in an incident that enraged many Sunnis.[20] By the time the four Blackwater contractors were ambushed in Fallujah on March 31, the south of the country was already on the brink, with tens of thousands of Shiites pouring into the streets. On April 2, during Friday prayers, Sadr declared, "I am the beating arm for Hezbollah and Hamas here in Iraq."[21] As U.S. forces prepared to lay siege to Fallujah, Bremer poured gas on the volatile situation by ordering the arrest of Sadr's top deputy, Sheikh Mustafa Yaqubi, who was taken into custody on Saturday, April 3, 2004.[22] For Sadr, it was the final straw. He urged his followers to openly and fiercely rise up against the occupation.

After Yaqubi's arrest, thousands of outraged Sadr followers boarded buses from Baghdad heading for their leader's spiritual headquarters in Kufa, next to the holy city of Najaf,[23] where many believed Yaqubi was being held by occupation forces. Along the way, they encountered jam-packed roads filled with thousands of men preparing to do battle. "We didn't choose the time for the uprising," said Fuad Tarfi, Sadr's Najaf spokesman. "The occupation forces did."[24] Shortly after dawn on Sunday, April 4, the Mahdi Army began to take over the administrative buildings in the area. Local police commanders immediately relinquished their authority, as did administrators in another government building. But then the massive crowd began moving toward its actual target—the occupation headquarters in Najaf, which was guarded by Blackwater.

04/04/04

On the morning of April 4, 2004, as the sun was rising over the Shiite holy city of Najaf, a handful of Blackwater men stood on the rooftop of the Coalition Provisional Authority headquarters they were tasked with protecting. At the time, the actual U.S. military presence in Najaf was very limited because of negotiations with Shiite religious leaders who had demanded that U.S. troops leave. As part of its contract in Iraq, Blackwater not only guarded Paul Bremer but also provided security for at least five regional U.S. occupation headquarters, including the one in Najaf.[25] Like most of the world, the Blackwater guards in Najaf were well aware of the fate of their colleagues a few days earlier in Fallujah. Now, with a national uprising under way, they watched as an angry demonstration of Muqtada al-Sadr's followers reached Camp Golf, formerly the campus of Kufa University, which had been converted to an occupation headquarters. Blackwater had just eight men guarding the facility that day, along with a handful of troops from El Salvador. By chance, there were also a few U.S. Marines at the complex.

U.S. Marine Cpl. Lonnie Young had been in Iraq since January 2004. The twenty-five-year-old native of Dry Ridge, Kentucky—population two thousand—was deployed in Iraq as a Defense Messaging System administrator. On the morning of April 4, he was in Najaf to install communication equipment at Camp Golf. "While entering the front gate, I noticed a small group of protesters out in the streets," Young recalled in an official Marine Corps account of the day.[26] "As we proceeded onto the base there were numerous coalition soldiers in 'riot gear' near the front gate." Young and his colleagues met with the local occupation commander, a Spanish official, and then proceeded to the roof of the building to install the communications equipment. About twenty-five minutes later, Young had finished his task.

Despite the beginnings of a protest at the camp, Young tried to catch a quick ten-minute nap in the back of his truck, "since we were about twenty-minutes from chow time." But a few moments later, a colleague of Young's woke him up and told him the equipment was not working properly. "I told him that I would be right in to help," Young said. "I got dressed, grabbed my weapon, and was about to get out of the truck when I heard the unmistakable sound of an AK-47 rifle fire a few rounds out in the street in front of the base." Young said he quickly grabbed his gear and headed into the CPA building, eventually making it to the roof, where he joined eight Blackwater mercenaries and the Salvadoran troops. Young assumed a position on the roof and readied his heavy M249 Squad Automatic Weapon. He peered through the scope of his gun, watching the action unfold below and awaiting orders. "After what seemed like an eternity, which was maybe just a few seconds, I could see people getting out of [a] truck and start running," Young recalled. "One of the Iraqis quickly dropped down into a prone position and fired several round[s] at us. I started yelling that I had one in my sights and asking if I could engage." But there was no commanding officer on hand from the U.S. military. Instead, Cpl. Lonnie Young, active-duty United States Marine Corps, would be taking his orders that day from the private mercenaries of Blackwater USA.

"With your permission Sir, I have acquired a target," Young recalled yelling out. "Finally, the Blackwater Security guys gave the call [to] commence firing." Young said he then "leveled the sights on my target and squeezed the trigger. I could see that the man had on an all white robe and was carrying an AK-47 rifle in his right hand. He seemed to be running as hard as he could when I fired off a short burst of 5.56 mm rounds. Through my sights I could see the man fall onto the pavement. I stopped for a second, raised my head from my gun, to watch the man lay in the street motionless."

"I had a weird feeling come over me," Young recalled. "I had many emotions kick in at once. I felt a sense of purpose, happiness, and sorrow, which all hit me at once."

While Young and Blackwater contend that the Iraqis initiated the shooting that day, other witnesses interviewed by journalists on the scene said it went down differently; they claimed the battle began when the forces guarding the occupation headquarters fired percussion rounds from atop the roof as the protesters assembled. "Alarmed to see the throng still moving toward them, [the forces on the roof] fired percussive rounds designed to break up the crowd, which instead enraged it," wrote *Washington Post* correspondent Anthony Shadid. "They may then have switched to live fire. Armed men in the crowd returned fire with small arms, rocket-propelled grenades, and mortars."[27] Estimates of the crowd size outside the occupation headquarters that day ranged from seven hundred to more than two thousand.

Regardless of how it started, once the shooting began, Blackwater's men, the Salvadorans, and Corporal Young were unloading clip after clip, firing thousands of rounds and hundreds of 40 mm grenades into the crowd.[28] They fired so many rounds that some of them had to stop shooting every fifteen minutes to let their gun barrels cool.[29] Sadr's men responded with rocket-propelled grenades and AK-47s.[30] Shadid reported, "At one point, witnesses saw a vehicle carrying four Salvadoran soldiers caught outside the gate. Demonstrators overwhelmed the terrified occupants, seizing and executing one prisoner on the spot by putting a grenade in his mouth and pulling the pin. Two of the other soldiers, their faces bruised from recent beatings, were [later] seen being led by armed men into the mosque."[31]

In the midst of the fighting, several active-duty military police officers joined the force on the roof being managed by Blackwater's men. During the battle, which would rage on for nearly four hours, a Blackwater contractor began videotaping the action. That video would make it onto the Internet and provide remarkable historical documentation of the events of April 4, 2004.[32] The home video opens with a deafening barrage of outgoing gunfire, as Blackwater's men, Corporal Young, and at least two other soldiers dressed in camouflage fire round after round. "You're aiming too high buddy," one contractor yells at the soldiers.

"You see a guy on the ground?" the voice yells. "RPG!"

"Where?"

"Right in front of the truck, right on the wall!"

Boom boom, rat-a-tat-tat. Explosive gunfire rips for thirty seconds. "Got more ammo?" someone yells. Then: "The truck's empty, the truck's empty."

The shooting stops as the men assess the situation below them. "Hold what you got, hold what you got right there," a voice commands. "Just scan your sectors. Scan your sectors. Who needs ammo?"

"We got mags, we got mags right here."

"Fuckin' niggers," says another voice as the men begin to reload their weapons. The camera then pans to what appears to be the cameraman—a goateed Blackwater contractor wearing sunglasses—who looks into the camera and smiles. As the camera pans back to the action, he quips laughingly, "What the fuck?" The camera then turns to a man who appears to be a U.S. soldier, and the cameraman asks him about his weapon, "That shit fuckin' hot, dude?"

"I spent all this time [unintelligible] in the fucking Marine Corps—never fired a weapon," the soldier replies. Another voice yells, "Mark your target!"

Men who appear to be Salvadoran troops can also be seen on the roof; a Blackwater contractor wearing a blue T-shirt and a baseball cap apparently instructs one Salvadoran on how to position the heavy weapon. "Hang tight, hang tight, hang tight," says another goateed man wielding a machine gun and wearing a T-shirt, bulletproof vest, and a blue baseball cap.

"Hey, all these fuckers right here," says another voice.

"Yeah, Mahdi ass!"

With that, the heavy firing once again begins as the men unload from the rooftop. Along with machine-gun fire, there is the methodical boom, boom, boom from heavier weapons. "Hey, get some!" someone yells as the deafening rip of gunfire explodes over Najaf. One of the Blackwater men appears to be directing three camouflaged soldiers firing from the roof.

As the battle raged on, Iraqi snipers hit a total of three of the men protecting the occupation headquarters. According to Young, a Blackwater contractor got hit and blood spurted five feet out from his face. "I could see a quarter-sized hole in his jaw," Corporal Young remembered. "By this time, the guy had lost about a pint of blood. I tried to press on the wound and stop the bleeding that way, but the blood was squirting out between my fingers." Young said he reached into the wound and pinched the man's carotid artery closed. He then picked him up and got him to Blackwater's medic before returning to his rooftop post. A picture taken that day shows Young on the rooftop aiming his SAW at the crowd with heavily armed Blackwater men in sunglasses positioned directly behind him and alongside him. "I gazed over the streets with straining eyes, only to see hundreds of dead Iraqis lying all over the ground," Young said. "It was an unbelievable sight; even though there were so many lying dead, the Iraqis were still running towards the front gate. I opened fire once again. Emptying magazine after magazine, I watched the people dressed in white and black robes drop to the ground as my sights passed by them. All I could think about at that time was that I had to either kill or be killed. It felt as if we were losing ground. In many senses we were, but that feeling just made me fight harder."

Blackwater later said that throughout the battle, its men tried to make contact with U.S. military commanders but were unsuccessful. A senior Blackwater executive, Patrick Toohey, told the *New York Times* that at one point the crowd was moving in fast on the compound, and Blackwater's men "were down to single digits of ammo, less than 10 rounds a man."[33] The besieged men eventually contacted Blackwater's headquarters in Baghdad. Within moments, Paul Bremer's staff gave the go-ahead for Blackwater to send in three company helicopters—known as "Ass Monkeys," the very ones used for Bremer's security—to deliver more ammunition.[34] The helicopter crews also rescued Corporal Young after he was wounded.[35] "We ran outside and I saw three Blackwater helicopters sitting there," Young recalled. "I ran to the farthest helicopter and got inside the front passenger seat. I felt very nervous as we took off from the ground. I didn't have any body armor at all, nor did I have a weapon. I looked all around the base and saw that everybody was firing their weapons. . . . I felt almost helpless sitting there." In the end, the Blackwater helicopter transported the Marine to safety. "It was OK with [Bremer] if they went out and saved some American lives," said Toohey.[36]

In another video filmed on the CPA roof in Najaf, Blackwater helicopters can be seen dropping off supplies.[37] The video then cuts to a closeup of what appears to be a Blackwater contractor aiming a large sniper-style weapon. "He slipped into a building," a man says off camera. "Guy on the wall runnin'?" asks the sniper. Before the man off camera says, "Yep," the sniper calmly pulls the trigger. Three shots ring out. He reloads his clip.

"We got a group of three. They're all runnin' now," says the man off camera. "Wow, we've got lots of—see the guy in white? He's goin' too fast—now they're haulin' ass." The sniper adjusts his scope. "We got a big group comin'. On the wall, squeezin' off," he calmly announces. Three more shots are fired off. "Wow, you got a whole group of 'em," says the man off camera, who appears to be acting as a spotter.

Another shot.

"We got a bunch of bad guys at twelve o'clock, 800 meters," says the man off camera into his walkie-talkie. "We've got about fifteen of 'em on the run up here." The spotter is asked for the location of the "bad guys" from a voice on the other end as the sniper continues firing. It was unnecessary, though. "Negative," he replies. "He cleaned 'em all out."

A short while later, the sniper indicates that U.S. forces have joined the battle, dropping a Joint Direct Attack Munition (JDAM)—a GPS-controlled air-to-surface missile, sometimes referred to as a "smart bomb"—in the vicinity. The sniper asks his colleague, "Who dropped the JDAM?"

"Marines."

"Yeah," the sniper says. "We were flyin' in right as that JDAM was hittin'." The sniper's reference to "flyin' in" as the JDAM missile was hitting indicates that in addition to ammunition, Blackwater also deployed more of its men to Najaf during the fighting.

"Another car haulin' ass out—blue Mercedes," the sniper says, firing a shot. "OK, I hit the car right in front of him." Another shot. The video then cuts to bursts of shooting and then back to the sniper again. "That guy with a green flag?" he asks. "Yeah. There you go," says his partner. A shot rings out. "That's Mahdi Army. Green flag is Mahdi Army—they're to be engaged at any opportunity." Three more shots. "OK, you see the road that goes straight out like that? That road right there?" asks the spotter.

"Yeah."

"Follow it out—straight out—about 800 meters," he instructs the sniper. As the sniper reloads, his partner exclaims, "Holy shit—look at all them fuckers." Then to the sniper: "All right, you're on 'em." The sniper begins picking people off. "You guys are dead on," says the spotter. Three more shots. As he shoots, the sniper declares, "Jesus Christ, it's like a fucking turkey shoot." Two more shots. "They're taking cover," says the spotter. Another shot. The Blackwater men then say they are receiving return fire and begin accelerating their firing pace. The video then cuts to a scene of heavy outgoing fire. "Smoke that motherfucker when he comes around the corner! Hit him now!" someone yells. Rat-a-tat-a-tat-a-tat.

Blackwater contractor Ben Thomas— the man who admitted to killing an Iraqi with the unapproved "blended metal" bullets in September 2003[38]— said he was on the roof in Najaf that day. Two years after the Najaf shootout, when the home videos had circulated widely around the Internet, Thomas lashed out at critics of the conduct of the Blackwater forces that day. "You wanna know what its like to be shoulder to shoulder with 8 teamates while 1,200 Mahdi troops hit the wire at 300 meters on three flanks? And then criticize the actions of my teamates based on a grainy video?" [sic] Thomas wrote in a posting on a private military contractor Web forum to which he is a frequent contributor.[39] "My seven teamates and our EL Salvadorian [SFODA] who fought with us are the only people who saw what happend. War is chronicaled and studied. Najaf is just another small battle in history but for us it was a place of alot of killing and dying. Its not a light dinner topic" [sic].[40] As for the man on the tape heard using the word "nigger," Thomas wrote: "My Teamate who had never been in direct combat and rarely swore can be heard making a racial slur. This is not his character. Its a man who has just killed 17 enemy troops who had slipped to within 70 meters of our Alamo. When my friend stopped the advance cold, alone and under direct fire, the worst word his mind could muster to yell at the dead bastards was 'nigger'. When he saw the video he cried. He isnt a racist. What you hear is a man terrified and victorious. But you dont see that in the video"[41] [sic].

Eventually, U.S. Special Forces moved into Najaf and the crowd was dispersed.[42] At the end of the battle, an unknown number of Iraqis were dead in the streets. According to Corporal Young, it was "hundreds." Other estimates put it at twenty to thirty dead with two hundred wounded.[43] Because Blackwater was guarding the building and coordinating its defense, there are no official military reports on how the incident started.[44] Blackwater admitted that its men fired thousands of rounds into the crowd, but vice president Patrick Toohey told the New York Times his men "fought and engaged every combatant with precise fire." Then, according to the Times, Toohey "insisted that his men had not been engaged in combat at all. 'We were conducting a security operation,' he said. 'The line,' he finally said, 'is getting blurred.'" At the end of one of the home videos of the Najaf battle, Iraqis are shown loaded on the back of a truck with hoods over their heads and plastic cuffs binding their hands. One of the men appears to be crying under his hood as he clutches his forehead.

What was clear from the video and from Corporal Young's recollections of that day was that Blackwater was running the operation, even giving orders to an active-duty U.S. Marine on when to open fire. "When there are rounds firing, coming at you from down range, everybody pulls together to do what needs to be done," said Blackwater's Chris Taylor. He praised Corporal Young after hearing how the Marine resupplied the ammunition of the Blackwater contractors on the roof. "He should be proud of the way he acted," Taylor said.[45] By afternoon, the top U.S. commander in Iraq, Lt. Gen. Ricardo Sanchez, and his deputy, Brig. Gen. Mark Kimmitt, had arrived on the scene. When Kimmitt later spoke about the battle, he did not mention Blackwater by name but praised the operation its men led. "I know on a rooftop yesterday in An Najaf, with a small group of American soldiers and coalition soldiers . . . who had just been through about three and a half hours of combat, I looked in their eyes, there was no crisis. They knew what they were here for," Kimmitt said. "They'd lost three wounded. We were sitting there among the bullet shells—the bullet casings—and, frankly, the blood of their comrades, and they were absolutely confident. They were confident for three reasons: one, because they're enormously well trained; two, because they're extremely good at what they're doing; and three, because they knew why they were there."[46] Blackwater's Toohey, acknowledging the growing use of private military contractors, concluded, "This is a whole new issue in military affairs. Think about it. You're actually contracting civilians to do military-like duties."[47]

To the Iraqis, particularly Sadr's followers, April 4 is remembered as a massacre in one of the holiest cities of Shiite Islam—indeed, clerics were among the casualties that day.[48] To the Blackwater men and Corporal Young, it was a day when—against all odds—they fended off hordes of angry, armed militia members intent on killing them and overtaking a building they were tasked by their government with protecting. "I thought, 'This is my last day. I'm going out with a bang,'" Corporal Young later told the *Virginian-Pilot*. "If I had to die it would be defending my country."[49] While scores of Iraqis were killed and Blackwater retained control of the CPA building, the battle emboldened Sadr's forces and supporters. By that afternoon "the loudspeakers of the Kufa mosque announced that the Mahdi Army held Kufa, Najaf, Nasiriyah and Sadr City, Baghdad's teeming Shiite slum," according to the *Washington Post*. "The checkpoint controlling access to the bridge into Kufa and Najaf was staffed by young militiamen. Many Iraqi police officers, paid and trained by the U.S.-led coalition, had joined the assault on its quarters."[50] That afternoon, Paul Bremer announced that he had appointed new Iraqi defense and intelligence ministers. In making the announcement, Bremer addressed the fight in Najaf. "This morning, a group of people in Najaf have crossed the line, and they have moved to violence," Bremer declared. "This will not be tolerated."[51]

Just before the sun set over Najaf, Muqtada al-Sadr issued a public call for an end to all protests, instead exhorting his followers to rise up. "Terrorize your enemy," he said. "God will reward you well for what pleases him. . . . It is not possible to remain silent in front of their abuse."[52] That night U.S. forces began moving into the Sadr City section of Baghdad. A U.S. military spokesman said U.S. fighter jets and helicopter gunships were striking back in response to the Najaf clash, and Reuters television footage showed images of tanks crushing civilian cars in the neighborhood.[53] As word spread of Sadr's orders, his followers carried out ambushes against U.S. forces, including in Sadr City, where Cindy Sheehan's son, Casey—a Specialist in the U.S. Army—was killed that day.[54] In all, eight U.S. soldiers died in Sadr City April 4 and fifty were wounded, along with an unknown number of Iraqis.[55] Maj. Gen. Martin Dempsey, commander of the First Armored Division, would later call the fighting in Sadr City that day "the biggest gunfight since the fall of Baghdad a year ago."[56] Ultimately, Sadr's followers staged uprisings in at least eight cities across Iraq.

On Monday, April 5, Paul Bremer officially labeled Muqtada al-Sadr an outlaw. "He is attempting to establish his authority in the place of the legitimate authority," Bremer declared. "We will not tolerate this. We will reassert the law and order which the Iraqi people expect."[57] Hours later, occupation authorities announced that there was a warrant for Sadr's arrest.[58] It would prove to be a disastrous decision that would boost Sadr's status tremendously. Along with the situation in Fallujah, the crackdown on Sadr would also briefly unite Shiites and Sunnis in a guerrilla war against the occupation.

Back in the United States, a debate was beginning to rage about the increasing use of private contractors—a development due in no small part to Blackwater's involvement in Fallujah and Najaf. In an unsigned editorial, the *New York Times* referred to the Fallujah ambush as evidence of "America's troubling reliance on hired guns" and the Najaf firefight as an indication that the "Pentagon seems to be outsourcing at least part of its core responsibilities for securing Iraq instead of facing up to the need for more soldiers."[59] The *Times* editorial said, "Defense Secretary Donald Rumsfeld has pledged that the Pentagon will keep looking for ways to 'outsource and privatize.' When it comes to core security and combat roles, this is ill advised. The Pentagon should be recruiting and training more soldiers, rather than running the risk of creating a new breed of mercenaries."[60] Amid mounting criticism of the use of private soldiers, Blackwater was lionized in some circles, particularly the Republican Congressional leadership. If there had been any question before, it was now clear that Blackwater was a major player in the war. The night of the Najaf firefight, hundreds of miles to the northwest, more than a thousand U.S. Marines had Fallujah surrounded and were preparing to exact revenge for the killing of the four Blackwater contractors five days earlier.

CHAPTER TEN

"THIS IS FOR THE AMERICANS OF BLACKWATER"

EVEN AS a Shiite rebellion spread across Iraq, the White House remained determined to crush Sunni Fallujah. The Blackwater ambush had provided the administration—enthusiastically encouraged by Paul Bremer in Baghdad—with the ideal pretext to launch a massive assault on a population that was fast becoming a potent symbol suggesting that the United States and its Iraqi proxies were not really in control of the country. To back down in the face of the boldest insurrection to date among antioccupation Sunnis and Shiites and talk of a Mogadishu redux, the administration reasoned, would have sent the message that the United States was losing a war that President Bush had already declared a "mission accomplished." Bremer and the administration had calculated that in "pacifying" Sunni Fallujah and making an example of the Shiite leader Muqtada al-Sadr, they could surgically

eliminate organized resistance in Iraq. While Washington's disastrous policies resulted in the deaths of thousands of Iraqis and hundreds of U.S. soldiers, they simultaneously facilitated an extraordinary business opportunity
for Blackwater and its mercenary friends (which will be discussed in depth
later in this book).

The first U.S. siege of Fallujah began on April 4, 2004, the day of the
Blackwater firefight at Najaf. It was code-named Operation Vigilant Resolve.
That night, more than a thousand Marines and two Iraqi battalions
surrounded Fallujah, a city of about 350,000 people. U.S. forces positioned
tanks, heavy machine guns, and armored Humvees at the major routes
running in and out of the city. They set up blockades with concertina wire,
effectively locking people in, and Marines set up "camps" for detainees.[1]
American forces commandeered the local radio station and began propaganda broadcasts telling people to cooperate with U.S. forces and to identify
resistance fighters and positions. Iraqi police distributed leaflets to mosques
in Fallujah announcing a weapons ban and a mandatory curfew from 7 p.m.
to 6 a.m.[2] and passed out "Wanted" posters featuring pictures of men alleged
to have been involved with the Blackwater attack.[3] On the city's outskirts,
the Marines dug trenches near a Muslim cemetery as sharpshooters took up
positions on the roof of a mosque.[4] "The city is surrounded," Lt. James
Vanzant of the First Marine Expeditionary Force told reporters. "We are
looking for the bad guys in town."[5] U.S. commanders announced their
intent to conduct house-to-house raids inside Fallujah to find the killers of
the four Blackwater contractors. "Those people are specially targeted to be
captured or killed," said Marine spokesman Lt. Eric Knapp.[6] U.S. commanders sent their Iraqi proxies into the city to instruct Fallujans not to
resist when U.S. forces entered their homes and to gather everyone in one
room during a raid.[7] If they wanted to speak with the invading troops, they
must first raise their hands.[8] Thousands of Fallujans fled the city ahead of
the imminent American onslaught.

The next morning, the U.S. forces made their first incursions into Fallujah—
first sending in special operators to hunt "high value targets." Then came the

full-on assault carried out by twenty-five hundred Marines from three battalions, backed up by tanks.[9] U.S. forces soon found themselves in fierce gun battles with resistance fighters. As the fighting raged on, the Marines called in for air support. On April 7, an AH-1W Cobra attack helicopter attacked the Abdel-Aziz al-Samarrai mosque compound, which the U.S. said was housing resistance fighters who were attacking the invading forces.[10] A Hellfire missile was launched at the base of the mosque's minaret.[11] Eventually, an F-16 warplane swooped in and dropped a five-hundred-pound bomb on the mosque compound,[12] an alleged violation of the Geneva Convention that prohibits the targeting of religious sites. The Marines issued a statement defending the attack, saying that because resistance fighters were inside it, "the mosque lost its protected status and therefore became a lawful military target."[13] Witnesses reported that as many as forty Iraqis were killed in the mosque attack,[14] while a handful of American soldiers died in the fighting that day.

Meanwhile, the military had seized Fallujah's main medical facility, preventing its use in treating the wounded.[15] "U.S. forces bombed the power plant at the beginning of the assault," recalled journalist Rahul Mahajan, one of the few unembedded journalists to enter Fallujah at the time. "[F]or the next several weeks, Fallujah was a blacked-out town, with light provided by generators only in critical places like mosques and clinics."[16] Food supplies were running out in the city, and a local doctor said that sixteen children and eight women had been killed in an air strike on a neighborhood on April 6.[17] The siege of Fallujah was under way. "We are solidly ensconced in the city, and my units are stiffening their grip," said Marine commander Lt. Col. Brennan Byrne.[18] If anyone resists, he said, "We will break their backs. We will drive them out."[19] Fallujah, Byrne said, had become a haven for resistance fighters and smugglers because "No one ever took the time to clean it out properly."[20] Byrne's battalion "was the first to persuade the U.S. Army Psychological warfare teams to initiate scatological warfare," recalled Bing West, a military author who was embedded with U.S. forces around Fallujah.[21] Platoons "competed to dream up the filthiest insults for translators to scream over the loudspeakers. When enraged Iraqis rushed from a mosque blindly firing their AKs, the Marines shot them down. The tactic of insult-and-shoot spread along the lines. Soon the Marines were mocking the city as 'Lalafallujah' (after the popular stateside concert Lollapalooza) and cranking out 'Welcome to the Jungle' by Guns 'n' Roses and 'Hell's Bells' by AC/DC."[22]

As images from inside Fallujah emerged, primarily via journalists from Arab television networks, portraying a dire humanitarian crisis in the city, protests began spreading across Iraq, with U.S. forces using violence in an effort to shut them down.[23] Mosques in Baghdad and elsewhere began organizing humanitarian convoys to Fallujah and stockpiling blood.[24] By April 8, local hospital officials inside the city painted a horrifying picture of the human suffering, saying that upwards of 280 civilians had been killed and more than 400 wounded.[25] "We also know of dead and wounded in various places buried under the rubble but we cannot reach them because of the fighting," said Dr. Taher al-Issawi.[26] The U.S. military denied it was killing civilians and accused resistance fighters of trying to blend into the broader population. "It is hard to differentiate between people who are insurgents or civilians," said Maj. Larry Kaifesh. "It is hard to get an honest picture. You just have to go with your gut feeling."[27]

Byrne, according to the *Washington Post*, "said any bodies were those of insurgents. He estimated that 80 percent of Fallujah's populace was neutral or in favor of the American military presence."[28] That optimistic pronouncement, however, did not match the ferocity of the resistance that succeeded—at an incredible human cost—in keeping the United States from totally capturing control of the city. "The enemy was better prepared than the Marines had been told to expect," wrote veteran *Washington Post* reporter Thomas Ricks.[29] He cited an internal Marine summary of the battle. "Insurgents surprise U.S. with coordination of their attacks: coordinated, combined, volley-fire RPGs, effective use of indirect fire," the summary stated. "Enemy maneuvered effectively and stood and fought."[30]

As the siege neared a week, bodies began piling up in the city and, according to witnesses, a stench of death spread across Fallujah. "Nothing could have prepared me for what I saw in Fallujah," recalled a doctor from Baghdad who made it into the city with a peace delegation. "There is no law on earth that can justify what the Americans have done to innocent people."[31] Independent U.S. journalists Dahr Jamail and Rahul Mahajan, meanwhile, managed to make it into Fallujah—unembedded—a week after the siege began. Upon entering the city with a humanitarian convoy, Jamail described the scene at a makeshift emergency room at a small health clinic. "As I was there, an endless stream of women and children who'd been sniped by the Americans were being raced into the dirty clinic, the cars speeding over the curb out front as their wailing family members carried them in. One woman and small child had been shot through the neck," Jamail wrote in a dispatch from inside the besieged city. "The small child, his eyes glazed and staring into space, continually vomited as the doctors raced to save his life. After 30 minutes, it appeared as though neither of them would survive."[32] Jamail said he saw one victim after another brought into the clinic, "nearly all of them women and children." [33] Jamail called Fallujah "Sarajevo on the Euphrates."[34]

Mahajan, meanwhile, reported: "In addition to the artillery and the warplanes dropping 500, 1000, and 2000-pound bombs, and the murderous AC-130 Spectre gunships that can demolish a whole city block in less than a minute, the Marines had snipers criss-crossing the whole town. For weeks, Fallujah was a series of sometimes mutually inaccessible pockets, divided by the no-man's-lands of sniper fire paths. Snipers fired indiscriminately, usually at whatever moved. Of 20 people I saw come into the clinic I observed in a few hours, only five were 'military-age males.' I saw old women, old men, a child of 10 shot through the head; terminal, the doctors told me, although in Baghdad they might have been able to save him. One thing that snipers were very discriminating about—every single ambulance I saw had bullet holes in it. Two I inspected bore clear evidence of specific, deliberate sniping. Friends of mine who went out to gather in wounded people were shot at."[35] Jamail reported that "the residents have turned two football fields into graveyards."[36]

The War on Al Jazeera

While most of the world came to understand the siege of Fallujah as an earth-moving development in the occupation, the story of the extent of the human suffering endured by Iraqis was downplayed in the "mainstream" U.S. press. Embedded corporate journalists reported exclusively from the vantage point of the invading U.S. forces and relied disproportionately on military spokespeople and their Iraqi proxies. The graphic verbiage that had peppered the media landscape following the ambush and killing of the Blackwater men days earlier was now absent from the reporting on the civilian consequences of the assault. As battles continued to rage on and spread to the outskirts of Fallujah, *New York Times* correspondent Jeffrey Gettleman—totally avoiding mention of the humanitarian disaster—wrote that the fierce fighting "showed not only the intensity of the resistance but an *acute willingness among insurgents to die*."[37] [Emphasis added.] Coming alongside U.S. military claims that "90 to 95 percent" of Iraqis killed in Fallujah were combatants,[38] such embedded reporting from the U.S. "paper of record" appeared almost indistinguishable from official U.S. military propaganda. "It's their Super Bowl," Maj. T. V. Johnson, a Marine spokesman, was quoted as saying in Gettleman's story. "Falluja is the place to go if you want to kill Americans."[39]

But while the embedded U.S. press focused on the "urban warfare" story, unembedded Arab journalists—most prominently from the popular Al Jazeera network—were reporting around the clock from inside the besieged city. Their reports painted a vivid picture of the civilian devastation and gave lie to U.S. commanders' pronouncements about precision strikes. Al Jazeera and Al Arabiya broadcast images of corpses in the streets and destruction of the city's infrastructure. In fact, when Brig. Gen. Mark Kimmitt was doing a phone interview on Al Jazeera, insisting the United States was observing a cease-fire, the network simultaneously aired live images of continued raids by U.S. fighter jets on residential neighborhoods inside Fallujah.[40] The images Al Jazeera's cameras captured in Fallujah were not only being broadcast widely in the Arab world but also on

TV networks across the globe. Veteran Al Jazeera journalist Ahmed Mansour and cameraman Laith Mushtaq had entered Fallujah on April 3 and were the primary source of footage of the civilian devastation in the city. They regularly filmed scenes of women and children killed by the U.S. offensive—in one case broadcasting a story about an entire family in the al Jolan neighborhood who had allegedly been killed in a U.S. airstrike. "The planes bombed this house, as they did for the whole neighborhood, and they brought the corpses and bodies to the hospital," Mushtaq recalled. "I went to the hospital. I could not see anything but, like, a sea of corpses of children and women, and mostly children, because peasants and farmers have usually a lot of children. So these were scenes that are unbelievable, unimaginable. I was taking photographs and forcing myself to photograph, while I was at the same time crying."[41]

Mansour, who is one of Al Jazeera's best-known personalities, said he realized early on that there were only a handful of journalists inside the city and believed he had a responsibility to remain in Fallujah, despite the enormous risk. "I wanted to report this reality to the whole world. I wanted the whole world to know what's happening to those besieged people. I wasn't thinking about leaving the city at all. I decided to stay and let my destiny be as those of people. If they die, I'll be with them; if they escape, I'll be with them. I decided not to think about any possibilities, what the U.S. forces will do with me if they catch me, and not to think about my family or anything. I only think about those people."[42] In the midst of the siege, Mansour reported live from Fallujah, "Last night we were targeted by some tanks, twice . . . but we escaped. The U.S. wants us out of Fallujah, but we will stay."[43] Despite its firm grip on embedded U.S. correspondents, Washington was losing the global propaganda war—so U.S. officials attacked the messenger. On April 9, Washington demanded that Al Jazeera leave Fallujah as a condition for a cease-fire.[44] The network refused. Mansour wrote that the next day "American fighter jets fired around our new location, and they bombed the house where we had spent the night before, causing the death of the house owner Mr. Hussein Samir. Due to the serious threats we had to stop broadcasting for a few days because every time we tried to broadcast the fighter jets spotted us [and] we became under their fire."[45]

On April 12, Kimmitt, facing questions about the footage being shown on Al Jazeera depicting a civilian catastrophe in Fallujah, called on people to "Change the channel. Change the channel to a legitimate, authoritative, honest news station." Kimmitt declared, "The stations that are showing Americans intentionally killing women and children are not legitimate news sources. That is propaganda, and that is lies."[46] Dan Senor, Bremer's senior adviser, asserted that Al Jazeera and Al Arabiya "are misreporting facts on the ground and contributing to a sense of anger and frustration that possibly should be directed at individuals and organizations inside of Fallujah that mutilate Americans and slaughter other Iraqis rather than at the Coalition."[47] On April 15 Defense Secretary Donald Rumsfeld echoed those remarks in still harsher terms, calling Al Jazeera's reporting "vicious, inaccurate and inexcusable."[48] A reporter asked Rumsfeld if the United States had a "civilian casualty" count. "Of course not," Rumsfeld shot back. "We're not in the city. But you know what our forces do; they don't go around killing hundreds of civilians. . . . It's disgraceful what that station is doing."[49] It was the very next day, according to a British government memo stamped "Top Secret" reported on in Britain's *Daily Mirror*, that President Bush allegedly told British Prime Minister Tony Blair of his desire to bomb Al Jazeera.[50] "He made clear he wanted to bomb al-Jazeera in Qatar and elsewhere," a source told the *Mirror*. "There's no doubt what Bush wanted to do."[51] Ahmed Mansour said he believed that what Al Jazeera was providing in its reports from inside Fallujah was balance to a story that otherwise was being told exclusively from the vantage point of embedded correspondents and U.S. military spokespeople. "Is it professionalism that the journalists wear U.S. [military] clothing and they go with them in the planes and tanks to cover this and report this?" Mansour asked. "The battles have to be reported from both sides. We were among the civilians, and we reported, and they had embedded journalists with those who launched this attack from the U.S. forces who occupied Iraq, and they reported what they wanted. We were trying to create an equilibrium or a balance, so that the truth is not lost."[52]

Collective Punishment

The horrors unfolding in Fallujah, coupled with the U.S. failure to take control of the city and the bold resistance of Fallujah's residents, was encouraging other Iraqis to rise up. As the siege went on, people from across Iraq began coming to Fallujah to help in the defense of the city. "The battle of Fallujah is the battle of history, the battle of Iraq, the battle of the nation," Harth al-Dhari, of the Muslim Scholars Association, told thousands of worshipers at Friday prayers in the midst of the siege. "Merciful God, take revenge for spilled blood. Take revenge for slaughter. Send your army against the occupiers. Kill all of them. Don't spare any of them."[53] By the time what U.S. officials called a "cease-fire" had set in the weekend of April 9, some thirty Marines had been killed. But it was Iraqis who paid the highest price. After the weeklong U.S. siege, some six hundred were dead in Fallujah, among them "hundreds of women and children."[54] On April 13, President Bush delivered a prime-time address on national television in the United States "Terrorists from other countries have infiltrated Iraq to incite and organize attacks," Bush declared from the East Room of the White House. "The violence we have seen is a power grab by these extreme and ruthless elements . . . it's not a popular uprising."[55]

But half a world away, as thousands of Fallujans escaped their city and fled to other parts of Iraq, they brought with them tales of horror and civilian death that no amount of propaganda could combat. Despite U.S. rhetoric about liberating Fallujah from "foreign fighters" and Baathists, it was not lost on Iraqis that the stated justification for the destruction of Fallujah and the deaths of hundreds of people was the killing of four U.S. mercenaries— seen by most Iraqis as the real foreign fighters. "For only four individuals, the Americans killed children, women, elderly, and now a whole city is under siege?" asked Haitham Saha, while at a Baghdad dropoff point for humanitarian supplies to Fallujah.[56] "We know who the people were who killed the American contractors," a cleric at a local mosque told a reporter.

"But instead of negotiating with us, Bremer has decided to have his revenge."[57] Even members of the U.S.-installed Iraqi Governing Council expressed outrage. "These operations were a mass punishment," said Governing Council president Adnan Pachachi,[58] who three months earlier sat next to First Lady Laura Bush, as her special guest, at the State of the Union address in Washington, D.C.[59] "It was not right to punish all the people of Fallujah, and we consider these operations by the Americans unacceptable and illegal."[60]

As Vigilant Resolve continued to exact a deadly toll on the people of Fallujah, Iraqis in the U.S.-created security force began deserting their posts; some joined the resistance to the siege, attacking U.S. forces around the city. "In all, as many as one in four of the new Iraqi army, civil defense, police, and other security forces quit in those days, changed sides, or stopped working," according to Anthony Shadid.[61] When the United States attempted hastily to hand over "responsibility" for Fallujah to an Iraqi force, some 800 AK-47 assault rifles, twenty-seven pickup trucks, and fifty radios the Marines gave the brigade ended up in the hands of the resistance.[62] Lt. Gen. James Conway would later admit, "When we were told to attack Fallujah, I think we certainly increased the level of animosity that existed."[63] In the midst of a worsening public relations disaster for the United States, Kimmitt said, "I would argue that the collective punishment on the people of Fallujah is those terrorists, those cowards who hunker down inside mosques and hospitals and schools, and use the women and children as shields to hide against the Marines, who are just trying to bring liberation from those cowards inside the city of Fallujah."[64] For most of the world, though, it was the United States that was responsible for the "collective punishment"—a phrase in Arabic that evokes images of the Israeli policy against Palestine—of the people of Fallujah. In fact, those were the exact words that the UN envoy to Iraq, Lakhdar Brahimi, used when he declared, "Collective punishment is certainly unacceptable, and the siege of the city is absolutely unacceptable."[65] Brahimi asked, "When you surround a city, you bomb the city, when people cannot go to hospital, what name do you have for that?"[66]

In the end, perhaps as many as eight hundred Iraqis died as a result of the first of what would be several sieges of Fallujah.[67] Tens of thousands of civilians fled their homes, and the city was razed. And yet the United States failed to crush Fallujah. Far from asserting U.S. supremacy in Iraq, Fallujah demonstrated that guerrilla tactics were effective against the occupiers. "Fallujah, the small city at the heart of the Sunni Arab insurrection, was considered something of a hillbilly place by other Sunni in Iraq," wrote veteran Middle East correspondent Patrick Cockburn in a dispatch from Iraq in late April. "It was seen as Islamic, tribal and closely connected to the former regime. The number of guerrillas probably totaled no more than 400 out of a population of 300,000. But by assaulting a whole city, as if it was Verdun or Stalingrad, the US Marines have managed to turn it into a nationalist symbol."[68]

Testifying before Congress on April 20, Gen. Richard Myers, chair of the Joint Chiefs of Staff, defended the operation. "As you remember, we went in because of the atrocities on the Blackwater security personnel, the four personnel that were killed and later burned, and then hung on the bridge. We went in because we had to and to find the perpetrators. And what we found was a huge rat's nest, that is still festering today—needs to be dealt with."[69] The April siege of Fallujah would be followed a few months later, in November 2004, by an even greater onslaught that would bring hundreds more Iraqi deaths, force tens of thousands of people from their homes, and further enrage the country. In all, U.S. forces carried out nearly seven hundred airstrikes, damaging or destroying eighteen thousand of Fallujah's thirty-nine thousand buildings.[70] Approximately 150 U.S. soldiers were killed in the operations. Meanwhile, the "perpetrators" of the Blackwater ambush "were never found,"[71] as political and military officials had vowed, further underscoring the vengeful nature of the U.S. slaughter in Fallujah. The Marines renamed the infamous bridge "Blackwater Bridge," and someone wrote in English in black marker on one of its beams: "This is for the Americans of Blackwater that were murdered here in 2004, Semper Fidelis P.S. Fuck You."[72] Journalist Dahr Jamail later concluded, "[I]n April of 2004, as a city was invaded and its residents were fleeing, hiding, or being massacred, there was considerable public awareness in the United States of human beings whose bodies had been mutilated in Iraq, thanks to our news media. But among thousands of references to mutilation in that month alone, we have yet to find one related to anything that happened after March 31. . . . [M]utilation is something that happens to Blackwater-hired mercs and other professional, American killers, not to Iraqi babies with misplaced heads."[73]

CHAPTER ELEVEN

MR. PRINCE GOES TO WASHINGTON

BEFORE THE invasion of Iraq, when most people heard the term "civilian contractors," they didn't immediately conjure up images of men with guns and bulletproof vests riding around a hellhole in jeeps. They thought of construction workers. This was also true for the families of many private soldiers deployed in Iraq and Afghanistan. Their loved ones were not "civilian contractors," in their minds but were often thought of and referred to in family discussions as "Special Forces" or being "with the military." Their actual employer or title was irrelevant because what they were doing in Iraq or Afghanistan was what they had always done—they were fighting for their country. The parents of one Blackwater contractor killed in Iraq said it was their son's "deep sense of patriotism and his abiding Christian faith that led him to work in Iraq,"[1] a common sentiment in the private military community. So on March 31, 2004, when news began to reach the United States that four "civilian contractors" had been ambushed in Fallujah, several of the men's families didn't draw any kind of connection. After all, their loved ones were not civilians—they were military. In Ohio, Danica Zovko, Jerry's mother, heard the news on the radio that "American contractors" had been killed.[2] After she saw the images coming out of Fallujah, she actually wrote her son an e-mail, telling him to be careful: "They're killing people in Iraq just like Somalia."[3]

Katy Helvenston-Wettengel, Scott's mother, was working at her home office in Leesburg, Florida, with the television on behind her.[4] "I was sitting here at my desk, doing research, and I had CNN on in the background," she recalled. "And the noon news just all of a sudden caught my attention, and I looked over there and I saw this burning vehicle and I thought, 'Oh, my God.'" It didn't cross her mind at the time that the footage she was watching was her own son's gruesome death. "When they said contractors, I was thinking construction workers working on pipelines or something. I changed the channel because I thought, This is just getting insane, I can't watch this anymore." Helvenston-Wettengel went on with her work, but then she heard the men described on the news as "security contractors," which made her nervous. "I said, 'My God, Scotty is a security contractor, but he's not in Fallujah. He's protecting Paul Bremer in Baghdad,'" she recalled. "I called my other son, Jason, and he told me, 'Mom, you worry too much.'" Anyway, she reasoned, her son had just arrived in Iraq a few days earlier. "He wasn't even supposed to be on any missions," she said. Helvenston-Wettengel went out that afternoon to a meeting, and when she returned home at seven o'clock that night, her answering machine was blinking like crazy: eighteen new messages. "The first four were from Jason, saying, 'Mom, it was Blackwater. They were Blackwater guys that got ambushed.'" Helvenston-Wettengel called Blackwater headquarters and got a woman on the other line. "This is Katy Helvenston, Scotty's mom," she said. "Is Scotty all right?" The Blackwater representative said she didn't know. "It's been twelve hours!" Helvenston-Wettengel exclaimed. "What do you mean you don't know?" She said the Blackwater representative told her that the company was in the process of doing a sort of "reverse 911" with its contractors in the field in Iraq. "She said there were about 400 of them and that 250 had checked in. I asked if Scotty was one of those and the woman said, 'No.'" Helvenston-Wettengel said she called Blackwater back every hour, desperate for any information. In the meantime, she found Fallujah on a map and realized that it wasn't that far from Baghdad. By midnight, she knew in her heart that her son was dead. "Scotty had been so good about calling me and e-mailing me, and I kept thinking, He would have called me and let me know he was OK, because he knew how worried I was," she recalled. "I just knew it."

While the families began to absorb the shock and horror of what had happened to their loved ones in Fallujah, the world—including many elected officials in Washington—was getting a window into just how privatized the war had become and how entrenched private contractors, like the dead Blackwater men, now were in the occupation. In the 1991 Gulf War, one in sixty people deployed by the coalition were contractors. With the 2003 occupation, the ratio had swelled to one in three.[5] For Erik Prince, the Fallujah killings and the Najaf firefight provided an almost unthinkable opportunity—under the guise of doing damage control and briefings, Prince and his entourage would be able to meet with Washington's power brokers and sell them on Blackwater's vision of military privatization at the exact moment that those very senators and Congressmen were beginning to recognize the necessity of mercenaries in preserving the occupation of (and corporate profits in) Iraq. With timing that would have been impossible to create, Blackwater was thrust into the fortunate position of a drug rep offering a new painkiller to an ailing patient at the moment the worst pain was just kicking in.

Blackwater's Lobbyists

The day after the Fallujah ambush, Erik Prince turned to his longtime friend Paul Behrends, a partner at the powerful Republican lobbying firm

Alexander Strategy Group, founded by senior staffers of then–majority leader Tom DeLay.[6] Behrends, a U.S. Marine Corps Reserve lieutenant colonel, had been a senior national security adviser to California Republican Congressman Dana Rohrabacher, a onetime aide to President Reagan. Prince and Behrends had a long history—in 1990–1991, young Prince worked for Rohrabacher alongside Behrends.[7] That marked the beginning of a close political, business, and religious partnership between the two men that would only strengthen as Blackwater grew.

Behrends first officially registered as a lobbyist for Blackwater in May 1998 and began advocating for the company in areas ranging from disaster planning to foreign relations.[8] That month, Behrends's firm Boland & Madigan "delivered" Representative Rohrabacher and another "staunch defender" of the Second Amendment, Representative John Doolittle, to Prince's Moyock compound for Blackwater's grand opening—at the company's expense.[9]

While Prince—with Behrends's lobbying assistance—built up his Blackwater empire, Behrends was simultaneously becoming deeply involved in areas of U.S. foreign policy that would become front lines in the war on terror and areas of revenue for Blackwater. Among these was a high-stakes Big Oil scheme, led by petrol giant Unocal, to run a pipeline through Taliban-governed Afghanistan. Behrends worked as a lobbyist for Delta Oil, Unocal's partner in the scheme, pushing for the United States to officially recognize the Afghan government.[10] Prince and Behrends's former boss, Rohrabacher, had long been interested in Afghanistan, since his days working as a senior speechwriter in the Reagan White House, when the United States was aggressively backing the mujahedeen against the Soviet occupation of the country. Rohrabacher, known as a fan of various U.S.-backed "freedom fighters," traveled to Afghanistan in 1988, personally joining the mujahedeen in the fighting against the Soviet forces before being officially sworn into Congress.[11] It was not surprising when Blackwater became one of the first private military firms contracted to conduct operations inside Afghanistan after 9/11.

Prince and Behrends have long served together on the board of directors of Christian Freedom International, the evangelical missionary organization founded and run by veterans of the Reagan administration—several of them major players in the Iran-Contra scandal. Its founder and president, Jim Jacobson, cut his political teeth working under Erik Prince's friend and beneficiary Gary Bauer, when Bauer served as the head of President Reagan's Office of Policy Development. Jacobson also served in the George H. W. Bush administration. CFI passionately supported the Bush administration's war on terror, faulting the White House's wars in Iraq and Afghanistan only for not doing enough to defend Christians.

At the time of the Fallujah ambush, there were few lobbying firms with more influence on Capitol Hill than Alexander Strategy, a centerpiece of the GOP's "K Street Project," under which lobbyists raised "enormous sums of money from their clients to ensure that Republicans remain the majority in Congress. For this fealty, the leadership grants the lobbyists access to the decision-makers and provides legislative favors for their clients," according to the Congressional watchdog group Public Citizen.[12] Behrends and his associates wasted no time in going to work for Prince and Blackwater. "[Blackwater] did not go out looking for the publicity and did not ask for everything that happened to them," said Chris Bertelli, a spokesman for Alexander Strategy assigned to Blackwater after the Fallujah killings. "We want to do everything we can to educate [the media and Congress] about what Blackwater does."[13]

A week to the day after the ambush, Erik Prince was sitting down with at least four senior members of the Senate Armed Services Committee, including chairman John Warner.[14] Former Navy SEAL turned Blackwater executive Patrick Toohey accompanied Prince to his Congressional meetings,[15] as did Behrends. Senator Rick Santorum arranged the meeting, which included Warner and two other key Republican senators—Appropriations Committee chairman Ted Stevens of Alaska and Senator George Allen of Virginia.[16] This meeting followed an earlier series of face-to-faces Prince had with powerful House Republicans who oversaw military contracts. Among them: Tom DeLay, the House majority leader and Alexander Strategy's patron; Porter Goss, chairman of the House Intelligence Committee (and future CIA director); Duncan Hunter, chair of the House Armed Services Committee; and Representative Bill Young, chair of the House Appropriations Committee.[17] What was discussed at these meetings remains a secret, as neither Blackwater nor the Congressmen have discussed them publicly. But there was no question: the company's moment had arrived.

With well-connected ASG operatives steering the publicity-shy Erik Prince and other company executives around, Blackwater was positioning itself to cash in on its newfound fame, while staking out a key role in crafting the rules that would govern mercenaries on U.S. government contract.[18] "Because of the public events of March 31, [Blackwater's] visibility and need to communicate a consistent message has elevated here in Washington," said ASG's Bertelli. "There are now several federal regulations that apply to their activities, but they are generally broad in nature. One thing that's lacking is an industry standard. That's something we definitely want to be engaged in."[19] By May, Blackwater was reportedly "leading a lobbying effort by private security firms and other contractors to try to block congressional or Pentagon efforts to bring their companies and employees under the same justice code" as active-duty soldiers.[20] "The Uniform Code of Military Justice should not apply to civilians because you actually give up constitutional rights when you join the armed forces," Bertelli said. "You're subject to a different legal system than you are if you are a civilian."[21] (Two years later, despite Blackwater's efforts, language would be slipped into the 2007 defense-spending authorization that sought to place contractors under the UCMJ.) In June, Blackwater would be handed one of the U.S. government's most valuable international security contracts to protect diplomats and U.S. facilities. [22] At the same time, Blackwater was given its own protection, as Bremer granted a sweeping immunity for its operations in Iraq.[23]

But while Blackwater executives worked the GOP elite on the Hill, others in Congress began to question what the Blackwater men were even doing in

Iraq, not to mention Fallujah that day. A week after the ambush, thirteen Democratic senators, led by Jack Reed of Rhode Island, wrote to Donald Rumsfeld, calling on the Pentagon to release an "accurate tally" of the number of "privately armed" non-Iraqi personnel operating in Iraq. "These security contractors are armed and operate in a fashion that is hard to distinguish from military forces, especially special operations forces. However, these private security companies are not under military control and are not subject to the rules that guide the conduct of American military personnel," the senators wrote.[24] "It would be a dangerous precedent if the United States allowed the presence of private armies operating outside the control of governmental authority and beholden only to those who pay them." The senators asserted that security in a "hostile fire area is a classic military mission" and "delegating [it] to private contractors raises serious questions." Rumsfeld did not respond to the letter.[25] Instead, the Iraq reconstruction floodgates opened wide and mercenary contracts poured out. As the *New York Times* bluntly put it, "The combination of a deadly insurgency and billions of dollars in aid money has unleashed powerful market forces in the war zone. New security companies aggressively compete for lucrative contracts in a frenzy of deal making."[26]

Two weeks after the Fallujah killings, Blackwater announced plans to build a massive new facility—a twenty-eight-thousand-square-foot administrative building—on its Moyock property for its operations.[27] The finished product would be sixty-four-thousand square feet, more than twice the originally projected size.[28] It was a major development for Blackwater, which had been denied permission for the project for six years because of objections by the local government. In the days after the ambush, county officials worked to amend local ordinances for Blackwater's expansion. With the new permissions, Blackwater was given the green light to build and operate firearms ranges and parachute landing zones, and to conduct explosives training as well as training in hand-to-hand combat, incendiary-type weapons, and automatic assault weapons.[29] "It will be our international headquarters," said company president Gary Jackson.[30]

Meanwhile, just two weeks after the Fallujah killings, Blackwater issued a press release announcing that it would be hosting the first-ever "World SWAT Conference and Challenge." The release declared, "Never before in the history of the world has there been such a need for men and women who can respond effectively to our most critical incidents. Blackwater USA, the world's largest firearms and tactical training facility, has put together a conference to meet that need that is unlike any other before it."[31] It boasted of workshops on a number of subjects, including "resolving hostage situations, suicide bomber profiling, and the psychology of operating and surviving critical incidents."[32] After the conference portion, there would be a SWAT Olympics, where teams from across the United States and Canada would compete in a series of events televised by ESPN. At the event's press conference, Gary Jackson refused to answer any questions about the Fallujah ambush, steering all discussion back to the SWAT challenge.[33] The only mention of Fallujah came during the chaplain's blessing of the event. "This is almost a vacation compared to what a regular week looks like," Jackson told reporters at the opening of the games.[34]

At the conference, retired Army Lt. Col. David Grossman, author of the book *On Killing* and founder of the Killology Research Group, addressed participants in a hotel ballroom, pacing around with a microphone.[35] He spoke of a "new Dark Age" full of Al Qaeda terrorism and school shootings. "The bad guys are coming with rifles and body armor!" he declared. "They will destroy our way of life in one day!" The world, Grossman said, is full of sheep, and it was the duty of warriors—the kind of men assembled at the Blackwater conference—to protect them from the wolves. "Embrace the warrior spirit!" he shouted. "We need warriors who embrace that dirty, nasty four-letter word *kill*!" Meanwhile, Gary Jackson sent out an e-mail to the Blackwater listserv encouraging people not to miss the "fantastic" dinner speaker at the challenge, one of the most experienced spies in recent U.S. history, J. Cofer Black, at the time the State Department's head of counterterrorism.[36] In the aftermath of 9/11, as head of the CIA's counterterrorism division, Black had led the administration's hunt for bin Laden. A year after the Fallujah ambush, he would join Blackwater as the company's vice chairman—one of several former senior officials the company would hire in building up its empire and influence.

As Blackwater plotted its tremendous expansion at home, it emerged as the mercenary industry trendsetter. "Increased violence this month has thrown a spotlight on the small army of private US security firms operating as paramilitaries in Iraq under Pentagon contracts," reported *PR Week*, a public relations trade journal.[37] "As calls for greater regulation over these companies increase, [they] are ramping up their presence in Washington to make their voices heard. . . . At the forefront is Blackwater USA, the North Carolina firm that lost four employees after an attack in Fallujah on March 31." After Blackwater started using well-connected ASG lobbyists to promote its services, other mercenary firms followed suit. All seemed to realize that the mercenary gold rush was on. The California-based Steele Foundation, one of the earliest private security companies to deploy in Iraq, hired former Ambassador Robert Frowick, a major player in the Balkans conflicts, on April 13, 2004, to help manage "strategic government relationships" in Washington.[38] Meanwhile, the London-based mercenary provider Global Risk Strategies rented office space in D.C. that month to base its own lobbying operations. "We are fully aware that D.C. operates in a totally different manner," said Global executive Charlie Andrews. "What we need to assist our company is a hand-holding organization basically who will guide us through procedures and D.C. protocols."[39] In the midst of the flurry of lobbying activity by private military companies, Senator Warner told the *New York Times* his view of the mercenaries. "I refer to them as our silent partner in this struggle," he said.[40]

The day after Erik Prince met with Warner and the other Republican senators, his new ASG spokesman, Chris Bertelli, boasted about a considerable spike in applications from ex-soldiers to work for Blackwater. "They're angry," Bertelli said, "and they're saying, 'Let me go over.'"[41] Bertelli said that with the graphic images of the Fallujah ambush, "it's natural to assume that the visibility of the dangers could drive up salaries for the folks who have to stand in the path of the bullets."[42] By late April, the

New York Times was reporting, "[S]ome military leaders are openly grumbling that the lure of $500 to $1,500 a day is siphoning away some of their most experienced Special Operations people at the very time their services are most in demand."[43]

In Iraq the situation was fast deteriorating. On April 13, in a dispatch from Baghdad, British war correspondents Robert Fisk and Patrick Cockburn reported, "At least 80 foreign mercenaries—security guards recruited from the United States, Europe and South Africa and working for American companies—have been killed in the past eight days in Iraq."[44] The violence rocking the country had brought "much of the reconstruction work" to a halt and contractors were being killed or abducted in record numbers.[45] Nearly fifty were kidnapped in the month after the March 31 Blackwater ambush.[46] The targeting of foreign contractors (brought in to support Washington's occupation and reconstruction operations), aid workers, and journalists would provide a major source of funding for the very forces fighting the United States in Iraq. Though the United States has an official policy of not paying ransoms, a classified U.S. government report estimated that resistance groups were taking in as much as $36 million annually from ransom payments.[47] In April 2004, Russia withdrew some eight hundred civilian workers from Iraq[48] and Germany followed suit,[49] while a senior Iraqi official said that month more than fifteen hundred foreign contractors had left the country.[50] As *Fortune* magazine reported, "[T]he upsurge in violence comes just as the government is awarding $10 billion in new contracts, and companies like Halliburton and Bechtel are trying to increase their presence there."[51] The United States was struggling to interest more business partners and organized a series of international conferences to entice new businesses. "In Rome there were over 300 companies and there was so much interest we had to use a spillover room," said Joseph Vincent Schwan, vice chair of the Iraq and Afghanistan Investment and Reconstruction Task Force.[52] He boasted that 550 businesses showed up at a similar conference in Dubai, and another 250 in Philadelphia. The U.S. Chamber of Commerce also distributed its "Doing Business in Iraq" PowerPoint presentation across the world, from Sydney to Seoul to London.[53]

At the conference in Dubai three weeks after the Fallujah ambush, described by the local press as an "opportunity to win billions of dollars in sub-contracted work in Iraq," Schwan told potential contractors, "Iraq presents an opportunity of a lifetime."[54] But to cash in on this opportunity, security was a necessity, and the contractors were being encouraged to add on new costs in their billing to hire mercenaries. As a public service the "Doing Business in Iraq" presentation included a list of mercenary companies for hire.[55]

Meanwhile, the newly appointed U.S. Special Inspector General for Iraq, Stuart Bowen Jr., explained the extent of the new demand for mercenary services in Iraq. "I believe that it was expected that coalition forces would provide adequate internal security and thus obviate the need for contractors to hire their own security," Bowen said. "But the current threat situation now requires that an unexpected, substantial percentage of contractor dollars be allocated to private security."[56] As a result of the ever-increasing demand for private security services from companies like Blackwater, corporations servicing the occupation began billing the CPA substantially more for their protection costs. "The numbers I've heard range up to 25 percent," Bowen said, versus the initially estimated 10 percent of the "reconstruction" budget that would go to pay for security for private companies like Halliburton.[57] The Pentagon official in charge of Army procurement contracts backed up Bowen's estimate.[58]

"The US military has created much of the demand for security guards," reported The Times of London. "It has outsourced many formerly military functions to private contractors, who, in turn, need protection."[59] Because the U.S. privatized so many of these essential services—like providing food, fuel, water, and housing for the troops—and made private corporations necessary components of the occupation, the Bush administration didn't even consider not using contractors when the situation became ultralethal. As one occupation official, Bruce Cole, put it, "We're not going to stop just because security costs go up."[60] Instead, the administration dug deeper into the privatization hole, paying out more money to more companies and encouraging an already impressive growth in the mercenary industry. "When Halliburton teams working to rebuild oil pipelines first arrived in the country, they had military protection," according to *Fortune* magazine. "But now they've had to hire private security. With armored SUVs running more than $100,000 apiece and armed guards earning $1,000 a day, big contractors like Bechtel and Halliburton are spending hundreds of millions to protect their employees. Since the government picks up the tab, ultimately that means fewer dollars for actual reconstruction work."[61] And many more dollars for private military companies.

What became clear after the Fallujah ambush and firefight at Najaf was that mercenaries had become a necessary part of the occupation. "With every week of insurgency in a war zone with no front, these companies are becoming more deeply enmeshed in combat, in some cases all but obliterating distinctions between professional troops and private commandos," reported the *New York Times*. "[M]ore and more, they give the appearance of private, for-profit militias."[62] A year after the invasion began, the number of mercenaries in the country had exploded. Global Risk Strategies, one of the first mercenary companies to deploy in Iraq, went from ninety men to fifteen hundred, Steele Foundation from fifty to five hundred, while previously unknown firms like Erinys thrived—hiring fourteen thousand Iraqis to work as private soldiers.[63] The global engineering firm Fluor—the largest U.S. publicly traded engineering and construction company—hired some seven hundred private guards to protect its 350 workers, servicing its nearly $2 billion in contracts.[64] "Let's just say there are more people carrying guns and protecting than turning wrenches," said Garry Flowers, Fluor's vice president.[65] "Established" mercenary firms—or those with connections to the occupying powers—began complaining about ramshackle operations offering security services in Iraq for cheaper and with far less "qualified" contractors. There was also controversy about former apartheid-era security forces from South Africa, whose presence came to light only after some were killed. "The mercenaries we're talking about worked for security forces that were synonymous with murder and torture," said Richard Goldstone, a retired justice of the Constitutional Court of South Africa who also served as chief prosecutor of the UN war crimes tribunals for the former Yugoslavia and Rwanda. "My reaction was one of horror that that sort of person is employed in a situation where what should be encouraged is the introduction of democracy. These are not the people who should be employed in this sort of endeavor."[66] A Pentagon official told *Time* magazine, "These firms are hiring anyone they can get. Sure, some of them are special forces, but some of them are good, and some are not."[67]

On April 28, 2004, the Abu Ghraib prison scandal was blown into the open when CBS's *60 Minutes II* broadcast graphic images depicting U.S. soldiers torturing and humiliating Iraqi prisoners.[68] It soon emerged that private contractors from two U.S. corporations—the San Diego–based Titan Corporation and the Virginia-based CACI—were allegedly involved in the torture, having provided interrogators for use at the prison during the period of alleged abuse. An Army investigative report by Maj. Gen. Antonio Taguba found that an interrogator at CACI and a translator for Titan "were either directly or indirectly responsible for the abuses at Abu Ghraib."[69] Both companies denied the allegations. CACI counted as one of its former directors Deputy Secretary of State Richard Armitage,[70] a key administration official in the war on terror. A subsequent class action lawsuit filed by the Center for Constitutional Rights charged that Titan and CACI conspired with U.S. officials to "humiliate, torture and abuse persons" to win more contracts for their "interrogation services."[71] Though a greater spotlight was being shone on private contractors, it was hardly having an adverse effect on business.

In Iraq, Blackwater, with its former Special Forces operators and political connections, billed some clients $1,500 to $2,000 per man per day, according to *Time* magazine.[72] The private military industry, meanwhile, used the Fallujah ambush to argue for overt approval from the United States for private soldiers to use heavier weapons in Iraq.[73] Even with the growing controversy and image problems, it was an incredible moment in mercenary history, blowing open a door to legitimacy that would have been difficult to fully imagine before the launch of the war on terror. A year after the Iraq invasion, shares in one of the largest private security firms, Kroll Inc.—which provided security for the U.S. Agency for International Development in Iraq—had soared 38 percent, while its profits had "skyrocketed" 231 percent with sales doubling to $485.5 million.[74] "Listen, it is the Gold Rush," said Michael Cherkasky, Kroll's president, warning, "This is what happens: People who don't know what they're doing can really get hurt."[75] The full magnitude of the industry-wide profits is difficult to gauge because many of the firms, like Blackwater, are ultrasecretive and not publicly traded. But some experts began estimating the value of the industry at $100 billion a year.[76] "We have grown 300 percent over each of the past three years," Blackwater's Gary Jackson bragged shortly before the Fallujah killings. "We have a very small niche market, we work towards putting out the cream of the crop, the best."[77]

In the aftermath of Fallujah and Najaf, some of the private military firms began to coordinate informally with one another, sharing information and intelligence. "Each private firm amounts to an individual battalion," a U.S. government official told the *Washington Post*. "Now they are all coming together to build the largest security organization in the world."[78] It became like a Frankenstein experiment in military and intelligence outsourcing, with Iraq as the laboratory. "[T]he power of the mercenaries has been growing," Robert Fisk wrote from Baghdad in the summer of 2004. "Blackwater's thugs with guns now push and punch Iraqis who get in their way: Kurdish journalists twice walked out of a Bremer press conference because of their mistreatment by these men. Baghdad is alive with mysterious Westerners draped with hardware, shouting and abusing Iraqis in the street, drinking heavily in the city's poorly defended hotels. They have become, for ordinary Iraqis, the image of everything that is wrong with the West. We like to call them 'contractors', but there is a disturbing increase in reports that mercenaries are shooting down innocent Iraqis with total impunity."[79]

Doing Kafka Proud

That summer, the United States began funding a large intelligence and operations center for the mercenaries, intended as a sort of privatized Green Zone within the Green Zone. It started in May 2004 with a massive

$293 million, three-year contract awarded to the newly formed UK firm
Aegis Defense Services, founded and run by the world's most well-known
mercenary, Tim Spicer, a former British Special Forces officer.[80] The firm
for which Spicer previously worked, Sandline, was hired by warring factions in Papua New Guinea and Sierra Leone in the late 1990s, sparking a
major controversy in Britain about the use of mercenaries.[81] He started the
new firm in September 2002 to shake the mercenary image of Sandline. "I
wanted to make sure that Aegis was a completely different animal," he
said.[82] Spicer became the godfather of sorts of the campaign to recast mercenary firms as "private military companies." That Spicer was awarded the
largest security contract to date in the Iraq occupation was an ominous
symbol of the dawning of a new era. What's more, the scale of the contract
and its timing made a bold statement about real U.S. intentions with the
"handover of sovereignty" a month away: *We—and our mercenaries—are
here to stay.* It was also a devastating commentary on the flimsiness of a key
part of the "handover" rhetoric—that Iraqis would be assuming responsibility for the country's security. Like the system that Halliburton used to
guarantee itself large-scale profits through its government contracts,
Spicer's contract was a "cost plus" arrangement. "In effect, this deal rewards
companies with higher profits the more they spend, and thus is ripe for
abuse and inefficiency," wrote Peter Singer, a Brookings Institution expert
on private military contracting. "It has no parallel in the best practices of
the business world, for the very reason that it runs counter to everything
Adam Smith wrote about free markets."[83]

The official intent of the contract was twofold: Aegis was to coordinate
and oversee the activities and movements of the scores of private military
firms in the country servicing the occupation, including facilitating intelligence and security briefings. Aegis would soon establish six control centers
across Iraq.[84] Under the contract, Aegis was also to provide up to seventy-
five "close protection teams" to protect employees of the occupation
authority's Program Management Office from "assassination, kidnapping,
injury and embarrassment."[85] The deal pushed Aegis from an unprofitable

company to one of the most successful ones operating in the war on terror. "The contract has taken us from a very small organization to a big one," said Spicer, the largest single shareholder in Aegis. "Now we want to consolidate. We will go wherever the threat takes us."[86] The awarding of the contract to Spicer sparked outrage from various sectors—including from other private military companies. Texas-based DynCorp, one of six original bidders for the contract, filed a protest with the U.S. Government Accountability Office.[87] Aegis was not even on the list of State Department–recommended private military firms in Iraq.[88] Even Republican lawmakers were up in arms over the deal. Texas Congressman Pete Sessions, in supporting DynCorp, wrote a letter to Defense Secretary Rumsfeld, saying, "It is inconceivable that the firm charged with the responsibility for coordinating all security of firms and individuals performing reconstruction is one which has never even been in the country."[89]

Then there was the issue of Spicer's past. In a letter to Rumsfeld shortly after the Aegis contract was announced, Senators John Kerry, Edward Kennedy, Hillary Clinton, Christopher Dodd, and Charles Schumer called on the Defense Secretary to order an Inspector General's review of the contract, labeling Spicer "an individual with a history of supporting excessive use of force against a civilian population" and a man "who vigorously defends [human rights abuses]."[90] As evidence, the senators cited a *Boston Globe* article charging that Spicer has "a reputation for illicit arms deals in Africa and for commanding a murderous military unit in Northern Ireland."[91] Spicer charges that his reputation regarding his work in both Africa and the north of Ireland had been consistently and unfairly maligned, saying his "involvement in certain historic events" are "generally inaccurately reported."[92] The senators' protests apparently fell on deaf ears, as Spicer's contract was renewed by the United States each of the following two years.[93] "The contract is a case study in what not to do," Peter Singer, the Brookings scholar, wrote in the *New York Times*.[94] Citing the already evident lack of coordination, oversight, and management of the mercenaries in Iraq, Singer asserted, "[O]utsourcing that very problem to another private company has a logic that would do only Kafka proud. In addition, it moves these companies further outside the bounds of public oversight."[95]

In late 2005 more controversy hit Aegis when a video was posted on a Web site run by a former Aegis employee that appeared to show private security contractors shooting at civilian vehicles driving on highways in Iraq.[96] The video looked as though it was filmed from a camera mounted in the rear window of an SUV. According to the *Washington Post*, "It contained several brief clips of cars being strafed by machine-gun fire, set to the music of the Elvis Presley song 'Mystery Train.' A version posted months later contained laughter and the voices of men joking with one another during the shootings. The scenes were aired widely on Arabic-language satellite television and prompted denunciations from several members of Congress."[97] Aegis had an "independent review board" investigate the video. The board alleged "the films were recorded during Aegis' legitimate operations" in Iraq and said "the incidents recorded were within the Rules for Use of Force," concluding "there was no evidence of any civilian casualities as a result of the incidents."[98] A subsequent investigation by the U.S. Army's Criminal Investigation Division determined there was a "lack of probable cause to believe that a crime was committed."[99] It also determined the incidents recorded were "within the rules for the use of force."[100]

The U.S. Special Inspector General for Iraq audited Aegis in 2005 and found "There is no assurance that Aegis is providing the best safety and security for the government and reconstruction contractor personnel and facilities."[101] Despite the controversy, what mattered to the industry was that "private military companies" were being brought closer to the fold and winning their legitimacy. "There have been a lot of changes in the way this industry works in the past ten years," Tim Spicer said in late 2006. "What I was doing ten years ago was way ahead of its time. The catalyst has been the war on terror. The whole period since 9/11 has highlighted the need for a private security sector."[102] By October 2006, there were an estimated twenty-one thousand mercenaries working for British firms in Iraq, compared to seventy-two hundred active duty British troops.[103]

Ambushed Again

In the summer of 2004, more private soldiers poured into Iraq, as the situation on the ground continued to deteriorate. In June, Blackwater commandos once again fell victim to an ambush that had echoes of the Fallujah killings. On the morning of Saturday, June 5, at about 10:30 a.m., two Blackwater sports utility vehicles were en route to the Baghdad airport.[104] Blackwater/Alexander Strategy spokesperson Chris Bertelli said the men were on a mission relating to Blackwater's ESS contract[105]—like the one the four men killed at Fallujah were working under when they died. Bertelli identified it as a subcontract with Halliburton subsidiary KBR.[106] Working the Blackwater detail that morning was a mixture of U.S. and Polish contractors. One of the Americans, Chris Neidrich, had previously worked the Bremer motorcade detail.[107] In one of his last e-mails sent before the mission, Neidrich had joked with his friends about needing to drive ninety miles per hour in Iraq to avoid roadside bombs. "You know when I get home I'll have to not drive for like two months," Neidrich wrote. "Can't remember the last time I drove slow, stopped for a light or stop sign or even a person."[108] The Poles on the Blackwater team that day were former members of their country's elite GROM ("Thunder") forces who had left Poland's official Iraq contingent and gone to work for Blackwater.[109] Gen. Slawomir Petelicki, former commander of the GROM, said Blackwater offered the Polish commandos $15,000 a month plus insurance.[110]

As the Blackwater convoy sped along the four-lane highway to the airport, resistance fighters began tailing them in their own vehicles. "They were set up by four to five vehicles, full of armed men, all with automatic weapons," said Bertelli. "It was a high-speed ambush."[111] The resistance fighters reportedly fired a rocket-propelled grenade at the trailing Blackwater vehicle, hitting the gas tank and engulfing the vehicle in flames.[112] The second Blackwater vehicle doubled back to assist, and a gun battle ensued. "It was a hell of a firefight," said K.C. Poulin, owner of Critical Intervention Services, a private security company that had employed Neidrich for years in the United States. "They engaged hostiles in multiple vehicles. They expended all their ammunition in the fight. The attack was well orchestrated. These weren't your run-of-the-mill terrorists."[113] Blackwater said its men were outnumbered about twenty to seven.[114] In the end, Neidrich and another American were killed, along with two of the Polish contractors.[115] The remaining three Blackwater guards reportedly managed to fight their way to the other side of the road, flag down a passing vehicle, and escape.[116]

The ambush took place on the main route from the Green Zone to the Baghdad airport and once again put Blackwater in the headlines. "Remember a year ago when Saddam's spokesman, the wacky 'Baghdad Bob,' claimed that U.S. forces didn't control the airport?" wrote New York Times columnist Thomas Friedman about the ambush. "We shouldn't have laughed. A year later, we still do not fully control the main road from Baghdad airport to Baghdad. You can't build anything under those conditions." Ironically, Blackwater would soon become one of the main high-paid taxi providers along this dangerous route—transporting clients in armored vehicles. The day after the ambush, with the chaos escalating in Iraq, the U.S.-installed Prime Minister-designate, Iyad Allawi, a former CIA asset, appeared to blame the violence on U.S. policy. He told Al Jazeera that "big mistakes" had been made by the United States in "dissolving the army, police services and internal security forces."[117] Allawi called for the Iraqi military to be reconstituted. The damage, though, had been done, and there were very few parties that benefited more from the violence than private military companies.

Paul Bremer snuck out of Iraq on June 28, 2004, two days ahead of the scheduled "handover of sovereignty." As Bremer made his final rounds in Baghdad, saying good-bye to his Iraqi allies, the head of Bremer's security detail, Frank Gallagher, insisted on increased security for the proconsul. "So this time he laid on seventeen extra Humvees to cover our convoy's route, ordered all three Blackwater helicopters—each with two 'shooters'—to fly just above our motorcade, and arranged with the military for a couple of Apache choppers to fly on our flanks and F-16 fighter bombers to fly top cover," Bremer recalled.[118] One of Bremer's last official acts was to issue a decree immunizing Blackwater and other contractors from prosecution for any potential crimes committed in Iraq. On June 27, Bremer signed Order 17, which declared, "Contractors shall be immune from Iraqi legal process with respect to acts performed by them pursuant to the terms and conditions of a Contract or any sub-contract thereto."[119] That same month, Senator Patrick Leahy attempted to attach an "Anti-War Profiteering" amendment to the Defense Authorization Bill that, among other provisions, would have created "extraterritorial jurisdiction over offenses committed overseas" by contractors.[120] It was voted down.

Paul Bremer's policies had left Blackwater firmly attached to the contract gravy train, not the least of which was the company's prized contract to guard senior U.S. officials in Iraq. Blackwater would soon be responsible for the security of Bremer's successor, Ambassador John Negroponte, a man notorious for his central role in the U.S. "dirty wars" in Central America in the 1980s.[121] Known as the "proconsul" when he was U.S. Ambassador to Honduras from 1981 to 1985, Negroponte helped oversee U.S. aid to the Contra death squads fighting to overthrow the left-wing Sandinista government in Nicaragua—a program Negroponte referred to as "our special project."[122] Negroponte was also accused of covering up widespread human rights abuses by the U.S.-backed Honduran junta.[123] Like several other officials from the Iran-Contra era, Negroponte was placed in a key position by the Bush administration. In Iraq, he would oversee the world's largest Embassy and the biggest CIA station anywhere.[124]

As Bremer left Iraq, there was a much bigger picture unfolding that Blackwater understood better, perhaps, than any other private military firm on the planet: a *kairos* moment was upon the new soldiers of fortune. Out of the carnage of Fallujah, Blackwater was leading the mercenary industry toward a level of legitimacy that years earlier would have seemed unimaginable. One of the broader goals of the neo-mercenary rebranding campaign has been acceptance as legitimate forces in the country's national defense and security apparatuses. For Blackwater, the Bremer contract in Iraq was undoubtedly far more valuable than its incredibly lucrative price tag. It was prestigious and an invaluable marketing tool to win more clients and high-value government contracts. The company could boast that the U.S. government had entrusted it with the protection of its most senior officials on Washington's hottest front line in the "war on terror." It also gave the unmistakable impression that Blackwater operations had a U.S. government seal of approval.

While private military firms on the ground in Iraq battled each other for contracts, Blackwater was quietly rewarded with the attachment of a U.S.-taxpayer funded I.V. to the company's headquarters in Moyock. In June 2004, at the end of Bremer's tenure, Blackwater was handed one of the most valuable and prestigious U.S. government contracts on the market, through the State Department's little-known Worldwide Personal Protective Service (WPPS) program.[125] State Department documents describe the WPPS program as a government "diplomatic security" initiative to protect U.S. officials and "certain foreign government high level officials whenever the need arises." In the government documents, the work is described as "providing armed, qualified, protective services details" and, if ordered, "Counter Assault Teams and Long Range Marksman teams." The companies might also provide translators and perform intelligence work. The State Department warned the companies to "Ensure that contractor-assigned protective detail personnel are prepared to, and in fact shall operate and live in austere, at times unsettled conditions, anywhere in the world." The contract also said that if necessary, "personnel, who are American citizens, will be issued an appropriate, official or diplomatic passport." Private contractors were also authorized to recruit and train foreign nationals and to "conduct protective security operations overseas with them."

In soliciting bids for the 2004 global contract, the State Department cited a need born of "the continual turmoil in the Mid East, and the post-war stabilization efforts by the United States Government in Bosnia, Afghanistan and Iraq." It said the government "is unable to provide protective services on a long-term basis from its pool of special agents, thus, outside contractual support is required."

The WPPS contract was divided among a handful of well-connected mercenary companies, among them DynCorp and Triple Canopy. Blackwater was originally slated to be paid $229.5 million for five years, according to a State Department contract list. Yet as of June 30, 2006, just two years into the program, it had been paid a total of $321,715,794. A government spokesperson later said the estimated value of the contract through September 2006 was $337 million.[126] By late 2007, Blackwater had been paid more than $750 million under the contract. A heavily redacted 2005 government-commissioned audit of Blackwater's WPPS contract proposal charged that Blackwater included profit in its overhead and its total costs, which would result "not only in a duplication of profit but a pyramiding of profit since in effect Blackwater is applying profit to profit."[127] The audit also alleged that the company tried to inflate its profits by representing different Blackwater divisions as wholly separate companies.[128]

For Blackwater, the WPPS contract was a milestone that solidified the company's role as the preferred mercenary firm of the U.S. government, the elite private guard for the administration's global war. In late November 2004, Blackwater president Gary Jackson sent out a mass e-mail celebrating President Bush's reelection and Blackwater's new contract: "Well, the Presidential elections are over, the masses spoke, the liberals are lined up at health clinics receiving treatment for Post Election Selection Trauma, and President Bush's war on terror will continue to move forward for the next four years. Our military is doing a fabulous job in fighting the war on terrorism as is apparent by the results of the most recent victory in the Battle of Fallujah. As Iraq continues to become more stable the Department of State will be sending in more U.S. Government Officials to assist Iraq in becoming a democracy. Even though the majority of Iraqis want democracy there will still be those terrorist[s] who do not, and they are a high-threat to the safety of our Officials. These Officials need professional protection and the Department of State, Bureau of Diplomatic Security has chosen and contracted Blackwater Security Consulting to assist their organization in providing that protection."[129] Jackson excitedly announced that for qualified candidates wishing to "get involved in stabilizing Iraq and supporting the President's war on terrorism . . . now is the time to join Blackwater."[130]

CHAPTER TWELVE

CASPIAN PIPELINE DREAMS

ALTHOUGH BLACKWATER'S name recognition in 2004 was almost exclusively centered on the Fallujah ambush and the company's role in Iraq, it was not the only "war on terror" front line where the Bush Administration dispatched the company. Beginning in July 2004, Blackwater forces were contracted to work in the heart of the oil- and gas-rich Caspian Sea region, where they would quietly train a force modeled after the Navy SEALs and establish a base just north of the Iranian border as part of a major U.S. move in what veteran analysts in the region call the "Great Game." As it won more contracts in Iraq in the aftermath of Fallujah, Blackwater simultaneously found itself helping to defend another high-stakes pet project of some of the most powerful figures in the U.S. national security establishment, including Henry Kissinger, James Baker III, and Dick Cheney.

The United States' quest for domination of the world's petrol reserves certainly did not begin with the 1991 Persian Gulf War or the subsequent 2003 invasion of Iraq. While Iraq and the war on terror have dominated the headlines, the U.S. government and American corporate interests have long been quietly engaged in a parallel campaign to secure another major prize, this one located on the territory of what was once the Soviet Union: the Caspian Sea, which is believed to house well over 100 billion barrels of oil.[1] After the collapse of the Soviet Union in 1991, Washington and its allies saw an opportunity to snatch one of the great deposits of valuable natural resources from Moscow's grip. Multinational oil giants swooped in like vultures as the United States and its allies moved quickly to shore up the repressive regimes of the littoral ex-Soviet republics of the Caspian region. Unocal spent much of the 1990s trying to run a pipeline from Tajikistan through Afghanistan, a project on which Erik Prince's friend (and Blackwater's lobbyist) Paul Behrends had worked, but there was also great interest in the nations of Kazakhstan and Azerbaijan, as well as the strategically important Republic of Georgia. While the route from Tajikistan proved very complicated, it was by no means the only one being explored by Big Oil, the White House, and a powerful cast of political players from past U.S. administrations.

Complicating a swift U.S. domination of the landlocked resources of the Caspian was the fact that two powerful nations—Russia and Iran—also border the sea and viewed the U.S. incursion into the area as a hostile threat. By 1997, a powerful U.S. consortium was hard at work exploring multiple ways to get to the Caspian resources. "American oil companies—including Amoco, Unocal, Exxon, Pennzoil—have invested billions of dollars in Azerbaijan and plan to invest billions more. As a result, they have developed a strongly pro-Azerbaijan position," reported *New York Times* correspondent Stephen Kinzer in a dispatch from Azerbaijan. "The list of private American citizens who are seeking to make money from Azerbaijani oil or to encourage investment here reads like a roster of the national security establishment.

Among the most prominent names are former Secretaries of State Henry A. Kissinger and James A. Baker 3d, former Defense Secretary Dick Cheney, former Senator and Treasury Secretary Lloyd Bentsen, former White House chief of staff John H. Sununu, and two former national security advisers, Brent Scowcroft and Zbigniew Brzezinski."[2]

While the Clinton administration worked feverishly to secure Caspian resources, hosting Azerbaijan's president at the White House for a two-hour meeting in August 1997 and courting his cooperation,[3] it was not until the Bush administration took power that these onetime "pipe dreams" became a reality. In May 2001, Dick Cheney's energy task force estimated that proven oil reserves in Azerbaijan's and Kazakhstan's sectors of the Caspian alone equaled "about 20 billion barrels, a little more than the North Sea and slightly less than the United States."[4] The Cheney group estimated that if the United States could get a major pipeline flowing west from the Caspian Sea—away from Moscow's control—daily exports from the Caspian to world markets could go as high as 2.6 million barrels per day by 2005, "as the United States works closely with private companies and countries in the region to develop commercially viable export routes."[5] By contrast, in 2005 Iran exported 2.6 million barrels of oil per day, Venezuela 2.2, Kuwait 2.3, Nigeria 2.3, and Iraq 1.3.[6]

Since the collapse of the Soviet Union, getting at the Caspian region's oil had proved extremely difficult for Washington. Dating back to the Clinton administration, the United States and its allies envisioned a plan wherein Washington would essentially prop up the repressive regime in Azerbaijan and establish a state-of-the-art oil exploitation operation off the coast of the Azerbaijani capital, Baku, a peninsula that juts into the western Caspian. The oil would then flow through a massive pipeline stretching from Baku to Tbilisi, Georgia, through Turkey to the Mediterranean port city of Ceyhan. From there, the Caspian oil could be easily transported to Western markets. The project would mean an end to Moscow's de facto monopoly on transporting Caspian oil, while at the same time providing Washington with an unparalleled opportunity to exert its influence in the ex-Soviet territories.

When the project began in 1994, some analysts celebrated it as a "new Persian Gulf"; estimates projected as much as 230 billion barrels of oil in the region—eight times the proven U.S. reserves.[7]

During the latter years of Clinton's tenure, however, the project came to be viewed as a white elephant likely to fail. The Caspian countries were governed by corrupt, unstable regimes that remained under Moscow's sway despite their nominal independence. The pipeline would be extremely costly and vulnerable to sabotage. To top it off, early Western explorations in the Caspian turned up estimates of the sea's potential resources far more modest than previous projections.[8] While the United States remained committed to tapping the Caspian, the program moved forward at a slow pace. That changed when Bush took office and oil executives were welcomed into the White House like cousins at a family reunion. By September 2002, construction on the massive eleven-hundred-mile Caspian pipeline was under way. The BBC described it as a project that U.S. officials favored because it would "weaken Russia's stranglehold on regional pipeline network and leave Iran on the sidelines."[9]

A potential problem for the project lay in what the White House saw as the dangerous geography of the neighborhood—located not far from Chechnya and Iran. The Bush administration, therefore, made a number of moves that would result in at least one regime change in the region and the deployment of forces from Blackwater and other U.S. war-servicing firms to protect what would be one of Washington's most ambitious power grabs on former Soviet territory.

In 2003, the Bush administration helped overthrow the government of a longtime U.S. ally, President Eduard Shevardnadze of Georgia. Once considered Washington's closest strategic partner in the region and affectionately referred to as "Shevy-Chevy" by U.S. officials like James Baker, Shevardnadze had fallen fast out of favor with the administration of George W. Bush, as Shevardnadze began increasingly doing business with Moscow after years of U.S. patronage.[10] Among his sins: granting new drilling and pipeline concessions to Russian firms and obstructing Washington's grand Caspian pipeline plan. Soon after those transgressions, he was forced to resign in November 2003 as the so-called "Rose Revolution" brought to power a more staunchly pro-U.S. regime. The first telephone call the new acting president, Nino Burdzhanadze, made when she took over from Shevardnadze was to oil giant BP to "assure them the pipeline would be OK."[11] Just prior to taking power in Georgia, the new U.S.-backed leader, Mikhail Saakashvili, announced, "All strategic contracts in Georgia, especially the contract for the Caspian pipeline, are a matter of survival for the Georgian state."[12] That regime change resulted in the closure of Russian bases in Georgia and an increase in U.S. military aid to the country. In early 2004, Defense Secretary Rumsfeld deployed private military contractors from the Washington firm Cubic on a three-year $15 million contract to Georgia "to equip and advise the former Soviet republic's crumbling military, embellishing an eastward expansion that has enraged Moscow," reported London's *Guardian*. "A Georgian security official said the Cubic team would also improve protection of the pipeline that will take Caspian oil from Baku to Turkey through Georgia. Georgia has already expressed its gratitude by agreeing to send 500 troops to Iraq."[13]

The Bush administration knew that the controversial pipeline would need to be protected in each country it passed through. While Washington increased its military aid to Georgia, it faced a decade-long U.S. Congressional ban on military assistance to Azerbaijan, where the oil would be extracted. In 1992, Congress banned such aid because of Azerbaijan's bloody ethnic and territorial conflict with Armenia in the Nagorno-Karabak region. But on January 25, 2002, President Bush "waived" that section of the Congressional Act, thereby allowing U.S. military aid to Azerbaijan to resume. The White House said the waiver was "necessary to support United States efforts to counter international terrorism [and] to support the operational readiness of United States Armed Forces or coalition partners to counter international terrorism"[14]—in other words, to protect oil interests. In the fall of 2003, the administration officially launched a project it called "Caspian Guard," under which the United States would significantly bolster the military capabilities of Kazakhstan and Azerbaijan.[15] Similar to the U.S. plan in Georgia, the $135 million program would create a network of commando and special operations forces that would protect the lucrative oil and gas exploitation being plotted out by transnational oil corporations and patrol the massive pipeline project that would allow an easy flow of the hydrocarbon resources of the Caspian to Western markets.

But oil and gas were only part of the story. While the Caspian's resources were undoubtedly viewed by Washington as a major prize to be secured, Azerbaijan's geographic proximity to the center of the administration's broader attempt at conquest of the Middle East was also incredibly valuable. With open talk of the possibility of a U.S. attack on Iran and several reports detailing military planning for such operations as part of the "war on terror," many of Tehran's neighbors, particularly those directly on its border such as Azerbaijan, were very resistant to the overt presence of U.S. forces on their soil. Iran had made clear that it would retaliate against any state that supported the United States in an attack. As the Caspian Guard program got under way in 2004, "the Azerbaijani parliament adopted a law prohibiting the stationing of foreign troops on the country's territory, a move widely believed to be a gesture towards Moscow and Tehran, which both oppose any strengthening of military ties between Azerbaijan and the US," reported the EurasiaNet news service.[16] But despite the overtures to Washington's foes, the reality was that Azerbaijan was on the receiving end of a massive new pipeline of U.S. military assistance.

Enter Blackwater

In early 2004, with the United States ratcheting up its rhetoric against "axis of evil" member Iran, Blackwater USA was hired by the Pentagon under Caspian Guard to deploy in Azerbaijan, where Blackwater would be tasked with establishing and training an elite Azeri force modeled after the U.S. Navy SEALs that would ultimately protect the interests of the United States and its allies in a hostile region. The $2.5 million Army contract for a one-year project indicated that it was open for competition but that Blackwater was the only company to bid on it.[17] On Pentagon documents, the nature of Blackwater's work in Azerbaijan was kept vague—only mentioning "training aids" and "armament training devices." Despite the secrecy, one thing was clear: Blackwater had once again found itself at the forefront of a pet Bush administration project. "We've been asked to help create, for lack of a more educated term, a SEAL team for Azerbaijan, both to help them with their oil interests in the Caspian but also to kind of monitor what goes on in the Caspian during the wee hours of the night," said Blackwater's Taylor. "These are very, very politically . . . sensitive issues."[18] Blackwater joined a U.S. corporate landscape in Baku that included other Bush administration–linked corporations such as Bechtel, Halliburton, Chevron-Texaco, Unocal, and ExxonMobil.

Some analysts viewed Caspian Guard and the Blackwater contract as a back-door U.S. military deployment. "We were hired to come in and build by the U.S. government, to build a maritime special operations capability in Azerbaijan," said Blackwater founder Erik Prince at a U.S. military conference in 2006. "We took over an old Spetsnaz (Soviet special forces) base and built about a ninety-man Azeri high-end unit."[19] Prince called Blackwater's Azerbaijan work "a great small footprint way to do it." Instead of sending in battalions of active U.S. military to Azerbaijan, the Pentagon deployed "civilian contractors" from Blackwater and other firms to set up an operation that would serve a dual purpose: protecting the West's new profitable oil and gas exploitation in a region historically dominated by Russia and Iran, and possibly laying the groundwork for an important forward operating base for an attack against Iran. "Compared with the U.S. efforts to train and equip troops in neighboring Georgia, training Azerbaijan's commandos was a relatively low-profile program," observed Central Asia correspondent Nathan Hodge. "It's understandable: The country is sandwiched between Russia and Iran, and sending a contingent of uniformed U.S. military trainers would be a provocative move. A private contractor helps keep things under the radar."[20]

One indication of the strategic importance of Azerbaijan comes from the list of names associated with the U.S. Azerbaijan Chamber of Commerce, an organization formed in 1995 to "facilitate and encourage trade and investment in Azerbaijan" and to "serve as a liaison between foreign companies and Azerbaijani businesses and officials."[21] Its "Council of Advisors" reads like a who's who of the hawks of the Reagan-Bush era: James Baker III, Henry Kissinger, John Sununu, and Brent Scowcroft.[22] The board of directors includes senior executives from ExxonMobil, Chevron, ConocoPhilips, and Coca-Cola, while the trustees include Azerbaijan's dictator, Ilham Aliyev, and top neoconservative Richard Perle. Listed as "former" officials of the organization are none other than Dick Cheney and Richard Armitage.[23] "These men are the power behind the throne in Azerbaijan," observed investigative journalist Tim Shorrock, adding that Blackwater's deployment would be "impossible to imagine . . . without a nod from one of these principals."[24]

A March 2004 Blackwater recruitment ad sought a manager to oversee the contract "to train, equip, and permanently establish a Naval Special Operations Unit in the Azerbaijan Armed Forces."[25] The announced salary was $130,000 to $150,000 annually. Blackwater referred to the project as part of a "Maritime Commando Enhancement" program. "The Caspian Sea is a region of interest for many, many reasons," said Blackwater vice president Chris Taylor at a conference on contracting in 2005, where he held up Blackwater's Azerbaijan work as evidence of successful U.S. government contracting to help allied governments build up their forces. "This is not a zero-sum game. We're not trying to take as much of the pie and leave the government with nothing so we can get as much money as we possibly can. It just doesn't work out that way. And if you want quote unquote repeat business, if you want to have a solid reputation, it's actually affecting the strategic balance in an area for the government or assisting in doing that, then you've got to be part of that give and take. And we like to think that we do that on a daily basis."[26]

Caspian Guard appeared to be part of a strategy Defense Secretary Rumsfeld had articulated publicly in a visit to the region in early 2004. At a press conference in Uzbekistan on February 24 of that year, Rumsfeld revealed that he and other senior U.S. officials had been discussing the establishment of "operating sites" in the area, which he described as facilities "that would not be permanent as a base would be permanent but would be a place where the United States and coalition countries could periodically and intermittently have access and support. . . . What's important to us is to be arranged in a way and in places that are hospitable, where we have the flexibility of using those facilities."[27] In Georgia, where the Pentagon has also deployed private military contractors, a Western diplomat told the *Guardian* that the United States was considering "creating a 'forward operational area' where equipment and fuel could be stored, similar to support structures in the Gulf."[28] "The two moves would combine to give Washington a 'virtual base'—stored equipment and a loyal Georgian military—without the diplomatic inconvenience of setting up a permanent base," according to the paper.[29]

That appeared to be the strategy with Blackwater in Azerbaijan as well. In strategically important Baku, Blackwater renovated a Soviet-era maritime special operations training facility that Pentagon planners envisioned as a command center modeled on those used by the Department of Homeland Security.[30] As part of Caspian Guard, the United States also contracted defense giant and Iraq War contractor Washington Group International to construct a radar surveillance facility in Astara, just north of the Iranian border, one of two such facilities built under the program.[31] The other was positioned atop a mountain south of Russia's North Caucasus region, not far from Chechnya.[32] Washington also renovated the nearby Nakhchewan airport to accommodate military aircraft, including from NATO.[33] In the meantime, encouraged by its cozy relationship with Washington, Azerbaijan dramatically increased its military spending by 70 percent in 2005 to $300 million.[34] By the end of 2006, it had reached a whopping $700 million, with the country's president pledging it would soon grow to $1 billion annually.[35]

In the event of a U.S. war against Iran, Azerbaijan would play a central role; to Tehran, the U.S.-orchestrated buildup along the Caspian was an ominous threat. Iran actually responded to word of Blackwater's involvement in the region by announcing the creation of its own special naval police force that would patrol the Caspian.[36] As an exclamation point to Iran's concerns, Ariel Cohen of the right-wing Heritage Foundation wrote in the *Washington Times* in 2005 that Caspian Guard was "significant . . . for any future conflict with Iran."[37] As *Jane's Defence Weekly* reported, the U.S. presence near the Caspian allowed Washington to "gain a foothold in a region that is rich in oil and natural gas, and which also borders Iran. 'It's good old US interests, it's rather selfish,' said US Army Colonel Mike Anderson, chief of the Europe Plans and Policies Division at US European Command (EUCOM). 'Certainly we've chosen to help two littoral states, Azerbaijan and Kazakhstan, but always underlying that is our own self interest.'"[38]

By April 2005, Rumsfeld had visited Azerbaijan, a small country of 8.5 million people, at least three times.[39] The visits were secretive, and U.S. and Azerbaijani officials would only speak in generalities about what exactly Rumsfeld was doing dropping into the country so often. After Rumsfeld's third visit, the popular daily newspaper *Echo* ran the headline "Rumsfeld Is Interested in Oil!"[40] Indeed, the flurry of U.S.-military-related activities in Azerbaijan, including the Blackwater deployment, was timed for the launch of one of the most diplomatically controversial Western operations on former Soviet soil since the fall of the Berlin Wall: the massive eleven-hundred-mile oil pipeline that for the first time would transfer oil out of the Caspian on a route that entirely circumvented Russia and Iran—a development both Moscow and Tehran viewed as a serious U.S. incursion into their spheres. The $3.6 billion pipeline project was heavily funded by the World Bank, the U.S. Export-Import Bank, and the Overseas Private Investment Corporation,[41] and spearheaded by a consortium led by oil giant BP along with U.S. companies Unocal, ConocoPhilips, and Hess. As originally planned, the pipeline would run from Baku, Azerbaijan through Tbilisi, Georgia to the Turkish port of Ceyhan, where the oil would then be shipped for Western consumption.

Known by its acronym, the BTC pipeline was labeled "a new round in the Great Game" by veteran Russia analysts, who viewed it as part of a wider plan to isolate Moscow. Analyst Vladimir Radyuhin said the "pipeline is a key element in the U.S. strategy to redraw the geopolitical map of the former Soviet Union and supersede Russia as a dominant force in the former Soviet Union. The U.S. has pushed through the project over more profitable pipelines via Russia and Iran to create an alternative export route for oil produced in Azerbaijan, Kazakhstan, Turkmenistan, and Uzbekistan, which have so far depended on Russian pipelines to export their oil to Europe."[42] Radyuhin said Washington's Caspian Guard program "together with the U.S.-promoted GUUAM alliance of Georgia, Ukraine, Uzbekistan, Azerbaijan and Moldova, will enable Washington to exercise control over an absolute majority of post-Soviet states and create a cordon sanitaire around Russia."[43] The head of the International Committee of Russia's upper house of parliament, Mikhail Margelov, said, "Russia will always oppose the presence of any foreign military contingents within the boundaries of the [Caspian region]. . . . First and foremost, it is a question of [Russia's] national security."[44]

Prior to the launch of the BTC pipeline, the United States had invested in the Russian-controlled Caspian Pipeline Consortium, a $2.6 billion project made up of a 935-mile crude oil pipeline that ran from the Tengiz oilfield in Kazakhstan to the Russian Black Sea port of Novorossiysk.[45] The White House called it "the largest single United States investment in Russia."[46] In November 2001, when the first tanker loaded with oil from the Caspian under the project was launched, Commerce Secretary Don Evans remarked, "It tells the world that the United States, Russia, and Central Asian states are cooperating to build prosperity and stability in this part of the world."[47] But once the new BTC pipeline became active in 2005, Bush publicly encouraged "companies producing oil [in Kazakhstan] and elsewhere in the Caspian region [to] embrace BTC as a gateway to global markets."[48] It seemed that was the plan from the start. Indeed, the Cheney energy task force had envisioned a scheme to allow multinational oil giants like Chevron and Exxon operating in Kazakhstan under the Russian pipeline to redirect oil through the BTC pipeline, effectively taking away from Russia's profits. It was all laid out in May 2001 in the recommendations made by the White House National Energy Policy Development Group, headed by Cheney. The group recommended that President Bush "direct the Secretaries of Commerce, State, and Energy to continue working with relevant companies and countries to establish the commercial conditions that will allow oil companies operating in Kazakhstan the option of exporting their oil via the BTC pipeline" instead of through the Russian controlled pipeline. It called for the Administration to "deepen [its] commercial dialogue with Kazakhstan, Azerbaijan, and other Caspian states to provide a strong, transparent, and stable business climate for energy and related infrastructure projects."[49]

The BTC pipeline was inaugurated in May 2005, and President Bush dispatched his new Energy Secretary Samuel Bodman to represent him at the ceremony. "BTC opens a new era in the Caspian Basin's development. It ensures Caspian oil will reach European and other markets in a commercially viable and environmentally sound way," Bush said in a letter read by Bodman at the ceremony.[50] The letter was addressed to the dictator of Azerbaijan, whom Bush praised. "As Azerbaijan deepens its democratic and market economic reforms, this pipeline can help generate balanced economic growth, and provide a foundation for a prosperous and just society that advances the cause of freedom," Bush wrote.[51] But as David Sanger of the *New York Times* reported, a few days before Bush's letter was read at the ceremony, "the Azerbaijani police beat pro-democracy demonstrators with truncheons when opposition parties, yelling 'free elections,' defied the government's ban on protests against President Ilham Aliyev. Mr. Aliyev is one of President Bush's allies in the war on terror, even though he won a highly suspect election to succeed his father, a former Soviet strongman."[52]

Azerbaijan's human rights record is dismal. "Torture, police abuse, and excessive use of force by security forces are widespread," according to Human Rights Watch.[53] The U.S. State Department, meanwhile, labeled Azerbaijan's human rights record "poor" and said President Aliyev, the ally of Kissinger, Baker, Cheney, et al., maintained power through an election "that did not meet international standards for a democratic election due to numerous, serious irregularities."[54] The State Department charged that in Azerbaijan there was: "restriction on the right of citizens to peacefully change their government; torture and beating of persons in custody; arbitrary arrest and detention, particularly of political opponents; harsh and life-threatening prison conditions; excessive use of force to disperse demonstrations; [and] police impunity."[55] It also determined, "Members of the security forces committed numerous human rights abuses."[56] Even still, the United States has spent millions of dollars to deploy Blackwater in the country with the explicit purpose of bolstering Azerbaijan's military capabilities, including creating units modeled after the United States most elite Special Forces, the Navy SEALs. As with other convenient allies of the administration, Azerbaijan was valued for its usefulness in securing oil profits and as a potential staging site for future wars. Blackwater's contract in the country strengthened the United States a foothold in a region that will only grow in importance to U.S. policy, and the company has publicly advertised its work in Azerbaijan as a model in seeking more business.[57] Journalist Tim Shorrock concluded, "Blackwater's project in Azerbaijan is clear evidence that contractors have crossed the line from pure mercenaries to strategic partners with the military-industrial complex."[58]

CHAPTER THIRTEEN

BLACKWATER'S MAN IN CHILE

WHILE THE Bush administration struggled and failed to build a "Coalition of the Willing" among nations for its invasion and occupation of Iraq, the private military firms Washington hired to support its Iraq operation recruited aggressively around the globe—often in nations whose military and security forces had horrible human rights records and reputations. Along with the workers from across the developing world—many of whose home countries strongly opposed the war—hired by Halliburton, Bechtel, Fluor, and other "reconstruction" megafirms, the mercenary companies in Iraq largely made up the "international" or multilateral nature of the occupation. The United States may not have been able to convince many governments to deploy forces in Iraq, but it certainly could entice their citizens with promises of significantly higher wages than they could earn at home. Unlike some other private military firms operating in Iraq—which contracted cheap Iraqi labor to staff security projects—Blackwater was viewed as an elite security company because of its high-profile contract guarding the top U.S. officials and several regional occupation headquarters. But while Blackwater encouraged this view, in both Baghdad and in Washington, of a highly professional all-American company patriotically supporting its nation at war, it quietly began bringing in mercenaries from shady quarters to staff its ever-growing security contracts in Iraq.

U.S. training of foreign forces to support covert operations and overtly repressive policies is hardly a new development, particularly in Latin America. Over its six decades of existence, the U.S. Army School of the Americas (renamed the Western Hemisphere Institute for Security Cooperation in 2001) trained more than sixty thousand Latin American soldiers "in counterinsurgency techniques, sniper training, commando and psychological warfare, military intelligence, and interrogation tactics."[1] According to Amnesty International, the SOA was "notorious for training and educating Latin American military personnel who went on to commit human rights violations in their own countries. . . . The SOA used manuals that advocated torture, extortion, kidnapping and execution."[2] Throughout the 1980s and '90s, the United States also fueled "dirty wars" by covertly arming, funding, and training death squads or repressive militaries to crush popular movements Washington deemed a threat to its interests. The Iraq occupation saw a greatly expanded use and training of foreign forces by the private sector. Latin American countries that had been victims of U.S.-sponsored death squads and repressive policies—and whose populations and governments opposed the 2003 Iraq invasion—became the new training grounds and recruitment centers for mercenaries enlisted in the Iraq War.

Among the largest contingents of non-U.S. soldiers imported to Iraq by Blackwater were former Chilean commandos, some of whom trained or served under the brutal military dictatorship of General Augusto Pinochet. The story of how nearly a thousand Chileans made their way to Iraq is in many ways the story of the ex–Chilean Army officer Erik Prince contracted to do Blackwater's recruiting in Chile: Jose Miguel Pizarro Ovalle.[3] Pizarro, a passionate defender of Pinochet, worked as a translator for the U.S. military in Latin America in the 1990s before becoming a liaison between more than a dozen Latin American governments and U.S. weapons manufacturers. When the U.S. invasion of Iraq began in 2003, Pizarro discovered Blackwater USA and almost overnight became a trailblazer in recruiting hundreds of low-cost Latin American mercenaries for it and other private military firms operating in Iraq. "From a Latin-American point of view, my story is not believable," Pizarro said in a lengthy two-and-a-half-hour interview. "From an American point of view it's the American story of success."

Pizarro, who prefers to be called "Mike," is a dual citizen of Chile and the United States, having been born in 1968 in Los Angeles, where his father worked at Paramount Pictures as an artist, drawing cartoon characters. His father also worked as a driver for UPS, and his mother worked as a teller for Bank of America. Shortly after Socialist presidential candidate Salvador Allende won the presidency in Chile in 1971, becoming the first democratically elected Marxist head of state in the hemisphere, the Pizarros returned to their native Santiago. Two years later, Allende's government would be overthrown in a U.S.-backed coup d'etat that brought to power one of the world's most notorious dictators. To understand the significance of Blackwater recruiting Chilean mercenaries for deployment in Iraq—and enlisting an apologist for Augusto Pinochet as Blackwater's point man—it is necessary to understand the U.S. government's role in Chile over the four decades that preceded the 2003 Iraq invasion.

When he launched his campaign for Chile's presidency, Salvador Allende had been a Chilean senator for twenty-five years; he campaigned with his "Popular Unity" movement on pledges to improve the lives of millions of impoverished Chileans.[4] On September 4, 1970, Allende narrowly—but freely and fairly—won a hotly contested presidential race in which right-wing parties, the CIA, and large transnational corporations aggressively backed his opponent. Allende had defied a decade-long "major covert effort," in the words of Secretary of State Dean Rusk, to "reduce chances of Chile being the first American country to elect an avowed Marxist president."[5] Allende's victory, a historic moment in Latin American politics, alarmed the Washington power structure and large U.S. corporations like PepsiCo, Anaconda Copper, and ITT, which had backed Allende's opponent. The Nixon White House immediately undertook a two-track covert plan to prevent Allende from being inaugurated or to overthrow his government if it took power.[6]

The Chilean Congress, however, overwhelmingly ratified Allende as president, and the Socialist leader moved quickly to implement his program, known as "La vía Chilena al socialismo" ("the Chilean Way to Socialism"). This included nationalization of large industries, the implementation of government-run healthcare and educational systems, land redistribution, literacy campaigns, and free milk programs for children. Allende reestablished diplomatic relations with Cuba in defiance of Washington and was close to Cuban leader Fidel Castro, who spent a month in Allende's Chile.

Throughout Allende's short-lived presidency, the Nixon administration—with the cooperation of large U.S. corporations and powerful media outlets in Santiago—aggressively fomented unrest within Chile and isolated it economically. In a cable to Washington, U.S. Ambassador Edward Korrey reported telling Chilean authorities: "Not a nut or bolt will be allowed to reach Chile under Allende. We shall do all within our power to condemn Chile and the Chilean to utmost deprivation and poverty."[7] Nixon, meanwhile, issued a directive saying the United States should "Make the [Chilean] economy scream."[8] By 1973, U.S.-influenced hyperinflation and strikes had gripped the country, while Washington supported a media campaign inside Chile aimed at blaming and ultimately bringing down the Allende government.[9]

On the morning of September 11, 1973, General Pinochet—Commander in Chief of the Army—coordinated a massive military operation that surrounded the presidential palace, La Moneda. In a radio recording of Pinochet instructing his troops during the coup, the General is heard saying, "Kill the bitch and you eliminate the litter."[10] Shortly after 9:00 a.m.—with gunfire and bombs in the background—Allende addressed the nation on one of the few radio stations still operating. "Having a historic choice to make, I shall sacrifice my life to be loyal to my people," Allende said. "I can assure you that I am certain that the seeds planted by us in the noble consciences of thousands and thousands of Chileans will never be prevented from growing."[11] Within hours, Salvador Allende was dead—allegedly having committed suicide—and one of the darkest eras in the country's history had begun. "The [U.S. government] wishes to make clear its desire to cooperate with the military Junta and to assist in any appropriate way," said a classified cable from the White House Situation Room dated two days after the coup. "We welcome General Pinochet's expression of Junta desire for strengthening ties between Chile and U.S."[12]

With the support of Washington, the junta quickly dissolved Congress and Pinochet was declared president. Thousands of Allende supporters and suspected "communist sympathizers" were hunted down by the junta's forces. Thousands were brought to Estadio Nacional de Chile between September and November 1973; hundreds were executed, thousands tortured.[13] The number of Chileans killed in the early days of the Pinochet regime will never be known, but the CIA station in Santiago reported that by September 20, "4,000 deaths have resulted so far from the [coup] and subsequent clean-up operations." Four days later, the CIA estimated the number at 2,000 to 10,000.[14] According to a secret briefing paper prepared in October 1973 for Secretary of State Henry Kissinger titled "Chilean Executions," the Junta had massacred some 1,500 civilians, summarily executing between 320 and 360 of them.[15] "During a ruthless seventeen-year dictatorship, the Chilean military would be responsible for the murder, disappearance and death by torture of some 3,197 citizens—with thousands more subjected to savage abuses such as torture, arbitrary incarceration, forced exile, and other forms of state-sponsored terror," wrote investigative researcher Peter Kornbluh in his groundbreaking book *The Pinochet File*. "Within weeks of the coup, Pinochet created a secret police force empowered to eliminate any and all enemies of his regime."[16] So brazen was the junta—and so confident in its backing by the United States—that it murdered U.S. citizens in Chile and targeted Chilean dissidents, such as Allende's foreign minister, Orlando Letelier, in Washington, D.C. Letelier and his U.S. research assistant, Ronni Karpen Moffitt, were killed in a 1976 car bombing fourteen blocks from the White House.[17]

Despite the overwhelming evidence of the brutality of the Chilean junta, Jose Miguel Pizarro, Blackwater's Chilean recruiter, remained a staunch defender of Pinochet and the coup. "It's exactly the same war on terror" that the Bush administration has waged, Pizarro argued. "I believe there was a major effort of the Chilean Army, the Chilean Navy, and the Chilean Air Force, to make sure that a lot of people got arrested in order to clear them up immediately, but very few people remained in actual custody after the first three or four weeks of the military putsch." Mass executions, Pizarro said, simply did not happen. He did not deny that there was a "military government" in Chile, but he asserted, "to claim that the amount, the scale of the corruption or the human right abuses, to claim that there was an actual, real military dictatorship, is a flat-out lie."

Pizarro grew up proud in Pinochet's Chile with dreams of serving in the Chilean Army: "I got a picture of myself when I was seven with a plastic rifle in my hands so—it's funny—I have never wanted to be anything else besides an Army officer." Despite the well-documented atrocities committed under the Pinochet regime in Chile, Pizarro said, "Funny because I spent those seventeen years of military government living in Santiago. I never saw troops shooting, arresting, killing, doing anything wrong in any way, in any shape, or in any form." He said allegations of Pinochet overseeing "human rights abuses at an institutional level" are "a flat-out lie." Instead, Pizarro painted a picture of Pinochet as a man who restored democracy to Chile, stamped out communism, and cracked down on Cubans from Fidel Castro's government who had filed into Chile as "advisers" after the election of Allende. As for allegations of mass torture, Pizarro said that, too, did not happen, adding that the Chilean definition of torture is liberal. When asked if he personally knew anyone who was tortured, he recalled a story told by a family friend whose father was taken in 1973 when they were in the midst of a barbeque, "and then the military stormed in, and they took my daddy prisoner. They keep him for forty-eight hours, and then they kicked him out on a highway." Pizarro said the official government documentation determined 2,871 people were killed under the dictatorship, adding, "After three years in Iraq, you have less than 3,000 casualties." Absolutely, he acknowledged, "there were human rights abuses" in Chile, but he asserted they were committed by "secret police, by little tiny groups of corrupted officials." There were human rights abuses "by Chilean standards," he said. "By Colombian standards, we were having, I mean, I don't know, a picnic."

Pinochet was, according to Pizarro, "A great patriot that was poorly advised by ill-prepared civilian and military advisers in terms of public relations, in terms of international image. Again, PR. Everything he was doing was right. He was building bridges, creating schools, creating new businesses. He was copying the model of the United States. He tightened up our ties with the U.S. He was fighting communism, fighting corruption, fighting the terrorism. He was doing exactly the right things that every president is supposed to be doing. However, he was so ill advised in terms of public relations that he didn't understand the importance of bringing on board the press, the media. He didn't understand the term *transparency*. We didn't have anything to hide." Pizarro called that his "negative assessment" of Pinochet.

Even though Allende was elected in an internationally recognized democratic election, Pizarro asserted that Pinochet's coup was necessary to restore democracy to Chile. "General Pinochet decided to rebuild the nation, divide the nation in regions, send the civilians to Chicago to study economy, change the traditional economical model of Chile up to 1973, to make a mirror image of the United States of America. So he did that," Pizarro recalled with pride. "And overnight, in less than ten years, this little, tiny banana, third-world nation turned out to be the model, and it is today still, the economical and political model of the region. The most stable nation, Spanish-speaking nation in Latin America." Pizarro says that the civilian governments that succeeded Pinochet's regime have feared that the Chilean military will once again take power, as it did in 1973, if the government is corrupt. As a result, he says civilian leaders in Chile have engaged in historical revisionism about the Pinochet era aimed at demonizing the Chilean armed forces to "destroy the image of the military, present them as corrupt, dumb, banana-oriented, whatever, just destroy their image and make sure they never come to power again." This history has endured, Pizarro argued, because "the right-wing parties of Chile are too calm, too silent, too comfortable, and they're not being aggressive and responsible enough to defend what really happened, to tell the people what really happened in Chile during those seventeen years."

Back in 1987, with Pinochet firmly in control of Chile, Pizarro finished high school and headed straight for the National Military Academy, where he graduated four years later as a second lieutenant. On graduation day, he shook General Pinochet's hand and began his career in Chile's armed forces. Pizarro moved around in various regiments and worked as a translator for the Army, translating for Chilean generals meeting with their foreign counterparts. That brought him in contact with military personnel from the U.S. Embassy in Santiago. In 1995, Pizarro said he struck up a friendship with one U.S. officer in particular, whom he declined to name. He listened to his new American friend and his colleagues speak of their adventures across the globe—from Panama to the Gulf War—with the U.S. military. Pizarro watched their videos and joined them at their homes for cookouts. "I was overwhelmed by their professionalism, their *esprit de corps*, their way of spreading good words, good news, their way of working. These guys were warriors," Pizarro recalled. "They went to a war, they won the war, they went back home, and they never went, you know, crazy, or cuckoo, or unreliable. They were normal people. And so it was very motivating for me to think, Maybe, maybe I can be a part of this, maybe." Pizarro began thinking of leaving the Chilean forces to join the U.S. military. "I love the Chilean Army," he said. But "I have an opportunity because I have dual citizenship to join an army of a nation that has the same goals of democracy of Western society that Chile [has], but they're actually deploying troops. I [felt] like a doctor that will study for thirty years and never, ever, ever operate [on] a single human being. I'm a professional. I want[ed] to deploy." About a month after informing his superiors in Chile, Pizarro joined the U.S. Marines, "guaranteed deployed within ninety days. I love it. I was the happiest guy."

Pizarro began his U.S. military career training at Paris Island, South Carolina, and then at the U.S. Armor School in Fort Knox, Kentucky. When he graduated in 1996, he says the commander of the Marine Detachment at Fort Knox called him into his office.

"Jose, is it true that you were a Chilean Army Officer?"

"Yes, sir."

"Do you speak Spanish?"

"Yes, sir. Better than English."

"Maybe we're going to have a career move for you," the commander told Pizarro. Shortly after that conversation, Pizarro was sent to Camp Lejeune in North Carolina before being ordered by the Second Marine Expeditionary Force to work for three years, from 1996 to 1999, "at the Marine unit specializing in military operations in South America, called the Unitas." Pizarro says that for the next three years, he traveled throughout Latin America working with U.S. Southern Command as a translator for "lieutenant colonels, colonels, and admirals from the U.S. Navy and the U.S. Marine Corps going down to South America. Either if they needed to go for a forty-eight-hours meeting with the Commander in Chief of the Brazilian Marine Corps, they took me as a translator, or if they needed to conduct a three-week military exercise in Colombia, I went over there with a lieutenant colonel, with a U.S. Marine lieutenant colonel as a translator. So I loved it. It was a super, super-interesting experience. I went to every single nation in Latin America, except Bolivia. I went to Brazil, Argentina, Chile, Ecuador, Colombia, Venezuela, you name it. I was having the time of my life learning how to present U.S. foreign policy, U.S. defense atmospheric policies to the armed forces in Latin America."

After three years working with Unitas and the U.S. Southern Command, Pizarro decided to take his experience to the private sector. In 1999, he said, he "offered my services" to the U.S. weapons manufacturer General

Dynamics. He said the connections he made during his work with the U.S. military in Latin America put him in a prime position to help General Dynamics expand its sales and marketing in the region. "I knew [Latin American governments'] needs for helicopters, weapon systems, etc.," Pizarro recalled. "I believe I grasped a certain degree of understanding of their needs, their budgets, their budget culture, etc." General Dynamics hired Pizarro and, he says, made him the head of its Latin American division. "I was in charge of sales of Mark 19, MK19, GOA19, which is automatic grenade launchers, rockets, and electric airborne, helicopter-borne, electric helicopter-borne machine guns," said Pizarro. He worked with General Dynamics for a year and a half and said he made so much money in salary and bonuses pushing weapons to Latin American governments that he was able to start his own company. "I realized, hey, I have enough money to, you know, create my own company and work for me instead of working for somebody else."

In 2001, Pizarro started Red Tactica (Tactical Network), a company that would serve as a liaison between Latin American governments and U.S. weapons manufacturers. "Because every single Latin American Government has a military attaché, a naval attaché, an air force attaché, and a police attaché on separate buildings actually, times sixteen countries, sixteen countries times four military attachés, that was a major, major market for me," Pizarro said. "So we went, for example, to the Argentinean Embassy. 'Good morning, my name is Mike Pizarro. I'm a U.S. citizen, and I'm also a Chilean citizen. I'm bilingual. I'm bicultural. I know exactly, sir, Admiral, what you're looking for. You're looking for submarines, torpedoes, radars, electronic communication system,' etc., etc." Eventually, Pizarro struck up a relationship with virtually every defense and military attaché from "friendly" Latin American nations and earned a reputation as a go-to guy for Latin American countries seeking to purchase specialized weapons systems from major defense companies.

Pizarro hotly denied that he was an arms dealer and scoffed at the label. Instead, he said, he was selling "business intelligence" to Latin American officials he characterized as essentially paying him to do their jobs. "A military attaché by definition is a gift, is a reward, is a promotion, is a vacation in Washington. You're not supposed to actually work," Pizarro said. "That is in the Latino world. For us, if you're a general and you get promoted to a senior general, you get a year of vacation, a paid vacation with your entire family in Washington, D.C. So having—and because I knew this—having a guy who can actually do the job for you for a few thousand dollars a month or less than that, it was a major advantage. It was very attractive to them." Pizarro says he worked with the military attachés from "every single" Latin American nation in good standing with the United States, "selling the information" to them on where they could purchase various weapons systems, military hardware, radars, spare parts—even rifles. Pizarro also sold his services to defense and weapons companies—in both the United States and in Europe—seeking to break into Latin American markets. He would tell these companies, "Well, let's say you pay me $10,000 a month times three months, I will provide you with enough information and enough business intelligence so your salespeople will know exactly which doors to knock, to which officers they're supposed to address, and how and when and for how much and for how long."

Pizarro said he made enough money selling "business intelligence" that he decided in early 2003 to "step away from the company and enjoy the money, enjoy my free time." Leaving the day-to-day operations of Red Tactica to his business partners, Pizarro began writing for a German magazine focused on military technology. In February 2003, as the United States prepared to invade Iraq, a producer at CNN's Spanish-language channel contacted Pizarro and asked him to come to the network's Washington bureau to apply for a possible position with the network as a commentator on the war. Pizarro said after testing him out, "They offered me a full-time job for the time of the war. So they put me in a hotel, at the CNN Hotel, at CNN headquarters in Atlanta for a month, plus the previous month in Washington, close to my house. I mean, I was showing up so many times per day that they thought it was necessary for me to be on call. So they provided [me] with a full salary." All the while, Red Tactica was on "auto pilot." Pizarro said that during his time in Atlanta, he struck up a friendship with

retired Gen. Wesley Clark, former Supreme Allied Commander of NATO
and future 2004 Democratic presidential candidate, who was doing commentary and analysis for CNN as well. "I'm so embarrassed to say this,"
Pizarro recalled, "but if I needed to ask, if I have a question from the public
or a major question from common sense, I just went to the coffee shop of
CNN in English," where he would ask Clark for advice on what analysis to
offer on air. Pizarro would then use Clark's analysis in his own commentary
on CNN en Español. "Love the guy," Pizarro says of Clark. "Love the guy."

Pizarro's full-time job with CNN en Español lasted until the end of April,
when he turned his attentions back to Red Tactica. With the Iraq occupation
underway, he began going to military shows and expos looking for new
business. In July 2003, Pizarro went to the Modern Marine Expo in Quan-
tico, Virginia, when a "very good-looking" woman at one of the booths
caught his eye. It turned out she was a rep for Blackwater USA, Pizarro said,
a former police officer in charge of selling Blackwater's target systems.
Pizarro had never heard of Blackwater and struck up a conversation with
the attractive representative about Red Tactica helping to market Blackwater's systems. Pizarro recalled that the Blackwater system was "fantastic.
It's absolutely fabulous. I told them, I can help you to sell that in Latin
America." After questioning Pizarro about his credentials, the Blackwater
representative suggested that Pizarro travel down to Blackwater's compound
in Moyock. What he would see on that trip would change Pizarro's life.

In describing his first visit to Blackwater in the summer of 2003, just as
the mercenary boom was getting under way in Iraq, Pizarro speaks with the
enthusiasm of a child describing Christmas presents to his friends at school.
"My hair was on fire," he recalled. "It's a private army in the twenty-first century. A private company with their own training, their own private forces to
protect U.S. government facilities in a war zone. It was like out of a *Dr. No*
movie. . . . It's like a movie. It's a gigantic facility with a military urban terrain. It's a mock city where you can train with real-life ammunition or
paintball, with vehicles, with helicopters. Gosh, impressive, very, very
impressive." Pizarro thought he was essentially going to a souped-up firing

and training range, but when he got there, "I saw people from all over the world training over there—civilians, military personnel, army personnel, naval, navy personnel, marines, air force, para-rescue. Wow, it was like a private military base."

Pizarro said that "within five seconds I dropped the idea of helping them in selling target systems" and began to dream of how he could fit into this incredible movie set. Pizarro said that he didn't want to blow his opportunity, so "I kept my mouth shut." In his head, though, he envisioned providing Chilean forces to Blackwater. "I didn't want to look like a walking suitcase," he said. "It was a hunch. Like maybe, maybe if I can get enough Chilean Navy SEALs, enough Chilean Army paratroopers, enough Chilean Marine Corps commandos, I know how professional they are, they're superyoung, they're recently retired, with twenty years or fifteen years of active duty, and working as a supermarket security guard—I mean, I should, in theory, I should be able to create something." Pizarro said after his first visit to Blackwater, he "spent a few weeks talking to people on the phone back in Chile. I called them from Washington. I hooked up with a few lieutenant colonels, a few retired majors. 'Can you get a hundred commandos?' 'Can you get a hundred paratroopers?' 'Can you get Navy SEALs, bilingual within a couple of weeks?' 'Yes,' 'No,' 'OK.' 'I can get twenty.' Another guy: 'I can get seven.' 'I can get twenty-five.'" The phone calls led to meetings in Santiago with military officials, but Pizarro said the reception was hardly enthusiastic. He heard the same things over and over: "That sounds illegal"; "That sounds dirty"; "That doesn't sound right"; "No, we're not interested"; "You're going [to] fail." But Pizarro said these responses "were actually fueling me more. I was convinced that I was doing the right thing."

A major reason Pizarro said he believed this is that he had been speaking regularly with Doug Brooks, president of the International Peace Operations Association, the private military trade group of which Blackwater is now a prominent member. "[Brooks] doesn't strike me as an illegal, evil bastard," recalled Pizarro. "He strikes me as a professional young man. And he told me this is perfectly legal. I mean, I spent countless meetings with his friends at his office. I mean, we both live in Washington, and after I was convinced that I was doing what's legal, what's right, what's correct, then I made up my mind. Nothing will stop me." In an e-mail, Brooks admitted he met with Pizarro "a few times" but said he didn't "recall discussion [of the] legality" of Pizarro's plan. Eventually, after "hundreds of meetings," Pizarro said he found people from Chile's military community who believed in his idea of supplying Chilean forces to U.S. companies: "I met the right colonel, the right lieutenant colonel, the right admiral, the right retired personnel." Pizarro and his comrades hired a private Chilean human resources firm to help recruit men for their plan. When Pizarro felt it was a go, he returned to the United States to make his pitch to Blackwater in October 2003. He said he spoke to Blackwater president Gary Jackson. "Gary didn't like the project," Pizarro recalled. "He kicked me out of his office, like, 'Hey, no way. We're not going to do this. It's just, it's too crazy. Get out of here.'" Then, Pizarro said, he landed a meeting with Erik Prince at Prince's office in Virginia. As Pizarro told it, he walked into the office and Prince said, "Who the hell are you?"

"My name is Mike Pizarro. Do we have five minutes, sir?"

"You got three," Prince shot back.

Pizarro said he presented Prince with a PowerPoint presentation on the Chilean forces he wanted to provide Blackwater. Within moments, Pizarro recalled, Prince warmed to the idea. "Guess what?" Pizarro recalled with excitement. "When [Prince] was a U.S. Navy SEAL, he was in Chile." Prince, he said, had a high regard for Chilean forces. "So he knew the Chilean Navy SEALs. He got friends over there. He knew our professionalism, the orientation of our training, how bilingual are our enlisted personnel, and the quality of our officers." Pizarro recalled that Prince said, "Mike, listen, you convinced me. If you can get one, just one Chilean Navy SEAL to work for me, this is worth it. Go ahead and impress me." Pizarro said as he was leaving the Virginia office, Prince told him, "Once you're ready for a demo, give us a call. I will send a few evaluators" to Chile. The next morning, Pizarro was on a plane back to Santiago.

Back in Chile, Pizarro moved quickly. He and his business partners established a company, Grupo Táctico, and rented a ranch in Calera de Tango, south of Santiago, where they could review prospective soldiers. Pizarro's commercial manager was Herman Brady Maquiavello, son of Herman Brady Roche, Pinochet's former defense minister.[18] On October 12, 2003, they placed an ad in the leading daily newspaper, El Mercurio: "International company is looking for former military officers to work abroad. Officers, deputy officers, former members of the Special Forces, preferably. Good health and physical condition. Basic command of English. Retirement documents (mandatory). October 20 to 24, from 8:45 am to 5 pm."[19] As applicants began showing up for interviews with Pizarro and his colleagues, word spread that salaries as high as $3,000 a month were being offered,[20] far greater than the $400 monthly pay for soldiers in Chile.[21] A former soldier who applied for the job told the Chilean newspaper La Tercera, "We were informed that a foreign security company needs around 200 former military officers to work as security guards in Iraq."[22] Another said, "I would like to get that job. They pay $2,500 and they told me at the fort that the job entailed going to Iraq to watch several facilities and oil wells."[23] It didn't take long for Pizarro to get flooded with applications from retired Chilean officers and those wishing to retire so that they could join this new private force.[24]

Before he knew it, Pizarro had more than a thousand applications to sort through.[25] But just as he was beginning to make progress, the Chilean press began to report on his activities. Reports emerged that a Chilean naval commander had allegedly violated military procedure and announced the job offer to soldiers, while some Socialist lawmakers accused Pizarro's colleagues of headhunting soldiers.[26] Within days of the ad's appearance in the paper, Chilean parliamentarians began calling for Pizarro to be investigated. "Lawmakers recalled that the Defense Ministry—not a private corporation—is the only body that, at the request of the UN, may select active military members to support the peacekeeping forces in that country. So any other method would be illegal," reported La Tercera shortly after Pizarro's project became public.[27] Pizarro responded at the time that his activities were "absolutely legal and transparent."[28] The Chilean press also recalled a controversy in July 2002 when Pizarro was quoted by a Brazilian paper, *Jornal do Brasil*, claiming that Chile's war academy was reviewing a plan for twenty-six hundred troops from the United States, Chile, Argentina, Uruguay, Ecuador, and Peru to intervene in Colombia's battle against FARC rebels, under the auspices of the United Nations.[29] The Chilean Defense Ministry was forced to issue a public denial, creating an awkward situation between Chile and Colombia.[30] There were also rumblings in Chile that Pizarro was working with the CIA. "Obviously, Mike Pizarro is a CIA agent, supported by the FBI and the Imperial Forces of the United States, and obviously, he's working for President Bush," Pizarro recalled with sarcasm. "There is a gossip that he also goes to the ranch of President Bush in Texas. I mean, the stories are absolutely flat-out ignorance."

In the midst of all of this, Pizarro forged ahead. He and his colleagues worked feverishly at their ranch to whittle down the number of men they would present to the Blackwater evaluators from one thousand to three hundred.[31] They purchased dozens of rubber and ceramic "dummy" rifles for training and painted them black.[32] By late October, Pizarro had his three hundred men, and he called Erik Prince. "We're ready," he told Prince. "Send your people." He said Prince told him that he was leaving for Switzerland but gave him Gary Jackson's cell phone number. Aware of Jackson's attitude about the project, Prince told Pizarro to wait a few minutes to call Jackson so that Prince could brief the Blackwater president, according to Pizarro. "Then I called Gary, and Gary was obviously not happy," Pizarro recalled. He said Jackson told him, "OK, I just talked to Erik. This is a fucking waste of time. I'll send my three evaluators there, but Mike, you better deliver on your promise because this is a complete waste of time," blah, blah, blah. He was very negative. But that's just the way Gary is."

Back at the ranch in Chile, Pizarro addressed the three hundred men he and his colleagues had chosen for evaluation by Blackwater. "You will be interviewed by American evaluators. They will ask you basic questions," Pizarro told the Chilean soldiers. "They will test the level of your leadership skills,

how smart you are, how well trained you are, etc., your physical ability."
Pizarro said they would be divided into three groups—one for each of the
three U.S. evaluators. "It will be a hundred guys per American. It will take
basically the entire day. So you need to be patient. I can make no promises.
If we can impress these guys, maybe, maybe we'll be hired to work in Iraq
protecting U.S. Consulates and Embassy," Pizarro said. In the last week of
November 2003, Pizarro said, the Blackwater evaluators arrived in Chile.
"The three of them, former U.S. Navy SEALs, impressive guys, six foot tall,
gigantic, excellent shape, very professional," Pizarro recalled. "The three of
them bilingual. I mean super-impressive. They evaluated 300 guys" in three
days. "They went back to the States, and those were the longest fourteen
days of my life because for fourteen days there was no news from Blackwater whatsoever."

In the meantime, the controversy in Chile about Pizarro's activities was
growing. Pizarro said that a few hours before the Blackwater evaluators
arrived at the ranch, a Chilean TV station showed up and ended up filming
the activities there. On national television in Chile, Pizarro was accused of
"training a private army," under the supervision of U.S. military people, he
said. "The news flash presented me like some sort of Arnold
Schwarzenegger—Latino version of—it was absurd," Pizarro recalled. "My
family was crying on the phone. My mom was calling, 'Mike, what are you
doing? We're going to jail.' 'No, mom. It's a dummy rifle.' 'It looks so real.
You're going down.' I mean, even my girlfriend kicked me out." Despite the
mounting controversy and the silence from Blackwater, Pizarro held out
hope that his plan would succeed.

Then on December 18, Pizarro said he got an e-mail from Gary Jackson.
*We're up. You're bringing 100 people in February to be evaluated in the United
States.* Pizarro said he chose his "best 100 guys" and prepared to head to
North Carolina. The Chilean soldiers were sequestered in Chile for forty-
eight hours before departing and were not allowed to call their families.[33]
They went to the U.S. Embassy in Santiago, which promptly issued them
multiple entry visas.[34] On February 4, 2004, Pizarro and seventy-eight

Chilean soldiers arrived at Moyock for "evaluation." Training, Pizarro asserted, "is illegal. You cannot train. They were *evaluated*." Pizarro said, "Every single one of them was evaluated for English skills, medical skills, first aid, rifle range, pistol range, driving skills, telecommunication skills, and leadership." Pizarro was particularly impressed with one exercise in which Blackwater evaluators used toy soldiers to present various scenarios that could occur in Iraq and quizzed the Chileans on how they would handle the situation. It was "very smart, very cheap," Pizarro recalled with amazement. "It didn't cost a penny, but it really tested my guys to extreme." In all, the first batch of seventy-eight Chileans spent ten days at Blackwater. Pizarro said the evaluators "were very impressed" with his men. Only one was sent home, he said, because of an attitude problem.

On February 14, 2004, Blackwater flew the first group of Chilean commandos from North Carolina to Baghdad. "They got deployed immediately," Pizarro said. "And then I got a contract for another group of seventy-eight within twenty-four hours. So I flew over [to Blackwater] again at the end of February with the second group." Pizarro recalled with great pride that Gary Jackson—who he said had doubted the project all along—was interviewed by a Chilean newspaper the day the first group of Chileans set off for Iraq, ahead of schedule. "They did incredibly well and they are absolute professionals," Jackson told *La Tercera*. "So they are leaving today on a flight that departs in the morning to the Middle East."[35] Jim Sierawski, Blackwater's director of training, said the deployment happened fast because the Chilean commandos did not need additional training beyond what they had received in the Chilean armed forces. "Their knowledge provides them with the necessary skills to do what they have to do in different missions," he said.[36] "The Chilean guys from group one were so highly trained, I mean the average age was forty-three years old," Pizarro recalled. "These were highly seasoned commandos."

Once in Iraq, the Chilean forces were tasked with doing "static protection" of buildings—generally headquarters of State Department or CPA facilities, Pizarro said. The first group of Chileans was deployed in

Samawah, where Pizarro said they guarded a CPA building, as well as a regional office in Diwaniyah. The second batch went straight for a hotel in Hillah that had been converted to an occupation building. They also guarded a CPA headquarters in the Shiite holy city of Karbala. "We are confident," former Chilean Army officer Carlos Wamgnet told *La Tercera*. "This mission is not something new to us. After all, it is extending our military career."[37] Former Marine John Rivas told the paper, "I don't feel like a mercenary."[38] Pizarro traveled to Iraq twice to observe his men on contract with Blackwater, remaining in the country for a month and traveling to all of the sites "from Baghdad to Basra" where Chileans were deployed. "We have been successful. We're not profiting from death. We're not killing people," Pizarro said. "We're not shooting. We're not operating on open streets. We're providing static security services. We do not interact with Iraqi people. We do not patrol the Iraqi street. We never touch, talk, or get involved in any way, shape, or form with civilians in Iraq." But, as journalist Louis E. V. Nevaer reported soon after the Chileans arrived in Iraq, "Newspapers in Chile have estimated that approximately 37 Chileans in Iraq are seasoned veterans of the Pinochet era. Government officials in Santiago are alarmed that men who enjoy amnesty in Chile—provided they remain in 'retirement' from their past military activities—are now in Iraq."[39]

Pizarro said that Blackwater was so impressed with the Chileans that the company stopped bringing them en masse for evaluation to North Carolina. Instead, Pizarro said he would bring twenty a month to Blackwater's compound and the rest would fly directly from Santiago to Jordan, where they would be evaluated by Blackwater officials in Amman before being deployed in Iraq. "We created such level of comfort, of professionalism, of trust. . . . Blackwater was addicted to us," Pizarro said. "Basically for the price of one U.S. former operator, they were getting four, sometimes five Chilean commandos." He described Blackwater's thirst for more Chileans as "very, very, very aggressive." In all, Pizarro said he provided 756 Chilean soldiers to Blackwater and other companies over two years and a month. By March 2004 Gary Jackson had become a public backer of the Chilean forces. In an interview with the *Guardian* newspaper, he explained that Chile was the only Latin American country where Blackwater had hired commandos for Iraq. "We scour the ends of the earth to find professionals—the Chilean commandos are very, very professional and they fit within the Blackwater system," Jackson said. "We didn't just come down and say, 'You and you and you, come work for us.' They were all vetted in Chile and all of them have military backgrounds. This is not the Boy Scouts."[40] Amid allegations from Chilean lawmakers that his activities were illegal and that the men Pizarro was recruiting were "mercenaries," Pizarro registered his firm in Uruguay to avoid legal troubles in Chile. So the contracting was eventually done between Blackwater and a Uruguayan ghost company called Neskowin.[41] "It is 110 percent legal," Pizarro said in April 2004. "We are bullet proof. They can do nothing to stop us."[42]

But as word spread about the use of Chilean commandos trained under Pinochet, it evoked strong condemnation in the country. As a rotating member of the UN Security Council, Chile opposed the war in Iraq.[43] "The presence of Chilean paramilitaries in Iraq has caused a visceral rejection in the population, 92% of which just a year ago rejected any intervention of the US in the country," said Chilean writer Roberto Manríquez in June 2004.[44] It also sparked outrage and horror from victims of the Pinochet regime. "It is sickening that Chilean army officers are considered to be good soldiers because of the experience they acquired during the dictatorship years," said Tito Tricot, a Chilean sociologist who was imprisoned and tortured under the dictatorship.[45] The Chilean commandos working for Blackwater "are valued for their expertise in kidnapping, torturing and killing defenseless civilians. What should be a national shame turns into a market asset due to the privatization of the Iraqi war. All this is possible, not only because of the United States' absolute disrespect for human rights, but also due to the fact that justice has not been done in Chile either. Therefore, members of the Armed Forces that should be in prison due to the atrocities they committed under the dictatorship, walk freely the streets of our country as if nothing had happened. Moreover, they are now rewarded for their criminal past."[46]

Journalist Gustavo González said that some of the Chileans working for Blackwater "form part of those displaced from active duty by a plan for the modernisation of the armed forces applied in the army by General Luis Emilio Cheyre, the current army chief. Cheyre, like his predecessor, General Ricardo Izurieta, who replaced Pinochet in 1998 as commander-in-chief of the army, carried out a discreet but effective purge, forcing into retirement officers and non-commissioned officers who played a role in the dictatorship's repression, in which some 3,000 people were killed or 'disappeared.'"[47]

Despite growing controversy in Chile over the export of "Chilean mercenaries" to fight a war the vast majority of Chileans—and the country's elected government—opposed, things were moving along smoothly for Pizarro, and he was predicting in the Chilean press that by 2006 he would have three thousand Chileans deployed in Iraq.[48] In September 2004, Pizarro's new company, Global Guards, which he says was modeled on Blackwater, placed another ad in El Mercurio—this time recruiting helicopter pilots and mechanics to operate "air taxis" for businesspeople going in and out of Iraq.[49] La Tercera reported that the pilots would be paid $12,000 a month, while mechanics would earn around $4,000. Within hours, forty pilots and seventy mechanics had sent in their résumés.[50]

But then Pizarro made a terrible miscalculation.

At the height of his operation, in late 2004, Pizarro branched out from Blackwater and began simultaneously working with its direct competitor, Triple Canopy. "Triple Canopy started asking me for hundreds and hundreds of former Chilean paratroopers for static security [in Iraq]," Pizarro recalled. Eager to expand his business, Pizarro said he provided the company with four hundred Chilean guards. "That was a bad mix. I never realized how much [Blackwater and Triple Canopy] hated each other." When Blackwater got wind of the deal with Triple Canopy, Pizarro said, Gary Jackson told him Blackwater was ending the partnership. "Gary told me that he felt betrayed, that my move was unforgivable. He couldn't forgive, he could not pardon me, that I betrayed his trust. He was the one who—which in a way is true—he basically helped me to create my own company." Pizarro said he deeply regrets that his Blackwater contracts fell through and pointed out that the men he was providing Blackwater were "Tier One" soldiers, "top-notch, fully bilingual, former special forces operators," while Triple Canopy was interested in cheaper "Tier Two" men, "an average former infantry person with limited language skills and limited operational experience." Even still, Pizarro said, Blackwater would no longer renew his contracts. "I ended up losing Blackwater," he recalled with obvious disappointment. "Blackwater is a fantastic company." To add insult to injury, Blackwater independently hired some of Pizarro's Chilean commandos directly. While he is "disappointed" in Blackwater, Pizarro said, "The good news is [the Chileans were] making a lot more money."

After he lost the Blackwater contracts, Pizarro continued to provide soldiers to Triple Canopy and Boots and Coots, a Texas company that specialized in fighting oil well fires. Pizarro's Chilean commandos became known as the "Black Penguins," a name he said Blackwater gave his men "because we came from a land from the Antarctica area, from the land of the snow; very short, very dark guys, very slow moving, fully equipped. They called us the penguins." Pizarro took that on as a brand for his forces and developed a logo around the concept. He also said "Black Penguins" was an effort to "emulate Blackwater." Beginning in July 2005, Pizarro said Blackwater began the process of replacing his Chileans with cheaper forces, "Tier Three, definitely. No English . . . no major military experience." Around the time his Blackwater relationship went sour, Pizarro said, competition had gotten stiff because the "Iraq reconstruction" was put on hold, meaning there were fewer projects for private forces to guard. Many firms, he said, began hiring less-trained, cheaper forces. "We were competing against Salvadorans, Peruvians, Nigerians, Jordanians, Fijians," he recalled. "We couldn't compete with them. Our prices were three times their price."

Blackwater's Plan Colombia

In the meantime, like many private military firms, Blackwater was internationalizing its force inside Iraq and had broadened out from Chileans, hiring Colombian forces for deployment in Iraq.[51] In July 2005, Jeffrey Shippy, who formerly worked for the private U.S. security company Dyn-Corp International, began trying to market Colombian forces to companies operating in Iraq. "These forces have been fighting terrorists the last 41 years," Shippy wrote in a Web posting advertising the benefits of hiring Colombian forces. "These troops have been trained by the U.S. Navy SEALs and the U.S. [Drug Enforcement Administration] to conduct counter-drug/counter-terror ops in the jungles and rivers of Colombia."[52] At the time, Shippy was offering the services of more than one thousand U.S.-trained former soldiers and police officers from Colombia. A U.S. Air Force veteran, Shippy said he came up with the concept after visiting Baghdad and seeing the market. "The U.S. State Department is very interested in saving money on security now," Shippy said. "Because they're driving the prices down, we're seeking Third World people to fill the positions."[53] At the time, according to the *Los Angeles Times*, Blackwater had deployed some 120 Colombians in Iraq.[54] While Gary Jackson refused to confirm that to the *Times*, Blackwater's use of Colombian troops became undeniable a year later, in June 2006, when dozens of Colombians blew the whistle on what they portrayed as Blackwater's cheating them out of their pay in Baghdad.

In late August 2006, thirty-five Colombian troops on contract in Iraq with Blackwater claimed in interviews with the Colombian magazine *Semana* that Blackwater had defrauded them and was paying them just $34 a day for a job that earned exponentially more for their U.S. counterparts.[55] Retired Colombian Army Captain Esteban Osorio said the saga began in Colombia in September 2005. "That was when I ran into a sergeant who told me, 'Sir, they are recruiting people to send to Iraq. They pay good money, like $6,000 or $7,000 a month, no taxes. Let's go and give them our resumes.' That number stuck in my head," Osorio told *Semana*. "Never in my life had I imagined so much money," said former National Army Major Juan Carlos Forero. "Who wouldn't be tempted by the prospect of a job where you earn six or seven times what they pay you?" After hearing about the prospect of working for big money in Iraq, Forero went to a recruitment office in Bogotá to hand in his resume. "The company was called ID Systems," he recalled. "This firm is a representative of an American firm called Blackwater. They are one of the biggest private security contractors in the world, and they work for the United States government." When he arrived at ID Systems, Forero said he was pleased to see several other ex-military officers—including Captain Osorio, whom he knew. Osorio said a retired Army Captain named Gonzalo Guevara greeted the men. "He told us that we were basically going to go provide security at military installations in Iraq," he recalled. "He told us that the salaries were around $4,000 monthly." No longer the rumored $7,000, but regardless, "it was very good money."

In October 2005, the men said they were told to report to a training camp at the Escuela de Caballeria (School of Cavalry) in the north of Bogotá, where they said ex–U.S. military personnel conducted courses ranging from country briefings about Iraq and the "enemy" to arms handling and a range of firing tests. A Colombian government official told Semana that the military had done a "favor" by lending one of its bases for the training operation. "It is a company backed by the American government that solicited the cooperation of the military, which consists of permitting the use of military facilities, under the condition that they will not recruit active personnel," the official told Semana. After the training, the men said they were told to be ready for deployment at a moment's notice. It wasn't until June 2006 that the call came from ID Systems that Blackwater was ready for them in Iraq—but instead of $4,000, they were now told they would be paid just $2,700 a month. While disappointing, it was still much more money than any of the men were making in Colombia. Major Forero says one evening at midnight they were given contracts to sign and told to be at the airport in four hours. "We didn't have a chance to read the contract," he recalled. "We just signed and ran because when they gave it to us they told us that we had to be at the airport in four hours and since everything was so rushed we hardly had time to go to say goodbye to our families, pack our suitcases and head to El Dorado [Bogotá's airport]." During a journey to Baghdad that took them to Venezuela, Germany, and Jordan, the men finally had time to read the contracts they had just signed. "That's when we realized that something was wrong, because it said they were going to pay us $34 a day, which is to say that our salary was going to be $1,000 not $2,700," recalled Forero.

When the Colombians arrived in Baghdad, they immediately raised the issue of their pay with their supervisors and were told to bring it up later. In Baghdad, they learned that they would be replacing a group of Romanian soldiers on contract with Blackwater. "When we joined with those Romanians they asked us how much we had been contracted for and we told them for $1,000." The Romanians were shocked. "No one in the world comes to Baghdad for only $1,000," the Romanians said, adding that they were being paid $4,000 to do the same work. The Colombians say they complained to both Blackwater and ID Systems and said that if they were not going to be paid at least the $2,700 a month they were promised, they wanted to be returned to Colombia. "When we got to the base, they took away all our return plane tickets. They brought us together and told us that if we wanted to get back we could do it by our own means," Captain Osorio recalled. "They told us that he who wanted to go back could do so, but we didn't have a single peso and where were we going to get in Baghdad the 10 or 12 million pesos for a ticket to Colombia?" He said the supervisors "threatened to remove us from the base and leave us in the street in Baghdad, where one is vulnerable to being killed, or, at best, kidnapped." Desperate, the men contacted journalists from *Semana*, which reported on their situation. "We want the people they are recruiting in Colombia to be aware of the reality and not allow themselves to be deceived," Forero told the magazine. Another alleged, "We were tricked by the company into believing we would make much more money." Blackwater vice president Chris Taylor confirmed that the Colombians were being paid as little as they alleged but said it was the result of recently revised contractual terms. "There was a change in contract, one contract expired, another task order was bid upon, and so the numbers are different," Taylor said. "Every single

Colombian signed a contract for $34 a day before they went over to Iraq."[56] Blackwater said it had offered to repatriate the men after they complained about their pay. In 2007, Captain Guevara, one of the Colombian recruiters who had hired the men for Blackwater, was gunned down in Bogatá.

Business as Usual

While the international mercenary market servicing the U.S. wars in Iraq and Afghanistan exploded, almost overnight, revelations of training camps and operations like Pizarro's in Chile surfaced across Latin America. In September 2005, news broke of a secret training camp in the remote mountain area of Lepaterique, Honduras, fifteen miles west of Tegucigalpa.[57] It was being operated by a Chicago-based firm called Your Solutions, reportedly headed by Angel Méndez, an ex-soldier from the United States.[58] In the 1980s, the army base at Lepaterique served as a CIA training ground for the Nicaraguan Contras and the headquarters of the notorious Battalion 316,[59] a U.S.-backed Honduran death squad responsible for widespread political killings and torture throughout the 1980s, when John Negroponte was U.S. Ambassador to Honduras. Two decades later, a private U.S. company was using it to prepare Honduran soldiers to work for U.S. mercenary companies in Iraq. The instructors "explained to us that where we were going everyone would be our enemy, and we'd have to look at them that way, because they would want to kill us, and the gringos too,"[60] said an unidentified trainee. Many of the Hondurans recruited by Your Solutions had been among the troops their country sent to Iraq in 2003.[61] The Honduran government subsequently pulled those troops out amid widespread domestic opposition to the war—and right after it was announced that Negroponte was to be the new U.S. Ambassador to Iraq. In September, it was revealed that it wasn't just Hondurans who were being contracted by Your Solutions. At the training camp were more than two hundred Chileans preparing for Iraq deployment.[62]

Among the Chileans working with Your Solutions overseeing the operation in Honduras was Oscar Aspe, a business partner of Pizarro's, who had headed one of the Chilean units in Baghdad on the Blackwater contract in

2004.[63] A former Chilean marine and Navy commando, Aspe said of his time in Iraq, "I felt more danger in Chile when I did high-risk operations."[64] Aspe was accused of being involved with questionable practices during his time in Chile's security forces. When Honduran authorities learned of the camp in September 2005 and that the Chileans had entered the country on tourist visas, Honduran Foreign Minister Daniel Ramos ordered the Chileans to leave the country, saying the Honduran Constitution prohibited security and military training of foreigners on its soil. "The foreigners better leave the country," Ramos declared at a news conference. "If not, we will be forced to take more serious measures."[66] There was nothing to suggest that Your Solutions had any business relationship with Blackwater. Reports said that the men were to deploy to Iraq with Triple Canopy as part of its contract to provide security for U.S. installations.[67] Your Solutions general manager Benjamin Canales, a former Honduran soldier,[68] defended the training in Honduras. "These people are not mercenaries, as some people have called them," he said. "This hurts because these are honorable people who aren't bothering anybody."[69] He added that the Chileans were being trained as "private bodyguards," not as a "national army."[70] At that point, Your Solutions had already successfully sent thirty-six Hondurans to Iraq and had planned to send another 353 Hondurans abroad, along with 211 Chileans.[71] The men were reportedly to be paid about $1,000 a month[72]—far less than Pizarro's Chileans. Aspe was defiant about the expulsion of Your Solutions from Honduras. "Our mission is to arrive in Iraq whether we are expelled or not from [Honduras]," he said.[73] By November, Your Solutions was reported to have sent 108 Hondurans, eighty-eight Chileans and sixteen Nicaraguans to Iraq—in just one day.[74] Similar operations were reportedly taking place in Nicaragua and Peru. In November 2006, the Honduran government imposed a $25,000 fine on Your Solutions for violating the country's labor laws. "The fine was imposed because the company was training mercenaries, and the act of being a mercenary is a form of violating labor rights in whatever country," said a government spokesperson, Santos Flores.[75] By then, Benjamin Canales had already fled the country.[76]

As for Jose Miguel Pizarro, in October 2005 a military prosecutor in Chile, Waldo Martinez, charged him with "organizing armed combat groups and illegally assuming functions that correspond to the armed forces and police."[77] The charge carried a maximum sentence of five years in prison. Pizarro responded publicly by saying that all of his activities were legal and that he had authorization from the U.S. State Department to operate in Iraq. "We are not mercenaries," Pizarro said. "We are private international security guards. Mercenaries are criminals who are prosecuted throughout the world."[78] He accused Socialist politicians of being behind what he called a "smear" campaign and complained of a "lack of laws here in Chile to file suit against defamation." Pizarro has maintained that he broke no laws; he has not been convicted of any crimes or violations.

As of late 2006, Pizarro said no action had been taken against him, and he sounded unconcerned about potential future legal troubles. He continued to operate Global Guards and still provided soldiers to Triple Canopy and other companies in Iraq, but it was hardly the "gold rush" it was at the height of his partnership with Blackwater, which ended in December 2005 when the last of his contracts with the company expired. In 2006, Pizarro's "Black Penguins" were operating at the U.S. regional headquarters in Basra and Kirkuk, as well as protecting Triple Canopy's offices in Baghdad.[79] He said he was also "exploring the possibility of working in Pakistan and Afghanistan." Pizarro said he was ready at a moment's notice to resume his partnership with Blackwater if the company called. Pizarro described what he does as "the most beautiful way of making a living," and he said he was waiting with great anticipation for the United States to restart its "reconstruction" operations in Iraq, which he said would bring back the "market" for private security. "We will sit tight, and wait for the political environment created by the U.S. government to rebuild Iraq, and we strongly believe that it is a matter of months, not even years, that the American people will realize that it's mandatory that the United States rebuild that nation," Pizarro said in October 2006. "And rebuilding means 400 civilian companies moving in," all of which will require significant security operations from companies like his.

For former Chilean political prisoner and torture victim Tito Tricot, the use of Chileans and other soldiers from countries with atrocious human rights records by the United States is "nothing new." But, he says, "There is something deeply perverse about the privatization of the Iraq War and the utilization of mercenaries. This externalization of services or outsourcing attempts to lower costs—'Third World' mercenaries are paid less than their counterparts from the developed world—and maximize benefits, i.e.: 'Let others fight the war for the Americans.' In either case, the Iraqi people do not matter at all. It is precisely this dehumanization of the 'enemy' that makes it easier for the private companies and the U.S. government to recruit mercenaries. It is exactly the same strategy used by the Chilean military to train members of the secret police and make it easy to annihilate opponents of the dictatorship. In other words, Chilean mercenaries in Iraq is business as usual."[80]

CHAPTER FOURTEEN

"THE WHORES OF WAR"

WHILE BLACKWATER plotted out its expansion in the aftermath of the Fallujah ambush and internationalized its force in Iraq, the families of the four men killed there on March 31, 2004, looked for answers. They wanted to know how their loved ones ended up in the middle of the volatile city that morning, not to mention in SUVs, short-staffed and underarmed. All of the families considered themselves patriotic Americans, military families— Special Forces people. For the Zovko family, life since Fallujah had become consumed with a quest to understand their son's life and death. Danica Zovko, Jerry's mother, spent months piecing together details and memories.[1] She recalled a week back in the summer of 2003, when Jerry was visiting her before heading off to Iraq. The national power crisis had left her family without electricity in their Cleveland, Ohio, home. "We had a lot of time to just spend at home—no TV, no radio, no nothing—just sitting outside and talking." She remembered conversing with her son about his work and travels. "While we sat there, my Jerry told me, 'The best thing that one can do in life is to sort of plant seeds and see what's going on so that no matter where you go, you never close the doors behind you—that you always have someone to be there that you can count on.' When I think about that now, all that talking and everything we did, that's what that comes out to."

At first, it didn't seem to Danica Zovko that anyone other than the insurgents in Fallujah were to blame for her son's gruesome death. In the immediate aftermath, she could not bring herself to read any news stories or look at the graphic images, but there was little doubt in her mind who bore the responsibility. From the start, Blackwater seemed on top of the situation. At 8 p.m. on March 31, 2004, Erik Prince showed up in person at the family home in Cleveland, accompanied by a state trooper, Danica recalled. "[Prince] told us that Jerry was one of the men killed that day," she said. "We were numb. Just numb. He also told me that as far as he was concerned, if anyone was going to survive the war in Iraq, he thought it was going to be my Jerry. He said he saw Jerry, he met with Jerry, he was in Baghdad with Jerry, that Jerry was—you would think he really, really liked Jerry." Danica Zovko said Prince handed them a form to fill out for $3,000 for funeral expenses, promised that Jerry's body would be coming home soon and that Prince would attend the funeral in person.

On April 6, Paul Bremer wrote the Zovkos a letter: "I would like to personally assure you that Jerry was serving an honorable cause. The Iraqi people will be successful in their long journey towards a democratic and free society," Bremer wrote. "Jerry was a dedicated individual and will remain an inspiration to all of us in Iraq whether civilian or military. In the line of duty, he gave his all. Rest assured that our authorities are actively investigating Jerry's murder and that we will not rest until those responsible are punished for this despicable crime. You[r] family will remain in our thoughts and prayers as you confront this terrible tragedy in the difficult days ahead. I will do my part to ensure Jerry's contribution to this county will be forever remembered by the Iraq people [sic]."[2] Three days later, Jerry Zovko's remains returned to the United States in an aluminum box at Dover Air Force base in Delaware.[3] True to his word, Danica Zovko said, Erik Prince came to the wake and funeral.

In Tampa, Florida, meanwhile, Scott Helvenston's family held a funeral at Florida National Cemetery. His godfather, Circuit Judge William Levens, eulogized Scott as "a warrior who wanted peace—peace in his heart, peace in the world."[4] In the obituary in the paper, Helvenston's family wrote, "Scott lost his life heroically serving his country."[5] A few weeks later, Scott Helvenston's high school buddies heard about an event in his hometown of Winter Haven, Florida, organized by Republican State Representative Baxter Troutman. The "Operation Troop Salute" event was to honor servicemen and -women deployed in the war zone and would be attended by eight thousand people, among them First Lady Laura Bush and the president's brother, Florida Governor Jeb Bush.[6] Helvenston's buddies hoped that their fallen friend, the ex-SEAL, could be mentioned from the podium in honor of his service in Iraq. But Troutman, the organizer, said no—because Scott was a private contractor, not an active-duty soldier. "This was for the servicemen and -women who are not there by choice; to me, that makes a difference," Troutman said. "If I am an employee of a company and don't like what I am being subjected to, then I can come back home."[7] To Scott's friends, it was devastating. "They'd be naming streets after him if he was still enlisted," said high school pal Ed Twyford.[8]

Katy Helvenston-Wettengel was finding that there were almost no resources available to families of private contractors killed in the war and decided to reach out to one of the few people she could think of who would understand what she was going through. She looked up Donna Zovko and called her. The two developed a friendship and mutual quest for the truth of what had happened to their sons. "For the first couple of months, we flew back and forth, like, every other week, and we were there holding each other up.

When one was struggling, the other would pick us up and vice versa," recalled Helvenston-Wettengel. "Those first few months after, I didn't quit crying—for almost a year. I cried every day. I just missed him so much and he's my baby. I know he's a big macho man, but he's my baby."[9]

As more details on the ambush emerged in the media, the families moved from grieving to questioning how it all happened. "Why weren't they escorted?" wondered Tom Zovko, Jerry's brother. "I don't believe my brother would have done that. He was definitely not careless."[10] When Danica Zovko learned details of the mission the men had been on in Fallujah, she said, "I couldn't believe it. I could not believe my son would be escorting trucks and protecting trucks. That was not my son. That made me believe that no, that's not my Jerry, it must be someone else. I just couldn't see him doing that, I just couldn't. Even we buried his casket and I didn't see the body and I'm going on the words of people—politicians and money-hungry people—that that's him in there. I still sometimes dream that my Jerry is somewhere and just can't call or doesn't have a computer. But you know, I know it isn't that. But you can't help but hope." Danica Zovko said that things started to feel strange when Blackwater returned Jerry's belongings and some of his things were missing. She said her efforts to get these items—or information about them—were curiously stymied by the company. She started reading some articles about the incident and about her son's mysterious employer, Blackwater. "When you want to find out things, when you start questioning yourself, when you are not content with saying, 'It's in God's hands,' when you think, well let me find out, your eyes open," she said. "I found out there were no rules and no laws that govern what my son was doing, that it was an open place, you know. He was working for a company that could do whatever they wanted to do and however they wanted to do it." She started thinking more about the ambush: *What were they even doing in Fallujah?*

But it wasn't just the families who sensed something was off. In fact, the very day of the ambush, questions arose about "who is driving around in unprotected SUVs" in Iraq.[11] On Fox News, retired Col. Ralph Peters said, "I have to give you a painful answer on this. Either the most foolish contractors in the history of mankind or frankly it may have been intelligence people doing intelligence work. I don't know. I was talking to a colonel friend of mine who is over in the Gulf right now, today, about this. And he said, 'If they're contractors, this is Darwinian selection at work.'"[12] Meanwhile, on NPR the next day, *New York Times* correspondent Jeffrey Gettleman came out of Fallujah asking the same questions. "What's really mysterious, though, is why two unescorted, unarmored cars would be driving through the downtown of one of the most dangerous cities in Iraq without any serious protection," Gettleman said. "If this could happen to these guys, who are, you know, well trained and had a lot of experience in dealing with things like this, you know, what does it mean for others like myself who walk into situations in places like Fallujah and don't have the military background?"[13] Other mercenary firms weighed in as well. "We have a policy with our international security division that requires that they use armored vehicles at all times," said Frank Holder of Kroll on Fox News. "We won't take an assignment unless there are armored vehicles."[14]

A few days later, London's *Observer* newspaper ran a story referencing the Fallujah ambush, headlined "Veiled Threat: Why an SUV Is Now the Most Dangerous Vehicle in Iraq."[15] The article labeled SUVs "the occupation car of choice." The *Observer's* correspondent noted, "Falluja is a centre of the anti-American resistance, where even the police don't support the Americans. US soldiers don't drive through Falluja much. When they do, they have helicopter back-up and heavy armour. 'Almost every foreigner who has been killed here is an idiot,' said one ex-Navy SEAL. Soldiers often show little sympathy for those who fail to follow the right procedure."[16] In a reaction piece written from Amman and Baghdad, Professor Mark LeVine wrote in the *Christian Science Monitor*, "[M]any here see last week's carnage of Americans in Fallujah as suspicious. To send foreign contractors into Fallujah in late-model SUVs with armed escorts—down a traffic-clogged street on which they'd be literal sitting ducks—can be interpreted as a deliberate

US instigation of violence to be used as a pretext for 'punishment' by the US military."[17] Amid the graphic scenes of mutilation and the dominant rhetoric of revenge emanating from the Pentagon and White House, the obvious questions about the Blackwater mission that day were overshadowed, but they certainly did not disappear. The company clearly knew it would have to offer some sort of an explanation.

A week after the ambush, Blackwater put forward a narrative that the *New York Times* said "could deflect blame for the incident from Blackwater."[18] "The truth is, we got led into this ambush," Blackwater vice president Patrick Toohey, a decorated career military officer, told the *Times*. "We were set up."[19] According to Blackwater's version of events, as reported by the *Times*, the four men killed in Fallujah "were in fact lured into a carefully planned ambush by men they believed to be friendly members of the Iraqi Civil Defense Corps . . . [who] promised the Blackwater-led convoy safe and swift passage through the dangerous city, but instead, a few kilometers later, they suddenly blocked off the road, preventing any escape from waiting gunmen."[20] According to the subsequent Congressional investigation, the CPA report on the ambush disputed this account, finding that "the evidence does not support the claim that the ICDC participated in the ambush, either by escorting the convoy into Fallujah or by using its own vehicle to block the convoy from escaping the ambush."[21] Despite the increasing hostilities in Fallujah at the time, the *Times* went along with the company's line, reporting that the Blackwater convoy "had little cause for suspicion." In the *Times* story, no questions were raised about the lack of armored vehicles or the fact that there were only four men on the mission instead of six. Lending credence to Blackwater's story, the *Times* declared that "the company's initial findings are in line with recent complaints from senior American officials about Iraqi forces":

> In testimony last month to the Senate Armed Services Committee, Gen. John P. Abizaid, the top American commander in the Middle East, spoke openly of his worries about the Iraqi security and police

forces, now numbering more than 200,000. "There's no doubt that terrorists and insurgents will attempt to infiltrate the security forces," he said. "We know it's happening, and we know it has happened. We attempt to do our best with regard to vetting people." Also, the Pentagon has received new intelligence reports warning that Sunni and Shiite militia groups have been ransacking Iraqi police stations in some cities, and then handing out both weapons and police uniforms to angry mobs, government officials said.[22]

But this story was soon directly contradicted by one of the most senior U.S. officials in Iraq at the time—Bremer's deputy, Jim Steele, who had been sent covertly into Fallujah to recover the bodies and investigate.[23] After Steele met with Jon Lee Anderson of The New Yorker magazine in Baghdad, Anderson reported that Steele had "concluded that there was no evidence that the Iraqi police had betrayed the contractors."[24] This was backed up by Malcolm Nance, a former naval intelligence officer and FBI terrorism adviser who headed a private security firm in Iraq at the time. "In Fallujah especially, an [Iraqi Civil Defense Corps] guarantee is of zero value," Nance said. "You would never trust the word of local forces in a place like that—especially if you were driving a high-profile convoy, as these people were."[25] Richard Perry, another former naval intelligence officer, who worked with Scott Helvenston when he was still in the service, said, "[E]verything that happened in Fallujah that day was a serious mistake. I simply cannot understand why the hell they were driving through the most dangerous part of Iraq in just two vehicles without a proper military escort. . . . They were lightly armed, and yet they would be up against people who regularly take on the U.S. Army."[26] Time magazine reported that "A former private military operator with knowledge of Blackwater's operational tactics says the firm did not give all its contract warriors in Afghanistan proper training in offensive-driving tactics, although missions were to include vehicular and dignitary-escort duty. 'Evasive driving and ambush tactics were not—repeat, were not—covered in training,' this source said."[27]

Meanwhile, the *San Francisco Chronicle* reported from Baghdad that Control Risks Group, the firm Blackwater had taken over the ESS contract from, had warned Blackwater at the time that Fallujah was not safe to travel through: "According to senior executives working with other Baghdad security companies, Blackwater's decision to press ahead anyway stemmed from a desire to impress its new clients. 'There has been a big row about this,' said one executive, who asked not to be named. 'Not long before the convoy left, Control Risks said, "Don't go through Fallujah, it's not safe." But Blackwater wanted to show . . . that nowhere was too dangerous for them.'"[28] In response, Blackwater spokesman Bertelli said, "It is certainly not out of the question that some of Blackwater's competitors would use this tragic occurrence as an opportunity to try and damage Blackwater's reputation and secure contracts for themselves."[29]

In what would turn out to be the most comprehensive statement Blackwater would provide on the incident, Bertelli told the *Chronicle*:

> While our internal investigation continues, we are not aware of any specific warnings by anyone, including other private security contractors, that the route being traveled the day of March 31 was not the safest route to the convoy's destination. The two men leading the convoy had extensive experience in Iraq prior to the trip that resulted in the ambush and were well aware of the areas that are considered to be highly dangerous. They were all highly trained former U.S. Navy SEAL and Special Forces troops. The ambush took place in such a way that it would not have made a difference if there had been additional personnel protecting the convoy.[30]

In the meantime, local reporters in North Carolina started digging for answers in Blackwater's backyard. A few months after Blackwater's alibi was published in the *New York Times*, Joseph Neff and Jay Price of the Raleigh *News and Observer* cast further doubt on Blackwater's narrative. "[C]ontractors who have worked with Blackwater in Iraq were skeptical that the team had arranged for an Iraqi Civil Defense Corps escort," the paper reported on August 1, 2004. "The Iraqi security force simply wasn't trusted, said the contractors, who asked not to be named to protect their jobs."[31] More important, the *News and Observer* had sources inside the company who were raising serious questions about the conditions under which the four men were sent into Fallujah:

> The contractors also said security teams on the ESS contract had insufficient firepower. And the team ambushed in Fallujah should have been the standard Blackwater team of three men in each car, not two, the contractors said. Days after the ambush, Helvenston's family got a copy of an April 13 [2004] e-mail message by someone who identified herself as Kathy Potter, an Alaska woman who had helped run Blackwater's Kuwait City office while Helvenston was there. Most of the lengthy message consisted of condolences. Potter, however, also said Helvenston's normal team, operating in relatively safe southern Iraq, had six members—not four like the group that entered Fallujah. Potter also wrote that Helvenston helped acquire "the backup vehicles and critical supplies for these vehicles . . . when the original plan for armored vehicles fell through." Company officials declined to say why there were no armored vehicles for the ESS contract.[32]

In Florida, Katy Helvenston-Wettengel, Scott's mom, had all sorts of questions running through her head. Finally, she decided to call Erik Prince directly. She said it was surprisingly easy to get him on the phone. "I said, 'I want an incident report on Scotty.' And I said, 'I want a copy of his contract that he signed with you,'" she recalled. "And he said, 'Why?' And I said, 'I just want to know what happened.' He said he would get it to me in the next few weeks. And I said, 'Well, you've already written a report. Why can't I have it tomorrow?' And I said, 'Are you going to rewrite it for my eyes only?'" She said she "never did get that report. I did get a call a few days later, and [Blackwater] all of a sudden [was] going to have this grand memorial."

Indeed, a memorial was scheduled for mid-October 2004 at the Black-water compound in North Carolina. But a week before the memorial, Blackwater held a different kind of ceremony—to inaugurate a new plant to manufacture military practice targets. Company president Gary Jackson beamed with pride as he discussed Blackwater's rapid expansion. "The numbers are actually staggering. In the last eighteen months we've had over 600 percent growth," Jackson said, adding that Blackwater's workforce in North Carolina would soon double.[33] The company, he said, had also opened offices in Baghdad and Jordan. "This is a billion-dollar industry," Jackson said of the target business. "And Blackwater has only scratched the surface of it."[34] The Associated Press noted, "Gov. Mike Easley said having the global security company headquartered in North Carolina is fitting for what he called the most military-friendly state in the country."[35]

A few days later, on October 17, the company flew most of the families of the Fallujah contractors to North Carolina, where Prince was to dedicate the company's memorial to the men killed in action.[36] In addition to the relatives of those men, there were three other families of Blackwater contractors who also had died in the line of duty.[37] The company put the families up in a hotel, and gift baskets of cheese and crackers were waiting in the rooms when they arrived. Danica Zovko said that from the moment they got to North Carolina, "It just felt uncomfortable. It's like sometimes somebody is watching you and you feel it but you don't know who it is. That's what it felt like. Stiff. You couldn't relax." She said that each family member was assigned a Blackwater minder that escorted them everywhere and was present for all conversations, sometimes changing the subject if the conversation moved onto one topic in particular: Both Zovko and Katy Helvenston-Wettengel said they had the distinct feeling that the company was trying to keep the families from talking with one another about the details of the Fallujah incident.

The memorial was held, trees were planted, small headstones with the men's names on them were laid in the ground around a pond on the company property. On October 18, the Zovkos said they were told there would be a meeting where they could ask questions about the Fallujah incident. "We assumed that everyone else was going to go to the meeting," Danica Zovko said. In the end, only she, her husband, Jozo, and their son, Tom, attended. "There was alcohol served at the luncheon [for the families] beforehand, so maybe people were too tired or they were taken for sight-seeing," she recalled. "Blackwater was very keen on showing everyone the compound, their training center." The Zovkos were escorted to a company building, and when they walked in, they saw two large flags, one of which bore the names of Jerry and his three colleagues. A company representative, they said, told them the flag was made by Blackwater staffers in Iraq.

The Zovkos said they were taken to a meeting room on the second floor, where they were seated at a large twenty-person conference table. Erik Prince was not in the room. At the head of the table, remembered Danica, was a young blonde-haired woman named Anne. A Blackwater executive, Mike Rush, was there, too, as was a gray-haired man introduced to the family as "the fastest gun in Iraq"—a man who they were told had just returned to the United States to "get divorced and sell his house" before heading back to Iraq. None of them, she recalled, said they knew Jerry. "The only person from Blackwater that admitted knowing my Jerry was Erik Prince," she said.

Danica said she began by asking for her son's missing belongings. She was told that he had taken them all with him to Fallujah that day and that they were destroyed. Eventually, the Zovkos began asking questions about the incident itself. "Annie [the Blackwater representative] did not even sit down at that point because I was asking for the contracts, asking at exactly what time my son had died. I was asking how he died. I was asking for his personal things," Danica said. "The tempers were not calm anymore. I mean, it's civilized, but it's not nice. You know, it's to where you see that they're not telling you what you want to know and they're not happy with what you're asking. So Annie actually stood up from her chair—she was at the head of the table, sitting all by herself. These other people were all sitting across from us. She was on the right-hand side of me at the head of the table. She stood up and said that was confidential and if we wanted to know those things, we'd need to sue them." Danica Zovko said, "I told them that's what we would do." At the time, Zovko did not know what that even meant, but she was now convinced that Blackwater was hiding something—something serious about her son's death.

Two weeks later, George W. Bush claimed victory in the 2004 presidential election. Blackwater executives, led by Prince, had poured money into Bush and Republican Party coffers and clearly viewed the reelection as great for business and necessary for the unprecedented expansion of the mercenary industry. On November 8, Gary Jackson sent out a celebratory mass e-mail with a screaming banner headline: "BUSH WINS FOUR MORE YEARS!! HOOYAH!!"[38] The U.S. military had just launched the second major siege of Fallujah, bombing the city and engaging in violent house-to-house combat. Hundreds more Iraqis were killed, thousands more forced from their homes, as the national resistance against the occupation grew stronger and wider. Despite the fierce attacks on the city, the killers of the Blackwater men were not apprehended.[39] On November 14, the Marines symbolically reopened the infamous bridge running over the Euphrates in Fallujah. It was then that the Marines wrote in black bold letters: "This is for the Americans of Blackwater that were murdered here in 2004, Semper Fidelis P.S. Fuck You."[40] Gary Jackson posted a link to the photo on Blackwater's Web site, saying, "OOHRAH . . . this picture is worth more than they know."[41] The families of the dead men, though, found little solace in revenge attacks or sloganeering.

When Katy Helvenston-Wettengel started complaining about Blackwater's conduct and lack of transparency about the Fallujah ambush, Scott's godfather, Circuit Judge William Levens, put her in touch with a lawyer who, he said, would help her seek answers. Eventually, a friend of Scott's, another Blackwater contractor who had been overseas with him, brought the case to the attention of the successful Santa Ana, California, law firm Callahan & Blaine, whose owner, Daniel Callahan, was fresh off a record-setting $934 million jury decision in a corporate fraud case.[42] Callahan jumped at the case. In North Carolina, Callahan enlisted the local help of another well-known lawyer, David Kirby—the former law partner of 2004 Democratic vice presidential candidate John Edwards. The new legal team began compiling evidence, talking to other Blackwater contractors, scouring news reports for every detail about the ambush, watching the precious few moments of the scene captured by insurgent video and news cameras. They got a hold of the Blackwater contracts the men were working under and also some contracts between Blackwater and its business partners in the Middle East. It took only a matter of weeks before they felt they had enough of a case to take action.

On January 5, 2005, the families of Scott Helvenston, Jerry Zovko, Wes Batalona, and Mike Teague filed a wrongful death lawsuit against Blackwater in Superior Court in Wake County, North Carolina. "What we have right now is something worse than the wild, wild west going on in Iraq," said Dan Callahan. "Blackwater is able to operate over there in Iraq free from any oversight that would typically exist in a civilized society. As we expose Blackwater in this case, it will also expose the inefficient and corrupt system that exists over there."[43] The suit alleged that the men "would be alive today" had Blackwater not sent them unprepared on that fateful mission.[44] "The fact that these four Americans found themselves located in the high-risk, war-torn City of Fallujah without armored vehicles, automatic weapons, and fewer than the minimum number of team members was no accident," the suit alleged. "Instead, this team was sent out without the required equipment and personnel by those in charge at Blackwater."[45]

After the suit was filed, the families felt empowered to begin publicly voicing their anger at the company. "Blackwater sent my son and the other three into Fallujah knowing that there was a very good possibility this could happen," charged Katy Helvenston-Wettengel. "Iraqis physically did it, and it doesn't get any more horrible than what they did to my son, does it? But I hold Blackwater responsible one thousand percent."

At first glance, the lawsuit may have seemed like a stretch. After all, the four Blackwater contractors were essentially mercenaries. All willingly went to Iraq, where they would be well paid, knowing that there was a solid chance they could be killed or maimed. In fact, it was all laid out very plainly in their contract with Blackwater in macabre detail. It warned that the men risked "being shot, permanently maimed and/or killed by a firearm or munitions, falling aircraft or helicopters, sniper fire, land mine, artillery fire, rocket-propelled grenade, truck or car bomb, earthquake or other natural disaster, poisoning, civil uprising, terrorist activity, hand-to-hand combat, disease, poisoning, etc., killed or maimed while a passenger in a helicopter or fixed-wing aircraft, suffering hearing loss, eye injury or loss; inhalation or contact with biological or chemical contaminants (whether airborne or not) and or flying debris, etc."[46] In filing its motion to dismiss the lawsuit, Blackwater quoted from its standard contract, insisting that those who signed it "fully appreciate[d] the dangers and voluntarily assume[d] these risks as well as any other risks in any way (whether directly or indirectly) connected to the Engagement."[47]

Callahan and his legal team did not deny that the men were aware of the risks they were taking, but they charged that Blackwater knowingly refused to provide guaranteed safeguards, among them: they would have armored vehicles; there would be three men in each vehicle (a driver, a navigator, and a rear gunner); and the rear gunner would be armed with a heavy automatic weapon, such as a SAW Mach 46, which can fire up to 850 rounds per minute, allowing the gunner to fight off any attacks from the rear.[48] "None of that was true," said Callahan. Instead, each vehicle had only two men and allegedly had far less powerful Mach 4 guns, which they had not even had a chance to test out.[49] "Without the big gun, without the third man, without the armored vehicle, they were sitting ducks," said Callahan.[50]

Contract Disputes

The contract the four men were working on the day they were killed in Fallujah was a newly brokered one between Blackwater and the Cypriot-registered company Eurest Support Services (ESS), a division of the British firm Compass Group. As previously discussed, Blackwater had teamed up with a Kuwaiti business called Regency Hotel and Hospital Company, and together the firms had won the job of guarding convoys transporting kitchen equipment to the U.S. military. Blackwater and Regency had essentially won the ESS contract over another security firm, Control Risks Group, and the lawsuit alleged Blackwater was eager to win more lucrative contracts from ESS in its other division servicing construction projects in Iraq.[51] "The ill-fated March 31, 2004 mission was an attempt by Blackwater to prove to ESS that it could deliver the security detail ahead of schedule, even though the necessary vehicles, equipment and support logistics were not in place," the suit alleged.[52]

Like many of the operations of private contractors in Iraq, the mission the four Blackwater men were on that day in Fallujah was shrouded in layers of subcontracts. In fact, determining whom they were ultimately working for remained a source of contention years after the ambush. Initially, it seemed as though the men were operating under ESS's subcontract with Halliburton subsidiary KBR, which was reported to be billing the federal government for Blackwater's security services. [53] In the primary contract between Blackwater/Regency and ESS, ESS reserved "the right to terminate this Agreement or any portion hereof, upon thirty (30) days prior written notice in the event that ESS's is given written notice by Kellogg, Brown & Root of cancellation of ESS's contracts, for any reason, or in the event that ESS receives written notice from Kellogg, Brown & Root that ESS is no longer allowed to use any private form of private security services [sic]."[54] After the Fallujah ambush, KBR/Halliburton would not confirm any relationship with ESS, despite the clear reference to KBR in the contract.

The story became even more complicated in July 2006, when the Secretary of the Army, Francis Harvey, wrote a letter to Republican Congressman Christopher Shays of the House Committee on Government Reform, stating, "Based on information provided to the Army by Kellogg, Brown and Root (KBR), KBR has never directly hired a private security contractor in support of the execution of a statement of work under any LOGCAP III Task Order. Additionally, KBR has queried ESS and they are unaware of any services under the LOGCAP contract that were provided by Blackwater USA . . . the U.S. military provides all armed force protection for KBR unless otherwise directed."[55] Harvey wrote that the theater commander had not "authorized KBR or any LOGCAP subcontractor to carry weapons. KBR has

stated they have no knowledge of any subcontractor utilizing private armed
security under the LOGCAP contract."[56] Testifying in front of the House
Committee on Government Reform in September 2006, Tina Ballard, an
undersecretary of the Army, said it was the Army's contention that Blackwater provided no services to KBR.[57]

For its part, KBR told the producers of PBS's *Frontline* program, "[W]e can
tell you that it is KBR's position that any efforts being undertaken by [ESS or
Blackwater] when the March 31, 2004, attack occurred were not in support
of KBR or its work in Iraq . . . this was not a KBR-directed mission."[58] KBR
also said it was not responsible for supplying kitchen equipment to Camp
Ridgeway, the Blackwater contractors' ultimate destination when they were
killed in Fallujah.[59] KBR's assertions had to be viewed in the context of what
the Pentagon's own auditors found regarding the company's practices in
Iraq. "KBR routinely marks almost all of the information it provides to the
government as KBR proprietary data . . . [which] is an abuse of [Federal
Acquisition Regulations] procedures, inhibits transparency of government
activities and the use of taxpayer funds," according to an October 2006
report by the Special Inspector General for Iraq Reconstruction.[60] "In effect,
KBR has turned FAR provisions . . . into a mechanism to prevent the government from releasing normally transparent information, thus potentially
hindering competition and oversight."[61] In Iraq, Halliburton/KBR has been
secretive to the point of not naming its subcontractors.[62] "All information
available to KBR confirms that Blackwater's work for ESS was not in support
of KBR and not under a KBR subcontract," said Halliburton spokesperson
Melissa Norcross in December 2006. "Blackwater provided services for the
Middle East Regional Office of KBR. This office is not associated with any
government contract. . . . These services were provided outside of the Green
Zone and were not directly billed to any government contract."[63] This all
raised crucial questions: Whom was Blackwater ultimately working for when
it sent those four men on that fateful Fallujah mission? And what was that
mission's official, documented connection to the U.S. military?

These were questions California Representative Henry Waxman, Congress's lead investigator, had been looking into since November 2004, when reports first emerged on the layers of subcontracts involved with the Fallujah mission. On December 7, 2006, the story took yet another twist when Waxman revealed that he had obtained a November 30, 2006, legal memo from Compass Group, ESS's British parent company, that asserted ESS had a subcontract under Halliburton's LOGCAP contract and used Blackwater "to provide security services" under that subcontract.[64] "If the ESS memo is accurate, it appears that Halliburton entered into a subcontracting arrangement that is expressly prohibited by the contract itself," Waxman asserted in a letter to Rumsfeld, adding that the memo appeared to contradict what Army Secretary Harvey had presented in his July 2006 letter, as well as Undersecretary Ballard's subsequent sworn testimony. The memo also appeared to introduce another major war contractor into the mix. "The ESS memo also discloses that Blackwater was operating under a subcontract with [KBR competitor] Fluor when four Blackwater employees were killed in Fallujah in March 2004," according to Waxman. He charged that Blackwater appeared to be "providing security services under the LOGCAP contract in violation of the terms of the contract and without the knowledge or approval of the Pentagon."[65]

Finally, in early February 2007, Waxman was able to get the answer to the question he had been asking for nearly three years. Following the Democrats' victory in the 2006 Congressional elections, Waxman became chair of the powerful Committee on Oversight and Government Reform and moved swiftly to hold a hearing on the ambush. What the public learned the day of that hearing was that the contract under which the Blackewater men killed in Fallujah were operating was indeed traceable to the largest war contractor in Iraq, KBR.

This was a complete about-face that contradicted many previous claims, including denials from KBR and the military that any such connection existed. Tina Ballard, the Army's head contracting officer, had assured the same committee six months earlier that Blackwater had not been hired under a KBR subcontract.

But during the February hearing, Ballard said that "after extensive research" it turned out that her earlier statements had been wrong. Further, she said that if KBR "knowingly or unknowingly incurred costs for private security subcontractors . . . the U.S. Army will take appropriate steps under the contract terms to recoup any funds paid for those services."[66] At the end of the hearing, Ballard announced that the Army would dock KBR $20 million now that it was clear that—under several layers of contracts—Blackwater had in fact been hired in violations of KBR's master contract with the military, which stated that only the official military could provide security services.[67] That it took nearly three years to get an answer to one simple question was an ominous commentary on the state of oversight of the mercenary industry in the United States.

At the same hearing, Blackwater attorney Andrew Howell told Congress the company would not turn over its incident report on the Fallujah ambush, saying, "We cannot turn over classified information. It would be a criminal act." Waxman shot back, "That's not an accurate statement. We are entitled to receive classified information in this committee."[68]

Waxman subsequently demanded that Blackwater hand over the document to the committee, and a company lawyer responded, "Blackwater lacks unilateral authority to provide the Committee with any classified incident reports."[69] Waxman, quite understandably, found it outrageous that a private company was telling him, a U.S. House committee chair, that it could not share "classified" information with him. As it turned out, the Congressional investigation found that "none of the documents about the Fallujah incident were classified."[70] Waxman alleged that Blackwater's chief operating officer, Joseph Schmitz, "acknowledged to Committee staff that rather than immediately produce the report by the Coalition Provisional Authority to the Committee, he instead hand-delivered it to [the] Defense Department and requested that it be reviewed to determine whether it should be classified. He took these steps even though the report was marked 'unclassified', no portion of it was marked as classified, and neither Blackwater nor its outside counsel had stored it in a classified manner. . . . [Later,] the Defense Department produced the report to the Committee and confirmed that it did not consider this document to be classified."[71]

Waxman alleged that Schmitz did this with another document as well, asking "that it be reviewed for classification purposes" by the Defense Department. The Pentagon informed Blackwater that it too was unclassified. In another instance, Waxman alleged, Blackwater refused to hand over documents under a subpoena and produced them only when "the Committee threatened a vote to hold Blackwater in contempt of Congress."[72] Blackwater later said it had "obtained the permission" to release the documents by "working with the Executive branch."[73]

"Whores of War"

Regardless of the controversy that later erupted over the various contractual relationships, the original contract between Blackwater/Regency and ESS, signed March 8, 2004, called for "a minimum of two *armored* vehicles to support ESS movements" [emphasis added] with at least three men in each vehicle because "the current threat in the Iraqi theater of operations" would remain "consistent and dangerous."[74] But on March 12, 2004, Blackwater and Regency signed a subcontract, which specified security provisions identical to the original except for one word: "armored." It was deleted from the contract. "When they took that word 'armored' out, Blackwater was able to save $1.5 million in not buying armored vehicles, which they could then put in their pocket," alleged another lawyer for the families, Marc Miles. "These men were told that they'd be operating in armored vehicles. Had they been, I sincerely believe that they'd be alive today. They were killed by insurgents literally walking up and shooting them with small-arms fire. This was not a roadside bomb, it was not any other explosive device. It was merely small-arms fire, which could have been repelled by armored vehicles."[75]

Before Helvenston, Teague, Zovko, and Batalona were sent into Fallujah, the omission of the word "armored" was brought to the attention of Blackwater management by Helvenston's friend John Potter, who was supervising the ESS contract, according to the lawsuit. Potter "insisted that the sub-contract include armored vehicles, not only to comply with the primary contract, but more importantly to protect the security contractors who would be working in the area. However, obtaining armored vehicles would not only be an expense to Blackwater, but would also cause a delay in commencing operations. Thus, on March 24, 2004, Blackwater fired Potter as Program Manager and replaced him with another Blackwater employee, Justin McQuown,"[76] the man Scott Helvenston identified as "Shrek," with whom he had allegedly clashed in both North Carolina and Kuwait.[77]

The suit alleged that there were six guards available for the Fallujah mission but that Blackwater managers ordered only the four to be sent "in direct violation of all of Blackwater's policies and agreements."[78] The other two contractors were allegedly kept behind at Blackwater's Baghdad facility to perform clerical duties.[79] A Blackwater official later boasted that the company saved two lives by not sending all six men, the suit alleged.[80]

Blackwater's Andrew Howell later said, "the vehicle that they went out in that day was believed appropriate based on the mission by everyone involved or . . . I don't believe the [the mission] would have been carried out at that point." Regarding the allegation that there should have been six men on the mission instead of four, Howell said, "The mission they were on that day, at that point in time, given the threat as it was known on the ground in Iraq, the norm was not to have the third person."[81] But a Regency official later told Congressional investigators that "although these vehicles included an armor plate behind the back seat, that level of protection was below the armor protection kit called for by the contract" between the companies.

On March 30, 2004, the day before the Fallujah ambush, Tom Powell, Blackwater's Baghdad opeations manager, sent an e-mail to Blackwater management with the subject line "Ground Truth." Powell wrote: "I need new vehicles. I need new COMs, I need ammo, I need Glocks and M4s. All the client body armor you got, guys are in the field with borrowed stuff and in harm's way. I've requested hard cars [armoured vehicles] from the beginning and, from my understanding, an order is still pending."[82]

The e-mail concluded, "Ground truth is appalling."

Another Blackwater team sent out that day faced a similar situation to that of Helvenston and his comrades—short-staffed, under-armed, and lacking adequate preparation time—and that group likewise protested these conditions to company managers. After allegedly being threatened by Blackwater officials with dismissal, the men went on their mission and managed to survive.[83] One of those men later said: "Why did we all want to kill [the Blackwater operations manager]? He had sent us on this f**ked mission and over our protest. We weren't sighted in, we had no maps, we had not enough sleep, he was taking 2 of our guys cutting off ou[r] field of fire. As we went over these things we [k]new that the other team had the same complaints. They too had their people cut. . . . Why were they sent into the hottest zone in Iraq in unarmored, under-powered vehicles to protect a truck? They had no way to protect their flanks because they only had four guys."[84]

The lawsuit also alleged that the men were not provided with a detailed map of the Fallujah area. A Blackwater official told Helvenston "it was too late for maps and to just do his job with what he had," the suit alleged. "The team had no knowledge of where they were going, no maps to review, and had nothing to guide them to their destination."[85] According to Callahan, there was a safer alternative route that went around the city, which the men were unaware of because of Blackwater's alleged failure to conduct a "risk assessment" before the trip, as mandated by the contract. The suit alleged that the four men should have had a chance to gather intelligence and familiarize themselves with the dangerous routes they would be traveling. Blackwater's internal report, which Waxman was finally able to obtain, acknowledged that the Fallujah team had "no time to perform proper mission planning" and was sent out "without proper maps of the city."[86] This was not done, attorney Miles alleged, "so as to pad Blackwater's bottom line" and to impress ESS with Blackwater's efficiency in order to win more contracts.[87] The suit also charged that Blackwater "intentionally refused to allow the Blackwater security contractors to conduct" ride-alongs with the teams they were replacing from Control Risks Group. In the CRG report on the incident, the company's project manager wrote that Blackwater "did not use the opportunity to learn from the experience gained by CRG on this operation, this leading to inadequate preparation for taking on this task, unfortunately the outcome was the loss of four lives. . . . I believe this incident could have been avoided or at least the risk minimised [sic]."[88] The suit contended that Blackwater "fabricated critical documents" and "created" a pre-trip risk assessment "after this deadly ambush occurred" to "cover-up this incident."[89] The day after the ambush, Erik Prince had directed his Baghdad managers "to perform an immediate internal audit and to keep the information close."[90] When that report finally made it to Waxman, it revealed that some Blackwater employees described the company's Baghdad office as "flat out a sloppy. . . . operation" and a "ship about to sink." One Blackwater operative said, "Some of these lazy f**ks care about one thing, money."[91]

After these and other statements were revealed by Waxman's committee, Blackwater issued its own report. "Stronger weapons, armored vehicles, ammunition, or maps would not have saved these Americans' lives," Blackwater declared. "[T]his event was a tragedy—for which only the terrorists are to blame."[92] The report repeated the discredited allegations about Iraqi police involvement in the ambush, said the four men had made the decision to proceed on the mission that day, and asserted, "Even if Blackwater had placed six men on the mission, the result would likely have been the same."[93]

Attorney Dan Callahan said that if Blackwater had done in the United States what it is alleged to have done in Iraq, "There would be criminal charges against them." Blackwater refused to comment on the case, but company vice president Chris Taylor said in July 2006, "We don't cut corners. We try to prepare our people the best we can for the environment in which they're going to find themselves."[94] Justin McQuown's lawyer, William Crenshaw, alleged that there are "numerous serious factual errors" in the lawsuit, asserting that McQuown lacked "involvement in the planning or implementation of that mission." In an e-mail, Crenshaw wrote: "Let there be no mistake that the murders of the Blackwater team members in Fallujah were tragic. On behalf of Mr. McQuown, we extend our sincerest sympathies to the families of the deceased. It is regrettable and inaccurate to suggest that Mr. McQuown contributed in any way to this terrible tragedy."[95]

In one of its few public statements on the suit, Blackwater spokesperson Chris Bertelli said, "Our thoughts and prayers were with them and their families then and are with them now. . . . Blackwater hopes that the honor and dignity of our fallen comrades are not diminished by the use of the legal process."[96] Katy Helvenston-Wettengel called that "total BS in my opinion," and said that the families decided to sue only after being stonewalled, misled, and lied to by the company. "Blackwater seems to understand money. That's the only thing they understand," she said. "They have no values, they have no morals. They're whores. They're the whores of war."

After its filing in January 2005, the case moved slowly through the legal system and sparked various battles over jurisdiction. From the start, Blackwater was represented by some of the most influential and well-connected lawyers and firms in the U.S. Its original lawyer on the Fallujah case was Fred Fielding, President Reagan's former counsel (among Fielding's assistants in that post was future Chief Justice John Roberts). Fielding had also served as a top lawyer under President Nixon and was a member of the 9/11 Commission. In an indication of how deep Fielding's connections ran, in early 2007 President Bush named him as his White House counsel, replacing Harriet Miers. Blackwater has also been represented in the case by Greenberg Traurig, the influential D.C. law firm that once employed disgraced lobbyist Jack Abramoff. The lawyers for the families charged that after the suit was filed, Blackwater attempted to stonewall the process.[97] While some of that may have been legitimate defense tactics, the lawyers alleged that Blackwater prevented court-ordered depositions from taking place, including taking steps to prevent a key witness from testifying: John Potter, the man who allegedly blew the whistle on the removal of the word "armored" from the subcontract, whom the suit alleged was subsequently removed from his position.[98]

Attorney Marc Miles said that shortly after the suit was filed, he asked the court in North Carolina for an expedited order to depose John Potter. The deposition was set for January 28, 2005, and Miles was to fly to Alaska, where he said the Potters were living. But three days before the deposition, Miles alleged, "Blackwater hired Potter up, flew him to Washington, where it's my understanding he met with Blackwater representatives and their lawyers. [Blackwater] then flew him to Jordan for ultimate deployment in the Middle East." Miles charged that Blackwater "concealed a material witness by hiring him and sending him out of the country." Miles said Blackwater subsequently attempted to have Potter's deposition order dissolved, but a federal court said no. In testimony before Congress in June 2006, Blackwater's Chris Taylor said, "I don't believe John Potter is in our employ right now."[99]

The Potter saga took another twist in November 2006 when Miles discovered Potter was back in the United States. After reaching Potter on the phone in his hometown in Alaska, Miles filed papers with the court seeking once again to depose him, sparking a rapid and forceful response from Blackwater. In its filing opposing the deposition, Blackwater argued that the "case involves issues of national security and classified information involving the United States military operations in Iraq" and that "any testimony [Potter] would give would necessarily involve the disclosure of classified information."[100] Miles and his colleagues responded that Blackwater's filing "reads like a good spy novel" with "claims of 'classified' information, state secrets and threats to national security."[101] In reality, they argued, the "Blackwater contractors were not acting as covert operatives for the CIA, but instead were working under a contract with a foreign hotel company to guard kitchen equipment." National security and espionage, they asserted, "have nothing to do with this case." In an indication of the significance of the lawsuit and, more significant, Blackwater's pull with the government, the U.S. Attorney General's office filed an opposition to the deposition of Potter, asking that— at a minimum—it be delayed so the government could review Potter's alleged possession of classified information or documents. The U.S. attorney cited a need to "protect the National Security interests of the United States."[102] The U.S. Army's chief litigator also filed a sworn declaration to "protect from improper disclosure any sensitive and properly classified information to which Mr. Potter may have been given access as a Government contractor."[103] What was remarkable was how quickly Blackwater was able to mobilize the government and military to go to bat for it—the day after Christmas—and help stop, at least for the moment, the deposition of a potentially crucial witness from going ahead.

The families have all maintained that their interest in suing Blackwater was not money but accountability. "There's not enough money in the world that can pay for my Jerry. There's not enough money that anyone can give me," said Danica Zovko. "If they made some rules and if they were obligated and if they treated those lives of those people the same way that I have to treat metal on the cars when I work for the city of Cleveland. It seems that there's more laws and rules made about how to fix a car than there is about a life. There's no amount of money that can do anything. It doesn't exist to pay for the death of my son. They're very, very foolish if they think that's an answer."

In the months after the suit was filed, Blackwater did not offer a rebuttal to the specific allegations made by the families, though the company denied in general that they were valid. Instead, Blackwater has argued that what is at stake in this case is nothing less than the ability of the President of the United States to conduct foreign policy as Commander in Chief of the armed forces. The company's lawyers argued that Blackwater's private soldiers have been recognized by the Pentagon as an essential part of the U.S. "Total Force," constituting the nation's "warfighting capability and capacity . . . in thousands of locations around the world, performing a vast array of duties to accomplish critical missions"[104]—and allowing Blackwater to be sued for deaths in the war zone would be to attack the sovereignty of the Commander in Chief. "[T]he constitutional separation of powers . . . preclude[s] judicial intrusion into the manner in which the contractor component of the American military deployment in Iraq is trained, armed, and, deployed" by the President, Blackwater argued in one of its court filings.[105] This argument, if successful, could have the added benefit of preemptively immunizing Blackwater from any liability when deploying its forces in U.S. war zones.

The company fought to have the case dismissed on grounds that because

Blackwater is servicing U.S. military operations, it cannot be sued for workers' deaths or injuries, and that all liability lies with the government. In its motion to dismiss the case in federal court, Blackwater argued that the families of the four men killed in Fallujah were entitled only to government insurance payments. Indeed, after the ambush, the families' lawyers alleged, the company moved swiftly to help the families apply for benefits under the federal Defense Base Act (DBA), government insurance that covers some contractors working in support of U.S. military operations. In its court filings in the Fallujah case, Blackwater asked the courts to recognize the DBA as the sole source of compensation for the men killed at Fallujah. Under the DBA, the maximum death benefits available to the families of the contractors was limited to $4,123.12 a month.[106] "What Blackwater is trying to do is to sweep all of their wrongful conduct into the Defense Base Act," said attorney Miles. "What they're trying to do is to say, 'Look—we can do anything we want and not be held accountable. We can send our men out to die so that we can pad our bottom line, and if anybody comes back at us, we have insurance.' It's essentially insurance to kill."[107]

Blackwater's primary argument, however, centered around what it portrayed as the bigger-picture ramifications for the future of U.S. war-fighting. "The question whether contractors may be sued, in any court, for war casualties while the military services may not . . . could determine whether the President, as Commander-in-Chief, will be able to deploy the Total Force decades into the future," Blackwater argued in an appellate brief filed October 31, 2005.[108] In a subsequent filing two months later, Blackwater cited Paul Bremer's Order 17—which officially immunized contractors in Iraq—arguing that since the order "reflects a foreign policy decision made or at least supported by the United States," Blackwater should be "immune from the claims stated" in the lawsuit.[109] The company's lawyers asserted that allowing the case to proceed against Blackwater could threaten the nation's war-fighting capacity: "In order for responsible federal contractors to accompany the U.S. Armed Forces on the battlefield, it is essential that their immunity from liability for casualties be federally protected and uniformly upheld by federal courts. Nothing could be more destructive of the all-volunteer, Total Force concept underlying U.S. military manpower doctrine than to expose the private components to the tort liability systems of fifty states, transported overseas to foreign battlefields. . . . How the President oversees and commands these military operations, including his decisions through the chain of command concerning the training, deployment, armament, missions, composition, planning, analysis, management and supervision of private military contractors and their missions, falls outside the role of federal—and perforce state—Courts."[110]

Blackwater argued that the courts could not interfere in its operations because they would be essentially interfering in the functioning of the military, something prohibited by the "political question doctrine," which "is one of the sets of principles that safeguard from judicial inquiry decisions made by civilian political leaders through the military chain of command, including, in this case, decisions to hire contractors to protect military supply lines from enemy attack."[111] In Fallujah, Blackwater argued, its men "were performing a classic military function—providing an armed escort for a supply convoy under orders to reach an Army base—with an authorization from the Office of the Secretary of Defense."[112] Because of this, Blackwater argued, it should be immune from any liability: "Any other result would amount to judicial intrusion into the President's ability to deploy a Total Force that includes contractors."[113]

In an indication of how great other war contractors viewed the stakes in the Fallujah lawsuit, KBR—the Pentagon's largest contractor in Iraq, with revenues from its work there totaling $16.1 billion[114]—filed an *amicus curiae* brief in support of Blackwater in September 2006. In filing the brief, KBR identified itself as "the Department of Defense's largest civilian provider of worldwide 'Stability Operations' logistical support services."[115] KBR backed up Blackwater's Total Force argument, asserting that the purpose of the LOGCAP program "is to facilitate Stability Operations by integrating military logistical support contractors like KBR into the US military's Total Force. KBR functions as a 'force multiplier' by performing mission-critical services, such as the driving of military supply convoys. Such services formerly were provided only by uniformed military personnel, but in every respect continue to operate under the direction and control of U.S. military commanders."[116]

From the start, the Blackwater lawsuit was viewed as a precedent-setting case on the role of and legal framework governing private forces in U.S. war zones. Blackwater enlisted no fewer than five powerhouse law firms to assist in its efforts to have the case dismissed or moved to federal court.[117] Lawyers for the four families believed they would have a more favorable playing field in state court, where there was no cap on damages and the families would not need a unanimous decision to win.[118] In October 2006, Blackwater hired one of the nation's heaviest-hitting lawyers to represent it—Kenneth Starr, the independent counsel in the 1999 impeachment of President Bill Clinton over the Monica Lewinsky sex scandal.[119] Starr's name first appeared in connection with the case in Blackwater's October 18, 2006, petition to U.S. Chief Justice John Roberts, asking him to put the state case on hold while Blackwater prepared to file its petition for writ of certiorari, which if granted would have allowed Blackwater to argue its case for dismissal before the U.S. Supreme Court, dominated by Republican appointees. Starr and his colleagues argued that Blackwater was "constitutionally immune" from such lawsuits and said that if the Fallujah case were allowed to proceed, "Blackwater will suffer irreparable harm."[120] In the eighteen-page petition to the Supreme Court, Blackwater argued that there are no other such lawsuits against private military/security companies in state courts "because the comprehensive regulatory scheme enacted by Congress and the President grant military contractors like Blackwater immunity from state-court litigation."[121] On October 24, Justice Roberts simply wrote "denied" on Blackwater's application, providing no reasoning for his decision. In late November 2006, over the objection of Blackwater's lawyers, Wake County Superior Court Judge Donald Stephens ordered the state case against Blackwater to proceed.[122] A month later, Starr and his colleagues appealed to the U.S. Supreme Court to hear the case, arguing that allowing it to proceed in state court "exposed U.S. civilian contractors carrying on their Defense Department-mandated operations in hostile territory to the destabilizing reach of fifty state tort sys-

tems in this country. . . . relegat[ing] civilian contractors serving in profoundly dangerous circumstances to the vagaries of a Balkanized regime of
conflicting legal systems among the several States."[123] In December 2006,
two years after the filing of the wrongful death lawsuit against it, Blackwater
filed a claim against the estates of the four men killed in Fallujah seeking
$10 million, charging that the families had breached their loved ones' con-
tracts with Blackwater, which stated the men could not sue the company.[124]
Attorney Callahan called the action "a meritless claim aimed at disrupting
the families' pursuit of justice."

After more than two years of losing legal battles in the case and with the
high-stake trial on the verge of commencing, Blackwater engaged in some
high-powered eleventh-hour legal maneuvering. In May 2007, the company's lawyers persuaded a senior federal judge in North Carolina to order
the case into closed-door arbitration, which Blackwater argued was the only
legitimate forum for the case under the contracts the four men slain had
signed with the company. The decision of the private panel of three arbitra-
tors would be binding and an appeal of their decision would be unlikely if
not impossible. "Anyone who supports the rule of law should be encouraged to see the written agreement finally being honoured and the dispute
heading to arbitration as the parties agreed," Blackwater spokesperson Anne
Tyrrell declared.[125] A Blackwater lawyer boldly proclaimed, "The state court
action is over."[126] This arbitration scenario would mean that there would be
no public trial, limited discovery and witnesses and that the decision could
be kept secret with a gag order imposed on the parties. As of spring 2008,
the families' lawyers were fighting the decision. "Blackwater has attempted
to move the examination of their wrongful conduct outside of the eye of the
public and away from a jury," Callahan and Miles said in a statement.
"Blackwater is trying to wipe out the families' ability to discover the truth
about Blackwater's involvement in the deaths of these four Americans and
to silence them from any public comment."[127]

As this case made its way through the legal labyrinth, Blackwater regularly switched legal teams and introduced new arguments and attempts to

beat the case before it could make its way to trial. In January 2008 Blackwater lashed out at Wiley Rein, the firm that originally represented the company in the Fallujah suit. Blackwater sued the firm for malpractice; if the attorneys had done their job, the company asserted, the "lawsuit would have been dismissed and the litigation involving plaintiffs would have ended."[128] Blackwater sought $30 million in damages. Wiley Rein said the claim was without merit.

Given the uncounted tens of thousands of Iraqis who have died since the invasion and the multiple U.S. sieges in Fallujah that followed the Blackwater incident, some might say this lawsuit was just warmongers bickering. In the bigger picture, the real scandal wasn't that these men were sent into Fallujah with only a four-person detail when there should have been six or that they didn't have a powerful enough machine gun to kill their attackers. It was that the United States had opened Iraq's door to mercenary firms whose forces roamed the country with apparent impunity. The consequences of this policy were not lost on the families of the four slain Blackwater contractors. "Over a thousand people died because of what happened to Scotty that day," said Katy Helvenston-Wettengel. "There's a lot of innocent people that have died." While the lawsuit didn't mention the retaliatory U.S. attack on Fallujah that followed the Blackwater killings, the case sent shockwaves through the corporate community that has reaped huge profits in Iraq and other war zones. At the time the lawsuit was filed, more than 428 private contractors had been killed in Iraq with U.S. taxpayers footing almost the entire compensation bill to their families. By February 2008, the U.S. Department of Labor adjusted the figure to 1,123 contractors killed and over 13,000 injured. "This is a precedent-setting case," said attorney Miles. "Just like with tobacco litigation or gun litigation, once they lose that first case, they'd be fearful there would be other lawsuits to follow."[129]

CHAPTER FIFTEEN

THE CRASH OF BLACKWATER 61

U.S. ARMY Spc. Harley Miller made his way out of the mangled wreckage of Blackwater 61, a turboprop plane that minutes earlier had slammed into Baba Mountain, 14,650 feet high in Afghanistan's Hindu Kush mountain range. He passed the two other soldiers who had been on the flight with him, both dead from the impact and still strapped into their seats. The twenty-one-year-old Miller was suffering from injuries just a shade less severe than those that had killed them. Miller was all alone on the snow-covered mountain, 2,000 feet below its peak. The two pilots—Blackwater contractors—had been ejected 150 feet in front of the plane after its 400-foot skid and had died from the impact. The body of the aircraft's engineer rested just outside the plane's bulkhead.[1]

Specialist Miller smoked a cigarette; urinated twice, once near the rear of the aircraft and once near the front; and unrolled two sleeping bags. He propped a metal ladder up against the fuselage, possibly so he could climb on top of it to call for help or to gauge his location. He lay down on the makeshift bed, suffering from massive internal bleeding, a broken rib, lung and abdominal trauma, and minor head injuries. Miller's injuries would be compounded by the lack of oxygen and the frigid temperatures, and after more than eight hours alive and alone atop Baba Mountain, the crash claimed its final casualty. It would be three days before his body was recovered.[2]

The November 27, 2004, crash of Blackwater 61, a privately owned plane on contract with the U.S. military, would attract scant media attention, mostly sugary obituaries in the hometown papers of those killed. While Blackwater had already become a familiar name because of the Fallujah ambush a few months earlier, the crash itself, a small speck of inaccessible wreckage in the rugged mountains of Afghanistan, was a nonstory. It could scarcely have created a more opposite impression than that of the iconic killings in Fallujah. There were no gruesome images broadcast internationally and no declarations from the White House. It was, for all practical purposes, a minor tragedy in what had become—at least in the eyes of the media—a secondary, if not forgotten, war in Afghanistan. But the crash would nonetheless become a serious legal problem for Blackwater, for this time, unlike in Fallujah, there was an official paper trail.

The U.S. Army's Collateral Investigations Board and the National Transportation Safety Board generated hundreds of pages of documents as they investigated the crash. A black box captured the final moments of the flight. Unlike in Fallujah, some of the victims of the incident were active-duty U.S. soldiers, and those who caused the deaths, even if not intentionally, were private contractors. On the surface, it would seem that with the exception of Blackwater being involved in both incidents, the crash atop Baba Mountain and the Fallujah massacre had little in common.

The similarities, though, began to reveal themselves after the families of the three U.S. soldiers killed in the crash filed a wrongful death lawsuit on

June 10, 2005. In fact, the issues surrounding the crash would prove to be much the same as those surrounding Fallujah, though they would draw far less attention. The families of the soldiers killed in the Blackwater 61 crash alleged that the company had cut corners, sidestepped basic safety procedures, and recklessly caused the deaths of their loved ones in the process.[3] At the center of the case, as in that of the Fallujah lawsuit, was once again Blackwater's claim that its forces were immune from any lawsuits because the company was part of the U.S. "Total Force" in the war on terror.[4]

Blackwater's aviation division, Presidential Airways, has largely operated off of the public radar, though its aircraft overseas have frequented the same airports as those used in the CIA's extraordinary rendition program.[5] Blackwater's pilots are required to have the same security clearances as those involved in renditions. David P. Dalrymple, the Bagram site manager for Presidential, said, "I, and all other Presidential personnel serving in Afghanistan, possess or are in the process of obtaining 'secret' or higher security clearances from the United States Government."[6] The company also asserted that it "holds a US DoD Secret Facility Clearance."[7]

The contract that Blackwater 61 operated under in Afghanistan had been inked in September 2004, just two months before the crash.[8] After three months of negotiations, the Air Force agreed to a $34.8 million contract for Presidential Airways to provide "short take-off and landing" (STOL) flights in Afghanistan, Uzbekistan, and Pakistan.[9] Presidential agreed to fly six regularly scheduled daily routes to small airfields throughout Afghanistan, and other flights as needed. It was estimated that Presidential's three aircraft would fly about 8,760 hours per year under the contract.[10] "With this contract, [Blackwater Aviation] has extended its reach out of Iraq and is providing much needed assistance to US Service men and women in Afghanistan and further into the southern countries of the former Soviet Union," Blackwater boasted in October 2004 in its *Tactical Weekly* newsletter.[11]

John Hight, Presidential's director of operations, explained that the company based its bid on its "experience operating in and out of unimproved landing strips and work for the military carrying sky divers."[12] Once the company got word that its bid was successful, Hight said he started recruiting "experienced CASA pilots" for the Afghanistan missions. Five days after the contract was signed, "we arrived in Afghanistan with our first aircraft," Hight recalled.[13]

But, experienced or not, flying in Afghanistan is substantially different from flying in most of the United States. Afghanistan is crisscrossed with mountain ranges that tower above even the highest point in the continental United States, which is California's Mt. Whitney at 14,495 feet. By contrast, Afghanistan's highest point is nearly 25,000 feet. Pilots also faced an additional hurdle in that there was limited communication with other aircraft and no air-traffic control to guide planes should they encounter a thick patch of clouds or other bad weather, which experts said could be incredibly variable in Afghanistan. This could cause serious problems very quickly because flights were often piloted using "visual flight rules"—in other words, pilots were on their own with little more than instinct and common sense to guide them. As one Blackwater pilot put it, "The flight crews know that if you can't get over it or under it, then you turn around and come home. There's no pressure to get the flight complete."[14]

While some bases in Afghanistan—like those at Kabul, Bagram, and Shindad—had ground control towers, others did not. Basically, according to Presidential's pilots, "once the aircraft are twenty miles out of radar coverage, they are on their own."[15] Flying in Afghanistan was low-tech to the point where pilots often had to use satellite phones to report their locations when they landed anywhere but the most frequented areas, and even the satellite phones often proved unreliable.[16] Aside from the impracticality of flying set routes, pilots also "don't want to fly set routes for force protection reasons"[17]—fear of being targeted by antioccupation or "enemy" forces.

Taken together, the weather, visual flight rules, threat of enemy fire, light turboprop aircraft with varying cargo and passenger loads, and extreme elevations made for a difficult combination even for experienced pilots. In essence, the Afghan skies were an unpredictable frontier. Indeed, all of Blackwater's flights in the country were piloted using visual flight rules.

"Therefore there were no prescribed routes of flight to and from Bagram or any of the other locations which we supported other than the sound aviation practice of flying as direct a route as possible while avoiding terrain and weather," said Paul Hooper, the site manager for Presidential. "Common practice was to fly the most direct route possible. Terrain, weather and a desire to avoid establishing a flight pattern in an environment with hostile ground forces, were some reasons our flight crews varied the specific ground track of each flight."[18]

Among those hired by Blackwater to fly under these unusual and dangerous circumstances were two experienced CASA pilots, thirty-seven-year-old Noel English and thirty-five-year-old Loren "Butch" Hammer. Both men had experience flying under unorthodox circumstances with little ground support in variable weather and terrain, as well as landing in nontraditional locations. English had logged nearly nine hundred hours in a CASA 212—most of it as a "bush pilot" in Alaska—while Hammer had spent years piloting and copiloting "smokejumpers" during the summer fire seasons in the United States, "dropping smoke divers and para-cargo on forest fires," according to Kevin McBride, another Blackwater pilot who had previously worked with Hammer. "He was a knowledgeable and skilled First Officer, with lots of experience in mountain flying and low level missions."[19]

After several weeks of training for the Afghanistan mission in Melbourne, Florida, Hammer and English arrived in Afghanistan on November 14, 2004.[20] According to the U.S. Army, Presidential had a policy of not pairing any two pilots with less than a month "in the theater."[21] Presidential, however, paired Hammer and English, both of whom had been in the country for only two weeks, because they were the only crew the company had who, in addition to the CASA planes, could fly an SA-227 DC, or Metro plane, which could be used for flights to Uzbekistan.[22] Presidential had two CASAs and one Metro plane in the theater. During their brief time in Afghanistan, Hammer and English had each logged thirty-three hours of flight time.[23]

On November 27, the pilots woke up at 4:30 a.m. to a crisp and clear forty-degree day at Bagram airport—the main prison facility for people

detained by U.S. forces in Afghanistan and an alleged site of prisoner torture.[24] The Presidential crew would be leaving the base in a little less than
three hours on a mission to transport a couple of U.S. soldiers and four
hundred pounds of 81 mm mortar illumination rounds. The route would
take them first to Farah, 450 miles southwest of Bagram, then to Shindad
to refuel, and then back to Bagram, where they were scheduled to return at
1:30 p.m. Neither Hammer nor English had flown the route before.[25]

Bunking with the men at Bagram the night before were two other Presidential pilots who would be leaving at about the same time as Blackwater
61 and traveling on a similar route. Like Hammer and English, pilots Lance
Carey and Robert Gamanche would fly a Blackwater CASA westward that
morning, stopping at Shindad to refuel. Carey, who shared a room at
Bagram with both English and Hammer for the three days prior to the
flight, said, "They were both looking forward to [it]." Gamanche ate breakfast with English on the morning of the flight. Both crews reviewed that
day's weather forecast. "Since our flights would eventually take us to the same
place [Shindad] and the forecast was marginal due to visibility, we decided
to make a group go–no go decision," Gamanche recalled. "If the current
weather at [Shindad] was not favorable, we would stay on the ground."
There were no weather problems reported at either of the crews' initial destinations. "The current weather was favorable so we all decided to go," said
Gamanche. Though there were indications that at Farah and Shindad
gusting winds and blowing dust could make landing difficult, at Bagram
"the weather was forecasted as clear with unlimited visibility."[26]

The flight was a go. Melvin Rowe, a forty-three-year-old flight mechanic,
joined the crew of Blackwater 61. Two passengers were slated to come on
the flight, Spc. Harley Miller and Chief Warrant Officer Travis Grogan. They
had loaded up the four hundred pounds of ammunition and begun to taxi
when a soldier ran along the runway toward their plane. A third passenger
would be joining them: Lt. Col. Michael McMahon, commander of the
twenty-five-thousand-soldier Task Force Saber, which was responsible for
the entire western region of Afghanistan—where Blackwater 61 was headed.[27]

McMahon, a Desert Storm veteran and West Point graduate,[28] "was just an extra guy that showed up and [asked] if he could get on the flight," one Blackwater employee explained. If they "ask us to do it and it's not out of the common sense category, then they'll do it."[29] There were now six people on board the plane.

At 7:38 a.m., Blackwater 61 took off from Bagram and headed northwest. The last thing the six of them would hear from anyone outside the flight was the Bagram tower telling them they would "talk to you later." Five minutes after that, the plane dropped off Bagram's radar, about nine miles out from the airport.[30] Hammer, Blackwater 61's copilot, quickly commented on the visibility, saying, "can't ask for a whole lot better than this." But it was apparent, even early in the flight, that the pilots didn't quite know exactly where to go, as evidenced from the flight's black box recording:[31]

Pilot English: "I hope I'm goin' in the right valley."
Copilot Hammer: "That one or this one."
English: "I'm just going to go up this one."
Hammer: "Well we've never or at least I've never done this Farah . . . from Bagram so it would be a valley up here."

The novice Afghanistan pilots clearly didn't have a command of the route they would be covering, and English ultimately said, "We'll just see where this leads." The pilots and Rowe spent the next several minutes fumbling through maps trying to determine their location and route. Hammer said that he hadn't brought a handheld global positioning system with them that would have issued a warning when the plane came close to the ground. About eight minutes into the flight, English expressed some concern about the weather in western Afghanistan, saying, "normally . . . on a short day like this we'd have time to play a little bit, do some explorin', but with those winds comin' up I want to [expletive] get there as fast as we can."

Despite the early indications of some complications, the pilots spent some time during the flight chatting with each other, making small talk. "I swear to God, they wouldn't pay me if they knew how much fun this was," English said. The pilots had been riding through the Bamian Valley, although from the transcript of their in-flight conversations, it seemed they were somewhat uncertain and unconcerned as to exactly where they were. "I don't see anythin' over about thirteen three is the highest peak in the whole route I think," said Rowe, the flight's engineer. "Plenty of individual valleys," English replied, "Yeah, so we'll be able to pick our way around it. Yeah, with this good visibility [expletive] it's as easy as pie. You run into somethin' big and you just parallel it until you find a way through. Yeah, like I said, this is the first good visibility day I've had in the CASA. It's not just good, it's outstanding."

At one point, the passengers asked the pilots what they'd be passing by on their way to Farah. Rowe, the man with the maps, replied, "I don't know what we're gonna see, we don't normally go this route." Seconds later, English said, "All we want to avoid is seeing rock at twelve o'clock." Then Hammer—the copilot—turned his attention to pilot English's apparent maneuvering of the plane: "Yeah, you're an X-wing fighter *Star Wars* man."

"You're [expletive] right," English shot back. "This is fun."

As the pilots started encountering some mountains and apparently swerving to avoid getting boxed in, they continued with their friendly, casual banter. They talked about getting an MP3 player wired into their headphones; English said he wanted to listen to "Phillip Glass or somethin' suitable New Age-y." No, Hammer shot back, "we gotta have butt rock— that's the only way to go. Quiet Riot, Twisted Sister."

But four minutes later, roughly twenty-five minutes into the flight, things started to go terribly wrong for Blackwater 61. When they emerged from the Bamian Valley, they found themselves flying along the Baba Mountain range. "Well, this, ah, row of mountains off to our left—I mean, it doesn't get much lower than about 14,000, the whole length of it, at least not till the edge of my map," Hammer informed English, as they discussed how to get past the mountain. "Well, let's kind of look and see if we've got anywhere we can pick our way through," English responded. "Doesn't really matter. It's gonna spit us out down at the bottom, anyway. Let's see, find a notch over here. Yeah, if we have to go to fourteen for just a second, it won't be too bad."

They soon decided to attempt a 180-degree turn. "Come on, baby. Come on, baby, you can make it," English said, as though willing the plane upwards. Nervously, the engineer Rowe asked the pilots, "OK, you guys are gonna make this, right?"

"Yeah, I'm hopin'," English replied.

The National Transportation Safety Board report said that at this point a sound similar to a "stall warning tone" could be heard on the black box recording. Inside the plane, chaotic conversation ensued before Rowe declared to the pilot, "Yeah, you need to, ah, make a decision." Heavy breathing could be heard inside the plane, as English exclaimed, "God [expletive deleted]." Rowe called out, "Hundred, ninety knots, call off his airspeed for him." At this point, the stall warning tone became constant, as the dialogue grew frantic, desperate.

"Ah [expletive] [expletive]," English called out.

Rowe said, "Call it off. Help him, or call off his airspeed for him . . . Butch."

Copilot Hammer: "You got ninety-five. Ninety-five."

Pilot English: "Oh, God. Oh [expletive]."

Engineer Rowe: "We're goin' down."

"God."

"God."

In the midst of attempting a 180-degree turn after it became clear that Blackwater 61 would not be able to clear the 16,580-foot Baba Mountain, the plane's right wing struck the mountain and was sheared off, causing the plane to tumble and skid for hundreds of feet, breaking apart the fuselage and crumpling the left wing under it. The pilots had been ejected 150 feet in front of the wreckage, and all of the passengers died on impact, except for Army Specialist Miller.[32]

Though the terrain on the route from Bagram to Farah was mountainous, Blackwater 61 had almost made it through the worst stretch of the flight. The plane cleared almost the entire Bamian Valley before the pilots decided to turn almost directly into Baba Mountain. As Blackwater pilot Kevin McBride later put it, "I really don't know how the pilots . . . got to the location where they were found. . . . The ridgeline where [Blackwater 61] crashed is the highest point in the highest ridgeline on our route."[33]

But the missteps involved in the accident were far from over. It wouldn't be until six hours after the plane reached Farah—and one hour after it was due back at Bagram—that any sort of rescue/recovery mission would even begin. The search for Blackwater 61 was immediately hampered by the lack of any tracking devices on the plane and an apparent absence of information about its intended route, as well as confusion over who was even responsible for finding the aircraft. "Lacking any coordinated rescue effort, and taking into account the probability that the aircraft flew to the south, my unit developed large search sectors, essentially covering the majority of Afghanistan," said Maj. David J. Francis, the operations officer for Task Force Wings, which was part of the Combined Joint Task Force 76. "There was some confusion as to who was going to run the rescue operation. At one point, the question was asked: 'Who owns this mission?'" Francis added, "There was no coordinated rescue plan until [eleven hours after the flight was due back at Bagram] on the day of the crash."[34]

It would be seventy-four hours before the wreckage was spotted and conditions allowed for CH-47 helicopters to reach the site and recover the remains, black box recorder, and the ammunition on board.[35] Though Specialist Miller had survived the initial impact, he didn't stand a chance of surviving the three days that passed before rescuers arrived. At the time of the crash, it was described in news reports as a basic accident—the kind of incident that ends up a small news item, if at all, in the papers. In fact, two weeks after Blackwater 61 went down, engineer Rowe's wife described it as "a plain-old regular plane crash."[36]

But as more details began to emerge and the military began to investigate, the families of the U.S. soldiers killed in the crash didn't view it as a fluke accident. On June 10, 2005, the families of Michael McMahon, Travis Grogan, and Harley Miller sued Blackwater's aviation subsidiaries, alleging negligence on the part of the flight crew and accusing the company of causing the soldiers' deaths. Blackwater's "gross and flagrant violations of safety regulations evince a reckless and conscious disregard of human life and for the rights and safety of their passengers," the lawsuit alleged, saying the actions of the company "evince reckless and wanton corporate policies, procedures, planning, and flight operations."[37] Robert Spohrer, the attorney for the families, alleged the company was "cutting corners" in its service to the armed forces. "If they're going to outsource to corporations services like flying personnel around Afghanistan, they must do it with corporations that put the safety of our men and women in uniform ahead of corporate profits. Sadly, that wasn't done here."[38]

Bolstering the families' case was the fact that the U.S. Army Collateral Investigations Board found Blackwater at fault for the crash, determining after a lengthy investigation that the crew suffered from "degraded situational awareness" and "inattention and complacency" as well as "poor judgment and willingness to take unacceptable risks."[39] The investigation also determined it was possible that the pilots were suffering from visual illusions and hypoxia, whose symptoms can include hallucinations, inattentiveness, and decreased motor skills. Further, the Army said there was demonstrated evidence of "inadequate cross-checking and crew coordination."[40] Presidential Airways said the report "was concluded in only two weeks and contains numerous errors, misstatements, and unfounded assumptions."[41]

In December 2006, nearly two years after Army investigators concluded their report, the National Transportation Safety Board issued a report of its own. The NTSB concluded that Blackwater's pilots "were behaving unprofessionally and were deliberately flying the nonstandard route low through the valley for 'fun.'" The board also found that the pilots' vision and judgment might have been impaired because they were not using oxygen, potentially in violation of federal regulations. "According to studies . . . a person without supplemental oxygen will exhibit few or no signs, have virtually no symptoms, and will likely be unaware of the effect," the board said.[42]

But perhaps the most significant finding, as a result of autopsies not mentioned in the earlier Army report, was that Specialist Miller had "an absolute minimum survival time of approximately eight hours" after the accident, and that if Miller "had received medical assistance within that time frame, followed by appropriate surgical intervention, he most likely would have survived." But, the board found, because Presidential Airways allegedly did not have procedures required by federal law to track flights, "by the time air searches were initiated, [Miller] had been stranded at the downed airplane for about seven hours," and "his rescue was further delayed when the subsequent five hours of aerial searches were focused in areas where the airplane had not flown."[43]

Joseph Schmitz, general counsel for Blackwater's parent company, The Prince Group, (who will be discussed in detail in a later chapter) described the report as "erroneous and politically motivated," according to the Raleigh *News & Observer,* and "said the report was intended to cover for the military's failures, but declined to elaborate on those failures. It was clear, he said, that the NTSB hadn't completed the rudiments of a proper accident investigation, which he called a disgrace to the victims and U.S. taxpayers," and added that the company would ask the NTSB to reconsider its findings.[44]

In fact, though the NTSB did blame the pilots and Presidential, it also blamed both the FAA and Pentagon for not providing "adequate oversight," and one NTSB member wrote a concurring opinion that highlighted the jurisdictional confusion in investigating "a civilian accident that occurred in a theater of war while the operator was conducting operations on behalf of the Department of Defense." The NTSB's Deborah Hersman called it "perplexing" that the Defense Department and FAA had not sorted out responsibility for "these types of flights" and added that even though the FAA was faulted for oversight, neither it nor the NTSB had personnel assigned to Afghanistan.[45] Those issues, combined with Hersman's description of Blackwater 61 as "clearly a military operation subject to DoD control," spoke directly to the tack Blackwater took in defending itself against the wrongful death lawsuit.

Blackwater's response strategy to the Afghanistan lawsuit closely paralleled that of its Fallujah defense: Blackwater and its subsidiaries are part of the Defense Department's "Total Force" and are therefore immunized against tort claims. Blackwater stiffly resisted acknowledging that the courts had any jurisdiction in the case and moved to stop the trial's discovery process at every turn, arguing that even allowing its employees to be deposed would interfere with its immunity. Blackwater's lawyers argued, "Immunity from suit does not mean just that a party may not be found liable, but rather that it cannot be sued at all and need not be burdened with even participating in the lawsuit. To require Presidential to engage in discovery thus would eviscerate the immunity that Presidential has."[46]

In fighting the lawsuit, Blackwater adopted a three-pronged approach to argue that it should be immune from such litigation: that its operations fall under the realm of a "political question" that must be addressed by either the executive or legislative branches, but not the judiciary; that Blackwater is essentially an extension of the military and thus should enjoy the same immunity from lawsuits that the government does when members of the military are killed or injured; and that Blackwater should be immune from lawsuits under an exception to the Federal Tort Claims Act that has in the past been granted to contractors responsible for the design and manufacturing of complex pieces of military equipment. Other military contractors closely monitored Blackwater's arguments in the Fallujah and Afghanistan cases, believing that the outcomes would have far-reaching implications for the entire war industry.

The Political Question Doctrine

In its court filings, Blackwater/Presidential cited the "political question doctrine," which relies on the idea that "the judiciary properly refrains from deciding controversies that the Constitution textually commits to another political branch and cases that are beyond the competence of the courts to resolve because of the lack of judicially manageable standards."[47] Referencing its contention that it was a recognized part of the U.S. "Total Force" and part of the Defense Department's "warfighting capability and capacity," Blackwater argued that "allowing civilian courts to consider questions of liability to soldiers who are killed or injured in operations involving contractors on the battlefield would insert those civilian courts directly into the regulation of military operations."[48]

This argument was not warmly received by the district court judge in the case. In rejecting Blackwater's argument, Judge John Antoon cited the 2006 ruling in *Smith v. Halliburton Co.* That lawsuit accused Halliburton of negligence for failing to secure a dining hall in Mosul, Iraq, that was hit by a suicide bomber on December 21, 2004, killing twenty-two people. Judge Antoon found:

> The proper inquiry, according to the court, was whether the claim would require the court to question the military's mission and response to an attack. If the military was responsible for securing the facility, resolving the matter would require "second-guessing military decision-making" and evaluating the conduct of the military—a political question. However, if the contractor was primarily responsible for securing the dining hall under its contract, the suit would be justiciable. Concluding that "there is a basic difference between questioning the military's execution of a mission and questioning the manner in which a contractor carries out its contractual duties," the court foreshadowed the conclusion drawn here: the former situation presents a political question, while the latter does not.[49]

Judge Antoon determined that because Blackwater 61 was "required to fly as [it] normally would, according to commercial, civilian standards, in a foreign, albeit treacherous, terrain" and could refuse to fly any mission they felt was too dangerous, "it does not appear . . . this Court will be called on to question any tactical military orders."[50]

The court ultimately rejected Blackwater's "political question" argument, saying it was "not a proper basis for dismissing this case." Antoon also questioned Blackwater's contention that it was essentially part of the military, pointing out that the federal government could have filed a brief supporting Blackwater in this case but had not. "Notably, the United States has not chosen to intervene on behalf of Defendants in this case," the judge wrote. " It has declined an opportunity to intervene and explain how its interests might be affected by this lawsuit."[51]

While rebuking Blackwater, the judge did seem to indicate that these situations could change for contractors in the future. "The extent to which for-profit corporations, performing traditional military functions, are entitled to protection from tort liability is an area of interest to the political branches."[52]

The Feres Doctrine

In arguing that it is immune from tort litigation, Blackwater cited the Feres Doctrine, which holds that the government has sovereign immunity from tort suits for "injuries to servicemen where the injuries arise out of or are in the course of activity incident to service."[53] Blackwater argued that "it is inconsequential here that the decedents died in aircraft hired by the Air Force, rather than in an aircraft operated by the Air Force—what matters is that they were military personnel who died while on war duty."[54] Blackwater alleged that even the families of the dead soldiers admitted their loved ones "(1) were deployed to Afghanistan, (2) died in a combat zone, and (3) did so while being transported on a DoD mission between two airfields in Afghanistan."[55]

Judge Antoon clearly took issue with Blackwater's interpretation of a fairly straightforward immunity granted to the military, pointing out that Blackwater's lawyers "cite no case in which the Feres doctrine has been held applicable to private contractors."[56] He said Blackwater/Presidential "essentially mask their request for this Court to stretch Feres beyond its established and logical bounds by citing cases which emphasize that it is the plaintiff's status as a member of the military and not the status of [Blackwater] that is significant."[57] The judge concluded, "Clearly, Defendants in this case are not entitled to protection under the Feres doctrine because they are private commercial entities. . . . Defendants entered into the contract as a commercial endeavor. They provided a service for a price. Simply because the service was provided in the mountains of Afghanistan during armed conflict does not render the Defendants, or their personnel, members of the military or employees of the Government."[58] In other words, Antoon determined that though the Pentagon might have referred to private military contractors as part of its "Total Force," that did not change Blackwater's status as a for-profit private company responsible for its actions.

Exception to Federal Tort Claims Act

Blackwater's third major argument for immunity from tort lawsuits was that, as a military contractor, it is immune from such litigation in the same way that certain producers of complex military equipment have been found immune. In one case, the family of a dead Marine sued a manufacturer for defects in its design of a helicopter escape system. The court concluded that "state tort law was preempted by the government's profound interest in procuring complex military equipment" and that the government had the "discretion to prioritize combat effectiveness over safety when designing military equipment."[59]

Judge Antoon decided that although that defense exists and it has been extended in some instances, there is no "authority for bestowing a private actor with the shield of sovereign immunity. Until Congress directs otherwise, private, non-employee contractors are limited" to exceptions like that involving the design of complex equipment. "This Court is skeptical that the combatant activities exception to the [Federal Tort Claims Act], which preserves the Government's traditional sovereign immunity from liability, has any application to suits against private defense contractors," Antoon wrote. "To the extent that it does apply, however, at most it only shields private defense contractors for products liability claims involving complex, sophisticated equipment used during times of war. It has never been extended to bar suits alleging active negligence by contractors in the provision of services, and it shall not be so extended by this Court."[60]

Blackwater's Curious Aviation Division

In late September 2006, Judge Antoon denied every single motion made by Blackwater to stop discovery and dismiss the case, and, as expected, Blackwater immediately began the appellate process. While Antoon decisively rejected Blackwater's claim that it is in effect an extension of the U.S. military because of its claimed status as part of the Pentagon's "Total Force," Blackwater may actually have been far more intertwined with the workings of the military and intelligence agencies than it would ever let on.

While what little attention that has been paid to Blackwater's aviation division has focused on the Afghanistan lawsuit, the company has multiple contracts with the U.S. government to provide pilots and aircraft. Information on the use of Blackwater's planes by the government is difficult to obtain, but it has been well documented that U.S. intelligence agencies and the military have used private aviation companies to "render" prisoners across the globe, particularly under the Bush administration's "war on terror." Under this clandestine program, prisoners are sometimes flown to countries with questionable or terrible human rights records, where they are interrogated far from any oversight or due process. To avoid oversight, the government has used small private aviation companies—many with flimsy ownership documentation—to transport the prisoners. "Terrorism suspects in Europe, Africa, Asia, and the Middle East have often been abducted by hooded or masked American agents, then forced onto a Gulfstream V jet," wrote investigative journalist Jane Mayer in *The New Yorker* magazine. The plane "has clearance to land at U.S. military bases. Upon arriving in foreign countries, rendered suspects often vanish. Detainees are not provided with lawyers, and many families are not informed of their whereabouts."[61] While there is nothing directly linking Blackwater to extraordinary renditions, there is an abundance of circumstantial evidence that bears closer scrutiny and investigation.

The rendition program was not born under the Bush administration but rather during the Clinton administration in the mid-1990s. The CIA, with the approval of the Clinton White House and a presidential directive, began sending terror suspects to Egypt, where, far removed from U.S. law and due process, they could be interrogated by *mukhabarat* agents.[62] In 1998, the U.S. Congress passed legislation declaring that it is "the policy of the United States not to expel, extradite, or otherwise effect the involuntary return of any person to a country in which there are substantial grounds for believing the person would be in danger of being subjected to torture, regardless of whether the person is physically present in the United States."[63] After 9/11, this legislation was sidestepped under the Bush administration's "New Paradigm," which stripped alleged terror suspects of basic rights.[64] This thinking was best articulated by Vice President Dick Cheney five days after 9/11, when he argued on NBC's *Meet the Press* that the government should "work through, sort of, the dark side." Cheney declared, "A lot of what needs to be done here will have to be done quietly, without any discussion, using sources and methods that are available to our intelligence agencies, if we're going to be successful. That's the world these folks operate in. And so it's going to be vital for us to use any means at our disposal, basically, to achieve our objective."[65] These sentiments were echoed by the CIA's number-three man at the time, Buzzy Krongard—the man allegedly responsible for Blackwater's first security contract in Afghanistan—who declared the war on terror would be "won in large measure by forces you do not know about, in actions you will not see and in ways you may not want to know about."[66]

The U.S. use of clandestine aviation companies dates back to at least the Vietnam War. From 1962 to 1975, the CIA used its secretly owned airline Air America (which simultaneously functioned as a commercial airline) to conduct covert or secretive operations that would have sparked even more investigation and outrage if made public. "Air America, an airline secretly owned by the CIA, was a vital component in the Agency's operations in Laos," according to a paper on the CIA Web site written by University of Georgia history professor William M. Leary. "By the summer of 1970, the airline had some two dozen twin-engine transports, another two dozen short-takeoff-and-landing (STOL) aircraft, and some 30 helicopters dedicated to operations in Laos. There were more than 300 pilots, copilots, flight mechanics, and air-freight specialists flying out of Laos and Thailand. . . . Air America crews transported tens of thousands of troops and refugees, flew emergency medevac missions and rescued downed airmen throughout Laos, inserted and extracted road-watch teams, flew nighttime airdrop missions over the Ho Chi Minh Trail, monitored sensors along infiltration routes, conducted a highly successful photoreconnaissance program, and engaged in numerous clandestine missions using night-vision glasses and state-of-the-art electronic equipment. Without Air America's presence, the CIA's effort in Laos could not have been sustained."[67]

In 1975, the Church Committee began investigating the legality of U.S. intelligence-gathering practices. The CIA's chief of cover and commercial staff told the Senate committee that if an operational requirement like the Vietnam War should again arise, "I would assume that the Agency would consider setting up a large-scale air proprietary with one proviso—that we have a chance of keeping it secret that it is CIA."[68]

Decades later, the Bush administration, waging a war many compared to Vietnam, clearly saw the need for a clandestine fleet of planes. Shortly after 9/11, the administration started a program using a network of private planes some began referring to as the "new Air America." The rendition program kicked into high gear, as the United States began operating a sophisticated network of secret prisons and detention centers across the globe, using the private aircraft to transport prisoners. Most of the planes alleged to have been involved in renditions under the Bush administration's war on terror were owned by shell companies. In contrast, Blackwater directly owns its aviation division and has been public and proud in promoting its military involvement.

Blackwater Aviation was born in April 2003, as the Iraq occupation was getting under way, when the Prince Group acquired Aviation Worldwide Services (AWS) and its subsidiaries, including Presidential Airways.[69] The AWS consortium had been brought together in early 2001 under the ownership of Tim Childrey and Richard Pere, who "focused on military training operations and aviation transport for the U.S. Government."[70] Presidential Airways was the licensed air carrier, and in addition to the Afghanistan contract, it has provided CASA 212 and Metro 23 aircraft for military training contracts, including some for the U.S. Special Operations Command.[71] STI Aviation was the maintenance company for the Blackwater fleet. And Air Quest Inc. provided Cessna Caravan planes equipped with aerial surveillance—it provided surveillance planes in 2000 and 2001 to U.S. Southern Command for operations in South America.[72]

"In addition to offering solutions for firearms training, steel targets and range construction and security needs, Blackwater now offers aviation and logistical solutions for its customers," Blackwater president Gary Jackson said in announcing the acquisition. The new aviation division "complements our strategic goal of providing a 'one stop' solution for all of our customer's security and tactical training needs."[73]

Blackwater also began developing a surveillance blimp that could be used to spy on "enemy" forces abroad or by the Department of Homeland Security to monitor the border.[74] In 2004, Blackwater announced plans to move the operations of its aviation division to North Carolina and in 2006 sought approval to build a private airstrip with two runways for its fleet of more than twenty planes.[75] "We have a fleet of aircraft that all have customers," Jackson said. "Every single aircraft has a contract."[76] While the role these planes have played in the war on terror is not clear, Blackwater's aviation wing fits the patterns of those companies that have been documented to be involved with renditions.

Blackwater aircraft have made stopovers at Pinal Airpark in Arizona, which used to be home to the Air America fleet.[77] After public scrutiny forced the CIA to dismantle its fleet and sell the airpark, a company called Evergreen International Aviation, whose board included the former head of the CIA's air operations, subsequently purchased it.[78] As of 2006, Evergreen still owned and operated the airpark primarily as a storage facility for unused aircraft, largely because the desert climate allowed planes to survive longer with less maintenance. Not surprisingly, the company boasted in April 2006 of "four years of consecutive growth."[79]

Aside from their stops at Pinal Airpark, Blackwater-owned planes frequented many airports alleged to be implicated in the rendition program. Aero Contractors, which has received much attention recently for its connections to the CIA, was headquartered in Johnston County, North Carolina, which "was deliberately located near Pope Air Force Base, where the CIA pilots could pick up paramilitary operatives who were based at Fort Bragg [home of the Special Forces]. The proximity to such an important military base was convenient for other reasons, too. 'That supported our principal cover,' one former pilot [said], 'which was, we were doing government contracts for the military, for the folks at Fort Bragg.'"[80] Former chief Air America pilot Jim Rhyne founded Aero Contractors for the CIA, and according to one pilot, he "had chosen the rural airfield [Johnston County] because it was close to Fort Bragg and many Special Forces veterans. There was also no control tower that could be used to spy on the company's operations."[81] Johnston County is just one of the airports frequented by CIA flights, according to experts. "Typically, the CIA planes will fly out of these rural airfields in North Carolina to Dulles," according to the authors of Torture Taxi.[82]

A glimpse of the flight records of planes registered to Blackwater subsidiaries Aviation Worldwide Services and Presidential Airways revealed numerous flights that follow these patterns and frequent CIA-linked airports:[83]

- Since February 2006, N964BW, a CASA 212, has flown the route from Johnston County to Dulles; been to Pinal Airpark three times; been to Pope Air Force Base twice; been to the Phillips Air Force Base and Mackall Army Air Field; and has also twice landed at the Camp Peary Landing Strip, home to the nine-thousand-acre CIA training facility known as "the Farm."[84]

- N962BW, a CASA 212, has made numerous trips between Johnston County and Dulles and has been to Camp Peary, Simmons Army

Airfield at Fort Bragg, and Blackstone Army Airfield near Fort Pickett. Its last reported flight was in September 2006, when it was headed from Goose Bay, Newfoundland, a NATO and Canadian Air Force Base, to Narsarsuaq, Greenland.

- N955BW, a SA227-DC Metro, is registered with Aviation Worldwide but has no recent flights. Nor does N961BW or N963BW, both CASA 212s. All of these planes have serial numbers that have not been assigned different N-numbers.

- N956BW fell off the radar in January 2006 just after beginning a flight from Louisiana to North Carolina.

- N965BW, a CASA 212, has traveled regularly to Pinal Airpark, the Southern California Logistics Airport, which is used by the military, and has made stops in Turks & Caicos, the Dominican Republic, Bahamas, St. Croix, and Trinidad and Tobago.

- N966BW, a CASA 212, has been to Pinal Airpark, many of the same Carribean stops as N965BW, Pope Air Force Base, and has made several Dulles-Johnston trips.

- N967BW, a CASA 212, was last recorded heading from Goose Bay to Narsarsuaq two weeks after N962BW.

- N968BW, a CASA 212, which regularly stops at Johnston County, Dulles, Phillips Airfield, and Camp Peary, has been to Pope Air Force Base, Pinal Airpark, and Oceana Naval Air Station.

In addition, though Blackwater's aircraft in Afghanistan flew normal circuits, the company was also charged with flying out of the country, including to Uzbekistan. Air Force Capt. Edwin R. Byrnes was quoted in the FAA report on the crash of Blackwater 61 as saying that one of the aircraft English and Hammer were trained to use, "[t]he Metro was going to be used like a private jet to fly to Uzbekistan."[85] Uzbekistan has been one of the "key destinations" for both U.S. military and CIA renditions. Prisoners are alleged to have been brought there both for interrogation and repatriation from Afghanistan.[86] Also, as it happens, Blackwater's planes in Afghanistan operate out of Bagram, a known U.S.-run detention and torture facility. According to Blackwater/Presidential's Afghanistan contract, all personnel "are required to possess a Secret security clearance."[87] The contract also outlined "operations security" requirements: "Information such as flight schedules, hotels where crews are staying, return trips, and other facts about the international mission shall be kept close hold and only communicated to persons who have a need to know this information. Flight crews should be aware of persons who are seeking information about the contractor, flights, etc. They should seek to maintain a low profile while operating DoD missions."[88] In June 2007, Blackwater released a statement in response to an article in London's *Daily Mail* (which the paper quickly retracted), which accused the company of engaging in renditions. "Blackwater and its affiliates do not now and have never conducted so-called 'rendition flights,' as the transport of detainees or terror suspects to interrogation centers has become known," the statement said.

It would take a far-reaching investigation to determine what, if any, involvement Blackwater has had in the government's secret rendition programs. Company president Gary Jackson has been bold in bragging of Blackwater's "black" and "secret" contracts, which are not publicly available or traceable; he claimed these contracts were so secret he could not tell one federal agency about Blackwater's work with another.[89] Under the war on terror, Blackwater's first security contract was a "black" contract with the CIA, an agency with which it has deep ties.[90] And then there was this development: In early 2005, Blackwater hired the career CIA spy many believe was responsible for jump-starting the Bush administration's post-9/11 rendition program: J. Cofer Black, the former chief of the CIA's counterterrorism center. In November 2001, when U.S. forces captured Ibn al-Shayk al-Libi, believed to have run the Al Qaeda training camp in Khalden, Afghanistan, Black allegedly requested and got permission, through CIA Director George Tenet, from the White House to render Libi, reportedly over the objections of FBI officials who said they wanted to see him dealt with more transparently. "They duct-taped his mouth, cinched him up and sent him to Cairo," a former FBI official told *Newsweek*. "At the airport the CIA case officer goes up to him and says, 'You're going to Cairo, you know. Before you get there I'm going to find your mother and I'm going to fuck her.'"[91]

CHAPTER SIXTEEN

COFER BLACK: THE GLOVES COME OFF

SINCE 9/11, few people have had the kind of access to President Bush and covert "war on terror" planning as Ambassador J. Cofer Black. A thirty-year CIA veteran, Black was a legendary figure in the shadowy world of international espionage, having been personally marked for death by Osama bin Laden in the 1990s. He rose to prominence in the spy world following the central role he played in Sudan in catching the famed international terrorist Ilich Ramirez Sanchez, known as "Carlos the Jackal." Black had spent his career in Africa and the Middle East, and when the 9/11 attacks happened, he enthusiastically seized a key role in plotting out the immediate U.S. response.

On September 13, 2001—two days after the planes crashed into the World Trade Center and the Pentagon—Black was sitting in the White

House Situation Room.[1] The career CIA veteran was there to brief the President on the kind of campaign he had prepared for since joining the agency in 1974 but had been barred from carrying out.[2] After clandestine operations training, Black had been sent to Africa, where he spent the bulk of his CIA career. He worked in Zambia during the Rhodesian War, then Somalia and South Africa during the apartheid regime's brutal war against the black majority.[3] During his time in Zaire, Black worked on the Reagan administration's covert weapons program to arm anticommunist forces in Angola.[4] After two decades in the CIA and a stint in London, Black arrived under diplomatic cover at the U.S. Embassy in Khartoum, Sudan, where he served as CIA Station Chief from 1993 to 1995.[5] There, he watched as a wealthy Saudi named Osama bin Laden built up his international network into what the CIA would describe at the end of Black's tour as "the Ford Foundation of Sunni Islamic terrorism."[6]

During much of the 1990s, agents tracking bin Laden worked under an "Operating Directive" that restricted them to intelligence collection on bin Laden and his network; they did not yet have authorization from the Clinton administration to conduct covert actions.[7] In bin Laden, Black saw a man who was a threat and who needed to be taken out. The administration, however, refused to authorize the type of lethal action against bin Laden and his cronies favored by Black. Some of Black's men were enthusiastic about killing the wealthy Saudi but were rebuffed. "Unfortunately, at that time permissions to kill—officially called Lethal Findings—were taboo in the outfit," according to CIA operative Billy Waugh, who worked closely with Black in Sudan. "In the early 1990s we were forced to adhere to the sanctimonious legal counsel and the do-gooders."[8] Among Waugh's rejected ideas was an alleged plot to kill bin Laden in Khartoum and dump his body at the Iranian Embassy in an effort to pin the blame on Tehran, an idea Waugh said Cofer Black "loved."[9]

But while Black and the CIA watched bin Laden, they, too, were under surveillance. In 1994, bin Laden's group in Khartoum had reportedly determined that Black, who maintained cover as a simple embassy diplomat, was indeed

CIA.[10] In his definitive book on the secret history of the CIA and bin Laden, *Ghost Wars*, Steve Coll wrote that bin Laden's men began to track Black's routes to and from the U.S. Embassy. "Black and his case officers picked up this surveillance and started to watch those who were watching them," Coll wrote. "The CIA officers saw that bin Laden's men were setting up a 'kill zone' near the US embassy. They couldn't tell whether the attack was going to be a kidnapping, a car bombing, or an ambush with assault rifles, but they were able to watch bin Laden's group practice the operation on a Khartoum street. As the weeks passed, the surveillance and counter-surveillance grew more and more intense. On one occasion they found themselves in a high-speed chase. On another the CIA officers leveled loaded shotguns at the Arabs who were following them. Eventually, Black dispatched the US ambassador to complain to the Sudanese government. Exposed, the plotters retreated."[11] When Black left Khartoum, bin Laden was more powerful than when the veteran spy had arrived; a fact that would help fuel what would become Black's professional obsession for years to come.

Black's greatest triumph in Sudan, therefore, resulted from the capture of an international fugitive whose notoriety long predated bin Laden's. Billy Waugh described how, in Sudan, he was pulled off surveillance of someone who "wasn't much of a big fish at the time"—Osama bin Laden—for "the biggest fish" in December 1993.[12] Waugh described a meeting at the Khartoum Embassy where Black announced their new target: "In this city of one million souls, we would be responsible for finding and fixing none other than Ilich Ramirez Sanchez, the man known far and wide as Carlos the Jackal, the world's most famous terrorist."[13] After the meeting, Waugh recalled, "Cofer Black pulled me aside and said, 'Billy, this is the man. You've got to get this guy.' At that moment, given the gravity evident in his voice, I knew the agency was making this a top priority. . . . I wanted to be the guy who caught this asshole."[14] Carlos was accused of a series of political killings and bombings throughout the 1970s and '80s and, while Cofer Black was in Sudan, was perhaps the most famous wanted man in the world.

Black, Waugh, and the Jackal team caught a break when Carlos called a trusted bodyguard from overseas to keep him out of trouble, after Carlos's guard had been thrown in a Khartoum jail for drunkenly waving a pistol at a local shopkeeper.[15] They were able to ID the new bodyguard and his vehicle when he arrived in Khartoum and eventually traced the Toyota Cressida to the Jackal's home. After months of careful and detailed surveillance from a rented apartment with a view of his home, the move was made in August 1994.[16] Waugh wrote of entering the CIA station that day, unsure of Carlos's fate: "Immediately, Cofer and the fine lady station manager handed me a glass of champagne. Cofer bellowed, 'Toast, Billy, you sweet son of a bitch. Carlos is in prison in France.'"[17] The arrest of the Jackal secured Cofer Black's legendary status in CIA circles and remains one of his top career bragging points. After Khartoum, Black was named in 1995 as CIA Task Force Chief in the Near East and South Asia Division, continuing his monitoring of bin Laden's network, before a brief stint in 1998 as Deputy Chief of the Agency's Latin America Division.[18] In 1999, Black was awarded a significant promotion, heading up the CIA's Counter-Terrorism Center (CTC).[19]

By the time Black officially took over at CTC, his nemesis, bin Laden, was a household name, publicly accused of masterminding and ordering the 1998 bombings of the U.S. Embassies in Kenya and Tanzania, which killed more than two hundred people, among them twelve U.S. citizens. Bin Laden left Sudan shortly after Black did, allegedly relocating to Afghanistan. Once a name known only in intelligence circles and in the Arab and Muslim world, bin Laden was now on FBI most-wanted posters. Among Black's duties beginning in 1999 was overseeing the special bin Laden unit of the CTC, known as Alec Station—internally referred to as the "Manson family," for its cultlike obsession with "the rising al Qaeda threat."[20] Black dove enthusiastically into planning and overseeing covert operations. "He would make pronouncements that were meant to be dramatic and tough-guy colloquial—to make you think, Oh, my God, this guy's got brass balls, and he knows the score," said Daniel Benjamin, head of the National Security

Council's counterterrorism team in the Clinton administration, in an interview with *Vanity Fair*. "He'd say things like, 'No more screwing around. This is going to get rough, and people are gonna come home in body bags. That's all there is to it. You guys gotta know that.' He'd talk about body bags all the time."[21]

Shortly after Black officially took over the CTC, the CIA made a damning admission to the White House in early December 1999. "After four years and hundreds of millions of dollars, Alec Station had yet to recruit a single source within bin Laden's growing Afghanistan operation," asserted investigative author James Bamford. "It was more than embarrassing—it was a scandal. . . . It was a dangerous time to be without intelligence. Within days, the 9/11 plotters began their operation."[22] While Black was technically in charge, he had only recently been named to that position, and he would later complain that he and his colleagues within the CTC were not given adequate support to take out bin Laden. "When I started this job in 1999, I thought there was a good chance I was going to be sitting right here in front of you," Black told the 9/11 Commission in April 2004. "The bottom line here, and I have to tell you, and I'll take part of the blame on this, I kind of failed my people despite doing everything I could. We didn't have enough people to do the job. And we didn't have enough money by magnitudes."[23] Black asserted that the CTC "had as many people as three infantry companies [that] can be expected to cover a front of a few kilometers" even though "our counterterrorism center has worldwide responsibilities."[24] Black said that before 9/11, when it came to "numbers of people, finances, and operational flexibility," these were "choices made for us. Made for the CIA and made for my counterterrorism center."[25]

There were indeed budget cuts happening during Black's tenure—in 1999, he faced a 30 percent reduction in the CTC's cash operating budget, including in the bin Laden unit.[26] Some analysts, though, said lack of resources was not the heart of the problem. Rather, they say, it stemmed from Black and his allies' strong emphasis on paramilitary covert operations over the more tedious work of infiltrating Al Qaeda or bin Laden's circle.[27] In 1999, briefing documents Black's office had prepared for the

Clinton White House acknowledged that "without penetrations of [the] UBL organization," the CIA was in trouble. Black's brief said that there was a need "to recruit sources" but added that "recruiting terrorist sources is difficult."[28] What was done (or not) about this problem would be the source of a substantial amount of finger-pointing after 9/11.

In the two years before 9/11, Black's strategy to fight Al Qaeda focused on using Afghanistan's neighbor, Uzbekistan, as a launching pad into Afghanistan.[29] Black clandestinely traveled to the capital of Tashkent and oversaw U.S. funding and training of an Uzbek paramilitary force that would supposedly try to kidnap bin Laden or his deputies through "covert snatch operations."[30] Uzbekistan's dictator, Islam Karimov, was fighting his own war against Islamic groups in the country and was adept at using threats of Islamic rebellion to justify wide-ranging repressive domestic policies, including arresting prodemocracy activists.[31] When the CIA came knocking, Karimov was happy to use the veneer of a war against bin Laden to justify covert military aid from Washington. While the CIA was able to use the country's air bases for some operations and install communications and eavesdropping equipment inside Uzbekistan, the end result of Black's covert U.S. support was that the brutal leader, Karimov, received millions of dollars of CIA money, which he used "to keep his torture chambers running," according to Bamford. "And the commando training would be useful to continue the repression of women and ethnic minorities."[32] Karimov was also known to have political enemies boiled to death; a practice the British ambassador in the country said was "not an isolated incident."[33]

Black also kicked up U.S. covert support for Ahmed Shah Massoud, the "Lion of Panjshir" and his Northern Alliance, which regarded bin Laden and Al Qaeda as enemies. On at least one occasion as CTC director, Black met face to face with Massoud—in Tajikistan in the summer of 2000.[34] Black and his units' heavy reliance on Massoud in confronting Al Qaeda was controversial— even within the intelligence world. Massoud's forces represented an ethnic minority in Afghanistan's complicated landscape and were based in the north, far from bin Laden's main operations. There were also broader concerns. "While one part of the CIA was bankrolling Massoud's group, another part, the CIA's Counter-Narcotics Center, was warning that he posed a great danger," according to Bamford. "His people, they warned, were continuing to smuggle large amounts of opium and heroin into Europe. The British came to the same conclusion."[35] White House countert-error expert Richard Clarke opposed the military alliance with Massoud, describing the Northern Alliance as "drug runners" and "human rights abusers."[36] Black, though, told his colleagues that this support was about "preparing the battlefield for World War Three."[37] Massoud would not live to see it, though. He was assassinated, allegedly by Al Qaeda operatives posing as journalists, on September 9, 2001.[38] During this time, Black was also pressing the Air Force to accelerate its production of an unmanned Predator spy drone that could be equipped with Hellfire missiles to launch at bin Laden and his lieutenants.[39]

Some former counterterrorism officials have alleged that during Black's time at CTC, there was more interest in using Al Qaeda to justify building up the bureaucracy of the CIA's covert actions hub, the Directorate of Operations, than the specific task of stopping bin Laden. "Cofer Black, he arrived, and he was the man, he was the pro from the D.O.," said veteran CIA official Michael Scheuer, who headed the bin Laden unit from 1995 to 1999 before Black's appointment.[40] Former counterterrorism czar Richard Clarke told *Vanity Fair*, "There's some truth to the fact that they didn't have enough money, but the interesting thing is that they didn't put any of the money they had into going after al-Qaeda." Clarke alleged, "They would say 'Al-Qaeda, al-Qaeda, al-Qaeda' when they were trying to get money, and then when you gave them money it didn't go to al-Qaeda. They were trying to rebuild the D.O. [Directorate of Operations], and so a lot of it went to D.O. infrastructure, and they would say, 'Well, you can't start by going after al-Qaeda, you have to repair the whole D.O.' . . . And what I would say to them is 'Surely there must be a dollar somewhere in C.I.A. that you could re-program into going after al-Qaeda,' and they would say 'No.' The other way of saying that is everything else they're doing is more important."[41]

The public blame war over who in the U.S. intelligence community and the Clinton and Bush administrations was responsible for the failure to prevent 9/11 intensified when Bob Woodward's book *State of Denial* was published in September 2006. In it, Woodward detailed a meeting that reportedly took place on July 10, 2001, two months before the 9/11 attacks. Then-CIA Director George J. Tenet met with Black, then head of the CTC, at CIA headquarters. The two men reviewed current U.S. intelligence on bin Laden and Al Qaeda. Black, Woodward reported, "laid out the case, consisting of communications intercepts and other top-secret intelligence showing the increasing likelihood that al-Qaeda would soon attack the United States. It was a mass of fragments and dots that nonetheless made a compelling case, so compelling to Tenet that he decided he and Black should go to the White House immediately."[42] At the time, "Tenet had been having difficulty getting traction on an immediate bin Laden action plan, in part because Defense Secretary Donald H. Rumsfeld had questioned all the National Security Agency intercepts and other intelligence. Could all this be a grand deception? Rumsfeld had asked. Perhaps it was a plan to measure U.S. reactions and defenses."[43] After reviewing the intelligence with Black, Tenet called National Security Adviser Condoleezza Rice from the car en route to the White House. When Black and Tenet met with Rice that day, according to Woodward, they "felt they were not getting through to Rice. She was polite, but they felt the brush-off." Black later said, "The only thing we didn't do was pull the trigger to the gun we were holding to her head."[44]

On August 6, 2001, President Bush was at his Crawford Ranch, where he was delivered a Presidential Daily Brief titled "Bin Ladin Determined to Strike in US." It twice mentioned the possibility that Al Qaeda operatives may try to hijack airplanes, saying FBI information "indicates patterns of suspicious activity in [the U.S.] consistent with preparations for hijackings or other types of attacks, including recent surveillance of federal buildings in New York."[45] Nine days later, Black addressed a secret Pentagon counterterrorism conference. "We're going to be struck soon," Black said. "Many Americans are going to die, and it could be in the U.S."[46]

While the debate on responsibility for 9/11 would continue for years—with Clinton and Bush administration officials hurling stones at one another—it was irrelevant to Cofer Black in the immediate aftermath of the attacks. Black found himself in the driver's seat with a Commander in Chief ready and eager to make Black's covert action dreams a reality. Black had long been frustrated by the restraints and prohibitions governing U.S. covert actions—namely a prohibition against assassinations—and the war on terror had changed the rules of the game overnight. "My personal emotion was, It is now officially started," Black said. "The analogy would be the junkyard dog that had been chained to the ground was now going to be let go. And I just couldn't wait."[47]

In his initial meeting with President Bush after the 9/11 attacks, Black came prepared with a PowerPoint presentation, and he threw papers on the floor as he spoke of deploying forces inside Afghanistan.[48] On September 13, he told Bush point-blank that his men would aim to kill Al Qaeda operatives. "When we're through with them, they will have flies walking across their eyeballs," Black promised, in a performance that would earn him a designation in the inner circle of the administration as "the flies-on-the-eyeballs guy."[49] The President reportedly loved Black's style; when he told Bush the operation would not be bloodless, the President said, "Let's go. That's war. That's what we're here to win."[50]

That September, President Bush gave the green light to Black and the CIA to begin inserting special operations forces into Afghanistan. Before the core CIA team, Jawbreaker, deployed on September 27, 2001, Black gave his men direct and macabre directions. "Gentlemen, I want to give you your marching orders, and I want to make them very clear. I have discussed this with the President, and he is in full agreement," Black told covert CIA operative Gary Schroen. "I don't want bin Laden and his thugs captured, I want them dead. . . . They must be killed. I want to see photos of their heads on pikes. I want bin Laden's head shipped back in a box filled with dry ice. I want to be able to show bin Laden's head to the President. I promised him I would do that."[51] Schroen said it was the first time in his thirty-year career he had been ordered to assassinate an adversary rather than attempting a capture.[52] Black asked if he had made himself clear. "Perfectly clear, Cofer," Schroen told him. "I don't know where we'll find dry ice out there in Afghanistan, but I think we can certainly manufacture pikes in the field."[53] Black later explained why this would be necessary. "You'd need some DNA," Black said. "There's a good way to do it. Take a machete, and whack off his head, and you'll get a bucketful of DNA, so you can see it and test it. It beats lugging the whole body back!"[54]

As the United States plotted its invasion of Afghanistan, Black continued with his apparent fixation with corporal mutilation when he accompanied Colin Powell's deputy, Richard Armitage, to Moscow for meetings with Russian officials. When the Russians, speaking from experience, warned Black of the prospect for a U.S. defeat at the hands of mujahedeen, Black shot back. "We're going to kill them," he said. "We're going to put their heads on sticks. We're going to rock their world."[55] Interestingly, the covert operations Black organized immediately after 9/11 relied heavily on private contractors, answering directly to him, rather than active-duty military forces. Black's men used their contacts to recruit about sixty former Delta Force, ex-SEALs, and other Special Forces operators as independent contractors for the initial mission, making up the majority of the first Americans into Afghanistan after 9/11.[56]

In late 2001, Black was exactly where he had wanted to be his entire career, playing an essential role in crafting and implementing the Bush administration's counterterror policies. "There was this enormous sense among the officers that had lived in this campaign before Sept. 11 that . . . finally, these lawyers and these cautious decision makers who had gotten in our way before can be overcome, and we can be given the license that we deserve to have had previously," said Steve Coll, author of Ghost Wars.[57] Black's CTC rapidly expanded from three hundred staffers to twelve hundred.[58] "It was the Camelot of counterterrorism," a former counterterrorism official told the Washington Post. "We didn't have to mess with others—and it was fun."[59] People were abducted from Afghanistan, Pakistan, and other hot spots and flown to the U.S. prison camp at Guantánamo Bay, Cuba—most held without charge for years, designated as enemy combatants and denied access to any legal system. Others were kept at hellish prison camps inside Afghanistan and other countries. In 2002, Black testified to Congress about the new "operational flexibility" employed in the war on terror. "This is a very highly classified area, but I have to say that all you need to know: There was a before 9/11, and there was an after 9/11," Black said. "After 9/11 the gloves come off."[60]

Black would later brag, in 2004, that "over 70 percent" of Al Qaeda's leadership had been arrested, detained, or killed, and "more than 3,400 of their operatives and supporters have also been detained and put out of an action."[61] As part of this new "operational flexibility," the CIA carried out "extraordinary renditions" of prisoners—shipping them to countries with questionable or blatantly horrible human rights records, where they were sometimes psychologically or physically tortured. The *Washington Post* reported that Black's CTC heavily utilized its "Rendition Group, made up of case officers, paramilitaries, analysts and psychologists. Their job is to figure out how to snatch someone off a city street, or a remote hillside, or a secluded corner of an airport where local authorities wait."[62] According to the *Post*'s Dana Priest:

Members of the Rendition Group follow a simple but standard procedure: Dressed head to toe in black, including masks, they blindfold and cut the clothes off their new captives, then administer an enema and sleeping drugs. They outfit detainees in a diaper and jumpsuit for what can be a day-long trip. Their destinations: either a detention facility operated by cooperative countries in the Middle East and Central Asia, including Afghanistan, or one of the CIA's own covert prisons—referred to in classified documents as "black sites," which at various times have been operated in eight countries, including several in Eastern Europe.[63]

The CIA would provide the host countries with questions it wanted answered by the prisoners. One anonymous U.S. official directly involved in rendering captives told the *Post*, "We don't kick the [expletive] out of them. We send them to other countries so they can kick the [expletive] out of them."[64] Another official who supervised the capture and transfer of prisoners told the paper, "If you don't violate someone's human rights some of the time, you probably aren't doing your job," adding, "I don't think we want to be promoting a view of zero tolerance on this. That was the whole problem for a long time with the CIA."[65]

Black played an integral role from the very beginning in the use of "extraordinary renditions" in the war on terror, beginning in November 2001 when the United States captured alleged Al Qaeda trainer Ibn al-Shayk al-Libi.[66] New York–based FBI agent Jack Cloonan felt that Libi could be a valuable witness against Zacarias Moussaoui and alleged would-be shoe bomber Richard Reid, both of whom had trained at the Khalden camp Libi allegedly ran. Cloonan told FBI agents to "handle this like it was being done right here, in my office in New York."[67] He said, "I remember talking on a secure line to them. I told them, 'Do yourself a favor, read the guy his rights. It may be old-fashioned, but this will come out if we don't. It may take ten years, but it will hurt you, and the bureau's reputation, if you don't. Have it stand as a shining example of what we feel is right.'"[68] But that didn't sit well with the CIA, which felt it could get more information out of Libi using other methods. Invoking promises of wider post-9/11 latitude in questioning suspects, the CIA Afghanistan station chief asked Black, then counterterrorism chief, to arrange for the agency to take control of Libi. Black in turn asked CIA Director George Tenet, who got permission for the rendition from the White House over the objections of FBI Director Robert Mueller.[69]

The White House, meanwhile, had its lawyers feverishly working to develop legal justifications for these ultraviolent policies. It "formally" told the CIA it couldn't be prosecuted for "torture lite" techniques that did not result in "organ failure" or "death."[70] Black had quickly earned an insider's pass to the White House after 9/11, and his former colleagues said he would return from meetings at 1600 Pennsylvania Ave. "inspired and talking in missionary terms."[71]

A year later, with Osama bin Laden still at large, releasing videotaped messages and praising anti-U.S. resistance, Cofer Black abruptly left the CIA. Some charged that Defense Secretary Donald Rumsfeld had him fired after Black allegedly served as a "deep background" source for a *Washington Post* story published on April 17, 2002, that described how the Pentagon allegedly allowed bin Laden to escape after being injured at Tora Bora in Afghanistan.[72] In its lead paragraph, the paper called it the administration's "gravest error in the war against al Qaeda."[73] A month later, buried within another *Post* story on May 19, came this announcement: "In other developments yesterday, CIA officials said Cofer Black, head of the agency's Counterterrorism Center for the past three years, has been assigned to another position. They described the move as part of normal turnover at the agency."[74] The UPI news agency later interviewed former CIA officials, one of whom said, "Black was fired. He was kicked out."[75] The news agency also reported, "Not only was Black fired, but he was barred from entering CIA headquarters. 'That's standard procedure if you've been fired,' former CIA Iraq analyst Judith Yaphe told UPI. Humiliated, Black was restricted to an agency satellite location at Tysons Corner, which separated him from old, trusted colleagues and the comfort of familiar surroundings."[76] Black, however, was not yet finished in government and clearly retained friends in high places. On October 10, 2002, President Bush appointed him as his coordinator for counterterrorism, with the rank of at-large ambassador at the State Department.[77]

Shortly after assuming his new post, Black spoke to a group of Egyptian journalists via satellite from Cairo, where he was pressed on several of the administration's new "war on terror" policies. "I have been to Guantánamo," Black told them. "I must say that I have been very well pleased. I mean, you know, you and I would be very lucky to be housed that way by our enemies."[78] It wouldn't take long for controversy to hit him.

During the 2003 State of the Union address, President Bush declared, "Tonight, I am instructing the leaders of the FBI, the CIA, the Homeland

Security, and the Department of Defense to develop a Terrorist Threat Integration Center, to merge and analyze all threat information in a single location. Our government must have the very best information possible."[79] As part of this mission, Black was to coordinate the government's annual report on "Patterns of Global Terrorism," which would serve as a report card of sorts for how the administration's "war on terror" was progressing. A few months later, on April 30, 2003, Black released the report and claimed that 2002 had seen "the lowest level of terrorism in more than 30 years."[80] While there was little public scrutiny of the statement at the time, that would not be the case when Black released the report a year later and made an almost identical claim.

On April 29, 2004, with anti-U.S. resistance in Iraq exploding, Black and Deputy Secretary of State Armitage unveiled "Patterns of Global Terrorism 2003," boldly claiming it showed that the United States was winning its loosely defined war on terror. "You will find in these pages clear evidence that we are prevailing in the fight," said Armitage. The report, he said, was prepared "so that all Americans will know just what we are doing to keep them safe."[81] For his part, Black said that 2003 "saw the lowest number of international terrorist attacks since 1969. That's a 34-year low. There were 190 acts of international terrorism in 2003. That's a slight decrease from the 198 attacks that occurred the previous year, and a drop of 45 percent from the 2001 level of 346 attacks."[82] For the White House, the report was held up as clear evidence of a successful strategy; after all, the Congressional Research Service called the State Department's annual report "the most authoritative unclassified U.S. government document that assesses terrorist attacks."[83]

The trouble was, it was a fraud. Congressional investigators and independent scientists soon revealed the truth. "The data that the report highlights are ill-defined and subject to manipulation—and give disproportionate weight to the least important terrorist acts," wrote Alan Krueger and David Laitin, two independent experts, from Princeton and Stanford, in the Washington Post shortly after the report was released. "The only verifiable information in the annual reports indicates that the number of terrorist events has risen each year since 2001, and in 2003 reached its highest level in more than 20 years. . . . The alleged decline in terrorism in 2003 was entirely a result of a decline in non-significant events."[84] Instead of a 4 percent decrease in terrorist acts, as Black's report claimed, there had actually been a 5 percent *increase*.[85] Attacks classified as "significant," meanwhile, hit the highest level since 1982.[86] What's more, the report stopped its tally on November 11, 2003, even though there were a number of major terrorist incidents after that date.[87] Despite the fact that in speeches, U.S. officials routinely referred to resistance fighters in Iraq and Afghanistan as "terrorists," in Black's report attacks on forces in Iraq were classified as combat, not terrorism. Black said they "do not meet the longstanding U.S. definition of international terrorism because they were directed at [combatants], essentially American and coalition forces on duty."[88] California Democratic Representative Ellen Tauscher later said this was evidence that the administration "continues to deny the true cost of the war and refuses to be honest with the American people."[89]

On May 17, 2004, in a letter to Black's direct supervisor, Secretary of State Colin Powell, California Democratic Representative Henry Waxman, the ranking member of the House Government Reform Committee, blasted the report, saying its conclusions were based on a "manipulation of the data" that "serve the Administration's political interests. . . . Simply put, it is deplorable that the State Department report would claim that terrorism attacks are decreasing when in fact significant terrorist activity is at a 20-year high."[90]

"The erroneous good news on terrorism also came at a very convenient moment," wrote *New York Times* columnist Paul Krugman. "The White House was still reeling from the revelations of the former counterterrorism chief Richard Clarke, who finally gave public voice to the view of many intelligence insiders that the Bush administration is doing a terrible job of fighting Al Qaeda. Meanwhile, Bush was on a 'Winning the War on Terror' campaign bus tour in the Midwest."[91] By June, the White House was forced to issue a major correction of the report, acknowledging there had actually been a significant *increase* in terror attacks since the launch of Bush's "war on terror." The revised report said that 3,646 people were wounded by terror attacks in 2003, more than double the number in Black's original report, while 625 were killed, dwarfing the report's original count of 307.[92] As Krugman observed, Black and other officials blamed the errors on "'inattention, personnel shortages and [a] database that is awkward and antiquated.' Remember: we're talking about the government's central clearinghouse for terrorism information, whose creation was touted as part of a 'dramatic enhancement' of counterterrorism efforts more than a year before this report was produced. And it still can't input data into its own computers? It should be no surprise, in this age of Halliburton, that the job of data input was given to and botched by private contractors."[93] Bush's Democratic challenger in the 2004 presidential election, John Kerry, charged through a spokesperson that Bush was "playing fast and loose with the truth when it comes to the war on terror," adding that the White House "has now been caught trying to inflate its success on terrorism."[94] There was talk of heads rolling at the State Department over the report, but not Black's. "It was an honest mistake," Black claimed, "not a deliberate deception."[95]

Despite the controversy, the State Department post allowed Black to remain at the center of United States counterterror policy. Black worked directly under Colin Powell, with whom he reportedly shared a common adversary within the administration—Donald Rumsfeld. As the Pentagon attempted to change U.S. policy after 9/11 to allow the military to insert Special Operations forces into countries without approval from the U.S. ambassador or CIA mission chief, Black became the point person in thwarting Rumsfeld's plan. "I gave Cofer specific instructions to dismount, kill the horses and fight on foot—this is not going to happen," Powell's deputy, Richard Armitage, told the *Washington Post*, describing how he and others had stopped a half dozen Pentagon attempts to weaken chief-of-mission authority.[96] (Interestingly, Black, Armitage, and Powell all resigned within two weeks of one another in November 2004 after Bush's reelection, while Rumsfeld continued on for another two years.)

Among Black's other duties in his new post was coordinating security for the 2004 Olympics in Greece. He traveled to Athens and oversaw the training of more than thirteen hundred Greek security personnel under the U.S. Anti-Terrorism Assistance (ATA) program.[97] More than two hundred of those trained were instructed in handling underwater explosives and responding to possible WMD attacks.[98] Blackwater was awarded a contract for an undisclosed amount of money in 2003 to train "special security teams" in advance of the international games.[99] The company denied there was anything untoward about that contract and that Black's subsequent hiring was unrelated.[100]

On April 1, 2004, a day after the Blackwater Fallujah ambush, Black was testifying before the House Committee on International Relations in a hearing on "The Al Qaeda Threat" when he made his first public comments about Blackwater. "I can't tell you how sad we all are to see that. And this takes me back; I have seen these things before," he said. "I think since it specifically happened in the Fallujah area, which is very Saddam Hussein–oriented, tribally oriented, they do see us as the enemy, and their natural inclination, until we prove them otherwise, is to vent their frustration, what they see as their humiliation and defeat against an outside force, against representatives of that entity. It's not that uncommon."[101] Black continued, "The people that did this were not, you know, three guys, you know, on an excellent adventure. You know, these are people that have had the training, have a vested interest." Asked about "any relationship you see between Al Qaeda and that kind of Islamic terrorism" evidenced in Fallujah, Black responded, "I think it is, from our perspective, it's associated, it's in proximity. There's not, specifically, a direct tie between that crowd and Al Qaeda as we know it. They just find themselves with the enemy of my enemy is my friend."[102]

The next month, Black was giving a keynote dinner address at Blackwater's World SWAT Challenge. In a mass e-mail announcing the speech, Blackwater president Gary Jackson wrote, "Dinner on Thursday night at Waterside has a fantastic guest speaker in Ambassador Cofer Black. Ambassador

Black's responsibilities include coordinating U.S. Government efforts to improve counterterrorism cooperation with foreign governments, including the policy and planning of the Department's Antiterrorism Training Assistance Program."[103]

In late 2004, two months before the U.S. presidential election, Black grabbed headlines after claiming on Pakistani television that the United States was near to capturing bin Laden. "If he has a watch, he should be looking at it because the clock is ticking," Black declared. "He will be caught."[104] These bold declarations were controversial and quickly put senior White House and Pakistani officials on the defensive in the media. In November 2004, Black resigned his State Department post, he said, to explore new professional opportunities. "He thought it would be a good time between administrations to go," said State Department spokesperson Adam Ereli. "He has a number of offers in the private sector, and he's going to take some time to think about them."[105]

For a brief moment after 9/11, Cofer Black had helped run an unprecedented covert war that some officials had salivated for their entire careers. That now was history as human rights groups and lawyers worked feverishly to dismantle the shadowy system Black had worked so diligently to build. In 2005, he was targeted for sanction, along with George Tenet and another CIA official, by the agency's Inspector General (IG) for bearing responsibility in the 9/11 intelligence failure.[106] The Bush Administration, however, worried that Tenet would retaliate and embarrass the White House by revealing damning information, buried the IG's report, saving Black in the process.[107]

Congressional Democrats would later use Black's covert program as evidence that the Administration had "outsourced" the job of hunting bin Laden. But while his work as a government official may have ended, Black found a gold mine of opportunity in the dramatically expanding world of private military, intelligence, and security contracting—where human rights oversight was optional at best. On February 4, 2005, Blackwater USA officially announced that it had hired Black as the company's vice chairman.

"Ambassador Black brings with him thirty years of experience in combating terrorism around the globe and absolute devotion to freedom and democracy and the United States of America," said Erik Prince. "We are honored to have him as part of our great team."[108]

For Blackwater, hiring Cofer Black was an unbelievable score. In marketing terms, it would be almost impossible to rival. The company moved swiftly to use him as a brand in and of himself. In August 2005, Black incorporated his own "consulting" practice, The Black Group, which would specialize in executive protection and security. "The 9/11 attacks were designed to damage the economy of the United States," Black said in a statement on his Web site. "To successfully inflict the greatest possible harm, terrorists will target the lifeblood of a nation: its economy. For that reason, Fortune 500 companies are especially attractive targets as governments continue to emphasize Homeland Security. We seek to anticipate and defeat the next terrorist tactic—disruptions of supply chains, coordinated attacks on key assets or customers, or even assassinations of top executives. Corporations are the most vulnerable targets. It's our job to keep them safe."[109] The Black Group boasted, "With leadership drawn from the Executive Branch of the United States Government, The Black Group has the practical experience and the network to mitigate any security issue. Ensure the security of your people and your assets."[110]

On The Black Group's Web site, various images of potential targets flash on the screen: a crowd gathered at the Mall in Washington, D.C., a power plant, a man in a suit using a device to inspect the bottom of a car in an underground garage, a Wall Street sign. On the contact page, the other main figure listed on the site is Francis McLennand, another career CIA officer, who worked alongside Black at the agency.[111] The contact phone number for the company was the same number used by Erik Prince's "Prince Group" in McLean, Virginia, not far from the CIA Counterterrorism Center Black once headed.

Few other Americans had their hands as deeply into the inner workings of U.S. covert operations in the post-9/11 world as Cofer Black. He soon would begin acting as a godfather of sorts to the mercenary community as it refined its rebranding campaign. Potential Blackwater clients could now assume they were getting direct access to the resources of the CIA and intelligence world from "a leadership team drawn from senior levels of the United States government"[112]—something few other private firms could boast or imply. Black was a heavy hitter among the heaviest of them, the man who caught Carlos the Jackal and brought down the Taliban. He would soon take the lead in promoting Blackwater as a privatized peacekeeping force that could deploy at a moment's notice in places like Darfur, Sudan, or domestically in U.S. Homeland Security operations. Other influential ex-government officials would soon join him at Blackwater as the company turned its sights on lucrative disaster contracting in the United States in the wake of Hurricane Katrina in late 2005. But just as Black was rolling up his sleeves in his fancy new digs, more Blackwater men were dying in Iraq in what would be the deadliest days to date for the company.

CHAPTER SEVENTEEN

DEATH SQUADS, MERCENARIES AND THE "SALVADOR OPTION"

WHEN PAUL Bremer skulked out of Iraq on June 28, 2004, he left behind a violent, chaotic mess that the White House called "a free and sovereign" Iraq.[1] Just how unstable the country was when Bremer departed was evident in the fact that he actually had to stage an exit in one plane for the press and then fly out of Baghdad in another to "get me out of here . . . preferably in one piece."[2] In real terms, this "sovereignty," which President Bush described as "the Iraqi people hav[ing] their country back,"[3] was a way to set the stage for U.S. officials to blame the puppet government in Baghdad for the worsening American-made disaster. When Bremer's secret flight fled Iraq, anti-U.S. attacks were increasing by the day as more mercenaries poured into the country—now officially operating with immunity. In the meantime, more Iraqi factions began arming militias, and talk of civil war began drowning out that of a united resistance to the U.S. occupation. It was in the midst of these developments that Bremer's successor arrived on the ground in Baghdad.

Ambassador John Negroponte was certainly no stranger to wanton blood-letting and death-squad-style operations, having cut his teeth working under Henry Kissinger during the Vietnam War.[4] Beginning in 1981, Negroponte was the Reagan administration's point man in fueling death squads in Central America.[5] As ambassador to Honduras, Negroponte had presided over the second largest embassy in Latin America at the time and the largest CIA station in the world.[6] From that post, Negroponte had coordinated Washington's covert support for the Contra death squads in Nicaragua and for the Honduran junta, covering up the crimes of its murderous Battalion 316.[7] During Negroponte's tenure in Honduras, U.S. officials who worked under him said the State Department human rights reports on the country were drafted to read more like Norway's than anything reflecting the actual reality in Honduras.[8] Negroponte's predecessor in Honduras, Ambassador Jack R. Binns, told the *New York Times* that Negroponte had discouraged reporting to Washington of abductions, torture, and killings by notorious Honduran military units. "I think [Negroponte] was complicit in abuses, I think he tried to put a lid on reporting abuses and I think he was untruthful to Congress about those activities," Binns said.[9] The *Wall Street Journal* reported that in Honduras, "Negroponte's influence, backed by huge amounts of U.S. aid, was so great that it was said he far outweighed the country's president and that his only real rival was Honduras's military chief."[10] He was "such a powerful ambassador in Honduras in the early 1980s that he was known as 'the proconsul,' a title given to powerful admin-istrators in colonial times," the *Journal* noted in a story published shortly after Negroponte's nomination to the Iraq post. "Now President Bush has chosen him to reprise that role in Iraq."[11]

Perhaps there was little irony, then, that shortly after Negroponte's appoint-ment as ambassador to Iraq, in April 2004, the Honduran government announced it was pulling its 370 troops out of the "coalition of the willing."[12] Despite Negroponte's well-documented record of involvement with a policy of horrible human rights abuses and killings, his confirmation as ambassador to Iraq went smoothly—he was approved by the Senate in a 95-3 vote on May 6, 2004. Senator Tom Harkin, who as a Congressman in the 1980s had investigated Negroponte's activities in Central America, said he wished he had done more to stop Negroponte's appointment. "I've been amazed at how this individual—from what he did in Central America, where under his watch hundreds of people disappeared—has moved up. He falsified reports and ignored what was happening," Harkin said. "This is going to be our ambassador to Iraq at this time?"[13]

Negroponte was guarded by Blackwater's forces upon his arrival in Baghdad in June and as he stepped up the development of the largest U.S. Embassy in the world—overseeing an estimated staff of thirty-seven hundred, including twenty-five hundred security personnel, "a unit only slightly smaller than a full Marine Corps regiment."[14] In an echo of his time in Honduras, the Baghdad Embassy would house some five hundred CIA operatives.[15] At the same time, Blackwater had just been awarded a vaunted diplomatic security contract worth hundreds of millions of dollars.[16] But it wasn't just American private armies that were making their mark in Iraq. In addition to the mercenary companies increasingly being employed by the occupation forces and reconstruction industry, there was also a sharp rise in death-squad-style activities in the country in the months directly following the brief joint uprising of Shiites and Sunnis in March/April 2004.

Six months after Negroponte arrived, on January 8, 2005, *Newsweek* reported that the United States was employing a new approach to defeating the insurgency in Iraq, one that harkened back to Negroponte's previous dirty work two decades earlier.[17] It was called "the Salvador option," which "dates back to a still-secret strategy in the Reagan administration's battle against the leftist guerrilla insurgency in El Salvador in the early 1980s. Then, faced with a losing war against Salvadoran rebels, the U.S. government funded or supported 'nationalist' forces that allegedly included so-called death squads directed to hunt down and kill rebel leaders and sympathizers."[18] The idea seemed to be that the United States would seek to use Iraqi death squads to hunt anti-occupation insurgents, while at the same time siphoning resources from the resistance and encouraging sectarian fighting. While Rumsfeld called the *Newsweek* report (which he admitted to not having read) "nonsense,"[19] the situation on the ground painted a different picture.

By February 2005, the *Wall Street Journal* reported from Baghdad that about fifty-seven thousand Iraqi soldiers were operating in "planned units" that were "the result of careful preparation this summer between the U.S. and Iraqi commanders."[20] At the same time, the country saw the emergence of militias "commanded by friends and relatives of [Iraqi] cabinet officers and tribal sheiks—[they] go by names like the Defenders of Baghdad, the Special Police Commandos, the Defenders of Khadamiya and the Amarah Brigade. The new units generally have the backing of the Iraqi government and receive government funding. . . . Some Americans consider them a welcome addition to the fight against the insurgency—though others worry about the risks."[21] U.S. commanders referred to them as "pop-up" units and estimated they numbered fifteen thousand fighters. "I've begun calling them 'Irregular Iraqi ministry-directed brigades,'" said Maj. Chris Wales, who was tasked in January 2005 with identifying the units.[22] The *Wall Street Journal* identified at least six of these militias, one with "several thousand soldiers" lavishly armed with "rocket-propelled-grenade launchers, mortar tubes and lots of ammunition." One militia, the "Special Police Commandos," was founded by Gen. Adnan Thabit, who took part in the failed 1996 coup plot against Saddam Hussein. Lt. Gen. David Petraeus, who in 2005 was "overseeing the massive U.S. effort to help train and equip Iraqi military units," told the *Journal* he gave Thabit's unit funding to fix up its base and buy vehicles, ammunition, radios, and more weapons. "I decided this was a horse to back," Petraeus said.[23]

Upon his arrival in Baghdad, Negroponte joined up with other U.S. officials who were veterans of the U.S. "dirty wars" in Central America—among them Bremer's ex-deputy, James Steele, who had been one of the key U.S. military officials managing Washington's brutal "counterinsurgency" campaign in El Salvador in the 1980s.[24] "The template for Iraq today is not Vietnam, to which it has often been compared, but El Salvador, where a right-wing government backed by the United States fought a leftist insurgency in a 12-year war beginning in 1980," wrote journalist Peter Maass at the time in *The New York Times Magazine*[25]:

The cost was high—more than 70,000 people were killed, most of them civilians, in a country with a population of just six million. Most of the killing and torturing was done by the army and the right-wing death squads affiliated with it. According to an Amnesty International report in 2001, violations committed by the army and its associated paramilitaries included "extrajudicial executions, other unlawful killings, 'disappearances' and torture. . . . Whole villages were targeted by the armed forces and their inhabitants massacred." As part of President Reagan's policy of supporting anti-Communist forces, hundreds of millions of dollars in United States aid was funneled to the Salvadoran Army, and a team of 55 Special Forces advisers, led for several years by Jim Steele, trained front-line battalions that were accused of significant human rights abuses. There are far more Americans in Iraq today—some 140,000 troops in all—than there were in El Salvador, but U.S. soldiers and officers are increasingly moving to a Salvador-style advisory role. In the process, they are backing up local forces that, like the military in El Salvador, do not shy away from violence. It is no coincidence that this new strategy is most visible in a paramilitary unit that has Steele as its main adviser; having been a key participant in the Salvador conflict, Steele knows how to organize a counterinsurgency campaign that is led by local forces. He is not the only American in Iraq with such experience: the senior U.S. adviser in the Ministry of Interior, which has operational control over the commandos, is Steve Casteel, a former top official in the Drug Enforcement Administration who spent much of his professional life immersed in the drug wars of Latin America. Casteel worked alongside local forces in Peru, Bolivia and Colombia.[26]

Newsweek described the "Salvador option" in Iraq as the United States using "Special Forces teams to advise, support and possibly train Iraqi squads, most likely hand-picked Kurdish Peshmerga fighters and Shiite militiamen, to target Sunni insurgents and their sympathizers."[27] The magazine also reported that then-interim Prime Minister Ayad Allawi "is said to be among the most forthright proponents of the Salvador option."[28] This was interesting, given that the *New York Times* reported, "Negroponte had taken a low-key approach, choosing to remain in the shadows in deference to Ayad Allawi."[29]

Though allegations that the United States was engaged in Salvador-type operations in Iraq predate Negroponte's tenure in Baghdad, they did seem to intensify significantly once he arrived. As early as January 2004, journalist Robert Dreyfuss reported on the existence of a covert U.S. program in Iraq that resembled "the CIA's Phoenix assassination program in Vietnam, Latin America's death squads or Israel's official policy of targeted murders of Palestinian activists."[30] The United States, Dreyfuss reported, had established a $3 billion "black" fund hidden within the $87 billion Iraq appropriation approved by Congress in November 2003. The money would be used to create "a paramilitary unit manned by militiamen associated with former Iraqi exile groups. Experts say it could lead to a wave of extrajudicial killings, not only of armed rebels but of nationalists, other opponents of the U.S. occupation and thousands of civilian Baathists."[31] The former CIA chief of counterterrorism, Vincent Cannistraro, said U.S. forces in Iraq were working with key members of Saddam Hussein's defunct intelligence apparatus. "They're setting up little teams of Seals and Special Forces with teams of Iraqis, working with people who were former senior Iraqi intelligence people, to do these things," Cannistraro said.[32] "The big money would be for standing up an Iraqi secret police to liquidate the resistance," said John Pike, an expert on covert military budgets. "And it has to be politically loyal to the United States."[33]

Veteran journalist Allan Nairn, who exposed U.S.-backed death squads in Central America in the 1980s, said whether Negroponte was involved with the "Salvador option" in Iraq or not, "These programs, which backed the killing of foreign civilians, it's a regular part of U.S. policy. It's ingrained in U.S. policy in dozens upon dozens of countries."[34] Duane Clarridge, who ran the CIA's "covert war against communism in Central America from Honduras," visited his old colleague Negroponte in Baghdad in the summer of 2004. In Iraq, "[Negroponte] was told to play a low-key role and let the Iraqis be out front," Clarridge told the *New York Times*. "And that's what he likes to do, anyway."[35] According to the *Times*, "Negroponte shifted more than $1 billion to build up the Iraqi Army from reconstruction projects, a move prompted by his experience with the frailty of the South Vietnamese Army."[36]

Negroponte called the connection of his name to the "Salvador option" in Iraq "utterly gratuitous."[37] But human rights advocates who closely monitored his career said the rise in death-squad-type activity in Iraq during Negroponte's tenure in Baghdad was impossible to overlook. "What we're seeing is that the U.S. military is losing the war [in Iraq], and so the Salvador option was really a policy of death squads," said Andres Contreris, Latin American program director of the human rights group Non-violence International. "It's no coincidence that Negroponte, having been the Ambassador in Honduras, where he was very much engaged in this kind of support for death squads, was the Ambassador in Iraq, and this is the kind of policy that was starting to be implemented there, which is not just going after the resistance itself but targeting for repression and torture and assassination the underlying support base, the family members, and those in the communities where the resistance is. These kinds of policies are war crimes."[38]

Negroponte's time in Iraq was short-lived—on February 17, 2005, President Bush nominated him as the first Director of National Intelligence. Some would say Negroponte had a job to do in Iraq, he did it, and then left. By May of that year, he was back in the United States, while reports increasingly appeared describing an increase in death-squad-style activity in Iraq. "Shiite and Kurdish militias, often operating as part of Iraqi government security forces, have carried out a wave of abductions, assassinations and other acts of intimidation, consolidating their control over territory across northern and southern Iraq and deepening the country's divide along ethnic and sectarian lines," the *Washington Post* reported a few months after Negroponte left Iraq.[39] "In 2005, we saw numerous instances where the behavior of death squads was very similar, uncannily similar to that we had observed in other countries, including El Salvador," said John Pace, a forty-year United Nations diplomat who served as the Human Rights Chief for the UN Assistance Mission in Iraq during Negroponte's time in the country. "They first started as a kind of militia, sort of organized armed groups, which were the military wing of various factions."[40] Eventually, he said, "Many of them [were] actually acting as official police agents as a part of the Ministry of Interior. . . . You have these militias now with police gear and under police insignia basically carrying out an agenda which really is not in the interest of the country as a whole. They have roadblocks in Baghdad and other areas, they would kidnap other people. They have been very closely linked with numerous mass executions."[41]

Shortly before Negroponte left Iraq, former chief UN weapons inspector Scott Ritter predicted that "the Salvador Option will serve as the impetus for all-out civil war. In the same manner that the CPA-backed assassination of Baathists prompted the restructuring and strengthening of the Sunni-led resistance, any effort by US-backed Kurdish and Shia assassination teams to target Sunni resistance leaders will remove all impediments for a general outbreak of ethnic and religious warfare in Iraq. It is hard as an American to support the failure of American military operations in Iraq. Such failure will bring with it the death and wounding of many American service members, and many more Iraqis."[42] Ritter's vision would appear prophetic in the ensuing months, as Iraq was hit with an unprecedented and sustained level of violence many began describing as an all-out civil war.

In October 2005, correspondent Tom Lasseter from the Knight Ridder news agency spent a week on patrol with "a crack unit of the Iraqi army— the 4,500-member 1st Brigade of the 6th Iraqi Division."[43] He reported,

"Instead of rising above the ethnic tension that's tearing their nation apart, the mostly Shiite troops are preparing for, if not already fighting, a civil war against the minority Sunni population." The unit was responsible for security in Sunni areas of Baghdad, and Lasseter reported that "they're seeking revenge against the Sunnis who oppressed them during Saddam Hussein's rule." He quoted Shiite Army Maj. Swadi Ghilan saying he wanted to kill most Sunnis in Iraq. "There are two Iraqs; it's something that we can no longer deny," Ghilan said. "The army should execute the Sunnis in their neighborhoods so that all of them can see what happens, so that all of them learn their lesson."

Lasseter reported that many of the Shiite officers and soldiers said they "want a permanent, Shiite-dominated government that will finally allow them to steamroll much of the Sunni minority, some 20 percent of the nation and the backbone of the insurgency." Lasseter described the First Brigade, which was held up by U.S. commanders as a template for the future of Iraq's military, like this: "They look and operate less like an Iraqi national army unit and more like a Shiite militia." Another officer, Sgt. Ahmed Sabri, said, "Just let us have our constitution and elections . . . and then we will do what Saddam did—start with five people from each neighborhood and kill them in the streets and then go from there." By November 2006 an estimated one thousand Iraqis were being killed every week[44], and the Iraqi death toll had passed an estimated six hundred thousand people since the March 2003 invasion.[45]

In retrospect, if one stepped back from the various substories playing out on the ground in Iraq in 2005, the big-picture reality was that the country was quickly becoming the global epicenter of privatized warfare with scores of heavily armed groups of various loyalties and agendas roaming Iraq. In addition to the U.S.-backed death squads, operating with some claim to legitimacy within the U.S.-installed system in Baghdad, there were the private antioccupation militias of various Shiite leaders, such as Muqtada al-Sadr, and the resistance movements of Sunni factions, largely comprised of ex-military officials and soldiers, as well as Al Qaeda–backed militias. The

Bush administration made it a policy to denounce *certain* militias. "In a free Iraq, former militia members must shift their loyalty to the national government, and learn to operate under the rule of law," Bush declared.[46] Yet at the top of this militia pyramid were the official mercenaries Washington had imported to Iraq—the private military companies, of which Blackwater was the industry leader. While calling for the dismantling of some *Iraqi* militias, the United States openly permitted its own pro-occupation mercenaries to operate above the law in Iraq.

"There Continues to Be the Need for This Kind of Security"

At the end of Negroponte's time in Baghdad, with militia violence on the rise, Blackwater's forces once again grabbed headlines in what would be—at the time—the deadliest incident the company acknowledged publicly in Iraq. On April 21, 2005, the day Negroponte was confirmed to his new position as Director of National Intelligence in Washington, some of his former bodyguards were dying in Iraq.[47] That day, a Bulgarian-operated Mi-8 helicopter on contract with Blackwater was flying from the Green Zone to Saddam Hussein's hometown of Tikrit.[48] On board were six American Blackwater troops on contract with the U.S. government's Bureau of Diplomatic Security.[49] With them were three Bulgarian crew members and two Fijian mercenaries.[50] A day before they left, one of the Blackwater men, twenty-nine-year-old Jason Obert of Colorado, had called his wife, Jessica. He "told me that he was going to be sent on a mission. He had a bad feeling about it," she recalled. "I begged him not to go. I just told him just to come home. But he would never quit; that's not him."[51] Jessica Obert said her husband did not tell her the nature of the mission. Like many who signed up for work with Blackwater in Iraq, Jason Obert viewed it as a chance to build a nest egg for his wife and their two young sons.[52] In February 2005, he quit his job as a police officer and signed up with Blackwater. "The financial gain was incredible," said Lt. Robert King, Obert's former boss at the El Paso County Sheriff's Department. "He had communicated to me and several other people that he would do one year, and his children and his wife would be taken care of. Their college education would be funded, houses paid off."[53] The day after he told his wife about his "bad feelings," he boarded the Mi-8 helicopter with his Blackwater colleagues, the Fijians, and the Bulgarian crew.

At about 1:45 in the afternoon, as the helicopter buzzed toward Tikrit, it passed near the Tigris River town of Tarmiya, a small community of Sunni Muslims twelve miles north of Baghdad.[54] The pilots were flying the craft low to the ground, a common military tactic to thwart potential attackers. On an elevated plain nearby stood an Iraqi who reportedly had been waiting three days for an occupation aircraft to come close enough so that he could carry out his mission.[55] When the chopper whizzed within range, the Iraqi fired off a Soviet-made Strela heat-seeking missile and directly hit the helicopter, setting it ablaze as it crashed into the flat desert.[56] The attacker and his comrades filmed the attack and kept the cameras rolling as they jogged toward the crash site. On their video, they can be heard out of breath repeating the chant "Allah-u-Akbar! Allah-u-Akbar!" When they arrive at the site, helicopter parts are spread across the open field and several small fires continue to burn. A badly charred body of one of the dead men lies on the ground with one arm raised in an L shape as though cowering from some form of attack.[57] "Look at this filth," says one of the attackers. "See if there are any Americans left."[58]

The attackers continue to explore the remains of the helicopter when they come across the Bulgarian pilot, Lyubomir Kostov, in a dark blue flight suit lying in a patch of tall grass. One of the men, realizing Kostov is still alive, shouts in Arabic and English, "Any weapons?" The camera pans to the pilot as he winces in pain. "Stand up! Stand up!" one of the attackers shouts in accented English. "I can't," replies the pilot. Motioning to his right leg, Kostov tells them, "I can't, it's broken. Give me a hand." One of the attackers replies, "Come here, come here," as he helps Kostov to his feet. "Go! Go!" someone shouts at the pilot. Kostov turns around and begins to limp away with his back to the camera. As he hobbles forward, Kostov turns his head around and puts his hand up as though to say, "Stop!" when someone suddenly yells,

"Carry out God's judgment." The attackers, shouting "Allah-u-Akbar," open fire on Kostov, filming the execution as they pump eighteen bullets into his body, continuing to shoot the pilot even after he has fallen.

Within two hours, a group identifying itself as the Islamic Army in Iraq provided the video to Al Jazeera, which broadcast it. "Heroes of the Islamic Army downed a transport aircraft belonging to the army of the infidels and killed its crew and those on board," the group said in a written statement that accompanied the video. "One of the crew members was captured and killed."[59] The group said it had executed the surviving pilot "in revenge for the Muslims who have been killed in cold blood in the mosques of tireless Fallujah before the eyes of the world and on television screens, without anyone condemning them."[60] The statement was interpreted as a reference to the apparent execution by a U.S. soldier of a wounded Iraqi in a Fallujah mosque in November 2004 (which was caught on tape) during the second U.S. assault on the city.[61]

In a statement released shortly after the helicopter was shot down, Blackwater said the "Six were passengers in a commercial helicopter operated by Sky Link under contract to Blackwater in support of a Department of Defense contract."[62] Despite its obvious military use, media reports overwhelmingly referred to the helicopter as a "civilian" or "commercial" aircraft. Reporters at the Pentagon, meanwhile, began reporting that "these commercial aircraft fly without the type of air protective measures that military aircraft fly with."[63] Shortly after the helicopter was downed, retired U.S. Air Force Maj. Gen. Don Shepperd, who once headed the Air National Guard, told CNN, "All of the airplanes over there, if possible, should have infrared countermeasures and flares to protect themselves against shoulder-fired missiles, which are the biggest threat to low-flying helicopters. . . . Once an infrared shoulder-fired missile is fired at you, you can confuse it and divert either with flares or with sophisticated maneuvers."[64] Shepperd added, "All those protect you."[65] At the Pentagon press briefing after the shoot-down, a reporter asked spokesman Larry Di Rita about the apparent lack of these "countermeasures" on the Blackwater-contracted helicopter:

REPORTER: The Department of Defense is contracting these folks. Are there any sort of restrictions that you have to force these contractors to make sure that the private individuals who are doing work on behalf of DOD have the same sort of protections that uniformed service members are getting? And shouldn't somebody who is doing the work of the Department of Defense, same mission, just because they're getting their paycheck from somewhere else, have the same—enjoy the same protections that somebody in a uniform would be?

DI RITA: I'm not sure that that premise is the basis on which people operate over there. In other words, there are contractors who assume a certain amount of risk. Everybody over there is—no, I don't say everybody—there are a number of contractors to the U.S. military, to the Department of Defense, some to the Department of State, and they assume a certain risk by being over there. And I wouldn't want to characterize exactly what status this particular—obviously we mourn the loss of life, and I'm sure that the contractor would have taken all of the appropriate precautions. I mean, I think that's what—they have the same regard for their employees as we do for our forces. But I can't say that that necessarily means they're going to be on the same status. I just don't think that's the case.

REPORTER: They have the same countermeasures. Shouldn't they have the same protective gear, shouldn't they have the same kind of ballistic gear, shouldn't they have the same—

DI RITA: As I said, I think contractors recognize the environment that they're operating in. It's like they're around the world, and they make appropriate adjustments on their own determination.[66]

Unlike the Pentagon—which was limited by budget constraints—Blackwater was limited in its ability to defend its personnel only by its own spending decisions and by how much it was willing to shell out for defensive counter-measures. "I have concerns for many of the contractors who are still over there," said Katy Helvenston-Wettengel, who already was suing Blackwater for her son's death in Fallujah. "Our government seems to be subcontracting out this war, and these companies have no accountability."[67]

The same day the helicopter was shot down, forty-two-year-old Curtis Hundley was working a Blackwater security detail outside the city of Ramadi, not far from the site of the helicopter shoot-down. He was just a few days away from a return trip home to his wife in Winston-Salem, North Carolina.[68] "When the war in Iraq started, he wanted to fight for our country," according to his father, Steve Hundley, a former helicopter pilot who fought in Vietnam. "Too old to rejoin the Army, he joined Blackwater Security. That put him on the roads in Iraq almost daily, the most dangerous place to be. I've never seen him more proud. He enjoyed throwing candy to kids along the road. Like me in Vietnam, at first, he thought progress was pretty good. But civilian miscalculations—such as not sending over enough troops to secure ammo dumps and borders, and then deactivating the entire Iraq army, which instantly created thousands of potential terrorists—began to take effect. I saw my happy-go-lucky son start to harden. His eyes, which always had had a twinkle, were different in the pictures he sent. When I could get him to talk about his job, he began to sound disgusted at the worsening situation. The last several weeks of his life, disgust had turned to anger."[69] Curtis Hundley died in Ramadi on April 21, when a bomb exploded near a company armored personnel carrier.[70] Hundley's death meant that with the helicopter crash, Blackwater had lost seven men in Iraq that day, its deadliest to date in the war. "Blackwater's Black Day," proclaimed one news headline.[71]

Back in Moyock, company executives quickly mobilized their response. "This is a very sad day for the Blackwater family," said president Gary Jackson. "We lost seven of our friends to attacks by terrorists in Iraq and our thoughts and prayers go out to their family members."[72] A company press release said, "Blackwater has a 15-member team of crisis counselors working with those family members to assist them in coping with the loss of their loved ones."[73] At the State Department, meanwhile, the seven men were eulogized as heroes. "These Blackwater contractors were supporting the State Department mission in Iraq, and were critical to our efforts to protect American diplomats there," said Assistant Secretary of State Joe Morton. "These brave men gave their lives so that Iraqis may someday enjoy the freedom and democracy we enjoy here in America."[74]

Once again, the killing of Blackwater forces in Iraq had cast the spotlight back on the secretive world of mercenary companies. "The fact of the matter is that private security firms have been involved in Iraq from the very beginning, so this is nothing new," said State Department spokesperson Adam Ereli, responding to questions from the press. "There's a need for security that goes beyond what employees of the U.S. Government can provide, and we go to private companies to offer that. That's a common practice. It's not unique to Iraq. We do it around the world."[75] In Iraq, Ereli said, "I think it's a statement of the obvious to say that the conditions . . . are such that it's not completely safe to go throughout the country at all parts, at all times, so there continues to be the need for security—for this kind of security protection."[76]

Those words must have been music to Blackwater's ears: *There continues to be the need for this kind of security.* Once again, the death of Blackwater contractors translated into more support for the mercenary cause. The day after the seven Blackwater mercenaries died in Iraq, the U.S. Senate approved a controversial $81 billion spending bill for the occupations of Iraq and Afghanistan, pushing the total cost of the wars to more than $300 billion.[77] More money was being allocated for "security" in Iraq. Some 1,564 U.S. soldiers had died since the invasion,[78] along with an uncounted number of mercenaries. It was a year after the Blackwater ambush in Fallujah, and business had never been better for Erik Prince and his colleagues, despite the confirmed deaths of eighteen Blackwater contractors in Iraq.[79] Back in the U.S., the Blackwater Empire was about to add another powerful former Bush administration official to its roster.

CHAPTER EIGHTEEN

JOSEPH SCHMITZ: CHRISTIAN SOLDIER

JOSEPH E. SCHMITZ had long been an ideological soldier for right-wing causes before he was appointed by President Bush to be the Pentagon's Inspector General, the top U.S. official in charge of directly overseeing military contractors in Iraq and Afghanistan. And he proved himself a loyal servant of the administration during his scandal-plagued tenure in that post from 2002 to 2005. By the time he resigned, Schmitz stood accused by Republicans and Democrats alike of protecting the very war contractors he was tasked with overseeing and of allowing rampant corruption and cronyism to go virtually unchecked. On Schmitz's watch, well-connected companies like Halliburton, KBR, Bechtel, Fluor, Titan, CACI, Triple Canopy, DynCorp, and Blackwater made a killing serving the occupations of Iraq and Afghanistan. By June 2005, the Defense Department had 149 "prime contracts" with seventy-seven contractors in Iraq worth approximately $42.1 billion.[1] According to Pentagon auditors, Halliburton "alone represent[ed] 52% of the total contract value."[2]

Allegations of contract fraud and war profiteering during this period could fill volumes, and lawmakers denounced the lack of transparency and open bidding. "It's been like Dodge City before the marshals showed up," declared Senator Ron Wyden.[3] In the midst of the brewing scandal over Halliburton's profiteering and corruption in Iraq, Schmitz said in July 2004, "I haven't seen any real deliberate gouging of the American taxpayer, but we are looking."[4] While there were many layers in the government system that facilitated such corporate misconduct, it was Schmitz whose singular task was overseeing the 1,250-person office with a $200 million budget charged with policing these lucrative U.S.-taxpayer-funded defense contracts.[5]

After three years of playing a key role in the system that indemnified well-oiled corporate profiteers, during which Schmitz went out of his way to demonstrate his loyalty to the Bush administration, the Pentagon's top cop found himself under investigation. The powerful Republican Senator Charles Grassley launched a Congressional probe into whether Schmitz "quashed or redirected two ongoing criminal investigations" into senior Bush administration officials.[6] Grassley also "accused Schmitz of fabricating an official Pentagon news release, planning an expensive junket to Germany, and hiding information from Congress."[7]

Finally, under fire from both Democrats and Republicans, Schmitz resigned as Inspector General, though his office denied it was a result of the investigations. Just before he resigned, Schmitz revealed his intention to pursue a career working for Erik Prince at Blackwater. In a letter stamped June 15, 2005, he officially informed the Defense Department and the White House that "I am disqualified from participating in any official matter that will have a direct and predictable effect on the financial interests" of Blackwater USA.[8] Schmitz wrote that he had "financial interests" in Blackwater "because I intend to discuss possible employment with them."⁹ During Schmitz's time at the Pentagon overseeing contractors, Blackwater had grown from a small private military and law-enforcement training facility to a global mercenary provider with hundreds of millions of dollars in U.S. government contracts.

But Schmitz's interest in Blackwater (or Blackwater's in Schmitz) was not simply about his dedication to the wars of the Bush administration, the fact that he worked for the Reagan administration, that he represented then–House Speaker Newt Gingrich, or his involvement in the murky, corrupt world of military contractors. All of these were certainly factors, but the connection ran deeper. Joseph Schmitz, like Erik Prince and other executives at Blackwater, was a Catholic and a Christian fundamentalist. Some would go so far as to say he was a religious fanatic obsessed with implementing "the rule of law under God." In numerous speeches given during his time as Pentagon Inspector General, Schmitz articulated his vision and understanding of the global war on terror, employing the rhetoric of Christian supremacy. "No American today should ever doubt that we hold ourselves accountable to the rule of law under God. Here lies the fundamental difference between us and the terrorists," Schmitz said in a June 2004 speech, just after returning from trips to Iraq and Afghanistan. "It all comes down to this—we pride ourselves on our strict adherence to the rule of law under God."¹⁰ On his official biography, Schmitz proudly listed his membership in the Sovereign Military Order of Malta,¹¹ a Christian militia formed in the eleventh century, before the first Crusades, with the mission of defending "territories that the Crusaders had conquered from the Moslems."¹² The Order today boasts of being "a sovereign subject of international law, with its own constitution, passports, stamps, and public institutions" and "diplomatic relations with 94 countries."¹³ In addition to his Christian zealotry, Schmitz was a fierce devotee and an awestruck admirer of one of the famed foreign mercenaries who fought on the side of Gen. George Washington during the American Revolutionary War: the Prussian militarist Baron Friedrich Wilhelm Von Steuben, whom Schmitz referred to as "our first Effective Inspector General."¹⁴ Von Steuben is one of four men often cited by Blackwater officials as founding mercenaries of the

United States, the others being Generals Lafayette, Rochambeau, and Kosciuszko, whose monuments stand across from the White House in what some Blackwater officials have taken to calling "Contractor Park."[15] All of this made Schmitz an ideal candidate to join the ranks of Prince and his cohorts at Blackwater, where Schmitz would sit directly at Prince's right hand as the Prince Group's chief operating officer and general counsel.[16] In a press release announcing the hire, Erik Prince referred to him as "General Schmitz."[17]

Joseph Schmitz comes from one of the most bizarre, scandal-plagued, right-wing political families in U.S. history. For decades they have operated on the fringes of a landscape dominated by the likes of the Kennedys, Clintons, and Bushes. The patriarch of the family, John G. Schmitz, was an ultra-conservative California state politician who raised his family in a strict Catholic household. As a state lawmaker, he railed against sex education in schools, abortion, and income tax, and he was a fierce supporter of states' rights. He regularly introduced measures supporting the "Liberty Amendment," which would have required the federal government to get out of businesses that would have competed with private industry.[18] At one point, he proposed selling the University of California.[19] In the late 1960s, he accused then–California Governor Ronald Reagan, a conservative Republican, of wanting to "run socialism more efficiently" after a tax increase.[20] A year after Martin Luther King Jr.'s 1968 assassination, John Schmitz led the opposition in the California State Senate to commemorating the slain civil rights leader. After winning a Congressional seat as a Republican from Orange County in the early 1970s, he soon "established himself as one of the country's most right-wing and outspoken congressmen."[21] He ran for President against Richard Nixon in 1972 as the candidate of the American Independent Party, founded in 1968 by segregationist politician George Wallace.[22] The elder Schmitz also served as national director of the anti-communist John Birch Society before being kicked out for being too extreme.[23] He made comments like, "Jews are like everybody else, only more so," "Martin Luther King is a notorious liar," "I may not be Hispanic, but I'm close. I'm Catholic with a mustache"[24] and described the Watts riot as "a communist operation."[25] After President Richard Nixon announced he would visit "Red China" in 1971, Schmitz—who represented Nixon's home district—called Nixon "pro-communist," saying the visit was "surrendering to international communism. It wipes out any chance of overthrowing the [Peking] government."[26] Schmitz also said he had "disestablished diplomatic relations with the White House"[27] and declared, "I have no objection to President Nixon going to China. I just object to his coming back."[28] Schmitz ultimately lost his seat in Congress and, after his failed presidential bid, returned to state politics. In 1981, he chaired a California State Senate committee hearing on abortion and described the audience as "hard, Jewish, and (arguably) female faces."[29] He also called feminist attorney Gloria Allred a "slick, butch lawyeress" during an attack on Allred's support for abortion rights.[30] Allred sued Schmitz, resulting in a $20,000 judgment against him and a public apology.[31] His political career, spent preaching about family values, came to a crashing end after he acknowledged fathering at least two children out of wedlock.[32] Eventually John G. Schmitz retired in the Washington, D.C., area, where he purchased the home of his hero, the anticommunist fanatic Senator Joseph McCarthy.[33] Schmitz wrote two books, *Stranger in the Arena: The Anatomy of an Amoral Decade 1964–1974* and *The Viet Cong Front in the United States*. He died in 2001 and was buried in Arlington National Cemetery with full military honors.[34]

Joseph Schmitz's older brother, John Patrick, also a lawyer, was deputy counsel to George H. W. Bush from 1985 to 1993, during Bush's time as both Vice President and President,[35] and he played a key role in protecting Bush from the Iran-Contra investigation. In 1987, Bush received a request from the Office of the Independent Counsel to produce all documents that might be related to the investigation, including "all personal and official records of [Office of the Vice President] staff members."[36] Bush delegated the responsibility for this to his counsel, C. Boyden Gray, and deputy counsel John P. Schmitz.[37] It wasn't until five years later—a month after Bush was elected President—that Gray and Schmitz disclosed that Bush had kept a personal diary during the scandal that was clearly covered under the earlier document request.[38] While they turned over the diary, Gray and Schmitz stalled in handing over documents related to the diary and failed to explain why it was not produced during the five crucial years of the investigation.[39] Investigators interviewed all those who had something to do with producing documents from Bush's office except Gray and Schmitz, who refused to comply.[40] Schmitz refused to turn over his own diary, which covered 1987 to 1992, claiming it was a privileged work product,[41] employing an obfuscatory tactic that would become de rigueur in George W. Bush's executive branch. Even after Gray and Schmitz were both essentially offered immunity, they still refused to be interviewed; Schmitz left the administration in 1993.[42] Joseph Schmitz had his own link to the Iran-Contra scandal, serving in 1987 as special assistant attorney general to Edwin Meese,[43] who served under Reagan as Attorney General and, in Meese's own words, tried "to limit the damage."[44] Prior to his time at the White House, John Patrick had clerked for then–U.S. Court of Appeals Judge Antonin Scalia.[45] John Patrick went on to become a lobbyist/attorney with the Washington, D.C., firm Mayer, Brown, Rowe & Maw.[46] Among his clients: the U.S. Chamber of Commerce, Lockheed Martin, Enron, General Electric, Pfizer, and Bayer.[47] He was also a "Major League Pioneer" funder of George W. Bush, donating thousands to his campaign coffers.[48]

Perhaps the most famous member of the Schmitz family, though, is the least political: Joseph Schmitz's sister, Mary Kay LeTourneau. In 1997, the married schoolteacher and mother of four grabbed headlines after being charged with the child rape of Vili Fualaau, her thirteen-year-old student.[49] Four months later, she gave birth to Fualaau's daughter.[50] The case was a tabloid obsession for years. After serving a seven-year prison term, during which time she gave birth to another child fathered by Fualaau, LeTourneau married her former sixth-grade student in 2004.[51] While her father—the hysterical family-values politician who railed against feminists, homosexuals, and abortion—vigorously defended her, other family members kept a much lower profile about the case, which ran parallel to Joseph Schmitz's ascension to a position in the Bush administration.[52]

Joseph Schmitz was a graduate of the U.S. Naval Academy who had served in the Navy, mostly in the reserves, for twenty-seven years at the time of his nomination in the summer of 2001 to be the Pentagon Inspector General.[53] His limited government work included the stint with Meese and as deputy senior inspector for the Naval Reserve intelligence program. Directly prior to his nomination, Schmitz was a partner at the high-powered and well-connected lobbying and law firm Patton Boggs, where he specialized in aviation law and international trade in high-tech goods, in militarily sensitive areas.[54] During Schmitz's time at the Pentagon, Patton Boggs launched its own "Iraq Reconstruction" practice, in June 2003.[55] "An insider's perspective is crucial . . . for companies seeking one of the many contracts to reconstruct Iraq," read the copy on Patton Boggs's reconstruction page, while the firm boasted of "an exceptionally high number of attorneys with extensive Hill experience and contacts, augmented by strong knowledge of key federal agencies involved in Iraq reconstruction" to help corporate clients procure lucrative contracts.[56] Like many Bush officials, Schmitz was a well-connected loyalist and a crony appointment. A glimpse into his extreme, at times bizarre, politics can be found in a series of antiabortion letters he wrote to various D.C.-area newspapers, beginning in 1989. In one letter, Schmitz wrote, "As a man, the plight of pregnant rape and incest victims may be hypothetical but as a former fetus, the plight of aborted innocent human life is as real to me as rape is to most women."[57] In another, Schmitz calls Roe v. Wade "illegitimate federal legislation by unelected judges," saying politicians should "leave political issues not addressed in the Constitution to the states and the people."[58] In yet another, Schmitz declared, "Most pro-lifers are not averse to taking an 'unpopular position' in the defense of human life, whether the life be that of a frozen embryo, a fetus, a vegetative old woman or a teen-age rape victim. After all, the God of most pro-lifers once said: 'Blessed are they who suffer persecution for justice's sake, for theirs is the kingdom of heaven.'"[59]

President Bush nominated Schmitz for the Pentagon IG position in June 2001, where he would be "responsible for conducting independent and objective audits and investigations of defense programs and impartial investigations of the allegations of misconduct by senior officers and civilian department employees."[60] The confirmation did not go smoothly, however. Schmitz's appointment was held up by Democratic Senator Carl Levin, chair of the Senate Armed Services Committee. During an October 2001 committee hearing, Levin questioned Schmitz about a letter he wrote to the right-wing *Washington Times* newspaper in 1992—three days before the presidential election between George H. W. Bush and Bill Clinton. "Clinton practically confessed to being a security risk during the Vietnam War," Schmitz wrote. "Now the same Bill Clinton wants to be commander in chief, but he won't even talk about his organizing anti-war activities in England and then traveling to Moscow at the height of the Vietnam War. The KGB apparently knows more about the shady side of Bill Clinton than the American people ever will. The American people deserve better."[61] Schmitz signed the letter with his official rank of lieutenant commander, U.S. Naval Reserve.[62] "Now, that was signed with your rank in the Reserves, which is the issue here," Levin said to Schmitz during the hearing. "It's not the views, whatever one thinks of those, but the fact that you signed it as a lieutenant commander in the US Navy Reserve."[63] Schmitz responded, telling Levin, "The letter was merely a venting exercise. It was not a reflection of my judgment at the time and it certainly is not a reflection of my judgment today." Careful with his words, Schmitz said, "The way the newspaper published my letter and highlighted my military rank obviously raises issues. I regretted it at the time and I regret it today. I learned a very good lesson for which I am now a better man. And, more importantly, I will be a much better inspector general for having learned that lesson if I am confirmed."[64] Levin also took issue with Schmitz's stated desire to remain on the board of a group called US English, Inc., while serving as Inspector General. "This is an organization that believes no government business should be done in any language other than English," Levin said. "Why would you think it would be appropriate for you as inspector general to remain on the board of an advocacy group that is—obviously takes positions that would be an anathema to at least some members of the military?" After a lengthy defense of the organization, during which he accused Levin of holding a "common misconception," Schmitz said, "It's just a practical issue. If you want to succeed in the United States, you ought to learn English."[65] Schmitz was required to resign from US English (which he had done just prior to the hearing) to be confirmed as Inspector General, which he was in March 2002.

Joseph Schmitz would be the top U.S. official in charge of policing the biggest corporate war bonanza in history during its most explosive period. His job description identified his mission as the "prevention of fraud, waste, and abuse in the programs and operations" of the Pentagon.[66] But unlike other IGs, the Pentagon's reported directly to Rumsfeld, creating what some critics say was an inherent conflict of interest—one that was compounded by Rumsfeld's ultracontrolling style. The Inspector General position should ideally be filled by an official determined to comb through the system looking for impropriety, corruption, and cronyism. Instead, what the Administration got in Schmitz was an official who seemingly admired the very parties he was supposed to be monitoring, not the least of whom was Rumsfeld himself. During his time at the Pentagon, Schmitz offered the following remarkable exaltation of his boss at the National Wrestling Coaches Association Coaches Clinic in St. Louis, during a speech entitled "Wrestling with Discipline: Life Lessons in Leadership:"

Secretary of Defense Donald Rumsfeld—my boss—is another former wrestler. He was famous for his grit and discipline on the mat. People still tell stories about the time when Don Rumsfeld dislocated his shoulder during a wrestling match. He was behind on points but he refused to quit. With one arm, he managed to take down his opponent—three more times—and emerge victorious from the contest. Secretary Rumsfeld's iron discipline is legendary within the five walls of the Pentagon. He never allows distractions, changing public opinion, or wishful thinking to mar his focus. He is so totally focused at the task at hand that he leaves others in awe at how much he can achieve on a given day. This former wrestler too, it can be said, reigns over himself. Reigning over ourselves—and answering only to God—is the key to living a virtuous, honorable, and purpose-driven life.[67]

Schmitz carried around Rumsfeld's famed twelve principles in his lapel pocket, of which the first sentence was, "Do nothing that could raise questions about the credibility of DoD."[68] Under Schmitz's watch, corporate profiteers, many with close ties to the administration, thrived as they burned through resources ostensibly allocated for the rebuilding of Iraq and Afghanistan. "Schmitz slowed or blocked investigations of senior Bush administration officials, spent taxpayer money on pet projects and accepted gifts that may have violated ethics guidelines," according to an investigation by T. Christian Miller of the *Los Angeles Times*.[69] Miller reported that investigators working under Schmitz were so concerned about his loyalties that, at times, they stopped telling him whom they were investigating—substituting letter codes for individual names during weekly briefings—in fear that Schmitz would tip off Pentagon superiors.[70] "He became very involved in political investigations that he had no business getting involved in," a senior official in Schmitz's office told the *Times*.[71] "I've seen this office become involved in many questionable projects despite strong and persistent opposition from senior staff," said Iowa Republican Senator Charles E. Grassley at the end of Schmitz's tenure. "It appears to me that this has created a lack of respect and trust, and has resulted in an ineffective Office of the Inspector General."[72]

In March 2003, a year after Schmitz took over as the Pentagon IG, and just as the Iraq invasion was beginning, he found himself responsible for investigating a scandal that rocked one of the key architects of the administration's Iraq policy: Richard Perle, a leading neoconservative activist, founder of the Project for a New American Century and chair of the Defense Policy Board. Perle was close to Deputy Defense Secretary Paul Wolfowitz and had an office right next to Rumsfeld's at the Pentagon.[73] As the Iraq invasion was getting under way, the *New York Times* and *The New Yorker* magazine revealed that

Perle was using his position to lobby for corporate clients in their dealings with the Defense Department.[74] "Even as he advises the Pentagon on war matters, Richard N. Perle, chairman of the influential Defense Policy Board, has been retained by the telecommunications company Global Crossing to help overcome Defense Department resistance to its proposed sale to a foreign firm," the *Times* reported.[75] Noting that Perle was "close to many senior officials, including Defense Secretary Donald H. Rumsfeld, who appointed him to lead the policy board," the *Times* revealed that Perle stood to make $725,000 from Global Crossing if the government approved the sale. The Pentagon and FBI opposed the sale because it would "put Global Crossing's worldwide fiber optics network—one used by the United States government— under Chinese ownership."[76] In legal documents obtained by the *Times*, Perle highlighted his Pentagon position to explain why he was uniquely qualified to help Global Crossing. "As the chairman of the Defense Policy Board, I have a unique perspective on and intimate knowledge of the national defense and security issues that will be raised" in the review process, Perle wrote.[77] Perle called the reference to the Defense Policy Board "inappropriate and irrelevant" and said it had only been left in the document because of "a clerical error." Perle also said that the defense Policy Board "has nothing to do with" the Global Crossing sale approval process.[78]

When the news broke, Perle quickly resigned his chairmanship of the advisory board, while maintaining his innocence. In resigning, Perle told Rumsfeld he didn't want the scandal to distract from "the urgent challenge in which you are now engaged" in Iraq.[79] Rumsfeld asked Perle to remain on the board, which he did. Representative John Conyers called for an investigation of Perle, and the case was sent to Joseph Schmitz. After a six-month investigation, Schmitz exonerated Perle of any wrongdoing, saying, "We have completed our inquiry regarding the conduct of Mr. Perle and did not substantiate allegations of misconduct."[80] Despite exposés in almost every leading news outlet in the country about Perle's multiple conflicts of interest, the Inspector General's report "found insufficient basis to conclude that Mr. Perle created the appearance of impropriety from the perspective of a reasonable person."[81] Perle said he was "very pleased"[82] with Schmitz's conclusion, while Rumsfeld declared, "The Inspector General's report confirms the integrity of the Defense Policy Board and Mr. Perle's participation."[83]

Not long after the revelations about Richard Perle's business dealings, another controversy erupted about a powerful senior official in Rumsfeld's inner circle, Army Lt. Gen. William Boykin, the Deputy Undersecretary of Defense for Intelligence. In October 2003, Boykin was revealed to have gone on several anti-Muslim rants, in public speeches, many of which he delivered in military uniform. Since January 2002, Boykin had spoken at twenty-three religious-oriented events, wearing his uniform at all but two.[84] Among Boykin's statements, he said he knew the United States would prevail over a Muslim adversary in Somalia because "I knew that my God was bigger than his. I knew that my God was a real God and his was an idol."[85] Boykin also charged that Islamic radicals want to destroy America "because we're a Christian nation"[86] that "will never abandon Israel."[87] Our "spiritual enemy," Boykin declared, "will only be defeated if we come against them in the name of Jesus."[88] As for President Bush, Boykin said, "Why is this man in the White House? The majority of Americans did not vote for him. Why is he there? And I tell you this morning that he's in the White House because God put him there for a time such as this."[89] In another speech, Boykin said other countries "have lost their morals, lost their values. But America is still a Christian nation."[90] He told a church group in Oregon that special operations forces were victorious in Iraq because of their faith in God. "Ladies and gentlemen, I want to impress upon you that the battle that we're in is a spiritual battle," he said. "Satan wants to destroy this nation, he wants to destroy us as a nation, and he wants to destroy us as a Christian army."[91]

Boykin was a career military officer, one of the first Delta Force commandos who rose through the ranks to become head of the top-secret Joint Special Operations Command. He had served in the Central Intelligence Agency, and during the war on terror, he had been in charge of Army Special Forces before joining Rumsfeld's close-knit leadership team, where he was placed in charge of hunting "high-value targets."[92] Boykin was one of the key U.S. officials in establishing what critics alleged was death-squad-type activity in Iraq. Asked in a Congressional inquiry about the similarities between the U.S. Phoenix program in Vietnam and special operations in the war on terror, Boykin said: "I think we're running that kind of program. We're going after these people. Killing or capturing these people is a legitimate mission for the department. I think we're doing what the Phoenix program was designed to do, without all of the secrecy."[93] Military analyst William Arkin, who first revealed Boykin's comments, wrote, "When Boykin publicly spews this intolerant message while wearing the uniform of the U.S. Army, he strongly suggests that this is an official and sanctioned view—and that the U.S. Army is indeed a Christian army. But that's only part of the problem. Boykin is also in a senior Pentagon policymaking position, and it's a serious mistake to allow a man who believes in a Christian 'jihad' to hold such a job. . . . Boykin has made it clear that he takes his orders not from his Army superiors but from God—which is a worrisome line of command. For another, it is both imprudent and dangerous to have a senior officer guiding the war on terrorism in Iraq and Afghanistan who believes that Islam is an idolatrous, sacrilegious religion against which we are waging a holy war."[94] When Boykin came under fire for his anti-Muslim comments, Rumsfeld and other Pentagon brass vigorously defended him. "Boykin was not removed or transferred. At that moment, he was at the heart of a secret operation to 'Gitmoize' . . . the Abu Ghraib prison," wrote former Clinton senior adviser Sidney Blumenthal. "He had flown to Guantanamo, where he met Major General Geoffrey Miller, in charge of Camp X-Ray. Boykin ordered Miller to fly to Iraq and extend X-Ray methods to the prison system there, on Rumsfeld's orders."[95]

Amid outcry from human rights groups and Arab and Muslim organizations, Boykin personally requested that Schmitz's department at the Pentagon conduct an investigation into any potential wrongdoing on his part.[96] Gen. Peter Pace, vice chairman of the Joint Chiefs of Staff, said Boykin "is anxious to have the investigator do the investigator's job."[97] After a ten-month review, Schmitz's office essentially cleared Boykin, concluding the general had violated three internal Pentagon regulations. "Although it was the substance of Boykin's remarks and not his regard for Pentagon rules that aroused controversy, the report pointedly steered clear of comment on the appropriateness of Boykin's injection of religion into his depiction of the military's counterterrorism efforts, including his claims that a 'demonic presence' lay behind the actions of radical Muslims," reported the *Washington Post*.[98] The paper quoted a senior Defense official who "said the report is seen as a 'complete exoneration' that ultimately found Boykin responsible for a few 'relatively minor offenses' related to technical and bureaucratic issues."[99]

In June 2004, Schmitz traveled to Iraq and Afghanistan and upon his return gave a major address titled "American Principles as Potent Weapons and Potential Casualties in the Global War on Terror."[100] At the time, the scandal over prisoner torture and abuse at Abu Ghraib was still fresh in the United States, and Schmitz, who was in charge of investigating the abuse, did his best to whitewash the scandal. He blamed Abu Ghraib on a few "bad eggs,"[101] saying, "I'm not aware of any illegal orders that came from any leaders."[102] He told an audience at the City Club of Cleveland, "The few systemic breakdowns, and the reprehensible actions of a few of our own people—who are even now being brought to justice—should not overshadow the sacrifices and accomplishments of the thousands of courageous Americans who continue to serve honorably in the best tradition of the United States Armed Forces."[103] Schmitz said that he had been to Abu Ghraib and "another detainee collection point" in Afghanistan "to learn more about the rules, standards, and procedures we use to collect intelligence and otherwise to deal with the known and potential terrorists we capture in the course of our ongoing military operations. The more time I spend with our forward-deployed troops, listening to their stories and watching them perform their duties, the more I understand why the terrorists hate us so much. Beyond any doubt, we owe our American men and women now serving overseas a debt of gratitude. I cannot begin to tell you what an awesome and honorable job American troops are doing in both Iraq and Afghanistan."[104] The terrorists, Schmitz said, "refuse to recognize the very standards of behavior that distinguish civilization from barbarism." Even after the revelations of systematic torture at Abu Ghraib, he said, "We are still, by the grace of God, the beacon of hope to the world."[105] While speaking at length about the "rule of law" that governs the United States, Schmitz told the audience, "We ought not let the bad news coming out of Abu Ghraib eclipse the fact that we've got some great American sons and daughters of regular Americans, farmers and whatever, and they're over there doing great work for you and for me."[106] In Afghanistan and Iraq, Schmitz said, "I saw American soldiers doing what we 'Yanks' have always done, being affable liberators, befriending the local people when they can, and chafing at the lack of contact when prevented from doing so by threats of violence from a shadowy and cowardly enemy."[107]

Like General Boykin, Schmitz often gave speeches during his tenure at the Pentagon that were overtly soaked in religious and Christian rhetoric and demeaning of other cultures and traditions. "The rule of law can scarcely be said to exist in tribal cultures, such as, for example, parts of Iraq and Afghanistan, where loyalty to one's own often trumps everything— honesty, the law, fairness, and even common sense," Schmitz said in a March 2004 speech.[108] In another, he declared, "The men and women of our armed forces today do not doubt the enduring principles that make America great—the same principles President Reagan mentioned in the midst of the Cold War: 'individual responsibility, representative government, and the rule of law under God.'"[109] Schmitz ended his address by quoting Donald Rumsfeld's "admonition" in the aftermath of 9/11: "We pray this day, Heavenly Father, the prayer our nation learned at another time of righteous struggle and noble cause—America's enduring prayer: Not that God will be on our side, but always, O Lord, that America will be on Your side." Schmitz then told the audience, "If we want to remain one nation, under the rule of law and under God, we must always hold ourselves to a higher standard."[110]

So prevalent was the religious rhetoric in Schmitz's speeches that after one, he was told by an audience member, "The flavor of your speech has kind of troubled me because I always believed that the Constitution is a secular document, and I thought government is supposed to be a secular organization. I find that the church/state separation has been blurred by this Administration."[111] Schmitz proceeded to ignore the question, babbling on about chaplains in the military, before the questioner said, "That wasn't the tenor that I had. I thought I was talking about—" At that point, Schmitz interrupted the man and declared, "The American people, unlike other people around the world, are profoundly religious. That's a historical and a current fact. So for us to pretend, somehow, that we shouldn't be acknowledging the existence of Almighty God is just—it ignores reality, Sir. I'm sorry to have to say that. But that's how I see it."[112]

Some of the most bizarre stories about Schmitz's time at the Pentagon stem from what colleagues described as his "obsession" with Baron Von Steuben, the mercenary who fought in the Revolutionary War.[113] Von Steuben reportedly fled Germany after learning that he was going to be tried for homosexual activities and was welcomed by George Washington in America as a key military trainer—one of several mercenaries who fought the British. Soon after Schmitz was appointed to his post at the Pentagon, according to the *Los Angeles Times*:

He spent three months personally redesigning the inspector general's seal to include the Von Steuben family motto, "Always under the protection of the Almighty." He dictated the number of stars, laurel leaves and colors of the seal. He also asked for a new eagle, saying that the one featured on the old seal "looked like a chicken," current and former officials said. In July 2004, he escorted Henning Von Steuben, a German journalist and head of the Von Steuben Family Assn., to a U.S. Marine Corps event. He also feted Von Steuben at an $800 meal allegedly paid for by public funds, according to [Sen.] Grassley, and hired Von Steuben's son to work as an unpaid intern in the inspector general's office, a former Defense official said. He also called off a $200,000 trip to attend a ceremony at a Von Steuben statue . . . . in Germany after Grassley questioned it.[114]

"[Schmitz] was consumed with all things German and all things Von Steuben," a former Defense official told the *Los Angeles Times*'s T. Christian Miller. "He was obsessed."[115] Schmitz also peppered many of his official speeches as Inspector General with references to Von Steuben, referring to him in almost messianic ways. "We all rely on his precedent and his wisdom to provide a compass for leadership within the Pentagon—to help find our way when things appear convoluted and distorted, as often is the case in large bureaucratic organizations, particularly in the heat of battle," Schmitz said in a May 2004 speech at a dedication ceremony for a Von Steuben monument in New Jersey.[116] In Iraq, Schmitz said in June 2004, "We must stay the course and stand behind our troops. For my part, I have deployed my very best 'Von Steubens' on the ground in Iraq to help train their new Inspectors General as champions of integrity and engines of positive change in each of the new Iraqi ministries."[117]

It didn't take long for Schmitz to be called to accounts by lawmakers of various political stripes and the critical in-depth investigative reporting of Miller in the *Los Angeles Times*. Perhaps the most serious heat Schmitz faced for his role in several scandals came from a powerful Republican—Senator Grassley. One centered on Rumsfeld aide John "Jack" Shaw, Deputy Undersecretary of Defense. A diehard, highly partisan Republican operative who had worked in every GOP administration going back to Gerald Ford, Shaw was put in charge of Iraq's telecommunications system by the White House once the occupation got under way, despite the fact that "he had no background in either defense contracting or telecommunications," wrote Miller.[118] Whistleblowers from the U.S.-led Coalition Provisional Authority in Iraq charged that Shaw attempted to use his position to steer lucrative contracts to corporate cronies, according to the *Los Angeles Times*.[119] Shaw worked behind the scenes with powerful Republican lawmakers in an effort to redirect lucrative mobile phone network contracts in Iraq to businesses run by people with whom Shaw had a personal relationship, according to Miller.[120]

In 2003, Schmitz, in his capacity as Inspector General, signed an agreement with Shaw that gave him investigative authority, which Shaw allegedly used to press for the redirection of the telecommunications contracts to his friends.[121] "In one case, Shaw disguised himself as an employee of Halliburton Co. and gained access to a port in southern Iraq after he was denied entry by the U.S. military," Miller reported, citing Pentagon officials. "In another, he criticized a competition sponsored by the U.S.-led Coalition Provisional Authority to award cell phone licenses in Iraq. In both cases, Shaw urged government officials to fix the alleged problems by directing multimillion-dollar contracts to companies linked to his friends, without competitive bidding, according to the Pentagon sources and documents. In the case of the port, the clients of a lobbyist friend won a no-bid contract for dredging."[122]

When the whistleblowers' allegations about Shaw came before Schmitz, rather than investigating the case himself, he sent it to the FBI, citing a potential conflict of interest because Schmitz had deputized Shaw. "It's a safe bet you can bury something at the FBI, because they won't have time to look at it," a Pentagon official told Miller.[123] "The [FBI] was far more interested in terrorism than in official corruption," Miller observed in his book *Blood Money*. "Schmitz's own senior investigators objected to the transfer, seeing the decision as a calculated move to help a fellow political appointee. Predictably, the FBI investigation never went anywhere, and it was eventually dropped."[124]

After Shaw's suspected corruption was revealed by the *LA Times*, Schmitz personally helped draft a Pentagon press release that sought to exonerate Shaw.[125] "The allegations were examined by DoD IG criminal investigators in Baghdad and a criminal investigation was never opened," the Pentagon release, dated August 10, 2004, read. "Shaw is not now, nor has he ever been, under investigation by the DoD IG."[126] The press release referred journalists to the FBI for further information. According to Miller's reporting, Schmitz deputy Chuck Beardall e-mailed his boss, saying the press release was "dead wrong and needs to be removed ASAP. Failure to do so reflects poorly on the DOD's and our integrity."[127] Schmitz, according to Miller, "told an assistant, Gregg Bauer, that he was inclined to 'let the sleeping dog lie.' 'We did the right thing by recommending a less-inclined-to-misinterpretation' version of the press release, Schmitz wrote in an e-mail response."[128] In a subsequent letter to Rumsfeld, Senator Grassley wrote, "What I find most disturbing about this situation is the alleged involvement of the IG, Mr. Schmitz, in this matter. First there is a paper trail that appears to show that Mr. Schmitz was personally and directly involved in crafting the language in this press release. And second, I understand that Mr. Schmitz was repeatedly warned by his own staff 'to take it down' because it was 'patently false.' Even the FBI weighed in on that score, I am told."[129] Grassley told Rumsfeld that after he informed Schmitz of his intention to investigate him and requested access to Schmitz's files on the matter, "I have been informed unofficially by sources within the IG's office that 'all papers related to Shaw and the other matter were stamped law enforcement sensitive to prevent my access.'"[130] Grassley also accused Schmitz of thwarting an investigation of a senior military official who Grassley believed may have lied under oath.[131] For his part, Shaw denied any wrongdoing and claimed allegations against him were a "smear campaign."[132]

During his time at the Pentagon, Schmitz spoke publicly and passionately about the scourge of human trafficking, focusing in particular on sex trafficking—a pet issue of the Christian right and the Bush administration. In September 2004, Schmitz presented to the House Armed Services Committee a paper he wrote called "Inspecting Sex Slavery through the Fog of Moral Relativism."[133] In it, he declared, "Moral relativism is an enemy of the United States Constitution" and "The President of the United States has identified 21st Century sex slavery as 'a special evil' under 'a moral law that stands above men and nations.'" Schmitz said, "Ostensible consent by the parties to immoral practices such as prostitution and sex slavery ought never to be an excuse for turning a blind eye," concluding, "Even as we confront the new asymmetric enemies of the 21st Century, those of us who take an oath to defend the Constitution of the United States (and similar principle-based legal authorities) should recognize, confront, and suppress sexual slavery and other 'dissolute and immoral practices' whenever and wherever they raise their ugly heads through the fog of moral relativism— 'so help [us] God.'"[134]

But while Schmitz railed against moral relativism and sex slavery, he simultaneously was accused of failing to investigate serious allegations of human trafficking by Iraq contractors, including KBR, which had thirty-five thousand "third country nationals" working in Iraq.[135] In a ground-breaking investigation, "Pipeline to Peril," Cam Simpson of the *Chicago Tribune* documented how twelve Nepalese citizens were sent into Iraq in August 2004 and subsequently abducted and executed.[136] The paper revealed how "some subcontractors and a chain of human brokers allegedly engaged in the same kinds of abuses routinely condemned by the State Department as human trafficking."[137] The *Tribune* also "found evidence that subcontractors and brokers routinely seized workers' pass-ports, deceived them about their safety or contract terms and, in at least one case, allegedly tried to force terrified men into Iraq under the threat of cutting off their food and water," and that KBR and the military "allowed subcontractors to employ workers from countries that had banned the deployment of their citizens to Iraq, meaning thousands were trafficked through illicit channels."[138]

According to the *Chicago Tribune*: "Separate records also show that similar allegations had been raised in September 2004 with Joseph Schmitz, who was then the Department of Defense inspector general. Schmitz did not respond in any detail until nearly a year later, saying in an Aug. 25, 2005, letter to Rep. Christopher Smith, R-N.J., that there was a 'list of corrective measures' ordered by coalition military officials in Iraq following 'a prelim-inary inquiry' into the allegations. The letter did not mention passport seizures or violations of U.S. laws against human trafficking, but said living conditions 'required further attention' and that officials were 'monitoring the status of corrections' purportedly under way."[139] Hardly the "moral rel-ativist," "special evil" condemnation, apparently reserved by Schmitz and his allies for more "immoral" crimes.

One of the greatest scandals involving Schmitz began in May 2003, when the Pentagon agreed to lease one hundred military tanker planes in a controversial deal with Boeing worth a whopping $30 billion.[140] Almost immediately, the unusual arrangement—the largest such lease in U.S. history—was blasted by government watchdog groups as "wasteful corporate welfare," as it boosted the struggling aerospace business.[141] Republican Senator John McCain slammed the deal as "a textbook case of bad procurement policy and favoritism to a single defense contractor."[142] McCain alleged that analyses by the General Accounting Office showed that it would be exponentially cheaper for the government to modernize existing tankers, rather than leasing additional ones from Boeing at several times the cost.[143] "I have never seen the security and fiduciary responsibilities of the federal government quite so nakedly subordinated to the interests of one defense manufacturer," McCain said.[144] In winning the controversial deal, Boeing reportedly had a string of powerful backers, among them House Speaker Dennis Hastert, a key ally of the White House and of senior White House aides Karl Rove and Andy Card. "What was unusual about Boeing's lobbying was that it gained complete access to all divisions of government from the president down, to having the key leadership of the House and Senate and dozens of lawmakers pushing their wares on the deal," said Keith Ashdown, director of Taxpayers for Common Sense.[145] According to the *Financial Times*, "Boeing also invested $20 million last year in a defence-related venture capital fund run by Richard Perle . . . [who] co-authored an editorial in *The Wall Street Journal* in August supporting the deal. He did not disclose the Boeing investment."[146]

The contract was approved by President Bush's chief weapons buyer at the Pentagon, Edward C. "Pete" Aldridge Jr.,[147] who just happened to be the former president of McDonnell Douglas Electronic Systems, which later became part of Boeing.[148] Aldridge approved the deal on his last day at the Pentagon before taking a job with weapons manufacturer Lockheed Martin.[149] The deal would soon go down as "the most significant defense procurement mismanagement in contemporary history," in the words of the Senate Armed Services Committee Chair, Republican John Warner,[150] resulting in a cancellation of the contract, amid widespread allegations of cronyism. Former Air Force procurement officer Darleen Druyun went to prison, as did a Boeing representative, while Air Force Secretary James Roche resigned.[151]

Ultimately, the case ended up on Joseph Schmitz's desk at the Pentagon for investigation. In June 2005, Schmitz released a 257-page report on the scandal, which critics charged concealed the possible role of senior White House officials in the deal—the report contained forty-five deletions of references to White House officials.[152] In fact, Schmitz had actually given the report to the White House for review before its release, where it appeared to have been scrubbed of possibly damning information.[153] In a letter to Schmitz, Republican Senator Grassley wrote, "By excluding pertinent evidence from the final report, certain potential targets were shielded from possible accountability." Grassley added that Pentagon officials "may have been acting in response to guidance and advice from the senior White House officials, whose names were redacted from the final report on your orders; those officials are not held accountable."[154]

Schmitz did not include the comments of Rumsfeld or Wolfowitz because, Schmitz said, they hadn't said anything "relevant." If so, asserted the *Washington Post* editorial board, "investigators must not have asked the right questions. To offer just one example: Mr. Roche recounted that Mr. Rumsfeld called him in July 2003 to discuss his then-pending nomination to be secretary of the Army and 'specifically stated that he did not want me to budge on the tanker lease proposal.'"[155] In a transcript of Schmitz's office's interview with Rumsfeld, obtained by the *Washington Post*, investigators asked the Defense Secretary whether he had approved the Boeing tanker lease despite widespread violations of Pentagon and government-wide procurement rules. "I don't remember approving it," Rumsfeld said. "But I certainly don't remember not approving it, if you will."[156] Investigators then asked Rumsfeld about the fact that in 2002 President Bush asked his Chief of Staff, Andy Card, to intervene in the Pentagon negotiations with Boeing (a major Bush contributor). "I have been told," Rumsfeld said, "that discussions with the President are privileged, and with his immediate staff."[157] The *Post* said much of the rest of the discussion was blacked out on the transcript. None of Rumsfeld's comments were included in Schmitz's report.[158]

What's more, Schmitz's team did not interview anyone outside the Defense

Department, despite the well-documented involvement of several high-profile lawmakers, administration officials, and the President himself.[159] Schmitz also failed to interview Edward Aldridge, the Pentagon official who approved the deal. His report noted that Aldridge failed to get proper approvals before moving forward with the deal, but said the approvals were in place anyway. In a Senate hearing on the scandal after the report was released, McCain said to Schmitz, "So, Mr. Aldridge basically lied," to which Schmitz replied, "We know generally that . . . he and others within the Air Force and [the Office of the Secretary of Defense] were trying to treat the appropriations language as if it had waived a whole bunch of legal requirements."[160] McCain was incredulous. "Don't you think it would have been important to have his testimony?" he asked Schmitz. "My staff couldn't reach him," Schmitz eventually asserted, saying he had sent him a registered letter and left him some voice mails. "You couldn't get a hold of him through Lockheed Martin?" asked a stunned McCain. Despite his subpoena power, Schmitz never used it to compel Aldridge to be interviewed. "I don't think it's a mystery," Senator John Warner told Schmitz. "He's on the board of a major defense contractor, it seems to me he's locatable." In fact, it is very difficult to imagine Schmitz could not reach him at Lockheed Martin. Schmitz's brother, John P. Schmitz, former deputy counsel for George H. W. Bush, served as a registered lobbyist for Lockheed Martin from July 2002 until January 2005,[161] overlapping the Boeing deal and probe. He served on a team of two to three lobbyists from Mayer, Brown, Rowe & Maw, which was paid at least $445,000 during that time.[162] There is nothing, however, to suggest that John P. Schmitz had any direct connection to the tanker deal or to Aldridge.

In the end, Senator Grassley told Joseph Schmitz that his handling of the scandal "raises questions about your independence" as Inspector General.[163] Ashdown of Taxpayers for Common Sense said, "We now know that at the highest levels of the Pentagon and the White House, the wheels were greased to direct billions in corporate welfare to the Boeing Company."[164] But, he added, because of "the inspector general's reluctance to grill the secretary of defense" and "overzealous redactions . . . we are now left with more questions than answers."

With his office embroiled in multiple scandals, Schmitz served his official notice in June 2005 that he was recusing himself from Blackwater-related issues because he was in talks with the company about possible employment. The brief memo did not reveal what led to the disclosure or his dealings with Blackwater, but it came exactly a year after Schmitz returned from a nine-day trip to Baghdad, where he worked with Blackwater's prized client Paul Bremer on establishing a network of twenty-nine inspectors general (with Schmitz's "very best Von Steubens") for Iraqi ministries ahead of the "handover" of sovereignty.[165] To some observers, having these two officials develop a system of oversight for a "new" Iraqi government would be like asking two foxes to decide how the chicken coop should be protected.

In November 2004, Schmitz gave Bremer the Joseph H. Sherick Award, given to an individual "who contributes to the mission of the inspector general."[166] Schmitz said he gave Bremer the award because he was "a man of vision and a man of principle."[167] In accepting the award, Bremer said, "I felt from the time I got [to Iraq] how important it was, given the history of corruption under Saddam Hussein . . . to try to get this concept of trust in government established right from the beginning."[168] In early 2005, Schmitz delivered a lecture to the Order of Malta Federal Association at Bremer's church in Bethesda, Maryland, during which he told a story from Frances Bremer's (Paul's wife) novel Running to Paradise.[169] A few months later, in November 2005, Schmitz and Paul Bremer would be united again, as Blackwater hosted Bremer at a "fundraiser" for victims of Hurricane Katrina.[170]

On August 26, 2005, Schmitz officially informed his staff that he was leaving the Pentagon to work with Blackwater. In an e-mail he sent out, he signed off, saying, "May the Creator acknowledged in our Declaration of Independence who has endowed each of us with those unalienable rights that we as Americans consider 'first things,' continue to bless each of you."[171] Just as Schmitz began his work at Blackwater, in September 2005, the company reeled in lucrative government contracts, deploying heavily armed Blackwater forces on U.S. soil, in the wake of the worst "natural disaster" in U.S. history.

CHAPTER NINETEEN

BLACKWATER DOWN:
BAGHDAD ON THE BAYOU

THE MEN from Blackwater USA arrived in New Orleans right after Hurricane Katrina hit on August 29, 2005. The company beat the federal government and most aid organizations to the scene as 150 heavily armed Blackwater troops dressed in full battle gear spread out into the chaos of New Orleans. Officially, the company boasted of its forces "join[ing] the hurricane relief effort."[1] But its men on the ground told a different story.[2] Some patrolled the streets in SUVs with tinted windows and the Blackwater logo splashed on the back; others sped around the French Quarter in an unmarked car with no license plates. They wore khaki uniforms, wraparound sunglasses, beige or black military boots, and had Blackwater company IDs strapped to their bulging arms. All of them were heavily armed—some with M-4 automatic weapons, capable of firing nine hundred rounds per minute, or shotguns. This despite police commissioner Eddie Compass's claim that "Only law enforcement are allowed to have weapons."[3]

The Blackwater men congregated on the corner of St. Peter and Bourbon in front of a bar called 711. From the balcony above the bar, several Blackwater troops cleared out what had apparently been someone's apartment. They threw mattresses, clothes, shoes, and other household items from the balcony to the street below. They draped an American flag from the balcony's railing. More than a dozen troops from the Eighty-second Airborne Division stood in formation on the street watching the action.

Armed men shuffled in and out of the building as a handful told stories of their past experiences in Iraq. "I worked the security detail of both Bremer and Negroponte," said one of the Blackwater men, referring to the former head of the U.S. occupation, L. Paul Bremer, and former U.S. Ambassador to Iraq John Negroponte. Another complained, while talking on his cell phone, that he was getting only $350 a day plus his per diem. "When they told me New Orleans, I said, 'What country is that in?'" he said. He wore his company ID around his neck in a case with the phrase "Operation Iraqi Freedom" printed on it. After bragging about how he drives around Iraq in a "State Department–issued" "explosion-proof BMW," he said he was "just trying to get back to [Iraq], where the real action is."

In an hour-long conversation in the French Quarter, four Blackwater troops characterized their work in New Orleans as "securing neighborhoods" and "confronting criminals." They all carried automatic assault weapons and had guns strapped to their legs. Their flak jackets were covered with pouches for extra ammunition. "This is a totally new thing to have guys like us working CONUS [Continental United States]," another Blackwater contractor said. "We're much better equipped to deal with the situation in Iraq." Blackwater president Gary Jackson told the *Virginian-Pilot* that his men were heavily armed "because of the intel that we received," adding, "We did a risk assessment and decided we're going to send guys in there for real."[4] Jackson claimed Blackwater "basically secured" the French Quarter—a claim hotly disputed by local law enforcement agents, one of whom said, "There may be some braggadocio involved" in Jackson's claim. Maj. Ed Bush of the Louisiana National Guard told the *Pilot*, "Every group wants to kind of thump their chest a little bit, but just think about it. We live here. Seems kind of naive to think Blackwater beat us to the French Quarter."[5]

Former Kentwood, Michigan, police officer Dan Boelens, another Blackwater contractor who had been to Iraq before deploying to New Orleans, was assigned by Blackwater to guard Bell South workers in New Orleans.[6] He said that for several days after he arrived, he and other Blackwater contractors had patrolled the streets in SUVs and armed with assault rifles. "The only difference between here and Iraq is there are no roadside bombs," he said. "It's like a Third World country. You just can't believe this is America." Boelens added, "We keep having this little flashback, like what we were doing in Iraq."[7] The only kill Boelens claimed in New Orleans was a pit bull he shot before it could attack him.

Blackwater was among a handful of well-connected firms that immediately seized the business opportunity not just in the rubble and devastation in the Gulf but also in the media hysteria. As the federal, state, and local government abandoned hundreds of thousands of hurricane victims, the images that dominated the television coverage of the hurricane were of looting, lawlessness, and chaos. These reports were exaggerated and, without question, racist and inflammatory. If you were watching from, say, Kennebunkport, Maine, you might imagine New Orleans as one big riot—a festival of criminals whose glory day had finally come. In reality, it was a city of internally displaced and abandoned people desperate for food, water, transportation, rescue, and help. What was desperately needed was food, water, and housing. Instead what poured in fastest were guns. Lots of guns.

Frank Borelli, a former military policeman who worked for Blackwater in the early days of the operation, recalled that when he arrived at the Blackwater camp in Louisiana, "I was issued a Glock 17 and a Mossberg M590A shotgun. I was also issued a shotshell pouch with ten rounds of slug and ten rounds of 00 Buck. There was (at that time) no 9mm ammo available, but I was blessed to be in a camp full of trigger-pullers. Before I racked out I had fifty-one rounds of 9mm ammo loaded into three magazines for the G17."[8] Clearly well armed, Borelli observed, "The logistics effort to support the operation is awesome, and I *know* ammo was just flown in on Monday. More came in on Wednesday. It is a comment on the spirit of the American cop/warrior that Blackwater can put *so many* men on the ground *so fast*. Supporting them is a daunting challenge."

In the early days of the hurricane, even with heavily armed Blackwater men openly patrolling the streets of New Orleans, a spokesperson for the Homeland Security Department, Russ Knocke, told the *Washington Post* he knew of no federal plans to hire Blackwater or other private security. "We believe we've got the right mix of personnel in law enforcement for the federal government to meet the demands of public safety," Knocke said on September 8.[9] But the very next day, the Blackwater troops on the ground put forward a very different narrative. When asked what authority they were operating under, one Blackwater contractor said, "We're on contract with the Department of Homeland Security." Then, pointing to one of his comrades, he said, "He was even deputized by the governor of the state of Louisiana. We can make arrests and use lethal force if we deem it necessary." The man then held up the gold Louisiana law enforcement badge he wore around his neck. Blackwater spokesperson Anne Duke also said the company had a letter from Louisiana officials authorizing its forces to carry loaded weapons.[10] Some of the men said they were sleeping in camps set up by Homeland Security.

"This vigilantism demonstrates the utter breakdown of the government," said Michael Ratner, president of the Center for Constitutional Rights, upon learning Blackwater forces were deployed in the hurricane zone. "These private security forces have behaved brutally, with impunity, in Iraq. To have them now on the streets of New Orleans is frightening and possibly illegal." A statement on Blackwater's Web site, dated September 1, 2005, advertised airlift services, security services, and crowd control and said the company was deploying its SA-330 Puma helicopter "to help assist in evacuating citizens from flooded areas."[11] The press release claimed "Blackwater's aerial support services" were being "donated" to the relief effort. "At this time, all Americans should band together and assist our countrymen who have been struck by this natural disaster," said founder Erik Prince. "Blackwater is proud to serve the people of New Orleans," said Blackwater's executive vice president Bill Mathews on September 13. "First and foremost, this is about Americans helping Americans in a time of desperation."[12] Cofer Black spun Blackwater's operations in Katrina as strictly humanitarian-motivated. "I think it's important to underscore that companies like ours are in servitude," Black later said, adding that when Katrina hit, "Our company launched a helicopter and crew with no contract, no one paying us, that went down to New Orleans. We were able to find out how to put ourselves under Coast Guard command—we got a Coast Guard call sign and we saved some 150 people that otherwise wouldn't have been saved. And as a result of that, we've had a very positive experience."[13] "We're always anxious to help our fellow citizens," Black said, "whether we get paid or not." But the fact is that Blackwater was indeed getting paid in New Orleans—big time.

On September 18, Blackwater estimated that it had 250 troops deployed in the region; a number Mathews said would continue to grow. "We are people who want to make a difference and help," he said. "It's time to set the record straight: We are not . . . skull-crushing mercenaries. We don't believe we will make a profit here. We ran to the fire because it was burning."[14] In another interview Mathews said that because Blackwater had donated more than $1 million in aviation services, "If we break even on the security services, our company will have done a great job."[15] By then, the company was aggressively recruiting for its New Orleans operations. It required applicants to have at least four years of military experience "with duties involving carrying a weapon." A Blackwater advertisement said, "This opportunity is for immediate deployment. Earning potential up to $9,000 a month."[16] Meanwhile, Blackwater floated a proposal to the Department of Homeland Security (DHS) that it set up a training facility to prepare local workers for security-industry jobs in New Orleans, either with Blackwater or other firms. "Security is going to be an issue during the entire reconstruction," said Mathews.[17]

While Blackwater may indeed have donated some "services" in New Orleans, some of its claims have been called into serious question by the U.S. Coast Guard, under whose direction Blackwater boasted it was operating. In early 2006, Erik Prince bragged that "after Hurricane Katrina hit, we sent one of our Puma helicopters. . . . I said, 'Start flying.' We got ourselves attached to the Coast Guard, actually became a Coast Guard call sign, and we flew, rescued 128 people."[18] That story doesn't appear to add up. "[Blackwater] offered to do rescues, but there were legal concerns. What if someone got hurt? So we asked them not to engage in pulling people out," said Coast Guard Cmdr. Todd Campbell, who directed a large part of the rescue operations. He told the *Virginian-Pilot* that Blackwater "debriefed me at the end of every day, and no one ever mentioned doing any rescues. If they were out there doing them, it was solely on their own."[19]

Moreover, despite its moralistic boasts, Blackwater hardly ran a pro-bono humanitarian operation in New Orleans. In addition to its work guarding private companies, banks, hotels, industrial sites, and rich individuals,[20] Blackwater was quietly handed a major no-bid contract with the Department of Homeland Security's Federal Protective Service, ostensibly to protect federal reconstruction projects for FEMA. According to Blackwater's government contracts, from September 8 to September 30, 2005—just three weeks— Blackwater was paid $409,000 for providing fourteen guards and four vehicles to "protect the temporary morgue in Baton Rouge, LA."[21] Documents show that the government paid Blackwater $950 a day for each of its guards in the area—some $600 more per man per day than the company was allegedly paying its men on the ground.[22] That contract kicked off a hurricane boon for Blackwater; by the end of 2005, in just three months, the government had paid Blackwater at least $33.3 million for its Katrina work for DHS.[23] All of these services were justified by the government's claim of not having enough personnel to deploy quickly in the hurricane zone, though spokespeople carefully avoided drawing a connection to the various U.S. occupations internationally. "We saw the costs, in terms of accountability and dollars, for this practice in Iraq, and now we are seeing it in New Orleans," said Illinois Democrat Jan Schakowsky, one of Blackwater's few critics in Congress. "They have again given a sweetheart contract—without an open bidding process—to a company with close ties to the Administration."[24] By June 2006, the company had raked in some $73 million from its Katrina work for the government—about $243,000 a day.[25]

Instead of a serious government relief operation in New Orleans, the forces that most rapidly mobilized were the Republican-connected corporations— many of the very companies making a killing off the Iraq occupation. To further aid these companies, President Bush repealed the 1931 Davis-Bacon Act, which required federal contractors to pay a prevailing wage to its workers[26] (he was later forced to restore it). This enabled the companies to pay bottom dollar to workers while reaping massive corporate profits. In the immediate aftermath of the hurricane, Vice President Dick Cheney's "former" company Halliburton/KBR (the greatest corporate beneficiary of the Iraq War) was given $30 million to "assess pumps and infrastructure in the city and construct a facility to support recovery efforts,"[27] while the Shaw Group (which was paid more than $135 million in Iraq) was given more than $700 million in Katrina contracts.[28] Both companies were represented by a lobbyist named Joseph Allbaugh, who just happened to be President Bush's former campaign manager and the former head of FEMA.[29] Eventually, the government significantly raised the ceilings of its contracts to Republican-connected firms: $950 million for Shaw, $1.4 billion for Fluor, and $575 million for Bechtel.[30] Fluor's Katrina project was run by Alan Boeckmann, the same manager who was in charge of the company's Iraq contracts. "Our rebuilding work in Iraq is slowing down," he told Reuters. "And this has made some people available to respond to our work in Louisiana."[31]

Some began referring to New Orleans and the surrounding disaster area as "Baghdad on the Bayou." As The Nation's Christian Parenti reported in a dispatch from New Orleans, "It seems the rescue effort is turning into an urban war game: An imaginary domestic version of the total victory that eludes America in Baghdad will be imposed here, on New Orleans. It's almost as if the Tigris—rather than the Mississippi—had flooded the city. The place feels like a sick theme park—Macho World—where cops, mercenaries, journalists and weird volunteers of all sorts are playing out a relatively safe version of their militaristic fantasies about Armageddon and the cleansing iron fist."[32] With U.S. forces spread thinly across multiple war zones, the landscape was ripe for some major-league disaster profiteering by the rapidly expanding world of private security and military companies.

Blackwater was hardly the only mercenary firm to take advantage of the tremendous profit opportunity in the great disaster. As business leaders and government officials talked openly of changing the demographics of one of America's most culturally vibrant cities, mercenaries from companies like DynCorp, American Security Group, Wackenhut, Kroll, and an Israeli company called Instinctive Shooting International (ISI) fanned out to guard private businesses and homes, as well as government projects and institutions. Within two weeks of the hurricane, the number of private security companies registered in Louisiana jumped from 185 to 235 and would continue to climb as the weeks passed. Some, like Blackwater, were under federal contract. Others were hired by the wealthy elite, like F. Patrick Quinn III, who brought in private security to guard his $3 million private estate and his luxury hotels, which were under consideration for a lucrative federal contract to house FEMA workers.[33]

A possibly deadly incident involving hired guns underscored the dangers of private forces policing American streets. One private security guard said that on his second night in New Orleans, where he was on contract with a wealthy business owner, he was traveling with a heavily armed security detail en route to pick up one of his boss's associates and escort him through the chaotic city. The security guard said their convoy came under fire from "black gangbangers" on an overpass near the poor Ninth Ward neighborhood. "At the time, I was on the phone with my business partner," he recalled. "I dropped the phone and returned fire." The guard said he and his men were armed with AR-15s and Glocks and that they unleashed a barrage of bullets in the general direction of the alleged shooters on the overpass. "After that, all I heard was moaning and screaming, and the shooting stopped. That was it. Enough said."

Then, he said, "the Army showed up, yelling at us and thinking we were the enemy. We explained to them that we were security. I told them what had happened and they didn't even care. They just left." Five minutes later, the guard said, Louisiana state troopers arrived on the scene, inquired about the incident, and then asked him for directions on "how they could get out of the city." The guard said that no one ever asked him for any details of the incident and no report was ever made. "One thing about security," he said, "is that we all coordinate with each other—one family." That coordination apparently did not include the offices of the Secretaries of State in Louisiana and Alabama, which said they had no record of his company.

A few miles away from the French Quarter, another wealthy New Orleans businessman, James Reiss, who served in Mayor Ray Nagin's administration as chairman of the city's Regional Transit Authority, brought in some heavy guns to guard the elite gated community of Audubon Place: Israeli mercenaries dressed in black and armed with M-16s. Reiss, who flew the men in by helicopter, told the *Wall Street Journal*, "Those who want to see this city rebuilt want to see it done in a completely different way: demographically, geographically and politically. The way we've been living is not going to happen again, or we're out."[34] Two Israelis patrolling the gates outside Audubon said they had served as professional soldiers in the Israeli military, and one boasted of having participated in the invasion of Lebanon. "We have been fighting the Palestinians all day, every day, our whole lives," one of them declared. "Here in New Orleans, we are not guarding from terrorists."[35] Then, tapping on his machine gun, he said, "Most Americans, when they see these things, that's enough to scare them."

The men said they worked for Instinctive Shooting International, which described its employees as "veterans of the Israeli special task forces from the following Israeli government bodies: Israel Defense Force (IDF), Israel National Police Counter Terrorism units, Instructors of Israel National Police Counter Terrorism units, General Security Service (GSS or 'Shin Beit'), Other restricted intelligence agencies."[36] The company was formed in 1993. Its Web site profile said: "Our up-to-date services meet the challenging needs for Homeland Security preparedness and overseas combat procedures and readiness. ISI is currently an approved vendor by the US Government to supply Homeland Security services."

As countless guns poured into New Orleans, there was a distinct absence of relief operations, food, and water distribution. The presence of the mercenaries raised another important question: given the enormous presence in New Orleans of National Guard, U.S. Army, U.S. Border Patrol, local police from around the country, and practically every other government agency with badges, why were private security companies needed, particularly to guard federal projects? "I don't know that there are any terrorist attacks being planned against FEMA offices in the Gulf Coast," said Illinois Senator Barack Obama. "It strikes me, with all the National Guardsmen that we've got down there, with a bunch of local law enforcement that are back on the job and putting their lives back together again, that that may not be the best use of money."[37] Shortly after *The Nation* exposed Blackwater's operations in New Orleans, Representative Schakowsky and a handful of other Congress members raised questions about the scandal. They entered the reporting into the Congressional Record during hearings on Katrina in late September 2005 and cited it in letters to DHS Inspector General Richard Skinner, who then began an inquiry.[38] In letters to Congressional offices in February 2006, Skinner defended the Blackwater deal, asserting that it was "appropriate" for the government to contract with the company. Skinner admitted that "the ongoing cost of the contract . . . is clearly very high" and then quietly dropped a bombshell: "It is expected that FEMA will require guard services on a relatively long-term basis (two to five years)."[39]

The hurricane's aftermath ushered in the homecoming of the "war on terror," a contract bonanza whereby companies reaped massive Iraq-like profits without leaving the country and at a minuscule fraction of the risk. To critics of the government's handling of the hurricane, the message was clear. "That's what happens when the victims are black folks vilified before and after the storm—instead of aid, they get contained," said Chris Kromm, executive director of the Institute for Southern Studies and an editor of Gulf Coast Reconstruction Watch.[40] Kromm alleged that while seemingly endless amounts of money were doled out to scandal-ridden contractors, vital projects had "gotten zero or little money" in New Orleans in the same period, including: job creation, hospital and school reconstruction, affordable housing, and wetlands restoration. Even in this context, DHS continued to defend the Blackwater contract. In a March 1, 2006, memo to FEMA, Matt Jadacki, the DHS Special Inspector General for Gulf Coast Hurricane Recovery, wrote that the Federal Protective Service considered Blackwater "the best value to the government."[41]

A month after Katrina hit, Blackwater's guards were also working the Hurricane Rita gravy train. At its high point the company had about six hundred contractors deployed from Texas to Mississippi.[42] By the summer of 2006, Blackwater's operations in New Orleans were staffed more by police types than the commandos of the early deployment. The paramilitary gear was eventually replaced by black polo shirts with the company logo, khaki pants, and pistols as Blackwater men patrolled the parking lot of a Wal-Mart that had been converted into a FEMA outpost.[43] In late August 2006, Blackwater was still guarding such vital public institutions as the city library—which was being used by FEMA—where one patron, after allegedly being refused entry by a Blackwater guard and finding himself unable to get an explanation as to why, said the "brazen representative declined to give his name and called a supervisor who declined to give his name or the name of the representative who denied [the man] access to the library."[44] In Baton Rouge, Blackwater set up a Katrina zone headquarters, renting space at the World Evangelism Bible College and Seminary, run by disgraced Christian televangelist Jimmy Swaggart (whose public career went up in flames in 1988 when he was caught with a prostitute in a motel).[45]

For Blackwater, Katrina was a momentous occasion—its first official deployment on U.S. soil. While it raked in a hefty sum for the domestic disaster operations, the greatest benefit to the company was in breaking into a new, lucrative market for its mercenary services—far from the bloodletting of Iraq. As the *Virginian-Pilot*, which is right in Blackwater's backyard, observed, the hurricanes of 2005 represented "a potential plug for a hole in Blackwater's business model. Private military companies thrive on war—an icy fact that could gut the now-booming industry when or if Iraq settles down. Katrina offered Blackwater a chance to diversify into natural disasters."[46] Erik Prince has said that prior to Katrina, "We had no plans to be in the domestic security business at all."[47] In the aftermath of the hurricane, though, Blackwater launched a new domestic operations division. "Look, none of us loves the idea that devastation became a business opportunity," said the new division's deputy, Seamus Flatley, a retired Navy fighter pilot. "It's a distasteful fact, but it is what it is. Doctors, lawyers, funeral directors, even newspapers—they all make a living off of bad things happening. So do we, because somebody's got to handle it."[48]

But critics saw the deployment of Blackwater's forces domestically as a dangerous precedent that could undermine U.S. democracy. "Their actions may not be subject to constitutional limitations that apply to both federal and state officials and employees—including First Amendment and Fourth Amendment rights to be free from illegal searches and seizures. Unlike police officers, they are not trained in protecting constitutional rights," said CCR's Ratner. "These kind of paramilitary groups bring to mind Nazi Party brownshirts, functioning as an extrajudicial enforcement mechanism that can and does operate outside the law. The use of these paramilitary groups is an extremely dangerous threat to our rights."

Blackwater and the Border

One quality Blackwater USA has consistently put on display is its uncanny ability to be in the right place at the right moment—especially when it comes to scooping up lucrative government contracts. Far from being a matter of simple luck, the company has dedicated substantial resources to monitoring trends in the world of law enforcement and military actions and has hired many well-connected ex-spooks, former federal officials, and military brass. Like the best entrepreneurs, Blackwater is always looking to provide what it refers to as "turnkey" solutions for problems ailing the government bureaucracy or to fill the seemingly endless "national security" holes appearing in the wake of the "war on terror." In the years following 9/11, Blackwater proved remarkably adept at placing itself in the middle of many of the prized battles the administration (and the right in general) was waging: rapid privatization of government, the occupations of Iraq and Afghanistan, and bolstering Christian/Republican friendly businesses.

While the hurricanes expedited Blackwater's domestic program, it was by no means the first time the company had considered the major profits to be made on the home front. In fact, in mid-2005, three months before Katrina hit—and with its forces firmly entrenched in Iraq and a taxpayer-funded I.V. running directly from Washington, D.C., to Moyock—Blackwater quietly threw its hat into the ring of another major front: immigration and "border security." After the launch of the "war on terror," anti-immigrant groups used the fear of further attacks to push for greater militarization of the U.S. borders—with some calling for a massive fence stretching hundreds of miles along the U.S./Mexico border—and to "crack down" on people they characterized as "illegal aliens."

In April 2005, the anti-immigrant/pro-militarized-border cause got a huge boost as the Minuteman Project Civil Defense Corps exploded onto the scene. The overwhelmingly white movement organized anti-immigrant militias to patrol the U.S. border with Mexico. The Minutemen, named after the militias that fought in the American Revolution, billed themselves as "Americans doing the jobs our Government won't do." They claimed to have hundreds of volunteers from thirty-seven states, among them many former military and law enforcement officers as well as pilots who would do aerial surveillance.

One of Blackwater's key Congressional allies, Representative Duncan

Hunter, began stepping up his campaign for a massive "border fence,"[49] while Erik Prince's old boss, Representative Dana Rohrabacher endorsed the Minutemen, saying the militias "demonstrated the positive effects of an increased presence on the southwest border. There's no denying that more border patrol agents would help create a stronger border and decrease illegal crossings that may include international terrorists."[50] T. J. Bonner, president of the National Border Patrol Council—a lobbying organization—echoed those sentiments, invoking the 9/11 attacks. "Even if a terrorist is a one-in-a-million occurrence, with several million people coming into the country every year, very soon they reach that critical mass necessary to carry out another attack on the magnitude of September 11," he said. "This is totally unacceptable from the standpoint of homeland security and national security. We have to gain control of our borders."[51]

On Capitol Hill, Republican operatives seized the opportunity to escalate their anti-immigrant, proprivatization, promilitarization campaign and push forward with an agenda that would have been difficult to popularize before 9/11. Now, the new national hysteria provided the ideal turf to wage the battle. In the midst of this, on May 18, 2005, the House of Representatives passed the first Department of Homeland Security Authorization Bill, which approved the hiring of some two thousand new border patrol agents. On May 24, the House Homeland Security Committee's management integration and oversight subcommittee held a hearing on the training of these new agents. One of the central purposes of the hearing seemed to be to promote outsourcing the border-training program to the private sector.

The first panel of the hearings consisted of two U.S. government immigration officials. The second panel represented the private industry. For this panel, there were just two speakers: T. J. Bonner and Gary Jackson.[52] "We need reinforcements desperately, and we need them yesterday," Bonner told the hearing. "There's a crying need for agents clearly, which is borne out by the call for citizen patrol groups, military on the border. Clearly we're not doing our job. But the reason we need more border patrol agents is to secure our borders. We need to spend whatever it takes, not try and do it on the cheap, not try and figure out how we can cut corners to hire as many border patrol agents as possible, but to spend whatever it takes to support these men and women so that they can go out there."[53] Jackson began his testimony by running through a brief, selective history of Blackwater. The company, he said, was founded "from a clear vision of the need for innovative, flexible training and security solutions in support of national and global security challenges. Both the military and law enforcement agencies needed additional capacity to fully train their personnel to the standards required to keep our country secure. Because these constraints on training venues continued to increase, Blackwater believed that the U.S. government would embrace outsourcing of quality training. We built Blackwater's facility in North Carolina to provide the capacity that we thought our government would need to meet its future training requirements. Over the years, Blackwater has not only become an industry leader in training but at the cutting edge." Jackson said that as the company grew, "We quickly realized the value to the government of one-stop shopping. While there were other companies who offered one or two distinct training services, none of them offer all of our services and certainly not at one location." The importance of this, Jackson said, "cannot be overstated. Being able to conduct training at a centralized locality is the most cost-effective, efficient way of ensuring that new federal law enforcement agents are trained to the level demanded by today's national and homeland security challenges."[54]

Alabama Republican Mike Rogers, who chaired the Congressional hearing, blasted the costs of government training programs for border agents, saying, "It's going to cost more to train a border patrol officer in a ten-month program than it is to get a four-year degree at Harvard University." Rogers asked: if Blackwater was given $100,000 per agent, did Jackson believe the company "would give them equal or better training than they're receiving" from the federal government's training program? "I could assure you of that," Jackson shot back. He told the lawmakers that Blackwater could train all two thousand new border patrol agents in one year. "Blackwater successfully conducts a similar public-private partnership with the

Department of State to recruit, train, deploy, and manage diplomatic security specialists in Iraq and other areas of interest. Securing our borders will continue to be a challenge for our nation," Jackson said. "The urgency is clear. History repeatedly demonstrates that innovation and efficiency are what alter the strategic balance, and Blackwater offers both in support of training new border patrol agents. Just as the private sector has responded in moving mail and packages around the world in a more efficient manner, so too can Blackwater respond to the CBP (Customs and Border Patrol) emerging and compelling training needs."

A few days later, Blackwater's *Tactical Weekly* newsletter carried the news headline "Border Patrol Should Consider Outsourcing Its Training, Lawmaker Says."[55] The article, from the *Federal Times*, reported that "[Congressman] Rogers said the government may need to turn to Blackwater USA or other contractor if they can do the job cheaper. 'We have a fiduciary obligation to taxpayers to look at other options,' Rogers said. 'It's irresponsible to go forward with that in the absence of supporting documentation.'"[56]

In November 2005, Blackwater and the American Red Cross held a joint "Gulf Region Relief" fundraiser that symbolically brought Blackwater's diverse federal contracts full circle. The keynote speaker, welcomed with a standing ovation, was Blackwater's once-prized client, L. Paul Bremer, whose book on Iraq had just been published. Blackwater claimed to have raised $138,000 that night[57]—about $100,000 shy of the company's estimated daily take from the Katrina contracting jackpot. "Tonight was a success because it was about Americans helping Americans," said Gary Jackson, repeating what had become Blackwater's new mantra. "Our great employees and our special relationship with Ambassador Bremer and the Red Cross made it possible to pull off this event."[58] It was reminiscent of the tobacco industry cheering its own meager contributions to antismoking campaigns, while at the same time aggressively marketing cigarettes with exponentially more resources. In reality, Blackwater gained far more from the hurricane than New Orleans's victims did from Blackwater's services.

President Bush used the Katrina disaster to try to repeal the Posse

Comitatus Act (the ban on using U.S. troops in domestic law enforcement), and Blackwater and other security firms initiated a push to install their paramilitaries on U.S. soil, bringing the war home in yet another ominous way. "This is a trend," said one Blackwater mercenary in New Orleans. "You're going to see a lot more guys like us in these situations." Blackwater had now solidified its position not only as one of the great beneficiaries of the "war on terror" but as a major player in several of the key arenas of the neoconservative agenda. On the one-year anniversary of Katrina, Gary Jackson used the opportunity to showcase Blackwater's services. "When the Department of Homeland Security called with an emergent and compelling requirement for a turnkey security solution for multiple federal assets, we responded," he wrote. "Our Rapid Response Enterprise has global reach and can make a positive difference in the lives of those who are affected by natural disasters and terrorist events."[59]

Shortly after Blackwater's Katrina profits started rolling in, Erik Prince sent out a memo on Prince Group letterhead to "all Blackwater USA officers, employees, and independent contractors." Its subject: "Blackwater USA National Security Oath and Leadership Standards." It required Blackwater workers to swear the same oath to the Constitution as Blackwater's "National Security-related clients" to "support and defend the Constitution of the United States against all enemies, foreign and domestic. . . . So help me God."[60]

K Street Collapse

In January 2006, as Blackwater continued to enjoy the great windfall from Hurricane Katrina, its powerful lobbying firm, the Alexander Strategy Group, was brought down in the flames of the Jack Abramoff lobbying scandal. Abramoff was a member of President Bush's 2001 Transition Team, a powerful Republican lobbyist, and a close associate of many of the most powerful political players in the United States. In March 2006, after months of sustained revelations about Abramoff's influence-peddling activities, he ended up pleading guilty to five felony counts in one of the greatest corruption scandals in Washington in recent history. ASG was one of several

Abramoff-related casualties. The well-connected Republican lobbying firm, founded and run by former senior staffers of ex-House majority leader Tom DeLay, was also entangled in several other scandals rocking Washington at the time. As Abramoff was going down, ASG's lobbyists feverishly scrambled to dissociate themselves from the sinking ship.

A few months earlier, it would have been difficult to predict ASG's downfall. The firm enjoyed a prosperous 2005, ranked as a Top 25 lobbying outfit by *National Journal*, with revenues on a steady rise—up 34 percent in one year, to $8 million from what the *Washington Post* termed "an A-list of about 70 companies and organizations."[61] In addition to powerhouses like PhRMA, Enron, TimeWarner, Microsoft, and Eli Lilly, ASG counted among its clients over the years several evangelical Christian causes and organizations—among them right-wing media operations like Salem Communications, the National Religious Broadcasters, and Grace News.[62] ASG was also a quiet workhorse in procuring lucrative military contracts for some of its clients. At the time of its downfall, ASG was on the cutting edge of one of the fastest-growing industries within the military world—private security. That was thanks in large part to the long-term relationship between ASG partner Paul Behrends and Blackwater owner Erik Prince.

While Behrends had been lobbying for Prince and Blackwater almost from the moment the business began, the key assistance Behrends provided came in the immediate aftermath of the Fallujah ambush in 2004. In November 2005, when Blackwater and other private security firms began a push to recast their mercenary image under the banner of the International Peace Operations Association, the mercenary trade association, it was Behrends and ASG they enlisted to help them do it.[63] Among those registered by ASG as lobbyists for IPOA were several former DeLay staffers, including Ed Buckham and Karl Gallant, former head of DeLay's ARMPAC, and Tony Rudy, DeLay's former counsel, who pleaded guilty in March 2006 to conspiracy to corrupt public officials and defraud clients.[64] Interestingly, Rudy had also worked alongside Behrends in Representative Dana Rohrabacher's office in the early 1990s—the same time Erik Prince claimed to have worked there as a defense analyst.[65]

According to Rohrabacher's office, Prince was actually an upaid intern. Rohrabacher remained an ardent defender of Jack Abramoff, whom he first met when Abramoff was a leading College Republican and Rohrabacher was an aide to President Reagan. When Abramoff was sentenced in 2006, Rohrabacher was the only sitting Congress member to write the sentencing judge asking for leniency. "Jack was a selfless patriot most of the time I knew him. His first and foremost consideration was protecting America from its enemies," Rohrabacher wrote. "Only later did he cash in on the contacts he made from his idealistic endeavors."[66]

Prince himself managed to escape scrutiny, despite his ties to Rudy and his connection to Abramoff. The Edgar and Elsa Prince Foundation, of which Erik Prince is a vice president and his mother is president, gave at least $130,000 to Toward Tradition,[67] an organization that described itself as a "national coalition of Jews and Christians devoted to fighting the secular institutions that foster anti-religious bigotry, harm families, and jeopardize the future of America."[68] Abramoff served as chairman of the organization, run by his longtime friend Rabbi Daniel Lapin, until 2000, and remained on the board until 2004.[69] Toward Tradition surfaced in Abramoff's plea agreement as a "nonprofit entity" through which "Abramoff provided things of value . . . [w]ith the intent to influence . . . official acts."[70] Abramoff clients eLottery, an Internet gambling company, and the Magazine Publishers of America each donated $25,000 to Toward Tradition.[71] The $50,000 was then paid to Tony Rudy's wife, Lisa, in ten $5,000 installments for consulting services.[72] At the time, Rudy was DeLay's deputy chief of staff and was helping eLottery to fight a bill that would outlaw Internet gambling and helping the MPA to fight a postal rate increase.[73]

Despite the ASG scandal in early 2006, the head of the IPOA, Doug Brooks, told *Roll Call* that the association with Behrends would continue, saying IPOA found him "helpful in terms of what we were working on."[74] While the ASG lobbyists scrambled to set up new shops with different names and clients tried to distance themselves from the scandal, Behrends began working for powerhouse law firm Crowell & Moring's lobbying arm, C&M Capitol Link—a company he had previously worked with on behalf of Blackwater in 2004.[75]

Still, some questioned the hiring of a DeLay-linked lobbyist. "We did our homework. We did all the right due diligence, as you might guess," said John Thorne, head of C&M Capitol Link. "[Behrends's] reputation is solid. Everyone we talked to said he was completely out of that other business."[76] But Behrends was not out of the mercenary business in general nor Blackwater's stake in it specifically. The bond between the influential lobbyist and Erik Prince was far too strong not to weather a mere political scandal. Besides, major projects were on the horizon.

The company would soon begin expanding its global reach and its appetite for international contracts, putting its forces forward as possible peacekeepers in places like Darfur—a crisis zone located in Cofer Black's old stomping ground, Sudan. Eight years after Blackwater's quiet beginnings, the company had become a major player in the neoconservative revolution and would enthusiastically act as the Pied Piper of the neo-mercenary rebranding movement.

CHAPTER TWENTY

"THE KNIGHTS OF THE ROUND TABLE"

BY THE time Defense Secretary Donald Rumsfeld resigned in late 2006, he had indeed, as President Bush declared, overseen the "most sweeping transformation of America's global force posture since the end of World War II."[1] By Rumsfeld's last day in office, the ratio of active-duty U.S. soldiers to private contractors deployed in Iraq had almost reached one to one,[2] a statistic unprecedented in modern warfare. Vice President Dick Cheney called Rumsfeld "the finest Secretary of Defense this nation has ever had."[3] The praise was understandable coming from Cheney. The dramatic military privatization scheme launched during Cheney's time as Secretary of Defense during the 1991 Gulf War had grown beyond his wildest expectations under Rumsfeld and has forever altered the way the United States wages its wars. And yet despite the unprecedented level of private sector involvement on the battlefield, the U.S. military has seldom been stretched more thinly or faced more perilous times. The Bush administration's occupations of Iraq and Afghanistan taxed U.S. forces to the point where former Secretary of State Colin Powell declared in late 2006 that "the active Army is about broken."[4] In the midst of such striking commentary from one of the country's most celebrated military figures, President Bush announced his intent to increase the size of the American armed forces to "position our military so that it is ready and able to stay engaged in a long war."[5] In his 2007 State of the Union address, Bush called for an increase of ninety-two thousand active duty troops within five years and proposed a Civilian Reserve Corps to supplement official U.S. forces.[6]

While the "bleeding" of the U.S. military was without question the result of the administration's aggressive policies and unpopular occupations, the new Democratic Congressional leadership, which swept to power in November 2006, seemed more than willing to go along with Bush's aspirations for an even larger military, rather than questioning the insatiable appetite for conquest that made it a necessity. Among the few forces that could take comfort in this situation are those that have benefited the most from the war on terror— the companies of the war industry. Few have gained as much in the Bush years and few stand to benefit more from the projected U.S. course in the future than Blackwater USA. Erik Prince knows this. In fact, he has offered up a remedy of his own for the numbers crisis in the military—the creation of a "contractor brigade." As for the official Army plan to increase its size by thirty thousand troops, Prince asserted, "We could certainly do it cheaper."[7] Those are the words of a man empowered by success and confident in his future. They are the words of a man with his own army, hailed by the neoconservative *Weekly Standard* as "the alpha and omega of military outsourcing."[8]

In the years since Blackwater began in 1997 as a firing range and lodge near the Great Dismal Swamp of North Carolina, it has grown to become one of the most powerful private military actors on the international scene. Blackwater in 2006 had some twenty-three hundred private soldiers deployed in nine countries around the world and boasted of a database of another twenty-one thousand additional contractors on whom it could call should the need arise. In 2006, one U.S. Congressperson observed that, in terms of military might, the company could single-handedly take down many of the world's governments. Its seven-thousand-acre facility in Moyock, North Carolina, has now become the most sophisticated private military center on the planet, while the company possesses one of the world's largest privately held stockpiles of heavy-duty weaponry. It is a major training center for federal and local security and military forces in the United States, as well as foreign forces and private individuals. It sells its own line of target systems and armored vehicles. Blackwater's state-of-the-art sixty-thousand-square-foot corporate headquarters welcomes visitors with door handles made from the muzzles of automatic weapons. It is developing surveillance blimps and private airstrips for its fleet of aircraft, which include helicopter gunships.[9]

Blackwater is building facilities in both Illinois ("Blackwater North") and California ("Blackwater West"), as well as a jungle-training center in the Philippines housed at the former U.S. naval base at Subic Bay, once the largest U.S. military base in Asia. The company holds hundreds of millions of dollars in U.S. government contracts, among them "black" contracts kept from public oversight, and has begun marketing aggressively to corporations. It has deep connections to the U.S. intelligence and defense apparatus and has become nothing short of the administration's Praetorian Guard in the war on terror. While Blackwater executives may have initially set their sights high in aiming to be a wing of the military—like the Marines or the Army—now, reeling from its successes, the company is no longer content to be subordinate to the United States. While it still maintains its pledge of loyalty and patriotism, Blackwater strives to be an independent army, deploying to conflict zones as an alternative to a NATO or UN force, albeit one accountable to Blackwater's owners rather than member nations.

Darfur Dreams

In late March 2006, Cofer Black flew to Amman, Jordan, where he represented Blackwater at one of the world's premier war bazaars, the Special

Operations Forces Exhibition and Conference (SOFEX). More than 220 companies ranging from weapons manufacturers and arms dealers to military consultants and trainers to full-blown mercenary outfits were on hand to peddle their goods and services to wealthy governments from across the Middle East, North Africa, and the world. The organizers boasted that SOFEX is "the world's leading special operations forces, homeland security, counter terrorism and security forces exhibition and conference serving the global defense market."[10] After the Cold War, the Middle East quickly became one of the world's hungriest markets for military equipment and training services, and the biennial conference was a valued chance for military commanders and planners to examine and purchase the latest wares international war contractors and military merchants had to offer. In attendance were military delegations from forty-two countries and more than seventy-five hundred visitors from across the globe. As the conference's promotional materials boasted, "In the last decade, the Middle East has emerged as the largest importing region for security and military defence equipment, representing approximately 60% of the global defence expenditure."[11] As though to give the affair an extra air of legitimacy, the managing director of the conference, Amer Tabbah, touted the fact that SOFEX had been "accredited by the US Department of Commerce . . . showing the global trust and belief held by many."[12]

The SOFEX conference was sponsored by one of President Bush's closest Arab allies, King Abdullah of Jordan. Unlike his father, the late King Hussein, who opposed the 1991 Gulf War, the U.S./U.K.–educated Abdullah provided key support to the Bush administration in the build-up and execution of the Iraq invasion. Jordan has also served as a major transit point and staging ground for war-servicing corporations supporting the occupation in neighboring Iraq. Blackwater, like the White House, developed a special relationship with Jordan, opening an office in Amman early on in the Iraq occupation.[13] Since King Abdullah took over from his deceased father in 1999, he has worked assiduously to modernize and Westernize Jordan's military capabilities and to bolster its prominence as a force in the region. When

King Abdullah—himself a former Special Operations commander[14]—decided in 2004 to create a five-hundred-man special operations counterterrorism aviation unit, Jordan hired Blackwater to conduct the training for the elite force.[15] The contract, however, was held up by the State Department because of export-control regulations governing the sensitive nature of training foreign military forces. In early December 2004, King Abdullah visited Washington and reportedly raised the issue of the stalled Blackwater contract with almost every U.S. official he met.[16] Soon thereafter the contract was given the go-ahead by the Bush administration. The Jordanian unit would receive training in operating various militarized assault helicopters, such as Blackhawks and Hughes MD500s, for use in counterterror operations, quick-air assaults, and forward reconnaissance. Jordan said it would pay for the training with part of its approximately $1 billion in annual U.S. military assistance.[17] "The Jordanians came to us," said Erik Prince. "They hired us to help build their squadrons, to teach them how to fly at night on goggles, to mount operations out of a helicopter."[18]

As an exclamation point to King Abdullah's drive to remake the Jordanian military, just ahead of the SOFEX conference, officials of the kingdom confirmed they had completed plans for what they called the King Abdullah Special Operations Training Center in Jordan, a $100 million project also funded by the U.S. government.[19] King Abdullah said the training center project was being supervised by the U.S. Army Corps of Engineers, and the monarch's description sounded as though he was constructing a facility modeled after Blackwater's Moyock training compound. Abdullah said the facility would be used for the "training of both national and regional special operations forces, counter-terrorism forces, security and emergency service units, and to act as the premier live-fire training center for the Middle East."[20] Indeed, members of Jordan's elite antiterror unit, Battalion 71, had participated in Blackwater's 2004 SWAT Challenge in Moyock and had seen the company's vaunted U.S. training facility firsthand.[21]

Blackwater's special relationship with Jordan and its king made the company a miniphenomenon at the international war bazaar in Amman in March 2006. Blackwater chose the SOFEX conference to unveil its newly formed parachute team, which performed publicly for the first time at the conference opening at King Abdullah I air base.[22] But while Blackwater's parachute team may have wowed spectators on the ground, it was Cofer Black who stole the show on the opening day. Black "astonished" international Special Forces representatives when he declared that Blackwater was prepared to deploy a private brigade-sized force to conflict or crisis zones worldwide.[23] "It's an intriguing, good idea from a practical standpoint because we're low-cost and fast," Black said. "The issue is, who's going to let us play on their team?"[24] As an example, Black suggested that Blackwater could deploy its force in the Darfur region of Sudan, adding that Blackwater had already pitched the idea to unnamed U.S. and NATO officials. "About a year ago, we realized we could do it," Black said. "There is clear potential to conduct security operations at a fraction of the cost of NATO operations." Black was mobbed after his remarks by throngs of defense suppliers excited about the prospect of new markets being described by one of the industry's star players, not to mention one of America's most legendary spies. Black explained that Blackwater is a self-sustained operation. "We've war-gamed this with professionals," he said. "We can do this." He was quick to add that the company would not contradict U.S. policy by renting its services to enemies of the government. "We're an American company," Black declared. "We would get the approval of the U.S. government for anything we did for our friends overseas."[25]

After Black's remarks in Jordan, Blackwater vice president Chris Taylor expanded on his firm's vision for a Sudan deployment. "Of course we could provide security at refugee camps, defensive security," Taylor said. "What we seek to do first is to be the best deterrent that we can possibly be."[26] He boasted that Blackwater could mobilize faster than the UN or NATO. "In the time that it takes to put an internationally recognized body unit on the ground, I can be there in a third of that time and I will be 60 percent cheaper," Taylor told National Public Radio.[27] But independent experts disputed

Blackwater's claims. "It's comparing real apples with fictional oranges," said P. W. Singer of the Brookings Institution. "NATO or UN operations represent a full array of political commitment and activities, not simply a small set of guys with guns and a CASA 212. That's why they are expensive and completely different."[28]

Blackwater wasn't just talking about Darfur. Taylor also broadened the private-army-for-hire theme, floating the idea of the Iraqi government hiring Blackwater's men to quell attacks by resistance groups. "We clearly couldn't go into the whole country of Iraq," Taylor told the *Virginian-Pilot*. "But we might be able to go into a region or a city." Cofer Black and other company officials spun their vision for "peacekeeping," "stabilization," and "humanitarian" operations as being born of moralistic outrage over human suffering. The international community, they argued, is slow to respond and ineffective, while, as Black said in Jordan, "Blackwater spends a lot of time thinking, How can we contribute to the common good?" What Blackwater executives rarely, if ever, discuss in public is the tremendous profit to be made in servicing disasters, crises, and wars. In Jordan Blackwater and other mercenary firms aggressively promoted an internationalization of the rapid privatization of military and security the benefits of which they now enjoy in the United States. Under the soft banner of "humanitarianism," these companies hoped to take "business" away from international governmental bodies like the UN, NATO, and the African and European Unions. For Blackwater, such a transformation would mean permanent profit opportunity, limited only by the number of international crises, disasters, and conflicts. "World stability and peacemaking/-keeping operations have been criminally cost-ineffective and operationally failed," said Blackwater's Taylor. "Send 10,000 UN troops to Darfur? A colossal waste of money. You do not create security and peace by throwing more mediocre, uncommitted people into the fray."[29]

Singer, who has extensively studied the role of private military firms in international conflicts, observed the following about Blackwater's Sudan pitch:

The firms go about talking about how they would save kittens in trees
if only the big bad international community would let them, but the
situation is just far more complex than that. This kind of lobbying
often attempts to confuse folks. . . . The issue preventing effective
action in Darfur is not simply a matter of financial costs. That is,
there is not some imaginary price point that only if such firms could
come in under, it would solve things. The real problem is that it is a
political mess on the ground, there is no effective UN mandate, no
outside political will to engage for real, plus a Sudanese government
that is obstructionist and effectively one of the sides (meaning if you
go in without a mandate, you gotta be willing to kick the doors down,
destroy air bases, etc. which no firm has the capacity to do, and sends
the issue back to US/NATO/UN), thus far preventing a useful deployment. So even if you got firms willing, you still have to solve those
problems.[30]

But Sudan's value to Blackwater stretched beyond a single peacekeeping
contract or purported humanitarian concerns for the victims in Darfur. It
was Blackwater's ticket into a whole new world of potential growth—Darfur
became the rallying cry for a rebranding operation aimed at winning massive international contracts for mercenary firms. Unlike the invasion and
occupation of Iraq, which was overwhelmingly opposed by a majority of
the world, calls for intervention in Darfur are much more widespread and,
therefore, an easier sell for Blackwater and its allies for increasing the use of
private soldiers. Indeed, even at antiwar rallies, scores of protesters held
signs reading, "Out of Iraq, Into Darfur."

A quick survey of Sudan's vast natural resources dispels any notion that
U.S./corporate desires to move into Sudan derive from purely humanitarian
motives. First off, because of Sudan's designation by the State Department
as a sponsor of terrorism, U.S. corporations are prohibited from investing
in Sudan. As a result, China has become the major player in exploiting
Sudan's tremendous oil supplies.[31] While Sudan is not a member of the

Organization of Petroleum Exporting Countries, it was granted observer status in August 2001, a distinction reserved for significant global oil producers.[32] Four years later, its proven oil reserves had expanded sixfold to 1.6 billion barrels, the thirty-fifth-largest in the world[33]—all inaccessible to U.S. oil corporations. The China National Petroleum Corporation owns 40 percent—the largest single share—of the Greater Nile Petroleum Operating Company, the consortium that dominates Sudan's oilfields.[34] Sudan also has a significant natural gas reserve, one of the three largest deposits of high-purity uranium in the world, and the fourth-largest deposits of copper.[35] Regime change in Sudan would open up extremely lucrative investment opportunities to U.S. corporations, potentially capturing them from Chinese companies. It would also mean the end of a strong Islamic government that has continued to modernize, despite tough U.S.-led sanctions. Sending in private U.S. forces, under the guise of an international humanitarian mission, could give Washington a major foothold in Sudan for future action.

At the time of Cofer Black's trip to Jordan, Darfur was very much in the headlines. Black himself had spent a significant amount of time in the country as part of his work for the CIA. "Cofer and I have been speaking about our ability to help in Darfur ad infinitum, and that just pisses off the humanitarian world," said Chris Taylor. "They have problems with private security companies, not because of performance but because they think that in some cases it removes their ability to cross borders, to talk to both sides, to be neutral. And that's great, but the age-old question—is neutrality greater than saving one more life? What's the marginal utility on one more life?"[36] In February 2005, the month Black joined Blackwater, Erik Prince publicly raised for the first time the prospect of private peacekeepers at a symposium of the National Defense Industrial Association. "In areas where the UN is, where there's a lot of instability, sending a big, large-footprint conventional force is politically unpalatable; it's expensive, diplomatically difficult as well," Prince told the military gathering. "We could put together a multinational, professional force, supply it, manage it, lead it, put it under

UN or NATO or U.S. control, however it would best be done. We can help stabilize the situation."[37] Prince suggested that Blackwater could deploy a "Quick Reaction Force" to protect nongovernmental organizations in Darfur or other conflict areas. "You talk about Darfur: I don't think you need an 8,000-peacekeeper force," he said. "If there's an atrocity in progress, it's the Janjaweed [militia] that has to be stopped, and we have to move and stop the problem, and solve the immediate threat. Not bring an 8,000- or 10,000-man force."[38]

Similar to the company's use of the Columbine "massacre" to win new business, Blackwater was taking advantage of a global crisis that found parties spanning the political spectrum calling for intervention and decrying the perceived indifference of the UN and other international bodies. Sudan has become a pet cause of many of the right-wing Christian forces Blackwater is in bed with, not the least of which is Christian Freedom International—on whose small nine-member board both Erik Prince and his lobbyist Paul Behrends sit. Christian Freedom, founded by a consortium of well-connected Republican evangelicals, has been accused of using its "humanitarian aid" designation as a cover for missionary activities. Despite operating largely in Muslim countries, the group publicly states, "We believe the Bible to be the inspired, the only infallible, authoritative Word of God."[39]

The leadership of Christian Freedom has had a long relationship with the crisis in Sudan because of the Christian/Muslim conflict. Early on in its work there, CFI engaged in the practice of "slave redemptions"—purchasing Christians it believed to be enslaved—but later denounced the practice, saying the "redemptions" had become a source of funding for rebel groups and that people were "faking their stories of enslavement in an attempt to make money."[40] For years, CFI has cast its vision for Sudan in the very economic terms that have fueled the Bush administration's global policies and Blackwater's corporate strategy. "Many Christians in Southern Sudan desire to break free from international handouts and learn free-market principles, useful skills and technologies that will move them from dependence to independence," wrote Christian Freedom founder Jim Jacobson, the former Reagan official, in a 1999 column. "It's time to help the Christians of Sudan begin to walk. When this day comes—and it will come—slavery in Sudan will end."[41] Like Blackwater executives, Jacobson has disparaged the work of the United Nations, charging that the UN has a vested interest in keeping refugees impoverished. "I consider a lot of the [UN] organizations to be merchants of misery," Jacobson said. "The UN welfare organizations need people in miserable conditions to justify their own existence. The more people they have depending on them, the more money they get. We are trying to promote self-sufficiency to get people off handouts."

As Blackwater continued to aggressively push its Sudan campaign, Behrends—the company's top lobbyist—hit the airwaves of conservative radio to push for support. "We can be a huge help and catalyst and enabler to save those people," said Behrends in a 2006 interview on *The Danger Zone*, the syndicated radio program of the neoconservative Foundation for Defense of Democracies. On the program, Behrends was simply identified as a representative of Blackwater. "I'd like to make a point that any money that we made, we would pour back into the community there, clinics, schools, roads, whatever, because this is not a place that we want to make any money, this is just a place that we feel very strongly about helping," he said.[42]

As with many of Blackwater's deployments under the Bush administration, the company could rake in profits while serving the political and religious agenda of the administration and Erik Prince's theoconservative allies. But aside from the political and religious motivations for Blackwater's push to deploy in Sudan, the proposal provided a vivid glimpse into the corporate strategy Blackwater sees as a key to its future—repackaging mercenaries as peacekeepers. "There's a lot of crises in the world," said Singer, author of *Corporate Warriors*. "If they could get their foot in the door in them, it potentially opens up an entire new business sector for them."[43] While media reports at the time of the Jordan military conference suggested that Cofer Black's "peacekeeping" proposal was a new development in Blackwater's strategic vision, it had actually been in the works for at least a year. Author Robert

Young Pelton said the company developed a detailed proposal for Blackwater deploying in Sudan soon after then–Secretary of State Colin Powell visited Darfur in June 2004. "If you look at the presentation, it includes not only men with guns. They're offering helicopter gunships, a fighter bomber that has the capacity to drop cluster bombs, and [satellite-guided weapons], armored vehicles," Pelton said. "You say: 'Wait a minute. That's a lot of offensive force. What does that have to do with peacekeeping?'"[44]

In January 2006, three months before Cofer Black was dispatched to Jordan, Prince spoke to yet another military conference attended by scores of U.S. military officials. "One of the areas we could help is peacekeeping, perhaps. In Haiti you have a 9,000-man peacekeeping brigade at a cost of $496 million a year, the garrison commander just committed suicide, it's in total disarray," Prince said. "List for me—if you could—any really successful UN peacekeeping operations. I mean, I see the movie *Hotel Rwanda* and I get sick, and I say, Why did we let that happen? We can do something about that next time without a huge U.S. footprint. We can build a multinational brigade of professionals vetted to the same kind of State Department standards that they use for guarding embassies so we know we're not employing war criminals and bad guys, train them, vet them, equip them, and now you have a multinational capability to do something with."[45] But, as Singer pointed out, "there is simply no support for such an overall privatized operation at the UN. The official line from the spokesperson is that it is 'a nonstarter.' I find it telling that two separate high-level panels of world leaders look at how to fix peacekeeping, and neither one even put privatizing peacekeeping as a point of discussion, let alone support it. They also didn't talk about Martians coming in and running the peacekeeping operations, but then again, I guess Martians don't have the same lobbying effort."[46] In a highly promotional cover story about Blackwater in 2006 in the neoconservative *Weekly Standard*, Mark Hemingway wrote, "Currently the U.N. Department of Peacekeeping Operations has an annual budget of $7 billion, to say nothing of the billions in private charities and foreign aid pouring in to the world's worst places. Even those suspicious of Blackwater's motives must realize it makes good business sense that they would be interested in the work. Why chase after shady corporate clients when the mother lode is in helping people?"[47] He called Blackwater "the alpha and omega of military outsourcing."[48]

Not long after Black's Sudan proposal in Jordan, Blackwater received boosts for its cause from several prominent commentators. Max Boot, a senior fellow at the Council on Foreign Relations, penned a widely distributed column in the Los Angeles Times called "Darfur Solution: Send in the Mercenaries."[49] Boot wrote:

If the so-called civilization nations of the world were serious about ending what the U.S. government has described as genocide, they would not fob off the job on the U.N. They would send their own troops. But of course they're not serious. At least not that serious. But perhaps there is a way to stop the killing even without sending an American or European army. Send a private army. A number of commercial security firms such as Blackwater USA are willing, for the right price, to send their own forces, made up in large part of veterans of Western militaries, to stop the genocide. We know from experience that such private units would be far more effective than any U.N. peacekeepers. In the 1990s, the South African firm Executive Outcomes and the British firm Sandline made quick work of rebel movements in Angola and Sierra Leone. Critics complain that these mercenaries offered only a temporary respite from the violence, but that was all they were hired to do. Presumably longer-term contracts could create longer-term security, and at a fraction of the cost of a U.N. mission. Yet this solution is deemed unacceptable by the moral giants who run the United Nations. They claim that it is objectionable to employ— sniff—mercenaries. More objectionable, it seems, than passing empty resolutions, sending ineffectual peacekeeping forces and letting genocide continue.[50]

Boot subsequently suggested that Blackwater or another mercenary firm could be deployed in Sudan after being hired "by an ad hoc group of concerned nations, or even by philanthropists like Bill Gates or George Soros."[51] But it wasn't just conservatives lining up to support Blackwater. One of the most venerable newsmen in U.S. history, Ted Koppel, wrote an op-ed for the *New York Times* published on May 22, 2006, called "These Guns for Hire," which opened with the line, "There is something terribly seductive about the notion of a mercenary army."[52] Koppel went on to provide "only a partial list of factors that would make a force of latter-day Hessians seem attractive:"

> Growing public disenchantment with the war in Iraq; The prospect of an endless campaign against global terrorism; An over-extended military backed by an exhausted, even depleted force of reservists and National Guardsmen; The unwillingness or inability of the United Nations or other multinational organizations to dispatch adequate forces to deal quickly with hideous, large-scale atrocities (see Darfur and Congo); The expansion of American corporations into more remote, fractious and potentially hostile settings.

After running through that list, which seemed to have been lifted from mercenary industry talking points, Koppel opined that "Just as the all-volunteer military relieved the government of much of the political pressure that had accompanied the draft, so a rent-a-force, harnessing the privilege of every putative warrior to hire himself out for more than he could ever make in the direct service of Uncle Sam, might relieve us of an array of current political pressures."

Koppel then spent a fair portion of his op-ed presenting a virtual advertisement for Blackwater:

> So, what about the inevitable next step—a defensive military force paid for directly by the corporations that would most benefit from its protection? If, for example, an insurrection in Nigeria threatens that nation's ability to export oil (and it does), why not have

Chevron or Exxon Mobil underwrite the dispatch of a battalion or two of mercenaries?

Chris Taylor, the vice president for strategic initiatives and corporate strategy for Blackwater USA, wanted to be sure I understood that such a thing could only happen with the approval of the Nigerian government and at least the tacit understanding of Washington. But could Blackwater provide a couple of battalions under those circumstances? "600 people in a battalion," he answered. "I could source 1,200 people, yes. There are people all over the world who have honorably served in their military or police organizations. I can go find honorable, vetted people, recruit them, train them to the standard we require."

It could have the merit of stabilizing oil prices, thereby serving the American national interest, without even tapping into the federal budget. Meanwhile, oil companies could protect some of their more vulnerable overseas interests without the need to embroil Congress in the tiresome question of whether Americans should be militarily engaged in a sovereign third world nation.

What Koppel neglected to mention in his piece was the likelihood that the type of insurrection that Blackwater's forces could potentially be fighting off in Nigeria in defense of Chevron or ExxonMobil could be a popular one, seeking to reclaim Nigeria's vast petrol-resources from the U.S. government/oil corporation–backed kleptocracy that has brutally governed Africa's most-populous nation for decades. Nor did Koppel mention that transnational oil corporations already use brutal forces to defend their interests from indigenous Nigerians, particularly in the oil-rich Niger Delta. Nigerian playwright Ken Saro-Wiwa was executed— hanged—with eight others in 1995 for his resistance to the Shell Oil Corporation, and Chevron has been deeply implicated in the killing of protesters in the Niger Delta.[53] What was most disturbing about Koppel's op-ed was that he appeared to be lending his credibility and reputation to the mercenary rebranding cause—at a crucial moment. In late 2006, Bush eased sanctions on Christian southern Sudan, paving the way for Blackwater to train the region's forces.

While Blackwater's campaign intensified, one of the company's few Congressional critics saw the talk of deployment in Darfur as an ominous sign. Blackwater "has the power and the influence with the administration that [leads Blackwater] to believe that it could be a force stronger than NATO, for example, in a place like Darfur," said Representative Jan Schakowsky. "Which means that suddenly you've got a for-profit corporation going around the world that is more powerful than states; can effect regime change, possibly, where they may want to go; that seems to have all the support that it needs from this Administration (that is also pretty adventurous around the world and operating under the cover of darkness). It raises questions about democracies, about states, about who influences policy around the globe, about relationships among some countries."[54] Maybe, Schakowsky said, it was Blackwater's goal "to render state coalitions like NATO irrelevant in the future, that they'll be the ones and open to the highest bidder. Who really does determine war and peace around the world?

"It's really disturbing and has enormous consequences," Schakowsky said. "Who are they loyal to? And it also empowers, then, an administration like the Bush administration—if they can engage in this kind of private warmaking or a private army, then what do they even need us for? They can operate in a totally separate arena and engage in conflicts all over the world, and it seems they don't much need to consult with us about it."

Blackwater and the Sleeping Lion

Cofer Black has advised others in the mercenary industry to "be opportunistic"[55]—a quality that has come naturally to Blackwater. "We have a dynamic business plan that is twenty years long," bragged Blackwater president Gary Jackson in the summer of 2006. "We're not going anywhere."[56] But while Blackwater has enjoyed almost unparalleled prosperity in the wake of 9/11, the rise of the Bush administration, and a Republican-controlled Congress, its executives know that such a moment, filled with such powerful backers in charge, may not present itself again soon, if ever. While the Bush administration enthusiastically encouraged the privatization of the military and the use of unsavory forces and tactics, future administrations may not be so thrilled about the idea of using mercenaries. An obvious part of that "dynamic business plan" Jackson spoke of is a sophisticated rebranding campaign aimed at shaking the mercenary image and solidifying the "legitimate" role of private soldiers in the fabric of U.S. foreign and domestic policy, as well as that of international bodies such as the UN and NATO. Though the Bush administration will govern for a finite period of time, Blackwater and its allies have taken full advantage of the overwhelming enthusiasm for their cause in the chambers of power during the Bush years to make swift headway in their long-term rebranding mission.

The rebranding is happening on many levels, and the terminology is already resonating in the broader discourse. Mercenary firms are now called "private military companies" or "private security companies." Rather than mercs, their men are now "private soldiers" or "civilian contractors." While there is fierce competition among the mercenaries, they clearly recognize the need to develop a common language to promote their cause. Many firms have their own lobbyists on contract. Blackwater was instrumental to the rapid growth of the mercenary trade association, the Orwellian-named International Peace Operations Association. Its logo is a cartoon sleeping lion that would fit perfectly in a Disney sequel to *The Lion King*. Under the auspices of the IPOA, Blackwater and its allies have become aggressive promoters of regulation of the "private security/military industry." IPOA boasts, "We are in the business of peace because peace matters," and spokespeople say the organization is made up of "the most professional forward-thinking and ethical companies in the industry."[57] Among its members are many of the leading mercenary firms operating in the "war on terror": Blackwater, ArmorGroup, Erinys, Hart Security, and MPRI.[58]

Though many corporations shun the idea of regulation and oversight, Blackwater assumed a leadership role in pushing for such policies—at least those that fit its agenda. Blackwater "has been a leading proponent of increased regulation, accountability and transparency, which undoubtedly is good for any industry," asserted IPOA spokesperson J. J. Messner.[59] The reason was simple: in the long run, it is better for business. But, more important, it also allows the mercenary companies to favorably shape the rules that govern their deployments, as Blackwater did in the aftermath of the Fallujah ambush when it was reported to be "leading a lobbying effort by private security firms and other contractors to try to block congressional or Pentagon efforts to bring their companies and employees under the same justice code as [active-duty] servicemen."[60]

Well aware of the severe image problems plaguing the mercenary industry, the IPOA has attempted to bring in representatives from Amnesty International and other respected human rights organizations as consultants.[61] The IPOA boasts of a "code of conduct" written with "the input of dozens of international and non-governmental organizations, human rights lawyers, and scholars."[62] In Congressional testimony in 2006, Chris Taylor pointed to his company's membership in the IPOA as evidence that Blackwater is "committed to defining the standards by which our independent contractors are credentialed as qualified to work in the industry, improving the federal contracting and oversight process, providing increased transparency in business operations, and encouraging discussion of our industry so that it can become more fully integrated into the process of finding solutions to difficult challenges."[63] Taylor has also suggested that "contracting agencies" use the IPOA as a "certification, somewhat like an ISO 9000 quality-management program."[64]

The IPOA Code, which all member companies are required to sign, commits its members to "agree to follow all rules of international humanitarian law and human rights law that are applicable as well as all relevant international protocols and conventions."[65] It has sections on transparency, ethics, and accountability, and IPOA warns: "Signatories who fail to uphold any provision contained in this Code may be subject to dismissal from IPOA at the discretion of the IPOA Board of Directors."[66] But the IPOA Code is not a binding document with any legal weight whatsoever. Moreover, the chair of the IPOA board of directors as of 2006 was Chris Taylor[67]—an unlikely candidate to oversee Blackwater's expulsion from the group in the event of a violation of human rights.

The crucial role the IPOA has played in the rebranding campaign has been to lobby lawmakers, journalists, and human rights groups to support greater privatization of military and peacekeeping operations by promoting the idea that society stands to benefit from a regulated mercenary industry. At the same time, its completely unenforceable, nonlegal code of conduct is used by the mercenary companies as a talking point to show how responsible and conscientious they are—voluntarily.[68] The IPOA has functioned as the political wing of the organized mercenary industry, which it has renamed the "peace and stability industry."[69]

Despite the fact that there were an estimated one hundred eighty thousand contractors operating in Iraq as of spring 2008, there remained no effective oversight system in place, nor was there a legal body with effective jurisdiction over the contractors. Paul Bremer's Order 17, which granted contractors immunity from prosecution in Iraq, remained the law of the land under successive puppet governments—from Iyad Allawi to Nouri al-Maliki—that ruled Iraq after Bremer departed and the CPA was dismantled. In theory, it is the responsibility of the home countries of contractors to police them. In reality, this has translated to impunity. That point was hit home in a dramatic way in one of the rare Congressional hearings on contractors in Iraq, which took place in June 2006. Representative Dennis Kucinich questioned Shay Assad, the Pentagon's director of Defense Procurement and Acquisition, the department in the DoD responsible for contractors. Kucinich pointed out that U.S. troops are subjected to enforceable rules of engagement and have been prosecuted for violations in Iraq, while contractors are not:

KUCINICH: Do you know what the statute of limitation is for murder in the United States?

ASSAD: No, I don't, Mr. Congressman.

KUCINICH: There isn't—there isn't one. Now, if someone connected
with a private contracting company was involved in the murder of
a civilian, would the Department be ready to recommend their
prosecution?

ASSAD: Sir, I'm just not qualified to answer that question.[70]

Incredulous, Kucinich asked Assad and the other government officials on
the panel, "Anybody here qualified to answer that, and if they're not, why
are you here, with all due respect?" Kucinich pointed out that as of the date
of the hearing in June 2006, "no security contractor has been prosecuted"
for crimes in Iraq (that remained the case as of spring 2008). He then
directly asked Assad, "Would the Department of Defense be prepared to see
a prosecution proffered against any private contractor who is demonstrated
to have unlawfully killed a civilian?"

"Sir, I can't answer that question," Assad replied.

"Wow," Kucinich shot back. "Think about what that means. These private
contractors can get away with murder." Contractors, Kucinich said, "do not
appear to be subject to any laws at all and so therefore they have more of a
license to be able to take the law into their own hands." (In late 2006, Senator Lindsey Graham quietly inserted language into the 2007 defense
authorization bill, which Bush subsequently signed, that sought to place
contractors under the Pentagon's UCMJ, but what effective impact—if
any—this could have remains unclear as of this writing, with experts predicting resistance from the private war industry.)

At that same hearing, Blackwater's Taylor and IPOA founder Doug
Brooks were the two primary defenders of the mercenary firms. "This
industry is highly responsible," Brooks told the Congressional hearing.
"IPOA includes the most professional forward-thinking and ethical companies in the industry, and all members are always publicly committed to our
code of conduct." But while Brooks was preaching from the accountability
gospel in front of the U.S. Congress, he was simultaneously fighting

attempts to rein in mercenaries on the African continent, where the industry stands to make substantial money if allowed to operate in Sudan and other crisis zones.

The South African Example

Perhaps the most visible work the IPOA has done in recent years was not actually in the United States, though it has far-reaching implications for Blackwater and other U.S. companies—particularly when it comes to their aspirations for peacekeeping deployments on the African continent. Despite their rhetoric about supporting regulation of the industry, the IPOA and Brooks were deeply engaged in a coordinated effort to defeat South Africa's groundbreaking antimercenary legislation, supported by the overwhelming majority of the country's elected legislators.

South Africa—indeed, the African continent—has had a long, bloody history with white mercenaries. After the fall of the apartheid regime in the early 1990s, many white South African soldiers and police, who had spent the past years terrorizing black Africans, found themselves looking for new jobs. An unknown number of these soldiers farmed out their services to companies, governments, and counterrevolutionary causes, bringing yet more infamy to South Africa—this time as a base of operations for mercenaries. Among the most notorious South African companies, Executive Outcomes was founded in 1989 by a former apartheid-era commander and operated openly until it was shut down in 1998. Among its clients were the diamond giant DeBeers and the government of Angola, where EO was contracted in 1993 to retake strategic oil-rich areas on behalf of government forces. But EO is perhaps best known for its operations in diamond-rich Sierra Leone, where its forces were contracted to defend the government from a rebellion by Foday Sankoh's Revolutionary United Front movement, which was committing widespread human rights abuses. The government paid EO approximately $35 million—a third of its annual defense budget—in 1995 to crush the insurgency after the U.S. and British governments and the UN declined to intervene.[72] It took EO just nine days to stop the rebellion and two days to retake the prized Kono diamond fields. Supporters of the mercenary industry have held up the work of EO and Sandline (Tim Spicer's old company) as evidence of the success of private forces.

But the ends do not always justify the means. EO's success was largely attributed to the fact that it was a descendant of elite South African apartheid forces from which it had inherited a vast system of corporate connections, underground networks, and counterinsurgency apparatuses throughout Africa that had been used to oppress black populations and dissidents.[73] Despite the touting of the tactical "successes" of EO in Angola and Sierra Leone, there was a broader issue raised by the involvement of mercenaries in international conflicts: who determines international order? The UN? Nation-states? Rich people? Corporations? And to whom are these forces accountable? This issue assumed a higher profile with the wide privatization present in the Afghanistan and Iraq occupations. While the United States largely avoided the issue of accountability for private forces, that was not the case in South Africa, with its firsthand tumultuous and lengthy experience playing host to mercenaries. After the apartheid government fell and the Truth and Reconciliation process began, calls spread for shutting down mercenary firms, especially given how closely linked many of them were to the apartheid regime. This led to the enactment of antimercenary legislation in South Africa in 1998.

But just a few years later, with reports of South African mercenaries deployed in Iraq, lawmakers in Johannesburg alleged that the law was not being applied effectively. They asserted the legislation had resulted in "a small number of prosecutions and convictions,"[74] notwithstanding the clear evidence of mercenary activities by South Africans—and not just in Iraq. The Prohibition of Mercenary Activities Act, introduced in the South African Parliament in 2005, was sparked not only by Iraq but also by the alleged involvement of more than sixty South Africans in an alleged plot to overthrow the government of Equatorial Guinea in 2004. The incident grabbed international headlines because of the alleged involvement of Sir Mark Thatcher, son of former British Prime Minister Margaret Thatcher.[75] The small country of five hundred thousand had recently discovered great oil reserves and at the time had become Africa's third-largest oil producer. The alleged leader of the coup attempt was Simon Mann, an ex–British SAS officer, a founder of both Executive Outcomes and Sandline, and a friend of Mark Thatcher's.[76]

The sponsors of the South African bill said that the coup plot demonstrated that "mercenary activities are undertaken from within the borders" of South Africa and pointedly noted, "There is a continuation in the recruitment of South Africans by so-called private military companies from outside the Republic, to provide military and security services in areas of armed conflict (such as Iraq)."[77] At the time, the South African government officially estimated that four thousand of its citizens were employed in conflict areas across the globe, including an estimated two thousand in Iraq.[78] Most of these were members of the country's white minority.[79] Other estimates put the number of South Africans deployed globally and in Iraq much higher.

The act sought to prevent any South African from participating "as a combatant for private gain in an armed conflict," or from involvement in "any act aimed at overthrowing a government or undermining the constitutional order, sovereignty or territorial integrity of a state."[80] It required South Africans seeking employment with private security or military firms to obtain permission from the government and provided for fines and imprisonment for violators. It also banned South Africans from serving in foreign armies if the South African government opposed that country's involvement in a war or conflict. At the time, some eight hundred South Africans were active in the British military, along with an unknown number serving in the Israeli military.[81] Interestingly, the act allowed South African participation in "legitimate armed struggles, including struggles waged, in accordance with international humanitarian law, for national liberation; self-determination; independence against colonialism, or resistance against occupation, aggression or domination by foreign nationals or foreign forces."

Among the most prominent forces to oppose South Africa's attempt to rein in mercenaries were Doug Brooks and the IPOA. Teamed with South African minority political parties and mercenary firms, Brooks and the IPOA worked feverishly to prevent its passage. In the year leading up to the vote on the legislation, Brooks wrote op-eds and policy papers and traveled to Johannesburg, where he met with members of Parliament. He expressed frustration that lawmakers had "eschewed" the participation of the mercenary industry in drafting the legislation[82] and said its passage could prove "disastrous" for private firms operating in hot spots and could undermine peacekeeping operations. "Many international efforts will be at risk . . . (some) will have to close their operations if they can't rely on South Africans," Brooks pleaded with lawmakers. "South Africans are more robust, able to live under more austere conditions, have increased flexibility and can adapt to changing conditions."[83] Brooks found himself on the side of white South African politicians who complained the act targeted white former members of the armed forces who would now find it "virtually impossible to find work."[84] While Brooks was mobilizing against South Africa's attempts to crack down on mercenaries, he was also showing his true agenda: aggressively promoting the use of mercenaries on the African continent, not just in Sudan, but also in the Congo and other crisis zones. "NATO is insanely expensive; it's not a cost-effective organization. Neither is the [African Union]. Private companies would be much, much cheaper," Brooks declared.[85]

On August 29, 2006, the Prohibition of Mercenary Activities Act passed by a whopping 211-28 vote in South Africa's National Assembly.[86] South Africa's Defense Minister Mosiuoa Lekota rejected the attempted rebranding of mercenaries, framing the debate by drawing on Africa's bloody history with mercenaries, which he said dated back to 1960 in the newly independent Congo. "No sooner than Congo achieved independence, the dogs of war were unleashed on the country," he said. "Mercenaries are the scourge of poor areas of the world, especially Africa," Lekota declared shortly before the act was passed. "These are killers for hire. They rent out their skills to the highest bidder. Anybody that has money can hire these human beings and turn them into killing machines or cannon fodder."[87] South Africa had dealt a rare blow to the rapidly expanding world of mercenary firms, but it was just one setback in a story of progress for the industry as a whole—and Blackwater in particular.

Greystone

Blackwater's plan wasn't just about breaking into the world of peacekeeping. Prince and his allies envisioned a total reshaping of the U.S. military, one that would fit perfectly into the aggressive, offensive foreign policy that had emanated from the White House since 9/11. The main obstacles that prevented the Bush administration from expanding its wars of occupation and aggression were a lack of military manpower and the on-the-ground insurgencies its interventions provoked. Domestic opposition to wars of aggression results in fewer people volunteering to serve in the armed forces, which historically deflates the war drive or forces a military draft. At the same time, international opposition has made it harder for Washington to persuade other governments to support its wars and occupations. But with private mercenary companies, these dynamics change dramatically, as the pool of potential soldiers available to an aggressive administration is limited only by the number of men across the globe willing to kill for money. With the aid of mercenaries, you don't need a draft or even the support of your own public to wage wars of aggression, nor do you need a coalition of "willing" nations to aid you. If Washington cannot staff an occupation or invasion with its national forces, the mercenary firms offer a privatized alternative—including Blackwater's twenty-one-thousand-man contractor database.[88] If the national armies of other states will not join a "coalition of the willing," Blackwater and its allies offer an alternative internationalization of the force by recruiting private soldiers from across the globe. If foreign governments are not on board, foreign soldiers can still be bought.

"The increasing use of contractors, private forces, or, as some would say, 'mercenaries' makes wars easier to begin and to fight—it just takes money and not the citizenry," said CCR's Michael Ratner. "To the extent a population is called upon to go to war, there is resistance, a necessary resistance to prevent wars of self-aggrandizement, foolish wars, and, in the case of the United States, hegemonic imperialist wars. Private forces are almost a necessity for a United States bent on retaining its declining empire."

With an adventurous President in the White House, mercenaries could enable an endless parade of invasions, covert operations, occupations, coups d'etat—all with the layers of bureaucratic protections, plausible deniability, and disregard for the will (or lack thereof) of the population. Moreover, private soldiers are not counted among the dead, providing yet another incentive for the government to utilize them. "These forces can be employed without a lot of publicity—and that's a very useful characteristic for any government. It's politically easier, and there is less red tape," said Thomas Pogue, a former Navy SEAL who enlisted in the Blackwater Academy. "We're expendable. If ten contractors die, it's not the same as if ten soldiers die. Because people will say that we were in it for the money. And that has a completely different connotation with the American public."[89]

While Blackwater's operations in Iraq and New Orleans have garnered the most attention and controversy, they are temporary deployments and only part of the company's global reach and aspirations. Despite the firm's projection as an all-American business ready to fight genocide at the drop of a hat, Blackwater is deeply invested in a secretive project that has the company recruiting mercenaries in some of the shadiest human-rights-abusing locales on the planet, some of whom could be repackaged as privatized international peacekeepers or ground forces in another military action of the coalition of the willing. The project is called Greystone.

About a month after the infamous 2004 Fallujah ambush, Blackwater's quietly registered "Greystone Limited" in the U.S. government's Central Contracting office, which listed its "business start date" as May 13, 2004.[90] But instead of incorporating it in North Carolina or Virginia or Delaware, like Blackwater's other divisions, Greystone was registered offshore in the Caribbean island-nation of Barbados.[91] It was duly classified by the U.S. government as a "tax-exempt" "corporate entity," listing as its services: "Security Guards and Patrol Services."[92] But this description, which evokes images of shopping mall guards, is nothing like the picture that emerges in Greystone's promotional literature and videos for prospective clients. Blackwater's original Web site for Greystone opened with a flash presentation where the word

"Greystone" appeared on the screen over a large rock. Suddenly from the top of the screen, a fancy silver medieval sword came smashing into the rock forming the "T" in GreysTone à la King Arthur. After this little intro, the site then jumped to a page with the sword in the stone next to the motto "In Support of Peace and Security Everywhere!"

On February 19, 2005, Blackwater held an extravagant, VIP, invite-only Greystone "inauguration" at the swank Ritz-Carlton hotel in Washington, D.C. The guest list for the seven-hour event was a revealing mixture of foreign embassy diplomats, weapons manufacturers, oil companies, and representatives of the International Monetary Fund.[93] The diplomats were from countries like Uzbekistan, Yemen, the Philippines, Romania, Indonesia, Tunisia, Algeria, Hungary, Poland, Croatia, Kenya, Angola, and Jordan. Several of those countries' defense or military attachés attended. "It is more difficult than ever for your country to successfully protect its interests against diverse and complicated threats in today's grey world where the solutions to your security concerns are no longer as simple as black and white," Greystone's promotional pamphlet told attendees. "Greystone is an international security services company that offers your country or organization a complete solution to your most pressing security needs. We have the personnel, logistical support, equipment, and expertise to solve your most critical security problems."[94] The invitation promised guests "the opportunity to meet with recognized experts from the global security industry. You will have the opportunity to see cutting edge capabilities presentations, and view tactical displays showcasing innovative equipment, and technology solutions for the global war on terror."[95] The keynote speaker was Cofer Black, who, on the invitation, was identified only as the "Former Ambassador for Counterterrorism Department of State and Former Director of CIA's Counterterrorism Center."

Materials distributed to prospective corporate and nation-state clients proclaimed, "Greystone is dedicated to providing the best physical security assets from around the world in support of freedom, peacemaking, and the maintenance of peace. Our international focus enables us to develop unique and creative solutions to match each client's individual needs." Greystone said its forces were prepared for "Ready Deployment in Support of National Security Objectives as well as Private Interests." Among the "services" offered were Mobile Security Teams, which, among other functions, could be employed for personal security operations, surveillance, and countersurveillance. Greystone's Proactive Engagement Teams could be hired "to meet emergent or existing security requirements for client needs overseas. Our teams are ready to conduct stabilization efforts, asset protection and recovery, and emergency personnel withdrawal." It also offered a wide range of training services, including in "defensive and offensive small group operations." Greystone boasted that it "maintains and trains a workforce drawn from a diverse base of former special operations, defense, intelligence, and law enforcement professionals ready on a moment's notice for global deployment."

A Greystone two-minute promotional video opens with the sword-in-the-stone graphic and quickly fades to a scene of a Blackwater helicopter delivering supplies to its troops on a rooftop.[96] Next it cuts to a scene of mercenaries in civilian clothes distributing aid by hand to a desperate crowd of people, perhaps Iraqis or Afghans. A cheesy Casio keyboard beat plays in the background. The video then runs through a montage of images: heavily armed commandos in camouflage and ski masks storming a room, paramilitaries patrolling a smoky street, troops busting down a door and throwing a smoke grenade inside. Then the words "Providing Protection" flash on the screen, and mercenaries are shown securing a perimeter with a K-9 unit before escorting a "principal" from his SUV to a building. The words "International Security" appear before dissolving into a smoke-filled corridor through which black-clad commandos storm forward, weapons raised. More images of VIP escorts, then a helicopter zooming over a body of water. The video cuts to scenes of jungle warfare, then to paratroopers jumping from planes, and back to the jungle. "Vulnerability Assessment" flashes on the screen. A camouflaged face appears, followed by white men in black T-shirts, khaki vests, and sunglasses wielding automatic weapons as they escort another VIP from her vehicle. The video cuts to a car aggressively cutting off another vehicle before the Greystone sword-in-stone logo reappears.

While Blackwater portrays itself as an all-American operation, even Greystone's name is a play on the moral and legal ambiguity of its mission and modern warfare, one backed up by its recruitment efforts. Greystone's application asked prospective mercenaries for their "recruitment source"— listing agencies with names like Beowulf, Spartan, and AVI. The countries from which Greystone claimed to draw recruits were: the Philippines, Chile, Nepal, Colombia, Ecuador, El Salvador, Honduras, Panama, and Peru. It asked applicants to check off their qualifications in weapons: AK-47 rifle, Glock 19, M-16 series rifle, M-4 carbine rifle, machine gun, mortar, and shoulder-fired weapons (RPG, LAAW). Among the qualifications the application sought: Sniper, Marksman, Door Gunner, Explosive Ordnance, Counter Assault Team.

Outside of its targeted marketing to prospective clients, Blackwater was quiet about Greystone. Not long after launching the project, Blackwater took down the original Web site, replacing it with a softer image and a new brand. The sword in the stone was gone, and so, too, was the overt combat imagery, replaced by a camouflaged soldier in a beret holding a small child on his lap with the phrase "Humanitarian Aid" above the photo. Another picture was of a man in a fancy suit speaking into a walkie-talkie—this picture was labeled "Security." The new slogan, "Fostering Stability, Promoting Peace," was splashed across the top of the page, and the services offered were security, training, logistics, and humanitarian aid/peacekeeping. Greystone's mission statement too had been revamped. "Greystone focuses on providing stability to locations experiencing turmoil whether caused by armed conflict, epidemics or natural or man-made disasters. Greystone has the ability to quickly and efficiently deploy anywhere in the world to create a more secure environment for our customers," the new statement read. Greystone could support "large scale stability operations requiring large numbers of people to assist in securing a region. Our goal is to foster a positive environment that promotes civilian security allowing commerce to flourish."

"The Knights of the Round Table"

The same month Blackwater launched Greystone, Erik Prince began, at least publicly, raising the prospect of creating what he called a "contractor brigade" to supplement the conventional U.S. military. "There's consternation in the DoD about increasing the permanent size of the Army," Prince told a military symposium in Washington, D.C., in early 2005. "We want to add 30,000 people, and they talked about costs of anywhere from $3.6 billion to $4 billion to do that. Well, by my math, that comes out to about $135,000 per soldier."[97] Prince confidently asserted Blackwater could do it cheaper. For Prince it was a rare public appearance, and like most of his speeches, it was based on the free-market gospel and delivered in front of a military audience.

That was the case in January 2006, when Prince addressed "West 2006," a massive conference of military commanders, weapons manufacturers and dealers, contractors, and other militarist entities. It was sponsored by the biggest names in war technology: Raytheon, Boeing, General Dynamics, Lockheed Martin, and Northrop Grumman.[98] Prince was the lone mercenary representative on a panel of senior military commanders including Dennis Hejlik, commander of the Marine Corps Special Operations Command; Sean Pybus, commander of the Naval Special Warfare Group; and Col. Edward Reeder, Commander of the Seventh Special Forces Group. "Why us? Why a private organization? Why am I even here?" Prince asked rhetorically. "This idea of private organizations doing things that used to be the sole realm of the U.S. government."[99] In his presentation, Prince outlined the rapid rise of Blackwater, speaking proudly of building his "field of dreams," Blackwater's massive compound in Moyock, North Carolina. "We now have 7,300 acres, it's a large private military facility," he said as he gave an overview of some of the company's operations, saying it trains about thirty-five thousand military and "law enforcement" representatives a year, including active-duty military, special operations forces, and personnel from the Department of Homeland Security as well as state, federal, and local governments. "We're vertically integrated up and down across the board," he said. "We have our own target business, we do full-on construction of tactical training facilities, we have our own aviation arm with twenty aircraft, canine operation with sixty dog teams deployed overseas, full-on construction, and a private intelligence service." At the time, Prince said Blackwater had eighteen hundred people deployed around the world, "all of them in dangerous places."

Prince also spoke with remarkable candor about his vision for the future of mercenaries. "When you ship overnight, do you use the postal service or do you use FedEx?" he asked the crowd and his fellow panelists. "It's kind of—our corporate goal is to do for the national security apparatus what FedEx did to the postal service—never going to replace it, but we want to make it run better, faster, smarter, make people think out of the box." The Department of Defense, Prince told the audience, consumes 48 percent of the world's military spending, "and it's very hard for an organization that large to transform itself. But if it has outside parties that are doing somewhat similar things, it gives people something to benchmark against." Comparing the military industry to the auto industry, Prince said, "General Motors can only get better if it looks at how Toyota and Honda do. It makes them think out of the box and it gives them a vehicle to perform against." Prince told a story of how in 1991, after the fall of the Berlin wall, he was driving down the Autobahn in Germany in a rented car. Suddenly, "a Mercedes S500 blew by me at about 140 mph. It was the latest and greatest Mercedes that was available, 300 horsepower, airbags, automatic transmissions, all the bells and whistles." But after the West German-manufactured Mercedes passed Prince, a slow-moving Tribant—the national car of communist East Germany—changed lanes in front of the Mercedes, almost causing an accident. "I thought, what a study in contrasts," Prince said. "You have the same two countries, the same language, same culture, same background, different command structure: one of them was central planning, one of them was much more free-market oriented, innovative, risk-taking, and efficient."

If you take Prince's message that day at face value, it all boils down to efficiency. At the end of his talk, Prince said he didn't want to "slight" the Pentagon. "The DoD has great numbers of fantastic people, but they get so trapped in so many bureaucratic layers that have been around for probably the last seventy years that it stifles a lot of innovation," he said. "We come with a different footprint." That "small footprint," which Prince loves to speak about, is growing larger by the day. And it is growing because of the very concerted effort of a powerful clique of modern-day mercenaries who understand public relations, hire lobbyists, and engage in spin, and who have been very effective at riding the tide of privatization. As the size of the pool of official active-duty U.S. soldiers has plummeted over the past twenty years, from 2.1 million in the 1980s to 1.3 million at the time of the 2003 Iraq invasion,[100] the payouts and contracting to mercenary firms have skyrocketed. Before the United States invaded Iraq, from 1994 to 2002, the Pentagon doled out more than three thousand contracts to U.S.-based firms worth more than $300 billion.[101] As P. W. Singer has observed, "While contractors have long accompanied U.S. armed forces, the wholesale outsourcing of U.S. military services since the 1990s is unprecedented."[102] This certainly escalated under the Bush administration with Defense Secretary Donald Rumsfeld pledging early on in the war on terror to "pursue additional opportunities to outsource and privatize,"[103] in part because of his personal obsession that the modern military has a "small footprint." As *New York Times* columnist Paul Krugman observed, "Conservatives make a fetish out of privatization of government functions; after the 2002 elections, George Bush announced plans to privatize up to 850,000 federal jobs. At home, wary of a public backlash, he has moved slowly on that goal. But in Iraq, where there is little public or Congressional oversight, the administration has privatized everything in sight."[104] Iraq was not the end of the trend but rather the model for the future. "Militaries are smaller than they were at the end of the Cold War," said IPOA's Doug Brooks. "So if anybody wants to do anything, essentially they have to go to the private sector now. And what they're finding is that it's faster, better, cheaper. Militaries are incredibly capable organizations, but they're not designed to be cost-effective."[105]

There is no question that the Fallujah killings in March 2004 boosted Blackwater's corporate success. On the one hand—some would say the cynical way of seeing things—you could say that Erik Prince cashed in on the deaths and saw right away the benefits of the highly publicized killings. Another way of looking at it is that the fortuitously timed killings happened to provide Blackwater the perfect venue and audience to further its already-active campaign to blaze a path toward greater privatization—with it, of course, at the forefront. The mercenary rebranding campaign, aimed at accelerating the pace of privatization to maximize profits, has allowed companies like Blackwater to build a permanent institutionalized presence for themselves within the structures of the state. The rebranding provides great PR opportunities and recruitment rhetoric while rolling out a ready-made justification scheme for politicians and various bureaucracies to outsource and privatize more and more taxpayer-funded military and security operations leading to added legitimacy and ever-growing profits. And this brings it all full circle: at the end of the day, it still boils down to money—a lot of it.

Exactly how much money the U.S. government has paid mercenary firms is nearly impossible to pin down—a fact due in no small part to the apparent lack of transparent or comprehensive bookkeeping. A June 2006 Government Accountability Office report acknowledged "neither the Department of State, nor DOD, nor the USAID—the principal agencies responsible for Iraq reconstruction efforts—had complete data on the costs associated with using private security providers."[106] But the report found that "as of December 2004, the agencies and contractors we reviewed had obligated more than $766 million for security services and equipment" in Iraq.[107] The GAO found that security often accounted for more than 15 percent of the cost of operating in Iraq, not including the security costs of subcontractors, and the State Department reported that security costs accounted for 16–22 percent of reconstruction projects.[108] Given estimates of the total reconstruction cost from 2004 to 2007 of $56 billion, even a conservative 10 percent allocation for security would mean $5.6 billion.[109] The bottom line is that the U.S. government has not provided publicly verifiable information on many of the private military companies it is increasingly hiring with taxpayer dollars.

Blackwater alone has won more than $500 million in publicly identifiable U.S. government contracts under the war on terror, not including much of its "black" or "urgent and compelling need" business or its work for private actors. And its rhetoric of saving taxpayer money through free-market efficiencies seems increasingly empty, given that its security division does not appear ever to have won a competitively bid contract.[110] With the U.S. government unable or unwilling to effectively tabulate its own expenditures on private security/military services, a worldwide estimate proves even more elusive. In 2003, just as the Iraq War was getting under way, and before the major mercenary boom had begun, P. W. Singer estimated the value of the private military industry at more than $100 billion globally.[111] Homeland Security Research, an industry tracking company, estimated that governments and businesses globally spent $59 billion in 2006 to fight terrorism, a figure that does not include many "passive" private security services and that represents a sixfold increase from 2000.[112]

What this means in practical terms is that the rebranding campaign is enabling the mercenaries to affix a permanent sieve to the most lucrative feeding trough in the world—the national budgets of the United States and its war-making allies. These "services" are no longer reserved for unstable nations struggling to maintain power but are being welcomed by the great powers of the world as an integral part of their national forces. In talking about the "expanding role" of the mercenary industry, Cofer Black said, "I think it is something that we all need to think about. We need to talk about and sort of agree. I do not see us going back. I do not see the national forces being increased exponentially, and I see [using companies like Blackwater] as a useful cost-effective tool."[113]

What is particularly disturbing about the "expanding role" of Blackwater specifically is the issue of the company's right-wing leadership, its proximity to a whole slew of conservative causes and politicians, its Christian fundamentalist agenda and secretive nature, and its deep and longstanding ties to the Republican Party, U.S. military, and intelligence agencies. Black-water is quickly becoming one of the most powerful private armies in the world, and several of its top officials are extreme religious zealots, some of whom appear to believe they are engaged in an epic battle for the defense of Christendom. The deployment of forces under this kind of leadership in Arab or Muslim countries reinforces the worst fears of many in the Islamic world about a neo-Crusader agenda masquerading as a U.S. mission to "liberate" them from their oppressors. What Blackwater seemingly advocates and envisions is a private army of God-fearing patriots, well paid and devoted to the agenda of U.S. hegemony—supported by far lower paid cannon fodder, foot soldiers from Third World countries, many of which have legacies of brutal U.S.-sponsored regimes or death squads. For its vaunted American forces, Blackwater has expanded the mercenary motivating factor (or rationalization) beyond simple monetary gain (though that remains a major factor) to a duty-oriented, patriotic justification. "This is not about business and widgets and making money, at least not in our company it is not," said Cofer Black.[114] "If you're not willing to drink the Blackwater Kool-aid and be committed to supporting humane democracy around the world, then there's probably a better place" to go work than Blackwater, "because that's all we do," Taylor told *The Weekly Standard*.[115]

In the bigger ideological picture, Blackwater executives fancy themselves part of a "just" mercenary tradition. "This is nothing new," asserted IPOA's Doug Brooks. "Even George Washington had contractors."[116] It is a line that Blackwater executives love. Indeed, they often cite the statues in Lafayette Park across the street from the White House as monuments to their trade and tradition. In the middle of the park is a statue of President Andrew Jackson on horseback. Flanking the four corners of the park are statues of mercenaries who fought on the U.S. side in the Revolutionary War: France's Gen. Marquis Gilbert de Lafayette and Maj. Gen. Comte Jean de Rochambeau; Poland's Gen. Thaddeus Kosciuszko; Prussia's Maj. Gen. Baron Frederich Wilhelm Von Steuben (the object of Prince Group general counsel Joseph Schmitz's obsession). "The idea of contractors on the battlefield, contractors doing this sort of thing, that it's a new idea, is just wrong," Erik Prince told a military conference in 2006.[117] Citing the statues at Lafayette Park, Prince said, "Those are four military officers, foreign officers, contractors if you will, that came here and built the capability of the continental army, the continental army was having a tough time until they showed up. On Von Steuben's statue it says he gave military training and discipline to the citizen-soldiers who achieved the independence of the United States. That's what we're doing in Iraq or Afghanistan, wherever we get hired and authorized to do so by the U.S. government, we're giving them the capability to defend themselves, and to clean out their own problems, so you don't have to send big conventional military to do that. You know, German mercenaries fought on behalf of the union in the civil war, even won the medal of honor." Cofer Black echoed the narrative: "There is nothing new in this. What we are really talking about is the management of this for the good of the country and to achieve the objective. Lafayette Park could be called Contractor Park for our heroes that came to this country that trained us, trained our forebears."[118]

In February 2006, the mercenary industry won a major victory in its rebranding campaign when private contractors were officially recognized in the Pentagon's Quadrennial Defense Review as part of the U.S. military's "Total Force." In releasing the report Defense Secretary Rumsfeld said the review "sets out where the Department of Defense currently is and the direction we believe it needs to go," adding, "Now in the fifth year of this global war, the ideas and proposals in this document are provided as a roadmap for change, leading to victory."[119] Cofer Black, was particularly pleased about the line in the report that explicitly recognized contractors like Blackwater:[120] "The Department's Total Force—its active and reserve military components, its civil servants, and its contractors—constitutes its warfighting capability and capacity. Members of the Total Force serve in thousands of locations around the world, performing a vast array of duties to accomplish critical missions."[121] Pentagon policy, according to the review, "now directs that performance of commercial activities by contractors . . . shall be included in operational plans and orders. By factoring contractors into their planning, Combatant Commanders can better determine their mission needs." It was a momentous occasion for the mercenary industry—one that Blackwater and other firms recognized as a watershed moment in the drive for the kind of integration and legitimacy they viewed as central to their survival and profitability. Hiring mercenaries was no longer an option; it was U.S. policy. That it was issued as an edict from Rumsfeld, without public debate, was irrelevant. By 2007, Blackwater had its forces deployed in at least nine countries. Some twenty-three hundred private Blackwater troops were spread across the globe along with another twenty-one thousand contractors in its database should the need for their services arise.[122] The rise of Blackwater's private army is nothing short of the embodiment of the ominous scenario prophesied decades ago by President Eisenhower when he warned of the "grave implications" of the rise of "the military-industrial complex" and "misplaced power."

Riding high on the privatization caravan aggressively pushed forward by the Bush administration, the right-wing think tank the American Enterprise Institute, which has long been at the forefront of the movement to privatize the government and military, sponsored a mercenary conference in Washington, D.C., in the summer of 2006. They called it "Contractors on the Battlefield: A Briefing on the Future of the Defense Industry." It featured two former Pentagon officials who were instrumental to privatization schemes, as well as Blackwater's vice chairman, Cofer Black. The conference room was packed with representatives from various private military companies, as well as the State Department, Pentagon, and a variety of NGOs. The event felt very much like a reeducation camp for mercenaries, with the godfather, Black, presiding over lessons in rebranding and marketing the product: mercenary services. "We are in a state, as a planet, of disorder," Black told the crowd. "I'm rather personally upset about this because coming out of the Cold War, I indeed thought that we would have a period of calm and relaxation and goodwill among men. This disorder is subversive."[123] Turning directly to the mercenary trade itself and with the room silent before him, Black spoke slowly, choppily, methodically, as though he were a hypnotist talking someone into a trance. "It may sound a little bit like the Knights of the Round Table, but this is what we believe," the veteran spy declared. "Focus on morals and ethics and integrity. This is important. We are not fly-by-night. We are not tricksters. We believe in these things. We believe in being represented. We believe in providing the support. We are ethical. We give training to our employees. This is something that will grow and grow. We want to be able to contribute for a significant period of time."[124]

BLACKWATER BEYOND BUSH

IN EARLY 2008, Blackwater's name had largely receded from the headlines save for the occasional blip on the media radar sparked by Henry Waxman's ongoing investigations into the company's activities. Its forces remained deployed in Iraq and Afghanistan, and despite the international infamy attached to the Blackwater name, business continued to pour in. In the two weeks directly following the Nisour Square massacre in September 2007, Blackwater signed more than $144 million in contracts with the State Department for "protective services" in Iraq and Afghanistan alone and, over the following weeks and months, won millions more in contracts with other federal entities like the Coast Guard, the Navy, and the Federal Law Enforcement Training Center.[1] Erik Prince continued to portray his company as the victim of a partisan witch hunt. "I met the president twice," he said after appearing before Waxman's committee. "Iraq is a controversial war—no question. If they can go after contractors and take some of them down . . . it's another way to embarrass the administration."[2]

While Blackwater's Iraq contract was extended in April 2008, the company was by no means betting the house on its long-term presence there. While quietly maintaining Blackwater's Iraq work, they aggressively pursued other business opportunities for the Prince Group empire. As Blackwater absorbed a barrage of incoming fire over its conduct in Iraq, there was a silver lining for the company. It had secured a very public reputation for being a badass operation that protected—and kept alive—its "principals" in the most hostile of settings by any means necessary. Its very presence in Iraq after Nisour Square, over the objections of the Iraqi prime minister and amid multiple Congressional, military, and Justice Department investigations, sent a clear message: Washington needed Blackwater more than the pretense of Iraqi sovereignty. Blackwater's boots on the ground were too important to lose, even in the face of growing outrage in the United States over the lack of accountability of Washington's private forces in Iraq. "I know we're there not only to be a protective screen," Prince said in late 2007, "but maybe the fall guy when something goes wrong. That's probably what's happened to us in this case."[3]

After Nisour Square, Prince hinted that Blackwater might quit Iraq, at least in its overt capacity there. "It's been a source of huge controversy and hassle for us," he said.[4] But Prince and Blackwater were clearly emboldened by the vivid demonstration of their centrality to the U.S. war machine, and in the days and weeks after Nisour Square, the Blackwater founder began speaking of his empire growing into "more of a full-spectrum" operation.[5]

A "One-Stop Shop" for the Government

In September 2007, it was revealed that Blackwater had been "tapped" by the Pentagon's Counter-Narcoterrorism Technology Program Office to compete for a share of a five-year $15 billion budget "to fight terrorists with drug-trade ties."[6] According to the *Army Times*, the contract "could include anti-drug technologies and equipment, special vehicles and aircraft, communications, security training, pilot training, geographic information systems, and in-field support."[7] A spokesperson for another company bidding for the work said that "80 percent of the work will be overseas."[8] As Richard Douglas, a deputy assistant secretary of defense, explained, "The fact is we use Blackwater to do a lot of our training of counternarcotics police in Afghanistan. I have to say that Blackwater has done a very good job."[9]

Such an arrangement could find Blackwater operating in an arena with the godfathers of the war industry, such as Lockheed Martin, Northrop Grumman, and Raytheon. It could also see Blackwater potentially expanding into Latin America, joining other private security companies who are well established in the region. The massive U.S. security company DynCorp is already deployed in Colombia, Bolivia, and other countries as part of the "war on drugs." In Colombia alone, U.S. defense contractors are receiving nearly half the $630 million in annual U.S. military aid for the country.[10] Just south of the U.S. border, the United States has launched Plan Mexico, a $1.5 billion counternarcotics program. This and similar plans could prove lucrative business opportunities for Blackwater and other companies. "Blackwater USA's enlistment in the drug war," observed journalist John Ross, would be "a direct challenge to its stiffest competitor, DynCorp—up until now, the Dallas-based corporation has locked up 94% of all private drug war security contracts."[11] The *New York Times* reported that the contract could be Blackwater's "biggest job ever."[12]

As populist movements grow stronger in Latin America, threatening U.S. financial interests as well as the standing of right-wing U.S. political allies throughout the region, the "war on drugs" becomes an increasingly central part of U.S. counterinsurgency efforts. It allows for more training of foreign security forces through the private sector—away from effective U.S. Congressional oversight—and a deployment of personnel from U.S. war corporations. With U.S. forces stretched thin, sending private security companies to Latin America offers Washington a "small footprint" alternative to the politically and militarily problematic deployment of active-duty U.S. troops. In a January 2008 report by the United Nations working group on mercenaries, international investigators found, "An emerging trend in Latin America but also in other regions of the world indicates situations of private security companies protecting transnational extractive corporations whose employees are often involved in suppressing the legitimate social protest of communities and human rights and environmental organizations of the areas where these corporations operate."[13]

In early 2008, Blackwater suffered a setback to its plans for work along the U.S. border. The company announced that it was abandoning its plans to build "Blackwater West" on 824 acres of land in Southern California, a stone's throw from Tecate, Mexico. Blackwater had planned to use the camp to train border patrol agents and other law enforcement and military in a major front line in the immigration debate.[14] Residents of the tiny town of Potrero—population 850—waged a heroic battle against the company's presence there for more than a year. They expressed a wide range of concerns—from the company's reputation in Iraq to environmental issues—and forced out local town officials who had attempted to push through Blackwater's deployment in their community. Finally, in March 2008, Blackwater had had enough; it released a muted statement that said, "The proposed site does not meet our business objectives at this time."[15] A company spokesperson said the decision had nothing to do with the protests against Blackwater. In the bigger picture, this was a minor defeat for Blackwater's growing business. Even without its desired California facility, Blackwater already annually trains more than 25,000 military and state, federal, and local law enforcement personnel at its Moyock headquarters. It also successfully established "Blackwater North" in Illinois.

If there is one quality that is evident from examining Blackwater's business history, it is the company's ability to take advantage of emerging war and conflict markets. Throughout the decade of Blackwater's existence, Prince has aggressively built his empire into a structure paralleling the U.S.

national security apparatus. "Prince wants to vault Blackwater into the major leagues of U.S. military contracting, taking advantage of the movement to privatize all kinds of government security," reported the *Wall Street Journal* shortly after Nisour Square. "The company wants to be a one-stop shop for the U.S. government on missions to which it won't commit American forces. This is a niche with few established competitors."[16]

Grizzlies and Polars

In addition to providing armed forces for war and conflict zones and a wide range of military and police training services, Blackwater does a robust multimillion-dollar business through its aviation division. It also has a growing maritime division and other national and international initiatives. Among these, Blackwater is in Japan, where its forces protect the United States' ballistic missile defense system, which, according to *Stars and Stripes*, "points high-powered radio waves westward toward mainland Asia to hunt for enemy missiles headed east toward America or its allies."[17] Meanwhile, in early 2008, *Defense News* reported, "Blackwater is training members of the Taiwanese National Security Bureau's (NSB's) special protection service, which guards the president. The NSB is responsible for the overall security of the country and was once an instrument of terrorism during the martial law period. Today, according to its Web site, the NSB is responsible for 'national intelligence work, special protective service and unified cryptography.'"[18] Former Pakistani Prime Minister Benazir Bhutto reportedly tried to hire Blackwater to protect her as she campaigned for the presidency in 2007.[19] Conflicting reports indicated that either the U.S. State Department or the Pakistani government vetoed the plan. She was assassinated in December 2007.

Back home, Blackwater has stepped up its work on creating military hardware and surveillance equipment and technology to be marketed to the Pentagon and Department of Homeland Security.

Blackwater is hoping to sell its Mine Resistant Ambush Protected (MRAP) armored vehicle, the Grizzly, to the U.S. Army and Marine Corps.[20] The company says it is already using three of the twenty-two-ton vehicles in Iraq.[21] The Grizzly is portrayed as combining the versatility of an SUV with the durability of a powerful armored car. It can be driven at speeds up to sixty-five miles per hour and is said to be able to deflect ordnance as large as .50 calibers.[22] In September 2007, the Pentagon received the green light to purchase more than 15,000 MRAP vehicles for about $11.3 billion.[23] Blackwater is hardly alone in producing them, but winning a share of that deal, which seems likely, would be yet another profitable arrangement. The company will manufacture the Grizzlies at its 70,000-square-foot plant, staffed in part by former Ford workers, in North Carolina, with company executives predicting it may eventually crank out as many as a thousand vehicles annually.[24] "We're going to see good, steady growth for at least ten years," Blackwater president Gary Jackson said.[25]

For Homeland Security operations, counterinsurgency, or "war on drugs" activities, Blackwater is manufacturing an unmanned aerial vehicle, the Polar 400. The surveillance blimp is remote-controlled and, unlike traditional drones, will be capable of remaining in the air for days at a time, operating at an altitude of up to 15,000 feet and a speed of sixty miles per hour. "We can sit it over the top of Baghdad at 18,000 feet and watch all that goes on," Jackson claimed. "The problem is if it really does work, it will be hard to produce them fast enough. I believe airships will be a multibillion-dollar business."[26] In late 2007, Blackwater conducted a test flight of a 170-foot prototype and predicted it would begin production in 2008.[27] Blackwater, once again, was placing itself in the middle of a rapidly expanding market. Defense spending on unmanned aerial vehicles rose from $284 million in 2000 to more than $2 billion in 2005, a trend analysts predicted would continue.[28] Blackwater, according to the *Virginian-Pilot*, is "touting its airship as a lower-cost, longer-operating alternative to the fixed and rotary-wing unmanned aerial vehicles now widely used by the Air Force and other military services." Alan Ram, the head of production and business development for Blackwater Airships, said, "We think it's a niche product with a lot of markets."[29]

Blackwater also continues to publicly agitate for a greater role in Homeland Security operations, disaster response, and international peacekeeping. Prince has consistently suggested Blackwater could be used in Darfur, saying in interviews after Nisour Square, "I mean, who can watch *Hotel Rwanda* and not want a different outcome?"[30] In a 2007 interview, Jackson said, "The question is not, 'Why would we use the private sector in humanitarian operations,' but, 'Why aren't we using the private sector to the fullest extent possible to reduce human suffering around the world?'"[31] Prince said a friend of his actually contacted actor George Clooney on Prince's behalf in an attempt to sell Clooney on a potential Blackwater role in Darfur. Clooney, who has been outspoken on the situation in Darfur, reportedly did not return the call.[32] The UN peacekeeping budget is estimated as being between $6 billion and $10 billion.[33] While private military companies have been used for years in UN operations for logistical support, the types of armed "services" Blackwater offers would undoubtedly spark major international controversy. "If you have now a marketplace for warfare, it is a commercial issue rather than a political issue involving a debate in the countries," said Hans von Sponeck, a thirty-two-year veteran UN diplomat, who served as a deputy secretary general. "To outsource security-related, military-related issues to nongovernment, nonmilitary forces is a source of great concern."[34] While Blackwater continues to push that project, another major one, involving one of the most sensitive sectors of U.S. national defense, is already well under way.

Spies Like U.S.

What could prove to be one of Blackwater's most profitable and enduring enterprises is one of the company's most secretive initiatives—a move into the world of privatized intelligence services. In April 2006, Prince quietly began building Total Intelligence Solutions, which boasts that it "brings CIA-style" services to the open market for Fortune 500 companies.[35] Among its offerings are "surveillance and countersurveillance, deployed intelligence collection, and rapid safeguarding of employees or other key assets."[36]

As the U.S. finds itself in the midst of the most radical privatization agenda in the nation's history, few areas have seen as dramatic a transformation to privatized services as the world of intelligence. "This is the magnet now. Everything is being attracted to these private companies in terms of individuals and expertise and functions that were normally done by the intelligence community," says former CIA division chief and senior analyst Melvin Goodman. "My major concern is the lack of accountability, the lack of responsibility. The entire industry is essentially out of control. It's outrageous."[37]

In late 2007, R.J. Hillhouse, a blogger who investigates the clandestine world of private contractors and U.S. intelligence, obtained documents from the Office of the Directorate of National Intelligence (DNI) showing that Washington spends some $42 billion annually on private intelligence contractors, up from $17.54 billion in 2000.[38] That means 70 percent of the U.S. intelligence budget is currently going to private companies. Perhaps it is no surprise, then, that the head of the DNI, as of the spring of 2008, was Mike McConnell, the former chair of the board of the Intelligence and National Security Alliance, the private intelligence industry's trade association.

Hillhouse also revealed that one of the most sensitive U.S. intelligence documents, the Presidential Daily Briefing, is prepared in part by private companies, despite having the official seal of the U.S. intelligence apparatus. "Let's say a company is frustrated with a government that's hampering its business or business of one of its clients. Introducing and spinning intelligence on that government's suspected collaboration with terrorists would quickly get the White House's attention and could be used to shape national policy," Hillhouse argued.[39]

Total Intelligence, which opened for business in February 2007, is a fusion of three entities bought up by Prince—the Terrorism Research Center; Technical Defense; and The Black Group, Blackwater vice chair Cofer Black's consulting agency.[40] The company's leadership reads like a who's who from the CIA's early "war on terror" operations after 9/11. In addition to the twenty-eight-year CIA veteran Black, who is chairman of

Total Intelligence, the company's executives include CEO Robert Richer, the former associate deputy director of the agency's Directorate of Operations and the second-ranking official in charge of clandestine operations. From 1999 to 2004, Richer was head of the CIA's Near East Division, where he ran clandestine operations throughout the Middle East and South Asia. As part of his duties, he was the CIA liaison with Jordan's King Abdullah, a key U.S. ally and Blackwater client, and briefed President Bush on the burgeoning Iraqi resistance in its early stages.[41] Total Intelligence's chief operating officer is Enrique "Ric" Prado, a twenty-four-year CIA veteran and former senior executive officer in the Directorate of Operations. He spent more than a decade working in the CIA's Counterterrorist Center and ten years with the CIA's "paramilitary" Special Operations Group.[42] Prado and Black worked closely together at the CIA.[43] Prado also served in Latin America with Jose Rodriguez, who would gain infamy in late 2007 after it was revealed that as director of the National Clandestine Service at the CIA he was allegedly responsible for the destruction of videotaped interrogations of prisoners, during which "enhanced" interrogation techniques, including waterboarding, were reportedly used.[44] Richer told the *New York Times* he recalled many conversations with his then boss, Rodriguez, about the tapes. "He would always say, 'I'm not going to let my people get nailed for something they were ordered to do,'" Richer said.[45] Before the scandal, there were reports that Blackwater had been "aggressively recruiting" Rodriguez.[46] He has since retired from the CIA.

Total Intelligence's leadership also includes Craig Johnson, a twenty-seven-year CIA officer who specialized in Central and South America, and Caleb "Cal" Temple, who joined the company straight out of the Defense Intelligence Agency, where he served from 2004 to 2006 as chief of the Office of Intelligence Operations in the Joint Intelligence Task Force—Combating Terrorism.[47] According to his Total Intelligence bio, Temple directed the "DIA's 24/7 analytic terrorism target development and other counterterrorism intelligence activities in support of military operations worldwide. He also oversaw 24/7 global counterterrorism indications and warning analysis for the U.S. Defense Department." The company also boasts officials drawn from the Drug Enforcement Agency and the FBI.[48]

Total Intelligence is run out of an office on the ninth floor of a building in the Ballston area of Arlington, Virginia.[49] Its "Global Fusion Center," complete with large-screen TVs broadcasting international news channels and computer stations staffed by analysts surfing the web, "operates around the clock every day of the year"[50] and is modeled after the CIA's counterterrorist center, once run by Black.[51] The firm now employs at least sixty-five full-time staff—some estimates say it is closer to 100.[52] "Total Intel brings the . . . skills traditionally honed by CIA operatives directly to the boardroom," Black said when the company launched. "With a service like this, CEOs and their security personnel will be able to respond to threats quickly and confidently—whether it's determining which city is safest to open a new plant in or working to keep employees out of harm's way after a terrorist attack."[53]

Black insists, "This is a completely legal enterprise. We break no laws. We don't go anywhere near breaking laws. We don't have to."[54] But what exact services Total Intelligence is providing and to whom remain shrouded in secrecy. What is clear is that the company is leveraging the reputations and inside connections of its executives. "Cofer can open doors," Richer told the *Washington Post* in 2007. "I can open doors. We can generally get in to see who we need to see. We don't help pay bribes. We do everything within the law, but we can deal with the right minister or person."[55] Black told the paper he and Richer spend a lot of their time traveling. "I am discreet in where I go and who I see. I spend most of my time dealing with senior people in governments, making connections."[56] But it is clear that the existing connections from the former spooks' time at the agency have brought business to Total Intelligence.

Take the case of Jordan.

For years, Richer worked closely with King Abdullah, serving as the CIA's liaison with the king. As journalist Ken Silverstein reported, "The CIA has lavishly subsidized Jordan's intelligence service, and has sent millions of dollars in recent years for intelligence training. After Richer retired, sources say, he helped Blackwater land a lucrative deal with the Jordanian government to provide the same sort of training offered by the CIA. Millions of dollars that the CIA 'invested' in Jordan walked out the door with Richer—if this were a movie, it would be a cross between *Jerry Maguire* and *Syriana*. 'People [at the agency] are pissed off,' said one source. 'Abdullah still speaks with Richer regularly and he thinks that's the same thing as talking to us. He thinks Richer is still the man.' Except in this case it's Richer, not his client, yelling 'show me the money.'"[57]

In a 2007 interview on the cable TV business network CNBC, Black was brought on as an analyst to discuss "investing in Jordan."[58] At no point in the interview was Black identified as working for the Jordanian government. Total Intelligence was described as "a corporate consulting firm that includes investment strategy," while "Ambassador Black" was introduced as "a 28-year veteran of the CIA," the "top counterterror guy" and "a key planner for the breathtakingly rapid victory of American forces that toppled the Taliban in Afghanistan." During the interview, Black heaped lavish praise on Jordan and its monarchy. "You have leadership, King Abdullah, His Majesty King Abdullah, who is certainly kind towards investors, very protective," Black said. "Jordan is, in our view, a very good investment. There are some exceptional values there." He said Jordan is in a region where there are "numerous commodities that are being produced and doing well."

With no hint of the brutality behind the exodus, he argued that the plight of Iraqi refugees, fleeing the violence of the U.S. occupation, was good for potential investors in Jordan. "We get something like six, 700,000 Iraqis that have moved from Iraq into Jordan that require cement, furniture, housing, and the like. So it is a—it is an island of growth and potential, certainly in that immediate area. So it looks good," Black said. "There are opportunities for investment. It is not all bad. Sometimes Americans need to watch a little less TV. . . . But there is—there is opportunity in everything. That's why you need situation awareness, and that's one of the things that our company does. It provides the kinds of intelligence and insight to provide situational awareness so you can make the best investments."

Black and other Total Intelligence executives have turned their CIA careers, reputations, contacts, and connections into profitable business opportunities. What they once did for the U.S. government, they now do for private interests. It is not difficult to imagine clients feeling as though they are essentially hiring the U.S. government to serve their private interests. "They have the skills and background to do anything anyone wants," said Hillhouse. "There's no oversight. They're an independent company offering freelance espionage services. They're rent-a-spies."[59]

In 2007 Richer told the *Post* that now that he is in the private sector, foreign military officials and others are more willing to give him information than they were when he was with the CIA. He recalled a conversation with a general from a foreign military during which Richer was surprised at the potentially "classified" information the general revealed. When Richer asked why the general was giving him the information, he said the general responded, "If I tell it to an embassy official I've created espionage. You're a business partner."[60]

"I Sleep the Sleep of the Just"

In 2008 Iraq was a leading issue in the U.S. presidential election. While the Democrats campaigned on a pledge to end the war, the Republican nominee, John McCain, suggested U.S. forces could remain in Iraq for "maybe a hundred" years, a scenario that he said "would be fine with me."[61] But hidden behind the rhetoric of political speeches, often framed as pro– versus anti–Iraq War, was a stark reality: the Iraq occupation will continue for years to come regardless of who resides at 1600 Pennsylvania Avenue. Erik Prince, who had previously donated more than $250,000 to Republican campaigns and causes, seems to have determined that his publicly traceable campaign contributions are a liability. "I don't know that I'll have much political involvement in either party going forward," he said in late 2007.[62] Whether that is a business decision or a political one, his company and the highly profitable industry in which it operates are so deeply embedded in the U.S. political system that they are here to stay.

Mercenary companies clearly have little to fear from Republican-dominated governance in Washington. But what about the Democrats? Despite their stated antiwar claims, the Democrats' dominant Iraq plan would keep in place tens of thousands of U.S. troops for an unspecified time, while escalating U.S. action in Afghanistan. For military contractors like Blackwater, this is welcome news. "Nobody is going to be able to throw the contractors out," said David Isenberg of the British-American Security Information Council. "They're the American Express card of the American military. The military doesn't leave home without them, because it can't."[63]

The 2007 Iraq supplemental spending bill opened a window onto what could happen in the first term of a Democratic administration. Along with the findings of the Baker-Hamilton Iraq Study Group analysis, it formed the basis for the Iraq plans of the leading Democratic contenders for the presidency. The bill was portrayed as the Democrats' withdrawal plan, and Senators Barack Obama and Hillary Clinton passionately supported it, with Obama saying it meant the country was "one signature away from ending the Iraq War."[64] But upon a careful reading of the legislation (which was vetoed by President Bush), that claim rings hollow. The plan would have redeployed some U.S. forces from Iraq within 180 days. But it also would have provided for 40,000–60,000 troops to remain in Iraq as "trainers," "counterterrorist forces," and for "protection for embassy/diplomats," according to an analysis by the Institute for Policy Studies.[65] "There was nothing in the legislation about contractors or mercenary forces," said IPS analyst Erik Leaver.[66] The truth is that as long as there are troops in Iraq, there will be private contractors.

In part, these contractors do mundane jobs that traditionally have been performed by soldiers, from driving trucks to doing laundry. These services are provided through companies such as Halliburton, KBR, and Fluor, and through their vast labyrinth of subcontractors. But private personnel, as Blackwater's history in Iraq has shown, are also consistently engaged in armed combat and "security" operations. Contractors interrogate prisoners,

gather intelligence, operate rendition flights, protect senior occupation officials—including some commanding U.S. generals—and in some cases have
taken command of U.S. and international troops in battle. In an admission
that speaks volumes about the extent of the privatization, Gen. David
Petraeus, who was charged with implementing the "surge," admitted that
he has, at times, not been guarded in Iraq by the U.S. military but by "contract security."[67] At least three U.S. commanding generals have been
guarded in Iraq by hired guns, including the general who oversees U.S. military contracting in Iraq and Afghanistan.[68]

In 2008 the number of private contractors in Iraq was at a one-to-one
ratio with active-duty U.S. soldiers, a stunning escalation compared with
the 1991 Gulf War. "To have half of your army be contractors, I don't know
that there's a precedent for that," said Congressman Dennis Kucinich, a
member of the House Oversight and Government Reform Committee.[69]

Some estimates actually put the number of contractors at higher than
active-duty soldiers in Iraq, but exact numbers are nearly impossible to
obtain.[70] According to a March 2008 report by the Government Accountability Office, the Pentagon "does not maintain departmentwide data on
the numbers of contractor employees working side-by-side with federal
employees."[71] But in a review of twenty-one Defense Department offices,
the GAO found that at "15 offices, contractor employees outnumbered
DOD employees and comprised up to 88% of the workforce. Contractor
employees perform key tasks, including developing contract requirements
and advising on award fees for other contractors."

Beyond the issues raised by private contractors hired by the Pentagon lies
the more troubling problem of the State Department's private armed forces.
A major part of the Democrats' plan calls for maintaining the massive U.S.
Embassy, the largest embassy in world history, as well as the Green Zone. At
present, much of the security work required by the embassy and the travel
of U.S. officials into and out of the Green Zone is done by three private
security firms: Blackwater, Triple Canopy, and DynCorp. This arrangement
reflects the simultaneous militarization and privatization of the State

Department's Bureau of Diplomatic Security. Created in the mid-1990s, the department's Worldwide Personal Protective Services was originally envisioned as a small-scale bodyguard operation, comprised of private security contractors, to protect small groups of U.S. diplomats and other U.S. and foreign officials. In Iraq, it has been turned into a sizable paramilitary force. Spending on the program jumped from $50 million in 2003 to $613 million in 2006.[72]

The looming question is: who would protect the Democrats' army of diplomats in Iraq? Some insist that it is possible to continue to rely on private forces to do this work as long as they are held accountable. As of March 2008, these private forces enjoyed a de facto "above the law" status, which both Obama and Clinton have decried. But it is hard to see how "accountability" is going to be achieved, at least in the short term.

In late 2007, in the aftermath of Nisour Square, the House overwhelmingly approved legislation that would ensure that all contractors would be subject to prosecution in U.S. civilian courts for crimes committed on a foreign battlefield.[73] The idea is: FBI investigators would deploy to the crime scene, gather evidence, and interview witnesses, leading to indictments and prosecutions. But this approach raises a slew of questions. Who would protect the investigators? How would Iraqi victims be interviewed? How would evidence be gathered amid the chaos and dangers of a hostile war zone like Iraq? Given that the federal government and the military seem unable—or unwilling—even to count how many contractors are actually in the country, how could their activities possibly be monitored? Apart from the fact that it would be impossible to effectively police such an enormous deployment of private contractors (such as in Iraq, where it is equal in size to the military presence), this legislation could give the private military industry a tremendous PR victory. The companies could finally claim that a legally accountable structure governed their operations. Yet they would be well aware that such legislation would be nearly impossible to enforce. Perhaps that is why the industry has passionately backed this approach. Prince called its passage in the House, "Excellent."

Others have proposed to address the problem simply by expanding the official U.S. government forces responsible for securing the embassy and Green Zone, thus reducing the market for mercenary companies. In an October 2007 letter to Secretary of State Condoleezza Rice, Senator Joe Biden, chair of the influential Foreign Relations Committee, suggested the United States should examine "whether we should expand the ranks of Diplomatic Security rather than continue to rely so heavily on contractors."[74] He called for hiring more agents, saying, "The requirement for extensive personal security to protect the employees of the U.S. mission will continue for several years to come—regardless of the number of U.S. forces in Iraq."

While an increase in funding to the Diplomatic Security division would ostensibly pave the way for a force made up entirely of U.S. government personnel, there are serious questions about how quickly that could happen. As of October 2007, the State Department had only 1,450 Diplomatic Security agents *worldwide* who were actual U.S. government employees and only thirty-six deployed in Iraq.[75] In contrast, as of March 2008, Blackwater had nearly 1,000 operatives in Iraq *alone*, not to mention the hundreds more working for Triple Canopy and DynCorp. The State Department has said it could take years to identify prospective new agents, vet them, train them, and deploy them.[76] In short, this would be no small undertaking and, even if the political will and funding was there, would take years to enact.

If the Democrats attempted to make diplomatic security a military operation, that would pose serious challenges as well. As the *New York Times* reported in late 2007, "the military does not have the trained personnel to take over the job."[77] Even if the military trained a specialized force for executive protection and bodyguarding in Iraq, this arrangement would mean more U.S. military convoys traveling inside Iraq, potentially placing them in deadly conflict with Iraqi civilians on a regular basis.

Realizing the practical challenges any transition away from private security forces in Iraq would entail, during the 2008 election campaign, a senior foreign policy adviser to Obama said, "I can't rule out, I won't rule out, private security contractors."[78] This must have been a difficult admission. While Obama has been at the forefront of attempts to legislate accountability for contractors on the battlefield—he introduced a contractor reform bill eight months before Nisour Square—his foreign policy team clearly understood that their support for maintaining a sizable U.S. presence in Iraq had painted them into a corner. On February 28, 2008, a day after I reported Obama's position in an article in *The Nation*, Hillary Clinton announced she would sign on to legislation to "ban the use of Blackwater and other private mercenary firms in Iraq."[79] The timing, in the middle of their hotly contested campaign for the Democratic nomination, was curious—Clinton, during her five years on the Senate Armed Services Committee, had been largely mute on the issue before the September 16 Blackwater shooting and did not issue her statement for a full six months after the massacre. How exactly she envisioned carrying out her Iraq plan without such private forces was also unclear.

Both Clinton and Obama indicated they supported increasing funding of Diplomatic Security, as advocated by Senator Biden in 2007. In the bigger picture, however, firms like Blackwater operate in a demand-based industry, and it is this demand, which derives from offensive, unpopular wars of conquest, that must be cut off. Even if a U.S. president determined to completely transfer diplomatic security jobs from companies like Blackwater to official U.S. government agents, which would be a major undertaking, the State Department has said it could take years to implement. The reality is that short of dramatically shrinking the size of the U.S. civilian and diplomatic presence in Iraq, which necessitates such a large "diplomatic" security force, the next president may have no choice but to continue the current contracting arrangements. And that is good news for Blackwater and other private security companies.

But Iraq and diplomatic security are only part of the picture. There is almost no discussion in Congress about the stunning growth of the operations of companies like Blackwater globally and at home. Their expansion into private intelligence, homeland security, military weapons, surveillance technology, the "war on drugs," and peacekeeping operations continues, largely free from the scrutiny of lawmakers and the media. Long ago, these companies began to stake out their role in future conflicts and a greater presence in highly sensitive and increasingly privatized government programs. It is in large part because of the lack of intense scrutiny by the media and Congress that their future appears both secure and bright.

Erik Prince certainly isn't losing sleep these days, not over the killings of Iraqi civilians by his forces or over his company's future status in the U.S. war machine and national security apparatus. Shortly after Nisour Square and facing a slew of Congressional, military, and Justice Department investigations over his company's actions, Prince said, "How can I sleep? Because I'm comfortable, and I know what we're doing. We're doing the right thing, so beyond that, I can't worry. I sleep the sleep of the just. I'm not feeling guilty."[80]

ACKNOWLEDGMENTS

I AM grateful to my parents, Michael and Lisa Scahill. They provided me with an education no university could ever rival. Their quiet humility, their dedication to justice, and their love for others amazes me. I have never met more decent people. They are my heroes and my friends. Thanks to my brother Tim and sister Stephanie for their lifetime love, companionship, and support, as well as my sister-in-law Jenny and my niece Maya. Ksenija, you are my heart and my world. Barb and Harry Hoferle, thank you for always believing and always being there. Also I wish to remember my late grandparents, two of whom were Irish immigrants who lived through the terror of the Black and Tans paramilitaries. Gratitude also to my aunts, uncles, and cousins for their love through the years.

This book is very much the product of the hard work and influence of scores of people who gave their time, commitment, friendship, love, and solidarity to this project and to me and my family. I would like to thank my editor Betsy Reed, who spent countless hours editing and revising this manuscript and who has supported my reporting through thick and thin. It has been a great gift to work with her over the past few years. Without her this project would never have happened. Thanks again to Garrett Ordower for everything. Gratitude to my friend and agent Anthony Arnove, who has believed in my work since we met. Naomi Klein for her undying friendship, solidarity, and support. Thank you to Daniela Crespo for her support. My *compañeros* Sharif Abdel Kouddous, Ana Nogueira,

Carmen Trotta, and Dave Mickenberg for being. Carl Bromley and Ruth Baldwin at Nation Books for their support, enthusiasm, and dedication from the jump—you guys were the glue. I would like to extend my deepest appreciation to the amazing team at Perseus: David Steinberger, John Shea, Michele Jacob, Nicole Caputo and Elena Guzman. At Avalon, Michele Martin for her faith, tenacity, and encouragement. The Avalon production team for pulling it all together: Peter Jacoby, Linda Kosarin, Jonathan Sainsbury, and Mike Walters. Also thanks to Anne Sullivan and Karen Auerbach. Mark Sorkin did an amazing job meticulously copyediting this book. Many thanks to the talented Joe Duax, who spent months combing through every sentence and footnote diligently fact-checking the manuscript.

I would like to extend *un abrazo fuerte* to Liliana Segura for her tireless work. She labored extensively on the original manuscript and has been central to completing the new edition. She had been a dedicated collaborator, ally, and strategist. Her love, companionship and friendship *en la lucha* leave me in awe always. Mercedes Camps González from Real World Radio and Russell Cobb ably translated many articles. I would also like to extend my gratitude to Hamilton Fish, Taya Kitman, and *The Nation* Institute for their crucial support and encouragement. Deep gratitude to Perry Rosenstein and the Puffin Foundation for backing this project and my work. Special thanks to Katrina vanden Heuvel, Victor Navasky, and *The Nation* magazine for supporting and publishing my reporting. I also wish to acknowledge Alan Kaufman, Sophie Ragsdale, Kim Nauer, Mike Webb, Roane Carey, Ben Wyskida, Suzanne Ceresko, and Andres Conteris for their assistance. Thanks to Jared Rodriguez for the pic and also to journalist Tim Shorrock for the tape. I would also like to thank all of the journalists whose work is cited in this book as well as those people who gave generously of their time in interviews and research, especially Katy Helvenston-Wettengel and Danica Zovko.

A special thanks to my friend, colleague, and mentor, Amy Goodman of *Democracy Now!* She took me under her wing and taught me to fly, and I will forever be in her debt. She is this country's finest journalist. Also to one of my media heroes and friends, Juan Gonzalez, for the example he has set and the battles he has waged. I also wish to acknowledge my rebel media comrades from my *Democracy Now!* family: Dan Coughlin, Maria Carrion, Sharif Abdel Kouddous, Ana Nogueira, Mike Burke, Elizabeth Press, Nell Geiser, Yoruba Richen, John Hamilton, Mike DiFilippo, and Aaron Mate. Also special thanks to: Rep. Jan Schakowsky and her staff, Dave Rapallo from Rep. Henry Waxman's office, Brenda Coughlin, Michael Moore, Elisabeth Benjamin, Kwame Dixon, Dave Isay, Verna Avery Brown, Dave Riker, Diana Cohn, Denis Moynihan, Mattie Harper, Isis Philips, Chuck Scurich, Karen Pomer, Vince Vitrano, Kareem Kouddous, the Antic family, Ian van Hulle, Laura Flanders, the Crespo family, Art Heitzer, William Worthy, the late Dave Dellinger, Tom Hayden, Errol Maitland, Dred Scott Keyes, Elombe Brath, Sharan Harper, Bernard White, Mario Murrillo, Deepa Fernandes, Karen Ranucci, Michael Ratner, Coach Goran Raspudic, St. Rose of Lima and Neighborhood House. For their support and encouragement: Carmen Trotta, Tom Cornell, Frank Donovan, Matt Daloisio, Bill and Sue Frankel-Streit, and the whole CW family. My deep gratitude to Philip, Daniel, and Frida Berrigan and Liz McAlister for their example, their community, and their love.

So much of what can truly be called independent journalism is produced by people and communities in struggle, and the labor is donated because of lack of financial resources and out of a deep commitment to a free media and a just world. I would like to thank the independent media outlets that have supported and published my work over the years: Pacifica Radio, its journalists and workers, and its five stations (WBAI, KPFA, KPFK, KPFT, and WPFW); *Democracy Now!*; Pacifica affiliates and community radio stations across the U.S. and the globe; *Free Speech Radio News*; Dennis Bernstein and *Flashpoints*; Norm Stockwell and WORT; Commondreams.org and Craig Brown; Antiwar.com; Alternet.org; *Z Magazine* and Michael Albert; Guerrilla News Network and Anthony Lappé; Jeffrey St. Clair and Alex Cockburn at Counterpunch.org; CorpWatch.org; the *Indypendent* newspaper and Independent Media Centers worldwide; Sam Husseini and the Institute for Public Accuracy; Brian Drolet and Free Speech TV; Dee Dee Halleck, the godmother of community TV; Danny Schechter and MediaChannel.org; John Alpert and DCTV; *The Progressive* magazine; *Dollars & Sense* magazine; the Grassroots Radio Conference; Ali Abunimah and Nigel Parry at ElectronicIraq.net; and HuffingtonPost.com and Arianna Huffington. Thank you also to independent journalists Dahr Jamail, Arun Gupta, Christian Parenti, Laila al-Arian, Alan Maass, Rosa Clemente, Norman Solomon, Josh Breitbart, Robert Greenwald, Pratap Chatterjee, John Tarleton, Andrew Stern, Kat Aaron, and Rahul Mahajan. To my friends and colleagues whom I worked with and struggled alongside in a place once called Yugoslavia: Ivana Antic, Ljiljana Smajlovic, Terry Sheridan, Katya Subasic, Nenad Stefanovic, Thorne Anderson, Kael Alford, Alex Todorovic, Josh Kucera, Vesna Peric Zimonjic, Ana Nikitovic, Ivan Benussi, Novak Gaijic, and Dusan Cavic. Thanks also to Oronto Douglas and Sowore Omoyele of Nigeria for taking big risks for justice.

I would like to express gratitude and admiration to my dear friend Kathy Kelly, who introduced me to the beautiful people of Iraq in 1998 and traveled that country with me many times thereafter. She is indeed a voice in the wilderness. Also, thanks to Cathy Breen and Abdul Sattar Jihad Jabbar for their friendship in times of struggle in Iraq over many years. Special thanks to Jacquie Soohen, Rick Rowley (and Big Noise Films), and Norm Stockwell for making the impossible happen and breaking down that technological and political firewall. Thanks also to Hans von Sponeck and Denis Halliday, whose courage in simply saying no has been a profound inspiration. Deep gratitude also to those Iraqis whom I cannot name for their own safety who have helped me on occasions too numerous to recount here. Finally, I wish to remember those journalists killed while serving as the eyes and ears of the world. May we have the courage to pick up their cameras, notebooks, and microphones and carry on the struggle and the work.

NOTES

INTRODUCTION

1. Steven R. Hurst and Qassim Abdul-Zahra, "Pieces Emerge in Blackwater Shooting," Associated Press, October 8, 2007.
2. Sudarsan Raghavan, "Tracing the Paths of 5 Who Died in a Storm of Gunfire," Washington Post, October 4, 2007.
3. Jennifer Daskal, "Blackwater in Baghdad: 'It Was a Horror Movie,'" Salon, December 14, 2007.
4. Videotaped interview with Ali Khalaf Salman.
5. Ibid.
6. Ibid.; Jennifer Daskal, "Blackwater in Baghdad," Salon, December 14, 2007.
7. James Glanz and Alissa J. Rubin, "From Errand to Fatal Shot to Hail of Fire to 17 Deaths," New York Times, October 3, 2007.
8. Videotaped interview with Ali Khalaf Salman; Jennifer Daskal, "Blackwater in Baghdad," Salon, December 14, 2007.
9. Ibid.
10. James Glanz and Alissa J. Rubin, "From Errand to Fatal Shot to Hail of Fire to 17 Deaths," New York Times, October 3, 2007.
11. Sudarsan Raghavan, "Tracing the Paths of 5 Who Died in a Storm of Gunfire," Washington Post, October 4, 2007.
12. Sudarsan Raghavan and Josh White, "Blackwater Guards Fired at Fleeing Cars, Soldiers Say," Washington Post, October 12, 2007.
13. James Glanz and Alissa J. Rubin, "From Errand to Fatal Shot to Hail of Fire to 17 Deaths," New York Times, October 3, 2007.
14. Steven R. Hurst and Qassim Abdul-Zahra, "Pieces Emerge in Blackwater Shooting," Associated Press, October 8, 2007.
15. Videotaped interview with Ali Khalaf Salman.
16. Ibid.
17. Jomana Karadsheh and Alan Duke, "Blackwater Incident Witness: 'It Was Hell,'" CNN.com, October 2, 2007.
18. Videotaped interview with Ali Khalaf Salman.
19. Jomana Karadsheh and Alan Duke, "Blackwater Incident Witness: 'It Was Hell,'" CNN.com, October 2, 2007.
20. Sabrina Tavernise and James Glanz, "Guards' Shots Not Provoked, Iraq Concludes," New York Times, September 21, 2007.
21. Videotaped interview with Ali Khalaf Salman.
22. Ibid.

23. Sudarsan Raghavan, "Tracing the Paths of 5 Who Died in a Storm of Gunfire," *Washington Post*, October 4, 2007.

24. Ibid.

25. Videotaped interview with Jawad al-Rubaie.

26. James Glanz and Alissa J. Rubin, "From Errand to Fatal Shot to Hail of Fire to 17 Deaths," *New York Times*, October 3, 2007.

27. Steven R. Hurst and Qassim Abdul-Zahra, "Pieces Emerge in Blackwater Shooting," Associated Press, October 8, 2007.

28. Ibid.

29. Videotaped interview with Ali Khalaf Salman; Jennifer Daskal, "Blackwater in Baghdad," *Salon*, December 14, 2007.

30. Sudarsan Raghavan, "Tracing the Paths of 5 Who Died in a Storm of Gunfire," *Washington Post*, October 4, 2007.

31. Ibid.

32. Kim Sengupta, "The Real Story of Baghdad's Bloody Sunday," *The Independent* (London), September 21, 2007.

33. Ibid.

34. Steven R. Hurst and Qassim Abdul-Zahra, "Pieces Emerge in Blackwater Shooting," Associated Press, October 8, 2007.

35. Jomana Karadsheh and Alan Duke, "Blackwater Incident Witness: 'It Was Hell,'" CNN.com, October 2, 2007.

36. Steven R. Hurst and Qassim Abdul-Zahra, "Pieces Emerge in Blackwater Shooting," Associated Press, October 8, 2007.

37. Ibid.

38. Jomana Karadsheh and Alan Duke, "Blackwater Incident Witness: 'It Was Hell,'" CNN.com, October 2, 2007.

39. Steven R. Hurst and Qassim Abdul-Zahra, "Pieces Emerge in Blackwater Shooting," Associated Press, October 8, 2007.

40. Richard Engel, "Blackwater's Ugly Americans," MSNBC World Blog http://worldblog.msnbc.msn.com/archive/2007/09/28/385833.aspx, September 28, 2007.

41. Sabrina Tavernise, "US Contractor Banned by Iraq Over Shooting," *New York Times*, September 18, 2007.

42. James Glanz and Sabrina Tavernise, "Blackwater Shooting Scene Was Chaotic," *New York Times*, September 28, 2007.

43. Ibid.

44. Richard Engel, "Blackwater's Ugly Americans," MSNBC World Blog, September 28, 2007.

45. James Glanz and Alissa J. Rubin, "From Errand to Fatal Shot to Hail of Fire to 17 Deaths," *New York Times*, October 3, 2007.

46. Jennifer Daskal, "Blackwater in Baghdad," *Salon*, December 14, 2007.

47. Steven R. Hurst and Qassim Abdul-Zahra, "Pieces Emerge in Blackwater Shooting," Associated Press, October 8, 2007.

48. Ned Parker, "Iraq Bans U.S. Security Firm After Deadly Incident," *Los Angeles Times*, September 18, 2007.

49. James Glanz and Alissa J. Rubin, "Blackwater Shootings 'Deliberate Murder,' Iraq Says," *New York Times*, October 8, 2007.

50. Sabrina Tavernise, "US Contractor Banned by Iraq Over Shooting," *New York Times*, September 18, 2007.

51. Ibid.

52. Jeremy Scahill, "Making a Killing," *The Nation*, October 15, 2007.

53. Steve Fainaru, "Four Hired Guns in an Armored Truck, Bullets Flying, and a Pickup and a Taxi Brought to a Halt. Who Did the Shooting and Why?," *Washington Post*, April 15, 2007.

54. Ibid.

55. John M. Broder, "Ex-Paratrooper Is Suspect in Drunken Killing of Iraqi," *New York Times*, October 4, 2007.

56. Committee on Oversight and Government Reform Majority Staff Report, "Additional Information About Blackwater USA," October 1, 2007.

57. John M. Broder, "Ex-Paratrooper Is Suspect in Drunken Killing of Iraqi," *New York Times*, October 4, 2007.

58. Committee on Oversight and Government Reform Majority Staff Report, "Additional Information About Blackwater USA," October 1, 2007.

59. Transcript, Hearing on Iraq Private Contractor Oversight, House Oversight and Government Reform Committee, February 7, 2007.

60. Bill Sizemore, "Blackwater Supports Inquiry into Fatal Shooting," *Virginian-Pilot*, July 25, 2007.

61. Transcript, Hearing on Iraq Private Contractor Oversight, House Oversight and Government Reform Committee, October 2, 2007.

62. John M. Broder, "State Dept. Plans Tighter Control of Security Firm," *New York Times*, October 6, 2007.

63. Transcript, Hearing on Iraq Private Contractor Oversight, House Oversight and Government Reform Committee, February 7, 2007.

64. Bill Sizemore, "Blackwater Supports Inquiry into Fatal Shooting," *Virginian-Pilot*, July 25, 2007.

65. Steve Fainaru, "How Blackwater Sniper Fire Felled 3 Iraqi Guards," *Washington Post*, November 8, 2007.

66. Ibid.

67. Ibid.

68. Ibid.

69. Steve Fainaru and Saad al-Izzi, "U.S. Security Contractors Open Fire in Baghdad," *Washington Post*, May 27, 2007.

70. Ibid.

71. "U.S. Ambassador Calls Blackwater Shooting Horrific, but Still Feels High Regard for Guards," Associated Press, October 25, 2007.

72. Steve Fainaru, "Warnings Unheeded on Guards in Iraq," *Washington Post*, December 24, 2007.

73. Sudarsan Raghavan and Steve Fainaru, "U.S. Repeatedly Rebuffed Iraq on Blackwater Complaints," *Washington Post*, September 23, 2007.

74. Steve Fainaru, "How Blackwater Sniper Fire Felled 3 Iraqi Guards," *Washington Post*, November 8, 2007.

75. Jeremy Scahill, "Making a Killing," *The Nation*, October 15, 2007.

76. "Iraq Makes U-turn on Blackwater," Al Jazeera, September 23, 2007.

77. "Iraq Official: Blackwater Exit Would Leave 'Vacuum,'" Associated Press, September 23, 2007.

78. Sudarsan Raghavan and Steve Fainaru, "U.S. Repeatedly Rebuffed Iraq on Blackwater Complaints," *Washington Post*, September 23, 2007.

79. Author interview, September 2007.

80. Steve Fainaru, "Where Military Rules Don't Apply," *Washington Post*, September 20, 2007.

81. Steve Fainaru, "Warnings Unheeded on Guards in Iraq," *Washington Post*, December 24, 2007.

82. Secretary of State Condoleezza Rice, State Department Press Conference, September 21, 2007.

83. Jeremy Scahill, "Making a Killing," *The Nation*, October 15, 2007.
84. Alissa J. Rubin and Andrew E. Kramer, "Iraqi Premier Says Blackwater Shootings Challenge His Nation's Sovereignty," *New York Times*, September 24, 2007.
85. James Glanz and Sabrina Tavernise, "Security Firm Faces Criminal Charges in Iraq," *New York Times*, September 23, 2007.
86. Ibid.
87. Ibid.
88. Jeremy Scahill, "Making a Killing," *The Nation*, October 15, 2007.
89. For more on this, see Chapter Four.
90. Author interview, September 2007.
91. Steve Fainaru, "Where Military Rules Don't Apply," *Washington Post*, September 20, 2007.
92. Ibid.
93. "U.S. Ambassador Calls Blackwater Shooting Horrific, but Still Feels High Regard for Guards," Associated Press, October 25, 2007.
94. Transcript, Hearing on Iraq Private Contractor Oversight, House Oversight and Government Reform Committee, October 2, 2007.
95. Ibid.
96. Matthew Lee, "Security Firm Is in Smuggling Probe; Blackwater May Be Charged for Bringing Weapons Into Iraq," Associated Press, September 22, 2007.
97. Author copy, letter from Representative Henry Waxman to Howard Krongard, September 18, 2007.
98. Ibid.
99. Jeremy Scahill, "Blackwater's Brothers," *The Nation*, November 15, 2007.
100. Warren P. Strobel, "Inspector General Krongard Resigns," McClatchy Newspapers, December 8, 2007.
101. Joseph Neff, "U.S. Probes Blackwater Weapons Shipments," *Raleigh News and Observer*, September 22, 2007.
102. Author copy, letter from the State Department to Blackwater, September 20, 2007.
103. Author copy, letter from Representative Henry Waxman to Condoleezza Rice, September 25, 2007.
104. Author copy, letter from the State Department to Blackwater USA, September 25, 2007.
105. Author interview, March 2007.
106. John Negroponte's statement before the Senate Appropriations Committee, September 26, 2007.
107. Jomana Karadsheh and Alan Duke, "Blackwater Incident Witness: 'It Was Hell,'" CNN.com, October 2, 2007.
108. "'They Protect People's Lives'—One Month After Baghdad Killings, Bush Defends Blackwater USA," *Democracy Now!*, October 18, 2007.
109. Unless otherwise noted, the description and quotes relating to Erik Prince's Congressional testimony on October 2, 2007, are drawn from the author's firsthand observations or the official transcript of the proceedings provided by the House Oversight and Government Reform Committee.
110. "Edwards Points to a Link," *Washington Post*, October 6, 2007.
111. Charles R. Black, Jr. biography, BKSH & Associates.
112. Committee on Oversight and Government Reform Majority Staff Report, "Additional Information About Blackwater USA," October 1, 2007.
113. Steve Fainaru, "Guards in Iraq Cite Frequent Shootings," *Washington Post*, October 3, 2007.
114. Committee on Oversight and Government Reform Majority Staff Report, "Additional Information About Blackwater USA," October 1, 2007.
115. Ibid.
116. Ibid.

117. Transcript, *Bill Moyers Journal*, February 1, 2008.

118. Dena Bunis, "Rohrabacher Stands Behind Blackwater Chief," *Orange County Register*, October 9, 2007.

119. Author copy.

120. "Blackwater Most Often Shoots First, Congressional Report Says," CNN.com, October 2, 2007.

121. David M. Herszenhorn, "House's Iraq Bill Applies U.S. Laws to Contractors," *New York Times*, October 5, 2007.

122. James Gordon Meek, "Blackwater to Guard FBI Team Probing It," *New York Daily News*, October 3, 2007.

123. Karen DeYoung, "Federal Guards to Protect Agents in Blackwater Investigation," *Washington Post*, October 4, 2007.

124. Author interview, September 2007.

125. James Risen and David Johnston, "Justice Department Briefed Congress on Legal Obstacles in Blackwater Case," *New York Times*, January 16, 2008.

126. Jonathan Karl and Kirit Radia, "ABC News Obtains Text of Blackwater Immunity Deal," ABCNews.go.com, October 30, 2007.

127. Author interview, October 2007.

128. Author interview, October 2007.

129. Ned Parker, "'Wall of Silence' Protects Security Contractor in Iraq," *Los Angeles Times*, September 21, 2007.

130. Committee on Oversight and Government Reform Majority Staff Report, "Additional Information About Blackwater USA," October 1, 2007.

131. Transcript, Hearing on Iraq Private Contractor Oversight, House Oversight and Government Reform Committee, October 2, 2007.

132. Committee on Oversight and Government Reform Majority Staff Report, "Additional Information About Blackwater USA," October 1, 2007.

133. Ibid.

134. Transcript, Hearing on Iraq Private Contractor Oversight, House Oversight and Government Reform Committee, October 2, 2007.

135. Committee on Oversight and Government Reform Majority Staff Report, "Additional Information About Blackwater USA," October 1, 2007.

136. Transcript, Hearing on Iraq Private Contractor Oversight, House Oversight and Government Reform Committee, October 2, 2007.

137. Steve Fainaru, "How Blackwater Sniper Fire Felled 3 Iraqi Guards," *Washington Post*, November 8, 2007.

138. Jennifer Daskal, "Blackwater in Baghdad," *Salon*, December 14, 2007.

139. Ibid.

140. Jomana Karadsheh and Alan Duke, "Blackwater Incident Witness: 'It Was Hell,'" CNN.com, October 2, 2007.

141. Sudarsan Raghavan, "U.S. Offers Cash to Victims in Blackwater Incident," *Washington Post*, October 25, 2007.

142. Ibid; Jennifer Daskal, "Blackwater in Baghdad," *Salon*, December 14, 2007.

143. Sudarsan Raghavan, "U.S. Offers Cash to Victims in Blackwater Incident," *Washington Post*, October 25, 2007.

144. Karen DeYoung, "Immunity Jeopardizes Iraq Probe," *Washington Post*, October 30, 2007.

145. David Johnston and John M. Broder, "F.B.I. Says Guards Killed 14 Iraqis Without Cause," *New York Times*, November 14, 2007.

146. Lara Jakes Jordan, "FBI Finds Blackwater Trucks Patched," Associated Press, January 12, 2008.

147. Author copy of the report.

148. Lara Jakes Jordan, "FBI Finds Blackwater Trucks Patched," Associated Press, January 12, 2008.
149. Ibid.
150. Max Boot, "Accept the Blackwater Mercenaries," *Los Angeles Times*, October 3, 2007.
151. Prepared Statement of Erik D. Prince for the House Committee on Oversight and Government Reform, October 2, 2007.
152. Sworn statement of "Paul," September 18, 2007; Ginger Thompson, "From Texas to Iraq, and Center of Blackwater Case," *New York Times*, January 19, 2008.
153. Sworn statement of "Paul," September 18, 2007.
154. Sudarsan Raghavan and Josh White, "Blackwater Guards Fired at Fleeing Cars, Soldiers Say," *Washington Post*, October 12, 2007.
155. Sworn statement of "Paul," September 18, 2007.
156. Prepared Statement of Erik D. Prince for the House Committee on Oversight and Government Reform, October 2, 2007.
157. Steve Fainaru and Sudarsan Raghavan, "Blackwater Faced Bedlam, Embassy Finds," *Washington Post*, September 28, 2007.
158. Sudarsan Raghavan and Josh White, "Blackwater Guards Fired at Fleeing Cars, Soldiers Say," *Washington Post*, October 12, 2007.
159. Transcript, interview with Erik Prince, *The Charlie Rose Show*, PBS, October 15, 2007.
160. David Johnston and John M. Broder, "F.B.I. Says Guards Killed 14 Iraqis Without Cause," *New York Times*, November 14, 2007.
161. Sudarsan Raghavan and Josh White, "Blackwater Guards Fired at Fleeing Cars, Soldiers Say," *Washington Post*, October 12, 2007.
162. Peter Spiegel, "Gates: U.S., Guards Are at Odds in Iraq," *Los Angeles Times*, October 19, 2007.
163. Karen DeYoung, "Security Firms in Iraq Face New Rules," *Washington Post*, October 24, 2007.
164. James Risen and David Johnston, "Justice Department Briefed Congress on Legal Obstacles in Blackwater Case," *New York Times*, January 16, 2008.
165. Executive Office of the President, "Statement of Administration Policy," October 3, 2007.
166. Author interview, January 2008.
167. Press Release from Representative Jan Schakowsky, "Schakowsky Condemns State Department for Offering Blackwater Immunity," October 30, 2007.
168. "Family Members of Slain Iraqis Sue Blackwater USA for Deadly Baghdad Shooting," *Democracy Now!*, October 11, 2007.
169. Author copy of the complaint.
170. Author interview, October 2007.
171. Transcript, *The Thom Hartmann Show*, Air America, January 29, 2008.
172. "Iraqi Shooting Victims' Families Sue Blackwater," *Virginian-Pilot*, October 12, 2007.
173. Transcript, interview with Erik Prince, *Late Edition With Wolf Blitzer*, CNN, October 14, 2007.
174. J. Michael Waller, "Lawyers for Terror," *New York Post*, October 17, 2007.
175. Author interview, January 2008.
176. Author copy of the complaint.
177. "Blackwater Sued Again for Sept. 9th Attack, Five Iraqis Dead, Ten Wounded," *Democracy Now!*, December 19, 2007.
178. Eric Schmitt and Paul von Zielbauer, "Accord Tightens Control of Security Contractors in Iraq," *New York Times*, December 5, 2007.
179. R.J. Hillhouse, "Blackwater Expanding State Department Contract," TheSpyWhoBilledMe.com, December 4, 2007.
180. Jeremy Scahill, "Blackwater's Business," *The Nation*, December 24, 2007.
181. Ibid.
182. Ibid.

183. August Cole, "Blackwater Vies for Jobs Beyond Guard Duty," *Wall Street Journal*, October 15, 2007.
184. Transcript, Hearing on Iraq Private Contractor Oversight, House Oversight and Government Reform Committee, October 2, 2007.
185. August Cole, "Blackwater Vies for Jobs Beyond Guard Duty," *Wall Street Journal*, October 15, 2007.
186. Ibid.
187. Jeremy Scahill, "Blackwater's Business," *The Nation*, December 24, 2007.
188. Senate Lobbying Records.
189. Author interview, February 2008.
190. Donald Bartlett and James Steele, "Washington's $8 Billion Shadow," *Vanity Fair*, March 2007.
191. Naomi Klein, "Outsourcing Government," *Los Angeles Times*, October 20, 2007.
192. Author interview, July 2007.
193. Jeremy Scahill, "*All* Cowboys Out Now," *The Nation*, November 26, 2007.
194. Committee on Oversight and Government Reform Majority Staff Report, "Additional Information About Blackwater USA," October 1, 2007.
195. Jennifer Parker, "Iraq Disputes Blackwater's Account of Baghdad Killings," ABC News, September 19, 2007.
196. T. Christian Miller, "Private Contractors Outnumber US Troops in Iraq," *Los Angeles Times*, July 4, 2007.
197. Ibid. and Jeremy Scahill, "A Very Private War," *The Guardian*, August 1, 2007.
198. Thom Shanker and Steven Lee Myers, "U.S. Asking Iraq for Wider Rights in Fighting War," *New York Times*, January 25, 2008.
199. White House Press Release, "President Bush Signs H.R. 4986, the National Defense Authorization Act for Fiscal Year 2008 into Law," January 28, 2008.
200. Jeremy Scahill, "*All* Cowboys Out Now," *The Nation*, November 26, 2007.
201. Transcript, interview with Erik Prince, *The Charlie Rose Show*, PBS, October 15, 2007.
202. Author interview, October 2007.
203. "On-the-Record Briefing with Acting Assistant Secretary of State for Diplomatic Security Gregory B. Starr," April 4, 2008. Transcript available at www.state.gov/r/pa/prs/ps/2008/apr/102999.htm.
204. Interview in *Private Armies*, Journeyman Pictures.

CHAPTER 1

1. Transcript, "Remarks as Delivered by Secretary of Defense Donald H. Rumsfeld," The Pentagon, September 10, 2001.
2. Donald H. Rumsfeld, "Transforming the Military," *Foreign Affairs*, May/June, 2002.
3. Erik Prince on *The O'Reilly Factor*, September 27, 2001.
4. Both Cheney and Rumsfeld were original signers of PNAC's "Statement of Principles," www.newamericancentury.org/statementofprinciples.htm, June 3, 1997.
5. *Rebuilding America's Defenses: Strategy, Forces and Resources for a New Century*, The Project for the New American Century, September 2000.
6. Ibid.
7. Renae Merle, "Census Counts 100,000 Contractors in Iraq," the *Washington Post*, December 5, 2006.
8. *Quadrennial Defense Review Report*, Department of Defense, February 6, 2006.
9. Erik Prince speaking at West 2006 conference, January 11, 2006.
10. John Helyar, "Fortunes of War," *Fortune*, July 26, 2004, as posted at http://money.cnn.com/magazines/fortune/fortune_archive/2004/07/26/377180/index.htm.
11. James Hider, "Soldiers of Fortune Rush to Cash in on Unrest in Baghdad," *The Times* of London, March 31, 2004.

12. Coalition Provisional Authority Order Number 17, signed by L. Paul Bremer, June 27, 2004.

13. Transcript, "Hearing of the National Security, Emerging Threats and International Relations Subcommittee of the House Government Reform Committee," June 13, 2006.

14. Blackwater appellate brief, filed October 31, 2005.

15. Erik Prince speaking at West 2006 conference, January 11, 2006.

16. National Defense Authorization Act for Fiscal Year 2007.

17. Report to Congressional Committees, "Military Operations: High-Level DOD Action Needed to Address Long-standing Problems with Management and Oversight of Contractors Supporting Deployed Forces," Government Accountability Office, December 2006.

18. Transcript, Face the Nation, CBS, December 17, 2006.

19. Nathan Hodge, "Washington Urged to Save Money by Raising Private Military 'Contractor Brigade,' " the Financial Times, February 10, 2005.

20. Author copy of Prince Group memo from Erik Prince dated September 16, 2005.

21. Author copy, Central Contractor registration documents for Greystone Limited.

22. Jonathan Franklin, "US Contractor Recruits Guards for Iraq in Chile," the Guardian (London), March 5, 2004.

23. E-mail to author, January 2007.

24. Author copy of contracts and government pay records.

25. Joanne Kimberlin and Bill Sizemore, "Blackwater: On American Soil," the Virginian-Pilot, July 27, 2006.

26. Ibid.

27. See Chapter 1.

28. Joseph E. Schmitz official biography, Department of Defense, February 10, 2005.

29. As stated on the website of the Order of Malta Federal Association, USA, www.smom.org/worldwide-history.php, captured December 4, 2006.

30. Ibid.

CHAPTER 2

1. "The Early History of Holland," www.holland.org/index.pl?paID=6, accessed November 14, 2006.

2. "Albertus Christiaan Van Raalte Papers," hope.edu/jointarchives/collections/registers/wts/vanraalt.html, accessed November 14, 2006.

3. Ibid.

4. "The Early History of Holland," www.holland.org/index.pl?paID=6, accessed November 14, 2006.

5. Peter Prince obituary, Holland area newspaper, May 21, 1943.

6. Michael Lozon, Vision on Main Street: Downtown Holland's Resurgence as the Heart of the Community, Lumir Corporation, 1994, p. 59.

7. Peter Prince obituary.

8. Michael Lozon, Vision on Main Street: Downtown Holland's Resurgence as the Heart of the Community, Lumir Corporation, 1994, p. 59.

9. Jim Timmerman, "Holland's Home-Grown Prince Corp. Has Big Role in Community," the Holland Sentinel, July 19, 1996.

10. "Prince Manufacturing Co. Builds Diecast Machines," the Holland Sentinel, June 5, 1969.

11. Ibid.

12. "Prince Corp. Constantly Expanding," the Holland Sentinel, May 16, 1973.

13. Caroline Vernia, "Prince's Jewel: Production of Illuminated Visors," the Holland Sentinel, January 26, 1980.

14. Letter from Family Research Council president Gary Bauer, April 13, 1995.

15. Ibid.

16. Caroline Vernia, "Prince's Jewel: Production of Illuminated Visors," the Holland Sentinel, January 26, 1980.

17. Ibid.

18. "Blackwater's Founder on the Record," the *Virginian-Pilot*, July 24, 2006.

19. Ibid.

20. Prince Corporation brochure, undated.

21. Katherine Sanderson, "Prince Expanding, Building New Office," the *Holland and Golden Sentinel*, January 29, 1983.

22. Diane Carmony, "Prince Corp. Plans Functional, Aesthetically Pleasing Facilities," the *Grand Rapids Press*, August 31, 1987.

23. Ibid.

24. "Edgar Prince: Spirit of Giving Defined a Giant," the *Grand Rapids Press*, March 3, 1995.

25. Katherine Sanderson, "Prince Expanding, Building New Office," the *Holland and Gold Sentinel*, January 23, 1983.

26. Robert Young Pelton, *Licensed to Kill: Hired Guns in the War on Terror*, Crown, New York, 2006, p. 3.

27. Letter from Family Research Council president Gary Bauer, April 13, 1995.

28. "Orlando Magic, NBA Team Valuations," *Forbes*, www.forbes.com/lists/2005/32/324583.html, accessed November 30, 2006.

29. Rachel Burstein and Kerry Lauerman, "She Did It Amway," *Mother Jones*, September/October 1996.

30. Ibid.

31. Ibid.

32. Ibid.

33. Ibid.

34. Author copy of Holland, Michigan, Polk directories.

35. Letter from Family Research Council president Gary Bauer, April 13, 1995.

36. Ibid.

37. Rachel Burstein and Kerry Lauerman, "She Did It Amway," *Mother Jones*, September/October 1996.

38. Ibid.

39. June Kronholz, "Big Test: In Michigan, Vouchers Get Money and Savvy and a Broad Coalition—Amway Chief and Wife Give Program Higher Profile, Better Shot at Success," the *Wall Street Journal*, October 25, 2000; "Biographical Information About Betsy DeVos," Associated Press, October 21, 2006.

40. Ward Harkavy, "The Bush-Cheney Gazillions Tour," *The Village Voice*, October 22, 2003.

41. Gordon Trowbridge, Charlie Cain, and Mark Hornbeck, "Granholm Wins Second Term," the *Detroit News*, November 8, 2006.

42. Ted Roelofs, "(Mostly) Conservative to the Core; Dutch Values Made Us This Way, But a Large Group Has Never Fit the Mold," the *Grand Rapids Press*, October 31, 2004.

43. Russ Bellant, *The Religious Right in Michigan Politics*, Americans for Religious Liberty, Silver Spring, Maryland, 1996, pp. 52–55, 63.

44. Ibid., p. 61.

45. Ibid., p. 33.

46. Ibid., p. 32.

47. Ibid., pp. 34–35.

48. Ibid., p. 35.

49. "Elsa Prince, DeVos Give Calvin College $10 Million Each," the *Holland Sentinel*, July 27, 1998; author copy of Edgar and Elsa Prince Foundation records.

50. Michael Lozon, *Vision on Main Street: Downtown Holland's Resurgence as the Heart of the Community*, Lumir Corporation, 1994, pp. 101–115, 136–140.

51. Ibid., pp. 102–103.

52. Ibid., pp. 86–87.

53. Ibid.

54. Letter from Family Research Council president Gary Bauer, April 13, 1995.

55. Ibid.

56. "Major Auto Suppliers in West Michigan," *Grand Rapids Business Journal*, May 26, 1992.

57. "The Prince Legacy," the *Grand Rapids Press*, March 3, 1995.

58. Michael Lozon, *Vision on Main Street*, p. 101; "Edgar Prince: Spirit of Giving Defined a Giant," the *Grand Rapids Press*, March 3, 1995.

59. "Edgar Prince: Spirit of Giving Defined a Giant," the *Grand Rapids Press*, March 3, 1995; Jim Harger, "Prince Corp. Will Continue to Prosper," the *Grand Rapids Press*, March 4, 1995.

60. Jim Harger, "Prince Corp. Will Continue to Prosper," the *Grand Rapids Press*, March 4, 1995.

61. "Edgar Prince: Spirit of Giving Defined a Giant," the *Grand Rapids Press*, March 3, 1995.

62. Ibid.

63. Jim Harger, "Prince Corp. Will Continue to Prosper," the *Grand Rapids Press*, March 4, 1995.

64. Ibid.

65. John Agar and John Burdick, "Eulogies Focus on Religious Side of Prince," the *Holland Sentinel*, March 6, 1995; Letter from Family Research Council president Gary Bauer, April 13, 1995.

66. John Agar and John Burdick, "Eulogies Focus on Religious Side of Prince," the *Holland Sentinel*, March 6, 1995.

67. "A Christian Man; Holland Philanthropist, Industrialist Edgar D. Prince Leaves Many Hometown Legacies," the *Grand Rapids Press* (Lakeshore supplement), March 3, 1995.

68. John Burdick, "Bil Mar Cofounder, Downtown Supporter Honored," the *Holland Sentinel*, October 19, 2002.

69. "Blackwater's Founder on the Record," the *Virginian-Pilot*, July 24, 2006.

70. John Agar, "Family Says He Always Put Them First," the *Holland Sentinel*, March 3, 1995.

71. John Agar and John Burdick, "Eulogies Focus on Religious Side of Prince," the *Holland Sentinel*, March 6, 1995.

72. John Agar, "Family Says He Always Put Them First," the *Holland Sentinel*, March 3, 1995.

73. Ibid.

74. Letter from Family Research Council president Gary Bauer, April 13, 1995.

75. Joseph Neff and Jay Price, "A Business Gets a Start," the *News & Observer* (Raleigh, North Carolina), July 29, 2004.

76. Ibid.

77. Author copy of Federal Election Commission records.

78. Ibid.

79. Erik Prince's official Prince Manufacturing biography.

80. Ted Roelofs, "Neither Party Well Off Here as Primary Nears," the *Grand Rapids Press*, February 23, 1992.

81. Ibid.

82. Author copy of Erik Prince's military records; Interviews 2006.

83. Interviews 2006.

84. Michael Lozon, "New Era Begins at Prince," the *Holland Sentinel*, October 2, 1996.

85. Ibid.

86. Ibid.

87. Richard Harrold, "City Officials Talked With Governor About Job Loss," the *Holland Sentinel*, March 31, 2004.

88. Mark Sanchez, "A Prince, by Any Other Name," the *Holland Sentinel*, October 16, 1998; Patrick Revere, "Analysts: Area Hit Hardest by JCI," the *Holland Sentinel*, June 2, 2006.

89. Ted Roelofs, "(Mostly) Conservative to the Core; Dutch Values Made Us This Way, But a Large Group Has Never Fit the Mold," the *Grand Rapids Press*, October 31, 2004.

90. John Burdick, "Bil Mar Cofounder, Downtown Supporter Honored," the *Holland Sentinel*, October 19, 2002; Russ Bellant, *The Religious Right in Michigan Politics*, p. 13.

91. John Burdick, "Bil Mar Cofounder, Downtown Supporter Honored," the *Holland Sentinel*, October 19, 2002.

92. Federal campaign records.

93. June Kronholz, "Big Test: In Michigan, Vouchers Get Money and Savvy and a Broad Coalition—Amway Chief and Wife Give Program Higher Profile, Better Shot at Success," the *Wall Street Journal*, October 25, 2000.

94. "Kerry Candaele's interview with Robert Pelton," www.iraqforsale.org/ robert_pelton.php, accessed November 28, 2006.

95. Joan Nicole Prince obituary from Herrick District Library obituary file; Obituary, the *Albany Times Union*, June 24, 2003.

96. Amazon.com page for *Christian Fatherhood*, www.amazon.com/exec/obidos/tg/detail/ 0965858227, accessed November 30, 2006.

97. "Voter's Guide for Serious Catholics," Catholic Answers Action, San Diego, 2006.

98. Ibid.

99. Karl Keating, "Karl Keating's E-Letter," April 29, 2003.

100. Author copy of Freiheit Foundation records.

101. Ibid.

102. David D. Kirkpatrick, "Club of the Most Powerful Gathers in Strictest Privacy," the *New York Times*, August 28, 2004.

103. Ibid.

104. Ibid.

105. Ibid.

106. Ibid.

107. Ibid.

108. Ibid.

109. Ibid.

110. Ibid.

111. Russ Bellant, *The Religious Right in Michigan Politics*, p. 13.

112. Ibid., p. 63.

113. Author copy of Freiheit Foundation records.

114. Ibid.

115. See Prison Fellowship Web site: www.prisonfellowship.org.

116. Joseph Loconte, "God's Warden; How Charles Colson Went From Watergate Villain to Christian Hero," *The Weekly Standard*, October 17, 2005.

117. David Plotz, "Charles Colson," *Slate* magazine, March 11, 2000.

118. Morton H. Halperin, "Bush Is No Nixon—He's Worse," the *Los Angeles Times*, July 16, 2006.

119. David Plotz, "Charles Colson," *Slate* magazine, March 11, 2000.

120. Ibid.

121. Prison Fellowship Web site, www.prisonfellowship.org/generic.asp?ID=138, accessed December 4, 2006.

122. Ibid.

123. Transcript, "America's Compassion in Action: Remarks by the President at the First White House National Conference on Faith-Based and Community Initiatives at the Washington Hilton and Towers," www.whitehouse.gov/news/releases/2004/06/ 20040601-10.html, June 1, 2004.

124. Ibid.

125. Gary Emerling, "Inmate Aid Project Grows," the *Washington Times*, March 20, 2005.

126. Charles Colson, "How Now Shall We Live," *Journal of Markets and Morality*, Spring 2002.

127. Chuck Colson, "What's Hidden in the Shadows: Radical Islam and U.S. Prisons," Town-Hall.com, September 26, 2006.

128. Ibid.

129. Ibid.

130. "Honoring Chuck Colson," www.acton.org/dinner/, accessed November 27, 2006.

131. Author copy of Freiheit Foundation records.

132. Acton Institute Board of Directors, www.acton.org/about/board/, accessed November 27, 2006; Joan Nicole Prince obituary from Herrick District Library obituary file.

133. Author copy of recording of Charles Colson's speech "War of the Worlds" at the Acton Annual Dinner, October 26, 2006.

134. "Evangelicals and Catholics Together: The Christian Mission in the Third Millennium," *First Things*, May 1994.

135. Damon Linker, *The Theocons: Secular America Under Siege*, Doubleday, New York, 2006.

136. "Evangelicals and Catholics Together: The Christian Mission in the Third Millennium," *First Things*, May 1994.

137. Ibid.

138. Ibid.

139. Damon Linker, *The Theocons*, p. 7.

140. "Evangelicals and Catholics Together: The Christian Mission in the Third Millennium," *First Things*, May 1994.

141. Ibid.

142. Ibid.

143. Ibid.

144. Ibid.

145. Ibid.

146. Damon Linker, *The Theocons*, pp. 85–86.

147. Charles Colson, "How Now Shall We Live," *Journal of Markets and Morality*, Spring 2002.

148. Nathan Hodge, "Blackwater CEO Touts Private Peacekeeping Model," *Defense Daily*, February 23, 2005.

149. Freiheit Foundation and Edgar and Elsa Prince Foundation records.

150. "Milestone Man," www.haggai-institute.com/News/NewsItem.asp?ItemID=990, accessed November 27, 2006.

151. "Where Christians are Persecuted Today," Christian Freedom International, www.christianfreedom.org/program_detail.aspx?id=77, accessed November 27, 2006.

152. Hans S. Nichols, "Jacobson Converts Faith Into Action," *Insight Magazine*, August 12, 2002.

153. "Christians Face Uncertain Future in Iraq, Says Christian Freedom International," *U.S. Newswire*, August 2, 2004; "Losing the Christian Right?" *The Hotline*, March 31, 2006; Hans S. Nichols, "Jacobson Converts Faith into Action," *Insight Magazine*, August 12, 2002.

154. "Christian Freedom International Urges Military Action to Protect the World's Persecuted Christians and Others," *PR Newswire*, October 8, 2001.

155. Christian Freedom International records; David R. Sands, "VOA Director Was Undermined by Doubts; 'Principled Conservative' Driven Out," the *Washington Times*, September 5, 2002; Mark Schapiro and Eric Burnand, "Keeping Faith," *The Nation*, January 17, 1987; Walter Pincus, "Army's Iraq Media Plan Criticized," the *Washington Post*, October 16, 2003.

156. June Kronholz, "Big Test: In Michigan, Vouchers Get Money and Savvy and a Broad Coalition—Amway Chief and Wife Give Program Higher Profile, Better Shot at Success," the *Wall Street Journal*, October 25, 2000.

157. Ibid.

158. Transcript, "Remarks by the President Upon Arrival at the South Lawn," www.whitehouse.gov/news/releases/2001/09/20010916-2.html, September 16, 2001.

CHAPTER 3

1. Interview, July 2006.

2. Ibid.

3. Ibid.

4. Author copy, Erik D. Prince military records.

5. Interview, July 2006.

6. "Blackwater's Founder on the Record," the *Virginian-Pilot*, July 24, 2006.

7. "Wife of Prince Founder Disappointed by Layoffs," the *Holland Sentinel*, April 1, 2004.

8. "Blackwater's Founder on the Record," the *Virginian-Pilot*, July 24, 2006.

9. Blackwater USA Web site, www.blackwaterusa.com/about/, accessed 11/14/2006.

10. "Blackwater's Founder on the Record," the *Virginian-Pilot*, July 24, 2006.

11. Interview, August 2006.

12. Dan Briody, *The Halliburton Agenda: The Politics of Oil and Money*, John Wiley & Sons, Hoboken, New Jersey, 2004, p. 195–196.

13. Ibid., p. 184.

14. Ibid.

15. Ibid., p. 196.

16. Interview, July 2006.

17. Interview, July 2006.

18. Jon Frank, "Best of the Best Arms Training Site Aims to Lure Gun Enthusiasts, Soldiers," the *Virginian-Pilot*, September 27, 1998.

19. "The End of Democracy?" *First Things*, November 1996.

20. Ibid.

21. Ibid.

22. Ibid.

23. Charles W. Colson, "Kingdoms in Conflict," *First Things*, November 1996.

24. James C. Dobson, "The End of Democracy? A Discussion Continued," *First Things*, January 1997.

25. "The End of Democracy?" *First Things*, November 1996.

26. Freiheit Foundation and Edgar and Elsa Prince Foundation records.

27. Erik D. Prince military records.

28. Delaware incorporation records.

29. Jon Frank, "Best of the Best Arms Training Site Aims to Lure Gun Enthusiasts, Soldiers," the *Virginian-Pilot*, September 27, 1998.

30. Blackwater USA Web site, captured April 5, 2004.

31. US Census.

32. Anna Saita, "Hearing Set on Beach Man's Plan for Shooting Range in Moyock," the *Virginian-Pilot*, December 5, 1996.

33. Ibid.

34. Anna Saita, "Currituck Rejects Outdoor Firing Range: An Ordinance Change Was Needed to Pave the Way for the Project," the *Virginian-Pilot*, January 8, 1997.

35. Ibid.

36. Ibid.

37. Ibid.

38. Ibid.

39. Jon Frank, "Best of the Best Arms Training Site Aims to Lure Gun Enthusiasts, Soldiers," the *Virginian-Pilot*, September 27, 1998.

40. Interview, July 2006.

41. Interview, July 2006.

42. www.navstanorva.navy.mil/history.htm, November 14, 2006.

43. Interview, July 2006.

44. Ibid.

45. Jon Frank, "Best of the Best Arms Training Site Aims to Lure Gun Enthusiasts, Soldiers," the *Virginian-Pilot*, September 27, 1998.

46. Ibid.

47. Interview, July 2006.

48. Steve Waterman, "Blackwater Lodge," http://williambowles.info/guests/blackwater.html, accessed June 23, 2006.

49. Ibid.

50. Kathy Scruggs, "Class Is In for SWAT Teams; North Carolina Facility Provides Realistic Setting to Train Officers for the Latest Type of Domestic Terrorism," the *Atlanta Journal-Constitution*, October 24, 1999.

51. Jon Frank, "Training Program Simulates a School Under Assault; Blackwater Lodge in Moyock Is Run by Former SEALs," the *Virginian-Pilot*, September 23, 1999.

52. Ibid.

53. Ibid.

54. Interview, July 2006.

55. Kathy Scruggs, "Class Is In for SWAT Teams," the *Atlanta Journal-Constitution*, October 24, 1999.

56. Jon Frank, "Training Program Simulates a School Under Assault," the *Virginian-Pilot*, September 23, 1999.

57. September 19, 2006 e-mail from General Services Administration spokesman Jon Anderson.

58. www.gsaadvantage.gov/ref_text/GS07F0149K/GS07F0149K_online.htm; www.gsaelibrary .gsa.gov/ElibMain/ContractorInfo?contractNumber=GS-07F-0149K&contractorName =BLACKWATER+LODGE+AND+TRAINING+CE&executeQuery=YES; accessed November 14, 2006.

59. Interview, August 2006.

60. Department of Defense records.

61. Federal Election Commission records.

62. September 19, 2006 e-mail.

63. Ibid.

64. Ibid.

65. Interview, July 2006.

66. Ibid.

67. FedBizOps Web site, www.fbo.gov/servlet/Documents/R/450249, accessed July 25, 2006.

68. Adm. Vern Clark testimony to the Senate Armed Services Committee , May 3, 2001.

69. 1998 Department of the Navy Posture Statement, chapter 7: "Efficiency: Exploiting the Revolution in Business Affairs."

70. Ibid.

71. Barry Yeoman, "Soldiers of Good Fortune," *Mother Jones*, May/June 2003.

72. Bill Sizemore and Joanne Kimberlin, "Profitable Patriotism," the *Virginian-Pilot*, July 24, 2006.

73. Chris Taylor speech at George Washington University Law School, January 28, 2005.

74. "Defense Contracts," *Defense Daily*, September 18, 2002.

75. Ibid.

76. Matthew Dolan, "Tough Duty: The Terror Watch; Protecting Their Own," the *Virginian-Pilot*, December 15, 2002.

77. Erik Prince on *The O'Reilly Factor*, September 27, 2001.

78. Federal Procurement Data System records.

79. Ibid.

80. Regent University Web site, www.regent.edu, accessed November 17, 2006.

81. Interview, August 2006.

82. Ibid.

83. Author copy, Delaware Department of State corporation records.

84. Interviews, August 2006; Robert Young Pelton, *Licensed to Kill: Hired Guns in the War on Terror*, Crown, New York, 2006, pp. 36–41.

85. Ibid.

86. "Former Alex.Brown Exec Becomes CIA's No. 3 Man," Associated Press, March 16, 2001.

87. Anita Raghavan, "Bankers Trust's Vice Chairman Resigns to Become Counselor to CIA Director," the *Wall Street Journal*, January 21, 1998.

88. Evan Thomas, "A James Bond Wanna-be? Buzzy Krongard Plans to Shake Up the Troubled CIA," *Newsweek*, May 28, 2001.

89. Ibid.

90. Ibid.

91. Ibid.

92. Chris Blackhurst, "Mystery of terror 'insider dealers,'" *Independent on Sunday* (UK), October 14, 2001.

93. Evan Thomas, "A James Bond Wanna-be? Buzzy Krongard Plans to Shake Up the Troubled CIA," *Newsweek*, May 28, 2001.

94. David Ignatius, "The CIA as Venture Capitalist," the *Washington Post*, September 29, 1999.

95. "It's Not Going to Be Pretty, CIA Says," the (Hobart) *Mercury*, October 20, 2001.

96. Tony Allen-Mills, "Let Bin Laden Stay Free, Says CIA Man," the *Sunday Times* (UK), January 9, 2005.

97. Ibid.

98. Pelton, *Licensed to Kill*, p. 37.

99. Interview, August 2006.

100. Ibid.

101. Interviews, August 2006; Pelton, *Licensed to Kill*, pp. 36–41.

102. Interview, August 2006.

103. Interviews, August 2006. Pelton, *Licensed to Kill*, pp. 36–37.

104. Interview, August 2006.

105. Ibid.

106. Ibid.

107. Pelton, *Licensed to Kill*, p. 38.

108. Ibid., pp. 36–41.

109. Ibid., pp. 38–41.

110. Ibid.

111. Ken Silverstein, "Revolving Door to Blackwater Causes Alarm at CIA," *Harper's Magazine* online, September 12, 2006.

112. Ibid.

113. Interview, August 2006.

114. Barry Yeoman, "Soldiers of Good Fortune," *Mother Jones*, May/June 2003.

CHAPTER 4

1. Anthony Shadid, *Night Draws Near: Iraq's People in the Shadow of America's War*, Henry Holt and Company, New York, 2005, p. 283.

2. Alfonso Rojo, "The Gulf War: Death Comes to a Town Almost Forgotten by War—Eyewitness," the *Guardian* (London), February 18, 1991.

3. Ibid.

4. David Fairhall, Kathy Evans, and Richard Norton-Taylor, "RAF Admits Bomb Hit Civilian Area—'50 Die' as Laser Aimer Fails," the *Guardian* (London), February 18, 1991.

5. David White, "Britain Admits Bomb Missed Target and Hit Town," the *Financial Times* (London), February 18, 1991.

6. Finlay Marshall, "RAF Regrets Civilian Deaths In Fallouja," The Press Association Limited, February 18, 1991.

7. Ibid.

8. "Pentagon Top Brass 'Admit Bomb Error,'" the *Courier-Mail* (Queensland, Australia), February 18, 1991.

9. This is based on the author's time spent in Fallujah in 2002.

10. Rajiv Chandrasekaran, "Troops Kill Anti-U.S. Protesters; Accounts Differ; 13 Dead, Many Hurt, Iraqis Say," the *Washington Post*, April 30, 2003.

11. Interview, November 2006.

12. Rajiv Chandrasekaran, "Troops Kill Anti-U.S. Protesters; Accounts Differ; 13 Dead, Many Hurt, Iraqis Say," the *Washington Post*, April 30, 2003.

13. Charles J. Hanley, "U.S. Troops, Conservative Religion a Fiery Combination in Heartland Town," Associated Press, May 1, 2003.

14. Rajiv Chandrasekaran, "Troops Kill Anti-U.S. Protesters; Accounts Differ; 13 Dead, Many Hurt, Iraqis Say," the *Washington Post*, April 30, 2003.

15. Charles J. Hanley, "U.S. Troops, Conservative Religion a Fiery Combination in Heartland Town," Associated Press, May 1, 2003.

16. Ibid.

17. Anthony Shadid, *Night Draws Near*, p. 233.

18. Charles J. Hanley, "U.S. Troops, Conservative Religion a Fiery Combination in Heartland Town," Associated Press, May 1, 2003.

19. Larry Kaplow, "U.S. Claims Defense in Killing 13, Iraqis Said Just Protesting," Cox News Service, April 29, 2003. Also: Rajiv Chandrasekaran, "Troops Kill Anti-U.S. Protesters; Accounts Differ; 13 Dead, Many Hurt, Iraqis Say," the *Washington Post*, April 30, 2003.

20. Ellen Knickmeyer, "U.S. Soldiers Fire on Iraqi Protesters After Reportedly Taking Fire; Hospital Chief Says 13 Iraqis Are Dead," Associated Press, April 29, 2003.

21. Ellen Knickmeyer, "U.S. Soldiers Fire on Iraqi Protesters After Reportedly Taking Fire; Hospital Chief Says 13 Iraqis Are Dead," Associated Press, April 29, 2003.

22. Among others: "US Troops Shoot Dead Three Iraqi Demonstrators," Xinhua News Agency (China), April 30, 2003.

23. Mohamed Hasni, "US Troops Shoot Dead 13 Iraqis at Anti-American Protest," Agence France-Presse, April 29, 2003.

24. Ellen Knickmeyer, "U.S. Soldiers Fire on Iraqi Protesters After Reportedly Taking Fire; Hospital Chief Says 13 Iraqis Are Dead," Associated Press, April 29, 2003.

25. Rajiv Chandrasekaran, "Troops Kill Anti-U.S. Protesters; Accounts Differ; 13 Dead, Many Hurt, Iraqis Say," the *Washington Post*, April 30, 2003.

26. Human Rights Watch Report, "Violent Response: The U.S. Army in Al-Falluja," June 2003.

27. These claims were very widespread and represented in virtually all on-the-ground media reports from Fallujah on the incident.

28. Rajiv Chandrasekaran, "Troops Kill Anti-U.S. Protesters; Accounts Differ; 13 Dead, Many Hurt, Iraqis Say," the *Washington Post*, April 30, 2003.

29. Alan Philps, "U.S. Troops Fire Into Crowd: 13 Iraqis Killed, 75 Wounded. U.S. Claims Protesters Fired First Shots," the *Daily Telegraph* (London), April 30, 2003.

30. Ibid.

31. Elizabeth Neuffer, "US, Iraqis at Odds on Protesters' Deaths," the *Boston Globe*, April 30, 2003.

32. Ibid.

33. Rajiv Chandrasekaran, "Troops Kill Anti-U.S. Protesters; Accounts Differ; 13 Dead, Many Hurt, Iraqis Say," the *Washington Post*, April 30, 2003.

34. Phil Reeves, "Iraq Aftermath: At Least 10 Dead As US Soldiers Fire on School Protest; US Put Under Pressure After Civilian Shooting, As Europe Forges Ahead," *The Independent* (London), April 30, 2003.

35. Ibid.

36. Ibid.

37. Ellen Knickmeyer, "U.S. Soldiers Fire on Iraqi Protesters After Reportedly Taking Fire; Hospital Chief Says 13 Iraqis Are Dead," Associated Press, April 29, 2003; Mohamed Hasni, "US Troops Shoot Dead 13 Iraqis at Anti-American Protest," Agence France-Presse, April 29, 2003.

38. Human Rights Watch Report, "Violent Response: The U.S. Army in Al-Falluja," June 2003.

39. Ibid.

40. Ellen Knickmeyer, "U.S. Soldiers Fire on Iraqi Protesters After Reportedly Taking Fire; Hospital Chief Says 13 Iraqis Are Dead," Associated Press, April 29, 2003.

41. "US Troops Kill 13 at Pro-Saddam Rally, Claim Self-defence," Agence France-Presse, April 29, 2003.

42. Elizabeth Neuffer, "US, Iraqis at Odds on Protesters' Deaths," the *Boston Globe*, April 30, 2003.

43. Phil Reeves, "Iraq Aftermath: At Least 10 Dead As US Soldiers Fire on School Protest; US Put Under Pressure After Civilian Shooting, As Europe Forges Ahead," *The Independent* (London), April 30, 2003.

44. Human Rights Watch Report, "Violent Response: The U.S. Army in Al-Falluja," June 2003.

45. Ibid.

46. Scott Wilson, "U.S. Forces Kill 2 More Civilians; Tensions Remain High in City in Central Iraq," the *Washington Post*, May 1, 2003.

47. Ian Fisher, "U.S. Force Said to Kill 15 Iraqis During an Anti-American Rally," the *New York Times*, April 30, 2003.

48. See, for example: Martin Sieff, "Falluja Fire-bell in the Night," United Press International, May 1, 2003.

49. P. Mitchell Prothero, "Second Day of Fighting at al-Falluja," UPI, April 30, 2003.

50. Ian Fisher with Michael R. Gordon, "G.I.s Kill 2 More Protesters in an Angry Iraqi City," the *New York Times*, May 1, 2003.

51. P. Mitchell Prothero, "Second Day of Fighting at al-Falluja," UPI, April 30, 2003.

52. Ian Fisher with Michael R. Gordon, "G.I.s Kill 2 More Protesters in an Angry Iraqi City," the *New York Times*, May 1, 2003.

53. Scott Wilson, "U.S. Forces Kill 2 More Civilians; Tensions Remain High in City in Central Iraq," the *Washington Post*, May 1, 2003.

54. Ibid.

55. Ibid.

56. Ian Fisher with Michael R. Gordon, "G.I.s Kill 2 More Protesters in an Angry Iraqi City," the *New York Times*, May 1, 2003.

57. "Rumsfeld Flies Into Iraq and Declares Iraqis Free," Agence France-Presse, April 30, 2003.

58. Ibid.

59. Phil Reeves, "Iraq Aftermath: Iraqi Rage Grows After Fallujah Massacre," *Independent on Sunday* (London), May 4, 2003.

60. As published on the *Guardian* (London) Web site, "Full text: The Saddam Hussein 'Letter,'" translated by Brian Whitaker, April 30, 2003.

61. Charles J. Hanley, "U.S. Troops, Conservative Religion a Fiery Combination in Heartland Town," Associated Press, May 1, 2003.

62. Niko Price, "U.S. Troops Again Fire on Anti-American Protesters; Rumsfeld Visits Baghdad," Associated Press, April 30, 2003.

63. Charles J. Hanley, "U.S. Troops, Conservative Religion a Fiery Combination in Heartland Town," Associated Press, May 1, 2003.

64. Sudarsan Raghavan, "Resistance Songs Urge Iraqis to Rise Up Against Occupiers," *Knight-Ridder*, December 28, 2003.

65. Ivan Watson, "Inexpensive Propaganda DVDs Being Produced by Insurgents in Fallujah, Iraq," *National Public Radio* Morning Edition transcript, March 31, 2004.

66. Sudarsan Raghavan, "Resistance Songs Urge Iraqis to Rise Up Against Occupiers," *Knight-Ridder*, December 28, 2003.

CHAPTER 5

1. Some of the best information on Paul Bremer's time in Iraq can be found in his book: L. Paul Bremer III with Malcolm McConnell, *My Year in Iraq: The Struggle to Build a Future of Hope*, Simon & Schuster, New York, 2006.

2. T. Christian Miller, "War's Aftermath: Stinging Report on Missing Funds; Audit Finds U.S.-led Coalition Managed Iraqi Money Poorly," the *Los Angeles Times*, January 31, 2005.

3. Bremer cochaired, with former Attorney General Edwin Meese, the Heritage Foundation's Homeland Security Taskforce.

4. Nixon Center program brief, "Countering the Changing Threat of International Terrorism; A Presentation by Ambassador L. Paul Bremer" at The Nixon Center, Washington, D.C., July 19, 2000. See: www.nixoncenter.org/publications/Program%20Briefs/vol6no19 Bremer.htm.

5. See Marsh & McLennan Web site www.mmc.com/about/history.php.

6. L. Paul Bremer, "What Now? Crush Them; Let Us Wage Total War on Our Foes," the *Wall Street Journal*, September 13, 2001.

7. *Fox Special Report with Brit Hume* transcript, "Terrorism Hits America," Fox News, September 11, 2001.

8. Naomi Klein, "Downsizing in Disguise," *The Nation*, June 23, 2003.

9. Ibid.

10. Ibid.

11. L. Paul Bremer, *My Year in Iraq*, pp. 6–7.

12. Knut Royce (*Newsday*), "Diplomat Expected to Take Charge in Iraq; Bremer to Replace Garner as Leader of Postwar Transition," *Seattle Times*, May 2, 2003.

13. Naomi Klein, "Downsizing in Disguise," *The Nation*, June 23, 2003.

14. Romesh Ratnesar with Simon Robinson, "Life Under Fire," *Time*, July 14, 2003.

15. David Leigh, "General Sacked by Bush Says He Wanted Early Elections," the *Guardian*, March 18, 2004.

16. Mike Allen, "Expert on Terrorism to Direct Rebuilding," the *Washington Post*, May 2, 2003.

17. Bremer, *My Year in Iraq*, p. 8.

18. Scott Wilson, "Bremer Adopts Firmer Tone for U.S. Occupation of Iraq," the *Washington Post*, May 26, 2003.

19. Bremer, *My Year in Iraq*, p. 4.

20. In *My Year in Iraq*, Bremer describes Defense Secretary Rumsfeld as giving him his "marching orders" regarding de-Baathification with Feith doing the groundwork, p. 39.

21. Naomi Klein, "Baghdad Year Zero," *Harper's*, September 2004.

22. Lara Marlowe, "Mission Impossible," the *Irish Times*, April 17, 2004.

23. Anthony Shadid, *Night Draws Near*, p. 152.

24. David Rieff, "Blueprint for a Mess," *The New York Times Magazine*, November 2, 2003.

25. Marc Lacey, "After the War: The Military; Jobs at Risk, Ex-Iraqi Soldiers Vow Fight If Allies Don't Pay," the *New York Times*, May 25, 2003.

26. Ilene R. Prusher, "Jobless Iraqi Soldiers Issue Threats," the *Christian Science Monitor*, June 5, 2003.

27. Edward Wong, "Beleaguered Premier Warns U.S. to Stop Interfering in Iraq's Politics," the *New York Times*, March 30, 2006.

28. Andrew Marshall (Reuters), "Sacked Troops, Tribes Threaten U.S. with War," *Toronto Star*, June 3, 2003.

29. Ibid.

30. Interview with Robert Frost, "Breakfast With Frost," BBC, as quoted on the BBC Web site, http://news.bbc.co.uk/2/hi/middle_east/3029538.stm, June 29, 2003.

31. Romesh Ratnesar with Simon Robinson, "Life Under Fire," *Time*, July 14, 2003.

32. Ibid.

33. Mark Zimmermann, "Iraq Envoy Says Faith Gives Him Strength," *Catholic Standard*, June 19, 2003.

34. Ed Sealover, "Candidates Talk Religion at Focus Forum," the *Colorado Springs Gazette*, August 1, 2006.

35. Dick Foster, "Bremer Says He Has Background Others Lack; Lawyer Running on His International Experience, Problem-solving Ability," *Rocky Mountain News* (Denver), July 26, 2006.

36. From Duncan Bremer's campaign blog: http://bremerforcongress.blogspot.com/2006/08/freedom-of-religion.html, accessed November 13, 2006.

37. Focus on the Family radio show hosted by James Dobson, "A Visit With Ambassador and Mrs. Bremer," June 27, 2006.

38. Mark Zimmermann, "Iraq Envoy Says Faith Gives Him Strength," *Catholic Standard*, June 19, 2003.

39. Naomi Klein, "Baghdad Year Zero," *Harper's*, September 2004.

40. Ibid.

41. Jeff Madrick, "Economic Scene; The Economic Plan for Iraq Seems Long on Ideology, Short on Common Sense," the *New York Times*, October 2, 2003.

42. Alissa J. Rubin, Mark Fineman, and Edmund Sanders, "Iraqis on Council to Get Guards," the *Los Angeles Times*, August 13, 2003.

43. Author copy, Special Inspector General for Iraq Reconstruction July 2004 Quarterly Report.

44. Bill Sizemore and Joanne Kimberlin, "Blackwater: On the Front Lines," the *Virginian-Pilot*, July 25, 2006.

45. L. Paul Bremer, *My Year in Iraq*, p. 148.

46. L. Paul Bremer, *My Year in Iraq*, p. 152.

47. Ibid.

48. Jonathan E. Kaplan, "Private Army Seeking Political Advice in D.C.," *The Hill*, April 14, 2004.

49. Dana Priest and Mary Pat Flaherty, "Under Fire, Security Firms Form an Alliance," the *Washington Post*, April 8, 2004.

50. John Helyar, "Fortunes of War," *Fortune*, July 26, 2004, as posted at http://money.cnn.com/magazines/fortune/fortune_archive/2004/07/26/377180/index.htm.

51. Chris Talor speaking at "Contractors on The Battlefield: Learning from The Experience in Iraq," George Washington University, January 28, 2005.

52. Ibid.

53. Ibid.

54. Energy Intelligence Group, Inc., "Perspective: Doing Business in Iraq," *Energy Compass*, October 16, 2003.

55. According to its filings with the North Carolina Secretary of State, Blackwater Security Consulting LLC was formed on September 29, 2003.

56. As stated on Blackwater's Web site, www.blackwatersecurity.com/dospsd.html.

57. Ibid.

58. "In his own words: 'The guys who do this are not money-hungry pigs,'" the *Virginian-Pilot*, July 28, 2006.

59. Tim Shorrock, "Contractor's Arrogance Contributed to Iraqi Rebellion, Marine Colonel Says," http://timshorrock.blogspot.com/2005/01/contractors-arrogance-contributed-to.html, posted January 31, 2005.

60. Ibid.

61. Ibid.

62. Interview with PBS *Frontline*, www.pbs.org/wgbh/pages/frontline/shows/warriors/interviews/hammes.html, posted June 21, 2005.

63. Michael Duffy, "When Private Armies Take to the Front Lines," *Time*, April 12, 2004.

64. Joanne Kimberlin, "Crash Course in Survival; Class Teaches Those Preparing for Iraq How to Defend Themselves Amid Danger," the *Virginian-Pilot*, June 30, 2004.

65. The full story of this incident is detailed in: T. Christian Miller, *Blood Money: Wasted Billions, Lost Lives, and Corporate Greed in Iraq*, Little Brown and Company, New York, 2006, pp. 169–171.

66. T. Christian Miller, *Blood Money*, p. 168.

67. Interview with PBS *Frontline*, www.pbs.org/wgbh/pages/frontline/shows/warriors/interviews/hammes.html, posted June 21, 2005.

68. As reported by CNN, "Purported bin Laden Tape Offers Gold for Bremer," http://www.cnn.com/2004/WORLD/asiapcf/05/06/bin.laden.message, posted May 7, 2004.

69. Robert Young Pelton, "Riding Shotgun in Baghdad," *Popular Mechanics*, April 2005.

70. "In his own words: 'The guys who do this are not money-hungry pigs.'" the *Virginian-Pilot*, July 28, 2006.

71. L. Paul Bremer, *My Year in Iraq*, p. 151.

72. Ibid., p. 245.

73. Ibid., p. 246.

74. Alan Sipress, "Bremer Survived Ambush Outside Baghdad; Officials Don't See Attack as Attempt at Assassination," the *Washington Post*, December 20, 2003.

75. Ibid.

76. Michele Faul, "Bremer Escaped Injury in Ambush on Convoy; Iraqi Woman Killed by Blast at Shiite Party Office," Associated Press, December 19, 2003.

77. Alan Sipress, "Bremer Survived Ambush Outside Baghdad; Officials Don't See Attack as Attempt at Assassination," the *Washington Post*, December 20, 2003.

78. Ibid.

79. Coalition Provisional Authority briefing transcript, Baghdad, December 19, 2003.

80. Sophie Claudet, "Coalition Removes First of Saddam's Four Infamous Heads Atop Baghdad Palace," Agence France-Presse, December 2, 2003.

81. Ibid.

82. "In his own words: 'The guys who do this are not money-hungry pigs,'" the *Virginian-Pilot*, July 28, 2006.

83. Jim Wolf (Reuters), "U.S. Tells Contractors to Bring Guards If They Use Work Sites in Iraq," *Orlando Sentinel*, November 20, 2003.

84. "The Baghdad boom; Mercenaries," *The Economist*, March 27, 2004.

85. Ibid.

86. James Hider, "Soldiers of Fortune Rush to Cash in on Unrest in Baghdad," *The Times* of London, March 31, 2004.

87. John G. Roos, "1-shot killer; This 5.56mm round has all the stopping power you need—but you can't use it," *The Army Times*, December 1, 2003.

88. Ibid.

89. Ibid.

90. Ibid.

91. Ibid.

92. "A Better Bullet; Blended-metal Ammo Rates Realistic Testing," *Armed Forces Journal*, December 2003 editorial.

93. Ibid.

94. John G. Roos, "1-shot killer," *The Army Times*, December 1, 2003.

95. "A better bullet," *Armed Forces Journal*, December 2003 editorial.

96. Ben Thomas's blog, http://blog.myspace.com/index.cfm?fuseaction=blog.view &friendID =63089073&blogID=107649210&MyToken=89c3dd1c-4760-4c6b-8e90-65039e474568, posted April 8, 2006.

97. See, for example: Michael Duffy, "When Private Armies Take to the Front Lines," *Time*, April 12, 2004.

98. Mary Pat Flaherty and Jackie Spinner, "In Iraq, Contractors' Security Costs Rise," the *Washington Post*, February 18, 2004.

99. Jackie Calmes, "Washington Wire: A Special Weekly Report From The *Wall Street Journal's* Capital Bureau," the *Wall Street Journal*, February 13, 2004.

100. Marego Athans, "Security Businesses, Black Market in Guns Thrive," the *Baltimore Sun*, March 18, 2004.

101. Walter Pincus, "More Private Forces Eyed for Iraq; Green Zone Contractor Would Free U.S. Troops for Other Duties," the *Washington Post*, March 18, 2004.

102. David Barstow, James Glanz, Richard A. Oppel Jr., and Kate Zernike, "Security Companies: Shadow Soldiers in Iraq," the *New York Times*, April 19, 2004.

CHAPTER 6

1. Nicolas Pelham, "Fear of Ambush Slows Urgent Drive to Rebuild," the *Financial Times*, January 13, 2004.

2. James Hider, "Soldiers of Fortune Rush to Cash in on Unrest in Baghdad," *The Times* (London), March 31, 2004.

3. Michael Stetz, "War Against Terror Gives Former SEALs the Chance to Resurrect Their Skills," the *San Diego Union-Tribune*, June 3, 2004.

4. Ted Roelofs, "Good Money, Constant Fear; Local Residents Stake Their Claim as Iraqi Civilian Contractors," the *Grand Rapids Press*, September 26, 2004.

5. Joanne Kimberlin, "Iraq 'Operators' Perform Duties in the Line of Fire," the *Virginian-Pilot*, April 15, 2004.

6. Michael Stetz, "War Against Terror Gives Former SEALs the Chance to Resurrect Their Skills," the *San Diego Union-Tribune*, June 3, 2004.

7. Ibid.

8. Joanne Kimberlin, "Iraq 'Operators' Perform Duties in the Line of Fire," the *Virginian-Pilot*, April 15, 2004.

9. Unless otherwise noted, all biographical information on Scott Helvenston is from the author's interviews with his mother, conducted throughout 2006, as are her quotes in this book.

10. Matt Crenson, "Military Experts Envision Lightning-Fast Special Forces Attack as Next Move in Afghanistan," Associated Press, October 11, 2001.

11. Samuel Lee, "War Is Hell, But It Makes for Good TV," the *Straits Times* (Singapore), January 21, 2002.

12. Mark A. Perigard, "'Missions' Accomplished—USA Reality Series Crowns a Champion Tonight," the *Boston Herald*, April 17, 2002.

13. Jay Price and Joseph Neff and Correspondent Charles Crain, "Series: The Bridge"; Chapter 5: "'Scotty Bod' Grows Up," the *News and Observer* (Raleigh, North Carolina), July 30, 2004.

14. Andrea Perera, "Mom Mourns Her Fallen Son; Leesburg Woman Saw TV Reports, Then Got Call; Ex-Seal Was Pentathlon Champ, Actor in Movies," the *Orlando Sentinel*, April 2, 2004.

15. Abby Goodnough and Michael Luo, "Amid Grief, They Focus on Pride; Iraq Ambush Victims' Kin Recall How Their Loved Ones Lived," the *New York Times*, April 4, 2004.

16. Andrea Perera, "Mom Mourns Her Fallen Son; Leesburg Woman Saw TV Reports, Then Got Call; Ex-Seal Was Pentathlon Champ, Actor in Movies," the *Orlando Sentinel*, April 2, 2004.

17. Jonathan Franklin, "US Contractor Recruits Guards for Iraq in Chile," the *Guardian*, March 5, 2004.

18. Ibid.

19. Author copy, Scott Helvenston e-mail; subject: extreme unprofessionalism, March 27, 2004.

20. Ibid.

21. Ibid.

22. Kathy Potter e-mail; subject: shared Conversations with Scott, April 13, 2004.

23. Ibid.

24. Joseph Neff and Jay Price, "Contractors in Iraq Make Costs Balloon; Extensive Paramilitary Work Earns Profit on Several Levels," the *News and Observer* (Raleigh, North Carolina), October 24, 2004.

25. Ibid.

26. Ibid.

27. Transcript, "Hearing on Iraq Private Contractor Oversight," House Oversight and Government reform Committee, February 7, 2007.

28. Author copy of contract.

29. *Richard P. Nordan v. Blackwater Security Consulting, LLC et al.*, filed January 5, 2005.

30. Jay Price and Joseph Neff, "Security Company Broke Own Rules; Four U.S. Civilians Ambushed and Killed in Fallujah, Iraq, Lacked Some Protection Their Contract Promised," August 22, 2004.

31. Ibid.

32. Ibid.

33. *Richard P. Nordan v. Blackwater Security Consulting, LLC et al.*, filed January 5, 2005.

34. Author copy, Scott Helvenston e-mail; subject: extreme unprofessionalism, March 27, 2004.

35. Ibid.

36. Ibid.

37. Ibid.

38. *Richard P. Nordan v. Blackwater Security Consulting, LLC et al.*, filed January 5, 2005.

39. E-mail to author April 14, 2006.

40. Author copy.

CHAPTER 7

1. Human Rights Watch Report, "Violent Response: The U.S. Army in Al-Falluja," June 2003.

2. Department of Defense Transcript, "82nd Airborne Division Commanding General's Briefing from Iraq," January 6, 2004.

3. Anthony Shadid, *Night Draws Near*, p. 235.

4. Patrick Graham, "23 Killed as Iraqi Rebels Overrun Police Station," the *Observer*, February 15, 2004.

5. L. Paul Bremer III, *My Year in Iraq*, pp. 314–15.

6. Associated Press, "A Year After Invasion, Some Iraqis Allege More Insecurities," March 20, 2004.

7. CNN, "General: It's 'Fun to Shoot Some People,'" CNN.com, February 4, 2005. See: www.cnn.com/2005/US/02/03/general.shoot/.

8. Hamza Hendawi, "Marines Seek to Pacify Fallujah With Show of Force, Residents Are Skeptical," Associated Press, March 30, 2004.

9. Rajiv Chandrasekaran and Anthony Shadid, "U.S. Targeted Fiery Cleric in Risky Move; As Support for Sadr Surged, Shiites Rallied for Fallujah," the *Washington Post*, April 11, 2004.

10. Ibid.

11. Christopher Torchia, "13 Killed in Iraq, Including US Marine," Associated Press, March 26, 2004.

12. "Four Killed, Seven Wounded in Iraq Battle: Hospital," Agence France-Presse, March 26, 2004.

13. Hamza Hendawi, "Marines Seek to Pacify Fallujah With Show of Force, Residents Are Skeptical," Associated Press, March 30, 2004.

14. Stephen Farrell and Richard Beeston, "Out of the Desert Darkness Came Hellfire," *The Times* of London, March 23, 2004.

15. Nayla Razzouk, "Iraqis Fear 'Resistance Leader' Yassin's Killing May Fuel Terrorism," Agence France-Presse, March 22, 2004.

16. Ibid.

17. Hamza Hendawi, "Marines Seek to Pacify Fallujah With Show of Force, Residents Are Skeptical," Associated Press, March 30, 2004.

18. Dexter Filkins (Associated Press), "2 Civilians Killed in Mosul Gunbattles," *Houston Chronicle*, March 27, 2004.

19. Hamza Hendawi, "Marines Seek to Pacify Fallujah With Show of Force, Residents Are Skeptical," Associated Press, March 30, 2004.

20. Ibid.

21. Transcript, *NewsHour With Jim Lehrer*, PBS, March 31, 2004.

22. Thomas E. Ricks, *Fiasco: The American Military Adventure in Iraq*, Penguin Press, New York, 2006, p. 331.

23. Transcript, press briefing, Brig. Gen. Mark Kimmitt, Baghdad, Iraq, March 30, 2004.

24. Unless otherwise noted, all biographical information on Jerry Zovko, as well as the comments of his mother, Danica Zovko, is from interviews conducted by the author, Summer 2006.

25. Joseph Neff and Jay Price, "A Private Driven man; A 1995 Tour in Bosnia Matured Jerry Zovko and Steered Him to the Contracting Business That Would Take Him to Iraq," the *News and Observer*, July 28, 2004.

26. Interview, Summer 2006.

27. Joseph Neff and Jay Price, "Army Molds a Future; During His 20 Years in the Service, Wesley Batalona Built Skills That Would Come Into Play Later for the Tough Former Sergeant," the *News and Observer* (Raleigh, North Carolina), July 27, 2004.

28. Ibid.

29. "Slain US Security Agents Once Served With Navy Seals, Special Forces," Agence France-Presse, April 2, 2004.

30. Ibid.

31. Jay Price, Joseph Neff, and Charles Crain, "Mutilation Seen Around the World," the *News and Observer* (Raleigh, North Carolina), July 25, 2004.

32. Bill Powell, "Into the Cauldron: The Murder of Four American Civilians in Fallujah Provokes a Vow of Retaliation. But Can Anything Defuse the Rage in Iraq?" *Time*, April 8, 2004.

33. Ibid.

34. The description of this mission and the details of it come largely from three sources: various Blackwater contracts obtained by the author; the lawsuit filed against Blackwater by the families of the four men in January 2005; and the groundbreaking investigative reporting done by Jay Price and Joseph Neff of the *News and Observer* newspaper.

35. PBS *Frontline* Web site, "Private Warriors: Contractors: The High-Risk Contracting Business," www.pbs.org/wgbh/pages/frontline/shows/warriors/contractors/highrisk.html, posted June 21, 2005.

36. Jay Price and Joseph Neff, "Families Sue Over Fallujah Ambush: Relatives Contend an N.C. Company Denied Necessary Equipment to Four Men Who Were Killed in the Iraqi City," the *News and Observer* (Raleigh, North Carolina), January 6, 2005.

37. Jay Prince and Joseph Neff, "Security Company Broke Own Rules; Four U.S. Civilians Ambushed and Killed in Fallujah, Iraq, Lacked Some Protection Their Contract Promised," the *News and Observer* (Raleigh, North Carolina), August 22, 2004.

38. Jay Price, Joseph Neff, and Charles Crain, "Graveyard; The Ambush Was So Sudden That the Four Private Contractors Had Little Chance to React. The Men had Driven Into Fallujah Rather Than Bypassing That Tinderbox in the Sunni Triangle. The City's Barely Suppressed Fury Boiled to the Surface," the *News and Observer* (Raleigh, North Carolina), July 31, 2004.

39. Jay Prince, Joseph Neff, and Charles Crain, "Ambush Kills 4 Workers in Iraq; Men Worked for N.C. Security Firm," the *News and Observer* (Raleigh, North Carolina), June 7, 2004.

40. *Richard P. Nordan v. Blackwater Security Consulting, LLC et. al.*, filed January 5, 2005.

41. Jay Prince and Joseph Neff, "Security Company Broke Own Rules; Four U.S. Civilians Ambushed and Killed in Fallujah, Iraq, Lacked Some Protection Their Contract Promised," the *News and Observer* (Raleigh, North Carolina), August 22, 2004.

42. Author copy of contract.

43. Jay Price, Joseph Neff, and Charles Crain, "Graveyard; The Ambush Was So Sudden That the Four Private Contractors Had Little Chance to React. The Men had Driven Into Fallujah Rather Than Bypassing That Tinderbox in the Sunni Triangle. The City's Barely Suppressed Fury Boiled to the Surface," the *News and Observer* (Raleigh, North Carolina), July 31, 2004.

44. Ibid.

45. Joshua Hammer, "Cowboy Up," *The New Republic*, May 24, 2004.

46. Committee on Oversight and Government Reform Majority Staff Report, "Private Military Contractors in Iraq: An Examination of Blackwater's Actions in Fallujah," September 2007.

47. Ibid.

48. Bill Powell, "Into the Cauldron; The Murder of Four American Civilians in Fallujah Provokes a Vow of Retaliation. But Can Anything Defuse the Rage in Iraq?" *Time*, April 8, 2004.

49. As quoted in the documentary *Shadow Company*, released 2006, produced and directed by Nick Bicanic, Purpose Films.

50. Robert Young Pelton, *Licensed to Kill*, p. 134.

51. David Barstow, "Security Firm Says Its Workers Were Lured Into Iraqi Ambush," the *New York Times*, April 9, 2004.

52. Thomas E. Ricks, *Fiasco*, p. 331.

53. Committee on Oversight and Government Reform Majority Staff Report, "Private Military Contractors in Iraq: An Examination of Blackwater's Actions in Fallujah," September 2007.

54. Bill Powell, "Into the Cauldron; The Murder of Four American Civilians in Fallujah Provokes a Vow of Retaliation. But Can Anything Defuse the Rage in Iraq?" *Time*, April 8, 2004.

55. Sewell Chan, "Descent Into Carnage in a Hostile City; In Fallujah, Mob Unleashes Its Rage," the *Washington Post*, April 1, 2004. Note: Subsequent autopsies determined that the men died immediately, disputing these accounts, but the bodies were horribly mutilated.

56. Bill Powell, "Into the Cauldron; The Murder of Four American Civilians in Fallujah Provokes a Vow of Retaliation. But Can Anything Defuse the Rage in Iraq?" *Time*, April 8, 2004.

57. Ibid.

58. Sameer N. Yacoub, "Insurgents Attack U.S. Convoy in Fallujah Day After Bodies of American Civilians Dragged Through Streets," Associated Press, April 1, 2004.

59. Sewell Chan, "Descent Into Carnage in a Hostile City; In Fallujah, Mob Unleashes Its Rage," the *Washington Post*, April 1, 2004.

60. Ibid.

61. Ibid.

62. Ibid.

63. Michael Georgy, "Iraqis Drag Bodies Through Streets After Attack," Reuters, March 31, 2004.

CHAPTER 8

1. Bing West, *No True Glory: A Frontline Account of the Battle for Fallujah*, Bantam Dell, New York, 2005, p. 58.

2. Transcript, "Deputy Director for Coalition Operations Hosts News Conference on Security Operations in Iraq," Department of Defense Press Briefing, March 31, 2004.

3. Tom Raum, "Stakes for U.S. Much Higher in Iraq Than They Were in Somalia," Associated Press, April 1, 2004.

4. Transcript, "Deputy Director for Coalition Operations Hosts News Conference on Security Operations in Iraq," Department of Defense Press Briefing, March 31, 2004.

5. Ibid.

6. Ibid.

7. Ibid.

8. Ibid.

9. Transcript, "Remarks by the President at Bush-Cheney 2004 Dinner Marriott Wardman Park Hotel Washington, D.C.," White House News Release, March 31, 2004.

10. L. Paul Bremer III, *My Year in Iraq*, p. 317.

11. Ibid.

12. Ibid.

13. Tom Raum, "Stakes for U.S. Much Higher in Iraq Than They Were in Somalia," Associated Press, April 1, 2004.

14. David Stout, "White House, With Support, Vows to Finish Mission in Iraq, the *New York Times*, April 1, 2004.

15. Ibid.

16. Transcript, *The O'Reilly Factor*, Fox News Network, March 31, 2004.

17. Ibid.
18. Transcript, *The O'Reilly Factor*, Fox News Network, April 1, 2004.
19. Ibid.
20. Transcript, *Scarborough Country*, MSNBC, March 31, 2004.
21. Claude Salhani, "Analysis: Mogadishu Revisited?" UPI, March 31, 2004.
22. Paul McGeough, "Shocked Iraqis Wait for US Retribution," *Sydney Morning Herald*, April 3, 2004.
23. Transcript, "Deputy Director for Coalition Operations Hosts News Conference on Security Operations in Iraq," Department of Defense Press Briefing, March 31, 2004.
24. Transcript, *CNN Crossfire*, CNN, April 1, 2004.
25. Transcript, "Coalition Provisional Authority Briefing With Brigadier General Mark Kimmitt," Department of Defense Press Briefing, April 1, 2004.
26. Ibid.
27. Ibid.
28. Transcript, "Coalition Provisional Authority Briefing With Brigadier General Mark Kimmitt," Department of Defense Press Briefing, April 12, 2004.
29. Jeffrey Gettleman, "4 From U.S. Killed in Ambush in Iraq; Mob Drags Bodies," the *New York Times*, April 1, 2004.
30. Transcript, *Larry King Live*, CNN, April 1, 2004.
31. Anne Barnard and Thanassis Cambanis, "Brutality, Cheers in Iraq: Mob Drags Burned Bodies of Four Slain American Civilians Through Streets," the *Boston Globe*, April 1, 2004.
32. Paul McGeough, "Shocked Iraqis Wait for US Retribution," *Sydney Morning Herald*, April 3, 2004.
33. Ibid.
34. Sewell Chan, "Descent Into Carnage in a Hostile City; In Fallujah, Mob Unleashes Its Rage," the *Washington Post*, April 1, 2004.
35. Kevin Johnson, "Fallujah Leaders Set Defiant Tone," *USA Today*, April 5, 2004.
36. Ibid.
37. Jack Fairweather, "American Dead Butchered 'Like Sheep,'" *The Telegraph* (London), April 1, 2004.
38. Transcript, White House Press Briefing, March 31, 2004.
39. Transcript, "Interview With Maybritt Illner of Zdf German Television," FDCH Federal Department and Agency Documents, April 1, 2004.
40. Transcript, "Coalition Provisional Authority Briefing With Brigadier General Mark Kimmitt," Department of Defense Press Briefing, April 1, 2004.
41. Transcript, *CNN Live Today*, CNN, April 1, 2004.
42. Joanne Kimberlin, "Three Slain Blackwater Workers Identified," the *Virginian-Pilot*, April 2, 2004.
43. Jonathan E. Kaplan, "Private Army Seeking Political Advice in D.C.," *The Hill*, April 14, 2004.
44. Gerry J. Gilmore, "U.S. Firm Mourns Slain Employees," American Forces Press Service, April 2, 2004.
45. Ibid.
46. Ben Deck, "N.C. Sheriff: Some Blackwater Workers Ex-Law Enforcement Officers," Cox News Service, March 31, 2004.
47. Transcript, "Hearing of the Emerging Threats & Capabilities Subcommittee of the Senate Armed Services Committee," Federal News Service, April 2, 2004.
48. D. R. Staton, "Chaplain Corner 04/05/04," *Blackwater Tactical Weekly*, April 5, 2004.
49. Sonja Barisic, "Deaths of North Carolina Company's Employees in Iraq Hit Stir Hometown," Associated Press, April 1, 2004.
50. Thomas E. Ricks, *Fiasco*, p. 332.

51. Alissa J. Rubin and Doyle McManus, "Why America Has Waged a Losing Battle on Fallouja," the *Los Angeles Times,* October 24, 2004.

52. Ibid.

53. Thomas E. Ricks, *Fiasco,* p. 332

54. Alissa J. Rubin and Doyle McManus, "Why America Has Waged a Losing Battle on Fallouja," the *Los Angeles Times,* October 24, 2004.

55. Jim Steele's "Premiere Speakers Bureau" bio.

56. Jon Lee Anderson, "Letter From Baghdad: The Uprising," *The New Yorker,* May 3, 2004.

57. Jim Steele's "Premiere Speakers Bureau" bio. Steele, of course, does not refer to them as "death squads" but rather a "counter-terrorist force."

58. Jon Lee Anderson, "Letter From Baghdad: The Uprising," *The New Yorker,* May 3, 2004.

59. Ibid.

60. Ibid.

61. Peter Maass, "The Salvadorization of Iraq?" *The New York Times Magazine,* May 1, 2005.

62. Ibid.

63. Jim Steele's "Premiere Speakers Bureau" bio.

64. Jon Lee Anderson, "Letter From Baghdad: The Uprising," *The New Yorker,* May 3, 2004.

CHAPTER 9

1. David Barstow, James Glanz, Richard A. Oppel Jr., and Kate Zernike, "Security Companies: Shadow Soldiers in Iraq," the *New York Times,* April 19, 2004.

2. One of the best and most comprehensive and credible histories of Muqtada al-Sadr can be found in Anthony Shadid's book *Night Draws Near.*

3. Robert Fisk, "Iraq on the Brink of Anarchy," *The Independent* (London), April 6, 2004.

4. This would later be official policy with the implementation of Coalition Provisional Authority Order 17, June 27, 2004.

5. Jeffrey Gettleman, "A Young Radical's Anti-U.S. Wrath Is Unleashed," the *New York Times,* April 5, 2004.

6. Rajiv Chandrasekaran and Anthony Shadid, "U.S. Targeted Fiery Cleric in Risky Move; As Support for Sadr Surged, Shiites Rallied for Fallujah," the *Washington Post,* April 11, 2004.

7. Jason Burke, Kamal Ahmed, Jonathon Steele, and Ed Helmore, "Ten Days That Took Iraq to the Brink," *The Observer* (London), April 11, 2004.

8. Rajiv Chandrasekaran and Anthony Shadid, "U.S. Targeted Fiery Cleric in Risky Move; As Support for Sadr Surged, Shiites Rallied for Fallujah," the *Washington Post,* April 11, 2004.

9. Jeffrey Gettleman, "A Young Radical's Anti-U.S. Wrath Is Unleashed," the *New York Times,* April 5, 2004.

10. Rajiv Chandrasekaran and Anthony Shadid, "U.S. Targeted Fiery Cleric in Risky Move; As Support for Sadr Surged, Shiites Rallied for Fallujah," the *Washington Post,* April 11, 2004.

11. Jeffrey Gettleman, "U.S. Accepts Responsibility, But Not Blame, in Deaths of 2 Iraqi Journalists," the *New York Times,* March 30, 2004.

12. Anthony Shadid, *Night Draws Near,* p. 367.

13. Rajiv Chandrasekaran and Anthony Shadid, "U.S. Targeted Fiery Cleric in Risky Move; As Support for Sadr Surged, Shiites Rallied for Fallujah," the *Washington Post,* April 11, 2004.

14. Ibid.

15. Dan Murphy, "Risks Rise for Iraqi Journalists," *Christian Science Monitor,* April 5, 2004.

16. Jeffrey Gettleman, "A Young Radical's Anti-U.S. Wrath Is Unleashed," the *New York Times,* April 5, 2004.

17. Mohamad Bazzi (*Newsday*), "U.S. Goes After the Cleric Who Incited Violence, Move Against Shiite Could Spark More Clashes in Iraq," the *Seattle Times,* April 6, 2004.

18. Rajiv Chandrasekaran and Anthony Shadid, "U.S. Targeted Fiery Cleric in Risky Move; As Support for Sadr Surged, Shiites Rallied for Fallujah," the *Washington Post,* April 11, 2004.

19. Ibid.

20. Ibid.

21. Jeffrey Gettleman, "A Young Radical's Anti-U.S. Wrath Is Unleashed," the *New York Times*, April 5, 2004.

22. Anne Barnard, "Cleric Followers Battle US Troops; Shi'ite Protests in Iraq Cities Turn Violent, Kill 8 Americans," the *Boston Globe*, April 5, 2004.

23. Anthony Shadid, *Night Draws Near*, p. 369.

24. Ibid.

25. David Barstow, "Security Firm Says Its Workers Were Lured Into Iraqi Ambush," the *New York Times*, April 9, 2004.

26. Unless otherwise noted, Corporal Lonnie Young's account of the battle at Najaf on April 4, 2004, is drawn from the following: U.S. Fed News, "True Grit: Real-Life Account of Combat Readiness," U.S. Marine Corps press release, September 2, 2004.

27. Anthony Shadid, *Night Draws Near*, p. 370.

28. Dana Priest, "Private Guards Repel Attack on U.S. Headquarters," the *Washington Post*, April 6, 2004.

29. Kate Wiltrout, "'If I Had to Die, It Would Be Defending My Country,'" the *Virginian-Pilot*, September 18, 2004.

30. Dana Priest, "Private Guards Repel Attack on U.S. Headquarters," the *Washington Post*, April 6, 2004.

31. Anthony Shadid, *Night Draws Near*, p. 370.

32. Author copy of video.

33. David Barstow, "Security Firm Says Its Workers Were Lured Into Iraqi Ambush," the *New York Times*, April 9, 2004.

34. Ibid.

35. Kate Wiltrout, "'If I Had to Die, It Would Be Defending My Country,'" the *Virginian-Pilot*, September 18, 2004.

36. David Barstow, "Security Firm Says Its Workers Were Lured Into Iraqi Ambush," the *New York Times*, April 9, 2004.

37. Author copy of video.

38. John G. Roos, "1-shot killer; This 5.56mm Round Has All the Stopping Power You Need—But You Can't Use It," *The Army Times*, December 1, 2003.

39. Ben Thomas aka "Mookie Spicoli," posting on "Get Off The X" forum, October 12, 2006. http://getoffthex.com/eve/forums/a/tpc/f/440107932/m/7871025602?r=6851057602#685105 7602, captured November 21, 2006.

40. Ibid.

41. Ibid.

42. Dana Priest, "Private Guards Repel Attack on U.S. Headquarters," the *Washington Post*, April 6, 2004.

43. Robert Fisk, "Three-Hour Gun Battle Leaves 22 Dead as Shia Join Iraq Conflict," *The Independent* (London), April 5, 2004.

44. Dana Priest, "Private Guards Repel Attack on U.S. Headquarters," the *Washington Post*, April 6, 2004.

45. Kate Wiltrout, "'If I Had to Die; It Would Be Defending My Country,'" the *Virginian-Pilot*, September 18, 2004.

46. Transcript, "Coalition Provisional Authority Briefing With Brigadier General Mark Kimmitt, Deputy Director for Coalition Operations," Department of Defense Briefing, April 5, 2004.

47. David Barstow, "Security Firm Says Its Workers Were Lured Into Iraqi Ambush," the *New York Times*, April 9, 2004.

48. "Deadly Clashes Erupt Between Iraqi Shiites and Coalition Troops," Agence France-Presse, April 4, 2004.

49. Kate Wiltrout, "'If I Had to Die, It Would Be Defending My Country,'" the *Virginian-Pilot*, September 18, 2004.

50. Rajiv Chandrasekaran and Anthony Shadid, "U.S. Targeted Fiery Cleric in Risky Move; As Support for Sadr Surged, Shiites Rallied for Fallujah," the *Washington Post*, April 11, 2004.

51. Robert Fisk, "Three-Hour Gun Battle Leaves 22 Dead as Shia Join Iraq Conflict," *The Independent* (London), April 5, 2004.

52. Anne Barnard, "Cleric Followers Battle US Troops; Shi'ite Protests in Iraq Cities Turn Violent, Kill 8 Americans," the *Boston Globe*, April 5, 2004.

53. Ibid.

54. Transcript, *Democracy Now!* August 31, 2005.

55. Melinda Liu, "Mean Streets: Inside the Brutal Battle of Sadr City. As a Venue for Urban Warfare, This Is As Bad As It Gets," *Newsweek* (Web exclusive), April 27, 2004.

56. Ibid.

57. Hala Boncompagni, "US Brands Radical Shiite Cleric an Outlaw Amid Anti-Coalition Uprising," Agence France-Presse, April 5, 2004.

58. "Warrant Outstanding for Arrest of Cleric Behind Iraq Unrest: Coalition," Agence France-Presse, April 5, 2004. Note: The CPA claimed that the warrant had been issued months earlier by an Iraqi judge insisting that the timing of the release of the warrant was a decision of that judge and not occupation officials.

59. "Privatizing Warfare," *New York Times* editorial, April 21, 2004.

60. Ibid.

CHAPTER 10

1. Seattle Times news services, "8 U.S. Troops Killed in Iraqi Shiite Revolt Anti-U.S. Cleric's Backers Riot; Coalition Calls in Jets, Copters; In Separate Action Today, Marines Move to Retake Control of Fallujah," the *Seattle Times*, April 5, 2004.

2. Bassem Mroue, "Marines Tighten the Noose on Rebel Town," the *Daily Telegraph* (Sydney, Australia), April 7, 2004.

3. Pamela Constable, "Marines, Insurgents Battle for Sunni City; Death Toll Disputed in Air Attack on Mosque," the *Washington Post*, April 8, 2004.

4. Bassem Mroue, "Marines Tighten the Noose on Rebel Town," the *Daily Telegraph* (Sydney, Australia), April 7, 2004.

5. Pamela Constable, "Marines, Insurgents Battle for Sunni City; Death Toll Disputed in Air Attack on Mosque," the *Washington Post*, April 8, 2004.

6. Bassem Mroue, "Marines Tighten the Noose on Rebel Town," the *Daily Telegraph* (Sydney, Australia), April 7, 2004.

7. Ibid.

8. Ibid.

9. Thomas E. Ricks, *Fiasco*, p. 333.

10. Rajiv Chandrasekaran, "Anti-U.S. Uprising Widens in Iraq; Marines Push Deeper Into Fallujah; Cleric's Force Tightens Grip in Holy Cities," the *Washington Post*, April 8, 2004.

11. Thanassis Cambanis, "Americans Advance on Fallujah," the *Boston Globe*, April 8, 2004.

12. Rajiv Chandrasekaran, "Anti-U.S. Uprising Widens in Iraq; Marines Push Deeper Into Fallujah; Cleric's Force Tightens Grip in Holy Cities," the *Washington Post*, April 8, 2004.

13. Ibid.

14. Bassem Mroue and Abdul-Qader Saadi, "US Bombs Fallujah Mosque; More Than 40 Worshippers Killed; Revolutionary Violence Engulfs Iraq," Associated Press, April 7, 2004.

15. Jack Fairweather, "'There Were Bodies by the Road But No One Stopped. We Just Wanted to Get Out of That Hellish Place;' Jack Fairweather Talks to Families Who Fled the Fighting in Fallujah," *The Daily Telegraph* (London), April 12, 2004.

16. Rahul Mahajan, "Fallujah and the Reality of War," Commondreams.org, November 6, 2004.

17. David Blair, Alec Russell, and David Rennie, "Urban Warfare Grips Iraq; US Forces Hit Mosque Compound in Fallujah With Bombs and Rockets; Britons Evacuated as Coalition HQ Is Abandoned to the Mahdi Militia," *The Daily Telegraph* (London), April 8, 2004.

18. Pamela Constable, "Troops Gaining Grip in Sections of Fallujah," the *Washington Post*, April 7, 2004.

19. Ibid.

20. Ibid.

21. Bing West, *No True Glory*, p. 176.

22. Ibid.

23. Thanassis Cambanis, "Americans Advance on Fallujah," the *Boston Globe*, April 8, 2004.

24. Ibid.

25. Patrick Cockburn, "Iraq: The Descent Into Chaos: US Has Killed 280 in Fallujah This Week, Says Hospital Doctor," *The Independent* (London), April 9, 2004.

26. Ibid.

27. Anne Barnard, "Anger Over Fallujah Reaches Ears of the Faithful," the *Boston Globe*, April 11, 2004.

28. Pamela Constable, "Marines Try to Quell 'a Hotbed of Resistance,'" the *Washington Post*, April 9, 2004.

29. Thomas E. Ricks, *Fiasco*, p. 333.

30. Ibid.

31. Jack Fairweather, "'There Were Bodies by the Road But No One Stopped. We Just Wanted to Get Out of That Hellish Place;' Jack Fairweather Talks to Families Who Fled the Fighting in Fallujah," *The Daily Telegraph* (London), April 12, 2004.

32. Dahr Jamail, "Americans Slaughtering Civilians in Falluja," *The New Standard*, April 11, 2004.

33. Ibid.

34. Dahr Jamail, "Sarajevo on the Euphrates: An Eyewitness Account From Inside the US Siege of Falluja," TheNation.com (Web only), April 12, 2004.

35. Rahul Mahajan, "Fallujah and the Reality of War," Commondreams.org, November 6, 2004.

36. Dahr Jamail, "Americans Slaughtering Civilians in Falluja," *The New Standard*, April 11, 2004.

37. Jeffrey Gettleman, "Marines Use Low-Tech Skill to Kill 100 in Urban Battle," the *New York Times*, April 15, 2004.

38. Joshua Hammer, "Fallujah: In the Hands of Insurgents," *Newsweek*, May 24, 2004: "Lt. Gen. James T. Conway, commander of the I Expeditionary Force, told NEWSWEEK that the Marines' use of 'precision' weaponry ensured that '90 to 95 percent' of Iraqis killed inside the city were combatants."

39. Jeffrey Gettleman, "Marines Use Low-Tech Skill to Kill 100 in Urban Battle," the *New York Times*, April 15, 2004.

40. Mustafa Abdel-Halim, "U.S. Forces Want Al-Jazeera Out of Fallujah," IslamOnline.net (Cairo), April 9, 2004.

41. Transcript, *Democracy Now!* February 22, 2006.

42. Ibid.

43. Melinda Liu, "War of Perceptions: The U.S. Military Is Devising a Plan to End the Siege of Fallujah. But Will It Win on the Battleground of Iraqi Public Opinion?" *Newsweek* (Web exclusive), April 29, 2004.

44. Mustafa Abdel-Halim, "U.S. Forces Want Al-Jazeera Out of Fallujah," IslamOnline.net (Cairo), April 9, 2004: "'American forces declared al-Jazeera must leave before any progress is made to settle the Fallujah stand-off,' al-Jazeera director general Wadah Khanfar told IslamOnline.net, citing sources close to the Iraqi Governing Council."

45. Author copy, "Letter From Ahmed Mansour," April 29, 2004.

46. Transcript, "Coalition Provisional Authority Briefing With Brigadier General Mark Kimmitt," Department of Defense Press Briefing, April 12, 2004.

47. Ibid.

48. Transcript, Defense Department Regular News Briefing, April 15, 2004.

49. Ibid.

50. Kevin Maguire and Andy Lines, "Exclusive: Bush Plot to Bomb His Arab Ally," the *Daily Mirror* (London), November 22, 2005.

51. Ibid. Note: The United States bombed Al Jazeera's offices in Afghanistan in 2001, shelled the Basra hotel where Al Jazeera journalists were the only guests in April 2003, killed Iraq correspondent Tareq Ayoub a few days later in Baghdad, and imprisoned several Al Jazeera reporters (including at Guantánamo), some of whom say they were tortured. In addition to the military attacks, the U.S.-backed Iraqi government banned the network from reporting in Iraq.

52. Transcript, *Democracy Now!* February 22, 2006.

53. Anne Barnard, "Anger Over Fallujah Reaches Ears of the Faithful," the *Boston Globe*, April 11, 2004.

54. Christina Asquith, "Refugees Tell of Rising Anger in Fallujah," the *Christian Science Monitor*, April 14, 2004.

55. Transcript, "President Addresses the Nation in Prime Time Press Conference," The White House, April 13, 2004.

56. Anne Barnard, "Anger Over Fallujah Reaches Ears of the Faithful," the *Boston Globe*, April 11, 2004.

57. Jack Fairweather, "'There Were Bodies by the Road But No One Stopped. We Just Wanted to Get Out of That Hellish Place;' Jack Fairweather Talks to Families Who Fled the Fighting in Fallujah," *The Daily Telegraph* (London), April 12, 2004.

58. Anne Barnard, "Anger Over Fallujah Reaches Ears of the Faithful," the *Boston Globe*, April 11, 2004.

59. White House News Release, January 20, 2004. The accompanying photo of Mrs. Bush and Pachachi read: "Mrs. Bush applauds her special guest, Dr. Adnan Pachachi, President of the Iraqi Governing Council, during President Bush's State of the Union Address at the U.S. Capitol Tuesday, Jan. 20, 2004. 'Sir, America stands with you and the Iraqi people as you build a free and peaceful nation,' said the President in his acknowledgement of Dr. Pachachi."

60. Anne Barnard, "Anger Over Fallujah Reaches Ears of the Faithful," the *Boston Globe*, April 11, 2004.

61. Anthony Shadid, *Night Draws Near*, p. 373.

62. Rajiv Chandrasekaran, "Key General Criticizes April Attack in Fallujah Abrupt Withdrawal Called Vacillation," the *Washington Post*, September 13, 2004.

63. Ibid.

64. Transcript, Coalition Provisional Authority Press Briefing, Department of Defense News Transcript, April 12, 2004.

65. Thanassis Cambanis, "U.N. Envoy Offers Plan for Interim Government," the *Boston Globe*, April 15, 2004.

66. Transcript, *This Week With George Stephanopoulos*, ABC, April 25, 2004.

67. Dahr Jamail, "Vigilant Resolve," DahrJamailIraq.com, February 15, 2005.

68. Patrick Cockburn, "The Failure in Iraq Is Even Deeper Than People Imagine," *The Independent* (London), April 17, 2004.

69. Transcript, Senate Armed Services Committee Hearing, April 20, 2004.

70. Bill Sizemore and Joanne Kimberlin, "Blackwater: When Things Go Wrong," the *Virginian-Pilot*, July 26, 2006.

71. Ibid.

72. Author copy of AFP/Getty photo of Fallujah bridge.

73. Dahr Jamail, "Vigilant Resolve," DahrJamailIraq.com, February 15, 2005.

CHAPTER 11

1. Whitney Gould, "Iraq Casualty Was a Born Leader; Gore, a St. John's Northwestern Graduate, Died in Helicopter Crash," *Milwaukee Journal Sentinel*, April 24, 2005.

2. Unless otherwise noted, all quotes attributed to Danica Zovko and information about her experiences are based on interviews conducted by the author in the summer of 2006.

3. Jay Price and Joseph Neff, "The Bridge; The Scene in Fallujah Was Unforgettable: Four Americans Shot, Their Bodies Defiled, Two of Them Hung From a Bridge. They Weren't Soldiers, But Private Guards Working For a North Carolina Company," the *News & Observer* (Raleigh, North Carolina), July 25, 2004.

4. Unless otherwise noted, all quotes attributed to Katy Helvenston-Wettengel and information about her experiences are based on interviews conducted by the author throughout 2006.

5. Bill Sizemore and Joanne Kimberlin, "Blackwater: On the Front Lines," the *Virginian-Pilot*, July 25, 2006.

6. Jonathan E. Kaplan, "Private Army Seeking Political Advice in D.C.," *The Hill*, April 14, 2004.

7. Erik Prince's Prince Manufacturing biography.

8. Federal lobbying records.

9. Bill McAllister, "Guns for Hire," the *Washington Post*, June 18, 1998; Dena Bunis, "U.S. Representatives Release Net-Worth Figures for '98," the *Orange County Register* (California), June 17, 1999.

10. Federal lobbying records.

11. Representative Dana Rohrabacher's speech on the floor of the U.S. House of Representatives, September 17, 2001.

12. Public Citizen report, "Rep. Roy Blunt: Ties to Special Interests Leave Him Unfit to Lead," January 2006.

13. Jonathan E. Kaplan, "Private Army Seeking Political Advice in D.C.," *The Hill*, April 14, 2004.

14. David Barstow, "Security Firm Says Its Workers Were Lured Into Iraqi Ambush," the *New York Times*, April 9, 2004.

15. Ibid.

16. Ibid.

17. Joseph Neff and Jay Price, "After the Horror, Strong Words Mask Inaction; Little Has Been Done to Determine the Facts of the Ambush in Fallujah That Cost Four Civilian Contractors Their Lives," the *News & Observer* (Raleigh, North Carolina), August 1, 2004.

18. Ibid.

19. Douglas Quenqua, "Security Firms in Iraq Look to Up US Political Support," *PR Week*, April 26, 2004.

20. James Rosen, "Contractors Operate in a Legal Gray Area; The Roles of an Interrogator and an Interpreter in the Abuse Scandal Are Murky. Even Less Clear Is Whom They Answer to," *Star Tribune* (Minneapolis), May 23, 2004.

21. Ibid.

22. See Jeremy Scahill, "Mercenary Jackpot," *The Nation*, August 28, 2006.

23. Coalition Provisional Authority Order Number 17, June 27, 2004.

24. Author copy of the letter dated April 8, 2004.

25. Office of Senator Jack Reed, "Statement by Senator Reed Regarding the Private Contractor Allegations," Press Release, February 16, 2005.

26. David Barstow, James Glanz, Richard A. Oppel Jr., and Kate Zernike, "Security Companies: Shadow Soldiers in Iraq," the *New York Times*, April 19, 2004.

27. Brenda Kleman, "Blackwater USA Eyes HQ Expansion," Cox News Service, April 16, 2004.

28. Transcript, "Inside the World of a Security Contractor in Iraq," CNN, June 18, 2006.

29. Brenda Kleman, "Blackwater USA Eyes HQ Expansion," Cox News Service, April 16, 2004.

30. Ibid.

31. Press Release, "Blackwater USA to Host 2004 World SWAT Conference and Challenge May 17–22, 2004," PR Web Newswire, April 14, 2004.

32. Ibid.

33. Kim O'Brien Root, "World Swat Challenge; Top-Ranked Teams Vie for National Tactics Title," *Daily Press* (Newport News, Virginia), May 22, 2004.

34. Ibid.

35. The description of David Grossman's presentation at the conference is drawn from Peter Carlson, "Sultans of SWAT; Competition Has Law Enforcement Assault Teams Gunning to Be the Best," the *Washington Post*, May 25, 2004.

36. Gary Jackson, *Blackwater Tactical Weekly*, May 17, 2004.

37. Douglas Quenqua, "Security Firms in Iraq Look to Up US Political Support," *PR Week*, April 26, 2004.

38. Ibid.

39. Jonathan E. Kaplan, "British Security Firm in Iraq Seeks K Street Input," *The Hill*, April 21, 2004.

40. David Barstow, James Glanz, Richard A. Oppel Jr., and Kate Zernike, "Security Companies: Shadow Soldiers in Iraq," the *New York Times*, April 19, 2004.

41. Joanne Kimberlin, "Blackwater Sees Increase in Applications," the *Virginian-Pilot*, April 10, 2004.

42. Ibid.

43. David Barstow, James Glanz, Richard A. Oppel Jr., and Kate Zernike, "Security Companies: Shadow Soldiers in Iraq," the *New York Times*, April 19, 2004.

44. Robert Fisk and Patrick Cockburn, "Deaths of Scores of Mercenaries Not Reported," *The Star* (South Africa), April 13, 2004.

45. Greg Griffin, "Reconstructing a Country: Civilians Face Increased Danger; U.S. Contractors Resolve to Stay in Iraq," the *Denver Post*, April 22, 2004.

46. Joshua Chaffin, James Drummond, and Nicolas Pelham, "Not Only Are Staff Being Moved to Safer Locations, But the Escalating Cost of Security Is Eating Into the Resources Available to Improve Infrastructure," the *Financial Times*, May 6, 2004.

47. John F. Burns and Kirk Semple, "U.S. Finds Iraq Insurgency Has Funds to Sustain Itself," the *New York Times*, November 26, 2006.

48. Greg Griffin, "Reconstructing a Country: Civilians Face Increased Danger; U.S. Contractors Resolve to Stay In Iraq," the *Denver Post*, April 22, 2004.

49. Jeremy Kahn and Nelson D. Schwartz, "Private Sector Soldiers: With Violence Escalating in Iraq, Tens of Thousands of U.S. Contractors Are Getting More Than They Bargained For," *Fortune*, May 3, 2004.

50. Greg Griffin, "Reconstructing a Country: Civilians Face Increased Danger; U.S. Contractors Resolve to Stay in Iraq," the *Denver Post*, April 22, 2004.

51. Jeremy Kahn and Nelson D. Schwartz, "Private Sector Soldiers: With Violence Escalating in Iraq, Tens of Thousands of U.S. Contractors Are Getting More Than They Bargained For," *Fortune*, May 3, 2004.

52. Sandip Roy, "U.S. to Worldwide Firms: Iraq Safer Than You Think," Pacific News Service, May 07, 2004.

53. Ibid.

54. Saifur Rahman, "Call to Take Advantage of Opportunities in Iraq," *Gulf News* (Dubai, United Arab Emirates), April 21, 2004.

55. Sandip Roy, "U.S. to Worldwide Firms: Iraq Safer Than You Think," Pacific News Service, May 07, 2004.

56. David Barstow, James Glanz, Richard A. Oppel Jr., and Kate Zernike, "Security Companies: Shadow Soldiers in Iraq," the *New York Times*, April 19, 2004.

57. Ibid.

58. Ibid.

59. James Hider, "Soldiers of Fortune Rush to Cash In on Unrest," *The Times* (London), March 31, 2004.

60. Joshua Chaffin, James Drummond, and Nicolas Pelham, "Not Only Are Staff Being Moved to Safer Locations, But the Escalating Cost of Security Is Eating into the Resources Available to Improve Infrastructure," the *Financial Times*, May 6, 2004.

61. Jeremy Kahn and Nelson D. Schwartz, "Private Sector Soldiers: With Violence Escalating in Iraq, Tens of Thousands of U.S. Contractors Are Getting More Than They Bargained For," *Fortune*, May 3, 2004.

62. David Barstow, James Glanz, Richard A. Oppel Jr., and Kate Zernike, "Security Companies: Shadow Soldiers in Iraq," the *New York Times*, April 19, 2004.

63. Ibid.

64. Diana McCabe, "Risky Business: Even in Baghdad's 'Green Zone,' Life Can Be Tough, But Big Paychecks and a Sense of Nation-Building Inspire Workers," the *Orange County Register*, April 21, 2004.

65. Ibid.

66. Barry Yeoman, "How South African Hit Men, Serbian Paramilitaries, and Other Human Rights Violators Became Guns for Hire for Military Contractors in Iraq," *Mother Jones*, November/December 2004 issue.

67. Michael Duffy, "When Private Armies Take to the Front Lines," *Time*, April 12, 2004.

68. CBS News, "Abuse of Iraqi POWs by GIs Probed," *60 Minutes II*, April 28, 2004.

69. Deborah Hastings, "Military Reports Match Some Lawsuit Details," Associated Press, October 24, 2004.

70. Tim Shorrock, "CACI and Its Friends," *The Nation*, June 21, 2004.

71. Press Release, "Lawsuit Charges Two U.S. Corporations Conspired with U.S. Officials to Torture and Abuse Detainees in Iraq," The Center for Constitutional Rights, June 9, 2004.

72. Michael Duffy, "When Private Armies Take to the Front Lines," *Time*, April 12, 2004.

73. David Barstow, James Glanz, Richard A. Oppel Jr., and Kate Zernike, "Security Companies: Shadow Soldiers in Iraq," the *New York Times*, April 19, 2004.

74. Paul Tharp, "Security Firms Get Boost From Rambo Work in Iraq," *New York Post*, April 8, 2004.

75. Seth Borenstein and Scott Dodd, "Private Security Companies in Iraq See Big Paychecks, Big Risks," *Knight Ridder/Tribune Business News*, April 2, 2004.

76. Jay Price, "Armed Security Business Booms," the *News & Observer* (Raleigh, North Carolina), April 2, 2004.

77. Jonathan Franklin, "US Contractor Recruits Guards for Iraq in Chile," *The Guardian*, March 5, 2004.

78. Dana Priest and Mary Pat Flaherty, "Under Fire, Security Firms Form an Alliance," the *Washington Post*, April 8, 2004.

79. Robert Fisk, "Saddam in the Dock: So This Is What They Call the New, Free Iraq," *The Independent on Sunday* (London), July 4, 2004.

80. Mary Pat Flaherty, "Iraq Work Awarded to Veteran of Civil Wars; Briton Who Provided Units in Asia and Africa Will Oversee Security," the *Washington Post*, June 16, 2004.

81. For Spicer's own account of these events, see: Lt. Col. Tim Spicer OBE, *An Unorthodox Soldier: Peace and War and the Sandline Affair*, Mainstream Publishing Company, Edinburgh, Great Britain, 1999.

82. Stephen Armstrong, "The Enforcer: Colonel Tim Spicer Is Effectively in Charge of the Second Largest Military Force in Iraq—Some 20,000 Private Soldiers. Just Don't Call Him a Mercenary," *The Guardian* (London), May 20, 2006.

83. P. W. Singer, "Nation Builders and Low Bidders in Iraq," the *New York Times*, June 15, 2004.

84. Jonathan Guthrie, "Tim Spicer Finds Security in the World's War Zones," the *Financial Times* (London), April 7, 2006.

85. Mary Pat Flaherty, "Iraq Work Awarded to Veteran of Civil Wars; Briton Who Provided Units in Asia and Africa Will Oversee Security," the *Washington Post*, June 16, 2004.

86. Jonathan Guthrie, "Tim Spicer Finds Security in the World's War Zones," the *Financial Times* (London), April 7, 2006.

87. Mary Fitzgerald, "U.S. Contract to British Firm Sparks Irish American Protest; Anger Over Iraq Deal Stems From 1992 Murder in Belfast," the *Washington Post*, August 9, 2004.

88. P. W. Singer, "Nation Builders and Low Bidders in Iraq," the *New York Times*, June 15, 2004.

89. Mary Fitzgerald, "U.S. Contract to British Firm Sparks Irish American Protest; Anger Over Iraq Deal Stems From 1992 Murder in Belfast," the *Washington Post*, August 9, 2004.

90. Senators Hillary Rodham Clinton, Edward M. Kennedy, Christopher J. Dodd, Charles E. Schumer, John F. Kerry, Letter to Defense Secretary Donald Rumsfeld, August 25, 2004.

91. Charles M. Sennott, "Security Firm's $293m Deal Under Scrutiny," the *Boston Globe*, June 22, 2004.

92. http://www.aegisworld.com/tim-spicer.html

93. James Boxell and Jimmy Burns, "Aegis Iraqi Contract Renewed," the *Financial Times* (London), April 19, 2006.

94. P. W. Singer, "Nation Builders and Low Bidders in Iraq," the *New York Times*, June 15, 2004.

95. Ibid.

96. Jonathan Finer, "Contractors Cleared in Videotaped Attacks; Army Fails to Find 'Probable Cause' in Machine-Gunning of Cars in Iraq," the *Washington Post*, June 11, 2006.

97. Ibid.

98. http://www.aegisworld.com/article.aspx?artID=5>

99. Ibid.

100. James Boxell, "Iraq Investigation Clears Aegis Defence," the *Financial Times* (London), June 15, 2006.

101. T. Christian Miller, "Federal Audit Criticizes Iraq Contract Oversight; Inspector General Finds That a Controversial Security Firm Failed to Meet its Obligations," the *Los Angeles Times*, April 23, 2005.

102. Matthew Lynn, "Men With Guns Are the New Dotcoms," *The Spectator* (London), November 4, 2006.

103. Kim Sengupta, "Blair Accused of Trying to 'Privatise' War in Iraq," *The Independent* (London), October 30, 2006.

104. "Four Hired Guns Killed in Baghdad Ambush Saturday," Agence France-Presse, June 6, 2004.

105. Danica Kirka, "Four Employees of U.S. Company Killed in Ambush in Baghdad," Associated Press, June 6, 2004.

106. Ibid.

107. William R. Levesque, "Clearwater Security Worker Killed in Iraq," *St. Petersburg Times* (Florida), June 8, 2004.

108. Ibid.

109. "Four Private Security Workers Killed in Iraq," Deutsche Presse-Agentur, June 6, 2004.

110. "Have Gun . . . Will Travel," *The Warsaw Voice* (Poland), June 23, 2004.

111. Joseph Neff and Jay Price, "Ambush Kills 4 Workers in Iraq; Men Worked for N.C. Security Firm," the *News & Observer* (Raleigh, North Carolina), June 7, 2004.

112. William R. Levesque, "Clearwater Security Worker Killed in Iraq," *St. Petersburg Times* (Florida), June 8, 2004.

113. Ibid.

114. Joseph Neff and Jay Price, "Ambush Kills 4 Workers in Iraq; Men Worked for N.C. Security Firm," the *News & Observer*, June 7, 2004.

115. Vickie Chachere, "Palm Harbor Man Among Dead in Ambush on Iraq Convoy," Associated Press, June 7, 2004.

116. Ibid.

117. Odai Sirri, "Allawi May Resort to Baathist Expertise," AlJazeera.net, June 7, 2004.

118. L. Paul Bremer III, *My Year in Iraq*, p. 384.

119. Coalition Provisional Authority Order Number 17, June 27, 2004.

120. Press Release, "Fact Sheet on the Anti-War Profiteering Amendment to the Defense Authorization Bill," Senator Patrick Leahy, June 15, 2004.

121. Scott Shane, "Cables Show Central Negroponte Role in 80's Covert War Against Nicaragua," the New York Times, April 13, 2005; Michael Dobbs, "Papers Illustrate Negroponte's Contra Role; Newly Released Documents Show Intelligence Nominee Was Active in U.S. Effort," the Washington Post, April 12, 2005.

122. Ibid.

123. Comprehensive coverage of Negroponte's time in Honduras can be found in the four-part series in the Baltimore Sun in June 1995 reported by Gary Cohn and Ginger Thompson.

124. Carol Rosenberg, "Weary Iraqis Losing Confidence in U.S.," the Miami Herald, April 8, 2004.

125. Author copy of the contract documents.

126. E-mail from State Department representative, August 2006.

127. Author copy of audit.

128. Ibid.

129. Gary Jackson, Blackwater Tactical Weekly, November 22, 2004.

130. Ibid.

CHAPTER 12

1. Jan H. Kalicki, "Caspian Energy at the Crossroads," Foreign Affairs, September/October 2001.

2. Stephen Kinzer, "Azerbaijan Has Reason to Swagger: Oil Deposits," the New York Times, September 14, 1997.

3. Ibid.

4. Report of the National Energy Policy Development Group, "Reliable, Affordable, Environmentally Sound Energy for America's Future," released by the White House in May 2001.

5. Ibid.

6. U.S. Department of Energy, "Top World Oil Net Exporters," www.eia.doe.gov/emeu/cabs/topworldtables1_2.html, accessed December 14, 2006.

7. Candace Rondeaux, "A Pipeline to Promise, or a Pipeline to Peril," the St. Petersburg Times, May 15, 2005.

8. Ibid.

9. "Caspian Pipeline Dream Becomes Reality," BBC News, September 14, 2002.

10. Eric Margolis, "Shevy's Big Mistake: Crossing Uncle Sam," the Toronto Sun, November 30, 2003.

11. Nick Paton Walsh, "Russia Accused of Plot to Sabotage Georgian Oil Pipeline," the Guardian, December 1, 2003.

12. Mevlut Katik, "Amid Risk, Baku-Ceyhan Pipeline Edges Forward," EurasiaNet, December 1, 2003.

13. Nick Paton Walsh, "US Privatises Its Military Aid to Georgia," the Guardian, January 6, 2004.

14. Presidential Determination on Azerbaijan, signed by George W. Bush on January 25, 2002.

15. John J. Fialka, "Search for Crude Comes With New Dangers—U.S. Strategic and Diplomatic Thinking Adjusts to Handle Hot Spots With Oil Potential," the Wall Street Journal, April 11, 2005.

16. Alman Talyshli, "Rumsfeld's Baku Trip Stirs Controversy," EurasiaNet, April 13, 2005.

17. Author copy of contract, dated July 28, 2004.

18. Chris Taylor speaking at "Contractors on the Battlefield: Learning from the Experience in Iraq," George Washington University, January 28, 2005.

19. Erik Prince's remarks at West 2006 Conference.

20. Nathan Hodge, "After the Gold Rush," Slate.com, February 9, 2006.

21. U.S. Azerbaijan Chamber of Commerce Web site, www.usacc.org/contents.php?cid=97, accessed December 5, 2006.

22. U.S. Azerbaijan Chamber of Commerce Web site, www.usacc.org/contents.php?cid=2, accessed December 5, 2006.

23. Ibid.

24. Tim Shorrock, "Contractor's Arrogance Contributed to Iraqi Rebellion, Marine Colonel Says," http://timshorrock.blogspot.com/2005_01_01_timshorrock_archive.html, accessed December 14, 2006.

25. Emery P. Dalesio, "NC Firm Was Providing Security for Food Delivery in Iraq," Associated Press, March 31, 2004.

26. Chris Taylor speaking at "Contractors on the Battlefield: Learning from the Experience in Iraq," George Washington University, January 28, 2005.

27. Transcript, "Secretary Rumsfeld and Ambassador Jon Purnell Press Conference in Uzbekistan," Department of Defense, February 24, 2004.

28. Nick Paton Walsh, "US Privatises Its Military Aid to Georgia," the Guardian, January 6, 2004.

29. Ibid.

30. Russ Rizzo, "Pentagon Aims to Bolster Security in Caspian Sea Region," Stars and Stripes (European edition), August 10, 2005.

31. Brett Forrest, "Azerbaijan Over a Barrel," Fortune (European Edition), November 28, 2005.

32. "US Working to Boost Sea Forces in Oil-Rich Caspian: Envoy," Agence France-Presse, September 21, 2005.

33. Kathy Gannon, "As Azerbaijan Democracy Struggles, Iran Makes Its Weight Felt," Associated Press, April 30, 2006.

34. "2005 In Review: Conflicts in Caucasus Still Characterized by Gridlock," Radio Free Europe/Radio Liberty, December 22, 2005.

35. "The Danger of a Military Buildup in the South Caucasus," Radio Free Europe/Radio Liberty, October 16, 2006.

36. "Caspian Hopes and Hazards," Africa Analysis (the Financial Times Limited), April 16, 2004.

37. Ariel Cohen, "Azerbaijan Intrigue," the Washington Times, October 25, 2005.

38. Joshua Kucera, "US Helps Forces, Gains Foothold in Caspian Region," Jane's Defence Weekly, May 25, 2005.

39. Alman Talyshli, "Rumsfeld's Baku Trip Stirs Controversy," EurasiaNet, April 13, 2005.

40. Ibid.

41. Candace Rondeaux, "A Pipeline to Promise, or a Pipeline to Peril," the St. Petersburg Times, May 15, 2005.

42. Vladimir Radyuhin, "Another Move in the Great Game," The Hindu, May 27, 2005.

43. Ibid.

44. Ibid.

45. White House press release, "Caspian Pipeline Consortium Fact Sheet," November 13, 2001.

46. Ibid.

47. Ibid.

48. U.S. Department of Energy press release, "Baku-Tbilisi-Ceyhan Pipeline First Oil Ceremony: Remarks of Secretary of Energy Samuel Bodman," May 25, 2005.

49. Report of the National Energy Policy Development Group, "Reliable, Affordable, Environmentally Sound Energy for America's Future," released by the White House in May 2001.

50. U.S. Department of Energy press release, "Baku-Tbilisi-Ceyhan Pipeline First Oil Ceremony: Remarks of Secretary of Energy Samuel Bodman," May 25, 2005.

51. Ibid.

52. David E. Sanger, "There's Democracy, and There's an Oil Pipeline," the New York Times, May 29, 2005.

53. Human Rights Watch, World Report 2005.

54. U.S. Department of State, *Country Reports on Human Rights Practices-2005*, released March 8, 2006.

55. Ibid.

56. Ibid.

57. www.BlackwaterUSA.com.

58. Tim Shorrock, "Contractor's Arrogance Contributed to Iraqi Rebellion, Marine Colonel Says," http://timshorrock.blogspot.com/2005_01_01_timshorrock_archive.html, accessed December 14, 2006.

CHAPTER 13

1. School of the Americas Watch, "What is the SOA?" www.soaw.org.

2. Amnesty International report, "United States of America: Human Dignity Denied; Torture and Accountability in the 'War on Terror,'" October 27, 2004.

3. Unless otherwise noted, all biographical information about and quotations from Jose Miguel Pizarro are drawn from an interview conducted in October 2006 by the author.

4. One of the most comprehensive accounts of the U.S. role in Chile can be found in Peter Kornbluh's incredibly detailed book, *The Pinochet File: A Declassified Dossier on Atrocity and Accountability*, The New Press, New York, 2003.

5. Peter Kornbluh, *The Pinochet File*, p. 5.

6. Ibid., "Project FUBELT: 'Formula for Chaos,'"pp. 1–35.

7. Ibid., p. 17.

8. National Security Archive, "Chile and the United States: Declassified Documents Relating to the Military Coup, 1970–1976"; "CIA, Notes on Meeting with the President on Chile, September 15, 1970."

9. Peter Kornbluh, *The Pinochet File*, p. 91.

10. Ibid., p. 113.

11. Jeff Cohen and Norman Solomon, "Chile Coup—Media Coverage Still Evasive 20 Years Later," Fairness & Accuracy In Reporting's *Media Beat*, September 8, 1993.

12. Peter Kornbluh, *The Pinochet File*, p. 234.

13. Ibid., p. 176.

14. Ibid., p. 153.

15. Ibid., p. 176

16. Ibid., p. 154.

17. Ibid., p. 344.

18. Marcelo Miranda, "Reclutamientos irregulares en Chile," *El Periodista* (Chile), January 30, 2004.

19. Gracia Rodrigo and Jorge Suez, "Parlamentarios rechazaron que en dependencias de la Armada se haya efectuado la inscripción de ex funcionarios interesados en trabajar para una firma en ese país en labores de seguridad," *La Tercera* (Chile), October 20, 2003.

20. "Ex comandos chilenos entrenan en EE.UU. antes de partir a Irak Los ex uniformados chilenos llegarán al Medio Oriente la próxima semana para prestar apoyo paramilitar a profesionales norteamericanos," *La Tercera* (Chile), February 24, 2004.

21. Pizarro interview, October 2006.

22. Isabel Guzmán, Mauricio Aguirre, and Jorge Suez, "La Armada suspendió el proceso de captación de personal para una empresa particular e inició sumario interno Ministra Bachelet pide investigar reclutamiento de chilenos para tareas de seguridad en Irak. La oferta laboral es para prestar servicios de vigilancia en instalaciones portuarias, petrolíferas y civiles en el Golfo Pérsico," *La Tercera* (Chile), October 21, 2003.

23. Gracia Rodrigo and Jorge Suez, "Parlamentarios rechazaron que en dependencias de la Armada se haya efectuado la inscripción de ex funcionarios interesados en trabajar para una firma en ese país en labores de seguridad," *La Tercera* (Chile), October 20, 2003.

24. Mauricio Aguirre, "El jueves, en dos vuelos de distintas aerolíneas, los militares (R) se embarcaron hacia EE.UU, para arribar a su destino final los primeros días de marzo. Ex comandos chilenos partieron a Irak a prestar labores de seguridad," *La Tercera* (Chile), February 22, 2004.

25. Author interview with Pizarro, October 2006.

26. Gracia Rodrigo and Jorge Suez, "Parlamentarios rechazaron que en dependencias de la Armada se haya efectuado la inscripción de ex funcionarios interesados en trabajar para una firma en ese país en labores de seguridad," *La Tercera* (Chile), October 20, 2003.

27. Gracia Rodrigo and Jorge Suez, "Parlamentarios rechazaron que en dependencias de la Armada se haya efectuado la inscripción de ex funcionarios interesados en trabajar para una firma en ese país en labores de seguridad," *La Tercera* (Chile), October 20, 2003.

28. Isabel Guzmán, Mauricio Aguirre, and Jorge Suez, "La Armada suspendió el proceso de captación de personal para una empresa particular e inició sumario interno Ministra Bachelet pide investigar reclutamiento de chilenos para tareas de seguridad en Irak. La oferta laboral es para prestar servicios de vigilancia en instalaciones portuarias, petrolíferas y civiles en el Golfo Pérsico," *La Tercera* (Chile), October 21, 2003.

29. Garry Leech, "Washington Targets Colombia's Rebels," *Colombia Journal*, July 29, 2002.

30. Gustavo González, "Chilean Mercenaries in the Line of Fire," Inter Press Service, April 7, 2004.

31. Pizarro interview, October 2006.

32. Pizarro interview; Héctor Rojas, "José Miguel Pizarro dice que recluta a efectivos para trabajar en labores de seguridad en el Medio Oriente, pero niega que se trate de mercenarios. Empresario asegura que enviará 3.000 ex militares chilenos a Irak en 2006," *La Tercera* (Chile), October 28, 2005.

33. Mauricio Aguirre, "El jueves, en dos vuelos de distintas aerolíneas, los militares (R) se embarcaron hacia EE.UU, para arribar a su destino final los primeros días de marzo. Ex comandos chilenos partieron a Irak a prestar labores de seguridad," *La Tercera* (Chile), February 22, 2004.

34. Ibid.

35. "Empresa estadounidense adelanta viaje de ex comandos chilenos a Irak Por razones de seguridad, los ejecutivos de Blackwater—entidad que contrató los servicios de los ex militares—no quisieron dar mayores detalles sobre el traslado de los ex uniformados al Medio Oriente," *La Tercera* (Chile), February 26, 2004.

36. "Ex comandos chilenos entrenan en EE.UU. antes de partir a Irak," *La Tercera* (Chile), February 24, 2004.

37. Mauricio Aguirre, "El jueves, en dos vuelos de distintas aerolíneas, los militares (R) se embarcaron hacia EE.UU, para arribar a su destino final los primeros días de marzo. Ex comandos chilenos partieron a Irak a prestar labores de seguridad," *La Tercera* (Chile), February 22, 2004.

38. Ibid.

39. Louis E.V. Nevaer, "For Security in Iraq, Corporate America Turns South," Pacific News Service, June 15, 2004.

40. Jonathan Franklin, "US Contractor Recruits Guards for Iraq in Chile," the *Guardian*, March 5, 2004.

41. Mauricio Aguirre, "De aprobar la evaluación a la que serán sometidos por la empresa estadounidense de seguridad Blackwater, los paramilitares se sumarán al contingente de avanzada que ya se encuentra en Irak desempeñando labores de vigilancia para el gobierno encabezado por George Bush," *La Tercera* (Chile), March 7, 2004.

42. Fiona Ortiz, "Chile Guards in Iraq, a Thorn for Government at Home," Reuters, April 20, 2004.

43. Gustavo González, "Chilean Mercenaries in the Line of Fire," Inter Press Service, April 7, 2004.

44. Roberto Manríquez, "Chile in Haiti & Iraq," Znet, June 2, 2004.

45. Interview by e-mail October 2006.

46. Ibid.

47. Gustavo González, "Chilean Mercenaries in the Line of Fire," Inter Press Service, April 7, 2004.

48. Carmen Gloria Vitalic, "Ejército investiga reclutamiento de ex militares para trabajar como 'guardias' en Irak," La Tercera (Chile), July 21, 2004.

49. Irene Caselli, "More Chilean Mercenaries to Be Sent to Iraq," The Santiago Times (Chile), September 9, 2004.

50. Ibid.

51. Ricardo Calderon, "Atrapados en Bagdad," Semana (Colombia), August 20, 2006.

52. Sonni Efron, "Worry Grows as Foreigners Flock to Iraq's Risky Jobs," the Los Angeles Times, July 30, 2005.

53. Ibid.

54. Ibid.

55. Unless otherwise noted, the quotes from the various Colombians speaking about their experiences with Blackwater are drawn from Ricardo Calderon, "Atrapados en Bagdad," Semana (Colombia), August 20, 2006.

56. Andy Webb-Vidal, "Colombian Ex-Soldiers in Iraq Pay Dispute," the Financial Times, August 21, 2006.

57. "Honduras Orders Chileans Training to Become Security Guards in Iraq to Leave Country," Associated Press, September 20, 2005.

58. Carmen Gloria Vitalic, "Ejército investiga reclutamiento de ex militares para trabajar como 'guardias' en Irak," La Tercera (Chile), July 21, 2004.

59. Ginger Thompson and Gary Cohn, "Torturers' Confessions: Now in Exile, These CIA-Trained Hondurans Describe Their Lives—and the Deaths of Their Victims," the Baltimore Sun, June 13, 1995.

60. Weekly News Update on the Americas #817, September 25, 2005.

61. "In Honduras, Former Soldiers Leave for Private-Security Work in Iraq," Associated Press, August 23, 2005.

62. "Honduras Orders Chileans Training to Become Security Guards in Iraq to Leave Country," Associated Press, September 20, 2005.

63. Hugo Infante, "Comandos chilenos en Irak relatan cómo han sobrevivido en ese país," La Tercera (Chile), June 6, 2004.

64. Ibid.

65. Darío Bermúdez, "Capítulos desconocidos de los mercenarios chilenos en Honduras camino de Iraq," La Nación (Chile), September 25, 2005; interviews October 2006.

66. "Honduras Orders Chileans Training to Become Security Guards in Iraq to Leave Country," Associated Press, September 20, 2005.

67. Carmen Gloria Vitalic, "Ejército investiga reclutamiento de ex militares para trabajar como 'guardias' en Irak," La Tercera (Chile), July 21, 2004.

68. Freddy Cuevas, "Honduras Fines U.S. Subsidiary Over Alleged Mercenary Training," Associated Press, November 25, 2006.

69. "Honduras Extends Deadline for Deporting Chileans After Nicaragua Refuses to Accept Them," Associated Press, September 24, 2005.

70. "Chileans Trained in Honduras to Be Shipped to Iraq," the Santiago Times, September 21, 2005.

71. Weekly News Update on the Americas #817, September 25, 2005.

72. "Honduras Deports Chileans Training for Private Guard Duty in Iraq," Associated Press, September 23, 2005.

73. "Chilean Security Guards Destined for Iraq, Training in Honduras," Honduras This Week, September 26, 2005.

74. "Engañados dos hondureños que trabajaban en Irak," EFE Agency (Spain), October 29, 2005.

75. Freddy Cuevas, "Honduras Fines U.S. Subsidiary Over Alleged Mercenary Training," Associated Press, November 25, 2006.

76. Ibid.

77. "Former Officer Accused of Recruiting Soldiers, Police, for Security Work in Iraq," Associated Press, October 21, 2005.

78. Héctor Rojas, "José Miguel Pizarro dice que recluta a efectivos para trabajar en labores de seguridad en el Medio Oriente, pero niega que se trate de mercenarios. Empresario asegura que enviará 3.000 ex militares chilenos a Irak en 2006," *La Tercera* (Chile), October 28, 2005.

79. Interview, October 2006.

80. Interview by e-mail, October 2006.

CHAPTER 14

1. Unless otherwise noted, all quotes and information from Danica Zovko come from author interviews in the summer of 2006.

2. Author copy.

3. Joseph Neff and Jay Price, "After the Horror, Strong Words Mask Inaction; Little Has Been Done to Determine the Facts of the Ambush in Fallujah That Cost Four Civilian Contractors Their Lives," the *News & Observer* (Raleigh, North Carolina), August 1, 2004.

4. "A Warrior Who Wanted Peace," *St. Petersburg Times* (Florida), April 14, 2004.

5. "Death and Funeral Notices," the *San Diego Union-Tribune*, April 9, 2004.

6. Renae Merle, "Contract Workers Are War's Forgotten; Iraq Deaths Create Subculture of Loss," the *Washington Post*, July 31, 2004.

7. Ibid.

8. Ibid.

9. Unless otherwise noted, all quotes and information from Katy Helvenston-Wettengel come from author interviews throughout 2006.

10. David Barstow, "Security Firm Says Its Workers Were Lured Into Iraqi Ambush," the *New York Times*, April 9, 2004.

11. Transcript, *The Big Story With John Gibson*, Fox News, March 31, 2004.

12. Ibid.

13. Transcript, *Morning Edition*, NPR, April 1, 2004.

14. Transcript, *The Big Story With John Gibson*, Fox News, April 2, 2004.

15. Patrick Graham, "Veiled Threat: Why an SUV Is Now the Most Dangerous Vehicle in Iraq," *The Observer* (London), April 4, 2004.

16. Ibid.

17. Mark LeVine, "Seeing Iraq Through the Globalization Lens," the *Christian Science Monitor*, April 5, 2004.

18. David Barstow, "Security Firm Says Its Workers Were Lured Into Iraqi Ambush," the *New York Times*, April 9, 2004.

19. Ibid.

20. Ibid.

21. Committee on Oversight and Government Reform Majority Staff Report, "Private Military Contractors in Iraq: An Examination of Blackwater's Actions in Fallujah," September 2007.

22. David Barstow, "Security Firm Says Its Workers Were Lured Into Iraqi Ambush," the *New York Times*, April 9, 2004.

23. Jim Steele's "Premiere Speakers Bureau" biography.

24. Jon Lee Anderson, "The Uprising," *The New Yorker*, May 3, 2004.

25. Colin Freeman, "Fallujah: Brutal Ambush Might Have Been Avoided," the *San Francisco Chronicle*, April 19, 2004.

26. Ibid.

27. Michael Duffy, "When Private Armies Take to the Front Lines," *Time*, April 12, 2004.

28. Colin Freeman, "Fallujah: Brutal Ambush Might Have Been Avoided," the *San Francisco Chronicle*, April 19, 2004.

29. Ibid.

30. Ibid.

31. Joseph Neff and Jay Price, "After the Horror, Strong Words Mask Inaction; Little Has Been Done to Determine the Facts of the Ambush in Fallujah That Cost Four Civilian Contractors Their Lives," the *News & Observer* (Raleigh, North Carolina), August 1, 2004.

32. Ibid.

33. "U.S. Security Contractor Cites Explosive Growth Amid Iraq War," Associated Press, October 13, 2004.

34. Ibid.

35. Ibid.

36. Interviews 2006.

37. Interviews 2006.

38. *Blackwater Tactical Weekly*, November 8, 2004.

39. Bill Sizemore and Joanne Kimberlin, "When Things Go Wrong," the *Virginian-Pilot*, July 26, 2006.

40. Author copy of photo.

41. *Blackwater Tactical Weekly*, November 22, 2004.

42. *Beckman Coulter v. Flextronics* (Orange County Superior Court, California). The verdict was the largest in California in 2003 and the largest in Orange County history.

43. Interview 2006.

44. *Richard P. Nordan v. Blackwater Security Consulting, LLC et. al.*, filed January 5, 2005.

45. Ibid.

46. Author copy of contract.

47. Blackwater Motion to Dismiss, filed January 31, 2005.

48. *Richard P. Nordan v. Blackwater Security Consulting, LLC et. al.*, filed January 5, 2005.

49. Ibid.

50. Interview 2006.

51. *Richard P. Nordan v. Blackwater Security Consulting, LLC et. al.*, filed January 5, 2005.

52. Ibid.

53. Joseph Neff and Jay Prince (the *News & Observer*), "Use of Private Contractors in War Zones Proves Costly," Associated Press, October 25, 2004.

54. Author copy of contract.

55. Author copy of letter.

56. Author copy of letter.

57. Transcript, Hearing of House Government Reform Committee, September 28, 2006.

58. E-mail to producers of PBS *Frontline*, www.pbs.org/wgbh/pages/frontline/shows/warriors/etc/response.html, posted June 21, 2005.

59. Ibid.

60. "Interim Audit Report on Inappropriate Use of Proprietary Data Markings by the Logistics Civil Augmentation Program (LOGCAP) Contractor," Office of the Special Inspector General for Iraq Reconstruction, October 26, 2006.

61. Ibid.

62. Jeff Gerth and Don Van Natta Jr., "Halliburton Contracts in Iraq: The Struggle to Manage Costs," the *New York Times*, December 29, 2003.

63. Halliburton Statement, December 7, 2006.

64. Letter from Representative Henry Waxman to Defense Secretary Donald Rumsfeld, December 7, 2006.

65. Ibid.

66. Transcript, Hearing on Iraq Private Contractor Oversight, House Oversight and Government Reform Committee, February 7, 2007.

67. See Jeremy Scahill and Garrett Ordower, "KBR's $400 Million Iraq Question!" *The Nation*, March 12, 2007.

68. Transcript, Hearing on Iraq Private Contractor Oversight, House Oversight and Government Reform Committee, February 7, 2007.

69. Committee on Oversight and Government Reform Majority Staff Report, "Private Military Contractors in Iraq: An Examination of Blackwater's Actions in Fallujah," September 2007.

70. Ibid.

71. Ibid.

72. Ibid.

73. Blackwater report, "Blackwater's Reponse to 'Majority Staff Report'," October 23, 2007.

74. Author copy of contract.

75. Interview 2006.

76. *Richard P. Nordan v. Blackwater Security Consulting, LLC et. al.*, filed January 5, 2005.

77. See Chapter 5.

78. *Richard P. Nordan v. Blackwater Security Consulting, LLC et. al.*, filed January 5, 2005.

79. Ibid.

80. Ibid.

81. Transcript, Hearing on Iraq Private Contractor Oversight, House Oversight and Government Reform Committee, February 7, 2007.

82. Committee on Oversight and Government Reform Majority Staff Report, "Private Military Contractors in Iraq: An Examination of Blackwater's Actions in Fallujah," September 2007.

83. Ibid.

84. Ibid

85. Transcript, Hearing on Iraq Private Contractor Oversight, House Oversight and Government Reform Committee, February 7, 2007.

86. Committee on Oversight and Government Reform Majority Staff Report, "Private Military Contractors in Iraq: An Examination of Blackwater's Actions in Fallujah," September 2007.

87. Interview 2006.

88. Committee on Oversight and Government Reform Majority Staff Report, "Private Military Contractors in Iraq: An Examination of Blackwater's Actions in Fallujah," September 2007.

89. *Richard P. Nordan v. Blackwater Security Consulting, LLC et. al.*, filed January 5, 2005.

90. Committee on Oversight and Government Reform Majority Staff Report, "Private Military Contractors in Iraq: An Examination of Blackwater's Actions in Fallujah," September 2007.

91. Ibid.

92. Blackwater report, "Blackwater's Response to 'Majority Staff Report'," October 23, 2007.

93. Ibid.

94. Bill Sizemore and Joanne Kimberlin, "When Things Go Wrong," the *Virginian-Pilot*, July 26, 2006.

95. E-mail to author April 14, 2006.

96. Scott Dodd, "Families of 4 Contractors Killed in Iraq Sue Security Company," Knight Ridder/Tribune News Service, January 6, 2005.

97. Interviews 2006.

98. Interviews 2006.

99. Transcript, "Hearing of the National Security, Emerging Threats and International Relations Subcommittee of the House Government Reform Committee," June 13, 2006.

100. Author copy, "Blackwater Defendants' Memorandum in Opposition," December 26, 2006.

101. Author copy, "Reply Brief in Support of Motion," December 27, 2006.

102. Author copy, "United States' Limited Opposition to Plaintiff's Motion," December 26, 2006.

103. Author copy, "Declaration Under Penalty of Perjury of Colonel Richard O. Hatch," December 26, 2006.

104. Quadrennial Defense Review Report, February 6, 2006.

105. Blackwater appellate brief, filed October 31, 2005.

106. Bernd Debusmann, "In Iraq, Contractor Deaths Near 650, Legal Fog Thickens," Reuters, October 10, 2006.

107. Interview 2006.

108. Blackwater appellate brief, filed October 31, 2005.

109. Blackwater petition, filed December 19, 2005. Note: Order 17 was signed by Bremer on June 27, 2004, three months after the Fallujah ambush.

110. Blackwater appellate brief, filed October 31, 2005.

111. Ibid.

112. Ibid.

113. Ibid.

114. "Halliburton/KBR the Lex Column," the *Financial Times* (London), November 16, 2006.

115. KBR amicus curiae, filed September 22, 2006.

116. Ibid.

117. Joseph Neff, "Blackwater Suit Can Go Forward; A Wake Judge Rules in Favor of Families of Four Killed in Iraq," the *News & Observer* (Raleigh, North Carolina), November 28, 2006.

118. Interviews 2006.

119. Jeremy Scahill and Garrett Ordower, "From Whitewater to Blackwater," TheNation.com, posted October 26, 2006.

120. Blackwater petition to U.S. Supreme Court, October 18, 2006.

121. Ibid.

122. Joseph Neff, "Blackwater Suit Can Go Forward; A Wake Judge Rules in Favor of Families of Four Killed in Iraq," the *News & Observer* (Raleigh, North Carolina), November 28, 2006.

123. Author copy, Blackwater's "Petition for a Writ of Certiorari," filed December 20, 2006.

124. Author copy, Blackwater's "Petition for Order Directing Arbitration," December 20, 2006; Author copy, Blackwater's "Demand for Arbitration," signed December 14, 2006.

125. Bill Sizemore, "Suit Against Blackwater Over Contractor Deaths Moves to Arbitration." *The Virginian-Pilot*, May 20, 2007.

126. Ibid.

127. Author copy of statement.

128. Attila Berry and Joe Palazzolo, "Blackwater Sues Wiley Rein for Malpractice; Former Client Claims Firm Botched Falluja Case," Legal Times, January 28, 2008.

129. Interview 2006.

CHAPTER 15

1. Many of the descriptive details on the crash of Blackwater 61 and its aftermath are drawn from the author's copy of the National Transportation Safety Board accident docket.

2. Author copy of National Transportation Safety Board accident docket.

3. Amended Complaint, filed October 4, 2005.

4. Presidential Airways' Emergency Motion to Quash Subpoena, February 24, 2006.

5. Flight records from flightaware.com accessed in October and November 2006; Federal Aviation Administration airplane registration records.

6. Author copy of National Transportation Safety Board accident docket.

7. Ibid.

8. Ibid.

9. Ibid.

10. Ibid.

11. *Blackwater Tactical Weekly*, October 18, 2004.

12. Author copy of National Transportation Safety Board accident docket.

13. Ibid.

14. Ibid.

15. Ibid.

16. Ibid.

17. Ibid.

18. Ibid.

19. Ibid.

20. Ibid.

21. Ibid.

22. Ibid.

23. Ibid.

24. Suzanne Goldenberg, "CIA Accused of Torture at Bagram Base; Some Captives Handed to Brutal Foreign Agencies," the *Guardian*, December 27, 2002.

25. Author copy of National Transportation Safety Board accident docket.

26. Ibid.

27. Author copy of National Transportation Safety Board accident docket; "Coalition Forces in Afghanistan as of Oct. 4, 2004, www.defenselink.mil/home/ features/1082004d.html.

28. Rafael A. Almeda, "A Soldier Until the End," the *Sun-Sentinel*, December 3, 2004.

29. Author copy of National Transportation Safety Board accident docket.

30. Ibid.

31. All in-flight dialogue from cockpit voice recorder transcript contained in "Specialist's Factual Report of Investigation," National Transportation Safety Board Vehicle Recorders Division, October 18, 2005.

32. Author copy of National Transportation Safety Board accident docket.

33. Ibid.

34. Ibid.

35. Ibid.

36. Jennifer Feehan, "Plane Crash Kills a Weston Man in Afghanistan," the *Toledo Blade*, December 2, 2004.

37. Amended Complaint, filed October 4, 2005.

38. Griff Witte, "Blackwater Broke Rules, Report Says," the *Washington Post*, October 5, 2005.

39. Author copy of National Transportation Safety Board accident docket.

40. Ibid.

41. Griff Witte, "Blackwater Broke Rules, Report Says," the *Washington Post*, October 5, 2005.

42. Author copy of National Transportation Safety Board Aircraft Accident Brief.

43. Ibid.

44. Jay Price and Joseph Neff, "Inquiry Pins Blackwater Crash on Pilot," the *News & Observer*, December 6, 2006.

45. Author copy of National Transportation Safety Board Aircraft Accident Brief.

46. Presidential Airways' Emergency Motion to Quash Subpoena, February 24, 2006.

47. Judge John Antoon, Order denying Blackwater motions, September 27, 2006.

48. Presidential Airways' Emergency Motion to Quash Subpoena, February 24, 2006.

49. Judge John Antoon, Order denying Blackwater motions, September 27, 2006.

50. Ibid.

51. Ibid.

52. Ibid.

53. Presidential Airways' Emergency Motion to Quash Subpoena, February 24, 2006.

54. Ibid.

55. Ibid.

56. Judge John Antoon, Order denying Blackwater motions, September 27, 2006.

57. Ibid.

58. Ibid.

59. Ibid.

60. Ibid.

61. Jane Mayer, "Outsourcing Torture," *The New Yorker*, February 14, 2005.

62. Ibid.

63. "United States Policy with Respect to the Involuntary Return of Persons in Danger of Subjection to Torture," Public Law 105–277.

64. Jane Mayer, "Outsourcing Torture," *The New Yorker*, February 14, 2005.

65. Ibid.

66. Jim Landers, "CIA Official Says War on Terrorism Will Be Won With Great Force," the *Dallas Morning News*, October 19, 2001.

67. William M. Leary, "Supporting the 'Secret War': CIA Air Operations in Laos, 1955–1974," CIA *Studies in Intelligence*, Winter 1999–2000.

68. Stephen Grey, *Ghost Plane: the True Story of The CIA Torture Program*, St. Martin's New York, 1996, p. 108.

69. Press release, "Blackwater USA Completes Acquisition of Aviation Worldwide Services," PRWEB, May 3, 2003.

70. Ibid.

71. Author copy of National Transportation Safety Board accident docket.

72. Ibid.

73. Press release, "Blackwater USA Completes Acquisition of Aviation Worldwide Services," PRWEB, March 3, 2003.

74. Jeffrey S. Hampton, "Blackwater Aviation Unit to Relocate," the *Virginian-Pilot*, March 29, 2006.

75. Ibid.

76. Ibid.

77. "Hangar Plaque Honors C.I.A.'s Air Operative," the *New York Times*, December 30, 1985.

78. David E. Hendrix, "CIA Got Burned on Airplane Deal, Suit Says Hemet City Councilman James Venable Ended Up with Some of the Planes," the *Press-Enterprise*, January 11, 1996.

79. Press Release, April 12, 2006.

80. Stephen Grey, *Ghost Plane: The True Story of the CIA Torture Program*, St. Martin's, New York, 1996, pp. 142–143.

81. Ibid., p. 125.

82. Aaron Sarver, "Tracking the CIA Torture Flights," *In These Times*, September 27, 2006.

83. All flight records from flightaware.com accessed in October and November 2006.

84. "To Catch a Spy," the *Washington Post*, March 26, 2006.

85. Author copy of National Transportation Safety Board accident docket.

86. Stephen Grey, *Ghost Plane*, p. 39.

87. Author copy of National Transportation Safety Board accident docket.

88. Ibid.

89. Barry Yeoman, "Soldiers of Good Fortune," *Mother Jones*, May/June 2003.

90. Interviews, July, August 2006; Ken Silverstein, "Revolving Door to Blackwater Causes Alarm at CIA," *Harper's*, www.harpers.org/sb-revolving-door-blackwater-1158094722.html, September 12, 2006; Robert Young Pelton, *Licensed to Kill*.

91. Michael Hirsh, John Barry, and Daniel Klaidman, "Interrogation: A Tortured Debate," *Newsweek*, June 21, 2006.

CHAPTER 16

1. Bob Woodward, *Bush at War*, pp. 50–52.

2. Biographical information on Cofer Black is largely drawn from Steve Coll, *Ghost Wars: The Secret History of the CIA, Afghanistan, Bin Laden, from the Soviet Invasion to September 10, 2001*, Penguin, New York, 2004.

3. Steve Coll, *Ghost Wars*, p. 267.

4. Ibid., p. 267.

5. Ibid., "Front Matter."

6. Ibid., p. 271.

7. Ibid., p. 267.

8. Billy Waugh with Tim Keown, *Hunting the Jackal: A Special Forces and CIA Ground Soldier's Fifty-Year Career Hunting America's Enemies*, William Morrow, New York, 2004, p. 143.

9. Robert Young Pelton, *Licensed to Kill*, p. 28.

10. Steve Coll, *Ghost Wars*, p. 271.

11. Ibid., pg. 271.

12. Billy Waugh with Tim Keown, *Hunting the Jackal*, p. 151.

13. Ibid., p. 150.

14. Ibid., p. 155.

15. Ibid., pp. 156–157.

16. Ibid., pp. 156–200.

17. Ibid., p. 198.

18. J. Cofer Black official biography, U.S. Department of State.

19. Ibid.

20. Steve Coll, *Ghost Wars*, p. 454.

21. Ned Zeman, David Wise, David Rose, and Bryan Burrough, "The Path to 9/11: Lost Warnings and Fatal Errors," *Vanity Fair*, November 2004.

22. James Bamford, *A Pretext for War: 9/11, Iraq, and the Abuse of America's Intelligence Agencies*, Doubleday, New York, 2004, p. 221.

23. J. Cofer Black testimony before the 9/11 Commission, April 13, 2004.

24. J. Cofer Black testimony before the Joint House/Senate Intelligence Committee Hearing into September 11, September 26, 2002.

25. Ibid.

26. Steve Coll, *Ghost Wars*, p. 455.

27. James Bamford, *A Pretext for War*, p. 219; Ned Zeman, David Wise, David Rose and Bryan Burrough, "The Path to 9/11: Lost Warnings and Fatal Errors," *Vanity Fair*, November 2004.

28. Steve Coll, *Ghost Wars*, p. 492.

29. Ibid., pp. 456–459.

30. Ibid., p. 457.

31. Ibid, pp. 456–457.

32. James Bamford, *A Pretext for War*, p. 219.

33. Nick Paton Walsh, "The Envoy Who Said Too Much: One Minute He Was Our Man in Tashkent, the Next He Was a Major Embarrassment for the Foreign Office," the *Guardian*, July 15, 2004.

34. Steve Coll, *Ghost Wars*, p. 502.

35. James Bamford, *A Pretext for War*, p. 220.

36. Steve Coll, *Ghost Wars*, p. 516.

37. Ibid., p. 518.

38. Jon Lee Anderson, "A Lion's Death: The Assassination of the Taliban's Most Important Afghan opponent," *The New Yorker*, October 1, 2001.

39. Steve Coll, *Ghost Wars*, p. 543

40. Ned Zeman, David Wise, David Rose, and Bryan Burrough, "The Path to 9/11: Lost Warnings and Fatal Errors," *Vanity Fair*, November 2004.

41. Ibid.

42. "Two Months Before 9/11, an Urgent Warning to Rice," the *Washington Post*, October 1, 2006.

43. Ibid.

44. Ibid.

45. Author copy of declassified memo titled "Bin Ladin Determined to Strike in US," August 6, 2001.

46. J. Cofer Black testimony before the Joint House/Senate Intelligence Committee Hearing into September 11, September 26, 2002.

47. Gordon Corera, "How Terror Attacks Changed the CIA," BBC News Online, March 12, 2006.

48. Bob Woodward, *Bush at War*, Simon & Schuster, New York, 2002, p. 52.

49. Ibid.

50. Ibid.

51. Gary Schroen, *First In: An Insider's Account of How the CIA Spearheaded the War on Terror in Afghanistan*, Ballantine, New York, 2005, p. 38.

52. Ibid.

53. Ibid.

54. Jane Mayer, "The Search for Osama," *The New Yorker*, August 4, 2003.

55. Bob Woodward, *Bush at War*, p. 103.

56. Robert Young Pelton, *Licensed to Kill*, pp. 30–32.

57. Transcript, Interview with Steve Coll, PBS Frontline, www.pbs.org/ wgbh/pages/frontline/darkside/interviews/coll.html, posted June 20, 2006.

58. Dana Priest, "Wrongful Imprisonment: Anatomy of a CIA Mistake German Citizen Released After Months in 'Rendition,'" the *Washington Post*, December 4, 2005.

59. Ibid.

60. Dana Priest and Barton Gellman, "U.S. Decries Abuse but Defends Interrogations; 'Stress and Duress' Tactics Used on Terrorism Suspects Held in Secret Overseas Facilities," the *Washington Post*, December 26, 2002.

61. Transcript, *Wolf Blitzer Reports*, CNN, April 30, 2004.

62. Dana Priest, "Wrongful Imprisonment: Anatomy of a CIA Mistake German Citizen Released After Months in 'Rendition,'" the *Washington Post*, December 4, 2005.

63. Ibid.

64. Dana Priest and Barton Gellman, "U.S. Decries Abuse but Defends Interrogations; 'Stress and Duress' Tactics Used on Terrorism Suspects Held in Secret Overseas Facilities," the *Washington Post*, December 26, 2002.

65. Ibid.

66. Michael Hirsh, John Barry, and Daniel Klaidman, "A Tortured Debate," *Newsweek*, June 21, 2004.

67. Jane Mayer, "Outsourcing Torture," The *New Yorker*, February 14, 2005.

68. Ibid.

69. Jane Mayer, "Outsourcing Torture," The *New Yorker*, February 14, 2005.

70. Evan Thomas and Michael Hirsh, "Torture and Terror: Interrogators Have Pondered the Uses of Torture for Centuries and in the Wake of 9/11 the US Has Embraced So-called Torture Lite," *Newsweek*, November 22, 2005.

71. Dana Priest, "Wrongful Imprisonment: Anatomy of a CIA Mistake German Citizen Released After Months in 'Rendition,'" the *Washington Post*, December 4, 2005.

72. Richard Sale, "Embarrassed Rumsfeld Fired CIA Official," United Press International, July 28, 2004.

73. Barton Gellman and Thomas E. Ricks, "U.S. Concludes Bin Laden Escaped at Tora Bora Fight; Failure to Send Troops in Pursuit Termed Major Error," the *Washington Post*, April 17, 2002.

74. Bob Woodward and Dan Eggen, "Aug. Memo Focused on Attacks in U.S. Lack of Fresh Information Frustrated Bush," the *Washington Post*, May 19, 2002.

75. Richard Sale, "Embarrassed Rumsfeld Fired CIA Official," United Press International, July 28, 2004.

76. Ibid.

77. White House press release, October 10, 2002.

78. Transcript, "Counterterrorism Chief Says Terrorist Attacks Fell Sharply in 2002," U.S. State Department, May 14, 2002.

79. Transcript, 2003 State of the Union Address, January 28, 2003.

80. Kathleen T. Rhem, "State Department: Terrorist Attacks Down 44 Percent in 2002," American Forces Press Service, April 30, 2003.

81. Transcript, "Release of the 2003 'Patterns of Global Terrorism' Annual Report," U.S. Department of State, April 29, 2004.

82. Transcript, "Rollout of 'Patterns of Global Terrorism 2003' Annual Report," U.S. Department of State, April 29, 2004.

83. Alan B. Krueger and David Laitin, "Faulty Terror Report Card," the *Washington Post*, May 17, 2004.

84. Ibid.

85. "Verbatim," *Time* (Asia), July 5, 2004.

86. Cam Simpson (*Chicago Tribune*), "Corrected Report Shows 2003 Terror Attacks the Highest in 2 Decades," *Knight Ridder/Tribune Business News*, June 23, 2004.

87. Alan B. Krueger and David Laitin, "Faulty Terror Report Card," the *Washington Post*, May 17, 2004.

88. Transcript, "Ambassador J. Cofer Black, Coordinator, Office of the Coordinator for Counterterrorism Foreign Press Center Briefing," U.S. Department of State, April 29, 2004.

89. Barry Schweid, "Revised State Department Report Shows Rise in Terror Incidents Worldwide," Associated Press, June 23, 2004.

90. Author copy of letter.

91. Paul Krugman, "White House Claims on Terrorism Don't Add Up," *International Herald Tribune*, June 26, 2004.

92. Salamander Davoudi, "US Re-Releases Flawed Global Terror Report," *Financial Times*, June 23, 2004.

93. Paul Krugman, "White House Claims on Terrorism Don't Add Up," *International Herald Tribune*, June 26, 2004.

94. Barry Schweid, "Revised State Department Report Shows Rise in Terror Incidents Worldwide," Associated Press, June 23, 2004.

95. Ibid.

96. Ann Scott Tyson and Dana Priest, "Pentagon Seeking Leeway Overseas; Operations Could Bypass Envoys," the *Washington Post*, February 24, 2005.

97. "US Supplies Three Patrol Ships to Boost Olympic Security," Agence France-Presse, June 26, 2004.

98. Ibid.

99. BlackwaterUSA.com, captured November 30, 2006.

100. "Blackwater's Top Brass," the *Virginian-Pilot*, July 24, 2006.

101. Transcript, "Hearing of the International Terrorism, Nonproliferation and Human Rights Subcommittee of the House International Relations Committee," April 1, 2004.

102. Ibid.

103. *Blackwater Tactical Weekly*, May 17, 2004.

104. Paul Wiseman, "The Hunt for Bin Laden: Dragnet Snares Many of His Men, But Terrorist Kingpin Still at Large," *USA Today*, September 10, 2004.

105. "US State Department Counter-Terrorism Chief Resigns," *AFX News*, November 7, 2004.

106. Douglas Jehl, "Officials Won't Be Disciplined for Actions Before Sept. 11," the *New York Times*, October 6, 2005.

107. John B. Roberts II, "Chinese Mole Hunt at CIA; Agency Keeps Human-Intelligence Apparatus, Barely," the *Washington Times*, October 14, 2005.

108. Blackwater USA Press Release, "Ambassador Cofer Black Becomes Vice-Chairman at Blackwater USA," February 4, 2005.

109. The Black Group Web site, www.blackgroupllc.com/services.html, captured November 30, 2006.

110. The Black Group Web site, www.blackgroundllc.com/about.html, captured November 30, 2006.

111. The Black Group Web site, www.blackgroupllc.com/contact.html, captured November 30, 2006.

112. The Black Group Web site, www.blackgroupllc.com/, captured November 30, 2006.

CHAPTER 17

1. Transcript, "President Bush Discusses Early Transfer of Iraqi Sovereignty," www.whitehouse.gov, June 28, 2004.

2. L. Paul Bremer III, *My Year in Iraq*, p. 395.

3. Transcript, "President Bush Discusses Early Transfer of Iraqi Sovereignty," www.whitehouse.gov, June 28, 2004.

4. Scott Shane, "Poker-Faced Diplomat, Negroponte Is Poised for Role as Spy Chief," the *New York Times*, March 29, 2005.

5. Ibid.

6. Carla Anne Robbins, "Negroponte Has Tricky Mission: U.S. Diplomat Is at Center of Debate Over Power of Iraq Envoy, the *Wall Street Journal*, April 27, 2004.

7. Jay Hancock, Gary Cohn, and Tom Bowman, "Contra-era Envoy Nominated to Be U.N. Ambassador; Diplomat Helped Hide Honduran Abuses from Congress in '80s; Vocal

Supporters, Critics," the *Baltimore Sun*, March 7, 2001; Michael Dobbs, "Papers Illustrate Negroponte's Contra Role; Newly Released Documents Show Intelligence Nominee Was Active in U.S. Effort," the *Washington Post*, April 12, 2005; Robert Parry, "Negroponte's Dark Past: The Case Against Bush's New Intelligence Czar," *In These Times*, March 28, 2005.

8. Jay Hancock, Gary Cohn, and Tom Bowman, "Contra-era Envoy Nominated to Be U.N. Ambassador; Diplomat Helped Hide Honduran Abuses from Congress in '80s; Vocal Supporters, Critics," the *Baltimore Sun*, March 7, 2001.

9. Scott Shane, "Poker-Faced Diplomat, Negroponte Is Poised for Role as Spy Chief," the *New York Times*, March 29, 2005.

10. Carla Anne Robbins, "Negroponte Has Tricky Mission: U.S. Diplomat Is at Center of Debate Over Power of Iraq Envoy, the *Wall Street Journal*, April 27, 2004.

11. Ibid.

12. "Honduras Rushes to Pull Out Troops," www.CNN.com, April 20, 2004.

13. Wil Haygood, "Ambassador With Big Portfolio: John Negroponte Goes to Baghdad With a Record of Competence, and Controversy," the *Washington Post*, June 21, 2004.

14. Tyler Marshall, "Operation Limited Freedom: The U.S. Embassy in Baghdad Is a Hub of 'Extreme Diplomacy.' All Moves Are Scripted, and There's Even a Hostage Negotiator on Site," the *Los Angeles Times*, January 22, 2005.

15. Transcript, *Democracy Now!* April 27, 2004.

16. Jeremy Scahill, "Mercenary Jackpot," *The Nation*, August 28, 2006.

17. Michael Hirsh and John Barry, "'The Salvador Option': The Pentagon May Put Special-Forces-Led Assassination or Kidnapping Teams in Iraq," *Newsweek* (Web exclusive), January 8, 2005.

18. Ibid.

19. Transcript, "Joint Media Availability With U.S. Secretary of Defense Donald Rumsfeld and Russian Defense Minister Sergey Ivanov Following Their Meeting," Department of Defense Briefing, January 11, 2005.

20. Greg Jaffe, "Bands of Brothers—New Factor in Iraq: Irregular Brigades Fill Security Void—Jailed by Hussein, Gen. Thavit Is Leading Thousands Now; Questions About Loyalty—'Toughest Force We've Got,'" the *Wall Street Journal*, February 16, 2005.

21. Ibid.

22. Ibid.

23. Ibid.

24. Peter Maass, "The Way of the Commandos," *The New York Times Magazine*, May 1, 2005.

25. Ibid.

26. Ibid.

27. Michael Hirsh and John Barry, "'The Salvador Option': The Pentagon May Put Special-Forces-Led Assassination or Kidnapping Teams in Iraq," *Newsweek* (Web exclusive), January 8, 2005.

28. Ibid.

29. Douglas Jehl and Elisabeth Bumiller, "Bush Picks Longtime Diplomat for New Top Intelligence Job," the *New York Times*, February 18, 2005.

30. Robert Dreyfuss, "Phoenix Rising," *The American Prospect*, January 1, 2004.

31. Ibid.

32. Ibid.

33. Ibid.

34. Transcript, *Democracy Now!* January 10, 2005.

35. Scott Shane, "Poker-Faced Diplomat, Negroponte Is Poised for Role as Spy Chief," the *New York Times*, March 29, 2005.

36. Ibid.

37. Michael Hirsh and John Barry, "'The Salvador Option': The Pentagon May Put Special-Forces-Led Assassination or Kidnapping Teams in Iraq," *Newsweek* (Web exclusive), January 8, 2005.

38. Transcript, *Democracy Now!* February 18, 2005.

39. Anthony Shadid and Steve Fainaru, "Militias on the Rise Across Iraq: Shiite and Kurdish Groups Seizing Control, Instilling Fear in North and South," the *Washington Post,* August 21, 2005.

40. Transcript, *Democracy Now!* February 28, 2006.

41. Ibid.

42. Scott Ritter, "The Salvador Option: By Any Standard, the Ongoing American Occupation of Iraq Is a Disaster," www.aljazeera.net , January 20, 2005.

43. Tom Lasseter, "Sectarian Resentment Extends to Iraq's Army," Knight-Ridder, October 12, 2005.

44. Patrick Cockburn, "Does Anyone in Washington or at Downing Street Know What's Really Happening in Iraq?" *CounterPunch,* November 28, 2006.

45. David Brown, "Study Claims Iraq's 'Excess' Death Toll Has Reached 655,000," the *Washington Post,* October 11, 2006.

46. Transcript, "President Discusses War on Terror and Rebuilding Iraq," www.whitehouse.gov, December 7, 2005.

47. Jim Warren, "Kentucky Buddies Are Killed in Iraq: 2 Ex-Soldiers Were With Security Firms Died in Separate Incidents," the *Lexington Herald Leader,* April 23, 2005.

48. Liz Sly, "6 Americans Die in Crash of Helicopter: Civilians Employed by Private Security Firm," the *Chicago Tribune,* April 22, 2005.

49. "Security Company Faces Loss of Seven in Iraq: 'A Very Sad Day for the Blackwater Family,'" Associated Press, April 22, 2005.

50. Ibid.

51. Transcript, *ABC World News Tonight,* April 23, 2005.

52. Hector Gutierrez, "Coloradan Killed in Iraq Crash Trying to Earn Family Nest Egg," *Rocky Mountain News,* April 23, 2005.

53. Ibid.

54. Liz Sly, "6 Americans Die in Crash of Helicopter: Civilians Employed by Private Security Firm," the *Chicago Tribune,* April 22, 2005.

55. John F. Burns, "Video Appears to Show Insurgents Kill a Downed Pilot," the *New York Times,* April 23, 2005.

56. Ibid.

57. Author copy of video.

58. John F. Burns, "Video Appears to Show Insurgents Kill a Downed Pilot," the *New York Times,* April 23, 2005.

59. Thomas Wagner, "Militant Group Says It Shot Down Helicopter in Iraq, Killed Sole Survivor," Associated Press, April 22, 2005.

60. Ibid.

61. Ibid.

62. Blackwater USA press release, April 21, 2005.

63. Transcript, *CNN Live From,* April 21, 2005.

64. Transcript, *CNN Wolf Blitzer Reports,* April 21, 2005.

65. Ibid.

66. Transcript, Defense Department Briefing, April 22, 2005.

67. Emery P. Dalesio, "N.C. Security Company Faces Largest Death Toll in Iraq," Associated Press, April 23, 2005.

68. Samiha Khanna, "Slain Guards' Lives Recalled: N.C. Company Loses 7 in Iraq," the *News & Observer* (Raleigh, North Carolina), April 24, 2005.

69. Steve Hundley, "U.S. Sends Soldiers Into a Meat Grinder," *Austin American-Statesman,* June 11, 2006.

70. Samiha Khanna, "Slain Guards' Lives Recalled: N.C. Company Loses 7 in Iraq," the *News & Observer* (Raleigh, North Carolina), April 24, 2005.

71. "11 Die As Missile Downs Copter—Blackwater's Black Day: 7 Employees Killed," the *Commercial Appeal* (Memphis), April 22, 2005.

72. Blackwater USA press release, April 21, 2005.

73. Ibid.

74. Joe D. Morton, Acting Assistant Secretary for Diplomatic Security and Director for the Office of Foreign Missions, Statement to Employees of the Bureau of Diplomatic Security, April 22, 2005.

75. Transcript, Daily Press Briefing, U.S. State Department, April 21, 2005.

76. Ibid.

77. "11 Die As Missile Downs Copter—Blackwater's Black Day: 7 Employees Killed," the *Commercial Appeal* (Memphis), April 22, 2005.

78. Thomas Wagner, "Car Bomb Kills 8 at Baghdad Mosque; Militant Group Says It Killed Survivor of Copter Crash," Associated Press, April 22, 2005.

79. Emery P. Dalesio, "N.C. Company Loses Seven in Iraq," Associated Press, April 23, 2005.

CHAPTER 18

1. U.S. House of Representatives Committee on Government Reform Minority Staff Special Investigations Division, "Halliburton's Questioned and Unsupported Costs in Iraq Exceed $1.4 Billion," June 27, 2005.

2. Ibid.

3. David Firestone, "Senate Votes to Require Open Bidding on Contracts," the *New York Times,* October 3, 2003.

4. Bloomberg News, "Pentagon Official Sees No Gouging," the *Houston Chronicle,* July 2, 2004.

5. Joseph Schmitz, "Improving Oversight at Defense; Mission Drives Overhaul of IG's Office," *Federal Times,* September 8, 2003; Department of Defense biography of Joseph Schmitz, www.defenselink.mil/bios/ schmitz_bio.html.

6. T. Christian Miller, "Pentagon Investigator Resigning: Joseph E. Schmitz, the Defense Department's Inspector General, Is Suspected of Blocking Investigations of Senior Bush Officials," the *Los Angeles Times,* September 3, 2005.

7. Ibid.

8. Author copy of Schmitz's letter.

9. Ibid.

10. Transcript of Joseph Schmitz's remarks as prepared for delivery at the City Club of Cleveland, June 25, 2004.

11. Joseph E. Schmitz official biography, Department of Defense, February 10, 2005.

12. As stated on the Web site of the Order of Malta Federal Association, USA, www.smom.org/worldwide-history.php, captured December 4, 2006.

13. Ibid.

14. Remarks delivered by Inspector General Joseph E. Schmitz of the Department of Defense to the 16th International Military Chaplains Conference, Ljubljana, Slovenia, February 9, 2005.

15. J. Cofer Black speaking at the American Enterprise Institute, May 17, 2006.

16. Blackwater USA press release, "Joseph E. Schmitz Becomes Chief Operating Officer and General Counsel for The Prince Group," September 13, 2005.

17. Ibid.

18. Howard Seelye, "Schmitz Striving for Moderate Image in Race for Utt's Seat," the *Los Angeles Times,* April 12, 1970.

19. Ibid.

20. Phil Kerby, "The Reagan Backlash," *The Nation,* September 25, 1967.

21. David Haldane and Jean O. Pasco, "Fiery O.C. Ultraconservative Schmitz Dies," the *Los Angeles Times,* January 11, 2001.

22. Ibid.

23. Adam Bernstein, "Conservative GOP Congressman John G. Schmitz, 70, Dies," the *Washington Post,* January 12, 2001.

24. David Haldane and Jean O. Pasco, "Fiery O.C. Ultraconservative Schmitz Dies," the *Los Angeles Times,* January 11, 2001.

25. "LeTourneau's Father Dies," the *Seattle Post-Intelligencer,* January 12, 2001.

26. Thomas J. Foley, "Rousselot, Schmitz Condemn Visit Plan," the *Los Angeles Times,* July 17, 1971.

27. Ibid.

28. Adam Bernstein, "Conservative GOP Congressman John G. Schmitz, 70, Dies," the *Washington Post*, January 12, 2001.

29. David Haldane and Jean O. Pasco, "Fiery O.C. Ultraconservative Schmitz Dies," the *Los Angeles Times*, January 11, 2001.

30. Adam Bernstein, "Conservative GOP Congressman John G. Schmitz, 70, Dies," the *Washington Post*, January 12, 2001.

31. Ibid.

32. David Haldane and Jean O. Pasco, "Fiery O.C. Ultraconservative Schmitz Dies," the *Los Angeles Times*, January 11, 2001.

33. Ibid.

34. Mark Martin, "John G. Schmitz, Former Congressman From Orange County," the *San Francisco Chronicle*, January 12, 2001.

35. John P. Schmitz, profile, www.mayerbrownrowe.com/lawyers/profile.asp?hubbardid =S884112239, accessed December 5, 2006.

36. Lawrence E. Walsh, "Final Report of the Independent Counsel for Iran/Contra Matters," Chapter 28, August 4, 1993.

37. Ibid.

38. Ibid.

39. Ibid.

40. Ibid.

41. Ibid.

42. Ibid.

43. Department of Defense biography of Joseph Schmitz, www.defenselink.mil/bios/ schmitz_bio.html.

44. Lawrence E. Walsh, "Final Report of the Independent Counsel for Iran/Contra Matters," Chapter 31, August 4, 1993.

45. John P. Schmitz profile, www.mayerbrownrowe.com/lawyers/profile.asp?hubbardid =S884112239, accessed December 5, 2006.

46. Ibid.

47. Author copy of Senate Office of Public Records lobbying records.

48. "Bush Donor Profile: John Patrick Schmitz," Texans for Public Justice, www.tpj.org/ docs/pioneers/pioneers_view.jsp?id=723, accessed December 5, 2006.

49. Alex Tresniowski, Lorenzo Benet, and Stacey Wilson, "One Year Later," *People*, May 15, 2006.

50. Ibid.

51. Ibid.

52. "LeTourneau's Father Dies," the *Seattle Post-Intelligencer*, January 12, 2001.

53. Department of Defense biography of Joseph Schmitz, www.defenselink.mil/bios/ schmitz_bio.html.

54. Ibid.

55. Patton Boggs's Iraq Reconstruction page, www.pattonboggs.com/practiceareas/a-z/ 104.html, as it appeared on June 15, 2003.

56. Ibid.

57. Joseph E. Schmitz, "Comments About Recent Veto of HHS Bill," letter published in the *Washington Times*, November 7, 1989.

58. Joseph E. Schmitz, "It's Not a Federal Matter," letter published in the *Washington Post*, July 13, 1990.

59. Joseph E. Schmitz, "Mr. Dershowitz's Dilemma Is No Dilemma," letter published in the *Washington Times*, July 6, 1992.

60. Transcript, "U.S. Senate Armed Services Committee Holds a Hearing on Defense Department Nominations," October 23, 2001.

61. Joseph E. Schmitz, "If you pull that lever for Clinton . . .," letter published in the *Washington Times*, October 30, 1992.

62. Ibid.

63. Transcript, "U.S. Senate Armed Services Committee Holds a Hearing on Defense Department Nominations," October 23, 2001.

64. Ibid.

65. Ibid.

66. As stated on the Department of Defense Inspector General's Web site.

67. Remarks as delivered by Inspector General Joseph E. Schmitz of the Department of Defense, "Wrestling with Discipline: Life Lessons in Leadership," National Wrestling Coaches Association Coaches Clinic, St. Louis, Missouri, March 20, 2004.

68. Remarks as delivered by Inspector General Joseph E. Schmitz of the Department of Defense, Association of Naval Aviators Defense Industry Leaders Breakfast, Tysons Corner, Virginia, June 10, 2004.

69. T. Christian Miller, "The Scrutinizer Finds Himself Under Scrutiny," the *Los Angeles Times*, September 25, 2005.

70. Ibid.

71. Ibid.

72. Ibid.

73. Transcript, White House Daily Press Briefing, March 25, 2003.

74. Stephen Labaton, "Pentagon Adviser Is Also Advising Global Crossing," the *New York Times*, March 21, 2003; Seymour M. Hersh, "Lunch With the Chairman: Why Was Richard Perle Meeting with Adnan Khashoggi?" *The New Yorker*, March 17, 2003.

75. Stephen Labaton, "Pentagon Adviser Is Also Advising Global Crossing," the *New York Times*, March 21, 2003.

76. Ibid.

77. Ibid.

78. Ibid

79. Janine Zacharia, "Pentagon Clears Richard Perle of Wrongdoing," the *Jerusalem Post*, November 19, 2003.

80. Stephen Labaton, "Report Finds No Violations at Pentagon by Adviser," the *New York Times*, November 15, 2003.

81. Janine Zacharia, "Pentagon Clears Richard Perle of Wrongdoing," the *Jerusalem Post*, November 19, 2003.

82. Jennifer C. Kerr, "Perle Didn't Violate Ethics Rules, IG Report Says," Associated Press, November 15, 2003.

83. "Investigation Clears Perle of Wrongdoing—Rumsfeld," Reuters, November 16, 2003.

84. R. Jeffrey Smith and Josh White, "General's Speeches Broke Rules; Report Says Boykin Failed to Obtain Clearance," the *Washington Post*, August 19, 2004.

85. William M. Arkin, "The Pentagon Unleashes a Holy Warrior," the *Los Angeles Times*, October 16, 2003.

86. Ibid.

87. R. Jeffrey Smith and Josh White, "General's Speeches Broke Rules; Report Says Boykin Failed to Obtain Clearance," the *Washington Post*, August 19, 2004.

88. William M. Arkin, "The Pentagon Unleashes a Holy Warrior," the *Los Angeles Times*, October 16, 2003.

89. Transcript, *NBC Nightly News*, October 15, 2003.

90. William M. Arkin, "The Pentagon Unleashes a Holy Warrior," the *Los Angeles Times*, October 16, 2003.

91. Ibid.

92. Ibid.

93. Michael Smith, "Donald Rumsfeld's New Killer Elite, *The Times* (London) Online, February 12, 2006.

94. William M. Arkin, "The Pentagon Unleashes a Holy Warrior," the *Los Angeles Times*, October 16, 2003.

95. Sidney Blumenthal, "The Religious Warrior of Abu Ghraib: An Evangelical US General Played a Pivotal Role in Iraqi Prison Reform," the *Guardian*, May 20, 2004. See also: John Barry, Michael Hirsh, and Michael Isikoff, "The Roots of Torture," *Newsweek*, May 24, 2004.

96. Jim Mannion, "General to Be Investigated for Anti-Muslim Remarks," Agence France-Presse, October 21, 2003.

97. Ibid.

98. R. Jeffrey Smith and Josh White, "General's Speeches Broke Rules; Report Says Boykin Failed to Obtain Clearance," the *Washington Post*, August 19, 2004.

99. Ibid.

100. Transcript of Joseph Schmitz's remarks as prepared for delivery at the City Club of Cleveland, June 25, 2004.

101. Joe Milicia, "Inspector General Says Prisoner Abuse Result of 'Bad Eggs,'" Associated Press, June 25, 2004.

102. Ibid.

103. Transcript of Joseph Schmitz's remarks as prepared for delivery at the City Club of Cleveland, June 25, 2004.

104. Ibid.

105. Ibid.

106. Ibid.

107. Ibid.

108. Remarks as delivered by Inspector General Joseph E. Schmitz of the Department of Defense, Information Assurance Industry Day, Arlington, Virginia, March 30, 2004.

109. Transcript of Joseph Schmitz's remarks as prepared for delivery at the City Club of Cleveland, June 25, 2004.

110. Ibid.

111. Ibid.

112. Ibid.

113. T. Christian Miller, "The Scrutinizer Finds Himself Under Scrutiny," the *Los Angeles Times*, September 25, 2005.

114. Ibid.

115. Ibid.

116. Remarks as delivered by Inspector General Joseph E. Schmitz of the Department of Defense, Von Steuben Monument Dedication: "The Role of Inspectors General in Defending American Values," Monmouth Battlefield, Monmouth, New Jersey, May 15, 2004.

117. Transcript of Joseph Schmitz's remarks as prepared for delivery at the City Club of Cleveland, June 25, 2004.

118. T. Christian Miller, *Blood Money*, p. 57.

119. T. Christian Miller, "The Scrutinizer Finds Himself Under Scrutiny," the *Los Angeles Times*, September 25, 2005.

120. T. Christian Miller, *Blood Money*, pp. 55–68.

121. T. Christian Miller, "Pentagon Investigator Resigning: Joseph E. Schmitz, the Defense Department's Inspector General, Is Suspected of Blocking Investigations of Senior Bush Officials," the *Los Angeles Times*, September 3, 2005.

122. T. Christian Miller, "The Conflict in Iraq: Pentagon Deputy's Probes in Iraq Weren't Authorized, Officials Say," the *Los Angeles Times*, July 7, 2004.

123. T. Christian Miller, "The Scrutinizer Finds Himself Under Scrutiny," the *Los Angeles Times*, September 25, 2005.

124. T. Christian Miller, *Blood Money*, p. 68.

125. T. Christian Miller, "The Scrutinizer Finds Himself Under Scrutiny," the *Los Angeles Times*, September 25, 2005.

126. Author copy of press release.

127. Ibid.

128. Ibid.

129. Author copy of letter dated July 27, 2005.

130. Ibid.

131. T. Christian Miller, "Pentagon Investigator Resigning: Joseph E. Schmitz, the Defense Department's Inspector General, Is Suspected of Blocking Investigations of Senior Bush Officials," the *Los Angeles Times*, September 3, 2005.

132. T. Christian Miller, "Pentagon Ousts Official Under FBI Investigation," Los Angeles Times, December 11, 2004

133. Author copy: Joseph E. Schmitz, "Inspecting Sex Slavery Through the Fog of Moral Relativism," September 18, 2004.

134. Ibid.

135. Cam Simpson, "Commander: Contractors Violating U.S. Trafficking Laws," the *Chicago Tribune*, April 23, 2006.

136. The series "Pipeline to Peril" by Cam Simpson was published in the *Chicago Tribune*, October 9–10, 2005.

137. Cam Simpson, "Commander: Contractors Violating U.S. Trafficking Laws," the *Chicago Tribune*, April 23, 2006.

138. Ibid.

139. Ibid.

140. Mike Allen, "Details on Boeing Deal Sought; Senators Raise Questions About White House Involvement," the *Washington Post*, June 8, 2005.

141. Greg Schneider and Renae Merle, "Pentagon to Lease Boeing Tanker Planes: Unusual Deal Saves Jobs; McCain Alleges Bias," the *Washington Post*, May 24, 2003.

142. Ibid.

143. Ibid.

144. Peter Spiegel, "Pentagon Gives Go-Ahead Over Boeing Deal," the *Financial Times*, May 24, 2003.

145. Caroline Daniel, James Harding, Joshua Chaffin, and Marianne Brun-Rovet, "A Cosy Relationship: Boeing's Pentagon Deal Bears Testament to Its Skilful Lobbying Efforts," the *Financial Times*, December 8, 2003.

146. Ibid.

147. Greg Schneider and Renae Merle, "Pentagon to Lease Boeing Tanker Planes: Unusual Deal Saves Jobs; McCain Alleges Bias," the *Washington Post*, May 24, 2003.

148. Renae Merle, "Lockheed Adds Director Fresh From the Pentagon," the *Washington Post*, June 27, 2003.

149. Caroline Daniel, James Harding, Joshua Chaffin, and Marianne Brun-Rovet, "A Cosy Relationship: Boeing's Pentagon Deal Bears Testament to Its Skilful Lobbying Efforts," the *Financial Times*, December 8, 2003.

150. "Holes in the Tanker Story," the *Washington Post*, June 20, 2005.

151. R. Jeffrey Smith, "Tanker Inquiry Finds Rumsfeld's Attention Was Elsewhere," the *Washington Post*, June 20, 2006.

152. Mike Allen, "Details on Boeing Deal Sought; Senators Raise Questions About White House Involvement," the *Washington Post*, June 8, 2005.

153. Author copy of Senator Grassley letter to Schmitz, dated August 8, 2005.

154. Ibid.

155. "Holes in the Tanker Story," the *Washington Post*, June 20, 2005.

156. R. Jeffrey Smith, "Tanker Inquiry Finds Rumsfeld's Attention Was Elsewhere," the *Washington Post*, June 20, 2006.

157. Ibid.

158. Mike Allen, "Details on Boeing Deal Sought; Senators Raise Questions About White House Involvement," the *Washington Post*, June 8, 2005.

159. "Holes in the Tanker Story," the *Washington Post*, June 20, 2005.

160. Transcript, "Hearing of the Senate Armed Services Committee," June 7, 2005.

161. U.S. Senate lobbying registration records.

162. Ibid.

163. Author copy of Senator Grassley letter to Schmitz, dated August 8, 2005.

164. Alicia Mundy, "Material Withheld from Tanker Report Angers Senate Panel; Many Names, Data Blacked Out—Key Pentagon Official Refused to Aid Probe," the *Seattle Times*, June 8, 2005.

165. Joe Milicia, "Inspector General Says Prisoner Abuse Result of 'Bad Eggs,'" Associated Press, June 25, 2004.

166. "DoD Inspector General Lauds Bremer," American Forces Information Service, November 15, 2004.

167. Ibid.

168. Ibid.

169. Remarks as delivered by Department of Defense Inspector General Joseph E. Schmitz to Order of Malta, Federal Association, USA, at the Church of the Little Flower, Bethesda, Maryland, February 5, 2005.

170. Blackwater USA press release, "Red Cross–Blackwater Fundraiser and Silent Auction a Huge Success!" November 23, 2005.

171. George Cahlink, "Defense IG Schmitz Leaves for Senior Post With Blackwater," *Defense Daily*, September 1, 2005.

CHAPTER 19

1. Blackwater USA press release, "Blackwater USA Continues to Support Katrina Devastated Areas; Aid Focuses on Humanitarian, Security and Clean Up Needs, September 13, 2005.

2. Unless otherwise noted, descriptions of Blackwater's operations and quotes from its personnel in New Orleans are from the author's time there in September 2005.

3. Alex Berenson and John M. Broder, "Police Begin Seizing Guns of Civilians," the *New York Times*, September 9, 2005.

4. Joanne Kimberlin and Bill Sizemore, "Blackwater: On American Soil," the *Virginian-Pilot*, July 27, 2006.

5. Ibid.

6. Ted Roelofs, "Iraq or New Orleans, It's All Part of the Job; Former Kentwood Cop Describes War-like Horrors from Security Assignment," the *Grand Rapids Press*, September 13, 2005.

7. Ibid.

8. Frank Borelli, "Blackwater in Louisiana," SwatDigest.com, September 8, 2005.

9. Griff Witte, "Private Security Contractors Head to Gulf," the *Washington Post*, September 8, 2005.

10. Bill Sizemore, "Blackwater Employees Create a Stir in New Orleans," the *Virginian-Pilot*, September 15, 2005.

11. Blackwater USA press release, "Blackwater Joins Hurricane Katrina Relief Effort!" September 1, 2005.

12. Blackwater USA press release, "Blackwater USA Continues to Support Katrina Devastated Areas; Aid Focuses on Humanitarian, Security and Clean Up Needs," September 13, 2005.

13. Interview, May 2006.

14. Lolly Bowean and Deborah Horan, "Outsiders Come Looking for Work," the *Chicago Tribune*, September 18, 2005.

15. August Cole, "From Green Zone to French Quarter," *MarketWatch*, September 18, 2005.

16. *Blackwater Tactical Weekly*, September 19, 2005.

17. August Cole, "From Green Zone to French Quarter," *MarketWatch*, September 18, 2005.

18. Author copy of Erik Prince's speech at West 2006 conference in San Diego, January 11, 2006.

19. Joanne Kimberlin and Bill Sizemore, "Blackwater: On American Soil," the *Virginian-Pilot*, July 27, 2006.

20. Ibid.

21. Author copy of contract.

22. Interviews, September 2005.

23. Author copy of government contract records.

24. Interview, June 2006.

25. Joanne Kimberlin and Bill Sizemore, "Blackwater: On American Soil," the *Virginian-Pilot*, July 27, 2006.

26. Bruce Alpert, "Democrats Fight Repeal of Prevailing Wage Law; Recovery Contractors Can Reduce Salaries," the *Times-Picayune* (New Orleans), September 27, 2005.

27. Pratap Chatterjee, "Big, Easy Iraqi-Style Contracts Flood New Orleans," *CorpWatch*, September 20, 2005.

28. Rita J. King, "A High-Stakes Game With Almost No Rules," *CorpWatch*, August 16, 2006.

29. Ibid.

30. Spencer S. Hsu, "$400 Million FEMA Contracts Now Total $3.4 Billion," the *Washington Post*, August 9, 2006.

31. "Fluor's Slowed Iraq Work Frees It for Gulf Coast," Reuters, September 9, 2005.

32. Christian Parenti, "New Orleans: Raze or Rebuild?" *The Nation* online, September 12, 2005.

33. Interviews, September 2005.

34. Christopher Cooper, "Old-Line Families Escape Worst of Flood and Plot the Future," the *Wall Street Journal*, September 8, 2005.

35. Interview, September 2006.

36. ISI Web site, www.isiusa.us/html/about.swf, captured December 7, 2006.

37. Transcript, "U.S. Senators Tom Coburn (R-Ok) and Barack Obama (D-Il) Hold a News Conference on Hurricane Katrina Relief Efforts," September 14, 2005.

38. Author copy of letter.

39. Author copy of letter.

40. Interview, 2006.

41. Author copy of memo.

42. Joanne Kimberlin and Bill Sizemore, "Blackwater: On American Soil," the *Virginian-Pilot*, July 27, 2006.

43. Renae Merle, "Storm-Wracked Parish Considers Hired Guns: Contractors in Louisiana Would Make Arrests, Carry Weapons," the *Washington Post*, March 14, 2006.

44. *LeRoy v. Blackwater USA*, filed August 25, 2005, U.S. District Court, Eastern District of Louisiana.

45. Joanne Kimberlin, "Fort Swaggart: Bible Campus Becomes Blackwater Base," the *Virginian-Pilot*, July 27, 2006.

46. Joanne Kimberlin and Bill Sizemore, "Blackwater: On American Soil," the *Virginian-Pilot*, July 27, 2006.

47. Author copy of Erik Prince's speech at West 2006 conference in San Diego, January 11, 2006.

48. Joanne Kimberlin and Bill Sizemore, "Blackwater: On American Soil," the *Virginian-Pilot*, July 27, 2006.

49. Terry Rodgers, "Finish the Fence, Congressmen Say; Republican Leaders Gather at Border to Promote 'Real ID Act,'" the *San Diego Union-Tribune*, March 30, 2005.

50. Press Release, "Rep. Rohrabacher Commends Minuteman Project," April 19, 2005.

51. Dan Robinson, "US Citizen Volunteers on Border Security: We Won't Stop," *Voice of America*, May 12, 2005.

52. Transcript, "Hearing of the Management, Integration, and Oversight Subcommittee of the House Homeland Security Committee. Subject: Training More Border Agents: How the Department of Homeland Security Can Increase Training Capacity More Effectively," May 24, 2005.

53. Ibid.

54. Ibid.

55. *Blackwater Tactical Weekly*, June 13, 2005.

56. Stephen Losey, "Border Patrol Should Consider Outsourcing its Training, Lawmaker Says," *Federal Times*, May 27, 2005.

57. Blackwater USA press release, "Red Cross–Blackwater Fundraiser and Silent Auction a Huge Success!" November 23, 2005.

58. Ibid.

59. *Blackwater Tactical Weekly*, August 28, 2006.

60. Author copy of memo dated September 16, 2005.

61. Jeffrey H. Birnbaum and James V. Grimaldi, "Lobby Firm Is Scandal Casualty; Abramoff, DeLay Publicity Blamed for Shutdown," the *Washington Post*, January 10, 2006.

62. Government lobbying records.

63. Judy Sarasohn, "Security Contractors Try Friendly Persuasion," the *Washington Post*, December 22, 2005; government lobbying records.

64. Government lobbying records.

65. Erik Prince bio from Prince Manufacturing.

66. Paul Kane and John Bresnahan, "Letters Depict a Softer Abramoff," *Roll Call*, March 29, 2006.

67. Author copy of Edgar and Elsa Prince Foundation records.

68. Toward Tradition Web site, www.towardtradition.org.

69. "The Rabbi Responds," *Seattle Weekly*, January 18, 2006.

70. Jack Abramoff plea agreement, January 3, 2006.

71. David Postman and Hal Bernton, "Abramoff Used Area Foundation as Conduit for Money," the *Seattle Times*, January 9, 2006.

72. Ibid.

73. Ibid.

74. Kate Ackley and Tory Newmyer, "Key Clients Quit Alexander Strategy Group; Others Weigh Options," *Roll Call*, January 11, 2006.

75. Anna Palmer, "Pickups," *Legal Times*, March 27, 2006.

76. Ibid.

CHAPTER 20

1. Transcript, President Bush speaking in the Oval Office, November 8, 2006.

2. Renae Merle, "Census Counts 100,000 Contractors in Iraq," the *Washington Post*, December 5, 2006.

3. Transcript, "Remarks By Vice President Dick Cheney at an Armed Forces Full Honor Review in Honor of Secretary of Defense Donald Rumsfeld," December 15, 2006.

4. Transcript, *Face the Nation*, CBS, December 17, 2006.

5. Peter Baker, "Bush to Expand Size of Military," the *Washington Post*, December 19, 2006.

6. President George W. Bush, "State of the Union," January 23, 2007.

7. Nathan Hodge, "Washington Urged to Save Money By Raising Private Military 'Contractor Brigade,'" the *Financial Times*, February 10, 2005.

8. Mark Hemingway, "Warriors for Hire: Blackwater USA and the Rise of Private Military Contractors," *The Weekly Standard*, December 18, 2006.

9. Mark Hemingway, "Warriors for Hire: Blackwater USA and the Rise of Private Military Contractors," *The Weekly Standard*, December 18, 2006.

10. Author copy of fact sheet from "6th International Special Operations Exhibition and Conference (SOFEX 2006)," held March 27–30, 2006, King Abdullah Air Base, Amman, Jordan.

11. Ibid.

12. "Record Number of Participants to Visit SOFEX 2006," DefenseWorld.net, captured November 2, 2006.

13. BlackwaterUSA.com.

14. Official biography, "His Majesty King Abdullah II," Jordanian Embassy to the United States, www.jordanembassyus.org/new/jib/monarchy/hmka.shtml, captured December 2, 2006.

15. Riad Kahwaji, "Jordan Forming Spec Ops Air Unit; Contracted U.S. Aviators Will Conduct Training," *Armed Forces Journal*, February 1, 2005.

16. Ibid

17. Ibid.

18. Author copy of Erik Prince's speech at West 2006.

19. Riad Kahwaji, "Jordan Leads Region in Spec Ops Capabilities," *Defense News*, March 20, 2006.

20. "Exclusive Interview: Partner for Peace. His Majesty King Abdullah II bin Al Hussein, King of The Hashemite Kingdom of Jordan," www.special-operations-technology.com/print_article.cfm?DocID=1361, undated.

21. Jonathan Franklin, "The SWAT Olympics: North America's Toughest, Most Heavily Armed Cops Go Head-to-Head in Live Ammo Games to See Who's the Ultimate Badass. What's Not to Love?" *Maxim*, September 2004.

22. Blackwater USA press release, "Blackwater USA Parachute Team Launched," March 21, 2006.

23. Kelly Kennedy, "Private Firm Pitches Army-for-Hire Plan," *Air Force Times*, April 10, 2006.

24. Ibid.

25. Ibid.

26. Transcript, "Private Military Firm Pitches Its Services in Darfur," National Public Radio, *All Things Considered*, May 26, 2006.

27. Ibid.

28. E-mail to author, December 2006.

29. Transcript, Chris Taylor, Vice President for Strategic Initiatives, Blackwater USA, speaking at George Washington University Law School, January 28, 2005.

30. E-mail to author, December 2006.

31. Peter S. Goodman, "China Invests Heavily in Sudan's Oil Industry; Beijing Supplies Arms Used on Villagers," the *Washington Post*, December 23, 2004.

32. Ibid.

33. C.I.A. World Factbook, https://cia.gov/cia/publications/factbook/rankorder/2178rank.html, captured December 6, 2006.

34. Peter S. Goodman, "China Invests Heavily In Sudan's Oil Industry; Beijing Supplies Arms Used on Villagers," the *Washington Post*, December 23, 2004.

35. Sara Flounders, "The U.S. Role in Darfur, Sudan: Oil Reserves Rivaling Those of Saudi Arabia?" The Centre for Research on Globalization, June 6, 2006.

36. Mark Hemingway, "Warriors for Hire: Blackwater USA and the Rise of Private Military Contractors," *The Weekly Standard*, December 18, 2006.

37. Nathan Hodge, "Blackwater CEO Touts Private Peacekeeping Model," *Defense Daily*, February 23, 2005.

38. Ibid.

39. Christian Freedom International "About Us," www.christianfreedom.org/about_cfi/Statement%20of%20Faith.html, accessed on November 26, 2006.

40. Jim Jacobson, "Slave Redemption Money Rewards the Slaver," the *Washington Times,* May 30, 1999.

41. Ibid.

42. "The Danger Zone" radio program, produced by the Foundation for Defense of Democracies, October 8, 2006.

43. Transcript, "Private Military Firm Pitches Its Services in Darfur," National Public Radio, *All Things Considered,* May 26, 2006.

44. Willis Witter, "Private Firms Eye Darfur," the *Washington Times,* October 2, 2006.

45. Author copy of Erik Prince's speech at West 2006.

46. E-mail to author, December 2006.

47. Mark Hemingway, "Warriors for Hire: Blackwater USA and the Rise of Private Military Contractors," *The Weekly Standard,* December 18, 2006.

48. Ibid.

49. Max Boot, "Darfur Solution: Send in the Mercenaries," the *Los Angeles Times,* May 31, 2006.

50. Ibid.

51. Max Boot, "A Mercenary Force for Darfur," the *Wall Street Journal,* October 25, 2006.

52. Ted Koppel, "These Guns for Hire," the *New York Times,* May 22, 2006.

53. See: *Democracy Now!* "Drilling and Killing: Chevron and Nigeria's Oil Dictatorship," September 30, 1998.

54. Unless otherwise noted, comments from Representative Schakowsky are drawn from an interview in June 2006.

55. Kelly Kennedy, "Private Firm Pitches Army-for-Hire Plan," *Air Force Times,* April 10, 2006.

56. Joanne Kimberlin, "Blackwater Eyes Creation of Private 'Brigade Force,'" the *Virginian-Pilot,* July 28, 2006.

57. Transcript, "Hearing of the National Security, Emerging Threats and International Relations Subcommittee of the House Government Reform Committee," June 13, 2006.

58. IPOA Member List, http://ipoaonline.org/php/index.php?option=com_content&task=view&id=18&Itemid=30, accessed December 7, 2006.

59. J. J. Messner, letter to the editor, "Don't Call Us Mercenaries!," *The Nation,* July 10, 2006.

60. James Rosen, "Contractors Operate in a Legal Gray Area; The Roles of an Interrogator and an Interpreter in the Abuse Scandal Are Murky. Even Less Clear Is Whom They Answer to," the *Star Tribune,* May 23, 2004.

61. Rebecca Ullam Weiner, "Peace Corp.; As the International Community Dithers Over Darfur, Private Military Companies Say They've Got What It Takes to Stop the Carnage; If Only Someone Would Hire Them," the *Boston Globe,* April 23, 2006.

62. IPOA History, http://ipoaonline.org/php/index.php?option=com_content& task=view&id=13&Itemid=30, captured December 7, 2006.

63. Transcript, "Hearing of the National Security, Emerging Threats and International Relations Subcommittee of the House Government Reform Committee," June 13, 2006.

64. Transcript, Chris Taylor, Vice President for Strategic Initiatives, Blackwater USA, speaking at George Washington University Law School, January 28, 2005.

65. IPOA Code of Conduct, Version 10, http://ipoaonline.org/php/index.php?option=com_content&task=view&id=35&Itemid=62, accessed December 7, 2006.

66. Ibid.

67. IPOA Executive Committee 2006, http://ipoaonline.org/php/index.php?option= com_content&task=view&id=40&Itemid=73, accessed December 7, 2006; Transcript, "Hearing of the National Security, Emerging Threats and International Relations Subcommittee of the House Government Reform Committee," June 13, 2006.

68. Transcript, "Hearing of the National Security, Emerging Threats and International Relations Subcommittee of the House Government Reform Committee," June 13, 2006.

69. IPOA Mission Statement, http://ipoaonline.org/php/index.php?option=com_content&task=view&id=14&Itemid=31, accessed December 7, 2006.

70. Transcript, "Hearing of the National Security, Emerging Threats and International Relations Subcommittee of the House Government Reform Committee," June 13, 2006.

71. P. W. Singer, *Corporate Warriors*, p. 114.

72. Ibid., pp. 116–117.

73. Republic of South Africa Prohibition of Mercenary Activities and Prohibition and Regulation of Certain Activities in Areas of Armed Conflict Bill, October 2005.

74. BBC News, "Q&A: Equatorial Guinea 'Coup Plot,'" http://news.bbc.co.uk/2/ hi/africa/3597450.stm, January 13, 2005.

75. BBC News, "Q&A: Equatorial Guinea 'Coup Plot,'" http://news.bbc.co.uk/2/hi/africa/3597450.stm, January 13, 2005; BBC News, "Profile: Simon Mann," September 10, 2004.

76. Republic of South Africa Prohibition of Mercenary Activities and Prohibition and Regulation of Certain Activities in Areas of Armed Conflict Bill, October 2005.

77. "South Africa Passes Controversial Mercenaries Bill," Reuters, August 29, 2006.

78. John Reed, "S. African Ban on Mercenaries Could Hit Conflict Zone Workers," the *Financial Times*, August 30, 2006.

79. Republic of South Africa Prohibition of Mercenary Activities and Prohibition and Regulation of Certain Activities in Areas of Armed Conflict Bill, October 2005.

80. John Reed, "S. African Ban on Mercenaries Could Hit Conflict Zone Workers," the *Financial Times*, August 30, 2006.

81. Doug Brooks, "New Legislation Will Undermine South Africa's Security Staff Abroad," the *Cape Times*, October 5, 2005.

82. "Defence Portfolio Committee Hears: Role of South Africans 'Critical for World Peace,'" the *Mercury* (South Africa), May 24, 2006.

83. Clare Nullis, "South Africa Assembly OKs Mercenary Bill," Associated Press, August 29, 2006.

84. Rebecca Ulam Weiner, "Peace Corp.; As the International Community Dithers Over Darfur, Private Military Companies Say They've Got What It Takes to Stop the Carnage; If Only Someone Would Hire Them," the *Boston Globe*, April 23, 2006.

85. Clare Nullis, "South Africa Assembly OKs Mercenary Bill," Associated Press, August 29, 2006.

86. Ibid.

87. Mark Hemingway, "Warriors for Hire: Blackwater USA and the Rise of Private Military Contractors," *The Weekly Standard*, December 18, 2006.

88. Joanne Kimberlin, "Blackwater Eyes Creation of Private 'Brigade Force,'" the *Virginian-Pilot*, July 28, 2006.

89. Author copy, Central Contractor registration documents for Greystone Limited.

90. Ibid.

91. Ibid.

92. Author copy of guest list.

93. Author copy of brochure.

94. Author copy of invitation.

95. Author copy of video.

96. Nathan Hodge, "Washington Urged to Save Money by Raising Private Military 'Contractor Brigade,'" the *Financial Times*, February 10, 2005.

97. West 2006 Web site, www.afcea.org/events/west/2006/intro.html, accessed December 7, 2006.

98. Author copy of Erik Prince's speech at West 2006.

99. Stephen Daggett and Amy Belasco, "Defense Budget for FY2003: Data Summary," Congressional Research Service, March 29, 2002.

100. P. W. Singer, *Corporate Warriors*, p. 15.

101. Ibid., p. 16.

102. Ian Traynor, "The Privatisation of War," the *Guardian*, December 10, 2003.

103. Paul Krugman, "Battlefield of Dreams," the *New York Times*, May 4, 2004.

104. Bill Sizemore, "The Layered Look: On Multi-level Contracts, Everyone Gets a Cut," the *Virginian-Pilot*, July 28, 2006.

105. "Rebuilding Iraq," Government Accountability Office, June 2006.

106. Ibid.

107. Ibid.

108. www.globalsecurity.org/military/ops/iraq_reconstruction_costs.htm.

109. Government contracts as listed on fedspending.org.

110. Peter W. Singer, "Peacekeepers, Inc." *Policy Review*, June 2003.

111. Gary Stoller, "Homeland security generates multibillion dollar business," *USA Today*, September 10, 2006.

112. Cofer Black's remarks at American Enterprise Institute Conference, "Contractors on the Battlefield: A Briefing on the Future of the Defense Industry," May 17, 2006.

113. Ibid.

114. Mark Hemingway, "Warriors for Hire: Blackwater USA and the Rise of Private Military Contractors," *The Weekly Standard*, December 18, 2006.

115. David Lerman and Stephanie Heinatz, "War in Iraq: For Contractors, War Is a Job, Not an Adventure," *Daily Press* (Newport News, Virginia), April 4, 2004.

116. Author copy of Erik Prince's speech at West 2006.

117. Cofer Black's remarks at American Enterprise Institute Conference, "Contractors on the Battlefield: A Briefing on the Future of the Defense Industry," May 17, 2006.

118. Quadrennial Defense Review report, February 6, 2006.

119. Cofer Black's remarks at American Enterprise Institute Conference, "Contractors on the Battlefield: A Briefing on the Future of the Defense Industry," May 17, 2006.

120. Quadrennial Defense Review report, February 6, 2006.

121. Mark Hemingway, "Warriors for Hire: Blackwater USA and the Rise of Private Military Contractors," *The Weekly Standard*, December 18, 2006.

122. Cofer Black's remarks at American Enterprise Institute Conference, "Contractors on the Battlefield: A Briefing on the Future of the Defense Industry," May 17, 2006.

123. Ibid.

EPILOGUE

1. Federal Procurement Data System records.

2. Joanne Kimberlin, "At Blackwater, Time Is Now Told in 'Before' and 'After,'" *Virginian-Pilot*, October 28, 2007.

3. Ibid.

4. Ibid.

5. August Cole, "Blackwater Vies for Jobs Beyond Security," *Wall Street Journal*, October 15, 2007.

6. Ibid.

7. Paul Richfield, "$15B Narcoterrorism War to be Outsourced," *Army Times*, September 14, 2007.

8. Ibid.

9. Solomon Moore, "Disputed in Iraq, Blackwater Now Splits California Town," *New York Times*, December 11, 2007.

10. Toby Muse, "U.S. Contractors Get Half of Aid to Colombia," *USA Today*, June 15, 2007.

11. John Ross, "Full Spectrum Mercenaries," CounterPunch.org, November 9, 2007.

12. Solomon Moore, "Disputed in Iraq, Blackwater Now Splits California Town," *New York Times*, December 11, 2007.

13. United Nations, "Report of the Working Group on the Use of Mercenaries as a Means of Violating Human Rights and Impeding the Exercise of the Right of People to Self-Determination," January 9, 2008.

14. Solomon Moore, "Disputed in Iraq, Blackwater Now Splits California Town," *New York Times*, December 11, 2007.

15. Anne Krueger, "Blackwater Pulls Application for Potrero Training Center," *San Diego Union-Tribune*, March 7, 2008.

16. August Cole, "Blackwater Vies for Jobs Beyond Security," *Wall Street Journal*, October 15, 2007.

17. Teri Weaver, "Tiny Base Assimilates Into Japanese Town," *Stars and Stripes*, October 8, 2007.

18. Wendell Minnick, "Blackwater Training Taiwanese," *Defense News*, February 12, 2008.

19. "Life-and-Death Repercussions of Blackwater Trashing," *Serviam*, January/February 2008 issue.

20. "ARES Systems Group Armor Applique Gets Thumbs Up From Army Aberdeen Test Center," Market Wire, March 3, 2008.

21. Kris Osborn, "Six Companies Compete for DoD MRAP II Contract," *Navy Times*, November 5, 2007.

22. David Macaulay, "Blackwater USA Hires Ford Workers to Build New APC," *Daily Advance*, February 20, 2007.

23. Kris Osborn, "Six Companies Compete for DoD MRAP II Contract," *Navy Times*, November 5, 2007.

24. David Macaulay, "Blackwater USA Hires Ford Workers to Build New APC," *Daily Advance*, February 20, 2007.

25. "Blackwater USA President Outlines Firm's Future Plans," Associated Press, July 31, 2007.

26. David Macaulay, "Blackwater USA Hires Ford Workers to Build New APC," *Daily Advance*, February 20, 2007.

27. Jon W. Glass, "Off the Ground," *Virginian-Pilot*, November 23, 2007.

28. Ibid.

29. Ibid.

30. Joanne Kimberlin, "At Blackwater, Time Is Now Told in 'Before' and 'After,'" *Virginian-Pilot*, October 28, 2007.

31. R.J. Hillhouse, "Exclusive Interview: Blackwater USA's President Gary Jackson," TheSpyWhoBilledMe.com, April 26, 2007.

32. Joanne Kimberlin, "At Blackwater, Time Is Now Told in 'Before' and 'After,'" *Virginian-Pilot*, October 28, 2007.

33. United Nations, "Report of the Working Group on the Use of Mercenaries as a Means of Violating Human Rights and Impeding the Exercise of the Right of People to Self-Determination," January 9, 2008.

34. Interview, July 2007.

35. Total Intelligence Solutions Press Release, "Former CIA and Counterterrorism Experts Respond to Security and Intelligence Demands of the Private Sector," February 20, 2006.

36. www.totalintel.com, accessed March 17, 2008.

37. Interview, July 2007.

38. R.J. Hillhouse, "The ODNI's Wal-Mart Approach to Intel," TheSpyWhoBilledMe.com, June 18, 2007.

39. R.J. Hillhouse, "Corporate Content and the President's Daily Brief," TheSpyWhoBilledMe.com, July 23, 2007.

40. Ben Hammer, "Blackwater Boss, Former CIA Execs Create New Firm," *Washington Business Journal*, March 12, 2007.

41. Richer's biographical details are drawn from multiple sources, including: Richer's official Total Intelligence biography; Ken Silverstein, "Revolving Door to Blackwater Causes Alarm at CIA," *Harper's* online, Washington Babylon column, September 12, 2006; Dana Hedgpeth, "Blackwater's Owner Has Spies for Hire," *Washington Post*, November 3, 2007; Ben Van Heuvelen, "The Bush Administration's Ties to Blackwater," *Salon*, October 2, 2007.

42. Prado's Total Intelligence bio.

43. Ibid.

44. Ken Silverstein, "Revolving Door to Blackwater Causes Alarm at CIA," *Harper's* online, Washington Babylon column, September 12, 2006.

45. Mark Mazzetti and Scott Shane, "Tape Inquiry: Ex-Spymaster in the Middle," *New York Times*, February 20, 2008.

46. Ken Silverstein, "Revolving Door to Blackwater Causes Alarm at CIA," *Harper's* online, Washington Babylon column, September 12, 2006.

47. Total Intelligence bios.

48. Ibid.

49. Dana Hedgpeth, "Blackwater's Owner Has Spies for Hire," *Washington Post*, November 3, 2007.

50. www.totalintel.com/dsp_gfc.php, accessed March 17, 2008.

51. Dana Hedgpeth, "Blackwater's Owner Has Spies for Hire," *Washington Post*, November 3, 2007.

52. Ben Hammer, "Blackwater Boss, Former CIA Execs Create New Firm," *Washington Business Journal*, March 12, 2007; Dana Hedgpeth, "Blackwater's Owner Has Spies for Hire," *Washington Post*, November 3, 2007.

53. Total Intelligence Solutions Press Release, "Former CIA and Counterterrorism Experts Respond to Security and Intelligence Demands of the Private Sector," February 20, 2006.

54. Dana Hedgpeth, "Blackwater's Owner Has Spies for Hire," *Washington Post*, November 3, 2007.

55. Ibid.

56. Ibid.

57. Ken Silverstein, "Revolving Door to Blackwater Causes Alarm at CIA," *Harper's* online, Washington Babylon column, September 12, 2006.

58. Kudlow & Company, "Ambassador Cofer Black Discusses Investing in Jordan," CNBC transcript, July 9, 2007.

59. Dana Hedgpeth, "Blackwater's Owner Has Spies for Hire," *Washington Post*, November 3, 2007.

60. Ibid.

61. John McCain speech in Derry, New Hampshire, January 3, 2008.

62. Joanne Kimberlin, "At Blackwater, Time Is Now Told in 'Before' and 'After,'" *Virginian-Pilot*, October 28, 2007.

63. Peter Grier and Gordon Lubold, "Private Security in Iraq: Whose Rules?" *Christian Science Monitor*, September 20, 2007.

64. Barrack Obama Press Release, "Obama Statement on Supplemental Bill That Sets a Target Redeployment Date," April 26, 2007.

65. Erik Leaver, "Iraq Supplemental Analysis," Institute for Policy Studies, March 14, 2007.

66. Interview, March 2007.

67. Transcript of Gen. David Petraeus's confirmation hearing before the Senate Armed Services Committee, January 24, 2007.

68. Steve Fainaru, "Iraq Contractors Face Growing Parallel War," *Washington Post*, June 16, 2007.

69. Interview, March 2007.

70. T. Christian Miller, "Private Contractors Outnumber US Troops in Iraq," *Los Angeles Times*, July 4, 2007.

71. Government Accountability Office, "Report to the Committee on Armed Services, US Senate," March 2008.

72. Jeremy Scahill, *"All* Cowboys Out Now," *The Nation*, November 26, 2007.

73. See Jeremy Scahill, "Bush's Shadow Army," *The Nation*, April 2, 2007.

74. Jeremy Scahill, *"All* Cowboys Out Now," *The Nation*, November 26, 2007.

75. Transcript, hearing on Iraq Private Contractor Oversight, House Oversight and Government Reform Committee, October 2, 2007.

76. Ibid.

77. John H. Broder and David Rohde, "State Department Use of Contractors Leaps in 4 Years," *New York Times*, October 24, 2007.

78. Jeremy Scahill, "Obama's Mercenary Position," *The Nation*, March 17, 2008.

79. Hillary Clinton Press Release, "Senator Clinton Cosponsors Legislation to Ban Use of Private Security Contractors in Iraq and Afghanistan," February 28, 2008.

80. Joanne Kimberlin, "At Blackwater, Time Is Now Told in 'Before' and 'After,'" *Virginian-Pilot*, October 28, 2007.

INDEX